D1201466

Role Models in the Roman World

Memoirs of the American Academy in Rome

Supplementary Volume VII

Support for this publication was provided by the Lucy Shoe Meritt, FAAR '37, '50, Publication Fund of the American Academy in Rome.

Role Models in the Roman World

Identity and Assimilation

edited by

Sinclair Bell
and
Inge Lyse Hansen

PUBLISHED FOR THE AMERICAN ACADEMY IN ROME
by
The University of Michigan Press
Ann Arbor, Michigan
2008

Copyright © by the University of Michigan 2008
All rights reserved
Published in the United States of America by
The University of Michigan Press
Manufactured in the United States of America
♾ Printed on acid-free paper

2011   2010   2009   2008   4   3   2   1

No part of this publication may be reproduced, stored
in a retrieval system, or transmitted in any form or by
any means, electronic, mechanical, or otherwise, without
the written permission of the publisher.

A CIP catalog record for this book is available from the British Library.

Library of Congress Cataloging-in-Publication Data applied for.

ISBN-13: 978-0-472-11589-1
ISBN-10: 0-472-11589-8

Every effort has been made to trace the ownership of all copyrighted
material in this book and to obtain permission for its use.

CONTENTS

ILLUSTRATIONS

ACKNOWLEDGMENTS

The papers in this volume originate from a conference, "Role Models: Identity and Assimilation in the Roman World and Early Modern Italy," held jointly at the American Academy in Rome and the British School at Rome from 17 to 19 March 2003. Thirty papers were delivered at the conference, and the present volume contains fifteen of the nineteen papers concerning ancient Rome, with the addition of one by Suzanne Dixon, who was unable to attend.

We would like to thank the staff of both institutions in Rome for their support. Ingrid Rowland, Andrew W. Mellon Professor of Humanities at the Academy, enthusiastically embraced the idea from the very start, and both Lester Little, then Director of the American Academy in Rome, and Andrew Wallace-Hadrill, Director of the British School at Rome, offered encouragement and assistance throughout. Our co-organizer in the conference, Helen Langdon, then Assistant Director of the British School, was a source of constant inspiration, not the least in the meeting of studies of antiquity and the early modern period. We warmly acknowledge here our debt to her in bringing about a seamless and truly interdisciplinary program. Joe Farrell, Elizabeth Fentress, Luisa Musso, Susan Walker, and Andrew Wallace-Hadrill—though not represented in the contents of this volume—played important roles as panel chairs.

The publication of the papers has been made possible through subventions from John Cabot University, the Loeb Classical Library Foundation, the Samuel H. Kress Foundation, and the Trustees' Publications Committee of the American Academy in Rome, all of whose generosity we are pleased to acknowledge here. At the University of Michigan and its Press, Elaine Gazda patiently shepherded us through the vetting process, Christy Byks and Chris Hebert offered logistical support, and Margaret Lourie lent fresh eyes in the final stages of copyediting. In addition, the detailed and insightful comments of two anonymous readers improved every aspect of the volume. We are grateful to all.

Lastly, we are pleased to acknowledge a special debt to Glenys Davies. There is little question that we, like many other former students of the University of Edinburgh, owe much to her, and to her intellectual curiosity, in our interests in and approaches to the study of antiquity. We hope that in reading this volume—an untraditional, interdisciplinary, and collaborative work—she will recognize traces of her own rich influence.

Sinclair Bell and Inge Lyse Hansen

ROLE MODELS IN THE ROMAN WORLD

Sinclair Bell

Consequently, with *virtus* held in such esteem, women too were incited to public honors. A maiden named Cloelia, one of the hostages, eluded her guards—since the Etruscan camp by chance was located not far from the Tiber's bank—and leading a band of maidens swam across the Tiber amidst the enemy's javelins, and restored them all safely to their kinsmen in Rome. . . . The truce re-established, the Romans rewarded this novel *virtus* in a woman with a novel form of honor, an equestrian statue; at the top of the Sacred Way was placed a *virgo* sitting upon a horse.

Livy, A History of Rome, 2.13.6; 2.13.11[1]

We, steadfast and devoted supporters, have from our own resources set up an altar-tomb for Fuscus of the Blue team, so that all might know the record and token of devotion. Your reputation is unsullied, you won for speed, you contended with many, though not rich you feared nobody, though you experienced envy you always bravely maintained silence, you lived a fine life, being mortal you died, but a natural death. Whatever sort of man you may be, you will miss such a one as Fuscus; halt, traveller, read, if you remember and know who the man was. Let men all fear Fortune, yet you will make one remark: "Fuscus has the epitaph and tomb that belong to death. The stone covers his bones. All is well with him. Away with you, Fortune. We poured our tears for this good man, now (we pour out) wine. We pray that you rest in peace. No one is like you."

    The ages will talk of your conquests.

CIL 2 4315[2]

F̲ar removed from each other in space and time, the protagonists of these two passages appear to share little in common. Cloelia, as Livy tells us in his *History*, was a young maiden who accomplished her feat of daring against the Etruscans in Rome of the early sixth century B.C. Fuscus,

Two individuals deserve top billing here: Ingrid Rowland, for her generous and enthusiastic support for the conference, and Tobias Sperlich, for his untiring assistance in the production of the book. I am indebted to Inge Lyse Hansen, Peter Holliday, Teresa Ramsby, and Francesca Tronchin for their insightful comments on an earlier version of this chapter, and to Marcia Calkowski for providing some crucial references. I would also like to thank Mary Boatwright, Henner von Hesberg, Janet Huskinson, Barbara Kellum, John Pollini, Matthew Roller, and Greg Woolf for sharing with me their work prepublication or in offprint. None should be held responsible for the views expressed here or for whatever errors may remain.

[1] (6) Ergo ita honorata virtute, feminae quoque ad publica decora excitatae, et Cloelia virgo una ex obsidibus, cum castra Etruscorum forte haud procul ripa Tiberis locata essent, frustrata custodes, dux agminis virginum inter tela hostium Tiberim tranavit, sospitesque omnes Romam ad propinquos restituit . . . (11) pace redintegrata Romani novam in femina virtutem novo genere honoris, statua equestri, donavere; in summa Sacra Via fuit posita virgo insidens equo (trans. M. Roller; Roller 2004, 29).

[2] D(is) M(anibus) / Factionis Venetae Fusco sacra- / vimus aram de nostro, certi stu- / diosi et bene amantes; ut sci- / rent cuncti monimentum / et pigus amoris. Integra / fama tibi, laudem cur- / sus meruisti; certasti / multis, nullum pauper timu- / isti; invidiam passus sem- / per fortis tacuisti: pul- / chre vixisti, fato morta- / lis obisti. Quisquis homo / es, quaeres talem. Subsiste / viator, perlege, si memor / es. Si nosti, quis fuerit vir, / fortunam metuant omnes, / dices tamen unum: Fus- / cus habet titulos mor- / tis, habet tumulum. Con- / tegit ossa lapis, bene habet / fortuna, valebis. Fundimus / insonti lacrimas, nunc vi- / na. Precamur, ut iaceas pla- / cide. Nemo tui similis. / Τοὺς σοὺς ἀγῶνας αἰὼν λαλήσει (trans. E. Courtney; Courtney 1995, 321–22, no. 112).

as his tombstone records, was an aged charioteer who raced with bravery at the circus in Tarragona in the second century A.D.[3] These biographical differences notwithstanding, their narratives share structural and conceptual parallels that speak to a larger, cultural process in which both participate: exemplarity.

The recursive tendency of Romans to recognize mythical and historical figures, actions, or events as *exempla* (or "role models," as we translate it here) was a characteristic cultural habit. Rome's literary and material culture was thick with precedent, its inscriptions and art signposting individuals and acts that the populace was enjoined to imitate in their own lives. Such role models were drawn from the contemporary and culturally familiar as well as the distant past and culturally remote, yet all were seen as bridging the gap between cultures and time frames. Seneca, for instance, advised Romans to "turn to better men: live with the Catos, with Laelius, with Tubero. But if it pleases you to live with the Greeks also, associate with Socrates, with Zeno . . ."[4] Although the preferences of elite adult males are by far the best attested, *exempla* were selected by all classes, ages, and genders. Where the nobility could turn inward into their homes, finding in their ancestral masks reflections of their own inborn greatness, those lower down the social ladder looked outward to Rome's rugged icons of masculinity, gladiators and charioteers—the "Marlboro Men" of their day.[5] And for the young as well as the old, *exempla* were a source of stability and comfort in the midst of headlong change. The ideals that they embodied found expression in diverse media: works of art, literature, and inscribed *monumenta* provided a lasting means for their glorification, while more ephemeral forms—triumphs, funerals, and other rhetorical set pieces—answered the needs of Rome's spectacle-driven society. Much like the great men of the past who paraded through Livy's *History*, the statues of the *summi viri* that filled the porticoes of the Forum of Augustus cast a long shadow over the city's inhabitants, especially its well-heeled youth. But there were other, less visible models too, ones that bore only fugitive traces or lay hidden in less familiar corners of the empire, that also prospered. *Exempla* were, in short, implicated in diverse aspects of Roman everyday life.

The mix of traditions out of which Rome's role models were fashioned, the media through which they were deployed, and the conditions under which they thrived (or faltered) are the subject of this book. The papers collected here seek out the *exemplum* across a broad range of genres, contexts, and periods and in this way probe the catholicity of its understanding within Roman culture. In so doing, this volume's central aim is not to push for a new orthodoxy in the study of exemplarity but rather to lay claim to a wider evidentiary base and diversity of approach than scholars have traditionally attempted. This introductory chapter places the volume within its wider academic context through discussion of its method, background, and content.

Between Role Modeling and Exemplarity

Before turning to the evidence of exemplarity in ancient Roman culture, it is useful to scrutinize the origins of the terminology employed here and to take stock of the theoretical and conceptual work that it performs. The term "role model" has assumed a prominent place in our cultural lexicon for more than half a century now, becoming a catchword in debates about multiculturalism and the

[3] Alföldy 1975, 238, no. 445, pl. 82:2.

[4] *Ep.* 104.21–22: "Ad meliores transi: cum Catonibus vive, cum Laelio, cum Tuberone. Quod si convivere etiam Graecis iuvat, cum Socrate, cum Zenone versare" (trans. L. Motto;

Motto 2000, 137). Her various *exempla* are collected in Motto 2000, 137 n. 31; cf. also Codoner 2005.

[5] Gleason 1999, 69–70, and see further below.

cult of celebrities, among others.[6] The range of individuals characterized as role models in modern society also ranges widely, from traditional figures of authority, such as heads of state, to iconic presences who loom large in the (pop-)cultural landscape, such as Barbie.[7] And while the concept is decidedly North American in origin, it is not without its analogues in other cultures, such as the French *modèle* or the German *Vorbild*.[8]

The American sociologist Robert Merton coined the term "role model" in a 1957 study of the socialization of medical students.[9] His formulation of this concept must be understood within the larger framework of his (structural) functionalist approach to social theory. Following Merton, an individual does not possess a single status and single role in society's structure; rather, society is made up of interrelated statuses and roles. Status can be explained as one's particular position in society, while a role is the behavior expected of occupants of a particular status. One's roles are oriented toward "reference groups," the larger categories or groups of people in society to which individuals compare themselves (but to which they may not necessarily belong). So for any given status (e.g., parent, educator), one assumes an array of roles calibrated to meet the specific, individual set of expectations of the reference groups in his or her orbit (e.g., children, colleagues). This is the essence of Merton's theory of the "role-set": that an individual has a status to which is attached the role or patterns of behavior expected by his or her respective reference groups.

Reference group theory leads directly to the concept of a role model, as the former investigates "the determinants and consequences of those processes of evaluation and self-appraisal in which the individual takes the values or standards of other individuals and groups as a comparative frame of reference."[10] As this passage makes clear, Merton understands "reference group" as shorthand for *both* a group and a particular "reference individual." However, he regards the latter as conceptually different from a "role model." For where reference individuals are identified with *completely*, in all of their multiple roles, role models are identified with in a more *restricted* sense, with only one (or two) roles selected for emulation. Thus "emulation of a peer, a parent or a public figure may be restricted to limited segments of their behavior and values and this can be usefully described as adoption of a role model. Or, emulation may be extended to a wider array of behaviors and values of these persons who can then be described as reference individuals."[11] So, for example, one may emulate an athletic hero for his particular skill in the arena, or one may want to assume that athlete's entire persona, to be identical to him in every aspect. In some instances, role models may develop into reference individuals, the initial identification with one role (e.g., musical ability, athletic skill) expanding into full identification with the totality of roles (i.e., to "be" him or her). But to reiterate, a role model is defined as "a person whose behavior *in a particular role* is imitated

---

[6] Multiculturalism: Allen 1994; media icons: Tierney 2001.

[7] Cf. Quan 1997, 122: "you did not have to own a Barbie to be touched by her, to know her as part of your childhood landscape to emulate her."

[8] Both of these words admit several degrees of interpretation and thus are not understood here to be strictly the same. For instance, as used in German, the concept of a role model has two distinct levels of meaning: pattern or template, in the sense of L. E. Baumer's *Vorbilder und Vorlagen. Studien zu klassischen Frauenstatuen und ihrer Verwendung für Reliefs und Statuetten des 5. und 4. Jahrhunderts vor Christus* (Baumer 1977), and exemplar, as in D. Michel's work *Alexander als Vorbild für Pompeius, Caesar und Marcus Antonius* (Michel

1967). However, the essential meaning exists in both cases and can be seen by, among other examples, the publication of Siegfried Lenz's (1976) autobiography *Das Vorbild* as *An Exemplary Life* or Tardy and Vallée's (1985) collection *Femmes: images, modèles* as *Women: Images, Role Models*.

[9] Merton, Reader, and Kendall 1957; Merton elaborates on this concept in his later work, *Social Theory and Social Structure* (Merton 1968, 302–3), from which this discussion is principally drawn. See Kendall 1975 for the theory's development since its original conception.

[10] Merton 1968, 355–56.

[11] Merton 1968, 357.

by others."[12] In this sense, it can be distinguished from its closest English relative, an exemplar, which can be defined as "a pattern; an example to; an example to be imitated."[13]

While the meaning of an *exemplum* in ancient Rome bears appreciable similarities to a modern "role model," there are also differences to be considered.[14] Scholars of the ancient world, including many of the contributors to this volume, consider an *exemplum* to be "something that was or could be copied; in Latin the word came to mean specifically a famous story or action or character that is held up as a specimen to others."[15] Similarly, in her study *Livy's Exemplary History*, Jane Chaplin treats an *exemplum* as "any specific citation of an event or an individual that is intended to serve as a guide to conduct [and offers] an opportunity to learn from the past."[16] In her analysis of mythological sarcophagi, Dagmar Grassinger notes the moralizing tenor of *exempla*, which she defines as "models or patterns of fixed characters, virtues or moral values. . . . They are explaining an ideal code of conduct in Roman society and, thus, have a normative character."[17] The moral aspect is also stressed by Alain Gowing, who in *Empire and Memory: The Representation of the Roman Republic in Imperial Culture* refers to them as "characters from the past whose deeds have been invested with certain moral authority, the use of which lay at the center of Roman thinking about ethics and morality."[18]

These definitions, which are taken from literary, historical, and art historical works, throw up a number of significant similarities and differences between Roman *exempla* and modern "role models" worth highlighting here. Both are (usually) applied in a restricted sense, so that "a person compared to one of the mythological [or historical] heroes is regarded only in one aspect to be *like* this hero."[19] They also both have a normative character and thus function as agents of social cohesion, the "motivated assimilation of the norms of the group or the standards of the group [acting] as a basis for self-appraisal."[20] But where the term "role model" carries a positive connotation,[21] an *exemplum* embraces a fuller spectrum of behavior, as it includes both "models of exemplary behavior and deterrent cases of reckless conduct";[22] an *exemplum* encompasses an *event* or *action* as well as an individual, reinforcing its narrative form and didactic function;[23] and an *exemplum* looks both backward and forward, as it "is deployed as a means of understanding, negotiating, and representing past and present alike."[24] It is this last aspect that affords perhaps

---

[12] Following Merriam-Webster. The obituaries that appeared after Robert Merton's death on 23 February 2003, less than a month before the conference in Rome, call attention to the way in which many of the terms that he coined (e.g., self-fulfilling prophecy) have passed into general use and resultingly have become more diffuse in meaning (e.g., see Holton 2004). A role model, for instance, is commonly understood as "any person who is an example to others" (cf. Wikipedia). There is not space here, however, for exploring all of the different shades of meaning that this term has come to assume since its coinage.

[13] Needham 1985, 1, following the definition of Samuel Johnson.

[14] On *exempla* generally, see Berlioz and David 1980; Skidmore 1996, 3–21; Chaplin 2000, 1–31.

[15] Kraus and Woodman 1997, 56.

[16] Chaplin 2000, 3.

[17] Grassinger 1994, 91, 92; see also Koortbojian 1995, 34–38,

who discusses them in the context of sarcophagi as well.

[18] Gowing 2005, 16.

[19] Grassinger 1994, 92.

[20] Merton 1968, 354.

[21] Merton does discuss the phenomena of positive and negative reference *groups*, acknowledging that the latter are little studied (Merton 1968, 354f.). The concept of a negative reference *individual* or idol (i.e., villain), however, has only recently been taken up; see Melnick 1998.

[22] D'Ambra 1993, 104.

[23] However, the reading of "individual" here as necessarily human is clearly no longer a given, as the term "role model" has gained elasticity through description of inanimate objects (e.g., dolls).

[24] Kraus 2005, 186.

the most salient distinction between role models and *exempla* for a contemporary audience since, as Suzanne Dixon notes in this volume, "cautionary examples are meat and drink to modern mass media but are seldom drawn from history."[25]

We can delineate still further gradients of meaning to this cultural practice by turning to Matthew Roller's "model of exemplary discourse," the most theoretically explicit approach yet to *exempla*.[26] Like other scholarship in this area, his study builds on the long-standing (and primarily) philological interest in the topic.[27] But in contrast to the majority of that work, his approach reaches out to social history and cultural studies. Roller's four-part model, which links "actions, audiences, values and memory," presents a comprehensive means for evaluating role models in all sectors of Roman society (i.e., not only among its much-studied elite core).[28] According to his scheme, an action is defined as something "held to be consequential for the Roman community at large, and admitting of ethical categorization—that is, regarded as embodying (or conspicuously failing to embody) crucial social values";[29] an audience consists of "eyewitnesses who observe this action, place it in a suitable ethical category (e.g., *virtus* or *pietas*, or *gratia*), and judge it 'good' or 'bad' in that category";[30] commemoration "must be not only of the action, but of its consequences to the community, and of the ethical evaluation it received from the primary audience. Commemoration occurs by means of a *monument*, a device that calls the deed to memory; monuments include narratives, statues, scars or other bodily marks, toponyms, cognomina, and even rituals, to name just a few";[31] and lastly, imitation, by which "any spectator to such a deed, whether primary or secondary, is enjoined to strive to replicate or surpass the deed himself, to win similar renown and related social capital—or, for negative examples, to avoid replicating an infamous deed."[32] Within this classificatory system there are still further nuances (especially as concerns the audience), many of which will be teased out throughout the course of this chapter.

The basic elements of Roller's scheme can be traced through the biographies of the two individuals who opened this chapter, the *virgo* Cloelia and *agitator* Fuscus. First, both individuals perform exemplary *actions* that associate them with Rome's cardinal values, from Cloelia's display of courage (*virtus*) to Fuscus's unwavering fortitude (*fortis*); an *audience* consequently recognizes the virtue of their actions, from Cloelia's Etruscan enemies and fellow Romans to Fuscus's compatriots; this recognition takes lasting form through monumental *commemoration*, both in the written (Livy's text, Fuscus's inscription) and visual record (Cloelia's statue, Fuscus's altar);[33] and, lastly, their *monumenta* (both textual and plastic) enlist the reader/viewer to *emulate* their virtues ("halt, traveller, read . . ."). Implicit in the inscription praising Fuscus's strength of character, for instance, is the suggestion that, for those who imitate his behavior, his epic-like *gloria* ("the ages will talk of your conquests") can in turn become their own.[34] Similarly, just as Cloelia was inspired into action by Mucius's bravery, so the public retelling of her story in image and text will inspire other Romans

---

[25] Dixon in this volume, p. 59.

[26] Roller 2004.

[27] Seen in such early work as Litchfield 1914 or Kornhardt 1936 (though the latter is not cited by Roller).

[28] Roller 2004, 4.

[29] Roller 2004, 4.

[30] Roller 2004, 5.

[31] Roller 2004, 5.

[32] Roller 2004, 5.

[33] The socle on Fuscus's altar appears originally to have been decorated but is now badly deteriorated. We can only speculate as to whether or not its decoration included a portrait of the deceased.

[34] Fuscus's inscription quotes from the verses of Ovid and Vergil and includes various epigraphical commonplaces; see further Rossetti 1999, 234–35.

to act accordingly. In this way, both stories perpetuate the cycle of emulation in which each generation draws upon old heroes in fashioning new ones.[35]

Both Merton's theory of role modeling and Roller's model of exemplary discourse offer two
useful and thought-provoking frameworks for approaching Roman exemplarity. While this volume
is informed throughout by a variety of theoretical approaches, its contributions cannot be said to
adhere to any single definition of exemplarity. Rather, the chapters represent a composite of approaches that are colored by the differing disciplinary traditions out of which their authors write.
An *exemplum* is therefore defined at some points broadly, as "an individual who displays notable
qualities worthy of imitation,"[36] and at other points particularly, as a figure meant "to offer a collective example to the Christian community in terms of beliefs and the conduct of their lives."[37] These
and other definitions employed here reflect the plurality of Roman society and the varied place and
wide scope of *exempla* within it. For the purposes of this volume as a whole, however, we can define
an *exemplum* as a model for imitation which provides contemporary society with lessons that are
informed by the past, inscribed into public memory, and catalyzed through replication.[38]

In summary, it is clear that an *exemplum* and a role model are not, strictly speaking, one and the
same.[39] However, having sketched the semantic and conceptual differences between them above,
we consider role modeling to be among those "interpretive tools that seem more or less familiar
to the ancient cultures that generated them."[40] We therefore employ these terms interchangeably
throughout this volume.[41]

Monuments, Memory, and the Mos Maiorum

Having clarified the terms of the discussion, we can now turn to the nature of the evidence.
That evidence, as mentioned above, is diverse in character as it encompasses permanent works
as well as ephemeral events, each with their own audience, context, and date to contend with.
In order to represent some measure of that diversity, this section forgoes offering an exhaustive
historiography of exemplarity, which can be found in both past and recent literature,[42] and instead
surveys some of its fundamental manifestations in Roman culture: literary works[43] (especially

---

[35] Cf. Habinek 2000.

[36] Dixon in this volume, p. 57.

[37] Huskinson in this volume, p. 288.

[38] It is the *performative nature* of the *exemplum* that bears
emphasis. E.g., Hölscher in this volume, p. 47: "taking these
[statuary] types as role models means that they imply some
performative qualities." Cf. Bartsch 2006, chap. 3.

[39] In addition to the issues outlined above, see also Suzanne Dixon's contribution, where she discusses how
"the superficial similarities obscure profound differences,
for the more public aspects of modern role-modeling are
based on presumptions of individualism and opportunity
that seem alien to ancient social attitudes"; Dixon in this
volume, p. 59.

[40] Bartsch 2006, 13.

[41] This is, of course, already common practice in classical
studies, and countless examples could be cited in support,
including studies in art history (Bergmann 1995, 89), literature (Ball 2002, 51), philosophy (Inwood 1995, 66), political
history (Bosworth 1999, 2), social history (Gray-Fow 1988,
184), etc. This applies in a Greek context as well: e.g.,
Siropoulos 2001.

[42] Berlioz and David 1980; Skidmore 1996, 3–21; Chaplin
2000, 1–31. The literature cited here and in what follows is
drawn mostly, but not exclusively, from the last decade.

[43] On Livy and Valerius Maximus, see below. Ammianus
Marcellinus: Wittchow 2001. Apuleius: Babo 2000. Cicero:
Bücher 2006; Lowrie 2007; Lowrie forthcoming a; Lowrie
forthcoming b. Pliny the Younger: Methy 2003. Plutarch:
Duff 2000; Perez Jimenez 2002. Propertius: Gazich 1999;

historiography[44] and epic[45]) and manuals of instruction, object-heirlooms (*imagines*) and rites of ancestral veneration (*laudatio funebris*), and works of sculptural commemoration (*monumenta*). As the thrust of this narrative should be familiar to most, a few brief examples will suffice.

Exempla, as Skidmore notes, were "the basic means of moral instruction in the ancient world from the earliest times."[46] The importance of such *paradeigmata* within Greek culture is well documented.[47] Studies of their appearance and function within Roman culture have focused upon their roots in republican ancestral custom, the *mos maiorum*,[48] its seat, the aristocratic household,[49] and its backdrop, the city's public spaces.[50] The conventional starting point to their discussion is provided by Livy,[51] who in the preface to his history declares that

> The study of history is beneficial and profitable for the following reasons. You behold the lessons of every historical event as clearly as if they were displayed on a stone monument. From these you may choose for yourself and for your own community what to imitate. From these you may decide what to avoid as shameful in cause or shameful in result. . . . No state was ever greater than Rome, none was more pious or richer in fine examples.
>
> *A History of Rome* 1, preface 10 and 11[52]

Here Livy sets out the ethical and social benefits that accrue from the close observance of history through the lens of *exempla*. For him, history is a narrative of striking paradigms that offers one moral orientation throughout the life course, from the pangs of youth to the vicissitudes of old age, and thus acts much as a map guides one in which path to follow (or reject).[53] But to take the "lessons" of history as one's guide is not to be beholden to the past; rather it is—as the Trojans learn in the *Aeneid*—to repeat it *"with a difference."*[54] As Chaplin notes, this is a process best characterized as a dialogue: "the past has lessons, but the student takes an active part in determining their relevance to his circumstances."[55] These lessons, however much they may assume an effect of permanence ("as if they were displayed on a stone monument"), are in fact malleable, easily suited to contemporary circumstance. Thus, during less salubrious times, like Livy's own, the tendency to seek refuge in the past through *exempla* became all the more acute, as did the historian's task to replenish it with new

Lowrie forthcoming c. Seneca: Mauch 1997; Motto 2000; Codoner 2005. Statius: Fantham 1999. Tacitus: Ash 1999 and Alston in this volume. On various matters literary-historical: Panitschek 1989; Bell 1994; Imbert 2002.

[44] Eigler et al. 2003; Roller forthcoming.

[45] E.g., Spentzou's contribution in this volume, with additional literature.

[46] Skidmore 1996, 3.

[47] Demoen 1997; Stewart 2005; cf. Styka 1991, on *exemplaria graeca* in a Roman context.

[48] Hölkeskamp 2004 [1996], 169–98; Linke and Stemmler 2000; and Hölscher 2004, on its transformation from the late republic onward.

[49] Hales 2003, 40–60; Stein-Hölkeskamp 2006; senatorial homes: von Hesberg 2005.

[50] Hölscher 2001; Hölkeskamp 2004, 137–68; Walter 2004;

Gowing 2005; Stein-Hölkeskamp and Hölkeskamp 2006; Boschung 2007.

[51] Generally, see Chaplin 2000, with earlier literature; note also Feldherr 1998; Langlands 2006; and Smith 2006, esp. 415–18, where he discusses Livy's vision of the utility of the Roman past.

[52] "Hoc illud est praecipue in cognitione rerum salubre ac frugiferum, omnis te exempli documenta in inlustri posita monumento intueri; inde tibi tuaeque rei publicae quod imitere capias, inde foedum inceptu, foedum exitu, quod vites . . . nulla umquam res publica nec maior nec sanctior nec bonis exemplis ditior fuit . . ." (trans. J. Shelton; Shelton 1998, facing p. 1).

[53] Roman lifecycle: Laurence and Harlow 2002; role models for youth: Daleas 1998; the elderly: Motto 2000.

[54] Quint 1993, 50.

[55] Chaplin 2000, 136.

ones.[56] In his *Histories*, for instance, Tacitus argues that through knowledge of the republic's *bona exempla* and an appreciation of contemporary Flavian role models, the elite could better negotiate their rocky present. As Richard Alston writes here, "Tacitus provided his audience with a new history for the new age, new role models, and a new way of constructing their identity in relation to imperial power and the Roman past."[57]

Besides the well-recognized role models that populated the historiographic and epic narratives, *exempla* also featured as "disembodied" anecdotes in manuals of moral instruction. Such collections, which are first attested in the triumviral period and include works by Nepos, Atticus, Varro, and Frontinus, among others, recall heroes and acts of bravery from Rome's history but largely lack any narrative framework.[58] Yet through their typological arrangement, manuals such as Valerius Maximus's *Memorable Deeds and Sayings* (*Facta et dicta memorabilia*) proved well suited to the needs of the exemplary discourse. That discourse, as Christina Kraus has described it, is a "process of evaluation and imitation [that] happens through thoughtful viewing, that is, spectacle used creatively, as *entertainment and education* at once."[59] The mix of education and entertainment value is stressed repeatedly by ancient commentators, including Quintilian,[60] who remark upon the vivid description (*enargeia*) and rhetorical flourish required for the successful communication of *exempla* (Valerius Maximus himself is thought to have been a professional rhetorician on account of his style).[61] In addition, the taxonomic arrangement of the material into ethical categories served "to free those who want to take an example from the labor of a long search."[62] Like their cousin genres, technical handbooks of this kind were likely intended for use in the schools of rhetoric and meant to inculcate prized social values among elite male Romans.[63] As Margaret Imber notes in her chapter here, exercises such as declamation "allowed Rome's future leaders to master the complexities and contradictions of Roman ideology and Roman practice."[64] And as the *exempla* they contained were seen as key to building character in Romans, the handbooks in which they were compiled also bore the warrant of ancestral custom. Indeed, *The Memorable Deeds and Sayings*, by far the most famous among these, has been characterized by some as a collection of "instant ancestors."[65]

An elite Roman's ancestors were not, of course, made up out of whole cloth or to be encountered only as anecdotes in texts.[66] Rather, they confronted their descendants daily, their "faces" (*imagines*) staring out from the cupboards (*armaria*) within the household atrium.[67] Wax masks of this kind are known to have sat cheek-by-jowl with other representations, including busts

---

[56] Cf. Chaplin 2000, 201: "For a generation undergoing severe dislocation . . . *exempla* had great advantages."

[57] Alston in this volume, p. 154; see also Haynes 2003; Gowing 2005.

[58] Kraus 2005, 197.

[59] Kraus 2005, 188 (my emphasis).

[60] *Inst.* 5.11.1–21; 12.4.1; *Rhet. Her.* 4.49, 62. See further Bloomer 2007.

[61] Valerius Maximus: Bloomer 1992; Guerrini 1994; Skidmore 1996; David 1998; Thurn 2001; Langlands 2006. There is dispute as to the target readership for this volume (bluebloods? social outsiders?) as well as its author's back-

ground, issues for which the limits of space prevent more detailed discussion.

[62] Val. Max. 1.1.1 (trans. M. Roller). See Roller forthcoming.

[63] Connolly 1998; Bloomer 2007.

[64] Imber in this volume, p. 168. See further Gunderson 2003; Schröder and Schröder 2003; Habinek 2004; and Bloomer 2007. On the influence of declamation and panegyric on historiographical narrative, see Kraus 2005.

[65] Kraus 2005, 198 n. 41.

[66] See further the papers collected in Højte 2002.

[67] Flower 1996.

Fig. 1. Marble statue of man with family portraits ("Barberini Togatus*"). From Italy, ca. late first century* B.C. *Palazzo dei Conservatori, Rome, Braccio Nuovo 2392 (© Araldo de Luca/Corbis).*

and statues and painted portraits of the type seen in the Barberini *Togatus* (fig. 1).[68] This marble statue, probably dating to the late first century B.C., depicts a nobleman framed by two ances- tors, one of which he cradles in his hand while the other he embraces on a support. Such kinship between past and present was on display in the house entrance too, where painted family trees (*stemmata*) provided the names and/or images of family members, the most illustrious connected to one another by strings or painted lines. Showcased in this way, ancestors served not only to advertise before his clients and friends an elite patron's "letters-patent of noble descent"[69] but also to impress upon members of the household itself (especially its youngest generation) their charge to realize their familial greatness. As Sallust writes of the ancestral masks, "the memory of great deeds kindles in the breasts of noble men this flame that cannot be quelled until they by their own prowess have equalled the fame and glory of their forefathers."[70] This challenge was reiterated in the rites of the public funeral, where the performative use made of these masks bore witness to the active, dialogic relationship between the generations.[71] Ancestral images of all kinds, then, served as "an external conscience for the present generation and the embodiment

[68] Stewart 2003, 47, 83, 256. The head of the standing figure is ancient but does not belong to this particular piece.

[69] Hanfmann 1973, 266.

[70] *BJ* 4.5–6: "sed memoria rerum gestarum eam flammam

egregiis viris in pectore crescere neque prius sedari, quam virtus eorum famam atque gloriam adaequaverit" (trans. J. C. Rolfe).

[71] Flower 2006a, with full literature; Pollini 2007, 240ff.

of traditional values. . . . They were also elevated as ethical exemplars in just the same manner as the portraits of famous men."[72]

The honorific statues of the *viri illustres*,[73] which likely first began to be erected in the latter part of the fourth century, were the most visible face of aristocratic virtue.[74] For unlike the shadowy figures who crowded the reception rooms of their homes, honorific statues and their texts (*elogia*) addressed the public at large: the inscriptions trumpeting their accomplishments in military and political life,[75] the "veristic" portrait faces brandishing their battle scars and creases of old age.[76] As Brian Rose argues in this volume, the veristic style's depiction of advanced age summoned associations with *dignitas*, thus distinguishing their subjects as role models to their fellow Romans and as morally superior to their enemies. In this way, the portraits "convey the impression of men who valued morals, character, and service to the state above classical ideals of beauty."[77] As Polybius reminds us in his *Histories*, immortality was achieved through such dedication: "accordingly, because the reputation for virtue of good men is continuously being renewed, the glory of those who performed something noble becomes immortal, while the repute of those who performed services for the fatherland becomes well known to many and is transmitted to posterity."[78] Thus, while poets raised bold claims for the immortality of their art,[79] the primacy of plastic works can hardly be overstated: it was statues that offered a highly visible and lasting means of *memoria*, transmitting *exempla* to posterity.[80]

Where their hard-won civic glory allotted aristocrats a special role in Roman society, including the right to a triumph,[81] their statues and other political monuments offered them a means of sedimenting that glory within the very fabric of Rome's exemplary past, its *bedrock*.[82] The expressive potential of works such as statues, for instance, must be understood as arising from not only the sculpted and scripted recollection of their own individual glories but also their juxtaposition with the esteemed ancestors and neighbors who fell along their horizon.[83] Seen together as a collective, these monuments of different eras and types functioned in counterpoint to the rigid annalistic records, forming instead an often haphazard tapestry in which the vicious rivalries of past politicos were belied by the close proximity of their images.[84] The city's topography was therefore stitched together into seamless "seats of memory," its monuments, buildings, and pathways echoing with the

---

[72] Stewart 2003, 256–57. According to a new theory, the procession of the ancestral masks (*pompa imaginum*) and the funeral oration (*laudatio funebris*) of which they were a part should be understood as "attempts to reactualize and extend the impression made by honorific statues with a focus on the family." Rüpke 2006, 274.

[73] On heroes and heroic deeds in the republic, see, e.g., Hölkeskamp 2003; Roller 2004.

[74] Rüpke 2006, 263, with earlier literature.

[75] Frisch 1980.

[76] In addition to the literature cited by Rose in his contribution, see also Kockel 2005 and Pollini 2007, 252ff.

[77] Rose in this volume, p. 102.

[78] 6.54.2: ἐξ ὧν καινοποιουμένης ἀεὶ τῶν ἀγαθῶν ἀνδρῶν τῆς ἐπ' ἀρετῇ φήμης ἀθανατίζεται μὲν ἡ τῶν καλόν τι διαπραξαμένων

εὔκλεια, γνώριμος δὲ τοῖς πολλοῖς καὶ παραδόσιμος τοῖς ἐπιγινομένοις ἡ τῶν εὐεργετησάντων τὴν πατρίδα γίνεται δόξα (trans. J. Pollini); see Pollini 2007, 241.

[79] Texts as monuments: Fowler 2000; Ramsby 2005.

[80] Hölscher 2001, 188–89; Rüpke 2006, 278–81, where he notes that "texts would offer even more possibilities [for achieving immortality], but they would not be as accessible to the general public as poets usually supposed" (279 n. 120) and that "statues embodied social eternity" (279).

[81] Flower 2005; Hölkeskamp 2006; Rüpke 2006.

[82] Hölscher 2001.

[83] See now Sehlmeyer 2000 (not cited in Stewart 2003, which is otherwise the standard work); also Haug 2001, esp. 118ff.

[84] Cf. Edwards 1996, 43; Hemelrijk 2005, 314.

heroic accomplishments and numinous presence of its ancestors (e.g., the "Hut of Romulus").[85] As Edwards suggests, "one might compare the city of Rome, in which buildings of different periods were everywhere juxtaposed, to the funeral of a Roman aristocrat, where living members of the family wore masks to represent prominent figures of previous generations, mingling with one another indifferently across the centuries."[86]

However much the republic's exemplary past may have felt anchored in place, weighted down by centuries-old tradition, its foundation ultimately proved weak. As is well known, the conceptual link between past and present ruptures with the ascension of Rome's first emperor, who insinuates into the center of power an Augustan past (*renovatio*) at the expense of its decaying republican one.[87] From the transfer of the old *viri lustres* from their home on the Capitol to the Field of Mars[88] to the increasingly "claustrophobic presence" of the emperor felt in historiographical narrative,[89] Augustus effectively wrests control of Rome's role models and, as a consequence, rewrites its collective memory.[90] With his "cultural revolution,"[91] the emperor situates himself as the "convergence of exemplary times," selectively channeling the role models from Rome's past and coercively deploying new ones for its future.[92] In his new pantheon, Aeneas and Romulus were elevated alongside other *summi viri* as symbols of eternal virtues (e.g., *pietas*), while the emperor and his family were promoted as their contemporary inheritors.[93] These and other actions by the emperor led to what Kraus terms a "representational crisis of empire"—that is, the question of how to represent an autocrat (exemplar) within the conventions set by a republican historiographical tradition (*exempla*)—an issue with which successive generations of subjects were forced repeatedly to grapple (see Alston's contribution here).[94] Kraus's analysis of how this new imperial system effects a change to the very structure of exemplary discourse is worth citing at length:

> When history's gaze is more or less forcibly directed at the emperor—especially (but not exclusively) to the emperor functioning as positive *role model*—the prescriptive function of *exempla* becomes dominant. The flexibility inherent in the *exemplum* thus becomes threatened or even lost, the audience's independent response to the spectacular suggestiveness of exemplarity is repressed or redirected, and its constructive use profoundly compromised.[95]

The redefinition of exemplarity in these terms results in an enduring ideological tug-of-war, as citizens are caught between accepting or rejecting the emperor as "the only *exemplum* in town, the model of all ideal leadership."[96] So where Pliny's *Panegyricus* labors in the fiction of a continuous connection between the republican past and imperial present, Tacitus's *Histories* and *Annales* offer a radical critique of state policy on account of the ideological break that it had wrought. In addition, this

---

[85] Memory: Flashar 1996; Walter 2004; Gowing 2005; and, more generally, Larmour and Spencer 2007; destruction of memory: Varner 2000; Flower 2006b.

[86] Edwards 1996, 42–43.

[87] The classic study is that of Zanker 1988; see also Wallace-Hadrill 2000; Haug 2001; Gowing 2005, 132ff.; Hölscher 2005, esp. 255ff.

[88] Haug 2001, 115.

[89] Kraus 2005, 182.

[90] Dueck 2000.

[91] Wallace-Hadrill 1997.

[92] Kraus 2005, 194–95; cf. Eder 1990.

[93] On the *summi viri*: Spannagel 1999; Itgenshorst 2004; on the place of Troy in Augustan art and literature: Barchiesi 2005, esp. 296ff.; Bettini 2006; Rose in this volume.

[94] Kraus 2005, 184; cf. Roller 2001.

[95] Kraus 2005, 188 (my emphasis).

[96] Kraus 2005, 186.

"imperial exemplary pressure" is applied by other members of its house and its message reverberates well outside Rome, as Suzanne Dixon discusses in this volume with reference to Pompeii.[97]

Thus, while we have earlier defined an *exemplum* as informed by the past, its lessons validated by tradition and inscribed into public memory, it bears reminding that those lessons and their standard-bearers were open to revision and rescripting in the present. For beginning with Augustus's reign, many of the characters familiar from the republican exemplary canon faded into the background and fell into disuse, their replacements drawn from amongst a new, imperial cast.

Finding an Audience

If we see Roman exemplarity as primarily constituted by the *mos maiorum* and the mental and physical spaces that it inhabited (memory and monuments), then we are left to interrogate the issue of audience to which Kraus and Roller refer above. For the picture of Roman exemplarity sketched thus far, which relies on our richest and most prominent source material (elite custom), is an admittedly lopsided one. But if we hold that exemplary discourse in fact "encompasses all of Roman society, from the loftiest aristocrats to the humblest peasants, laborers and slaves," then how can we recover the full range of their voices?[98] In this section, I outline briefly two ways in which the scholarly picture of exemplarity is changing, both in our methods as well as our objects of study. As a result of these changes, our picture is broadening, the conventional role models of earlier work yielding to new and less familiar ones.

IMAGE VERSUS TEXT

As the majority of the scholarship cited in the preceding section makes clear, *exempla* have been primarily studied through a vast supply of texts, be they works of literature or inscriptions.[99] This tendency continues to be supplemented by new work in this area, which picks apart conventional sources in new ways and also explores undercapitalized corpora. For instance, in his forthcoming *Untersuchungen zum "Exemplum" als normbildender Größe im klassischen römischen Recht unter spezieller Berücksichtigung kaiserlicher Entscheide*, Nikolaus Benke collects and analyzes a vast body of underused material that bears witness to the normative influence *exempla* exerted upon Roman life through their enshrinement in law.[100] That such material is crucial to the enterprise of under-standing exemplarity goes without saying. However, in continuing to pursue a largely text-based approach, we run the risk of overlooking other types of evidence that may prove equally valuable to our understanding of this discourse. In short, there are two issues upon us here: first, that we must recognize the limits of the literary evidence, as its perspective is planted firmly in positions of social and economic privilege and thus bias; second, that visual evidence—while beset by similar problems—can offer us complementary as well as competing perspectives onto exemplarity.

The first issue requires little elaboration here, as it is well known that Latin literature principally represents the interests and preoccupations of its patrons, producers, and readers, the nobility. As

---

[97] Dixon in this volume, p. 66. On Livia/Concordia, see further Flory 1984.

[98] Roller 2004, 6.

[99] As Roller acknowledges in his study, the stories of Horatius Cocles and Cloelia are paradigmatic of exemplary discourse

not least because they are well documented, allowing them to function in turn "as models for how other, less richly at-tested exemplary figures might—ought to—have functioned socially and ethically, and might be seen to function, had more monuments survived" (Roller 2004, 52).

[100] Benke forthcoming; cf. also Benke 1995.

Thomas Habinek notes, "many of the characteristics of Latin literature can be attributed to its production by and for an elite that sought to maintain and expand its dominance over other sectors of the population through reference to an authorizing past."[101] This means, of course, that the role models that appear within these narratives are prescriptive, predominantly retailing the values of their elite readers and in some cases speaking directly to their contemporary situation. This is nicely brought out in Effi Spentzou's contribution to this volume, where she discusses how in *Punica*, Silius Italicus's retelling of the Second Punic War, Hannibal surprisingly surfaces as the epic's lead figure through his parallelism with Aeneas. Spentzou explains this role reversal and Silius Italicus's habit of blurring Roman epic's traditional polarities (Roman versus barbarian, virtue versus vice) as products of the writer's social position: a senator living in an "Age of Monarchy" who voiced his insecurities by eulogizing republican *libertas*. As she notes, Silius's "'exemplary' Roman exists in the aftermath of recent traumas that are still present in the collective as well as personal memory."[102] Thus, while not all readers were noble, their texts were by and large heavily invested in an elite perspective, one paramount to our understanding of their exemplary message.

This can be said to be less the case with works of art and architecture since, taken collectively, they represent a wider cross-section of Roman society. To be sure, objects and monuments are also burdened by questions of elite bias: so much of the material that art historians and archaeologists are traditionally drawn to is the product of noble patronage and therefore conditions how we "read" its messages. As Paul Zanker notes, "our interpretations always presuppose a conventional spectator who interprets the message in the way intended by the patron. We do not consider the observations of those who did not share the perspective represented, nor of those who read and deconstructed the message from the point of view of the opposition."[103] That tendency, however, has very much begun to change.[104] John Clarke's recent work, including his chapter here, places the "everyday Roman" in the seat of the critical analyst, offering us quite a different view onto Roman society than that which the elite would have us see, especially in texts.[105] In her contribution to this volume, Shelley Hales elucidates the ways in which the images of Aphrodite and Dionysus and their devices (masks, mirrors) shaped the viewer's experience of the home as a *contested* social space. She argues that by commissioning and displaying these protean deities as decoration for their homes, Roman patrons resisted the closure and polarization encouraged by moralist rhetoric in favor of the instability and frisson of ambiguity.[106] Questions of intentionality are equally crucial in the world of the dead. As Inge Lyse Hansen discusses here, the Muse and philosopher figures depicted on sarcophagi express not only inward, mirrored gestures toward one another but outward gestures of communication with the living viewers of the tomb: the internal dialogue between Muse and man is mirrored by an external dialogue between viewer and *exempla*.[107] The sarcophagus is therefore a "transitive" artwork: it is completed only by means of the viewer's presence and participation.[108]

[101] Habinek 1998, 3.

[102] Spentzou in this volume, p. 144.

[103] Zanker 1994, 289: "nos interprétations présupposent toujours un spectateur conventionnel qui voudrait interpréter le message dans le sens recherché par le commanditaire. Nous le pensons pas au regard de celui qui ne partageait pas le point de vue représenté, ni à celui qui lisait le message avec les yeux de l'opposant, et déconstruisait ce message."

[104] Cf. Zanker's own most recent contribution in this new direction: Neudecker and Zanker 2005.

[105] Clarke 2003; for the big picture: Kampen 2003.

[106] Cf. also Muth 1998, on mosaics; Elsner 1999, on painting.

[107] On gender roles as represented on sarcophagi in late antiquity, see Ewald 2005.

[108] Cf. Shearman 1992, on the concept of the transitive. On the importance of the role of the viewer to sarcophagi, see now Bielfeldt 2003.

None of this or related work, which seeks to rethink the usual hierarchy of viewing Roman art, denies the relevance of the traditional objects and monuments of our study or obscures the powerful hold that they exerted over public as well as private life.[109] Rather, it simply compels us to consider them and their exemplary messages from a wider array of perspectives. As Peter Holliday and Michael Koortbojian have stressed in recent studies of funerary and state art, it was through their generality that *exempla* gained such wide currency and authority in the republic.[110] Whether communicated through painting, "historical" relief sculpture, or coins, exemplary messages about *virtus*, *pietas*, or *concordia* could be reproduced to speak to a broad range of social classes.[111] In his chapter here, Tonio Hölscher discusses how imperial values were mass-marketed to a diverse audience in similar fashion: there were degrees of "permeability" and "exclusiveness" to these images, some of which admitted close association to the state (i.e., emperor) by way of the viewer's performance of select roles.[112] So on sarcophagi, for instance, Romans outside the imperial family symbolized their shared values (e.g., *concordia*) with him through imitation of the gestures and postures that he adopted on state monuments and media.[113] While we may question the sincerity of these acts of emulation, the benefits to be had from their observance were clearly understood at all rungs of Rome's society, especially by those seeking integration into it. As Barbara Kellum argues in a forthcoming study of wealthy Roman freedmen of the first century A.D., "more often than not, it was the emperor himself whom freedpeople emulated, staging a presentation of themselves *representationally* playing all the roles: emperor and former slave, aristocrat and commoner, worker and bon vivant."[114]

In summary, images offer us the means to deprivilege the literary sources and reinstate the voice of a wider cross-section of Roman society. In doing so, we are better able to appreciate how the exemplary impulse played out in diverse ways through Roman culture: state art and architecture, for instance, encouraged the fulfillment of prescribed roles, but these roles might be contested or subverted to suit the needs of members within its highly pluralistic society.[115] We can redress the tendency of earlier scholars to subordinate the visual to the verbal by remaining sensitive to the advantages (and biases) of both.[116]

MODEL ROMANS?

It is a commonplace in the literature on *exempla* that they were generated by the elite, for the elite. But if it was the responsibility of the *nobiles*, those who possessed ancestors, "to know, imitate and transmit the *mos maiorum*,"[117] what role could the middling or lower classes play beyond respectful observance and imitation? Were they compelled to share in *only* the same role models as the elite, *exempla* that must have often appeared to sit at a distant remove from their own lives? As Suzanne

[109] This is not to overlook the fact that there is also work being done with textual sources in this same direction: e.g., various papers collected in De Blois et al. 2003; Weber and Zimmermann 2003.

[110] Holliday 2005, on the Tomb of the Statilii; Koortbojian 2002, on the Temple of Victory.

[111] E.g., Koortbojian 2002, 41: "As such an *exemplum*, the banquet scene offered a quotidian vehicle for the representation of Roman values, as this particular historical event was employed to give both form and substance to a general sense of what the Romans understood as *virtus*."

[112] Cf. Aldrete 1999.

[113] E.g., on coins: Noreña 2001.

[114] Kellum forthcoming; for an epigraphic perspective, see Witzmann 2003.

[115] This is admittedly painting with a broad brush, overlooking plurality among the elite themselves: see Dench 2005 and Farney 2007.

[116] See further Smith 2002 and Kampen 2003; also Rives 2006, for interdisciplinary approaches, including Roman art. Cf. also Storey 1999 and Laurence 2004 on the relation between archaeology and text.

[117] Wallace-Hadrill 1997, 13.

Dixon asks, "Did the common man, woman, or child perceive them as something to live up to?"[118] This raises the fundamental problem of how to classify individuals within an exemplary framework who, despite their age, gender, or social status, nonetheless achieved wider recognition and thus became, in a less conventional sense, exemplary Romans. The subjects of children, women, and slaves offer complementary sources of evidence for weighing *exempla* from a subaltern perspective.[119]

Children offer a logical starting point, as it is they who embody the values and self-understanding that underwrite any given society.[120] In this sense, the study of their funerary commemoration can prove highly illuminating, as is seen in the texts and imagery of a group of altars, urns, and *stelai* from the first and early second centuries A.D. in Rome.[121] On these monuments, parents use idealizing representations and gilded language in order to recast their prematurely deceased children as mature, model Romans. Deprived of the opportunity to make their mark on the urban stage, these infants and children appear instead as statesmen or soldiers, outfitted in ceremonial togas or military cloaks.[122] On the funerary stele to Marcus Valerius Masculus and Marcus Valerius Verus, for instance, the brothers are seen in miniature above the dedicatory inscription, which lists their ages—4 years, 3 months and 20 days and 3 years, 4 months and 21 days, respectively (fig. 2).[123] Despite their youth, their full-length bodies are depicted nude with cloaks draped over their left shoulders, the folds of which they grasp in their left hands. This iconography ascribes mature qualities to the boys but with a poignancy and economy that the text could not: namely, that these "most dutiful sons" were already in possession of the virtues befitting soldiers and that, given the chance, they would have realized those roles in heroic fashion.[124] In modeling the images of their children on adult roles in this way, parents enunciated the ideal qualities that Roman males ought to embody—*virtus*, *pietas*, and learning.[125]

Yet in spite of the rigid rhetoric advocating a clear separation between male and female gender roles, evidence would suggest that these roles and the respective honors that accrued to them were, in practice, negotiable. For instance, as Eve D'Ambra explores in this volume, images of *virtus* were not confined to boys and men alone.[126] Her contribution concentrates on a relatively small but remarkable corpus of funerary altars, portrait busts, and statuary in which the deceased is depicted in the guise of the hunting goddess Diana. On the cusp of assuming normative sexual and social roles as brides and matrons, these young women are memorialized instead as maiden huntresses who take inspiration from a figure known for her emasculate appearance and socially transgressive behavior (*virginitas severa*).[127] D'Ambra argues that "the deceased girls were endowed with *virtus* in compensation for the loss of their lives or for their unfulfilled state as virgins . . . [they] have bypassed the

---

[118] Dixon in this volume, p. 60.

[119] For recent approaches to these groups as a unity, see Joshel and Murnaghan 1998; Dixon 2001; Balch and Osiek 2003.

[120] Roman children: Daleas 1998; Rawson 2003a; Uzzi 2005.

[121] These commemorate children who died aged four years or younger: see King 2003 and Huskinson 2005.

[122] Toga: Kleiner 1987, 87, 195–96, no. 68, pl. 40. *Chlamys*: Kleiner 1987, 188–89, no. 62, pl. 37; 246–47, no. 108, pl. 61.

[123] Giuliano 1984, 52–53, no. 2.34 (*CIL* 6 28055).

[124] On funerary inscriptions for children, see further King 2000 and McWilliam 2001. For the use of "heroic nudity" in

representing children on funerary monuments, see Kleiner 1987, 188, 247; on this phenomenon in Roman art generally, Hallett 2005.

[125] On epigraphic evidence for "Kinderkarrieren," see Horster 1996. The conceit of the precocious child can be traced in other, later genres as well, such as sarcophagi, which similarly illustrate how children's "short lives had lacked the opportunity to reach the events which celebrated their father's careers, yet they still needed the same role models and chance to display social virtues" (Huskinson 2008).

[126] On *virtus* more generally, see McDonnell 2006.

[127] Ovid *Met.* 3.254–55. For Diana as *exemplum* in Ovid: Schmitzer 2001, esp. 306, 317; and see further Green 2007.

Fig. 2. Funerary stele of Marcus Valerius Masculus and Marcus Valerius Verus. Rome, late first to early second century A.D. *Rome, Museo Nazionale Romano, inv. no. 124572 (© M. King, 2004. Published with kind permission of Ministero per i Beni e le Attività Culturali— Soprintendenza Archeologica di Roma).*

usual accolades accorded to exemplary women and, despite their gender, have been accorded a heroic portrait reserved for daughters who didn't get a chance to live up to their parents' expectations."[128] The depiction of girls as Diana thus enabled them to transcend the borders of gender hierarchy and display military valor like that of Cloelia, another heroic *virgo* and "manly maiden."

Cloelia and other such transgressive Roman women (and men) have been the subject of much study of late because of the way in which they point up contradictions within the seemingly monolithic cast of Roman gender roles.[129] Studies of Roman art, for instance, have called attention to the processes of "transgendered" assimilation, whereby images of imperial women were blended with those of their husbands or images of goddesses were amalgamated with those of emperors through subtle adaptations to their facial features or hairstyles. In his study of this phenomenon in this volume, Eric Varner references both imperial and private works of art in order to illustrate how such agglomerative strategies ran close to the surface at Rome and were not confined to elite commissions alone (seen in statuary, coins, and gemstones). Parallels to this process, a sort of "divine transvestism," can also be traced in Latin literature (e.g., Propertius's Hercules).[130] Like D'Ambra's study, Varner's and related work illustrate how certain female *exempla* were not only resistant to gender categorization but lent unique authority to their users.

While female empowerment clearly exists,[131] we cannot always trust its signs. As Emily Hemelrijk has recently pointed out, Augustus's introduction of public statues for exemplary women was

[128] D'Ambra in this volume, p. 181.

[129] E.g., Cloelia: Hemelrijk 2004, 190ff.; Roller 2004, 28ff. Generally: Hartmann, Hartmann, and Pietzner 2007.

[130] See the papers by Maurizio, Duncan, and Connolly in Stehle 2001; Welch 2004 (on Hercules); note also Corbeill forthcoming.

[131] Späth 1994; D'Ambra 2007.

achieved by a sleight of hand—that is, as part of his bid to manufacture an ideal model of femininity.[132] The monument to Cornelia in the Porticus Octaviae, for instance, functioned in parallel to those of the *summi viri* in the Forum Augustum, except that the former drew especial charge from her juxtaposition with a cautionary example (Tarpeia).[133] Such *exempla* were not extracted from Rome's history alone: as Sarah Pomeroy discusses here, "the famous mothers of Sparta as well as those of their own early and middle republic served as exemplars to 'new-style' Roman women, who left the rearing of their children to outsiders or rejected motherhood completely."[134] The enforcement of these ideal codes of female behavior was particularly felt within the circle of the court, especially toward those whose behavior appeared to challenge the convention of exemplary femininity (e.g., Agrippina Minor, *dux femina*).[135] But even for those who achieved a canonization of sorts, any sense of personality can be lost through the filter of imperial propaganda: the empress Faustina, for instance, has been described as "one of many *silent* 'role models' of history who are commemorated in art but remain unknown as individuals."[136]

The exemplary model that imperial women set, especially as seen in the dress[137] and body language[138] of their statues, was targeted at all levels of Roman society.[139] The *stola*, as Kristina Milnor observes, was "not simply a woman's garment, but a *good* woman's garment, associated not just with female members of the upper classes, but with female members who correctly performed their duties as wives, mothers, daughters and sisters."[140] While women received public praise for their exemplary performance of these roles, it came through literary and artistic representations that depicted them as self-restrained, uniform, and inactive counterparts to their husbands.[141] So where the elaborate iconography, lavish material, and prominent display of female statuary appear to honor and beautify its subjects, the body language and garments of these works serve instead to regulate and disable them (see further Glenys Davies's chapter).[142] These female prototypes spread throughout the empire, but their translation into new contexts often results in a "peculiar duality." As Henner von Hesberg writes of female and familial imagery in the northwest provinces, "provincials definitely hold on to their own forms but, at the same time, accept the paradigms of the existing Roman role models."[143] In this way, the female qualities most highly prized in Roman society, such as

[132] Hemelrijk 2005; see also Severy 2003; Ramsby and Severy 2007.

[133] Woodhull 2003; Ruck 2004.

[134] Pomeroy in this volume, p. 223.

[135] See further the papers in Kunst and Reimer 2000 and Temporini-Grafin 2003.

[136] Bergmann 1999, 22 (my emphasis).

[137] See generally De Brouhn 2001; Edmondson and Keith 2008.

[138] Corbeill 2004; Cairns 2005.

[139] Schade 2003; Alexandridis 2004.

[140] Milnor 2005, 113; cf. Sebesta 1997; Olson 2002; Dixon 2004. As Milnor argues, this ideal code of conduct carried over into country life as well, as where the *vilicus* and *vilica* in Columella's *De re rustica* were seen to work in harmony and

thus serve as moral exemplars; see Milnor 2005, 267.

[141] Cf. Olson 2002, 392: "The literary record describes what the *matrona* should look like and how her clothing should embody her moral stance; she seems to be described in terms of exemplary (not actual) appearance."

[142] Shumka 2001; Alexandridis forthcoming. Statues are but one among many possible examples: cf. Kleiner and Matheson, who write how "the proximity of Livia and Mother Earth [on the Ara Pacis] forcefully presented the public with a striking image of a fertile and productive role model for all other Roman women. Goddesses like Venus, Juno, and Ceres were amply endowed with the characteristics most prized in a Roman woman, and the near assimilation of Roman imperial women to their divine alter egos was openly advertised on the official Roman coinage" (Kleiner and Matheson 2000, 8).

[143] Von Hesberg in this volume, p. 266. Cf. Rawson 2003b and the contributions to George 2005, esp. Boatwright 2005, which considers related material.

modesty, fertility, and domesticity, came to be adopted and ingrained into local patterns of behavior across the empire.[144] Thus, while the visibility of women in Roman society generally testifies to a greater degree of parity with men than that seen in some other ancient civilizations, "their equality is expressed in very traditional (unequal) virtues, like silence."[145]

While one can draw many parallels between the social situation of women and slaves, especially in their representation as outsiders in *exemplum* literature,[146] the latter were by far the more tightly controlled and heavily censored.[147] Slaves are a category of individual who, from the elite master's perspective, represent the immoral non-Roman: that is, they were anti-models. But we should not let this influential and deeply ingrained belief deter us from appreciating how slaves possessed their own exemplary figures, ones deeply invested with meaning to those inside the group even if those meanings were not comprehensible to or sanctioned by those outside it. Roberta Stewart's contribution to this volume suggests one of the ways in which such role models can be recuperated. Her chapter looks at Plautus's *Pseudolus*, a comedy of manners that features a roguish slave who orchestrates a scam with another slave to con his family masters, a curmudgeonly father and witless son, out of various commodities (money, wine, etc.). Stewart argues that, since the story was circulated amongst slaves, approaching the play from the perspective of exemplarity opens it up in new ways: that is, "as an analytical category, the concept of the 'role model' helps first to identify and assess the role of Plautus's tricksters in the moral logic of the slave society and second to explore the problem of identifying the slave's agency in a system of domination."[148] In his role as trickster, Pseudolus overturns his position of marginality and so "offers the possibility of radical perspectives from which to see and create, to imagine alternatives, new worlds."[149]

These "alternatives" clearly went beyond strategies for mere survival but instead extended to freedom, fame, and wealth. In his study of the social role of the gladiator in Petronius's novel, Marc Kleijwegt considers how this subhuman figure, seen in the person of Petraites, functions as an *exemplum* for the wealthy freedman Trimalchio. He calls attention to the resonance that such an athletic hero must have held for a manumitted slave, in both his acclaim and (presumed) riches. Kleijwegt notes that "the parallels that can be drawn on a general level between their respective roads to freedom and their social circumstances . . . prove instructive for an evaluation of Petronius' strategy of choosing a famous gladiator as Trimalchio's favourite role-model."[150] A parallel case is offered by charioteers, who, despite the stigma of their servile status, might rise to a higher station and become role models through their freedom, wealth, or character.[151] The inscription extolling Fuscus's virtues is of particular interest, for instance, since it demonstrates how diverse individuals

---

[144] Cf. Woolf 2003–2004, where he notes how, following Alfred Gell, "earlier works do not determine the shape of their successors but they provide essential resources for their creation, and in time the power of tradition or much imitated archetypes can be difficult to resist. This dynamic can be envisaged operating at different levels in Roman material culture" (unpaginated ms.). On the application of Gell's ideas to ancient art history, see further Osborne and Tanner 2006.

[145] Sharrock 1997, 608. The strictures placed upon the female body in art can be read alongside efforts in other media, such as the silencing of the feminine voice in poetry, as a "mechanism of censorship"; Habinek 1998, 131. See also Farrell 2001, 52–83, on the "gender of Latin."

[146] Parker 1998.

[147] The literature on ancient slavery is vast: see most recently Serghidou 2007 and the bibliography in Roberta Stewart's chapter in this volume.

[148] Stewart in this volume, p. 70.

[149] Hooks 1992, 341.

[150] Kleijwegt 1998, 92. Compare work on pugilists (e.g., Mike Tyson) as role models in our own society: Wacquant 1995, esp. 515 (on parallels to Roman gladiators).

[151] See further Horsmann 1998.

from across the empire saw fit to tap into a common language of exemplarity, however shopworn or bastardized its expression.[152]

The high visibility of figures such as Petraites and Fuscus is echoed by Maud Gleason's statement that "we simply do not know what mythic images of maleness appealed to ordinary Romans, although the tremendous popularity of successful chariot-racing drivers and gladiators offers a clue."[153] This is not to argue that these figures, whose actions and status went largely (or wholly) against the grain of Roman social norms, were officially sanctioned or perceived as role models in the way we have spoken of, say, the *summi viri*. Popularity, to be sure, does not confer moral authority. But they and others, like Pseudolus, spoke to particular social classes and ethnic communities, some quite considerable in size (slaves, for instance, or Christians),[154] in ways that offered hope and inspiration and that invited imitation. In this way, they present something of a quandary to our traditional understanding of *exempla*, which are by definition figures or actions that reinforce the accepted standards of the time; they are normative, not countercultural. But when successful athletes, upstart slaves, and heroic daughters are seen from the inside—that is, from the perspective of the individual, the parent, or the group—it becomes clear that we would do well to expand our definition of exemplarity to embrace not just those in Rome's center but those at its margins as well.

The Book

This volume aims to provide a sampling of the broad spectrum of actors and actions, historical and mythological, that functioned as *exempla* at various levels of Roman society. As we have seen, the study of exemplarity is already well established in literary and historical scholarship and is central to current debates about cultural memory, among other subjects. Yet much recent work demonstrates that the gallery of models that Romans looked to was far more crowded and diverse than that portrayed in our traditional sources. This collection of essays goes well beyond the city of Rome and its urban aristocracy, and its contents speak to the necessity and advantages of doing so. In particular, it inserts into the wider discourse about exemplarity a number of topics that have suffered neglect, including gender and sexuality, slavery, and "Romanization." In addition, visual culture is given a far larger role to play here than it has in earlier studies. In many senses, then, this is an untraditional book about a very traditional topic, and we hope that these contributions will energize its study in new ways.

While the chapters here approach Roman exemplarity from a multiplicity of perspectives, they are united by an interest in promoting further debate. Some of the questions that they raise include: What are the different media for disseminating *exempla* (e.g., oral, visual, literary, epigraphic), and how do their target audiences vary accordingly? What factors (age, gender, social status) determine the extent of an individual's identification with an exemplary figure? To what extent is the choice of a role model decided from amongst one's own social circle or from a public, more distant figure, and thus influenced by an individual's degree of social interaction? In what ways are *exempla* employed by persons or groups (ethnic, religious, etc.) in opposition to the accepted standards of the time? Can we map the shifts in people's preferences for particular types of exemplary figures over the course of their life cycle and across cultures? Can we develop a diachronic

---

[152] See Rossetti 1999, esp. 235, on its wide appeal.

[153] Gleason 1999, 69–70.

[154] For a literary perspective on the creation of Christian "identity," see Lieu 2004; for an overview of the role of art in "inventing Christian Rome," see Elsner 2003; and on Christian *exempla*, see Janet Huskinson's chapter in this volume.

framework through which the whole of Roman exemplary practice can be understood? And lastly, what degree of influence have modern perceptions of the past had upon our interpretations of the evidence for exemplarity?

Identity and Assimilation

A closing concern here is that of the relation between the concepts of roles and identity, another term that is invoked frequently in this volume. The issue that I would like to foreground here briefly, one that is addressed at greater length in the chapter by Tonio Hölscher, is what he refers to as the "malaise of identity." Simply stated: why do we *need* the concept of identity? What ends does it serve that the concept of roles cannot achieve on its own?

In the last two decades the subject of identity—"the practice of self-description through categorization"[155]—has assumed a central place in scholarship within the humanities and social sciences.[156] Disciplines with widely divergent interests and methods now communicate through a common, if sometimes garbled, "identity discourse." We are all well acquainted with (or at least cognizant of) the manifold dimensions to this discourse, especially as it surfaces in matters of race, ethnicity, gender, sexuality, and the all-embracing "culture." Over time, roles have increasingly become tied to the concept of identity (as intimated by the subtitle to this volume). Their apparent kinship was by no means a natural development, however: as Frederick Cooper and Rogers Brubaker note, "The notion of identification was pried from its original, specifically psychoanalytic context (where the term had been initially introduced by Freud) and linked to ethnicity on the one hand . . . and to sociological role theory and reference group theory on the other (through figures such as Nelson Foote and Robert Merton)."[157] This forced marriage has led scholars to treat role modeling and identity as part and parcel of the same approach, as both lay claims to explicating "the ways in which human persons are imagined to assimilate elements of collective identities into their unique personal identities."[158]

The general perception of their cause as shared or at least overlapping can be seen in the realm of classical studies as well. In recent work on Roman religion, for instance, studies have focused on the role of charismatic individuals in the formation of Jewish and Christian identities (e.g., Poorthuis and Schwartz's *Saints and Role Models in Judaism and Christianity*),[159] while others have wrestled with the pagan identities against which Christians defined themselves (e.g., Piepenbrink's *Christliche Identität und Assimilation in der Spätantike*).[160] Similarly, studies in Roman art have probed the self-perceptions of citizens who modeled their portraits after rulers, looking "positively for the roles and identities they seek to portray beside the imperial image."[161] Examples can be seen in the contributions to the present volume as well, both on literature and art. In short, much current scholarship holds that an exemplary figure or type "provides a way of thinking about greatness that is relevant to contemporary Rome and Roman *identity*."[162]

---

[155] The definition is from Chapman 2000, 172.

[156] On "identity" generally, see Appiah and Gates 1995 and Cooper 2005, both with copious bibliography.

[157] Cooper 2005, 60–61 (my emphasis).

[158] Handler 1994, 28 (this is Handler's definition of the third function of "identity" but one that I understand here as closely allied to Merton's own conception of role modeling).

[159] Poorthuis and Schwartz 2004; cf. Hartney 2005; Diefenbach 2007.

[160] Piepenbrink 2005; cf. Lieu 2004.

[161] Smith 1998, 92; cf. now Stewart 2006.

[162] Kraus 2005, 199 (my emphasis), discussing the use of Alexander the Great in a Roman context.

On a certain level, the kinship between identity and role models appears beyond contest: for if we define identity as a "narrative of inclusions and exclusions," then role models—the individuals and behaviors that we strive to replicate within ourselves—surely lie at the heart of our attempts to unmask identity, be it an individual's or a group's.[163] But where a role model operates in similar fashion to an ancient *exemplum* (however approximately), identity finds no corresponding analogue within the Roman value system. Nor should it, since "as historical analysis and ethnographic data suggest, the concept of 'identity' is peculiar to the modern Western world."[164] This is further complicated by its semantic ambiguity within our culture, since its (over) use as an umbrella term has largely drained it of any of its former analytic power. As Cooper and Brubaker note, identity "tends to mean too much (when understood in a strong sense), too little (when understood in a weak sense), or nothing at all (because of its sheer ambiguity)."[165] The problematic nature of identity, its semantic and conceptual muddiness, has increasingly been highlighted by scholars working in diverse disciplines, who have argued for employing the term with more discrimination or even avoiding it altogether.[166] At the same time, the authors of several recent studies of the cultural and linguistic history of "identity" have called for its abandonment as a theoretical category, particularly within the context of cross-cultural studies. For instance, Richard Handler argues that

> We cannot simply appropriate from our own, mid-twentieth-century discourse the term "identity" to use as a cross-cultural analytic operator. People in [Jane] Austen's world, and *many other people from even more distant times and places, do not use the concept of identity as we do, or at all*; nor do they understand human personhood and social collectivities in terms of what identity implies. Our examination of these other worldviews should give us occasion to recognize what is peculiar in our own discourse rather than to discover elsewhere what we imagine to be the universality of our own ways of thinking.[167]

Following Handler's lead, I would argue that classicists, too, should not treat identity as a "cross-culturally neutral conceptual tool,"[168] one that we can uncritically import and seamlessly insert into our own literary, art historical, or archaeological tool kit. Rather, we should recognize that identity is an analytical device that demands self-reflexivity, something that can be found wanting from even the most current, self-avowedly "critically aware" literature on this topic. This is illustrated, among other places, by the contributions to the recently published collection on *Coinage and Identity in the Roman Provinces*.[169] In his introduction, Christopher Howgego outlines the many different ways that provincial coinage, through its imagery, inscriptions, and manufacture, is revealing of Roman concepts of religion, time, geography, and so forth, and thus affords insight into diverse Roman "identities." But while seemingly grounded in evidence from the past, his narrative in fact hangs upon the present: "'Identity is *now* seen not as an eternal given, but as something actively constructed and contested in a particular historical context, based on subjective, not objective criteria.' For all that it may be a contingent construct, identity is a

[163] Chapman 2000, 172.

[164] Handler 1994, 27.

[165] Cooper 2005, 59; see 64–65 for a breakdown of five of its key uses and 67–70 for discussion of its strong and weak understandings.

[166] Valentin Groebner, for one, discusses how the term's

"vagueness" and its conflicting applications by historians persuaded him against using it in his own work; see Groebner 2007.

[167] Handler 1994, 37 (my emphasis).

[168] Handler 1994, 27.

[169] Howgego, Heuchert, and Burnett 2005.

powerful driver of action, *as we know all too well from our own experience.*[170] Howgego offers the disclaimer that "naturally there are major differences between now and then" and that, among other things, we need "to think away nationalism" but offers only vague, presentist justification for why we need to think *with* an equally anachronistic category.[171] Indeed, the primary backing for his approach comes through recourse to the emphatic claim of identity: that is, that every individual (and group) is entitled to the right to have, maintain, and safeguard its own "identity."[172] But as Tonio Hölscher observes in this volume, "an emphatic concept of 'identity' is not a universal and timeless anthropological fact but a specific phenomenon of certain historical societies."[173] Furthermore, framing identity in the language of "soft" constructivism (i.e., as a "contingent construct") rather than of "hard" essentialism (the old paradigm) doesn't mean that one skirts the critical dilemma that this tool creates (as Howgego and others appear to assume).[174] Rather, by it one simply picks a side in that now all too familiar game "in current scholarly analyses of collective identities, [in which] there is a tension between the notion that identity is essential, fundamental, unitary, and unchanging, and the notion that identities are constructed and reconstructed through historical action."[175]

In his chapter on "Aspects of Identity" in the same volume, George Williamson declares that Roman "identity was more than an academic game."[176] His essay calls attention to the discrepancies between the modern historian's and the individual Roman's perspectives on identity in local contexts, points of view that he straddles helpfully. But like Howgego, at no point does he opt out of this "game," his essay instead turning on the specious commonplace that "the issues treated by the study of identity—senses of belonging and community, sameness and difference—have *of course* as much a *contemporary relevance* as they did under the Roman empire."[177] Furthermore, in making liberal use of its terminology, his repeated enjoinders to his reader that the concept is elusive to pin down since individuals possessed "multiple and overlapping" putative identities serve only to reify identity as orthodoxy, not to call into question its assumptions.[178] That said, neither author appears aware of any dissenting voices in the contemporary literature on identity, reflecting how both deep-seated and unexamined this concept has become in classical studies today.[179] While the volume contains much to recommend it, its theoretical contribution is hampered by its authors'

[170] Howgego 2005, 1 (my emphasis): the first part of this (his definition) quotes from Preston 2001, 87.

[171] "But it will be obvious that there is potentially considerable *contemporary interest* in the opportunity to explore through coinage the assertion of local, regional, and imperial identities in a multi-cultural and multilingual world with overarching political and military structures" (Howgego 2005, 2, my emphasis).

[172] Howgego 2005, 1: "Identity has been a major focus of research in recent decades, for the obvious reason that *it is particularly an issue when under threat.* That consideration applies as much to our own scholarly context as it does to our subject, the Roman empire" (my emphasis).

[173] Hölscher in this volume, p. 53.

[174] See further Cooper 2005, 63–64: "Nor is the solution to be found in more consistent constructivism, for it is not clear why that which is routinely characterized as 'multiple, fragmented, and fluid' should be conceptualized as identity at all" (64).

[175] Handler 1994, 28.

[176] Williamson 2005, 24.

[177] Williamson 2005, 20 (my emphasis); cf. Howgego's claim in n. 171, above.

[178] Williamson 2005, 27. This is not to suggest that he is alone in this point of view; cf. Jones 2004, one among many other examples.

[179] In the case of the introduction, for instance, the intellectual debts accrued for ideas about identity are paid almost entirely to other classicists (e.g., Laurence 1998; Preston 2001) and contributors (e.g., "As argued with authority by Williamson": Howgego 2005, 1 n. 2), and far less so to anthropological, sociological, or other theorists. Martin Pitts's recent (2007) study of the utility of identity for Roman archaeologists goes further in this regard but still fails to engage fully the objections raised by scholars outside Classics, especially Brubaker and Cooper (glossed by Pitts on 693).

lack of critical reflection about their shared tool of analysis, one that is treated as a self-evident *fact* of antiquity (e.g., "Identity matters").[180]

What, then, is the way forward? The arguments of Cooper, Handler, and others outlined above, which originate largely within the sphere of postcolonial studies, are mirrored in Tonio Hölscher's contribution here, in which he weighs the term's validity within the context of classical studies. There he tackles head on the question of using roles as a framework for analyzing the textual and material traces of ancient Roman society, especially its visual culture. Hölscher calls for a paradigm shift away from "identity" to "roles": for where roles are rational and communicative, rooted in social conventions, identity makes claims for individuals, social groups, and political communities that are idealistic, irrational, and egocentric. These emphatic claims are the product of twentieth-century ways of thinking about the world, in which discussions about so-called crises of personal and national "identity" rose to the fore, especially in the face of colonialism and globalization. Roles, by contrast, make no such claims but instead are concerned with how a person is socially constructed and perceived by others.[181] Thus, given that roles "may be judged, as good or bad, on the basis of ethical categories, without questioning the individual or the community in its inner self . . . is it not more appropriate, and less burdened by anachronistic assumptions, to speak of concrete public and private roles and qualities, merits and deficiencies in social communication?"[182] Role modeling, when pulled from under the shadow of identity, represents a promising way forward.

In spite of its seeming ubiquity, identity is a concept that "does not travel well"—especially into antiquity.[183] But given the growth industry that it has spurred, one that shows especially few signs of abating in Roman studies,[184] identity will continue to find adherents within the discipline for some time to come.[185] To be sure, not all of the contributors to this volume are agreed on the need to interrogate, let alone abandon, this concept (see in particular Richard Alston's contribution for an alternate viewpoint). This does not alter the basic methodological rule of thumb, however, that in order to make judicious use of contemporary critical theory in our own analyses (be it role modeling or identity), we must first diagnose its prevailing understanding within the period of its production (i.e., the twentieth century).[186] By contrast, the concept of identity remains little scrutinized in the humanities generally and in classics especially, "despite the fact that the epistemological presuppositions that the concept carries are similar, if not identical, to those that have made other terms suspect."[187] Whether an analysis sufficiently convincing to unseat identity has yet to appear[188] or whether due time has not yet passed

[180] Howgego 2005, 1. Where self-reflexivity makes appearances (outside of Williamson's chapter), it is directed at the coinage, not its analysts: e.g., "Butcher in this volume stresses the self-reflexive nature of the evidence" (Howgego 2005, 17).

[181] Cf. Von den Hoff and Schmidt 2001, on roles and the social construction of reality in antiquity; also Mauss 1985, on the emergence of the concept of the person from antiquity.

[182] See his chapter in this volume, p. 54.

[183] Cooper 2005, 81.

[184] E.g., I note that the forthcoming *Oxford Handbook of Roman Studies* will include a chapter on "Identity" under "Approaches" (Dench 2008).

[185] Two important qualifications: first, I am not suggesting

that identity is not being critically handled at all, just not very often; e.g., I note the recent work of Breckner 2004 and Woolf 2005; second, the use of identity is by no means an exclusively Anglo-American phenomenon (e.g., see Borca 2001; Faller 2001, etc.); the concerns expressed here could therefore be applied much more widely than they have.

[186] On the balance between theory and method in classical archaeology, for instance, see Zanker 1994, esp. 290–91.

[187] Handler 1994, 27.

[188] Hölscher, for instance, believes that "a critical analysis of the *emphatic* concept of individual 'identity' has to be awaited"; see p. 53 below (my emphasis). However, he does not cite Handler's or Cooper's work, for instance, and it may be that such work has so far failed to gain a wider following due to its relatively recent publication, as well as disciplinary boundaries and cultural/linguistic barriers.

to allow for its arguments to settle remains open for debate.[189] But in the meantime, we ought to ask ourselves what we stand to gain *and* to lose in repeatedly invoking the same analytic categories. It is in this last, added capacity that we hope this volume will raise awareness and contribute to future debates about not only role modeling and exemplarity but also "identity."

Chapter Summaries

The chapters that follow are arranged by theme, be it methodology, medium, period, or geographical area. The volume begins by looking at approaches to role modeling within Roman culture, paying particular attention to issues of anachronism (Hölscher, Dixon); these are followed by a consideration of the variety and appearance of *exempla* in the republic, including their revival in some cases under the empire (Stewart, Rose, Spentzou, Alston); the next contributions investigate the role of exemplarity in the formation of gender roles, including instances of their monolithic nature (Imber, Davies) as well as signs of slippage in their categorization (D'Ambra, Varner); three papers on the provinces then explore the diverse and shifting nature of *exempla* across the empire (Pomeroy, Hales, von Hesberg); the next two chapters use the medium of the sarcophagus to survey the appearance of emergent subcultures (and their role models) at Rome (Hansen and Huskinson), while the concluding chapter takes a look back at methodology (Clarke).

The first two chapters share in a driving concern with methodology. Tonio Hölscher and Suzanne Dixon each contend with the shadow of modernity, giving historical perspective to the issues involved in using the categories of roles and identity to study antiquity. In his survey of images of leaders, ancient and modern, Hölscher explores how the roles that these leaders inhabit are limited and fixed, as are the values assigned to them. The fixed nature and lucid expression of approved roles and behavior encourage stability at many levels of imperial society: they assist individuals in integrating themselves within their social setting and provide communities with a clear grasp of the social pecking order and value system. But as Hölscher stresses, the function of role behavior in this way also has its problems, even dangers, as it collapses the messy and infinite complexity of reality into fixed, finite patterns of ideology. The representation of imperial roles, such as in state art (relief sculpture, coins), makes clear that these works function in the service of ideology, not reality. There are, however, degrees of permeability and exclusivity in representations of these roles and values. Some are accessible to all citizens and made the individual essentially indistinguishable from the emperor, while others are directed at particular groups, such as married couples, many of whom follow the imperial example (e.g., matrimonial harmony, or *concordia*). The representation of still other roles and values is reserved for a select few, such as the senatorial elite's military *virtus* or the emperor's world dominion. In this system, the emperor is the role model par excellence, the bridge between ideal values and everyday reality.

Suzanne Dixon's chapter shifts the focus away from the person of the emperor in order to examine how both marginal and elite Romans distinguish themselves as role models. She identifies four individuals whose accomplishments or acts of beneficence are regarded as exemplary and considers how the monumental records of their lives speak to different social groups. Dixon's choices give

---

[189] It is worth noting that Cooper and Brubaker's arguments find echoes elsewhere in the social sciences, where some scholars forecast a discipline-wide shift "beyond identity." The latter is the title of essays by both Cooper 2005 (first published in 2000) and Field 2005, who raises similar questions about the problematic application of this concept in Latin American studies.

shape and detail to the range of local and regional role models that existed in Roman Italy, including civic worthies (Eumachia of Pompeii, Pliny the Younger of Como), social upstarts (the baker Vergilius Eurysaces of Rome), and lesser-knowns (the shoemaker Septimia Stratonice of Ostia). Her four case studies illustrate how the superlative actions and behaviors of these individuals were determined by a matrix of influences—family, community, state—and that their reputations were molded in no small part by the individuals and groups that they aided. Some were clearly influenced by the *exemplum* of the imperial house, while others' decisions were affected by local factors, including personal relationships, family traditions of supporting the community, or political necessity. But as Dixon elaborates, individuals' reputations as role models were not simple by-products of their agency as patrons; rather, it was an individual's or community's material acknowledgment of their beneficence that proved crucial in shaping and sealing their memory as *exempla*. The various forms that this "social reciprocity" took (honorific inscriptions, reliefs, statuary) take us to Dixon's second major concern: context: Septimia Stratonice's forlorn tombstone did not reach as wide an audience as Eumachia's statue in Pompeii's forum, but its message underlines the aspirational potential of *any* monument. A full comprehension of that exemplary message is conditioned not only by the viewer's physical context but also by his or her historical framework: so Eurysaces' rise to wealth through industry, chronicled in the narrative panels and statuary on his tomb, reads to some scholars like a modern success story. As such anachronism is inescapable, Dixon argues that we must strive to reconstruct the fullness of context and to take stock of our own biases in order to project less of modernity onto antiquity.

The next four chapters turn to the evidence of republican *exempla*. In the first contribution, Roberta Stewart uses Plautus's *Pseudolus* to reveal how the actions and behavior of a slave, a category of person considered unworthy of emulation in Roman society, assume an exemplary status in Plautus's early second-century B.C. work. According to Stewart, in staging *Pseudolus* for the public, Plautus popularized a story typically circulated amongst slaves and thus one guided by the *slave's* agency. As a consequence, Stewart argues that its representations may be interpreted from a different register than that determined by the plays themselves. In this reading, ambivalence is key: the play not only presents the expected manipulation of the slave's voice to gird the social hierarchy and provide reassurance to the elite of its stability; it also discloses the slave's manipulation of that hierarchy to his own ends. Stewart illustrates how Pseudolus's mastery of word play parallels the behavior of other tricksters in the Plautine *œuvre* and in the larger literary tradition, including Aesop's *Fables* and slave songs from the American South. In all of these narratives, the trickster is a folk hero who manipulates language to assert his selfhood and to question the morality of the slave system. Through his deceitful self-assertion, Pseudolus the trickster served as a role model to subordinate groups struggling to survive their enslavement in republican Rome.

Brian Rose's chapter focuses on the sculptural and numismatic representation of republican Rome's male elite and its Trojan ancestry. His contribution analyzes the ways in which both models, historical and mythological, reflect an inherent ambiguity in their formulation of *Romanitas*. When iconography depicting Trojans was first coined around the early third century B.C., it carried a positive significance at Rome, where eastern associations were already privileged (e.g., the *lusus Troiae*). But as a result of conflicts with the Parthians and Celts from the later republican period onward, eastern costume came to assume a negative meaning as well. The Trojan statuary group dedicated as part of the Forum of Augustus brought clarity to this "bilingual" visual language, as it set a fixed iconography for representing Rome's ancestral role model, Aeneas (outfitted as a contemporary general), and his family (with little Ascanius in eastern costume). This balancing act between foreign versus Roman and past versus present is also visible in the style of republican portraiture known as verism. While the corpus of these portraits does not lack in scale, none of the some 350 examples derives from a secure archaeological context, prompting some scholars to search for the style's origins in the vernacular traditions of Egypt and Etruria, among others. On the basis of clay bullae recently discovered in situ at the site of Kedesh, the portraits of which bear unmistakably veristic characteristics, Rose argues that it is now possible to date securely the origin of the style to ca. 200 B.C. This is also the period at which the Romans were heavily involved in foreign wars and thus faced a crossroads in their own self-definition, the rising tide of urbane Hellenistic culture threatening to overwhelm "barnyard Latium" (*agresti Latio*: Horace *Ep.* 2.1.157). Rose makes a determined case for seeing the birth of verism as the natural outgrowth of this crisis in Roman "identity." But while the veristic style armed Rome's most prominent citizenry with a "badge" of *Romanitas*, it did so by grafting elements from *two* visual traditions, those of the *imagines* (the victor) and those realistic images of Greek intellectuals (now the vanquished). Like the imagery of Trojan ancestry, the "bilingual" iconography of verism defined Roman culture through both its emulation of and opposition to the "Other"—in this case, Hellenism.

The discussion of the redefinition of republican *Romanitas* is continued in Efi Spentzou's chapter on Silius Italicus's epic retelling of the Second Punic War, *Punica*. Filled with a cast of characters redolent of the republic's old-fashioned heroism, tellingly including "a senate rivaling the gods in virtue" (*aequantem superos virtute senatum*), the *Punica* is not in short supply of legendary role models (Regulus, Fabius Cunctator, etc.). Yet Spentzou argues that it is the very presence of and conflicts between the *multos viros* that unhinges the reader's sense of *Romanitas*. Lacking a clear mouthpiece through which to articulate prized Roman values, the *Punica* becomes an "epic in search of a hero," the single "great man" replaced by a cacophony of competing voices. This muddled definition of *Romanitas* is further garbled by the role of Hannibal, who functions not simply as the antihero but as a sympathetic, even heroic figure as well. While the barbaric nature of his character is in little doubt—the gruesome scenes of slaughter expose his "wrath and menace" (*iramque minasque*)—Hannibal emerges as the epic's dominant figure through his parallelism with Aeneas. Seen against a war-torn canvas like that of the *Aeneid*, Hannibal's virtue, patriotism, and marital bonds are carefully sketched in order to assimilate (or at least closely associate) him with his Vergilian antithesis. Spentzou explains the destabilization of the conventional epic hero as a manifestation of the author's own sense of unease and disenchantment within an unsettled political climate. This explains why the reader who comes to the *Punica* expecting a paean to Roman values finds instead the opposite: a "dark reflection" on *Romanitas* that plumbs the hollow, inconsistent categories of hero and Other. In the figure of Hannibal, the Roman state's legendary archenemy, the impotent Roman elite found an unlikely role model: a barbarian transgressor whose struggle against tyranny they could identify with all too closely.

Richard Alston's chapter also considers the ways in which anxious aristocrats of the late first and early second centuries used history and memory to counter the emperor's increasingly despotic hold over them. His contribution outlines three responses that were available to the elite of the period: openly opposing the emperor, withdrawing from political life, or shifting the terms of the discourse. Alston's subject is the third option, the creation of an alternative narrative to imperial monarchy, which he surveys through the lens of Tacitus's *Histories* and *Annales*. In these works, Tacitus argues that, despite the death of the *res publica* at the hands of the principate, history's charge is still able to be fulfilled: namely, to encourage responsive behavior through the promulgation of moral *exempla*. Tacitus's *exempla* are drawn from a pantheon of republican heroes, but their stories are considered anachronistic and thus not directly suitable for emulation by imperial elites. Rather, the unsettled political climate of their time demands that elites understand Brutus, Cassius, and others as belonging to an age now past and that they seek their role models from amongst their contemporaries—valiant mothers, dutiful wives, loyal slaves, and courageous men. Thus, in an era fraught with anxiety for elite males, their fortunes in flux, Tacitus's position allayed fears by offering new role models to emulate in the emergent empire.

The next four papers consider *exempla* in the light of gender roles and sexuality, drawing heavily upon the evidence of art as well as literature. Margaret Imber's chapter looks at the critical role that rhetorical education played in negotiating the relationships between elite fathers and sons. Declamation occupied a central place in the education of upper-class male Romans, who rehearsed in their classrooms the starchy, mock courtroom speeches (*controversiae*) about irresolvable, imaginary family and social conflicts. Imber's chapter demonstrates how these speeches—far from being innocent pedagogical exercises—were devices inscribed within the dominant ideologies that reinforced the role of schools, like other social institutions, as bastions of male solidarity. Furthermore, they were employed in a society where the fathers of sons of elite status were often absent from their daily lives, especially in the provinces, and at a time in their lives, the so-called *lubrica aetas*, when they were particularly vulnerable to external influence. In the figure of the *vir bonus*, declamation offered an imaginary paternal role model or stepfather for adolescents to embody and emulate. By performing these speeches, elite youth rehearsed and reconciled the contested roles of *pater* and *civis* that they would occupy as adults and so ensured the regeneration of the male hierarchy of power.

Imber's discussion of gender roles is complemented by the chapter by Eve D'Ambra, who considers them through the lens of commemorative practices for girls and young women who died prematurely. The monuments represent their subjects with varying degrees of assimilation to the divinity, whose *persona* is evoked through hairstyle, ornament, and dress as well as various props redolent of a sacro-idyllic setting. The exposed breast and expressionistic facial features on many girls, the latter perhaps suggestive of their headstrong character, further amplify the divine identification. As D'Ambra notes, our understanding of these works has been poorly served by the scholarly tendency to divorce the realistic portrait heads from the ideal body types. Her chapter redresses this imbalance by demonstrating how it is the very tension between the ideal and the specific, the ambiguity between goddess and girl, that reflects powerfully back upon the slippery status of the deceased. On one level, parents' invocation of these heroic qualities was culturally appropriate for their daughters, whose deaths had prevented the realization of their sexual maturity and the development of traditional feminine virtues. But, as D'Ambra argues, the selection of Diana as a heroic *exemplum* had a further resonance: equipped as a warrior, the deceased is empowered to stake a claim of manly virtue.

Eric Varner's chapter is similarly concerned with the borrowing of gendered features or motifs in art in order to appropriate particular qualities or virtues, in this case for patrons of the opposite sex. The wide remit of Varner's contribution provides for a useful synthesis of this phenomenon, known as "transgendered assimilation," as it encompasses representations in the imperial as well as the private realm. Varner's chapter also projects the evidence of the historical sources against Rome's political scenery, bringing greater nuance to our understanding of numerous accounts of the feminized behavior of emperors as well as a number of widely misunderstood works of art (such as the mannish numismatic representations of Cleopatra VII). He argues that transgendered representations should not be seen as necessarily making a claim of historical accuracy; rather, they were primarily intended to communicate social or political messages, such as imperial virtue, marital concord, or dynastic legitimacy. Transgressive representations of this kind appear to run counter to our expectations about the rigidity of the gender hierarchy in Roman culture. But as

Varner demonstrates, their long-standing employment in diverse media reflects the fact that, in certain cases, Romans tolerated, even exploited, ambiguity in their gender taxonomy. In this way, hybridized or transgendered images served as role models for the successful resolution of conflicting, ambiguous gender roles at many levels of Roman society.

Where Varner discusses the instability of gender norms in Roman art, Glenys Davies considers the monolithic qualities of gendered representation. Her chapter on portrait statuary from the imperial period demonstrates that, while these works frequently lack inscriptions or attested contexts, their prototypes and gestures ("body language") have much in themselves to tell us about ingrained understandings of men's and women's roles in Roman society. She begins by clarifying how the prototype employed for female statues was Hellenistic Greek in origin and that, apart from the use of portrait heads with contemporary hairstyles and variations in dress (e.g., addition of the *stola*), the statue bodies underwent relatively little adaptation by Roman sculptors. Yet Roman culture also wrote rank, status, and morality onto these "bodies" through a subtle language of gesture, stance, and dress. Here Davies offers a series of translations of the body language of female statuary, focusing in particular on what she refers to as their "disguised barrier gestures": abundant, cumbersome drapery; restricted or preening hand gestures; compressed, defensive postures; and, in some cases, down-turned, submissive gazes. She details how Romans overwhelmingly chose from this same small cluster of stereotyped statue types, images that advertised and rewarded the pursuit of "appropriate" (if clichéd) female roles: faithful wives, devoted mothers, stoic widows. Thus, while their high visibility in a public, privileged medium elevated their subjects as *exempla* and intimated their parity with men, their statue types communicated the limited range and restricted nature of the roles available to them. The visual language of female statuary therefore deals in a paradox, for in supplying women with role models of their own, men were provided with a powerful tool for their social control.

The next three chapters catapult us far from Rome and into the provinces. The first contribution, by Sarah Pomeroy, is framed as a case study of provincial women in the Roman imperial period and concerns the most ethnically visible of the Greeks—the Spartans. In contrast to Glenys Davies's examples, the literary and lapidary representations of women discussed by her celebrate their difference. Pomeroy's chapter charts how women negotiated new social, religious, and legal roles as Sparta was subsumed into Rome's empire. The tension that developed between Spartan women's own, resistant voices and those that Romans and others sought to impose upon them is, as she notes, reflective of the wider cultural "conversation" that was taking place between Rome and the provinces. A woman's character as "Spartan" was neither fixed nor necessarily preeminent, as foreign domination meant catering to Spartan, Greek, and Roman influences simultaneously. In fine-tuning their roles to the shifting circumstances, Spartan women consciously drew upon their cultural heritage, such as their distinctive dialect and archaic religious images, in order to invoke their glorious past and so revitalize their sense of group origins. In other cases, different political realities proved more pressing: for instance, they rejected Helen, their traditional role model for married women, and instead chose Penelope so as to conform with anti-Roman, pan-Hellenic mores. Similarly, eulogies for women tended toward the same hackneyed superlatives as other honorary inscriptions set up in the eastern Mediterranean, reflecting how Spartans prized the virtues of modesty and chastity like other Greeks. But as Pomeroy demonstrates, Spartan women *were* distinctive—whether in their roles as empowered and sometimes heroic mothers or as brave and victorious athletes. Even as their society was in flux, their inherited cultural traits marked them out as revered *exempla* and unrivaled foils to others.

The following chapter by Shelley Hales ranges widely over the empire as she accounts for the popularity of images of Aphrodite and Dionysus, the two dominant motifs in domestic art from the early to late empire. For some scholars, the imagery's long-lived and widespread use in domestic wall paintings, mosaics, and sculpture has pointed toward the deities' interpretation as positive role models of *Romanitas*, finite and stable in meaning. Hales, however, argues that the opposite held true: it was the manifold and fugitive nature of these figures and their accouterments—the masks and mirrors by which they were manipulated in domestic assemblages—that gave them their cultural currency. Masks, for instance, extended to the viewer the vicarious opportunity to assume not one fixed persona but rather an endless array of them (as in the Theater Room of the terraced houses at Ephesus). The elision of boundaries between the represented world and the actual viewer is also effected by the device of the mirror, whereby viewers' attention is consumed and their persona lost in Narcissus-like self-reflection (e.g., the Marine Venus mosaic from Cuicul). In this way, the imagery of these deities and their devices did more than answer the formal needs of Roman domestic design; it afforded purchase of complex, even subversive personae within an increasingly pluralistic society.

Henner von Hesberg's chapter shifts the focus to the northwest provinces, where he considers how the representation of the ideals of family life and family structure changed over the course of three centuries. In his analysis, he traces the way in which the depiction of emotional ties between family members—as expressed by their dress, body language, and proxemics—evolved from being a peripheral concern on monuments of the first century A.D. to their defining quality in the second and third centuries. To this end, he concentrates on three issues: the general conventions of the two types of imagery, stately versus sentimental; the points of similarity (and difference) between the representations on provincial monuments with those from Rome, especially in their visualization of female roles; and the comprehensive social change underlying this iconographic shift. The contrast between the two generations of sculptured monuments that he distills is a striking one: the abstraction and self-restraint seen in the first-century examples is replaced by an emphasis on the anecdotal and affective in the second- and third-century monuments. Von Hesberg argues that the growth in the display of emotional gestures and interaction (and the valorization of domestic bonds that this connotes) resulted from a redefinition of Roman societal norms, and not from any alteration to the structure of the nuclear family itself. Whereas the community, or larger social group, was the framework through which individuals arranged their concerns in the first century, it was the Roman family, the smallest social group, that assumed that role in the second and third centuries.

The next two chapters return us to Rome, where the authors also address questions about gender roles and community but do so through the lens of sarcophagi produced and displayed in its metropolitan area. Inge Lyse Hansen's chapter is an exploration of how gender roles and exemplary models were visualized in late antique art. She takes as her focus the motif of the philosopher and Muse, one of the most popular choices for the decoration of metropolitan sarcophagi produced from the mid-third to early fourth century A.D. Hansen argues that the pronounced interest in the imagery of the learned couple was due to its appeal to an emergent clientele: upwardly mobile individuals of largely middle-class social status who had embraced the ideal of classical learning (*paideia*) and sought to advertise their acculturation. These traits were in turn reflected in the labile personae that they assumed within the narratives of their tombs: for instance, in the third century the "philosopher" functioned as visual shorthand for a host of social positions, ranging from domestic pedagogues to celebrity *rhetors*. The guise of the philosopher or the Muse thus gave only diffuse expression to the social role of the patron as a learned individual while upholding the distinct but complementary ideals of his or her gender. Yet the act of honoring the patron through such identification was not intended to promote him or her as the narrative's primary *exemplum*. Rather, the individuality of the Muse and philosopher figures, which are often depicted with portrait features, resolves itself through the unity of their interaction, their eye contact and gestural reciprocity. The narrative arrangement thus privileges the reading of these figures as in *concordia*, a harmonious and dialogic relationship. For one emerging class of sarcophagus patrons, then, the salient aspect to the imagery of the learned couple was its evocation of *auctoritas*: the cultural literacy (Greek *paideia*) and social respectability (Roman *dignitas*) that they aspired to in late antique Rome.

The social-historical significance of sarcophagi produced for another emergent community, the Christians, provides the focus of Janet Huskinson's chapter. She analyzes two of the ways in which role models were differentiated in late antique funerary art and how these competing visions, reflected in contemporary writings as well, testify to the fluid and discursive construction of Christian character and community. She first considers how certain Christians quietly aligned themselves with pagans by drawing upon a shared symbolic language in the decoration of their sarcophagi. She then looks at how other Christians openly defined themselves in opposition to pagans through visual quotations of scripture that spoke directly to their salvation. In the first instance, Huskinson explains how Christians used the rich allusive structure of the sarcophagus as a veil of legitimacy, the familiar (but slightly altered) pagan motifs creating an appearance of continuity with mainstream values. Here the learned couple and other familiar tropes of classical learning provided filters through which Christians presented their own brand of exemplary behavior, such as neighborly respect (the Good Shepherd) and devout learning (the *orans*). For other Christian patrons, the scenes on their sarcophagi offered *exempla resurrectionis*, historical proofs of their salvation. To this end, the narratives of such home-grown role models as Jonah or the Three Young Hebrews in the fiery furnace afforded little purchase for self-identification by non-Christian viewers. The messages of inclusion and exclusion that characterize the decoration of these sarcophagi reflect how the formation of Christian character was a public act of mediation between the (Christian) self and (pagan) other but also among Christians themselves. A case study of the evolution of visual culture in one of ancient Rome's most prominent "subcultures," Huskinson's chapter also highlights the ambivalence underlying the selection of role models within social groups generally.

The volume concludes with the contribution by John Clarke. As in Tonio Hölscher's and Suzanne Dixon's chapters at the start of this volume, the role models discussed by Clarke are both the big men and bit players of Roman history as well as the modern scholars who have helped to shape their narratives. His chapter is a case study of the painted decoration on a commercial establishment in Pompeii that demonstrates how earlier approaches were methodologically blinkered in their analysis of its (in)famous imagery: a scene of an ass mounting a lion and crowned by winged Victory. Clarke charts the way in which its interpretation has evolved in parallel with changes in the social and literary *Zeitgeist*: from an early school of thought (ca. 1860–1950) that sought to explain the wall painting as allegorical of a historical event (Antony versus Augustus at the battle of Actium) to a later circle of scholars (ca. 1950–1980) who advanced "folkloric" explanations that situated its imagery of upset in the same tradition as southern Italian folk tales or artistic representations of reversals of animal behavior. But neither the tenuous historical connections nor the sweeping folkloric comparisons in themselves establish a dependency between the painting and the suggested templates. Rather, what is necessary, as Clarke illustrates, is a "site-specific" approach. In this, he pins his own interpretation to a judicious analysis of the *context* of the image and produces the first reconstruction of the painting in situ. His social-historical interpretation reclaims the image's function as street-side art, seen and constantly reinterpreted by a multiplicity of viewers, and thus emphasizes the contingency of its "meaning." As both an art historical case study and a disciplinary reflection on its progress, Clarke's chapter offers a timely reappraisal of old methodologies while outlining ways forward in the writing of social histories from literary and visual evidence.

Works Cited

Aldrete, G. S., *Gestures and Acclamations in Ancient Rome* (Baltimore 1999).

Alexandridis, A., *Die Frauen des römischen Kaiserhauses. Eine Untersuchung ihrer bildlichen Darstellung von Livia bis Iulia Domna* (Mainz 2004).

———, "Neutral Bodies? Female Portrait Statue Types from the Late Republic to the 2nd Century C.E.," in *Local and Global Identities: Rethinking Identity and Material Culture in the Ancient World*, ed. S. Hales and T. Hodos (forthcoming).

Alföldy, G., *Die römischen Inschriften von Tarraco*, 2 vols. (Berlin 1975).

Allen, A. L., "On Being a Role Model," in *Multiculturalism: A Critical Reader*, ed. D. T. Goldberg (Oxford 1994) 180–99.

Appiah, K. A., and H. L. Gates, Jr., eds., *Identities* (Chicago 1995).

Ash, R., "An Exemplary Conflict: Tacitus' Parthian Battle Narrative (*Annals* 6.34–35)," *Phoenix* 53 (1999) 114–35.

Babo, M., "Mythologische *Exempla* als teleologische Elemente in den *Metamorphosen* des Apuleius," *Maia* 52 (2000) 485–96.

Balch, D. L., and C. Osiek, eds., *Early Christian Families in Context: An Interdisciplinary Dialogue* (Grand Rapids 2003).

Ball, R., "*Legiturque Tibullus et placet*: Ovid's Tribute to a Role Model," in *Hommages à Carl Deroux I—Poésie*, ed. P. Defosse, Société d'Études Latines de Bruxelles, 5 vols. (Brussels 2002) 48–53.

Barchiesi, A., "Learned Eyes: Poets, Viewers, Image Makers," in *A Companion to the Augustan Age*, ed. K. Galinsky (Cambridge 2005) 281–305.

Bartsch, S., *The Mirror of the Self: Sexuality, Self-Knowledge, and the Gaze in the Early Roman Empire* (Chicago 2006).

Baumer, L. E., *Vorbilder und Vorlagen. Studien zu klassischen Frauenstatuen und ihrer Verwendung für Reliefs und Statuetten des 5. und 4. Jahrhunderts vor Christus*, Acta Bernensia 12 (Berne 1977).

Bell, A. A., Jr., "Fact and *Exemplum* in Accounts of the Deaths of Pompey and Caesar," *Latomus* 53 (1994) 824–36.

Benke, N., "Women in the Courts. An Old Thorn in Men's Sides," *Michigan Journal of Gender & Law* 3 (1995) 195–256.

———, Exempla Sequimur—*Untersuchungen zu "Exemplum" als normbildender Größe im klassischen römischen Recht unter spezieller Berücksichtigung kaiserlicher Entscheide* (forthcoming).

Bergmann, B., "Greek Masterpieces and Roman Recreative Fictions," in *Greece in Rome: Influence, Integration, Resistance*, ed. C. P. Jones, C. Segal, R. J. Tarrant, and R. F. Thomas, *Harvard Studies in Classical Philology* 97 (Cambridge, Mass. 1995) 79–120.

———, "The Moon and the Stars. Afterlife of a Roman Empress," in B. Bergmann and W. M. Watson, *The Moon and the Stars. Afterlife of a Roman Empress* (South Hadley, Mass. 1999) 5–24.

Berlioz, J., and J.-M. David, "Rhétorique et historie. L'*exemplum* et le modèle de comportement dans le discours antique et médiéval," *Rhétorique et historie. L'exemplum et le modèle de comportement dans le discours antique et médiéval, Mélanges de l'École française de Rome* 92 (1980) 1–31.

Bettini, M., "Forging Identities. Trojans and Latins, Romans and Julians in the *Aeneid*," in *Herrschaft ohne Integration? Rom und Italien in republikanischer Zeit*, ed. M. Jehne and R. Pfeilschifter, Studien zur Alten Geschichte 4 (Frankfurt am Main 2006) 269–92.

Bielfeldt, R., "Orest im Medusengrab. Ein Versuch zum Betrachter," *Römische Mitteilungen* 110 (2003) 117–50.

Bloomer, W. M., *Valerius Maximus and the Rhetoric of the New Nobility* (Chapel Hill 1992).

———, "Roman Declamation: The Elder Seneca and Quintilian," in *A Companion to Roman Rhetoric*, ed. J. Hall and W. Dominik (Malden, Mass. 2007) 297–306.

Boatwright, M., "Children and Parents on the Tombstones of Pannonia," in *The Roman Family in the Empire: Rome, Italy and Beyond*, ed. M. George, vol. 4 (Oxford 2005) 287–318.

Borca, F., "Identità e suono: modalità espressive dei morti nella cultura romana," *Latomus* 60 (2001) 864–76.

Boschung, D., "Die Präsentation von Geschichte im Stadtbild der Kaiserzeit," in *Arte e memoria culturale nell'eta della Seconda Sofistica*, ed. O. D. Cordovana and M. Galli (Catania 2007) 103–8.

Bosworth, B., "Augustus, the *Res Gestae* and Hellenistic Theories of Apotheosis," *Journal of Roman Studies* 89 (1999) 1–18.

Breckner, R., "Die gesellschaftliche Produktion von Identität(en)—eine soziologische Perspektive," in *Lokale Identitäten in Randgebieten des Römischen Reiches*: *Akten des Internationalen Symposiums in Wiener Neustadt, 24.–26. April 2003*, ed. A. Schmidt-Colinet, Wiener Forschungen zur Archäologie 7 (Vienna 2004).

Bücher, F., *Verargumentierte Geschichte.* Exempla Romana *im politischen Diskurs der späten römischen Republik*, Hermes Einzelschrift 96 (Stuttgart 2006).

Cairns, D. L., ed., *Body Language in the Greek and Roman Worlds* (Swansea 2005).

Chaplin, J. D., *Livy's Exemplary History* (Oxford and New York 2000).

Chapman, J., "Tensions at Funerals: Social Practices and the Subversion of Community Structure in Later Hungarian Prehistory," in *Agency in Archaeology*, ed. M.-A. Dobres and J. E. Robb (London 2000) 169–95.

Clarke, J. R., *Art in the Lives of Ordinary Romans: Visual Representations and Non-Elite Viewers in Italy, 100 B.C.–A.D. 315* (Berkeley 2003).

Codoner, C., "Seneca: *exemplum*, similitudo," *Pallas* 69 (2005) 143–56.

Connolly, J., "Mastering Corruption: Constructions of Identity in Roman Oratory," in *Women and Slaves in Greco-Roman Culture: Differential Equations*, ed. S. R. Joshel and S. Murnaghan (London 1998) 130–51.

Cooper, F., *Colonialism in Question: Theory, Knowledge, History* (Berkeley 2005).

Corbeill, A., *Nature Embodied: Gesture in Ancient Rome* (Princeton 2004).

———, *The Boundaries of Sex and Gender in Ancient Rome* (forthcoming).

Courtney, E., *Musa Lapidaria: A Selection of Late Verse Inscriptions*, American Classical Studies 36 (Atlanta 1995).

Daleas, B. C., "Children in the Roman World: Status and Growth of Identity" (Ph.D. diss., Indiana University 1998).

D'Ambra, E., *Private Lives, Imperial Virtues: The Frieze of the Forum Transitorium in Rome* (Princeton 1993).

———, *Roman Women* (Cambridge 2007).

David, J.-M., ed., *Valeurs et mémoire à Rome: Valère Maxime ou la vertu recompsée* (Paris 1998).

De Blois, L., P. Erdkamp, G. de Kleijn, and S. Mols, eds., *The Representation and Perception of Imperial Power. Proceedings of the Third Workshop of the International Network Impact of Empire (Roman Empire, c. 200 B.C.–A.D. 476), Netherlands Institute in Rome, March 20–23, 2002* (Amsterdam 2003).

De Brouhn, J. B., "Power Dressing in Ancient Greece and Rome," *History Today* 51 (2001) 18–25.

Demoen, K., "A Paradigm for the Analysis of Paradigms: The Rhetorical *Exemplum* in Ancient Imperial Greek Theory," *Rhetorica* 15 (1997) 125–58.

Dench, E., *Romulus' Asylum: Roman Identities from the Age of Alexander to the Age of Hadrian* (Oxford 2005).

———, "Identity," in *The Oxford Handbook of Roman Studies*, ed. A. Barchiesi and W. Scheidel (Oxford 2008).

Diefenbach, S., *Römische Erinnerungsräume. Heiligenmemoria und kollektive Identitäten im Rom des 3. bis 5. Jahrhunderts n. Chr.* (Berlin 2007).

Dixon, S., ed., *Childhood, Class and Kin in the Roman World* (London 2001).

———, "Exemplary Housewives or Luxurious Sluts? Images of Roman Women in Commerce," in *Women's Influence on Classical Civilization*, ed. F. McHardy and E. Marshall (London 2004) 56–74.

Dueck, D., "Historical '*Exempla*' in Augustan Rome and Their Role in a Geographical Context," in *Studies in Latin Literature and Roman History X*, ed. C. Deroux, Collection Latomus 254 (Brussels 2000) 176–96.

Duff, T., *Plutarch's Lives: Exploring Virtue and Vice* (Oxford 2000).

Eder, W., "Augustus and the Power of Tradition: The Augustan Principate as a Binding Link between Republic and Empire," in *Between Republic and Empire*, ed. K. Raaflaub and M. Toher (Berkeley 1990) 71–122.

Edmondson, J., and A. Keith, eds., *Roman Dress and the Fabric of Roman Culture* (Toronto 2008).

Edwards, C., *Writing Rome: Textual Approaches to the City* (Cambridge 1996).

Eigler, U., U. Gotter, N. Luraghi, and U. Walter, eds., *Formen römischer Geschichtsschreibung von den Anfängen bis Livius: Gattungen—Autoren—Kontexte* (Darmstadt 2003).

Elsner, J., "The Viewer in the Roman Landscape," *Apollo* (1999) 13–17.

———, "Inventing Christian Rome: The Role of Early Christian Art," in *Rome the Cosmopolis*, ed. C. Edwards and G. Woolf (Cambridge 2003) 71–99.

Ewald, B., "Rollenbilder und Geschlechterverhältnis in der römischen Grabkunst. 'Archäologische' Anmerkungen zur *Geschichte der Sexualität*," in *Neue Fragen, Neue Antworten. Gender Studies in der Klassischen Archäologie*, ed. N. Sojc (Münster 2005) 24–42.

Faller, S., ed., *Studien zu antiken Identitäten* (Würzburg 2001).

Fantham, E., "'Chironis *exemplum*': On Teachings and Surrogate Fathers in 'Achilleid' and 'Silvae'," *Hermathena* 167 (1999) 59–70.

Farney, G. D., *Ethnic Identity and Aristocratic Competition in Republican Rome* (Cambridge 2007).

Farrell, J., *Latin Language and Latin Culture from Ancient to Modern Times* (Cambridge 2001).

Feldherr, A., *Spectacle and Society in Livy's History* (Berkeley and Los Angeles 1998).

Field, L. W., "Beyond Identity? Analytic Crosscurrents in Contemporary Mayanist Social Science," *Latin American Research Review* 40 (2005) 283–93.

Flashar, M., H.-J. Gehrke, and E. Heinrich, eds., *Retrospektive. Konzepte der Vergangenheit in der griechisch-römischen Antike* (Berlin 1996).

Flory, M. B., "*Sic Exempla Parantur*: Livia's Shrine to Concordia and the Porticus Liviae," *Historia* 33 (1984) 309–30.

Flower, H. I., *Ancestor Masks and Aristocratic Power in Roman Culture* (Oxford 1996).

———, "Spectacle and Political Culture in the Roman Republic," in *The Cambridge Companion to the Roman Republic*, ed. H. I. Flower (Cambridge 2005) 322–343.

———, "Der Leichenzug—die Ahnen kommen wieder," in *Erinnerungsorte der Antike: Die römische Welt*, ed. E. Stein-Hölkeskamp and K.-J. Hölkeskamp (Munich 2006a) 321–39.

———, *The Art of Forgetting: Sanctions against Memory in Ancient Rome* (Chapel Hill 2006b).

Fowler, D., "The Ruin of Time: Monuments and Survival at Rome," in *Roman Constructions: Readings in Postmodern Latin* (Oxford 2000) 193–217.

Frisch, P., "Zu den Elogien des Augustusforums," *Zeitschrift für Papyrologie und Epigraphik* (1980) 91–98.

Gazich, R., *"Exemplum" ed esemplarità in Properzio*, Scienze filologiche e storia, Brescia 6 (Milan 1999).

George, M., ed., *The Roman Family in the Empire: Rome, Italy and Beyond* (Oxford 2005).

Giuliano, A., ed., *Museo Nazionale Romano. Le sculture* (Rome 1984).

Gleason, M., "Elite Male Identity in the Roman Empire," in *Life, Death and Entertainment in the Roman Empire*, ed. D. S. Potter and D. J. Mattingly (Ann Arbor 1999) 67–84.

Gowing, A. M., *Empire and Memory: The Representation of the Roman Republic in Imperial Culture* (Cambridge 2005).

Grassinger, D., "The Meaning of Myth on Roman Sarcophagi," in *Fenway Court 1994: Isabella Stewart Gardner Museum* (Boston 1994) 91–107.

Gray-Fow, M. J. G., "A Stepfather's Gift: L. Marcius Philippus and Octavian," *Greece & Rome* 35 (1988) 184–99.

Green, C. M. C., *Roman Religion and the Cult of Diana at Aricia* (Cambridge 2007).

Groebner, V., *Who Are You? Identification, Deception, and Surveillance in Early Modern Europe*, trans. M. Kyburz and J. Peck (New York 2007).

Guerrini, R., "*L'exemplum* in contesto di variazione: vocaboli nuovi e *nomina agentis* in Valerio Massimo," *Materiali e discussioni per l'analisi dei testi classici* 33 (1994) 207–19.

Gunderson, E., *Declamation, Paternity and Roman Identity: Authority and the Rhetorical Self* (Cambridge 2003).

Habinek, T., *The Politics of Latin Literature: Writing, Identity and Empire in Ancient Rome* (Princeton 1998).

———, "Seneca's Renown: Gloria, Claritudo, and the Replication of the Roman Elite," *Classical Antiquity* 19 (2000) 264–303.

———, *Ancient Rhetoric and Oratory* (Oxford 2004).

Hales, S., *Roman Houses and Social Identity* (Cambridge 2003).

Hallett, C. H., *The Roman Nude: Heroic Portrait Statuary 200 B.C.–A.D. 300* (Oxford 2005).

Handler, R., "Is 'Identity' a Useful Cross-cultural Concept?," in *Commemorations: The Politics of National Identity*, ed. J. Gillis (Princeton 1994) 27–40.

Hanfmann, G. M. A., "Personality and Portraiture in Ancient Art," *Proceedings of the American Philosophical Society* 117 (1973) 259–85.

Hartmann, E., U. Hartmann, and K. Pietzner, eds., *Geschlechterdefinitionen und Geschlechtergrenzen in der Antike* (Stuttgart 2007).

Hartney, A. M., *Gruesome Deaths and Celibate Lives: Christian Martyrs and Ascetics* (Bristol 2005).

Haug, A., "Constituting the Past—Forming the Present. The Role of Material Culture in the Augustan Period," *Journal of the History of Collections* 13 (2001) 111–23.

Haynes, H., *The History of Make-Believe: Tacitus on Imperial Rome* (Berkeley 2003).

Hemelrijk, E. A., "Masculinity and Femininity in the *Laudatio Turiae*," *Classical Quarterly* 54 (2004) 185–97.

———, "Octavian and the Introduction of Public Statues for Women in Rome," *Athenaeum* 93 (2005) 309–17.

Hesberg, H. von, "Die Häuser der Senatoren in Rom: gesellschaftliche und politische Funktion," in *Senatores populi Romani. Realität und mediale Präsentation einer Führungsschicht.* Kolloquium der Prosopographia Imperii Romani vom 11.–13. Juni 2004, ed. W. Eck and M. Heil, *HABES* 40 (Stuttgart 2005) 19–52.

Højte, J. M., ed., *Images of Ancestors*, Aarhus Studies in Mediterranean Antiquity 5 (Aarhus 2002).

Hölkeskamp, K.-J., "Ikonen der Virtus—exemplarische Helden(-taten) im monumentalen Gedächtnis der römischen Republik," in *Modelli eroici dall'Antichità alla cultura europea*, ed. A. Barzanò, C. Bearzot, F. Landucci, L. Prandi, and G. Zecchini (Rome 2003) 213–37.

———, "*Exempla* und *mos maiorum*: Überlegungen zum kollektiven Gedächtnis der Nobilität," in *Vergangenheit und Lebenswelt: soziale Kommunikation, Traditionsbildung und historisches Bewusstsein*, ed. H.-J. Gehrke and A. Möller (Tübingen 1996) 301–38 = *Senatus Populusque Romanus. Die politische Kultur der Repubulik—Dimensionen und Deutungen* (Stuttgart 2004) 169–98.

———, *Senatus Populusque Romanus. Die politische Kultur der Republik—Dimensionen und Deutungen* (Stuttgart 2004).

———, "Der Triumph—'erinnere Dich, daß Du ein Mensch bist'," in *Erinnerungsorte der Antike: Die römische Welt*, ed. E. Stein-Hölkeskamp and K.-J. Hölkeskamp (Munich 2006) 258–76; 745–47.

Holliday, P., "The Rhetoric of *Romanitas*: The 'Tomb of the Statilii' Frescoes Reconsidered," *Memoirs of the American Academy in Rome* 50 (2005) 89–129.

Hölscher, T., "Die Alten vor Augen: Politische Denkmäler und öffentliches Gedächtnis im republikanischen Rom," in *Institutionalität und Symbolisierung: Verstetigungen kultureller Ordnungsmuster in Vergangenheit und Gegenwart*, ed. G. Melville (Cologne 2001) 183–211.

———, "Provokation und Transgression als politischer Habitus in der späten römischen Republik," *Römische Mitteilungen* 111 (2004) 83–104.

———, "Greek Styles and Greek Art in Augustan Rome: Issues of the Present versus Records of the Past," in *Classical Pasts: The Classical Tradition of Greece and Rome*, ed. J. I. Porter (Princeton 2005) 238–59.

Holton, G., "Robert K. Merton," *Proceedings of the American Philosophical Society* 148 (2004) 506–17.

hooks, b., "marginality as site of resistance," in *Out There: Marginalization and Contemporary Cultures*, ed. R. Ferguson, M. Gever, T. Minh-ha, and C. West (Cambridge, Mass. 1992) 341–43.

Horsmann, G., *Die Wagenlenker der römischen Kaiserzeit. Untersuchungen zu ihrer sozialen Stellung* (Stuttgart 1998).

Horster, M., "Kinderkarrieren?," in *Satura Lanx. Festschrift für Werner A. Krenkel zum 70. Geburtstag*, ed. C. Klodt, Spudasmata 62 (Hildesheim 1996) 223–37.

Howgego, C., "Coinage and Identity in the Roman Provinces," in *Coinage and Identity in the Roman Provinces*, ed. C. Howgego, V. Heuchert, and A. Burnett (Oxford 2005) 1–17.

Howgego, C., V. Heuchert, and A. Burnett, eds., *Coinage and Identity in the Roman Provinces* (Oxford 2005).

Huskinson, J., "Disappearing Children? Children in Roman Funerary Art of the First to the Fourth Century A.D.," in *Hoping for Continuity: Childhood, Education, and Death in Antiquity and the Middle Ages*, ed. K. Mustakallio, J. Hanska, H.-L. Sainio, and V. Vuolanto, Acta Instituti Romani Finlandiae 33 (Rome 2005) 101–14.

———, "Constructing Childhood on Roman Funerary Memorials," in *Constructions of Childhood in the Ancient World*, ed. A. Cohen and J. B. Rutter, *Hesperia* Suppl. 41 (Princeton 2008).

Imbert, C., "Sertorius, *exemplum* politique et figure litteraire au seuil de l'age classique," *Pallas* 60 (2002) 133–45.

Inwood, B., "Seneca in His Philosophical Milieu," in *Greece in Rome: Influence, Integration, Resistance*, ed. C. P. Jones, C. Segal, R. J. Tarrant, and R. F. Thomas, *Harvard Studies in Classical Philology* 97 (Cambridge, Mass. 1995) 63–76.

Itgenshorst, T., "Augustus und der republikanische Triumph: Triumphalfasten und *summi viri*—Galerie als Instrumente der imperialen Machtsicherung," *Hermes* 132 (2004) 436–58.

Jones, C. P., "Multiple Identities in the Age of the Second Sophistic," in *Paideia: The World of the Second Sophistic / Die Welt der Zweiten Sophistik*, ed. B. Borg (Berlin 2004) 13–21.

Joshel, S. R., and S. Murnaghan, eds., *Women and Slaves in Greco-Roman Culture: Differential Equations* (London 1998).

Kampen, N. B., "On Writing Histories of Roman Art," *Art Bulletin* 85 (2003) 371–86.

Kellum, B., "Playing All the Roles: The Social Authorship of Wealthy Roman Freedpeople," article manuscript (forthcoming).

Kendall, P., "Theory and Research: The Case Studies in Medical Education," in *The Idea of Social Structure*, ed. C. A. Coser (New York 1975) 301–21.

King, M., "Commemoration of Infants on Roman Funerary Inscriptions," in *The Epigraphy of Death: Studies in the History and Society of Greece and Rome*, ed. G. J. Oliver (Liverpool 2000) 117–54.

———, "Whose Identity? Whose Role Model? Representations of Young Children on Roman Funerary Memorials," unpublished paper delivered at the conference "Role Models in the Roman World and Early Modern Italy," American Academy in Rome, 17 March 2003.

Kleijwegt, M., "The Social Dimensions of Gladiatorial Combat in Petronius' *Cena Trimalchionis*," in *Groningen Colloquium on the Novel*, ed. H. Hofmann and M. Zimmerman (Groningen 1998) 9:75–96.

Kleiner, D. E. E., *Roman Imperial Funerary Altars with Portraits*, Archaeologica 62 (Rome 1987).

Kleiner, D. E. E., and S. B. Matheson, "Introduction: 'Her Parents Gave Her the Name Claudia'," in *I Claudia II: Women in Roman Art and Society*, ed. D. E. E. Kleiner and S. B. Matheson (Austin 2000) 1–14.

Kockel, V., "Typus und Individuum: Zur Interpretation des 'Realismus' im Porträt der Späten Republik," in *Realität und Projektion. Wirklichkeitsnahe Darstellung in Antike und Mittelalter*, ed. M. Büchsel and P. Schmidt (Berlin 2005) 73–86.

Koortbojian, M., *Myth, Meaning, and Memory on Roman Sarcophagi* (Berkeley 1995).

———, "A Painted *Exemplum* at Rome's Temple of Liberty," *Journal of Roman Studies* 92 (2002) 33–48.

Kornhardt, H., "Exemplum. Eine bedeutungsgeschichtliche Studie" (Ph.D. diss., Universität Göttingen 1936).

Kraus, C. S., "From *Exempla* to *Exemplar*? Writing History around the Emperor in Imperial Rome," in *Flavius Josephus and Flavian Rome*, ed. J. Edmondson (Oxford 2005) 181–200.

Kraus, C. S., and A. J. Woodman, *Latin Historians* (Oxford 1997).

Kunst, C., and U. Reimer, eds., *Grenzen der Macht. Zur Rolle der römischen Kaiserfrauen*, Potsdamer altertums-wissenschaftliche Beiträge 3 (Stuttgart 2000).

Langlands, R., *Sexual Morality in Ancient Rome* (Cambridge 2006).

Larmour, D. H. J., and D. Spencer, eds., *The Sites of Rome: Time, Space, Memory* (Oxford 2007).

Laurence, R., "Introduction," in *Cultural Identity in the Roman Empire*, ed. J. Berry and R. Laurence (London 1998) 1–9.

———, "The Uneasy Dialogue between Ancient History and Archaeology," in *Archaeology and Ancient History*, ed. E. Sauer (London 2004) 99–113.

Laurence, R., and M. Harlow, *Growing Up and Growing Old in Ancient Rome: A Life Course Approach* (London 2002).

Lenz, S., *An Exemplary Life*, trans. D. Parmée (New York 1976).

Lieu, J. M., *Christian Identity in the Jewish and Graeco-Roman World* (Oxford 2004).

Linke, B., and M. Stemmler, eds., Mos maiorum*: Untersuchungen zu den Formen der Identitätsstiftung und Stabilisierung in der römischen Republik* (Stuttgart 2000).

Litchfield, H. W., "National *Exempla Virtutis* in Roman Literature," *Harvard Studies in Classical Philology* 25 (1914) 1–71.

Lowrie, M., "Making an *Exemplum* of Yourself: Cicero and Augustus," in *Classical Constructions. Papers in Memory of Don Fowler, Classicist and Epicurean*, ed. S. J. Heyworth, with P. G. Fowler and S. J. Harrison (Oxford 2007) 91–112.

———, *The* Exemplum*, the Exception, and Self-Authorization in Cicero, Caesar, and Augustus* (forthcoming a).

———, "The Law and the *Exemplum*: Cicero on the Gracchi," *Law and the Humanities* (forthcoming b).

——, "Cornelia's *Exemplum*: Form and Ideology in Propertius 4.11," in *Elegy and Narrativity*, ed. G. Liveley and P. B. Salzman-Mitchell (Columbus forthcoming c).

Mauch, M., *Senecas Frauenbild in den philosophischen Schriften* (Bern 1997).

Mauss, M., "A Category of the Human Mind: The Notion of Person, the Notion of Self," in *The Category of the Person: Anthropology, Philosophy, History*, ed. M. Carrithers, S. Collins, and S. Lukes (Cambridge 1985).

McDonnell, M., *Roman Manliness: "Virtus" and the Roman Republic* (Cambridge 2006).

McWilliam, J. C., "Children among the Dead: The Influence of Urban Life on the Commemoration of Children on Tombstone Inscriptions," in *Childhood, Class and Kin in the Roman World*, ed. S. Dixon (London 2001) 74–98.

Melnick, M. J., "The Villain as Reference Idol: Selection Frequencies and Salient Attributes among New Zealand Teenagers," *Adolescence* 33 (1998) 543–54.

Merton, R. K., *Social Theory and Social Structure* (New York 1949, repr. 1968).

Merton, R. K., G. G. Reader, and P. Kendall, eds., *The Student Physician* (Cambridge, Mass. 1957).

Methy, N., "'*Ad exemplar antiquitatis.*' Les grandes figures du passé dans la correspondance de Pline le Jeune," *Revue des études latines* 81 (2003) 200–214.

Michel, D., *Alexander als Vorbild für Pompeius, Caesar und Marcus Antonius*, Collection Latomus 94 (Brussels 1967).

Milnor, K., *Gender, Domesticity, and the Age of Augustus: Inventing Private Life* (Oxford 2005).

Motto, L., "Seneca on Old Age," *Cuadernos de filología clásica: Estudios latinos* 19 (2000) 125–39.

Muth, S., *Erleben von Raum—Leben im Raum: Zur Funktion mythologischer Mosaikbilder in der römisch-kaiserzeitlichen Wohnarchitektur*, Archäologie und Geschichte 10 (Heidelberg 1998).

Needham, R., *Exemplars* (Berkeley 1985).

Neudecker, R., and P. Zanker, eds., *Lebenswelten. Bilder und Räume in der römischen Stadt der Kaiserzeit*, Symposium am 24. und 25. Januar 2002 zum Abschluß des von der Gerda Henkel Stiftung geförderte Forschungsprogramms "Stadtkultur in der römischen Kaiserzeit," *Palilia* 19 (Wiesbaden 2005).

Noreña, C., "The Communication of the Emperor's Virtues," *Journal of Roman Studies* 91 (2001) 146–68.

Olson, K., "*Matrona* and Whore: The Clothing of Women in Roman Antiquity," *Fashion Theory* 6 (2002) 387–420.

Osborne, R., and J. Tanner, eds., *Art's Agency and Art History* (Malden, Mass. 2006).

Panitschek, P., "Sp. Cassius, Sp. Maelius, M. Manlius als *exempla maiorum*," *Philologus* 133 (1989) 231–45.

Parker, H., "Loyal Slaves and Loyal Wives. The Crisis of the Outsider-within and Roman *Exemplum* Literature," in *Women and Slaves in Greco-Roman Culture: Differential Equations*, ed. S. R. Joshel and S. Murnaghan (London 1998) 152–73.

Perez Jimenez, A., "*Exemplum*: The Paradigmatic Education of the Ruler in the Lives of Plutarch," in *Sage and Emperor: Plutarch, Greek Intellectuals, and Roman Power in the Time of Trajan (98–117 A.D.)*, ed. P. A. Stadter and L. Van der Stockt (Leuven 2002) 16–35.

Piepenbrink, K., *Christliche Identität und Assimilation in der Spätantike. Probleme des Christseins in der Reflexion der Zeitgenossen*, Studien zur Alten Geschichte 3 (Frankfurt 2005).

Pitts, M., "The Emperor's New Clothes? The Utility of Identity in Roman Archaeology," *American Journal of Archaeology* 111 (2007) 693–713.

Pollini, J., "Ritualizing Death in Republican Rome: Memory, Religion, Class Struggle, and the Wax Ancestral Mask Tradition's Origin and Influence on Veristic Portraiture," in *Performing Death: Social Analyses of Funerary Traditions in the Ancient Near East and Mediterranean*, ed. N. Laneri, Oriental Institute Seminars 3 (Chicago 2007) 237–85.

Poorthuis, M., and J. Schwartz, eds., *Saints and Role Models in Judaism and Christianity*, Jewish and Christian Perspectives Series 7 (Leiden 2004).

Preston, R., "Roman Questions, Greek Answers: Plutarch and the Construction of Identity," in *Being Greek under Rome: Cultural Identity, the Second Sophistic, and the Development of Empire*, ed. S. Goldhill (Cambridge 2001) 86–119.

Quan, T., "The Littlest Harlot: Barbie's Career as a Role Model," in *Whores and Other Feminists*, ed. J. Nagle (New York 1997) 119–24.

Quint, D., *Epic and Empire: Politics and Generic Form from Virgil to Milton* (Princeton 1993).

Ramsby, T., "Striving for Permanence: Ovid's Funerary Inscriptions," *Classical Journal* 100 (2005) 365–91.

Ramsby, T., and B. Severy, "Gender, Sex, and the Domestication of the Empire in Art of the Augustan Age," *Arethusa* 40 (2007) 43–71.

Rawson, B., *Children and Childhood in Roman Italy* (Oxford 2003a).

———, "The Roman Family in Recent Research: State of the Question," *Biblical Interpretation* 11 (2003b) 119–38.

Rives, J. B., "Interdisciplinary Approaches," in *A Companion to the Roman Empire*, ed. D. S. Potter (Malden, Mass. 2006) 98–112.

Roller, M. B., *Constructing Autocracy: Aristocrats and Emperors in Julio-Claudian Rome* (Princeton 2001).

———, "Exemplarity in Roman Culture: The Cases of Horatius Cocles and Cloelia," *Classical Philology* 99 (2004) 1–56.

———, "Exemplarity," in *The Cambridge Companion to Roman Historiography*, ed. A. Feldherr (Cambridge forthcoming).

Rossetti, A. M., "Committenze e monumenti funerari nella Hispania Tarraconensis," *Anales de arqueología cordobesa* 10 (1999) 231–62.

Ruck, B., "Das Denkmal der Cornelia in Rom," *Römische Mitteilungen* 111 (2004) 477–94.

Rüpke, J., "Triumphator and Ancestor Rituals between Symbolic Anthropology and Magic," *Numen* 53 (2006) 251–89.

Schade, K., *Frauen in der Spätantike—Status und Repräsentation. Eine Untersuchung zur römischen und frühbyzantinischen Bildniskunst* (Mainz 2003).

Schmitzer, U., "Strenge Jungfräulichkeit. Zur Figur der Göttin Diana in Ovids Metamorphosen," *Wiener Studien* 114 (2001) 303–21.

Schröder, B.-J., and J.-P. Schröder, eds., *Studium declamatorium. Untersuchungen zu Schulübungen und Prunk-reden von der Antike bis zur Neuzeit*, Beiträge zur Altertumskunde 176 (Munich and Leipzig 2003).

Sebesta, J. L., "Women's Costume and Feminine Civic Morality in Augustan Rome," *Gender & History* 9 (1997) 529–41.

Sehlmeyer, M., "Die kommunikative Leistung römischer Ehrenstatuen," in *Moribus antiquis res stat Romana: Römische Werte und römische Literatur im 3. und 2. Jh. v. Chr.*, ed. M. Braun, H. Haltenhoff, and F. H. Mutschler, Beiträge zur Altertumskunde 134 (Munich and Leipzig 2000) 271–84.

Serghidou, A., ed., *Fear of Slaves—Fear of Enslavement in the Ancient Mediterranean. Peur de l'esclave—Peur de l'esclavage en Mediterranee ancienne (Discours, représentations, pratiques)*. Actes di XXIXe Colloque du Groupe International de Recherche sur l'Esclavage dans l'Antiquité (GIREA). Rethymnon 4–7 November 2004 (Franche-Comté 2007).

Severy, B., *Augustus and the Family at the Birth of the Roman Empire* (New York and London 2003).

Sharrock, A., "Re(ge)ndering Gender(ed) Studies," *Gender & History* 9 (1997) 603–14.

Shearman, J., *Only Connect . . . Art and the Spectator in the Italian Renaissance* (Princeton 1992).

Shelton, J., *As the Romans Did: A Sourcebook in Roman Social History*, 2nd ed. (Oxford 1998).

Shumka, L. J., "Designing Women: Studies in the Representation of Femininity in Roman Society" (Ph.D. diss., University of Victoria 2001).

Siropoulos, S. D., "An Exemplary 'Oikos': Domestic Role-models in Euripides' 'Alcestis'," *Eirene* 37 (2001) 5–18.

Skidmore, C., *Practical Ethics for Roman Gentlemen: The Work of Valerius Maximus* (Exeter 1996).

Smith, R., "The Construction of the Past in the Roman Empire," in *A Companion to the Roman Empire*, ed. D. S. Potter (Malden, Mass. 2006) 411–38.

Smith, R. R. R., "Cultural Choice and Political Identity in Honorific Portrait Statues in the Greek East in the Second Century A.D.," *Journal of Roman Studies* 88 (1998) 56–93.

——, "The Use of Images: Visual History and Ancient History," in *Classics in Progress: Essays on Ancient Greece and Rome*, ed. T. P. Wiseman (Oxford 2002) 59–102.

Spannagel, M., *Exemplaria Principis. Untersuchungen zu Entstehung und Ausstattung des Augustusforums* (Heidelberg 1999).

Späth, T., "'Frauenmacht' in der frühen römischen Kaiserzeit?," in *Reine Männersache? Frauen in Männer-domänen der antiken Welt*, ed. M. Dettenhofer (Cologne and Vienna 1994) 159–205.

Stehle, E., ed., "Unmasked Performances," special edition of *Helios* 28 (2001).

Stein-Hölkeskamp, E., "Das römische Haus—die memoria der Mauern," in *Erinnerungsorte der Antike: Die römische Welt*, ed. E. Stein-Hölkeskamp and K.-J. Hölkeskamp (Munich 2006) 300–321.

Stein-Hölkeskamp, E., and K.-J. Hölkeskamp, eds., *Erinnerungsorte der Antike: Die römische Welt* (Munich 2006).

Stewart, A., "Baroque Classics: The Tragic Muse and the *Exemplum*," in *Classical Pasts: The Classical Tradition of Greece and Rome*, ed. J. I. Porter (Princeton 2005) 127–70.

Stewart, P. C. N., *Statues in Roman Society: Representation and Response* (Oxford 2003).

——, "The Image of the Roman Emperor," in *Presence: The Inherence of the Prototype within Images and Other Objects*, ed. R. Shepherd and R. Maniura (London 2006) 243–58.

Storey, G., "Archaeology and Roman Society: Integrating Textual and Archaeological Data," *Journal of Archaeological Research* 7 (1999) 203–48.

Styka, J., "Die Bedeutung der *exemplaria graeca* in den Kunstansichten römischer Autoren der augusteischen und der Kaiserzeit," *Klio* 73 (1991) 143–56.

Tardy, É., and M. Vallée, eds., *Femmes: images, modèles; actes du Colloque de l'Institut de recherches sur les femmes = Women: Images, Role Models; Proceedings of the Canadian Research Institute for the Advancement of Women Conference* (Ottawa 1985).

Temporini-Grafin, H., ed., *Die Kaiserinnen Roms von Livia bis Theordora* (Munich 2003).

Thurn, N., "Der Aufbau der Exemplasammlung des Valerius Maximus," *Hermes* 129 (2001) 79–94.

Tierney, S., "Media Icons: Dangerous Role Models or Innocent Scapegoats?," *Journal of Gender Studies* 10 (2001) 323–27.

Uzzi, J. D., *Children in the Visual Arts of Imperial Rome* (Cambridge 2005).

Varner, E., ed., *From Caligula to Constantine: Tyranny and Transformation in Roman Portraiture* (Atlanta 2000).

Von den Hoff, R., and S. Schmidt, "Bilder und Konstruktion: Ein Interdisziplinäres Konzept für die Altertumswissenschaften," in *Konstruktionen von Wirklichkeit*, ed. R. von den Hoff and S. Schmidt (Stuttgart 2001) 11–25.

Wacquant, L. J. D., "The Pugilistic Point of View: How Boxers Think and Feel about Their Trade," *Theory and Society* 24 (1995) 489–535.

Wallace-Hadrill, A., "*Mutatio morum*: The Idea of a Cultural Revolution," in *The Roman Cultural Revolution*, ed. T. Habinek and A. Schiesaro (Cambridge 1997) 3–22.

———, "The Roman Revolution and Material Culture," in *La Révolution Romaine après Ronald Syme. Bilans et Perspectives*, ed. A. Giovannini and B. Grange, *Entretiens sur l'Antiquité Classique* 46 (Geneva 2000) 283–321.

Walter, U., Memoria *und* res publica. *Zur Geschichtkultur im republikanischen Rom*, Studien zur Alten Geschichte 1 (Frankfurt am Main 2004).

Weber, G., and M. Zimmermann, eds., *Propaganda—Selbstdarstellung—Repräsentation im römischen Kaiserreich des 1. Jhs. n. Chr.*, *Historia* Einzelschrift 164 (Stuttgart 2003).

Welch, T. S., "Masculinity and Monuments in Propertius 4.9," *American Journal of Philology* 125 (2004) 61–90.

Williamson, G., "Aspects of Identity," in *Coinage and Identity in the Roman Provinces*, ed. C. Howgego, V. Heuchert, and A. Burnett (Oxford 2005) 19–27.

Wittchow, F., *Exemplarisches Erzählen bei Ammianus Marcellinus: Episode, Exemplum, Anekdote*, Beiträge zur Altertumskunde 144 (Munich 2001).

Witzmann, P., "Integrations- und Identifikationsprozesse römischer Freigelassener nach Auskunft der Inschriften (1. Jh. v. Chr.)," in *O tempora, o mores! Römische Werte und römische Literatur in den letzten Jahrzehnten der Republik*, ed. A. Haltenhoff, A. Heil, and F.-H. Mutschler (Munich 2003) 289–321.

Woodhull, M., "Engendering Space: Octavia's Portico in Rome," *Aurora* 4 (2003) 13–33.

Woolf, G., "Cultural Change in Roman Antiquity: Observations on Agency," *Kodai* 13/14 (2003–2004) 157–67.

———, "Some Problems in the Archaeological Theorization of Identity," unpublished paper delivered at the conference "Crossing Cultures. Identities in the Material World," 7–9 January 2005, Bristol.

Zanker, P., *The Power of Images in the Age of Augustus*, trans. A. Shapiro (Ann Arbor 1988).

———, "Nouvelles orientations de la recherche en iconographie. Commanditaires et spectateurs," *Revue Archéologique* (1994) 281–93.

1 ◆ THE CONCEPT OF ROLES AND THE MALAISE OF "IDENTITY": ANCIENT ROME AND THE MODERN WORLD

Tonio Hölscher

Fixed Roles, Ancient and Present

On the column of Trajan the emperor appears no less than nine times in a scene of *adlocutio*, a speech to his army.[1] He is always represented standing on a high podium, surrounded or followed by a group of officers, and directing his words with a deictic gesture towards his soldiers (fig. 1).[2] Very similarly President George Bush is pictured in American newspapers in a television speech to his nation, which is suggested as his audience by two microphones (fig. 3).[3] The Roman emperor demonstrates by his entourage that he conducts the war against the Dacians in accordance with good advisors; in some scenes of the war council, this aspect even becomes an autonomous topic (fig. 2).[4] Likewise, the American president emphasizes the fact that he wages the war against Iraq in total agreement with a group of influential senators. The similarity of attitudes is striking: the protagonist being more emphatically directed toward the audience, with an expression of great determination, the others in part looking at him, in part repeating and enhancing his determined expression, in part complementing it by physiognomies of seriousness and thoughtfulness.

In Roman art such scenes of *adlocutio* appear also on other monuments celebrating successful wars, most similarly on the column of Marcus Aurelius and on the arch of Septimius Severus. It was a stock type of political representation, in art as well as in real war, stressing some fundamental aspects of Roman aggressive warfare, above all the emperor's quality of political and military leadership, his personal determination to wage the war, his capacity to mobilize the ideological program of Roman virtues, his confidential reliance on his military staff, and his good relations, *concordia* and *fides*, with his army.[5] The emperor, his officers, and the soldiers played a precise role in this event, by which they enacted these ideological concepts as a public performance. All this seems to have changed little in the last nearly 2,000 years.

Great emphasis is laid in such scenes on visual staging. Often Trajan is delivering his speech in

---

This contribution was given on the morning of Monday, 19 March 2003, following the night in which the war against Iraq was started. It is not only with the intention of an accurate record of that situation that I did not modify the text into a timeless scientific product. The text was written during a research stay at the German Archaeological Institute in Rome for a group project, "Bilderwelt—Lebenswelt im antiken Rom und im Römischen Reich," financed by the Gerda Henkel Stiftung, Düsseldorf.

[1] Scenes of *adlocutio* on the column of Trajan: Baumer 1991; David 2000.

[2] Lepper and Frere 1988, pl. LXXVII, cf. also pls. XI, XXVII, XXXXIX; Coarelli 1999, pl. 125, cf. also pls. 10, 26, 46, 56, 84, 90.

[3] *The Boston Globe*, 3 October 2002, p. 1.

[4] Lepper and Frere 1988, pl. IX, cf. other groups of advisors: pls. XXV, XXVI, XLII, XLIX, LX, LXXVIII; Coarelli 1999, pl. 7; for numerous other groups of advisors: pls. 33, 35, 62, 76, 95, 127.

[5] Campbell 1984, 69–88.

Fig. 1. Trajan in
adlocutio. *Rome,*
Column of Trajan
(photo Anger,
DAIR, inst. neg.
1989.0583).

Fig. 2. Trajan
seated amidst his
war council. Rome,
Column of Trajan
(photo Anger,
DAIR, inst. neg.
1991.0150).

front of his army's insignia, the holiest symbols of Roman sovereignty,[6] very much like his American counterpart, before beginning a fundamental speech on attacking Iraq (fig. 4).[7] The president's "vision for the Near and the Middle East," as it is advertised in the newspapers, must be a vision of

---

[6] Other scenes with the representative use of ensigns: Lepper and Frere 1988, pls. X, XI, XXI, XXV, XXXIII, XXXVII, XXXIX, XLII; Coarelli 1999, pls. 10, 26, 32, 46, 49, 53, 55, 56, 63, etc.

[7] *Süddeutsche Zeitung*, 28 February 2003, p. 1.

Fig. 3. President George W. Bush speaking
at the White House alongside members of Congress
(photo © AP Images/Doug Mills).

Fig. 4. President George W. Bush
preparing to address an audience (photo ©
Agence France-Presse/Getty Images).

Fig. 5. Trajan receiving
the submission of Dacians.
Rome, Column of Trajan
(photo Anger, DAIR, inst.
neg. 1989.0746).

enemy defeat similar to that accomplished by Trajan in a scene of submission in front of his army's
ensigns (fig. 5).[8] Performative roles call for appropriate strategies and types of visibility.

Another means of giving impressive visibility to public events is staging them in front of the
appropriate public scenery.[9] Before entering the theater of war on the Balkans, Trajan performs a

[8] Lepper and Frere 1988, pls. LIV–LV; Coarelli 1999, pls.   [9] See Grunow 2002.
86–88.

great sacrifice in front of the magnificent facades of a theater, a temple, and other public buildings, representing the kind of Roman urban culture that is to be saved against the assault of the Dacians.[10] In the same sense, Trajan's great administrative acts of money distribution and debt release are represented on the Anaglypha Traiani in front of public buildings of the Forum Romanum, the public burning of the debt records being placed below the temple of Saturnus, where the public treasury was housed.[11] Even more impressive is the great speech of Constantine on a relief on his arch, displayed on the rostra of the Roman Forum, in front of the five-columned monument of Diocletian and his co-emperors, and framed by statues of Hadrian and Marcus Aurelius.[12] Here the architecture of the huge platform, the columns with statues of Jupiter and his imperial predecessors, the images of "ideal" emperors of the past, and, last but not least, the real entourage of the emperor as well as the audience of citizens add up to a magnificent tableau of Roman greatness. From written sources we know that this staging of public acts in significant public spaces was a device not only of art but also of political reality. Symbolic architecture and significant images are the visual space in which the real actors play their symbolic roles.

The most important common denominator between the ancient war and its contemporary counterparts is the reduction of the adversaries' resistance to an individual foe. While all Dacians are continually defeated, in flight and submitting to the victorious Romans, Decebalus is the only enemy who stubbornly offers resistance to them. His role, however, as well as that of his actual doubles, is characterized by a dramatic lack of visibility, acting as he is from the woods and other hidden places.[13] War, therefore, necessarily ends in the pursuit and hunt of the great personification of evil.[14]

The Roles of a Roman Emperor

On Trajan's column, the scenes of *adlocutio* are part of a precisely calculated scheme of military activities. Each of the three great offensive campaigns is described as an almost stereotyped sequence of a limited number of stock scenes.[15] It starts with a *profectio* of the emperor and the army, followed by a war *consilium* (fig. 2), a ritual *lustratio* of the army, and an encouraging *adlocutio*. After these initial rituals, fortifications, camps, and roads are built, and the first captives are brought to the emperor. Then the army sets out to fight, a great battle is waged and of course won, and the brave soldiers are praised by the emperor in a second *adlocutio*. The subsequent scenes demonstrate the consequences of victory, a collective *submissio* of further groups of the enemy, a final speech, and a description of the more or less cruel consequences for the rest of the enemies' population. Within this general scheme there occur, during these three sequences of Roman initiatives, some minor modifications according to the specific character of the different campaigns, and moreover some individual scenes are inserted here and there. But on the whole, the concept remains remarkably stable. The same holds true for the two defensive campaigns, which follow a somewhat diverse pattern.

[10] Lepper and Frere 1988, pl. LXIII; cf. other imperial acts in front of impressive facades of significant buildings: pls. X (left), XXVI (right), XXXVII, LXXII; Coarelli 1999, pl. 101, cf. pls. 8, 35, 53, 118.

[11] Hannestad 1986, 192–94; Kleiner 1992, 248–50.

[12] Hannestad 1986, fig. 127.

[13] Particularly notable: Lepper and Frere 1988, pl. XCIX;

Coarelli 1999, pl. 163.

[14] After these lines were written, history continued its play of analogies: the sons of the actual foe Saddam Hussein being captured and executed, like those of Decebalos on the column, their corpses publicly exposed, which in the relief account is the destiny of Decebalos himself (Lepper and Frere 1988, pls. CVI–CVIII; Coarelli 1999, pls. 171–73).

[15] Hölscher 1991; Hölscher 2002.

Obviously, in all such scenes the emperor, the officers, the various parts of the army, and even the enemies play fixed roles. In these roles they perform a number of fixed values, which constitute the ideological framework of Roman warfare and Roman politics. The emperor demonstrates in the *profectio* his *virtus* of leading the army against the enemy; in the council scene, his quality of deliberating and consulting with his officers; in the *lustratio*, his *pietas* and *providentia*, securing the favor of the gods; in the *adlocutio*, his good relations, *concordia* and *fides*, with his soldiers; in the building scenes, his capacity to induce the soldiers to hard labor, *labor*, and to organize the military infrastructure of war; in the battle pieces, his *virtus* of supreme command; and in the *submissio*, his *clementia*, his *iustitia*, or his determination to punish hostile rebels.[16]

Almost all of these scenes, with their respective roles and values, also appear on other monuments of war and victory, referring to other emperors, other enemies in other parts of the world, and other courses of actual events. Almost regardless of historical differences, various war campaigns are conceived in official monuments according, more or less, to the same general patterns.

These results can be transferred and enlarged to the whole range of political representation on Roman state monuments, ranging from the solemn *adventus* of the emperor in Rome at the beginning of his reign to public sacrifices in civic spaces and to scenes of *liberalitas* toward the poorer sections of the population.[17] The whole political business of the Roman emperor is represented on his monuments as a limited number of stock scenes in which he performs in public a limited number of stock ideals of a Roman statesman and war hero.

The Functions and Ambivalence of Role Behavior

The function of social roles is to provide the individual person in specific situations with patterns of behavior in accordance with collective expectations. Roles connect the individual person with three fundamental spheres of their existence: with the structural system of their society, where they have their social position; with the cultural system from which they receive their behavioral norms and values; and with the reality of social life, where social positions and values are brought into action. By performing a specific role, individuals incorporate specific values of their cultural repertoire that are linked to their specific position in significant social situations, giving them validity and visibility in the space of social reality.

There have been long and fruitless discussions among archaeologists about whether Roman "historical reliefs" are to be read as historical reports or as timeless representations of ideological values—*virtus*, *clementia*, *iustitia*, *pietas*, and so forth—as they were proclaimed on the *clupeus virtutis* of Augustus.[18] Indeed, this exclusive opposition of reality and ideology is conceptually misleading since it neglects the basic dialectics between these two spheres. The function of the Roman emperor was precisely to enact these ideological values in real public life, to give them presence, effectiveness, and visibility in specific situations of social reality. Salvatore Settis has demonstrated that the basic Latin concept of *exemplum* serves as a conceptual link between ideal values and the reality of life.[19] We may add the concept of the public "role," which emphasizes the dynamic, the active and performative aspect of this mediation between ideology and reality.

[16] Hölscher 1980, 290–97.

[17] *Adventus*: Koeppel 1969. Sacrifice: Ryberg 1955. *Liberalitas*: Hamberg 1945, 32–41; Spinola 1990.

[18] See Fittschen 1972; Hölscher 1980. *Clupeus virtutis*: Hölscher 1967, 102–5.

[19] Settis 1985.

Thus, the relative standardization of political scenes in Roman state monuments does not mean, as many scholars have thought, that these monuments do not refer to specific acts, events, and situations of public life and military campaigns. On the contrary, it indicates that political and military enterprises were actually conceived and experienced according to these fixed patterns of public behavior and ideological values.

Therefore, the force—and the danger—of such roles lies in their capacity to reduce the complexity and variety of the world and of human life to a limited repertoire of manageable issues. The infinite variety and complexity of collective and individual life is reduced to a small number of "significant" situations. The wide and highly differentiated range of social and ethical issues is reduced to an imperative spectrum of clear-cut values. The infinite multiplicity and complexity of potential human actions, reactions, and attitudes are reduced to a calculable number of behavioral patterns, of social "roles."

It is obvious that this conception of social reality, of social ideals, and of social behavior in distinct units is extremely helpful for individuals, on the one hand, in order to orient and integrate themselves into their society and, on the other hand, for the community to assign the individual an appropriate place within its social and ethical system. The Roman emperor knew thereby how to present himself within the public space and how to represent himself in public monuments. Roman citizens knew equally well according to which patterns and parameters they might behave toward the emperor and assess his rule. This is one of the basic foundations of the interior stability and the aggressive force of Roman imperial rule.

On the other hand, the simplifying reduction of complexity and variety that is inherent in this whole system tends to exclude the complexity of real experience dramatically. Reducing three entire war campaigns to a sequence of twelve stereotyped stock scenes each leaves very little space for contingent and individual reality. Accordingly, the specific culture of the Dacians, their particular means of resistance, and even their forms of being defeated, are almost nowhere taken into consideration. Conversely, under this condition, ideological claims could become predominant all the more easily: the more ideological concepts are developed in a vacuum of reality, the more they tend to become autonomous and self-sufficient. Needless to say, this combination of ideological self-assertion with ignorance of the adversary and neglect of reality has today reached a disastrous peak.

Complementary Roles, Divergent Roles

The importance accorded such role models in ancient Rome is particularly evident from the statuary types of Roman emperors. As Paul Zanker has demonstrated, there was a limited number of fixed statuary types by which the various qualities and aspects of imperial rule could be represented.[20] The togate type shows the emperor as a Roman citizen on various levels, from the *toga praetexta* of the curule magistrates to the *toga triumphalis* of the *triumphator*; the toga with *velatio capitis* defines him as a religious functionary, representing the quality of *pietas*; and from written sources we know even of the *statua auguralis* type, defining the specific function of the *augur* and the quality of religious *providentia*.[21] On the other hand, the cuirass type showed him as an army leader, incorporating *imperium* and *virtus*.[22] Moreover, there were ideal types, like the seated half-nude type

[20] Zanker 1979.

[21] Goette 1990.

[22] Stemmer 1978.

in the guise of Jupiter, that suggest sovereign rule over the world or the standing nude type with a dynamic turn of the head, after the model of the classical hero Diomedes, that signifies heroic *virtus* combined with superhuman power in the tradition of Alexander the Great.[23]

Individual patrons who intended to set up an image of the emperor had the choice of what specific aspect they wanted to honor him with through their particular statue. Taken together, however, such images of the emperor in all major cities must have quickly become so numerous that the various types of representation added up to a rich spectrum of his qualities, which could be perceived more or less simultaneously, one beside the other. If there existed in Rome by 28 B.C. eighty images of Augustus in silver alone, which he ordered melted down in an act of conspicuous "modesty," then we have an indication of how many portraits in other, more frequently used materials we have to reckon with.[24]

That such images—in various places, of heterogeneous functions, set up by diverse commissioners—may have been viewed by ancient spectators together and in relation to one another is suggested also by single and coherent groups of images where the same person was represented in various statuary types and roles. From the *Historia Augusta* we know of a painting representing the third-century A.D. emperor Tacitus five times: in a Roman toga, in a Greek *chlamys*, in a military cuirass, in a *pallium*, and in the habit of a hunter.[25] An approximately contemporary group of marble statues shows an unknown person in a civic toga and twice as a hunter in "ideal" nudity.[26]

This practice can be traced back with some probability to the first phase of public images in Rome and its surrounding cities in the middle republican period. From Livy we know of a certain M. Anicius from Praeneste who, together with 570 soldiers under his command, bravely defended the city of Casilinum in 216 B.C. against Hannibal and was honored with a portrait statue in his city's forum.[27] This image is described very strangely as *loricata, amicta toga, velato capite*. If this is taken literally, it shows with utmost clarity that in this image the two aspects of religious *pietas* and military *virtus* were combined in an unusually forced iconography. Most probably, however, the explanation must go one step further since the combination of a toga, and even a *velatio*, with a cuirass is materially impossible. Therefore, it seems reasonable to suppose some misunderstanding by Livy or his source of this "statue," which in fact must have been a group of two or even three images showing him once in a toga *capite velato*, perhaps a second time in a normal toga, and certainly another time in a military cuirass.

Taking these types as role models means that they imply some performative qualities. Indeed, all such statuary types could be extended by further elements, step by step, into scenes of more complex and more narrative content. To the figure type with *velatio* and sacrificial *patera*, as restored on a portrait statue of Tiberius in Naples (fig. 6), there could be added, on a coin of Septimius Severus (fig. 7), a small altar by which the static figure is activated within a scene of sacrifice.[28] In relief sculpture, for example on the arch of Trajan at Beneventum or on a small altar in Milan (fig. 8), such reduced scenes may be extended into larger compositions, in which the emperor retains his statue-like posture.[29] Similarly, the static image of the emperor with a cuirass can be activated

---

[23] Maderna 1988, 18–55, 56–80.

[24] *RG* 24.

[25] Tac. *SHA* 16.2. Further examples: Fittschen 1977, 325–26.

[26] Von Heintze 1962; Kleiner 1992, 381, figs. 351–53.

[27] Livy 23.19.17–18. See Hölscher forthcoming.

[28] Portrait statue of Tiberius in Naples: Goette 1990, pl. 8, 2. Coin of Septimius Severus: *BMCRE* 1950, 5.79, no. 311, 97, no. 387–88; Hölscher 1980, fig. 19.

[29] Ryberg 1955, figs. 27, 29, 33d, 39a, 41d, 45e, 51, 64, 83; cf. 93, 95, 97c.

Fig. 6. *Portrait statue of Tiberius. Naples,*
Archaeological Museum, inv. no. 5615
(photo DAIR, inst. neg. 06717).

Fig. 8. *Altar with a scene of a*
sacrifice of a sevir. Milan, Musei Civici
(photo Rossa, DAIR, inst. neg. 1975.0848).

Fig. 7. Denarius *with the emperor sacrificing, reign*
of Septimius Severus (photo Vögele, Archaeological
Institute, University of Heidelberg).

by a gesture of his hand, as in the famous portrait statue of Augustus from Prima Porta.[30] By this potential activity, such images of the emperor in *tunica* and *paludamentum* can be integrated into larger scenes of *adlocutio*, where they may be slightly adapted to the situation.[31] But even then the emperor always keeps a static, "statuary" character on his high podium.

From these observations there results a double ambivalence. On the one hand, statues and other images contain a certain potential activity that can be made explicit by further narrative elements but that must be inherent in the figure type itself as well. On the other hand, the representative character that is best expressed in an autonomous statue type is also transferred to the narrative scenes of public activity. This reciprocal dialectic between active statues and static activities is determined by the relation between a symbolic representation of ideal values and the dynamic activity of performing them in real life.

A second ambivalence concerns the relation between image and reality. As the statuelike emperor enacted political values in public life, his statues were also effective factors in public life.[32] His images presided over public jurisdictions, lending their authority to the legal decisions of Roman magistrates; they were the object of soldiers' oaths, and so forth. The image, in this sense, *was* the emperor, in his various roles.

Permeability and Exclusiveness

Regarding the entire range of Roman society, as far as it is present in works of art, there is an interesting balance between such roles and values that are shared by and accessible to the whole community and others that are reserved for the emperor, on the one hand, and special social groups, on the other.

Shared ideals of the emperor and other groups are those that belong to the civic sphere. The most general case is the role of a Roman citizen, represented by the toga that is common to all Romans, including the emperor.[33] Of course, there were differences in status indicated by colors, seen above all in the *toga praetexta* and *triumphalis*, but these appear as variations of the common status of Roman citizenship. More specific is the ideal role of *pietas*, indicated by the *velatio* and scenes of sacrifice, which again is shared by all members of the cultural community of the Roman Empire. Beginning with Augustus, the emperor appears as the exemplary protagonist of this pious attitude toward the gods. But in his typological appearance, he is indistinguishable from the members of all other social classes down to the level of the middle class and the *liberti*, who frequently adopted such roles of *pietas*, thereby aspiring to some kind of public dignity (fig. 8).[34] Even the ambitious type of equestrian statues was at least accessible to all the upper classes, from the emperor through the senatorial and equestrian elite down to the local *decuriones*.[35] The same holds true for the military type of cuirassed statues.[36]

Particularly revealing is the role of married couples, demonstrating their *concordia* by clasping hands. In the Antonine period, imperial couples are represented as exemplary models of matrimonial

[30] Hannestad 1986, 50–56; Kleiner 1992, 63–67.

[31] Ryberg 1967, fig. 37.

[32] Generally, on the use of imperial portrait statues in specific topographical contexts, see Pekáry 1985.

[33] On social differentiation, see Goette 1990, 4–7.

[34] See in particular the altars of the *vicomagistri*: Ryberg 1955, 53–63; Hano 1986.

[35] Bergemann 1990, 14.

[36] Stemmer 1978, 147–48.

Fig. 9. Sestertius *with the emperor and his wife and couple of Roman citizens in the gesture of* dextrarum iunctio, *reign of Antoninus Pius (photo Vögele, Archaeological Institute, University of Heidelberg).*

harmony, to be imitated by civic couples throughout the empire.[37] Again there was a reciprocal transfer from images to reality and vice versa. In the temple of Venus and Roma, images of Marcus Aurelius and Diva Faustina Minor were erected together with an altar where all newly married couples were supposed to offer a sacrifice to the imperial model of matrimonial harmony.[38] The same procedure is supposed to have been in existence by the time of Antoninus Pius since a decree of the *decuriones* of Ostia prescribing an analogous sacrifice of brides and bridegrooms to the local images of Pius and Faustina Maior *ob insignem eorum concordiam* must go back to a model in the capital.[39] This is represented on Antonine *sestertii* that, in large format, show the emperor holding a statuette of Concordia and clasping hands with his wife. In front of them, in much smaller size but in exactly the same attire and attitudes, a married couple offers a sacrifice at an altar (fig. 9).[40] We may question whether human couples imitated the postures of imperial statues in their actual ceremonies. But at a minimum, the real persons on the coin repeat the model of the imperial images, enacting the ideological concept of *concordia* that is represented as an ideal statuette type in the hands of the emperor. On hundreds of Roman sarcophagi and other monuments, this scheme is adopted for all strata of Roman society. This is a clearly evident instance of the exemplary visual character of the concept of the "role" permeating all social strata.

Hierarchy of political and social status is introduced in public images by subtler devices, above all by format and placing.[41] On the whole, therefore, the typology of roles must have appeared rather homogeneous. This homogeneity in iconography and public visibility between the emperor and his subjects, in images that could be seen everywhere in public places and sepulchral areas of Roman cities, must have been an important bond of reciprocal coherence—all the more so since it concerns some central roles of collective behavior.

Only very few roles were reserved for specific groups or persons. On a famous pair of silver cups from Boscoreale, Augustus and Tiberius perform a set of stock roles of military character.[42]

---

[37] *BMCRE* 1940, 4.44 nos. 298–300, 65, no. 466; *BMCRE* 1950, 5.206–7 nos. 272–74, etc.

[38] Cass. Dio 71.31.1.

[39] *CIL* 14 5326.

[40] *BMCRE* 1940, 4.198–99 nos. 1236–40.

[41] Alföldy 1979; Alföldy 1984; Zimmer 1989.

[42] De Villefosse 1899, 133–68; Hölscher 1980, 281–90; Kuttner 1995.

Fig. 10. Sarcophagus with scenes of deceased receiving the submission of enemies, performing a sacrifice, and united with his wife with clasped hands. Mantua, Palazzo Ducale (photo Alinari Archives, Florence).

Augustus, on the first cup, appears in one scene as the ruler of the world, holding a globe, to whom Venus offers a small Victoria, while Mars leads a group of provinces toward him. In the opposite scene he receives, with a gesture of clemency, the submission of the Gaulish tribes. Tiberius, on the second cup, is represented on one side in a scene of sacrifice before leaving for war, on the other as a *triumphator* after a victorious campaign. Of the four imperial virtues that were praised on Augustus's *clupeus virtutis*, three are demonstrated here in a ritual performance: *virtus*, *clementia*, and *pietas*.

One and a half centuries later, a group of sarcophagi of Roman senatorial officers shows a sequence of three or four very similar ritual scenes: a battle-piece (replaced on a sarcophagus in Mantua by a figure of Virtus, on another chest in Florence by a hunting scene), followed by the deceased receiving the submission of enemies, performing a sacrifice, and united with his wife by clasped hands (sarcophagus in Mantua: fig. 10).[43] Here, therefore, we meet again the performance of *virtus*, *clementia*, and *pietas*, and, in addition, of *concordia*. This is at once a striking demonstration of the relative stability of the Roman value system and a good example of the ambivalence between permeability and exclusiveness of these exemplary values. Most of these virtues, taken as abstract

[43] Rodenwaldt 1935; Hölscher 1980, 288–90; Reinsberg 1984; Kleiner 1992, 303; Reinsberg 1995; Wrede 2001, 21–43.

concepts, are shared between the emperor and the military elite. Only the highest expressions in ritual and allegory are excepted: while "ordinary" men demonstrate their military *virtus* in scenes of fighting and hunting, the honor of the triumph and the allegory of world dominion are reserved for the emperor.

The only statuary types that were exclusively adopted for the emperor are those derived from images of Jupiter, seated or standing.[44] On the other hand, there was one sphere that was never used in public monuments for the representation of the emperor, although it was of utmost importance in real policy: the organization and presentation of public games. This was one of the major themes exploited in the self-representation of members of the local elites, *decuriones* and *liberti* in the *coloniae* and *municipia* all over Italy, beginning in late republican and early imperial times.[45] It would be a rewarding task to compare systematically imperial and upper-class public self-presentation in actual public life and in public monuments, asking how far these two spheres are interconnected or independent semantic systems of social symbolization.

Roles and "Identity"

The various roles performed by single persons may complement one another—for example, *pietas* in religious rituals and *virtus* in military activity. Yet they may also be more contradictory. A famous sarcophagus in Naples from the time of Gallienus shows the deceased in four different roles: in the consular *processus*, as a Greek philosopher, in the habit of a magistrate, and in matrimonial harmony.[46] The two central figures, incorporating Roman *dignitas* and Greek *paideia*, would—at least in earlier periods—have been a conflicting pair. This divergence between public self-presentation in the capital and semi-private lifestyle in rural and seaside villas is well known. In art it is evident in the divergent styles of urban public monuments, following the tradition of classical dignity, and private residences, decorated according to the taste for Hellenistic *luxuria*.

Such divergences can easily be described as "roles," and Roman art has developed efficient means to represent such roles performed by one and the same person. Should we go further? This brings us to the notion of "identity." Roles are said to create and confirm "identity." What do we mean by this notion? Is it anything more than a modernistic expression for "personality," "quality," "role"? What does "identity" imply? And why do we need it?

The term "identity," individual as well as collective, is a creation of the twentieth century, increasingly in use after World War II and in particular during the last generation, when it became a fundamental catchword of social and cultural studies.[47] This universal and wholehearted adoption of not only the term but also the notion and concept of "identity" suggests, however, a kind of self-evident validity that contrasts markedly with its relatively recent origin. Therefore, we may at least ask to what extent we are dealing with a universal category of cultural anthropology or rather with a limited phenomenon of specific historical societies. Why could earlier scholars and entire societies do without the concept of "identity"? What did we win by introducing it into and placing it at the center of our heuristic terminology and cultural notions? What are its consequences for our understanding of historical and contemporary societies, not least of our own society and our social behavior?

[44] Maderna 1988, 18–55.

[45] Coarelli 1966; Franchi 1966; La Regina 1966.

[46] Himmelmann-Wildschütz 1962; Wrede 2001, 70–76.

[47] Niethammer 2000.

"Identity" is a basic category by which the questions "who am I?" and "who are we?" are answered. Of course, there is no doubt every historical society adopted definitions of who it was, for the entire body of its members as well as for particular groups and individuals. Otherwise there would not be any possibility of marking social structures. But "identity" is more than that: it means that every individual person, every social group or political community, is supposed not only to have but also to develop and strengthen, preserve and defend its "identity." It is this emphatic character of the notion of "identity" that goes beyond mere definitions of social entities, collective as well as individual.

Obviously, this emphasis on "identity" was conditioned by a crisis of contemporary societies that was diagnosed as a loss of this very "identity": first, a crisis of the concept of the "person," which is a main topic of early twentieth-century literature; then, a crisis of the "nation" and of cultural communities in recent trends toward "globalization." In this context, "identity" is conceived as a basic foundation, a driving force, and a leading principle of individual persons, social groups, and large-scale communities. All such entities, whether they feel in conscious possession of their "identity" or are in search of it, are claiming emphatically their right to "identity," advancing it against rival claims of alternative "identities." It is an essentially egocentric concept of individual persons, social groups, and political communities.

Like all terms of ubiquitous diffusion, the term "identity" has often become a *passe partout* for all sorts of social and cultural qualities. In a precise sense, however, it is meant to be a category of the highest rank, defining an irreducible, pre-rational core of individual persons and collective entities, which again are conceived according to the model of individual personality—in short, a core "behind" all manifestations of the specific person or community.

The basic—and most problematic—feature of this concept of "identity" is its fundamental idealism, irrationalism, and self-centeredness. "Identity" is different from "character," individual or collective, since it transcends good or bad. It is also different from "cultural habitus" since it is founded on underlying values and patterns of behavior that are not subject to debate: something between an individual's or a community's basic essence and its destiny.[48] From any aspect, "identity" means a given fact that cannot be criticized but must be acknowledged. Moreover, the notion of "identity" implies a strong emphasis on introspection, self-definition, and self-assertion; every goal can be strongly legitimized, without any further reasoning, by the claim to a right of "identity." This is, of course, not to deny categorically the validity of the term and the notion of collective and individual "identity," which exists and has therefore to be dealt with appropriately. Rather, it is to stress two points: first, that an emphatic concept of "identity" is not a universal and timeless anthropological fact but a specific phenomenon of certain historical societies; second, that it is a basically problematic and potentially dangerous concept that is of doubtful use and benefit when placed at the center of our own social system.

Regarding the situation of the contemporary world, the disastrous consequences to which the claims of collective "identity" of national, cultural, and religious communities almost necessarily lead need not be elaborated here. Kofi Annan warned against them many years ago, while the historian Lutz Niethammer has heavily criticized their scientific abuses. A critical analysis of the emphatic concept of individual "identity" has to be awaited.

Regarding historical approaches, the notion of "identity" seems to involve a kind of reflection on the individual or collective self that accords more with twentieth-century obsessions than with

[48] Bourdieu 1979. For further discussion of habitus, see Richard Alston's contribution in this volume.

the concerns of premodern societies. This is why I would like to ask whether in antiquity individual persons and social or political communities were really concerned with the question of who they were in the same sense as their modern counterparts.

The concept of "roles" is of a much more rational character. It is not based on an unquestionable core of an individual or collective self but on social conventions. Roles are not self-centered but communicative and socially oriented. They may be judged, as good or bad, on the basis of ethical categories, without questioning the individual or the community in its inner self. Persons and groups may adopt various roles; they may change their roles according to various social situations and their specific requirements. Therefore, is it not more appropriate, and less burdened by anachronistic assumptions, to speak of concrete public and private roles and qualities, merits and deficiencies in social communication?

Works Cited

Alföldy, G., "Bildprogramme in den römischen Städten des Conventus Tarraconensis. Das Zeugnis der Statuenpostamente," in *Homenaje a García Bellido* 4 (Madrid 1979) 177–275.

———, *Römische Statuen in Venetia et Histria, Abhandlungen der Heidelberger Akademie der Wissenschaften zu Berlin* 3 (Heidelberg 1984).

Baumer, L., "Adlocutio," in L. Baumer, T. Hölscher, and L. Winkler, "Narrative Systematik und politisches Konzept in den Reliefs der Traianssäule. Drei Fallstudien," *Jahrbuch des deutschen archäologischen Instituts* 106 (1991) 278–87.

Baumer, L., T. Hölscher, and L. Winkler, "Narrative Systematik und politisches Konzept in den Reliefs der Traianssäule. Drei Fallstudien," *Jahrbuch des deutschen archäologischen Instituts* 106 (1991) 261–95.

Bergemann, J., *Römische Reiterstatuen. Ehrendenkmäler im öffentlichen Bereich* (Mainz 1990).

Bourdieu, P., *La distinction: critique sociale du jugement* (Paris 1979).

Campbell, J. B., *The Emperor and the Roman Army* (Oxford 1984).

Coarelli, F., "Il rilievo con scene gladiatorie," in *Sculture municipali dell'area sabellica tra l'età di Cesare e quella di Nerone*, ed. R. Bianchi Bandinelli, L. Franchi, and A. Giuliano, *Studi miscellanei. Seminario di archeologia e storia dell'arte greca e romana dell'Università di Roma* 10 (Rome 1966) 85–99.

———, *La colonna Traiana* (Rome 1999).

David, J., "Les contiones militaires des colonnes Trajane et Aurélienne: les nécessités de l'adhésion," in *Autour de la colonne Aurélienne: Geste et image sur la colonne de Marc Aurèle à Rome*, ed. J. Scheid and V. Huet, Bibliothèque de l'école des hautes études section des sciences religieuses 108 (Turnhout 2000) 213–26.

Fittschen, K., "Das Bildprogramm des Trajansbogens zu Benevent," *Archäologischer Anzeiger* (1972) 742–88.

———, "Siebenmal Maximinus Thrax," *Archäologischer Anzeiger* (1977) 319–26.

Franchi, L., "Rilievo con pompa funebre e rilievo con gladiatori al museo dell'Aquila," in *Sculture municipali dell'area sabellica tra l'età di Cesare e quella di Nerone*, ed. R. Bianchi Bandinelli, L. Franchi, and A. Giuliano, *Studi miscellanei. Seminario di archeologia e storia dell'arte greca e romana dell'Università di Roma* 10 (Rome 1966) 23–32.

Goette, H. R., *Studien zu römischen Togadarstellungen* (Mainz 1990).

Grunow, M. D., "Architectural Images in Roman State Reliefs, Coins, and Medallions: Imperial Ritual, Ideology, and the Topography of Rome" (Ph.D. diss., University of Michigan, Ann Arbor 2002).

Hamberg, P. G., *Studies in Roman Imperial Art* (Copenhagen 1945).

Hannestad, N., *Roman Art and Imperial Policy* (Aarhus 1986).

Hano, M., "À l'origine du culte imperial. Les autels des Lares Augusti," in *Aufstieg und Niedergang der römischen Welt*, ed. H. Temporini et al., 2.16.3 (1986) 2333–381.

Heintze, H. von., "Drei spätantike Porträtstatuen," *Antike Plastik* 1 (1962) 7–32.

Himmelmann-Wildschütz, N., "Sarkophag eines gallienischen Konsuls," in *Festschrift für Friedrich Matz*, ed. N. Himmelmann-Wildschütz and H. Biesantz (Mainz 1962) 110–24.

Hölscher, T., *Victoria Romana* (Mainz 1967).

———, "Die Geschichtsauffassung in der römischen Repräsentationskunst," *Jahrbuch des deutschen archäologischen Instituts* 95 (1980) 265–321.

———, "Einleitung" and "Vormarsch und Schlacht," in L. Baumer, T. Hölscher, and L. Winkler, "Narrative Systematik und politisches Konzept in den Reliefs der Traianssäule. Drei Fallstudien," *Jahrbuch des deutschen archäologischen Instituts* 106 (1991) 261–66, 287–95.

———, "Bilder der Macht und Herrschaft," in *Traian. Ein Kaiser der Superlative am Beginn einer Umbruchzeit?*, ed. A. Nünnerich-Asmus (Mainz 2002) 127–44.

———, "Eine mehrfache Statuenehrung zur Zeit der mittleren römischen Republik?" *Archäologischer Anzeiger* (forthcoming).

Kleiner, D. E. E., *Roman Sculpture* (New Haven and London 1992).

Koeppel, G., "Profectio und Adventus," *Bonner Jahrbücher des rheinischen Landesmuseums in Bonn und des Vereins von Altertumsfreunden im Rheinlande* 69 (1969) 130–94.

Kuttner, A. L., *Dynasty and Empire in the Age of Augustus* (Berkeley 1995).

La Regina, A., "Monumento funebre di un Triumviro Augustale al museo di Chieti," in *Sculture municipali dell'area sabellica tra l'età di Cesare e quella di Nerone*, ed. R. Bianchi Bandinelli, L. Franchi, and A. Giuliano, *Studi miscellanei. Seminario di archeologia e storia dell'arte greca e romana dell'Università di Roma* 10 (Rome 1966) 39–53.

Lepper, F., and S. Frere, *Trajan's Column: A New Edition of the Cichorius Plates* (Gloucester 1988).

Maderna, C., *Iuppiter, Diomedes und Mercur als Vorbilder für römische Bildnisstatuen* (Heidelberg 1988).

Niethammer, L., *Kollektive Identität* (Reinbek bei Hamburg 2000).

Pekáry, T., *Das römische Kaiserbildnis in Staat, Kult und Gesellschaft* (Berlin 1985).

Reinsberg, C., "Das Hochzeitsopfer—eine Fiktion," *Jahrbuch des deutschen archäologischen Instituts* 99 (1984) 291–317.

———, "Senatorensarkophage," *Mitteilungen des deutschen archäologischen Instituts, römische Abteilung* 102 (1995) 353–78.

Rodenwaldt, G., *Über den Stilwandel in der antoninischen Kunst*, *Abhandlungen der deutschen Akademie der Wissenschaften zu Berlin* 3 (Berlin 1935).

Ryberg, I. S., *Rites of the State Religion in Roman Art*, *Memoirs of the American Academy in Rome* 22 (Rome 1955).

———, *Panel Reliefs of Marcus Aurelius* (New York 1967).

Settis, S., "La colonne trajane. Invention, composition, disposition," *Annales. Économie, sociétés, civilisations* 40 (1985) 1165–94.

Spinola, G., *Il "congiarium" in età imperiale. Aspetti iconografici e topografici*, *Rivista di archeologia* Supplement 6 (Rome 1990).

Stemmer, K., *Untersuchungen zur Typologie, Chronologie und Ikonographie der Panzerstatuen* (Berlin 1978).

Villefosse, H. de, "Le trésor de Boscoreale," *Monuments et mémoires. Fondation E. Piot* 5 (1899) 7–290.

Wrede, H., *Senatorische Sarkophage Roms. Der Beitrag des Senatorenstandes zur Kunst der hohen und späten Kaiserzeit* (Mainz 2001).

Zanker, P., "Prinzipat und Herrscherbild," *Gymnasium* 86 (1979) 353–68.

Zimmer, G., *Locus datus decreto decurionum. Zur Statuenaufstellung zweier Forumsanlagen im römischen Afrika*, Bayerische Akademie der Wissenschaften, München, Philosophisch-historische Klasse. Abhandlungen N. F. 102 (Munich 1989).

2 ◆ GRACIOUS PATRONS AND VULGAR SUCCESS STORIES IN ROMAN PUBLIC MEDIA

Suzanne Dixon

Introduction

We are all—yes, even scholars—creatures of our time. Convinced that we see more clearly than our Renaissance or twentieth-century predecessors, we continue to rediscover and reinvent the ancient world in our own terms. Yet when we look upon ancient self-presentations, perhaps we ourselves are looking for role models, unwittingly favoring readings that suit our own cultural prejudices, for we have our own received styles of role model and of narratives connected with them.[1] Today's sports and entertainment celebrities not only model (*sic*) running shoes and makeup but ostentatiously support selected charities/causes and are paid huge sums on the lecture circuit for "motivational" talks which reinforce the dogma that, given the right attitude, *any*one can achieve *any*thing. It is hard to imagine such arguments being promoted in classical antiquity, where social mobility and gender-crossing were possible but by no means favored in dominant discourse.[2] Romans did nonetheless have a variety of role models: by the time of Augustus's death in A.D. 14, every public space in the Roman Empire was replete with buildings, honorific statues, and inscriptions that trumpeted the virtues of central and local dignitaries; the *necropoleis* outside town walls sent messages about the dead and their families. We have to work out how to read those messages, terse and emblematic, embedded as firmly in their temporal, generic, and geographic locations as modern advertising and political clichés of today—the dreaded McDonald's arches, "terror," the Gucci "G"—which may well puzzle future readers of this volume.

Implicit in the notion of a role model is an individual who displays notable qualities worthy of imitation. This study therefore treats four individuals associated with monumental records that highlighted specific virtues and were visible to a general public. The examples, all from the early empire, are from different parts of Roman Italy: Septimia Stratonice of Ostia, Vergilius Eurysaces of Rome, Eumachia of Pompeii, and Pliny the Younger in his role as benefactor of his native Como.[3] All four individuals are represented by inscriptions that were publicly displayed. I consider ways in which these iconographic and epigraphic representations of work and generosity might have been viewed as role models by contemporaries.

Context is, we know, all-important to the analysis of monuments, so it is a pity that we cannot locate Septimia's memorial or Pliny's commemorative inscription and the buildings he donated or adorned with the same confidence that applies to the location of Eurysaces' monument and Eumachia's

---

[1] For additional perspectives on the methodological concerns faced by modern scholars, see the chapters by Tonio Hölscher and John Clarke in this volume.

[2] On the fluidity of the Roman gender taxonomy, see the contributions by Eve D'Ambra and Eric Varner.

[3] Septimia Stratonice's memorial probably dates, like Pliny's, to the early second century A.D. Both were apparently erected posthumously. Eurysaces' monument is usually dated by its orthography to ca. 30 B.C., and Eumachia's building was probably erected ca. 9–3 B.C. See the detailed discussion and notes below, with references.

building. It is ironic that Pliny, who was doubtless honored for his numerous benefactions with statues throughout Italy, is the only one of this sample without a surviving portrait.[4] He is also the only one who speaks at some length in a literary medium of his own qualities and motivations. Lacking the iconographic expertise of other contributors to this volume, I have necessarily consulted scholarship on art historical and architectural aspects of these monuments crucial to issues of dating and intent, but the emphasis of this study is on social analysis, and descriptive detail has therefore been tailored to this purpose.[5]

The monument erected by a grateful friend of the Ostian shoemaker Septimia Stratonice, which stands out in obvious ways from the rest of the selection, raises interesting questions. It is by no means the stock epitaph of a lower-class woman. Septimia shares with all the subjects but Eurysaces the merit of being commemorated by others for her generosity—in her case, for a personal favor, not a civic benefaction. Divorced from its original setting, her chiseled marble relief was probably recycled from the necropolis outside the walls of Ostia. Image and text would have been readily visible to a passerby, who could identify her sex and work from a glance at the seated figure in simple costume holding up a shoe or last in a gesture familiar from shop signs.[6] Only the interested and literate observer might have read that she shared the monument with the dedicator's son. Probably a tombstone, the monument is the least "public" of the examples studied here and easily the least lavish, but it is still a far cry from the terse tablet in an underground locus. It represents a conscious attempt by someone—dedicator or dedicand—to single out aspects of Septimia not commonly projected in funerary genres by women of this social group. Given the dedicator's care and expense, it is interesting that he has not added any epithet to his son's name or recorded the stock lament that he was predeceased by the child who ought by rights to have survived him. The dedicator therefore displays his own *pietas*, paternity, friendship, and gratitude but visually and textually highlights Septimia's work and generosity. The roles presented thus draw on recognizable images and values. Their display represents conscious choices to reinforce, manipulate, and extend familiar, admired characteristics.

Such characteristics contributed to the construction of identity in Roman Italy, a complex, lifelong process. Many of its elements must have been transmitted primarily within the overlapping contexts of the family unit, household or workplace, in domestic settings. The examples studied here, via these selected buildings and funerary or honorific sculpture and their related written texts, largely relate to more public aspects of identity, including regional affiliation, gender, status, social obligation, and relationship with the central imperial power.[7] Interaction with these visible, concrete

---

[4] Woolf (1996, 24) stresses the need to treat "both the monumental and the written aspects of inscriptions seriously," while Jas Elsner (1996) emphasizes the interplay of image and text in the introduction to his edited collection. In that collection, Koortbojian (1996, 233) concludes his excellent discussion of funerary monuments with the affirmation of the important role they played in the culture of memory "because the monuments speak, not merely with their texts, but with their imagery." See also Nielsen 1996 and Eck 1997. On the general need to draw on all aspects for the interpretation of ancient visual material, readers are referred to the superb discussion of N. B. Kampen (2003). My thanks to Sinclair Bell for drawing my attention to this important statement of the need for interdisciplinary cooperation.

[5] Bibliographic guidance is therefore supplied in the notes, but I have avoided lengthy discussion of controversies that

were not germane to my purpose. Even I (whose eyes cross at the art historical preoccupation with acanthus leaves and hairstyles) have seen the light and understood their importance in assessing the building of Eumachia and the sculptural/relief portraits of Septimia, Atistia, Eumachia, and Eurysaces.

[6] See below for a description of the reconstructed memorial and a discussion of the implications of the chosen portrait styles of the other women in this study. The two fragments were recovered in the early twentieth century from the Via della Fontana and from the Antonine Baths at Ostia (Kampen 1981, 139–40).

[7] I am simplifying categories here. The domestic and public were not so distinct (Lomas and Cornell 2003b, 4). "Private" virtues (of marital and filial affection, e.g.) were displayed

statements involves a number of parties—the person celebrated, the recipients of benefactions, the person who commissions a monument, and, at a slight remove, the audience who glances at a statue or relief, who reads the script or enjoys a public amenity (Eumachia's building and its porch; Pliny's baths and library). There are other levels, too: the role models we study might in turn base their choice of portrait and building style or of the type of civic piety or benefaction they display on imperial models. And, just as noble proprietors in the classical revival copied (and transformed) the design and architectural models of Pompeii, so modern audiences continue to reprocess the virtues and narratives they read into these ancient monumental advertisements.[8]

Since I am suggesting that differences between ancient and modern notions of self-promotion, civic virtue, and propriety might influence the ways in which we read such ancient monuments, I need to state my understanding of modern "modeling," as elaborated in twentieth-century sociology and popular culture. Modern discourse characterizes children and youth as the prime targets of role models in the public and private sphere: sons who follow fathers' blueprint of masculinity, girls who look up to trail-blazing professional women, ghetto children who imbibe capitalist values from self-made entrepreneurs. Roman literature made fun of such entrepreneurs, and low-born celebrities of the Roman world like gladiators and mime artistes were not held up as models to be emulated, but children of noble Roman families were reared on stories about distinguished ancestors, a practice institutionalized in the funerary rituals first recorded by Polybius.[9] At all social levels, Roman boys and girls would have modeled their behavior on the same-sex parent in a way that we would recognize.

Outside the home, Roman children gained inspiration from the heroic figures of the distant past, learning stories connected with the overthrow of the kings (Lucretia, Iunius Brutus). Historians and biographers proclaimed the importance of presenting readers, particularly young men, with instances of particularly good (inspirational) or bad (cautionary) behavior.[10] These *exempla* were reinforced in public art and oratory and formed part of community culture. Augustus associated himself with Apollo, and his architectural program involved the public display of famous figures—*summi viri*—from Rome's history and heroized Aeneas and Romulus as a permanent, public inspiration to all onlookers while displaying imperial family members as contemporary manifestations of these inherited virtues.[11]

Cautionary examples are meat and drink to modern mass media but are seldom drawn from history. Unwitting role models—drug-taking rock stars and badly behaved cricketers—can be castigated by tabloid moralists for setting a bad example to their youthful admirers. The twenty-first century News Limited editor or the exposé-anchor who highlights exemplary/cautionary aspects of a public figure thus assumes the role of the biographer of classical antiquity. But the superficial similarities obscure profound differences, for the more public aspects of modern role-modeling are based on presumptions of individualism and opportunity that seem alien to ancient social attitudes. Confronted with affirmations of the status quo by an establishment lady in an Italian *colonia*, or of

---

in arguably public venues. See the considerable literature on this topic, such as Nielsen 1996 and Eck 1997, and my introduction to Dixon 2001b. On refinements of identity and its variable representation, see Joshel 1992 and my discussion in Dixon 2001a (113–32), as well as some of the discussions in the collection edited by Alison Cooley (2000), including Valerie Hope's thoughtful analysis of gladiators' funerary inscriptions.

[8] Trevelyan (1976, 39–73) outlines the eighteenth-century European response to Pompeii.

[9] See now Garland (2006) on the possibility of influence by such low-ranking "celebrities."

[10] See, for instance, Margaret Imber's chapter in this volume on the role of declamation in educating boys through the emulation of prescribed, paternal *exempla*.

[11] See Zanker's influential study (1988). On the role of Aeneas, see the contribution by Charles Brian Rose; on the imperial family, see the chapter by Tonio Hölscher, both in this volume.

aspirations to elite standards by a Rome baker, we insist on seeing proclamations of female economic power or pride in self-made status.

So my first question is whether—or in what sense—we might apply this construct of the role model to the reception by an ancient audience of public representations such as funerary monuments and civic statues of living or recently deceased members of the community. Did the common man, woman, or child perceive them as something to live up to? This question applies not only to the monuments of Vergilius Eurysaces of Rome and Septimia Stratonice of Ostia, both workers outside the elite, but to those celebrating the distinction and generosity of the two elite figures, Eumachia of Pompeii and Pliny the Younger of Como. A survey of the people and sources I am examining provides the basis for my suggestions.

EUMACHIA OF POMPEII

Eumachia was a member of an elite Pompeian family network that did not aspire, as far as we know, to a position of influence in the central Roman structure. Her background was more typical of the regional elites of Roman Italy than the more ambitious families like Pliny's that competed for court and senatorial favor and have therefore left a greater mark on historical consciousness via consular *fasti* and literary records. She was a member by birth and marriage of the Pompeian office-holding establishment.[12] We can infer Eumachia's husband's name from that of her son, Marcus Numistrius Fronto. These Numistrii were established within the office-holding elite, which typically cemented its position with benefactions and general patronage. Thus Eumachia herself held a priesthood, benefited the fullers' guild, and apparently supported her son's candidacy for office.[13] The survival of a family tomb, of a statue dedicated to her by the fullers, and the inscription honoring her donation of a building are a relatively rich source of information for this woman—too often, we have less than this on which to base our knowledge of Italian town elites or of the distinguished women of Roman Italy.[14] Apart from the conventional lines on the tomb outside the Porta Nocerina ("Eumachia, daughter of Lucius, [built this] for herself and for her household"), the relevant inscriptions are grouped under *CIL* 10 810–12. The full-length statue of her, depicting her in formal garb with covered head as befits her religious office, probably graced the rear niche of the building on the eastern side of the Pompeiian forum conventionally termed the *aedificium Eumachiae*. The base bears a dedication typical of honorific inscriptions throughout Roman Italy: "The fullers [erected it] to Eumachia, daughter of Lucius, public priestess."[15] The public building giving onto the forum, possibly linked

[12] Castrén 1975, 165–66. On the basis of her name, it has sometimes been argued that she herself came from a wealthy but not long-standing family, which had risen to prosperity and respectability, linking itself with more distinguished families such as the Lassii and Numistrii (cf. the comment on entry 196 in Lefkowitz and Fant 1982). Professor Fant has confirmed (pers. comm.) that this judgment derived from J. D'Arms's prosopographic analysis, based on inscriptions and the "h" in her family name, a common index of Campanian social mobility (cf. *CIL* 10 8042.47, 48: Campanian *figlinae*). On the status of her natal and conjugal families, see *CIL* 10 899–900; D'Arms 1988, 63 n. 14. Castrén (1975, 71, 95, 165–66), however, regards her as a member of the inner elite; cf. Andreau 1974, 213.

[13] Cf. MacMullen 1980, 209: "To be chosen priestess brought one before the public eye very sharply. For Eumachia, as for

others we know of, election was connected with great wealth, wide business associations, a husband an office-holder, and forebears the same. We can only guess that certain personal qualities were needed as well." Cf. Castrén 1975, 70–72.

[14] Full descriptions can be found in Fantham et al. 1994, 332–36 and Zanker 1998, 97–101. Both have photographs of the statue (now in Naples, Archaeological Museum, inv. no. 6232), and Zanker has a plan of the building and plates of other artifacts from the site.

[15] *CIL* 10 813: EVMACHIAE L F / SACERD PVBL / FULLONES. Castrén (1975, 165–66) suggests that intermarriage with the Numistrii gave the Eumachii Lucanian grazing lands, which led to their patronal relations with the Pompeian woolen industry. Moeller (1972) challenged earlier assumptions about the function of the building and the nature of

to her son's successful campaign for the office of *duovir*, bears the inscription "Eumachia, daughter of Lucius, public priestess, in her own name and that of her son Marcus Numistrius Fronto, built the *chalcidicum* [porch] and cryptoporticus with her own money and dedicated them to Augustan Concord and Piety."[16] Other inscriptions and building fragments confirm the tendency, which was to become stronger in the next century, for the town elites to embrace the favored religious and mythological motifs of the imperial family.[17]

PLINY THE YOUNGER

Pliny is a figure familiar to students from his published letters, many of which detail his generosity to peers and other groups. Here I focus on his testamentary provision for his male *liberti*, the less lavish (but still substantial) foundation established in his lifetime for some poor children of his region and his donation of a library and school for Como.[18] Some of these benefactions are detailed in an inscription (*CIL* 5 5262 = *ILS* 2927) assembled from fragments, which seems to have been erected in his honor by the people of Como after his death. Some are also known from the *Letters*, particularly 1.8, in which Pliny elaborates on the rationale for his generosity to the town, the particular forms it took, and the influence on him of his family tradition of civic munificence.[19]

EURYSACES FROM ROME

Just outside the Porta Praenestina (modern *Porta maggiore*), the baker Marcus Vergilius Eurysaces has left a striking monument that has happily survived the vicissitudes of time and continues to proclaim his success as a self-made man who apparently rose from lowly status to become a successful entrepreneurial baker, *pistor redemptor* (*CIL* 1.2 1203–4). Full-length statues of Eurysaces and his wife A[n]tistia were found nearby and almost certainly intended for a high niche, facing the busy Viae Praenestina and Labicana roads.[20] Inscriptions on the monument and statues are brief, their import supplemented by scenes of bread preparation.

Eurysaces—and his monument—would be a fitting icon of the modern Roman slow food movement. I am not the only scholar to point out that his memorial counters Cicero's assertion (*Off.* 1.150–51) that trades catering to the senses rank low in the Roman social and moral

---

Eumachia's relationship with the fullers. Cf. Will 1979; Castrén 1975, 101–2; Jongman 1988, 179–84. Current thinking stresses the role of the building as a public amenity modeled on the Porticus Liviae at Rome—e.g., Richardson 1978, 267–69; D'Arms 1988, 53–54; Zanker 1998, 93–102; Dobbins 1996, 113; and Dobbins 1997, his Pompeian forum website.

[16] *CIL* 10 810: EVMACHIA L F SACERD PVBL NOMINE SVO ET / M NVMISTRI FRONTONIS FILI CHALCIDICVM / CRYPTAM PORTICVS CONCORDIAE / AVGVSTAE PIETATI SVA PEQVNIA FECIT EADEMQVE DEDICAVIT. *CIL* 10 892, restored after the earthquake of 62, probably refers to Numistrius Fronto as *duovir*; cf. Richardson 1988, 194–98. It is less likely that the *duovir* of that period was her husband of the same name. But see *contra* D'Arms 1988, 63 n. 14.

[17] The trend is best attested in Pompeii: see Castrén 1975, 101–2; Richardson 1988, xx–xxi; D'Arms 1988; Zanker 1998, 78–124. Dobbins (1996) gives some of the developments a

later Julio-Claudian date. Lomas (2003) takes issue with Zanker's "top-down" view of civic building by Italian towns, seeing it as driven by internal elite competition and the public assertion/maintenance of status. Whatever the motive, there is a clear response (if only in superficialities like fashion) to the central, imperial example in such cases.

[18] Once Pliny's *liberti* died, the fund was to be used for a feast for the urban poor of Como: 5.5262, lines 12–13. The discussion of these benefactions in Duncan-Jones (1974, 17–32) is still very valuable, and see Nicols 1980.

[19] See also 7.18, on his scheme for the children of the rural poor, and 4.13 on the school at Como.

[20] For pictures and discussion, see Toynbee 1971, 128 (fairly basic) with pls. 34 and 35; Kleiner 1992, 105–9 with excellent plates; and Koortbojian 1996, 216 on the statues only. Kleiner and Koortbojian locate the portraits in the art of the very early principate.

hierarchy.[21] Eurysaces proudly proclaims his own success and celebrates its source: the provision of bread. His self-made status and his social elevation are both emphasized by the combination of work scenes—apparently depicting his employees or slaves rather than himself—and the status of himself in a citizen's *toga* and of his wife in the matron's *palla.* Atistia's association with the family business is confined to the epigraphic claim that her remains are "in this bread basket."[22]

The monument can almost be read as a modern success story, the familiar self-made man narrative viewed with favor in modern dominant discourse and with amused scorn in the dominant elite discourse of classical antiquity.[23] Eurysaces both states his own background and work and separates himself from it by stressing his current superior position, much as an Australian might take pride in juxtaposing his early struggles as a recent immigrant with his current prosperity and new citizenship status. Eurysaces' wife Atistia is shown in the statue as a modest matron, an extension of his own success. In her case the only arguable reference to any background of menial work is confined to the marble *panarium* (bread bin) that, according to its inscription, housed her remains: FVIT ATISTIA VXOR MIHEI / FEMINA OPITVMA VEIXSIT / QVOIVS CORPORIS RELIQVIAE / QVOD SVPERANT SVNT IN / HOC PANARIO.[24]

SEPTIMIA STRATONICE FROM OSTIA

This woman is known to us only from a monument, convincingly pieced together from two fragments by Calza.[25] The commemoration includes a semi-relief of a seated woman holding up a shoe or last.[26] If we follow Calza's reconstruction, the memorial is dedicated both to her and to Acilius Fortunatianus, son of the dedicator, (*Marcus Acilius Is . . .*), who celebrates Septimia as a shoemaker (*sutrix*), as his very dear friend (*amica carissima*), and as his benefactress. Her favors to him are the reason for her inclusion in the monument (*ob benefacta ab ea in se*) and her paramount position in the text (*CIL* 14 Suppl. 4698).

Reading the Roles

All of these monuments represent, in varying degrees, the conversion of financial capital into social goods: either status in its most obvious form (a working baker becoming an entrepreneur whose children or grandchildren can perhaps aspire to elite status) or with all the moral ramifications of patronage conferred on groups or individuals. Whether commemorated by themselves or others, the four chosen individuals have left varying models for their contemporaries and for posterity. In each case, physical monuments attest their material success and, usually, their liberality. Indeed, liberality always implies

---

[21] See Kampen 1981, esp. 114–15; Kampen 1982; Joshel 1992, 66–71, 80–81; Dixon 2001a, 91, 126. Petersen (2003) has the most thorough discussion of the statues and the original composition of the monument, the significance of its location, and, particularly, its likely impact on passersby.

[22] *CIL* 1.2 1206. This claim (lines 3–5) has puzzled scholars but is only marginal to this discussion. The inscription also celebrates the wifely virtues of Atistia: *fuit Atistia uxor mihei /- femina opitvma veixsit* (lines 1–2). Petersen (2003) discusses in detail whether the Atistia material properly belongs with the Eurysaces monument. I follow the conventional grouping of Eurysaces and Atistia, associating them with

this inscription and with the portrait statues.

[23] Joshel 1992, 82–83.

[24] *CIL* 6 1958. "She was my wife Atistia. She lived her life as an excellent woman, whose surviving bodily remains are in this breadbin."

[25] *CIL* 9 568 + 487; Calza 1978, nos. 37–38.

[26] Mus. Arch. Ostiense, inv. no. 1418. Kampen (1981, 63–65) discusses the imagery in some detail, with consideration of its mixed genre elements.

prosperity as well as virtue and status—at the least, a status superior (if only temporarily) to that of the beneficiary, who was required to offer some form of public acknowledgment of the benefit. Within the Roman system of social reciprocity, a monumental token of gratitude was more typical of significant status distinctions between the two parties and was sometimes funded by the beneficiary.[27]

In the most general sense, any monument could have been inspirational. An imposing tomb with elaborate work scenes, dignified statues, an image of the deceased at work in the trade that had brought prosperity and opportunity—all of these show the onlooker what can be achieved in life and rewarded by a textual or material souvenir. The gratitude of a friend (in the case of Septimia Stratonice), a guild (in the case of Eumachia and her son), or a town (in the case of Pliny), thus immortalized in concrete form, gives the audience some notion of how one might be remembered.

Perhaps the monuments to Septimia and Eurysaces speak most directly to modern notions of modeling. In each case, a practitioner of a skilled craft is remembered for the material benefits of industry: in the case of Septimia, the monument displays a friend's gratitude and therefore her moral and financial ability to benefit others with the surplus. Eurysaces himself seems to speak with his tomb of his own industry and status and, by implication, of the ladylike status enjoyed by his wife Atistia, who—unlike Septimia—is depicted in classic matron's dress and posture.[28] He, too, is shown in his statue as a citizen, not a worker like the slaves/employees whose activities adorn the monument.[29]

The typical elite pattern of conspicuous benefit to social inferiors is displayed in the tributes to Pliny and Eumachia, both clearly embedded in the politics of giving in two disparate Italian regions. Both individuals were associated with already prominent families, and their significant donations to groups fall into established patterns. They affirm upper-class status in the most public way.[30]

Once we move beyond the usual interest in self-presentation and reciprocity to ask about the expected impact of these representations on others—that is, modeling—our quest becomes more complex. Eumachia's lavish celebration of the cult of *Concordia Augusta* shrine (and the related cult of *Pietas Augusta)* is almost certainly linked to her son's inevitable elevation to office: *CIL* 10 810 stresses her wealth, her own office as public priestess, and the connection with her son, in whose name, as well as her own, she finances the public structure.[31] Even the brief dedication by the fullers stresses her priestly office and patronymic. Such tributes and reminders, reinforced by buildings and the full-length statue all within the same area, would be (and are) today read by women as models directed at them. But it is not clear that the same messages would be apparent to an ancient audience, imbued with rather differing concepts of status and gender. Perhaps to a deferential electorate, the abiding message was of the importance of leading families, of suitable conjugal matches, of the appropriateness of electing a known name to office. The idealized portraiture style reinforces the

---

[27] As in the case of orphans or recipients of alimentary largesse, e.g. Pliny must have received many such statues; cf. the statue erected by the fullers to Eumachia.

[28] Septimia is depicted wearing a simple belted *tunica* without the addition of a cloak of any kind. Such simplicity, usually associated with slaves and attendants or shopkeepers, emphasizes the woman's working status rather than her wealth or marital standing, as does her hairstyle (Kampen 1982, 64–65).

[29] The structure is conventionally referred to as the "Tomb of Eurysaces." For the purposes of this chapter, it is not important whether it is actually a monument of a more general kind erected by Eurysaces in his lifetime (Petersen 2003), a folly, as

J.-T. Bakker believes, or, indeed, whether it is in the shape of an oven, as some have thought (cf. Toynbee 1971, 128).

[30] Verboven's summary, though referring to personal gifts, is worth quoting: "The social nature of the obligation to give was deeply rooted in the social identity of the Roman aristocrat. A notable was primarily a *homo liberalis* and by the time of the Late Republic this implied first and foremost showing generosity. Numerous donations were meant to uphold the much-cherished image of *liberalitas*. A substantial donation enhanced or upheld the giver's social status" (2002, 100).

[31] Zanker 1988, and compare the introduction to Kleiner and Matheson 2000, 1–16.

reminiscences in the building decoration of the Augustan Ara Pacis and of Livia herself, so strongly associated with the cult of Concordia.[32] The priestly and proper attire of Eumachia—like that of Atistia in Rome, near the Porta Praenestina—is a general affirmation of womanly qualities such as modesty in dress as well as a particular example of motherly virtue: a woman of means and position using both to benefit the town and her son while showing that proper female concern for an imperial cult associated with an imperial model of conjugal harmony and virtue. Eumachia was a successful woman by the standards of her time, but this possible reading would make her more like an English titled lady opening a church bazaar in the 1920s during her son's candidacy for the local Conservative constituency, which he was expected to take by virtue of family tradition. Eumachia might thus have stood for continuity and stability.

It may be significant that modern readings progressively move away from this kind of interpretation. Inevitably, we all read history and its characters in terms of the preoccupations of a particular age. A 2003 review of on-line courses and resources thrown up by a search engine quest for "Eumachia" soon shows the shift toward viewing Eumachia herself as a "merchant" or businesswoman, almost sliding into a "working woman."[33] What interests me about this is not—for the moment—the "truth" of these varying readings (Eumachia as established elite woman; Eumachia as socially mobile, from a family with ignoble origins; Eumachia as entrepreneur; Eumachia as worker). All can be justified, challenged, or subject to modification in terms of the same evidence. But it seems the impulse to view Eumachia as upwardly mobile and as a businesswoman in her own right is driven in part by the understandable desire of academics not only to help students to "relate" to the ancient world but, more specifically, to present young female students with a sympathetic role model.[34]

The process of modeling is therefore dynamic, part of a continuing process of historical reassessment. Since the 1970s, scholars have linked the conceptualization of Eumachia's building to the Augustan program of civic munificence. The building itself is modeled on the Porticus Liviae in Rome and therefore—like the building dedication—associates Eumachia and her son with the famous imperial mother and son. The strong echoes of the Ara Pacis and the Porticus Liviae in the statuary—including the idealized portraiture of Eumachia's own statue on the premises—identified her, her family, and her town with the imperial style of piety and civic display.[35] Dobbins reads this as a kind of manipulation of the imperial cult for self-aggrandizement by Eumachia and her son, a "co-opting of imperial imagery."[36] In following Livia's model, Eumachia thus provided a model of local prominence that could be taken up in turn by other Pompeian notables, especially women.

[32] Argued in convincing detail by Zanker 1998, 93–101, who refers to architectural "quotations" from the Ara Pacis Augustae and Porticus Liviae in Rome and points to the parallelism of the statues of Concordia (/Livia) and Eumachia in the structure. And see references above n. 11.

[33] In the "Feminae Romanae" resources section, under the "Women of Influence" heading, we find the following statement about Eumachia: "she used the fortune inherited from her merchant father to marry well and provide the guild's headquarters" (Cross 2001). In their introduction, Kleiner and Matheson (2000, 3–4) describe her thus: "Eumachia achieved wealth and power as a priestess and successful businesswoman in Pompeii."

[34] Consider the wording on the private website of "the Cole family," which groups Eumachia with the New Testament *purpuraria* Lydia (Acts 16:14–15): "History has tended to

overlook that there were smart and influential women during the first century" (Cole Family 2001). Castrén (1975, 102) explains the dedication of the statue by the fullers as being "because she was their patroness and employer." D'Avino (1967, 19) is characteristically colorful: "Eumachia lived among the male and female workers, and her indefatigable efforts were worthy of any great industrial manager."

[35] Castrén 1975, 101–2; Richardson 1978, 267–69; Richardson 1988, xx–xxi; Zanker 1998, 97–102.

[36] Dobbins 1996, 99–104. This reading reflects the recent shift in scholarship on the imperial cult from the imposition of centralized policy to the response and participation of subjects, pioneered by D'Arms (1988, 52): "Ideology and policy are reducible, ultimately, to persons." Cf. Lomas and Cornell 2003b, 5, 10.

Farther north and at least two generations later, Pliny the Younger was also performing in a continuous Italian tradition of civic benefaction and its celebration that he explicitly linked to his own family's past practice, *munificentia parentum nostrorum* (*Ep.* 1.8.5).[37] He was also following an imperial model. We know that Nerva, then Trajan, specifically encouraged the Italian elites to emulate his alimentary schemes, so Pliny, like others, was responding to the imperial example and exhortation.[38] Did he in his turn expect less wealthy and distinguished members of the Como elite to imitate *him*? Very likely. His concern for self-advertisement has ensured that his letters give us more insight into his intentions than the starker monumental testimonials. We might not take his words about his motives at face value, but at the least they help us to appreciate what he wanted to be known for, how he hoped his peers at least might view his example. He stresses his preference for cultural benefactions rather than the usual donations of games and feasts.[39] This preference strikes a sympathetic note today, but we should acknowledge that he did make such donations (*sportulae*), which—being ephemeral and not usually directed at the needy—might strike moderns as rather pointless. In ancient terms, however, this was equivalent to corporate sponsorship of public events and advertised the willingness of the elite to engage with the wider community. The inscriptional excerpts from Pliny's will thus display his participation in expected forms of display and generosity—substantially benefiting his own *familia* and, less crucially, the *plebs* of his region. By implication, they display the rewards that can be won by deserving servants and perhaps by a population that appreciates the local hero. His concern for youth is displayed in different ways: the provision of a foundation to enable the local poor to rear their children is also a sign of respectability and a declaration of his closeness to the imperial example; the donation of a library and school displays his wealth and dedication to culture in a way that will ensure his memory (in fact, he is still remembered and immortalized in statuary and inscriptions in modern Como). His provision of one-third of a teacher's salary is even more interesting—clearly, he could have donated the whole stipend, but he chose to insist on the involvement of local elite parents in the enterprise (a process quite recognizable to anyone engaged in fundraising for modern preschools).

The role-modeling implicit in Pliny's substantial gifts is thus quite varied. Peasant children and former slaves would be expected to remember his generosity and perhaps to act on it in their own, lesser sphere. It was a model of a well-established virtue, *liberalitas*, not confined to Pliny's class but having the most significant results and memorials when practiced by it. One might imagine that he was a more direct model for the kind of boys who would attend the new school. His expressed intention was that the school would keep talented boys in the region for longer. If they hoped, like Pliny himself, to make their literary and political name in the capital, they would have to move on. But perhaps even those who moved on might draw inspiration from Pliny's continued loyalty to his hometown of Como. Regional identity was in some sense a choice for elite landowners. Both Eumachia and Pliny possessed land outside the towns they favored, but both endorsed their own regional identity by means of substantial and conspicuous civic donations that provided public amenities. Eumachia thereby marked herself (and her family members) as Pompeian, and Pliny even more significantly proclaimed his continuing identity with a *patria* he could only visit at intervals.

[37] Pliny's gentile name appears in *CIL* 5 745, which documents a temple to AETERNITAS ROMAE ET AUGUSTI, with its porticoes and *ornamenta*, dedicated by one Caecilius in the name of his daughter Caecilia and begun by his father L. Caecilius Secundus. *CIL* 5 5279 records a testamentary gift by the officeholder L. Caecilius Cilo to the citizens of the Como municipality (Sherwin-White 1966, 732–33).

[38] See Currie 1996 and Rawson 2001; 2003, 59–61 on the imperial example and the supporting iconography relating specifically to *alimenta* for poor children. Cf. Patterson 2003, 97, 99 on imperial alimentary schemes.

[39] Cf Cic. *Off.* 2.60–61; Sen. *Ben.* 1.2.4.

Eumachia's building was clearly part of a concerted beautification in the Augustan style of the Forum area, of a piece with the *genius Augusti* building adorned by her fellow priestess Mamia or the Sanctuary of the Lares undertaken in the same period and the building a little farther away, north of the Forum, of the Temple of Fortuna Augusta by M. Tullius.[40] These projects were elite expressions of a new identity, following imperial models and providing models for current and subsequent elite observers of imperial loyalty and civic munificence.[41] For the populace at large, Eumachia's public displays provided the reassurance of continuity and the specific inspiration of her own example, echoing that of Livia/Concordia in the capital, and the inspiration of great figures of the past—the *chalcidium* was certainly adorned by semi-reliefs of Aeneas and Romulus, and it seems likely that the statue bases supported the kind of *summi viri* Augustus had displayed in Rome.

Each of these records expresses something about the identity of the individual celebrated and of certain actions or aspects of their lives. Portraiture of the early empire by definition attested to the impact of imperial role models. Augustus began the process, followed by his successors, of presenting themselves and their family members on coins and civic statues as ideals of virtues. Not only did this lead emerging social groups to include their children in funerary sculptural groups, but it encouraged elites to represent themselves in certain idealized styles and to identify iconographically and architecturally with specific religious and moral icons.[42] Their identity—as aspiring, prosperous *libertini* or as established regional elites—absorbed, then passed on in public form these new values and symbols.

Modern ideologies stress merit and notional egalitarianism. The enduring powers of the establishment, inherited wealth and position, are not perceived as moral values. But they were part of the dominant value system of the Roman world. It was no shame to be "patronizing," only to be ungrateful to a patron.[43] The recognition of Eumachia by the fullers, of Pliny by the Comienses, and of Septimia by her friend provided models of gratitude and proper behavior for beneficiaries of all status groups. So potential beneficiaries and benefactors were both provided with models through these displays. We take heart today from Eurysaces' undoubted pride in his material success and his willingness to display work of a kind decried in literary representations. He had also guaranteed by the placing of the monument that a large and varied audience could see the distinguished images of Atistia and himself in proper, formal garb that effectively proclaimed their distance from the work that funded the edifice. He went to considerable lengths to make an impression, but its precise character is not clear—and, even if it were, there is no certainty that it had its desired effect on its intended audience: there is no doubt what a modern advertiser hopes for from promotion of its product by a high-profile sports figure, but the most frenetic market research cannot substantiate its success. As scholars, we have refined our studies of public display, the interaction of image and text in ancient spaces, issues of audience reception and iconographic nuances, but, in the end, we can only speculate about the particular motives behind these enduring representations of individuals and about their possible impact on members of their own class or on their client groups.

[40] Richardson 1988, xx–xxi; Zanker 1998, 78–107. *CIL* 10 816 for the Mamia inscription. Lavish reconstruction was undertaken again after the earthquake of 62.

[41] Suet. *Aug.* 29.4. On the role of individual donors in reshaping the townscape of Pompeii and other Italian municipal centers in the early principate, see Zanker 1998, 101–2 and Lomas and Cornell 2003a.

[42] Kleiner (1977) outlines the impact on family portrayals, especially the inclusion of children in tomb reliefs. Kleiner 1992, 118 and Koortbojian 1996, 318 n. 9 both provide good guides to the considerable bibliography on developments in libertine monumental representations, a typology that Petersen (2003) challenges. Eck (1984) discusses the senatorial styles of self-representation of Augustus's day.

[43] Dixon 1993. The language of benefaction and reciprocity is subtle and complex (Hellegouarc'h 1963), and it is difficult to draw a hard and fast line between civic and personal patronage.

Works Cited

Andreau, J., *Les affaires de Monsieur Iucundus* (Rome 1974).

Calza, R., *Scavi di Ostia IX: I Ritratti II* (Rome 1978).

Castrén, P., *Ordo Populusque Romanus* (Rome 1975).

Cole Family, *Pompeii Virtual Tour. Building of Eumachia.* http://www.thecolefamily.com/italy/pompeii/slide24. htm (3 August 2005) 2001, 5 July.

Cooley, A., ed., *The Epigraphic Landscape of Roman Italy* (London 2000).

Cross, S., *Feminae Romanae. The Women of Ancient Rome.* http://dominae.fws1.com/Influence/Index.html (3 February 2004) 2001.

Currie, S., "The Empire of Adults," in *Art and Text in Roman Culture*, ed. J. Elsner (Cambridge 1996) 153–81.

D'Arms, J., "Pompeii and Rome in the Augustan Age and Beyond. The Eminence of the *Gens Holconia*," in *Studia Pompeiana et Classica in Honor of Wilhelmina F. Jashemski*, ed. I. Curtis (New Rochelle, N.Y. 1988) 51–73.

D'Avino, M., *The Women of Pompeii* (Naples 1967).

Dixon, S., "'A Lousy Ingrate': Honour and Patronage in the American Mafia and Ancient Rome," *International Journal of Moral and Social Studies* 8.1 (1993) 61–72.

————, *Reading Roman Women: Sources, Genres and Real Life* (London 2001a).

————, ed., *Childhood, Class and Kin in the Roman World* (London 2001b).

Dobbins, J., "The Imperial Cult Building on the East Side of the Forum at Pompeii," in *Subject and Ruler: The Cult of the Ruling Power in Classical Antiquity. Papers Presented at a Conference Held in The University of Alberta on April 13–15, 1994, to Celebrate the 65th Anniversary of Duncan Fishwick*, ed. A. Small, *Journal of Roman Archaeology* Supplement 17 (Ann Arbor 1996) 99–115.

————, *Pompeii Forum Project.* http://pompeii.virginia.edu/pompeii/ (3 February 2004) 1997.

Duncan-Jones, R., *The Economy of the Roman Empire* (Cambridge 1974).

Eck, W., "Senatorial Self-representation: Developments in the Augustan Period," in *Caesar Augustus: Seven Aspects*, ed. F. Millar and E. Segal (Oxford 1984) 129–67.

————, "Rome and the Outside World: Senatorial Families and the World They Lived in," in *The Roman Family: Status, Sentiment, Space*, ed. B. Rawson and P. R. C. Weaver (Oxford 1997) 74–100.

Elsner, J., ed., *Art and Text in Roman Culture* (Cambridge 1996).

Fantham, E., H. P. Foley, N. B. Kampen, S. Pomeroy, and H. A. Shapiro, *Women in the Classical World: Image and Text* (New York 1994).

Garland, R., *Celebrity in Antiquity: From Media Tarts to Tabloid Queens* (London 2006).

Hellegouarc'h, J., *Le vocabulaire latin des relations et des partis politiques sous la république* (Paris 1963).

Hope, V., "Fighting for Identity: The Funerary Commemoration of Italian Gladiators," in *The Epigraphic Landscape of Roman Italy*, ed. A. Cooley (London 2000) 93–113.

Jongman, W., *The Economy and Society of Pompeii* (Amsterdam 1988).

Joshel, S. R., *Work, Identity and Legal Status at Rome: A Study of the Occupational Inscriptions* (Norman 1992).

Kampen, N. B., *Image and Status. Roman Working Women in Ostia* (Berlin 1981).

————, "Social Status and Gender in Roman Art: The Case of the Saleswoman," in *Feminism and Art History: Questioning the Litany*, ed. N. Broude and M. Garrard (New York 1982) 62–77.

————, "On Writing Histories of Roman Art," *Art Bulletin* 85 (2003) 371–86.

Kleiner, D. E. E., *Roman Group Portraiture: The Funerary Reliefs of the Late Republic and Early Empire* (New York 1977).

————, *Roman Sculpture* (New Haven 1992).

Kleiner, D. E. E., and S. B. Matheson, "Introduction: 'Her Parents Gave Her the Name Claudia'," in *I Claudia II: Women in Roman Art and Society*, ed. D. E. E. Kleiner and S. B. Matheson (Austin 2000) 1–16.

Koortbojian, M., "*In commemorationem mortuorum:* Text and Image along the 'Streets of Tombs'," in *Art and Text in Roman Culture*, ed. J. Elsner (Cambridge 1996) 210–33.

Lefkowitz, M., and M. Fant, *Women's Life in Greece and Rome* (London 1982).

Lomas, K., "Public Building, Urban Renewal and Euergetism in Early Imperial Italy," in *"Bread & Circuses." Euergetism and Municipal Patronage in Roman Italy*, ed. K. Lomas and T. Cornell (London and New York 2003) 28–45.

Lomas, K., and T. Cornell, eds., *"Bread & Circuses." Euergetism and Municipal Patronage in Roman Italy* (London and New York 2003a).

——, "Introduction. Patronage and Benefaction in Ancient Italy," in *"Bread & Circuses." Euergetism and Municipal Patronage in Roman Italy*, ed. K. Lomas and T. Cornell (London and New York 2003b) 1–11.

MacMullen, R., "Woman in Public in the Roman Empire," *Historia* 29 (1980) 208–18.

Moeller, W. O., "The Building of Eumachia: A Reconsideration," *American Journal of Archaeology* 76 (1972) 323–27.

Nicols, J., "Pliny and the Patronage of Small Communities," *Hermes* 108 (1980) 365–85.

Nielsen, H. S., "The Physical Context of Roman Epitaphs and the Structure of the Roman Family," *Analecta Romana Instituti Danici* 23 (1996) 35–60.

Patterson, J. R., "The Emperor and the Cities of Italy," in *"Bread & Circuses." Euergetism and Municipal Patronage in Roman Italy*, ed. K. Lomas and T. Cornell (London and New York 2003) 89–104.

Petersen, L. H., "The Baker, His Tomb, His Wife, and Her Breadbasket: The Monument of Eurysaces in Rome," *Art Bulletin* 85 (2003) 230–57.

Rawson, B., "Children as Cultural Symbols: Imperial Ideology in the Second Century," in *Childhood, Class and Kin*, ed. S. Dixon (London 2001) 21–42.

——, *Children and Childhood in Roman Italy* (Oxford and New York 2003).

Rawson, B., and P. R. C. Weaver, eds., *The Roman Family: Status, Sentiment, Space* (Oxford 1997).

Richardson, jr., L., "*Concordia* and *Concordia Augusta*: Rome and Pompeii," *La parola del passato* 33 (1978) 260–72.

——, *Pompeii: An Architectural History* (Baltimore 1988).

Sherwin-White, A. N., *The Letters of the Younger Pliny: A Historical and Social Commentary* (Oxford 1966).

Toynbee, J. M. C., *Death and Burial in the Roman World* (London 1971).

Trevelyan, R., *The Shadow of Vesuvius: Pompeii, A.D. 79* (London 1976).

Verboven, K., *The Economy of Friends: Economic Aspects of* Amicitia *and Patronage in the Late Republic*, Collection *Latomus* 269 (Brussels 2002).

Will, E. L., "Women in Pompeii," *Archaeology* 32 (1979) 34–43.

Woolf, G., "Monumental Writing and the Expansion of Roman Society in the Early Empire," *Journal of Roman Studies* 86 (1996) 22–39.

Zanker, P., *The Power of Images in the Age of Augustus*, trans. A. Shapiro (Ann Arbor 1988).

——, *Pompeii: Public and Private Life*, Revealing Antiquity 11, trans. D. L. Schneider (Cambridge, Mass. and London 1998).

3 ◆ WHO'S TRICKED:
MODELS OF SLAVE BEHAVIOR IN PLAUTUS'S *PSEUDOLUS*

Roberta Stewart

In Plautus's *Pseudolus* a young and conventionally witless free male hasn't the necessary funds (20 *minae*) to buy a slave woman who is about to be sold away by a sadistic slave-dealing pimp. The witless youth is rescued by the clever family slave, who orchestrates a scam whereby a second trickster tricks the pimp to give the girl away. The mean father, who wants to whip the family slave because of the son's excesses, attempts to thwart the clever slave's designs and is literally made to pay for his obstruction. The clever slave celebrates his success by getting drunk, dancing, and falling flat on his face. Characterization and plot in this play are conventional for New Comedy and typical of Plautus: witless young free lover, curmudgeonly old man, dishonorable pimp, wily slaves who show verbal wizardry; scam in the interests of the young lover, drunken celebration by the clever slave, doubling and so dramatic mirroring of two scams of two masters by two slaves.[1] Yet the trickster figure in *Pseudolus* also represents a larger tradition of trickster tales, the universal tales of the weaker besting the stronger and gaining control of desirable social goods, in this instance food, women, wine, and money. Although the trickster tale is ubiquitous and the transgression of normally functioning social restraints its essential feature, individual tales vary in historically significant and revealing ways in their details: which cultural restraints are surpassed, by whom, and by what means.[2] Moreover, trickster tales have particular currency in slave societies (e.g., the tales of Br'er Rabbit and John tales from the American South; the tale of Aesop from the Roman imperial slave society), where they have provided role models—the topic of this volume—for subordinated groups on how to survive enslavement and its concomitant dehumanization.[3] Yet the trickster tales, like the publicly performed *Pseudolus*, have also had a public function to articulate the resistance of dominated groups to their domination.[4] The tales thus embedding two perspectives and the dynamic interaction of two interconnected groups can provide crucial insight into the perspectives of masters and slaves.

In this chapter I want to analyze *Pseudolus*, and the stereotyped images of Plautus's tricksters, as an example of a trickster tale, and I want to contextualize the comportment of Plautus's slave tricksters as a staged public performance in a developing slave society.[5] My historical questions are

---

[1] For a survey of Plautus's plots and characters in relation to their New Comic literary tradition, see Anderson 1993; Duckworth 1994, 139–76, 236–71. On parallel plots, scenes, and characters, see Sharrock 1996, 167; Moore 1998, 93, 95.

[2] See Joyner 1986, 150–51.

[3] For the "Tale of Aesop," see Hopkins 1993, 3–27. For a provocative exploration of the trickster as a cultural, mythic artifact, see Hyde (1998, 226–51), who interprets Frederick Douglass as trickster. On the trickster tales of the American South, see Joyner 1986; Levine (1977, 102–35) emphasizing

the function of the tales in the slave society of the American South to educate young slaves in the skills necessary to survive slavery. Cf. Abrahams (1992, 110–11) cautioning against a simplifying perspective.

[4] For the political significance of the trickster tales as public documents emanating from a dominated group, see Scott 1990, passim, esp. 162–66.

[5] Finley (1998, 135–60) emphasized the slave society as a historically occurring phenomenon and correlated Roman conquest and enslavements in Italy and the Punic wars with

three: What qualities distinguish the trickster in Plautus? How do these characteristics correlate with the legal and social conditions of the slave in Plautine Rome? What can these characteristics suggest about the slave's sense of him- or herself as agent in Plautine Rome? The discussion is focused on the individual text of *Pseudolus* while drawing broadly from the Plautine corpus to corroborate particular features of slave behavior and conceptual representations of slave experience. In this way I have tried not only to exploit the dramatic tensions of the particular play as evidence but also, in collecting groups of similar representations across the plays, to create an argument about slave behavior, not a particular reading.[6] The tale of Aesop studied by Hopkins offers comparative material from the Roman slave society for identifying details of Plautus's representations as characteristic of a Roman experience, not simply unique to Plautus. As an analytical category, the concept of the "role model" helps first to identify and assess the role of Plautus's tricksters in the moral logic of the slave society and second to explore the problem of identifying the slave's agency in a system of domination.

Latin New Comedy and Roman Social History

The use of Plautus's drama in order to explore problems of Roman history faces two preliminary objections: Plautus's work derived from Greek New Comedy and so reflects the details of his originals or the traditions of a highly conventionalized genre and not the images of the slave that existed in the minds of elite and non-elite Roman audiences.[7] For the Greek model of *Pseudolus*, there is no extant Greek original nor any agreement on what the original looked like.[8] Nevertheless, the textual studies of Frankel, followed by Stärk, Anderson, and Lowe among others, have demonstrated that

---

a demand for labor caused by the freeing of the person of the citizen, ostensibly by the *lex Plaetoria* of 326/313 (though Finley does not mention the law: 1998, 154–58). Hopkins (1978, 8–25) emphasizes the increasing use of slaves and the reemployment of citizens as soldiers as necessary correlates in the evolution of the slave society during the Mediterranean conquest, though he doubts, by his own admission without evidence, the prevalence of slavery in the third century. Crucially, however, the *lex Aquilia* first defined the slave as chattel (ca. 287 B.C.), implying a significant redefinition of the slave; see Watson 1987, 46. By contrast, the *Twelve Tables*, in defining a legal remedy for damage to a slave, compared the slave with a free man, i.e., not yet as chattel; see table 8.2 with the comments of Wieacker 1988, 364–65 and n. 64. Watson (1975, 81–97) imagines a considerable slave presence at Rome already in the fifth century because of the legal provisions made for testamentary manumission. He does not distinguish, however, between Roman and non-Roman slaves, though he does recognize the military weakness of Rome in the first half of the fifth century. The *Twelve Tables* prescribe the sale of Romans as slaves *trans Tiberim* and so suggest the existence of extra-communal sources of slavery; see table 3 (Gell. 20.1.47). As William Harris (1979, 59 with n. 4) observed in another context (1990), records of large enslavements begin in the late fourth and early third century, precisely when the *lex Plaetoria* abolished debt slavery at Rome.

[6] On the method, see Lowe's comments (1992, 152–55,

esp. 155) on the work of Leo (1912, 87–187) and Fraenkel (1960).

[7] LeFèvre (1997, 9–22) gives a historiography of scholarly opinion on *Pseudolus* and Plautus's originality in the play. For a summary survey of the changing assessments of Plautus's originality, see Lowe (1992), who also correlates valuations of Plautus's Romanness with the interests (Greek or Roman) with which the text is approached. For Plautus's value for history, cf. the dismissals of, e.g., Parker 1989, 234 ("Plautus is not a reliable source for Roman social history"); Halporn 1993, 210 n. 24 ("In the absence of supporting external evidence, it would be a contravention of standard historical methodological principles to attempt to write social history from these comedies"). For finding the Greek in Plautus, Leo (1912, 87–187) carefully correlated Latin legal terminology with its Greek equivalents to show how Plautus was translating, established patterns of thought in Plautus's drama and sought parallels in earlier literature, and classified types of dramatic action and sought parallels particularly in Greek New Comedy. Fraenkel 1960 used similar methods to determine the Plautine: close comparison of Plautus's language over against known parallels, classification of types of speech, types of dramatic action, and character types.

[8] LeFèvre (1997, 23–92) carefully considers discontinuities in plot and inconsistencies in characterization to suggest the original Greek plot.

Plautus did not simply reproduce the characters, plot, or language of the originals (most of the originals are lost) but that he instead worked consciously within the literary tradition of Greek New Comedy and made it his own, suppressing and developing elements of the tradition (the characters of the dowered wife, the clever slave, and the parasite; metatheatrical elements of performance; the development of deception).[9] Fraenkel also showed how Plautus added allusions to Greek myth or institutions in order to exploit Roman sensibilities about Greekness.[10] Performance studies have emphasized the theatrical event as a further variable in the Romanization of the New Comic tradition at Rome, where both actors and audience converged with shared theatrical experience and expectations.[11] We thus need to think of Plautus's drama as the product of conscious and careful appropriation rather than simple reproduction, and we need to consider the Roman significance of both obviously Greek and obviously Roman allusions. From a Greek comic tradition Plautus made a play in Latin, which Roman actors performed and which Roman audiences understood with Roman eyes and Roman ears.[12] More important for the study of the *Pseudolus* and of Plautus's trickster plays, the literary studies of Fraenkel and especially of Anderson have emphasized the role and the character of the clever slave as a Plautine development.[13] Yet although literary and performance studies can help us to isolate the Plautine and so what is Greek and what is Roman in particular representations of slaves, they do not explain the fascination with slaves or their characterization as tricksters. We still need to wonder why Plautus—or the Roman tradition of New Comedy and *palliata* of which Plautus is one example—developed the character of the slave in order to create the trickster figure and did not develop, for example, the poor free male, who is instead developed as the character of the parasite (in fact, there is some conflation of these roles in *Captivi*).[14]

[9] Literary studies of Plautus's originality have centered not only on identifying Roman or recurrent non-Greek imagery or idiom (e.g., Fraenkel 1960; Perna 1955, 1–37; Paratore 1975) but also on his careful selection and omission of New Comic plots in order to develop his own literary purposes, both themes and characters. Anderson (1993, 3–29) gives a close analysis of comparable passages of Menander and Plautus to show how Plautus turned Menander's realistic melodrama into comic caricature. More briefly, see Halporn 1993. For the structural studies of plot and character (dis)continuities, see, e.g., Lowe 1992; Lowe 1999; Stärk 1990. For an attempt to identify elements of Italic drama in *Pseudolus*, see Barsby 1995, who emphasizes recurrent routines of accosting, of question-and-answer, and monologues of panic and congratulation.

[10] Fraenkel (1960, 55–94) already observed this about Plautus's use of Greek myth.

[11] For the fullest exposition of performance interpretation, see Slater 1985, 3–18. Slater (1985, 8) interprets Plautus as a fusion of Greek, south Italian, and Roman traditions. On performance and meaning in *Pseudolus*, see Moore 1998, 92–107; Slater 1985, 118–46; most smartly, Sharrock 1996, who sees *Pseudolus* as a series of staged, seeming improvisations. Konstan (1983, 25) acknowledges the influence of literary predecessors ("The sympathy of the Roman dramatists with the themes of their Greek models is revealed by their coherent symbolism and terminology which reproduced or embellished the style of the original in a specifically Roman guise"), but his assessment of Plautus as evidence for social and political value systems emphasizes the performance dimension, and he argues that the drama was topical: "In a period when foreign campaign, the rise of slavery on a mass scale, and growing class divisions among the citizens threatened the solidarity of the Roman community, comedy portrayed a natural harmony in the society, in which its members, despite contrary impulses, were ultimately united through the fundamental bond of kinship."

[12] Segal (1968, 1–7, esp. 7) insisted that, regardless of source, the acts of translation and performance made the comedies "Plautine": "Plautus made them laugh and the laughter was Roman." On translation and evidence for social history, see Stehle 1984, 240.

[13] On the character type of the clever slave, see Fraenkel 1960, 223–41; Segal (1968, 99–169), who interprets the comportment of the slave as carnival functioning to affirm normal real constraints; Anderson (1993, 92–106), who emphasizes the development of Plautus's clever slave as one of a "rogue" type. Cf. Gatwick 1982, 93, assigning the innovative use of slaves to Naevius. Literary studies of Pseudolus as trickster have emphasized the slave's use of language to create multiple identities and the poet Plautus's use of language to develop a metaphor conflating the roles of trickster and poet; see Wright 1975; Slater 1985, 118–46; Sharrock 1996. On Menander's slaves, see MacCary 1969.

[14] On Plautus's predilection for slaves, see Stehle 1984. On the prevalence and variety of Plautus's slave characters, see the survey by Stace 1968.

Assessing the value of Plautus's drama as historical evidence depends not only on the assessment of his originality but also on the definition of history. The major narratives of Roman society were produced by elites using records (pontifical, familial) of the elite state and document a history construed as *res gestae* with names, dates, and actions. Such histories of "facts" tend to emphasize action, rather than interactions, and to leave out the non-elite, the women, and the slaves (i.e., those who rarely accomplished "facts" but whose lives and personal experience were nevertheless framed by Roman social conditions (norms and institutions). Plautus, unlike the writers of the major historical narratives, has written a comedy of manners that draws from daily life.[15] He repeatedly conjures up social interactions that presume moral codes and in which standards of judgment are made real. He stages conflicts and conflict resolution within families, within the status hierarchy of patrons and clients, and within the political community of elite peers; and he exploits expectations of appropriate and inappropriate behavior associated with age, status, and gender.[16] Even as the drama claims to present a Greek social milieu, the production presumes shared ways of thinking and feeling within a Roman milieu.[17] Simply, the representations of slaves carry assumptions about slavery.

But whose Roman history does Plautine drama attest? In staging the trickster, Plautus has appropriated for the public stage a story typically told among slaves.[18] The historical study of Roman political and moral ideology provides a framework for interpreting elite perspectives, particularly the master's perspective of himself as master and of the slave, and for considering the significance of Plautus's appropriation of the trickster tale. This framework is often necessarily synchronic (*Twelve Tables* to Justinian's *Digest*), even for elite sensibilities and models, and the value of Plautus resides partly in his situating in time particular sensibilities and problems.[19] Delineating the elite master's perspective as it is represented in the drama is important for understanding the social conditions framing the life of the slave. Identifying the perspectives of slaves as represented in the plays requires, however, a definition of the slave that is not defined by the master. In the absence of Roman slave autobiography, the understanding of the dynamic of slavery as a system of domination—an understanding articulated by Hegel and informing the studies of American slavery—itself supplies the definition of the slave perspective.[20] Slavery

[15] Cf. Hopkins (1993, 4 n. 3) on the tale of Aesop: "My intention here is not to squeeze fiction for facts, but to interpret fiction as a mirror of Roman thinking and feelings."

[16] On dramatic narrative as historical evidence, see Konstan 1983, 9: "Stories, which are narratives of purposive actions, necessarily project an image of a social code, though not always a simple or harmonious one."

[17] Comic caricature is also good evidence; see Hopkins 1993, 7: "The interpretation of comic caricature is necessarily individualistic and error-prone, but it would be dangerous to assume that serious newspapers or the minutes of the Roman senate are more secure guides to the partial recovery of a lost reality than creative fiction."

[18] The same appropriation of trickster tales is evident in the slave society of the American South: see Scott 1990, 163.

[19] See Konstan's study (1983) of elite sensibilities in Plautus. For Roman sensibilities the evidence to construct the models is largely first century, and historians seek details of the attested sensibilities in earlier periods. E.g., in Hölkeskamp's

synchronic reconstruction (1987, 206) of the elite drive to public service, Plautus's materials offer important evidence for gauging sensibilities in the late third and early second century and sometimes afford the earliest documentation.

[20] Studies of the roles of slaves have tended to adopt, consciously or not, the master's definition of the slave. So, for instance, Segal (1968, 99–169), discussing the ubiquity of torture jokes in Plautus, concludes that the slaves are whip-worthy, a judgment that (whether true or not) has assumed the perspective of the master in defining the slave. Again, in defining the comic scheme as "the victimization of the ruling class by the lowly slaves" (1968, 152), Segal's analytical perspective goes no further than the perspective of the masters within the plays. McCarthy (2000, 27) recognized the limitation of perspective created within the play but did not move beyond it: "Thus we can explain the slave-master relations in Plautine comedy as the conjunction of two pictures: the good slave embodies the view that masters would like slaves to have of slavery, and the clever slave embodies the view that masters themselves would like to have of their own lives." The analytical perspective needs to step back from the perspective of the plays and treat the slave's perspective implied by the representations.

involved a twofold assault on the slave, for physical domination by the master but also and more important a struggle for survival (physical and especially cognitive) from the perspective of the slave. The actions of the slave may thus be understood as a form of self-assertion within a contest for domination and survival.[21] This definition of the slave perspective does not deny the master's definition of the slave as "chattel" but attempts to look through it. Whether Plautus worked in a mill (Gell. 3.3.14) and so gained his perspective on slavery is ultimately unprovable and, while interesting, unimportant.[22] More important, Plautine drama, as a comedy of manners, provides representations of slave behavior that reflect the slave's agency because the slave *acts* and actions reflect conceptions of the individual as an agent.[23]

Pseudolus *as a Trickster Narrative*

The play *Pseudolus* identifies the trickster as subscribing to the system of domination. The play opens with a dialogue between the slave Pseudolus and his young master, who is forlorn at the imminent loss of his beloved.[24] In the first words of the play, the slave identifies himself as solicitous for his master's well-being and an intimate of his master's counsels (14–15: "For you before now have considered me the greatest confidante for your affairs").[25] Pseudolus offers his assistance (16–17: "Let me know what's the matter. I will help you with material support or work or with a good idea"), and he ultimately promises to get the master's slave girlfriend from the pimp (112).[26] Fraenkel has remarked the Plautine elements in the language with which Pseudolus expatiates upon his servile concern, thereby embellishing his dramatic role as helpful subordinate.[27] Comparison of Plautus's text with opening dialogues from Greek drama emphasizes the Plautine developments, particularly the use of language to enact a contest for power between master and slave.[28] So in reading the letter that his master Calidorus received from his girlfriend, Pseudolus interprets the personal name of the girlfriend literally and concretely in order to conjure up the image of her as sprawling in the

[21] On the master-slave dialectic, see Gadimer 1976, 54–74; Rauch 1999. Recognition of the master-slave dialectic has been foundational for American slavery studies: see Genovese 1974; Berlin 1998; Bontemps 2001. Bontemps emphasizes objectification (i.e., being treated as not human) as an equally violent attack on the slave's sense of self. Blassingame (1978, 137–39) strongly rejects using Hegel's dialectic to interpret American slave experience because, he reasons, slave sources provide direct testimony with which to interpret behavior and motives. This is precisely the material lacking for antiquity.

[22] Cf. the authenticating stories for blackface minstrelsy and Br'er Rabbit tales collected and told by whites: Abrahams 1992, 142–43.

[23] On reading descriptions of slave behavior as "action-statements," see the appendix on method in Isaac 1982, 323–57.

[24] For a summary of proposed Roman and Greek elements in act 1.1, see LeFèvre 1997, 39–42.

[25] *nam tu me antidhac / supremum habuisti comitem consiliis tuis.*

[26] *face me certum quid tibist; / iuvabo aut re<d> aut opera aut consilio bono.*

[27] Fraenkel (1960, 390–93) compares a Menandrian opening with Plautus.

[28] Arnott (1982, 130) likens the dramatic technique of question and answer to Greek drama and concludes that Plautus "has adapted his Greek model with unusual fidelity." Arnott's *comparanda* are important for showing the differences with Plautus: the dialogue in Menander's *Heros* of two slaves concerns one slave's love for a slave girl, whereas in *Pseudolus* the dialogue develops a hierarchical interaction of slave and master concerning the master's love of a slave prostitute; the dialogue of slave and master in Menander's *Misoumenos* slowly reveals the history of a love affair but does not enact with words the contest for hierarchy between master and slave; the question and answer between slave and master in the Freiburg fragment concludes with the slave offering assistance to the master. None of the *comparanda* develops the characterization of the slave, and none enacts the contest for verbal one upmanship that is characteristic of Plautus; see the general discussion in Anderson 1993, 92. On the Freiburg fragment, see the discussion of Fraenkel 1964.

writing tablet, so undermining Calidorus's romantic image of his beloved and of himself as romantic lover (35–36; cf. 38–39):[29]

> PS: *Tuam amicam video, Calidore.* CA: *Ubi ea est, opsecro?*
> PS: *Eccam in tabellis porrectam: in cera cubat.*

> PS: I see your girl-friend, Calidorus. CA: Where is she, I beg you?
> PS: Here she is spread out on the writing tablet: she is reclining in the wax.

When Calidorus attempts to respond to the insult, Pseudolus interrupts his curse and finishes it as a prayer for his own personal well-being (37):

> CA: *At te di deaeque quantumst*—PS: *Servassint quidem.*

> CA: You, may the gods and goddesses, as much as they can . . . PS: May they preserve me, of course.

Pseudolus consistently exploits the range of meaning of words or conflates concrete and abstract meanings in order to get the upper hand in his interactions with his master.[30] So, for instance, at 711, when Caldiorus enters and claims to have brought around (*attuli*) a helper for Pseudolus, Pseudolus interprets the verb literally in order to question his master's physical strength and establish himself as arbiter of meaning:

> CA: *attuli hunc.* PS: *quid, attulisti?* CA: *"adduxi" volui dicere.*

> CA: I brought him around. PS: What do you mean, you carried him?
> CA: I meant to say, "I led him around."

Language thus becomes a vehicle with which the slave challenges the master's authority to define empirical reality, even as the master controls the slave's reality and indeed his very definition as "chattel" or thing.[31] Yet although in the opening lines of the play the trickster's trickery—and so his challenge to the master—is developed for humor, the plot locates the trickery ultimately as serving the interests of the master.

The opening further emphasizes Pseudolus's self-proclaimed identification with the standards of judgment of the ruling elite. With the entry of the pimp Ballio, Pseudolus seconds his master's negative judgment of Ballio's behavior, where the master emphasizes Ballio's arrogance and Pseudolus the violence of the pimp's treatment of his slaves (190–94):[32]

> BA: *fac sis sit delatum huc mihi frumentum, hunc annum quod satis,*
> *mihi et familiae omni sit meae, atque adeo ut frumento afluam,*

---

[29] On the Plautine character of the lines, see LeFèvre 1997, 41; Jachmann 1933, 452. On the rhetorical devices deployed here, see Willcock (1987, 18), who classifies the device as *paraprosdokian*, or a surprise turn, what describes the final curse turned prayer but not the literal interpretation of an abstraction, on which see below.

[30] Sharrock (1996, 159) sees the verbal skills as reflecting Pseudolus's identification with the poet.

[31] The clever slave does not challenge directly the master's authority to define punishment; cf. McCarthy 2000, 26–27.

[32] For this scene, see Fraenkel 1960, 136–40; LeFèvre 1997, 43–46. Fraenkel (1960, 139) observes that the repetition of commands at lines 170 and 241 marks out a Plautine addition to the dramatic action.

ut civitas nomen mihi commutet meque ut praedicet
lenone ex Ballione regem Iasonem. CALI: *audin? furcifer [quae loquitur?]*
satin magnificus tibi videtur? PS: *pol iste atque etiam malificus.*

BA: Make sure that grain is brought here to me, enough grain for this year,
for me and for my entire household, so much that I am abounding in grain,
that the citizenry change my name and proclaim me
as King Jason instead of Pimp Ballio. CALI: Do you hear him? Do you hear what the low-class
   is saying?
Does he seem to you to make himself sufficiently grand? PS: Yes, by god and the villain seems
   sufficiently evil-doing as well.

It is Pseudolus, moreover, who wonders aloud at the absence of elite sanction against the pimp
(201–4):

CALI: *nimi'sermone huius ira incendor.*
PS: *huncine hic hominem pati*
colere iuventutem Atticam?
ubi sunt, ubi latent quibus aetas integra est, qui amant a lenone?
quin conveniunt? quin una omnes peste hac populum hunc liberant?

CALI: I am burning with anger at this man's talk.
PS: That this man live here, how can the young men of Attica endure it?
Where are they? Where are they hiding, those men of flourishing youth, who take lovers from
   the pimp?
Why do they not form a plan? Why do they not all together free the people from this moral
   blight?

In a subsequent monologue, Pseudolus reaffirms his judgment of Ballio and identifies himself as fighting a common public enemy, where the use of a military metaphor to describe the slave's actions suggests Plautine authorship (584–85: "Now I will elegantly take by storm Ballio, this common enemy of mine and of all of you").[33] The statement in monologue—the stage device for expressing privately held and so hidden sentiments[34]—once again allows Roman masters to hear a slave sincerely defining himself as subordinate to the system of slavery and acting in its interests.

The avowed subordination to slavery is characteristic of Plautus's trickster. Of the eight Plautine plays with dominant, wily slaves, five (including *Pseudolus*) begin with the trickster slave identifying his subordinate position in relation to the coercive punishment of the slave system (the beginning of the *Bacchides* is lost): *Asinaria* begins with the clever slave fearfully asking his master about his intentions to send him to the mill, and the scene ends with jokes about the slave's fear even to mention the name of the mill (24–42); *Epidicus* begins with a dialogue in which the trickster learns that his young master has brought home a slave girl/lover, and the scene ends with the trickster discoursing with himself about the punishment his older master will give him because of the young master's new love interest (73–79); *Persa* begins with a monologue of a slave trickster just returning from penal slavery in the mines and avowing his readiness to endure again such punishment (7–12, 20–23); *Poenulus* begins with the trickster reminding his master of the whipping he had received from him the previous day (129–39). A sixth play, *Mostellaria*, begins with a dialogue between the

---

[33] *nunc inimicum ego hunc communem meum atque vostrorum omnium / Ballionem exballistabo lepide.* On the passage, see Fraenkel 1960, 59, 68–69.

[34] The stage monologue has been considered as a theatrical device to build rapport with the audience by bringing the audience in on the trickster's intentions: Moore 1998, 36.

trickster and another household slave who promises the imminent punishment of the trickster with the anticipated return of the master (55–57). Moreover, as in *Pseudolus*, the trickster risks the coercive authority of the system for the sake of the master: so in *Epidicus* the slave Epidicus risks punishment from his older master because of the young master's love interest and risks a beating from the young master if he fails to help him (*Epid.* 120–23, 139–47); in *Mostellaria*, Tranio takes the blame for promoting his master's love affair (16–19, 27–33; see also *Asinaria*, 52–53; *Poenulus* 159–65). Finally, as in *Pseudolus*, the stage device of the monologue is used in both *Persa* and *Epidicus* to suggest the authenticity of the trickster's self-conception as a subordinate within a system of domination. Thus Plautus's plays with dominant tricksters begin with reminders of the system of domination, and they show the trickster subordinate—often consciously and willingly—to the system of domination and risking its punishment in the interests of the master. The trickster is represented as cooperative labor displaying concerned obedience to his master's needs and interests, exactly what the slave system demanded of the slave. The stage characterization of the trickster thus distills the Roman problem with slavery not as a problem of obedience, which could be forcibly exacted, but as a problem of the slave's subjectivity.

The opening scenes introduce two masters who differ in social status and acceptability but share a belief in their ability to dominate their slaves by means of the whip.[35] The slave dealer Ballio makes his first appearance brandishing and probably cracking a whip in a scene that Slater has rightly described as sadistic (153–55).[36] Ballio believes he can control his slaves by means of the whip. He accuses them of classic forms of slave resistance—that is, of not obeying orders, of working poorly or slowly, and of pilfering food and drink (137–41):[37]

> BA: *eo enim ingenio hi sunt flagitribae,*
> *qui haec habent consilia, ubi data occasiost, rape clepe tene*
> *harpaga bibe es fuge: hoc*
> *est eorum opus, ut mavelis lupos apud ovis linquere,*
> *quam hos domi custodes*

> BA: For these whip-wasters are of this sort, they have these designs, when opportunity is given,
> take, steal, grab, rob, drink, eat, run.
> This is their work, so that you would prefer to leave wolves with sheep,
> than leave these as guardians of your home.

He uses the violence of the whip to counter the slaves' behavior and avows that the whip is more powerful than they are (153–55):

> BA: *huc adhibete auris quae ego loquor, plagigera genera hominum.*
> *numquam edepol vostrum durius tergum erit quam terginum hoc meum.*
> *quid nunc? doletne? em sic datur, si quis erum servos spernit.*

> BA: Turn your ears here to what I am saying, you blow-bearing race of men.

---

[35] On the legitimacy of the whip as coercive instrument against slaves, see Saller 1994, 133–53.

[36] Slater 1985, 122. Fraenkel (1960, 135–42) gives detailed analysis of Plautine elements and a structural argument for identifying Ballio's addresses to the courtesans as Plautine. According to Fraenkel (1960, 138), both staging (Ballio calls out his slaves for what should have been an interior scene) and

particular details of Ballio's speech (the extended description of whipping) point to Plautine expansion of a scene in which the master ordered his slaves to clean house and prepare for his birthday party.

[37] On the slave behaviors and an attempt to assess Roman masters' attitudes regarding them, see Bradley 1987, 27–30.

Never will your back be tougher than my whip.
What now? Does it hurt? Take that, that for any slave who disdains his master.

The accompanying dialogue of Calidorus and Pseudolus, who eavesdrop and provide asides to the audience, establishes the play's judgment of Ballio as intolerable.[38] Ballio's offensiveness is probably, however, a matter of his status and not of his whip. For when Pseudolus's master Simo first encounters Pseudolus, his first words concern his desire to hurt him physically (445–48):

> SI: *quis hic loquitur? meus hic est quidem servos Pseudolus.*
> *hic mihi corrumpit filium, scelerum caput;*
> *hic dux, hic illist paedagogus, hunc ego*
> *cupio excruciari.*

> SI: Who is speaking here? He is my slave Pseudolus.
> This man has corrupted my son, the criminal.
> This man is the guide, the slave in charge of my son, this man I
> want to torture.

Simo's friend urges his restraint from anger (448–52):

> CALL: *iam istaec insipientiast,*
> *iram in propromptu gerere. quanto satius est*
> *adire blandis verbis atque exquirere*
> *sintne illa necne sint quae tibi renuntiant!*
> *bonus animus in mala re dimidiumst mali.*

> CALL: Now that is folly,
> to act publicly in anger. How much better it is
> to approach him with agreeable words and ask
> whether those things which have been reported to you are or are not so!
> Noble self-possession in a bad circumstance is a half of misfortune.

The friend's advice reflects a discourse about elite standards of behavior in punishing slaves.[39] Simo's friend does not deny the legitimacy of physical coercion as the instrument of the master's power; he only insists on its timely and calm application. Like Ballio, Simo identifies the whip as the instrument of a master's anger (471–75):

> PS: *Age loquere quidvis, tam etsi tibi suscenseo.*
> SI: *Mihin domino servos tu suscenses?* PS: *tam tibi*
> *mirum id videtur?* SI: *Hercle qui, ut tu praedicas,*
> *cavendum est mi aps te irato, atque alio tu modo*
> *me verberare atque ego te soleo cogitas.*

> PS: Say what you will, although I am angry at you.

---

[38] On the use of the eavesdropping to unite the perspectives of audience and eavesdroppers, see Slater 1985, 123.

[39] See Garnsey (1996, 90–94), whose earliest reference for this Roman thought is Cicero. Harris (2001, 321–35) traces the Roman discourse about the master's anger from the historical accounts of the first Sicilian slave rebellion in the 130s through the formulation of imperial policy regulating the punishment of slaves by their masters. Harris emphasizes the formulation of the discourse as practical slave management with financial benefits.

SI: You, a slave, are angry at me your master?
PS: Does it seem so surprising to you? SI: By Hercules, by your account,
I should beware of you in your anger, and you are thinking to whip me in some other way than
I am wont to whip you.

Like Ballio, Simo wants to punish his slave for disobedience: he accuses Pseudolus of not informing him of his son's transgressions and claims that Pseudolus therefore merits penal servitude (490–94). Both masters are thus represented as believing they can dominate their slaves by means of physical coercion.

The two masters are shown to differ in their responses to Roman practices of public shaming, or *flagitatio*, which difference would underscore their difference in status.[40] When Pseudolus and Calidorus learn that the pimp Ballio has forsworn his oath to sell the slave girl to Calidorus, they attempt to censure him with reproaches drawn from the political and moral vocabulary of the Roman elite (357–69): they censure Ballio as shameless (*inpudice*), criminal (*sceleste*), a grave robber (*bustirape*), a deceiver of dependents (*sociofraude*), a father or citizen murderer (*parricida*), a temple robber (*sacrilege*), a false oath swearer (*peiiure*), a lawbreaker (*legerupa*), a corrupter of the youth (*permities adulescentum*), a thief (*fur*), a fugitive (*fugitive*), a deceiver of the people (*fraus populi*), a parent beater (*verberavisti patrem atque matrem*).[41] Conspicuously, Pseudolus's otherwise overwhelming power with words has here no effect, perhaps highlighting the inappropriateness of the slave's invoking Roman standards of morality but certainly underscoring Ballio's characterization as shameless and so unmovable by conventional Roman forms of shaming.[42] For, by contrast, when Pseudolus promises a public clamor (*flagitabere*) should his elite master Simo fail to live up to a promise, the Roman audience may have found humorous the slave's presumption even to promise the public censure of a free person, but the elite Simo insists on the integrity of his word (554–56; cf. 1313–29).[43] The doubling and mirroring of the two masters thus produce contrast and highlight commonality. The text focuses on contrasting the status and character of the masters as honorable elite (Simo) and disreputable outcast (Ballio). But their commonality is important for the position of the slave: the slave is subordinate to the master's coercive authority, whether sadistically or calmly inflicted.

The Trickster in Cross-Cultural Perspective

The assumptions about slavery implicit in Pseudolus's opening find a parallel first in the trickster tale of Aesop, a composite of tales about a slave and his master, preserved in a text dating between 100 B.C. and A.D. 200.[44] Although the tale focuses on the unremitting contest of wits between master

[40] On Roman procedures of folk justice, see Lintott 1968, 6–9.

[41] On the scene, see Fraenkel 1960, 380 n. 1; LeFèvre 1997, 53–54. Fraenkel does not discount a Greek kernel in the scene; LeFèvre doubts such.

[42] Wright 1975; Slater 1985, 118–46; Sharrock 1996, 155. Wright (1975, 409) suggests Pseudolus's lack of command because he wields "conventional insults." Slater (1985, 124–25) notes that the unsuccessful *flagitatio* was not Pseudolus's idea and emphasizes the staging, that the scene of the *flagitatio* with Pseudolus and Calidorus on either side of Ballio would create a stage image of Ballio as the "apex of power."

[43] On the humor of Pseudolus's threatened *flagitatio*, see LeFèvre 1997, 108; Willcock 1987, 117.

[44] On the text of the tale of Aesop, see Holzberg 1992; Hopkins 1993; Hägg 1997. Holzberg showed that the apparently composite text of Aesop betrays careful organization and suggested parallels for the overall structure in Greek Romance. For the particular literary motives coloring the interactions of the master Xanthus and the slave Aesop, Holzberg (1992, 47–51) adduced parallels from the Greek New Comedy of Menander for the dramatic function of the divine prologue (1992, 47–48), from New Comedy for the character of the clever slave ("Der Verfasser . . . dürfte . . . durch Komödien vom Typ des plautinischen *Epidicus* wichtige Anregungen

and slave, the slave Aesop, like Pseudolus, affirms his sincere subordination to the master and to the rightness of slavery. Aesop instructs his master on the slave's loyalty to the good master (chap. 26), and he ultimately subordinates his own interest in freedom to his master's honor (chap. 85). Like Pseudolus, Aesop repeatedly uses his control of language in order to challenge the authority of the master, even as he displays concerned obedience to his master's will.[45] Thus Aesop accompanies his master to the baths with an empty oil flask because the master ordered him to bring the flask but did not command him to put oil in it (chap. 38). Again Aesop boils one lentil for supper because the master ordered Aesop to cook a collective singular noun "lentil" and Aesop interpreted the singular form literally (chaps. 38, 41). Like both Ballio and Pseudolus's master Simo, Aesop's master continually seeks a pretext to beat him (chap. 56; cf. chaps. 42, 49, 58).[46] Hopkins has emphasized the function of the tale to enact the typically obscured hostility between masters and slaves and to diffuse Roman anxiety about their clever slaves.[47] The characterization of Plautus's trickster as a self-consciously insubordinate subordinate could have functioned similarly for Roman republican masters, to reduce anxiety and diffuse hostility with humor. Such historical interpretation gives greater significance to what Segal saw as comedy's inversion of normally functioning social restraints and what Holt Parker interpreted as comedy's function to relieve Roman anxiety about the physical oppression of the slave society.[48] Yet the repeated avowals of subordination in monologue in *Pseudolus*, *Epidicus*, and *Persa* underscore a further function for the humor, namely to diffuse Roman anxiety about the deference of their slaves as a performance of forced compliance. The dramatic representations of the trickster presume a world that defined slaves as "chattel" but lived with the problem of an independent slave subjectivity.[49]

Although *Pseudolus* stages anxieties about clever Greek slaves, both the historical data of Roman enslavements and comparative data from slave societies allow us to view the comportment as reflecting the dynamics of slavery as a system of domination and not necessarily a Greek (slave) capacity with language or a Roman experience with intelligent Greeks.[50] First, although the staging of Pseudolus in 192 occurred amidst Roman wars with and enslavements of Greeks (e.g., 5,000

erhalten haben": 1992, 50), and from Old Comedy for the motif of a slave who criticizes his master and for the character of the comic philosopher (1992, 50). On the comic philosopher type in Aesop and Old Comedy, see also Goins 1989. Hägg provides a careful study of the history of the text and particular elements in the tradition of Aesop. But the clever slave is a Roman, not Greek, New Comic feature (see Holzberg 1992, 50), or at least not Menander (see MacCary 1969). The trickster slave Xanthias in Aristophanes' *Frogs* shows universal features of resistance with respect to his master: grumbling as an aside to his master (*Frogs* 87–88; cf. 107) and playing with words in an attempt to subvert power relations (*Frogs* 25–26). But Aristophanes represents the master getting the better of the slave in verbal reasoning (*Frogs* 25–30); see the comments on line 25 of Dover 1993, 193. Again, although the dialogue of the two slave tricksters at *Frogs* 738–55 creates a list of standard trickster behaviors (cursing the master secretly, grumbling, being noisy, eavesdropping, and being a chatterbox to the neighbors), the dramatic action focuses on (and makes humor of) the blurring of the slave's and master's identities, what is announced thematically at the beginning of the play, when Xanthias avows that he might have been free had he rowed at the Battle at Arginusae (*Frogs* 33–34), and invoked in the parabasis (*Frogs* 686–705).

[45] See Hopkins 1993, 19–21.

[46] On the role of whipping in the tale of Aesop, see the comments of Hopkins 1993, 23. On the whip and Roman slavery in general, see Hopkins 1993, 7–10.

[47] Hopkins 1993, 22–23.

[48] On torture jokes in Plautus, see Parker 1989, esp. 240–41.

[49] McCarthy (2000, 27) recognizes the fundamental feature of the clever slave as "the ability to be free from another's subjectivity." But she uses this literary representation of freedom as evidence for the master's perspective about being a master. This chapter does not deny the interrelation of complementary definitions of "master" and "slave" but tries to explore representations of "slave" to consider the perspective of slaves rather than masters.

[50] Cf. Stehle 1984, emphasizing Roman anxieties about Greek rhetoric in the early second century B.C.

Macedonians in 197 at Kynoskephalai), Roman enslavements of conquered peoples, including Greeks, had begun a century earlier with recorded enslavements of at least 60,000 Italic peoples (Etruscans, Samnites, and Greeks) in the years 297–93; of at least 85,000 Carthaginians and assorted Greeks in Sicily during the First Punic War; of 60,000 in Italy, Africa, and the Spains during the Second Punic War.[51] Although any particular recorded figure from antiquity is notoriously unreliable, the sources nevertheless suggest Roman experience with a composite slave population and, more important, suggest that the Romans had enslaved cultured Greeks long before the 190s. How many slaves ended up in Roman service is again a matter of conjecture, but Brunt reckoned a Roman slave population of 500,000 providing labor and so enabling the massive Roman military deployments during the Second Punic War.[52] Thus when Pseudolus's master likens his verbal skills to those of the philosopher Socrates (464–65), the reference may reflect a fashion among the Roman aristocracy to affect Greek culture without necessarily reflecting on the ethnic origins of the current slave population.[53]

Moreover, Pseudolus's verbal skills—both their forms and their purposes—have parallels in comparative material from the slave societies of the Caribbean and the American South. Although the particular circumstances of Roman, Caribbean, and American slave societies were arguably very different, the trickster is the folk hero of subordinated groups, and a basic feature of the trickster across cultures is the capacity to manipulate language, its literal and figurative meanings.[54] The language of the folktale hero has, moreover, documented parallels in the verbal strategies whereby subordinated groups euphemize their insubordination.[55] Of the corn-shucking songs in the slave society of the American South, Abrahams has emphasized the use of rhyming and allusive language to create commentary on slave life and on the behavior of individual masters.[56] In a separate study of expressive culture in the Caribbean, Abrahams has emphasized how the verbal skills for speaking to power become a mechanism for asserting a common identity within the subordinate community. Abrahams distinguished two modes of speech with particular functions: "talking sweet," deploying an assimilated standard English, served to affirm the family and its rituals; "talking broad" or "talking bad," emphasizing wit and verbal skill, worked to socialize young men as men and impart verbal skills necessary for life.[57] But Henry Louis Gates, in a study of African-American rhetorical expression from slavery to its contemporary forms, has argued that the very act of displaying verbal dexterity itself represents a form of resistance to forced subordination. That is, the obvious verbal skills characteristic of African-American expressive culture (such as metaphor, punning, or irony) presume a subtler recognition of language as a system of signification and are designed to challenge the verbal system of the dominant culture.[58] Gates cites examples from literature that offer important *comparanda* for Plautus. So, in Chester Himes's *Hot Day, Hot Night*, when a white supervisor questions two black

[51] On enslavements 297–93, see Harris 1979, 59 and n. 4. On their political and social significance, see Harris 1990, 498–99. On enslavements during the First and Second Punic Wars, see Pritchett 1991, 5:232–33 (a summary table of numbers and sources); Toynbee 1965, 2:170–72; Brunt 1971, 67 n. 2.

[52] Brunt 1971, 67. Frank (1933, 1:101–2) guesstimated from the recorded returns on the 5% manumission tax that Romans were manumitting more than 1,000 slaves per year.

[53] Cf. McDonnell (2003, 245 n. 30), who suggests that the Roman preference of Greek names for slaves indicates their prestige value at Rome.

[54] On the trickster and his use of language in Venezuelan myth, see Hill 2002.

[55] See Scott (1990, 136–82, esp. 152–56, 162–66), whose citations from various cultures demonstrate the universality of the strategies for resisting domination.

[56] Abrahams 1992, 107–30.

[57] Abrahams 1983, 21–39, 47–76.

[58] Gates 1988, 44–88, esp. 47.

detectives about the person(s) responsible for a riot, they, like Pseudolus and Aesop, first insist on the precise meaning of the superior's words and give a precise but logically unexpected answer:

> "I take it you've discovered who started the riot," Anderson said.
> "We knew who he was all along," Grave Digger said.
> "It's just nothing we can do to him," Coffin Ed echoed.
> "Why not, for God's sake?"
> "He's dead," Coffin Ed said.
> "Who?"
> "Lincoln," Grave Digger said.
> "He hadn't ought to have freed us if he didn't want to make provisions to feed us," Coffin Ed said. "Anyone could have told him that."

When the superior recasts his question more precisely to disallow an historically correct but situationally useless response, the detectives play with the concrete and abstract meanings of words and names:

> "All right, all right, who's the culprit this night, here, in Harlem? Who's inciting these people to senseless anarchy?"
> "Skin," Grave Digger said.

As Gates observes, the humor of the final response depends on the "multiple irony implicit in the metaphor of skin."[59] Verbal play, as well as the content of the speech, serves to challenge authority and to insinuate an independent self. Similarly, Pseudolus had played with the concrete and figurative sense of the master's girlfriend's name written in the writing tablet (35–36).

Conspicuously, such verbal skill in Plautus characterizes the slave, and, in the two instances when a master displays verbal acuity, either the slave or the master identifies the skill as properly belonging to the slave. So when Pseudolus and the master Charinus discuss the qualifications of an assistant for Pseudolus's scam, the master puns, creates a metaphor, and extends it to hyperbole, prompting Pseudolus to exclaim that Charinus bests him at his own game (737–43):[60]

> PS: *sed iste servos ex Carysto qui hic adest ecquid sapit?*
> CH: *hircum ab alis.* PS: *manuleatam tunicam habere hominem addecet.*
> *ecquid is homo habet aceti in pectore?* CH: *atque acidissumi.*
> PS: *quid, si opu'sit ut dulce promat indidem, ecquid habet?* CH: *rogas?*
> *murrinam, passum, defrutum, mellam, mel quoiuismodi;*
> *quin in corde instruere quondam coepit pantopolium*
> PS: *eugepae! lepide, Charine, meo me ludo lamberas.*

> PS: But this slave of yours from Carystus, who is here on hand, is he sensible (or does he smell)?
> CH: He smells of goat from his armpits. PS: The man needs a long-sleeved tunic.
> Does he have any wit in his breast? CH: The sharpest.
> PS: What if he needs to bring forth sweetness from the same place. Does he have it? CH: You ask?
> He has myrrh wine, raisin-wine, grape must, mead, honey of all sorts,
> indeed once he began to set up a drink-shop inside himself.
> PS: Good job! Delightfully, Charinus, you tear me up at my own game.

---

[59] Gates 1988, 96–97.

[60] Fraenkel (1960, 122–23) identifies the lines as characteristically Plautine.

Again, in *Poenulus* when the master Agorastocles puns on his slave's answer to his summons and his slave remarks on his verbal play, Agorastocles claims to have learned the verbal skill from his slave (279–80; cf. 292–96):[61]

> AG: *Milphio, heus, ubi es?*
>   MI: *Assum apud te, eccum.*
>   AG: *At ego elixus sis volo.*
>   MI: *Enim vero, ere, facis delicias.*
>   AG: *De tequidem haec didici omnia.*

> AG: Milphio, hey there, where are you?
>   MI: Here I am, at your side (or "Here I am, roasted brown")
>   AG: But I want you boiled.
>   MI: Master, you are surely making word-play.
>   AG: I learned all these things from you.

The subsequent dialogue plays on the master's allowance of verbal play where the slave selectively interprets the meaning of the master's words, and the master's initial admission of verbal play becomes a mechanism whereby the master undermines his own authority. So when the master Agorastocles uses a metaphor to describe his respect for his beloved's sexual purity and Milphio interprets the metaphor concretely for humor, the master orders the slave to disappear "immediately" or "eternally," and the slave chooses to interpret the ominous command as a further instance of verbal play (292–97):

> AG: *At vide sis, cum illac numquam limavi caput.*
> MI: *Curram igitur aliquo ad piscinam aut ad lacum, limum petam.*
> AG: *Quid eo opust?*
> MI: *Ego dicam: ut illi et tibi limem caput.*
> AG: *I in malam rem.*
>   MI: *Ibi sum equidem.*
>   AG: *Pergis* (or *perdis*).
>   MI: *Taceo.*
>   AG: *At perpetuo volo.*
> MI: *Enim vero, ere, meo me lacessis ludo et delicias facis.*

> AG: But consider this, if you will. I have never dirtied her person.
> MI: Then I will run somewhere, to a pool or lake, and I will look for mud.
> AG: What for?
> MI: I'll tell you, so that I might dirty her head and your own.
> AG: Go to hell.
>   MI: I am indeed there.
>   AG: Go on! (or drop dead).
>   MI: My lips are sealed.
>   AG: I wish them to be so forever.
> MI: Ho, Master, you truly make word-play and slay me with your puns.

Once again, the humor comes in the challenge to the master's power to define reality with words. Whether or not the lines in *Poenulus* represent a metatheatrical intrusion and a nod to Roman experience, Plautus shows us slaves consistently deploying verbal skills similar to those used by

---

[61] On the lines as a Plautine addition, see Fraenkel 1960, 208–10.

forcibly subordinated groups in order to critique and subvert dominant power relations.[62] The verbal skills, played for humor in Plautus, nevertheless create a space for an independent slave subject.

The plot turns on the problem of the slave as an independent agent. The scam against the pimp drives the plot, although it is only one of at least three scams in the play.[63] The focus on Pseudolus's tricking the pimp allows the trickster to appear to serve good over evil, for the pimp was a recognized social outcast in Roman society, and in the play he is represented to have forsworn his oath to Calidorus about the sale of the slave girl (352–53), to be willing to forswear his second oath to the Macedonian about the sale of the slave girl (376–77), and to be unheeding to the words of shaming that are applied to him throughout the play (972–75, 1130, 1225).[64] Moreover, just before Ballio is scammed, one of his young slave boys delivers a monologue in which he contemplates his own sexual exploitation as his only recourse for getting a birthday gift for Ballio (781–89).[65] The monologue recalls Ballio's threats to his slaves at the beginning of the play and his sadistic, overwhelming violence with the whip, underscoring by contrast the daring of the slave Pseudolus, who presumes to challenge him.[66] The trickster thus becomes superficially a hero, and Plautus develops a military metaphor of campaign and triumph to describe the scam. So when Pseudolus in monologue identifies Ballio as a common, civic enemy, he describes his intended scam in the language of Roman militarism and political aspiration (579–90):

> PS: *nam ego in meo pectore prius ita paravi copias,*
> *duplicis, triplicis dolos, perfidias, ut, ubiquomque hostibu' congrediar*
> *(maiorum meum fretus virtute dicam, mea industria et malitia fraudulenta),*
> *facile ut vincam, facile ut spoliem meos perduellis meis perfidiis.*
> *nunc inimicum ego hunc communem meum atque vostrorum omnium*
> *Ballionem exballistabo lepide: date operam modo;*
> *hoc ego oppidum admoenire ut hodie capiatur volo.*
> *atque hoc meas legiones adducam; si hoc expugno facilem hanc rem meis civibu'faciam,*
> *post ad oppidum hoc vetus continuo meum exercitum protinus obducam:*
> *ind'me et simul participes omnis meos praeda onerabo atque opplebo,*
> *metum et fugam perduellibus meis me ut sciant natum.*
> *eo sum genere gnatus: magna me facinora decet ecficere quae post mihi clara et diu clueant.*

> PS: For I earlier prepared my forces in my breast in this way,
> two-fold, three-fold tricks and treacheries, so that, wherever or whenever I engage with the
>   enemy,
> (I speak relying on the manly courage of my ancestors, on my hard work, and on my treacher-
>   ous badness),
> I will easily conquer, I will easily despoil my enemies with my tricks.
> Now I will elegantly overcome Ballio, the common enemy of me and all of you. Just pay at-
>   tention.

[62] On parodies of slave speech in the American South, see Gates (1988, 90–94) identifying examples from the early nineteenth century.

[63] On the schemes and Plautus's addition of the trick against Simo to the original, single trick against Ballio, see Lowe 1999. Le Fèvre (1997, 23–27) argues that the wagers are Plautine additions based on inconsistencies in characterization and on resemblance to the Roman form of wager or *stipulatio*. Sharrock (1996, 155–57) insightfully argues that the inconsistencies reflect not structural problems but a plot that is being presented as improvisation.

[64] Williams (1956, 429–30) argues that the forsworn oath not to sell Calidorus's girl worked to evoke greater audience sympathy for the scam against the pimp.

[65] On the sexual imagery in the *puer*'s monologue, see Kwintner 1992.

[66] On the structural linking of Ballio's entrance monologue and the *puer*'s monologue, see Slater 1985, 135.

I want to invest this town in order that it be captured today.
And I will lead my legions against it. If I conquer it, I will easily accomplish this business for
    my citizens,
Afterwards I will lead my army immediately against this old town:
From there I will heap up both myself and all of my partners with booty,
and I will fill my enemies with fear and flight so that they know that I am I.
I am sprung from this stock: it is fitting that I accomplish great deeds, which lustrous deeds will
    bring me repute for a long time afterwards.

Fraenkel first observed the ubiquity in Plautus of such exaggerated military language describing the trickster and his tricks, and he identified the slave's vaunt as characteristically and authentically Plautine.[67] Anderson has suggested the theatrical function of the language to conflate the slave's tricks with elite ideology and thereby render the trickster "a heroic rogue."[68] From the perspective of the master, the humor could arise from a double irony playing on the legal definition of the slave as deracinated outsider and the moral definition of the slave as naturally inferior. First, the slave trickster defines himself by what he is not and can never be: not possessing family, which is here defined as a source of politico-military virtue (*maiorum meorum fretus virtute dicam*, 581), and not possessing the manly valor that, according to Roman elite ideology, brings status in the Roman community.[69] Second, the slave vaunts of deceitful action (*malitia fraudulenta . . . meis perfidiis*, 581–82), which could never be an honorable action to boast about, especially in the politico-military context conjured up here.[70] The slave thus identifies himself as fundamentally lacking in the capacity for honorable interaction (*fides*) and so "other" or non-Roman.[71] The military metaphors continue throughout the play to define and to undermine with irony the trickster's characterization of himself and of his success. So, finally having scammed Ballio, Pseudolus declares his triumph (1051), which results in the drunken debauch that ends the play, where Pseudolus becomes overly drunk, demonstrates to the audience his dance steps, falls down, and belches in his master's face (1270–83, 1295–1301).[72] The stereotype of unrestrained servile behavior allows a conventional resolution of the play in terms of the status hierarchy: the master possessing moral restraint and constancy shows himself a worthy master, and the unrestrained slave displaying unrestraint deserves his status as morally inferior slave. Plot and characterization

[67] On the military imagery, see Fraenkel 1960, 223–33. Lowe (1999, 11) gives a structural argument for identifying the lines as Plautine.

[68] Anderson 1993, 88–106, esp. 95–96.

[69] On deracination and the lack of recognized family ties creating the legal definition of the slave, see Finley 1998, 142–45. On these ideals, see Earl (1967, 11–43), who emphasizes the conflation of moral and political vocabulary and thinking. On their currency among the Roman people, see Harris (1979, 9–53, esp. 41–53), who identifies the political morality with Roman militarism and delineates its particular configuration among the larger citizen body.

[70] *Fraus* by an elite is defined as a crime meriting his exclusion from the community and sanctioning his murder (*sacer esto*) in the *Twelve Tables*: see Table 8.10 (Crawford) and Crawford's comments (1996, 690). Petrone (1983, 94–98) surveys the Plautine terms for trickery (*dolus, machinor/*

machina) and their Greek literary antecedents. The argument here does not deny the literary pedigree of the terms but insists only on the multiple meanings, particularly in a political or military context.

[71] On Roman (written) thinking about faithful slaves and the moral capacity of slaves, see the summary survey of Vogt 1975, 129–45. For the social and historical context of the idea of (un)faithful slaves at Rome, see Parker 1998, esp. 155–63. Bradley (1987, 29) suggests that the regular association of Plautus's slaves with deceit represents a popular conception of slave behavior. On the topicality of *fides* for the Plautine audience, see Franko 1995, who argues that Plautus exploits the Roman meaning of *fides* to show how foreigners, specifically Greek Aetolians, may be made better by assimilating Roman *fides*. Focusing on ethnicity, Franko does not extend his analysis to status and slavery.

[72] For the scene as a Plautine addition, see Williams 1956, 440; Barsby 1995, 69.

thus exploit the trickster as an anti-model of Roman elite behavior and ideals, and the play as performance naturalizes the arbitrary logic of the slave system.[73]

The trickster tricks everyone in this play regardless of status or morality, thereby affirming the master's judgment of him as morally inferior. In addition to the slave-dealing pimp and his older master, the trickster tricks his fellow slave, who is identified as a good slave seeking to be obedient to his master's command. Before Harpax learns that he has been tricked by Pseudolus and will therefore be unable to fulfill his master's orders, he is made to deliver a monologue—a theatrical device to identify sincerity of sentiment—asserting his concerned obedience to his master's will (1103–15):

> HA: *Malus et nequamst homo qui nihili eri imperium sui servos facit,*
> *nihilist autem suom qui officium facere inmemor est nisi est admonitus.*
> *nam qui liberos esse ilico se arbitrantur,*
> *ex conspectu eri si sui se abdiderunt,*
> *luxantur, lustrantur, comedunt quod habent, i nomen diu servitutis ferunt.*
> *nec boni ingeni quicquam in is inest,*
> *nisi ut inprobis se artibu' teneant.*
> *cum his mihi nec locu' nec sermo*
> *convenit neque is [umquam] nobilis fui.*
> *ego, ut mi imperatumst, etsi abest, hic adesse erum arbitror.*
> *nunc ego illum metuo, quom hic non adest,*
> *ne quom adsiet metuam.*

> HA: The man is bad and worthless, who as a slave counts the command of his own master for nothing.
> Of no value, moreover, is he who is unmindful to do his job unless he is reminded.
> For they who consider themselves to be free on the spot,
> if they have removed themselves from the sight of their master,
> who are extravagant, frequent brothels, consume whatever they have, these bear the name of slave for a long time.
> Nor is there any bit of good character in them,
> except that they persist in shameless ways.
> I have no contact nor conversation with these,
> nor have I been well known to them.
> I [do] as I was ordered; even though the master's absent, I consider that he is present.
> Now I fear him, when he is not here,
> lest I fear him when he is here.

Fraenkel identified these sentiments as a category of Plautine dialogue in which a slave delivers a "catechism" of good slave behavior.[74] Harpax is furthermore identified as a captured slave. The detail underscores his status as a nobler slave in the eyes of the slave society (1170–71) because he had experienced freedom and the opportunity for volitional action.[75] The trickster thus tricks the

---

[73] On Roman thinking about natural slavery, see Garnsey (1996, 38–43, esp. 38), emphasizing that Roman thinking needs to be distinguished from Aristotle's philosophical arguments. Garnsey's earliest evidence for the thinking at Rome is Cicero. See too the brief comments concerning the representation of slavery in *Captivi*: McCarthy 2000, 169–70, esp. n. 5. But the contrasting terms "slave by nature" and "slave by condition" are used by the master to designate how a slave accommodates slavery, not the essential definition of

the slave as "chattel" and labor.

[74] Fraenkel 1960, 234: "una specie di catchismo dei doveri d'un bravo servitore." Fraenkel emphasizes the distinctively Plautine meter of the passages.

[75] Cf. *Captivi* 110–25, in which the master Hegio contrasts the desire for freedom in new and seasoned slaves.

good slave, thereby making him fail in his duty and making him liable to the physical coercion of the whip. From the perspective of the master, the trickster has no moral compass and is thus once again shown to be a natural slave. Most important, the slave's own behavior (and not the arbitrary logic of the slave system) makes him so. But from the perspective of the slave trickster (at least as represented in this play), morality doesn't figure.

From the perspective of the slave, the arbitrary logic of the slave society defines the problem of action: all action must be a trick. That is, the slave's agency must be cloaked. Obviously, overt disobedience met with the coercive physical punishments that were deemed legitimate within the Roman system: whipping to penal servitude to capital execution.[76] More subtly, the slave's capacity for action from volition was denied by the slave society, in the definition of the slave as an *instrumentum vocale* or "talking tool" (Varro's phrase),[77] in the Aquilian law of delict, which defined the slave as a chattel and classified injury to the slave's person together with damage to four-footed herd animals,[78] and in the Roman legal principle of noxal surrender, which implicitly recognized the agency of the slave while insisting on the slave's definition as chattel (the master was legally liable for the actions of the slave but in the event of a civil liability might surrender the slave to a plaintiff in lieu of a civil penalty).[79] Plautus's play exploits the slave's cloaked agency for humor, while it also shows a slave creating a sphere for independent action from volition.

The Trickster Slave as His Own Agent

In the first and crucial scam of the play, Pseudolus tricks his older master by playing on the master's sense of sure domination by means of the whip. Superficially, Pseudolus tricks his older master in the interests of his younger master. (This is the typical trickery of the trickster in Plautus's comedy,[80] though there are several revealing exceptions—for instance, in *Captivi* when the trickery secures the former master's freedom from bondage and in *Persa* when the trickster tricks to secure the freedom of his own slave-girlfriend.) The accompanying dialogue acknowledges the profound moral problem of the slave with two masters but recasts the problem in terms of the slave's contingent morality. Thus when Simo accuses Pseudolus of disobedience, Pseudolus first claims to have acted from a moral consideration not to put master against master and only belatedly admits that he consciously preferred a postponed to an immediate punishment (502–3).[81] From the perspective of the master, Pseudolus thus betrays himself as morally inferior and a natural slave.

But from the perspective of the slave, Pseudolus's trick emerges as a form of self-assertion. Pseudolus convinces his master Simo to make a series of wagers, by the terms of which the prize in the second wager (524–45) becomes the fulfillment of the terms of the first wager (508–14). First, Pseudolus wagers Simo that he will get money from him (508–14):

---

[76] On the thinking about punishing slaves, see Saller 1994.

[77] Varro, *RR* 1.17.1: *instrumenti genus vocale . . . vocale, in quo sunt servi.*

[78] Watson (1975, 86) comments on the contrast between remedies for injury to a slave in the *Twelve Tables* and in chap. 3 of the *lex Aquilia*.

[79] On noxal liability, see Watson 1987, 67–75. On the com-

plexities of the law defining the slave as chattel yet regulating slave families, see Bradley 1988, 485–87.

[80] See Anderson 1993, 90–91.

[81] Cf. McCarthy (2000, 169), who recognizes in the plot and characterization of *Captivi* a fundamental contrast "that links principled moral behavior with the freeborn and short-sighted, contingent moral behavior with slaves." These basic assumptions about slavery extend beyond *Captivi*.

PS: *tu mi hercle argentum dabis,*
aps te equidem sumam. SIMO: *tu a me sumes?* PS: *strenue.*
SIMO: *excludito mi hercle oculum, si dedero.* PS: *dabis*
iam dico ut a me caveas. CALL: *certe edepol scio,*
si apstulerius, mirum et magnum facinus feceris.
PS: *faciam.* SIMO: *si non apstuleris?* PS: *virgis caedito.*
sed quid si apstulero? SIMO: *do iovem testem tibi te aetatem inpune habiturum.*

PS: You will give the money to me, by god.
I will take it from you yourself. SIMO: You will take it from me? PS: Absolutely.
SIMO: Knock my eye out, by Hercules, if I will have given it to you. PS: You
will give it. Now I tell you, beware of me. CALL: Certainly I know, by god,
if you take the money from him, you will have done a great and wondrous deed.
PS: I will do it. SIMO: If you don't get the money? PS: Beat me.
But if I shall have taken it from you. SIMO: I give Jupiter as my witness to you that you will
      have it with impunity for your lifetime.

Then he wagers Simo the value of the young master's beloved that he will get the girl from the
pimp (524–45):

PS: *priu'quam istam pugnam pugnabo, ego etiam prius dabo aliam pugnam claram et commemorabilem.*
SIMO: *quam pugnam?* PS: *em ab hoc lenone vicino tuo*
per sycophantiam atque per doctos dolos
tibicinam illam tuo'quam gnatus deperit,
ea circumducam lepide lenonem. SIMO: *quid est?*
PS: *ecfectum hoc hodie reddam utrumque ad vesperum.*
SIMO: *siquidem istaec opera, ut praedicas, perfeceris,*
virtute regi Agathocli antecesseris.
sed si non faxis, numquid caussaest ilico
quin te in pistrinum condam? PS: *non unum diem,*
verum hercle in omnis quantumst; sed si ecfecero,
dabin mi argentum quod dem lenoni ilico
tua voluntate? CALL: *ius bonum orat Pseudolus;*
"dabo" inque. SIMO: *at enim scin quid mihi in mentem venit?*
quid si hisce inter se consenserunt, Callipho,
aut de compecto faciunt consutis dolis,
qui me +argento circumvortant?+ PS: *quis me audacior*
sit, si istuc facinus audeam? immo sic, Simo:
si sumu' compecti seu consilium umquam iniimus
aut si de istac re umquam inter nos convenimus,
quasi in libro quom scribuntur calamo litterae,
stilis me totum usque ulmeis conscribito.

PS: Before I fight that engagement, I first will make another illustrious and memorable battle.
SIMO: What battle is this? PS: Well, from the pimp your neighbor
through cheating and skillful tricks,
that flute girl over whom your son is perishing in love,
I will elegantly relieve the pimp of her. SIMO: What's this?
PS: I will render each feat accomplished at dusk today.
SIMO: If indeed you will have accomplished these things, as you say,
you will have surpassed King Agathocles in manly valor.
But if not, is there any reason
that I not put you in penal servitude at the mill? PS: Not for one day,

but by Hercules for all my days, as many as there are. But if I shall accomplish this, you will
forthwith give me the money to give the pimp
of your own free will? CALL: Pseudolus asks what's fair.
Say "I will." SIMO: But do you know what has come into my mind?
What if they have made a compact amongst themselves, Callipho,
or they are acting on agreement with tricks all crafted,
and turn me in circles for money. PS: Who would be more daring than me, if I dared to do
such a deed? No way, Simo:
If we have made a pact or have at any time entered into an agreement,
or if about this matter at any point among us we have come together,
just as into a book when letters are written with a reed-pen,
so write all over my whole back with your elm-wood pen.

Sharrock has emphasized that Pseudolus accomplishes the deception by the power of words, of
which power Simo announces himself fully conscious and wary from his first appearance on stage
(464–65).[82] But for each wager Pseudolus offers to pay with his body. He wagers his master a whipping that he will get money from him (513), wagers him life-long penal servitude in the mill that he
will get the slave girl from the pimp (534), and finally he wagers yet another whipping that he and
the pimp are not in cahoots (545). Pseudolus lures his master Simo with an offer that the accompanying dialogue shows Simo to be extremely desirous of, that is, an excuse to whip him. Pseudolus
turns the master's strength into his weakness, thereby making the scam a double scam. The wagers
define Pseudolus's actions in the play as actions to avoid the whip, but the double scam defines
Pseudolus's trick as defiance of the slave system. The wager proposed by Pseudolus and agreed to
by Simo would have been impossible for a slave at Rome, thereby creating humor from the slave's
presumption to the legal privilege of action from volition.[83] But from the perspective of the slave,
the trick is its own goal and a means of self-assertion.

The trickster transforms the skills for surviving slavery into mechanisms of self-assertion. When
Pseudolus defines the qualities he needs in an assistant for scamming Ballio (724–28, 737–49), he
catalogues the qualities driving the scams in this play and defining his own character: capacity for
witty and beguiling words (739–43), capacity for flexibility in action (745), capacity for cunning
(746, 748), and capacity to cloak his agency (747):

> PS: *si modo mihi hominem invenietis propere.* CH: *qua facie?* PS: *malum*
> *callidum, doctum, qui quando principium prehenderit,*
> *porro sua virtute teneat quid se facere oporteat;*
> *atque qui hic non visitatus saepe sit.* CH: *si servos est,*
> *numquid refert?* PS: *immo multo mavolo quam liberum. . . .*
> PS: *sed iste servos ex Carysto qui hic adest ecquid sapit?*
> CH: *hircum ab alis.* PS: *manuleatam tunicam habere hominem addecet.*
> *ecquid is homo habet aceti in pectore?* CH: *atque acidissumi.*
> PS: *quid, si opu'sit ut dulce promat indidem, ecquid habet?* CH: *rogas?*
> *murrinam, passum, defrutum, mellam, mel quoiuismodi;*
> *quin in corde instruere quondam coepit pantopolium.*
> PS: *eugepae! lepide, Charine, meo me ludo lamberas.*
> *sed quid nomen esse dicam ego isti servo?* CH: *Simiae.*
> PS: *scitne in re advorsa vorsari?* CH: *turbo non aeque citust.*
> PS: *ecquid argutust?* CH: *malorum facinorum saepissume.*

---

[82] Sharrock 1996, 174. On the dramatic logic of the wagers,   [83] Williams 1956, 435.
see Slater 1985, 130 and n. 16; Sharrock 1996, 160.

PS: *quid quom manufesto tenetur?* CH: *anguillast, elabitur.*
PS: *ecquid is homo scitust?* CH: *plebi scitum non est scitius.*
PS: *probus homo est, ut praedicare te audio.*

PS: If only you will find a person for me quickly. CH: With what appearance? PS: Bad,
clever, skilled, who when he has made a beginning,
holds steady with his own manly courage to what he has to do,
and who has not been seen often here. CH: If he is a slave,
does it matter? PS: On the contrary, I would much prefer a slave to a free person. . . .
PS: But this slave of yours from Carystus, who is here on hand, is he sensible?
CH: He smells of goat from his armpits. PS: The man needs a long-sleeved tunic.
Does he have any wit in his breast? CH: The sharpest.
PS: What if he needs to bring forth sweetness from the same place. Does he have it? CH: You
    ask?
He has myrrh-wine, raisin-wine, grape must, mead, honey of all sorts,
indeed once he began to set up a drink shop inside himself.
PS: Great! Delightfully, Charinus, you tear me up at my own game.
But what should I call this slave of yours? CH: Simia.
PS: Does he know how to turn himself about in a tough situation? CH: A whirlwind is not
    equally swift.
PS: Is he cunning? CH: He has been charged for bad behavior most often.
PS: What happens when he is caught in the act? CH: He is an eel; he slips away.
PS: Is he shrewd? CH: Shrewder than a piece of popular legislation.
PS: He is an excellent man, as I hear from your account.

From the perspective of the master, what the trickster calls flexibility in action (*in re adversa vorsari*;
possessing both sweet and sharp in the same place) reflects contingent moral behavior, and the
humor could arise from the slave defining his own moral inferiority and so the moral logic of his
enslavement. From the perspective of the trickster, these are the survival skills of slavery. Fraenkel
first identified a series of monologues in which a slave opines on the proper comportment of the
slave, and he observed how the speeches developed similar themes of loyal obedience with similar
terms of expression: the good slave's obligation to remember his *officium*,[84] not to need repeated
admonition,[85] to act with industry when the master was absent as well as present,[86] to fear the master and so to act well.[87] But the same passages also highlight another skill, namely the slave's skill
of accommodation, which is identified in Plautus with the Latin word *frugi*. So the slave Strobilus
asserts that the *frugi* slave needs to perform useful actions for the master, to subordinate his own
interest to the master's will, and to recognize the master's will from his very expression (*Aulularia*,
587–91, 599–602):

STROBILUS: *Hoc est servi facinus frugi, facere quod ego persequor,*
ne morae molestiaeque imperium erile habeat sibi.
nam qui ero ex sententia servire servos postulat,
in erum matura, in se sera condecet capessere.
sin dormitet, ita dormitet servom sese ut cogitet . . .
eri ille imperium ediscat, ut quod frons velit oculi sciant;
quod iubeat citis quadrigis citius properet persequi.

[84] *Pseud.* 1103; *Rud.* 920.

[85] *Aul.* 587; *Persa* 7.

[86] *Men.* 968; *Pseud* 1113; *Stich.* 9.

[87] *Men.* 983; *Pseud.* 1114; *Most.* 858; Fraenkel 1960,
234–36.

qui ea curabit apstinebit censione bubula,
nec sua opera rediget umquam in splendorem compedis.

STROBILUS: This is the behavior of a successful slave, that which I hasten to do.
Let the master's order hold for him no hindrance or annoyance.
For the slave who claims purposefully to be a slave to his master
let him properly hasten for his master and later busy himself about himself.
If he sleeps, thus let him sleep, that he contemplate himself being a slave . . .
Let him learn the authority of the master, so that his eyes know whatever desire the master's
     face indicates,
so that more swiftly than swift four-horse chariots, he hasten to accomplish whatever the master
     orders.
He who will take care for these things will abstain from whippings.
Nor will he apply his own labor towards the luster of a shackle.

Again, the trickster slave Chrysalus asserts that the *frugi* slave must accommodate himself to changing moral circumstance (*Bacchides*, 651–60):

CHRYSALUS: *nequiu' nil est quam egens consili servos, nisi habet*
multipotens pectus:
ubi quomque usus siet, pectore expromat suo.
nullus frugi esse potest homo,
nisi qui et bene et male facere tenet.
inprobis cum inprobus [sit,] harpaget furibus,
[furetur] quod queat; vorsipellem frugi convenit
esse hominem, pectus quoi sapit:
bonu' sit bonis, malu' sit malis;
utquoumque res sit, ita animum habeat.

CHRYSALUS: There is nothing more worthless than a slave lacking in prudence, unless he has
a multipowerful understanding.
Whenever there is need, let him produce it from his own native wit.
No man is able to be successful
except him who is able to act both well and badly.
Let him be dishonorable with the dishonorable, let him rob with the thieves,
let him steal what he can.
It is appropriate for a successful man to be a chameleon,
he who has wisdom and understanding, let him be good with the good and bad with the bad,
whatever the situation, let him be thus in his thinking.

The passages—whether or not they represent a humorous and comfortable denigration of slave behavior for a Roman audience—presume a recognized, independent slave subjectivity and underscore the slave's contingent morality as a necessary skill for surviving slavery. The use of the word *frugi* to describe slaves elsewhere in Plautus corroborates the slave's contingent morality as a skill of accommodation. *Frugi* occurs to describe the judgment of the slave by others, particularly the master, and seems to designate an upright slave (e.g., *Cas.* 255, contrasting with *nequam*; *Cas.* 268, contrasting with *improbus*; *Cas.* 283, joined with *probus*).[88] Yet when the slave uses it of himself, it

---

[88] Cf. *frugi* describing elites: *Asin.* 856, joined with *continens*; *Men.* 579, contrasting with *nequam*; *Most.* 133, joined with *probus*; *Persa* 453–54, contrasting with *malus* and *nequam*; *Trin.* 321–22, joined with *probus*.

describes the capacity to recognize and mirror the different emotional states of the master (*Amphitruo*, 958–61):

> SOSIA. *atque ita servom par videtur frugi sese instituere:*
> *proinde eri ut sint, ipse item sit; voltum e voltu comparet:*
> *tristis sit, si eri sint tristes; hilarus sit, si gaudeant.*

> SOSIA: And so it seems best that a slave manage himself as a successful slave
> just as the masters are, let him himself likewise be, and let him arrange his facial expression in
>   accordance with their countenance.
> Let him be sad, if they are sad; let him be merry if they rejoice.

The catechisms of good behavior in slaves and the usage of *frugi* offer parallels for the trickster's behavior and identify the behavior as an extreme use of the set of behaviors enjoined by slavery.

Conspicuously, Plautus stages the ambivalence of the trickster's behavior only in the comportment of two slave tricksters with each other (another instance of doubling and mirroring), suggesting again the ideological function of Plautus's trickster tale to allay Roman anxiety about their slaves. The two tricksters enact with each other a contest for domination in which the capacity to trick defines domination and subordination (932–33: "I will surpass you, who are my master, with tricks and guiles, just to show you").[89] Underscoring their enactment of the master/slave dynamic, Simia offers Pseudolus the right to whip him, should he fail of the scam.

The trickster exploits the arbitrary definitions of his own lack of agency as a source of power. Dallying has been observed as a classic form of slave resistance (in Rome, in the *Digest*; in America), a behavior that insinuates the slave's volition into the performance of nonvolitional, compulsory action. Simia is made to deploy it repeatedly with Pseudolus.[90] When Pseudolus first encounters Simia and questions him about his delayed arrival, Simia responds that it is his job to create uncertainty about his compliance (912–13):

> PS: *ehem, te hercle ego cicumspectabam, nimi' metuebam male ne abiisses.*
> SIMIA: *fuit meum officium ut facerem, fateor.*

> PS: Uh-hum, I was looking about for you, by Hercules. I was dreadfully afraid, that you had
>   slipped away.
> SIMIA: It was my duty, that I should act so, I admit.

When Pseudolus urges his haste, Simia avows he prefers to move slowly (920; cf. 923):

> PS: *ambula ergo cito.* SIMIA: *immo otiose volo.*

> PS: Well then, walk quickly. SIMIA: No way, I prefer calmly.

A similar thought is expressed at 923. Slavery views the slave as a talking tool, denying the slave's subjective self. Simia uses reticence as a mechanism of resistance.[91] When Pseudolus asks where he delayed, Simia answers him without supplying the requested information:

---

[89] *te quoque etiam dolis atque mendaciis, qui magister mihi est, antidibo, ut scias.*

[90] On dallying and absconding, see Bradley 1987, 27–28,

32; Bradley 1990, 143–44. On the American experience, see Levine 1977, 121–22.

[91] On reticence among American slaves, see Levine 1977, 99–101.

PS: *ubi restiteras?* SIMIA: *ubi mi lubitum est.*

PS: Where did you stop? SIMIA: Where I wanted.

Simia's refusal to supply specific knowledge of his whereabouts identifies knowledge as a slave's strategic asset, an asset that the slave refuses to disclose. Within the world of the play, Pseudolus's master had accused him of similar reticence (about his younger master's transgressions) and identified that reticence as disobedience. Simia also refuses to tell Pseudolus how he plans to accomplish the trick (930–31):

> PS: *qui potest?*
> SIMIA: *occidis me quom istuc rogitas.*

> PS: How are you going to be able to do this?
> SIMIA: You kill me when you ask that question.

Similarly, Pseudolus had himself refused to explain how he had scammed Harpax.

But the response ("where I wanted") reveals another form of reticence, about sentiment. Wright, Slater, and Sharrock have all observed that Pseudolus deploys a surfeit of words in this play, and Sharrock has shown how the abundance of words aids the scams. But there is also a silence at work in the play, and that too aids the scams. When Pseudolus suggests that Simia doesn't respect him and so the scam, Simia claims that he acts apart from his sentiment and leaves his sentiment undefined (916–19):

> PS: *nimi'tandem ego aps te contemnor.*
> SIMIA: *quippe ego te ni contemnam,*
> *stratioticus homo qui cluear?* PS: *iam*
> *hoc volo quod occeptumst agi.* SIMIA: *numquid agere aliud me vides?*

> PS: Really, I am too much disdained by you.
> SIMIA: Certainly if I did not disdain you,
> how would I be a famous soldier? PS: Now
> I want that which has been begun to be done. SIMIA: Do you see me doing anything else?

Simia rejects Pseudolus's repeated promises of material reward, and when Pseudolus attempts to flatter him, Simia responds that he too knows how to flatter and won't take the bait (944–45).

> PS: *ut ego ob tuam, Simia, perfidiam te amo et metuo et magni facio.*
> SIMIA: *ego istuc aliis dare condidici: mihi optrudere non potes palpum.*

> PS: How I love you, Simia, for your faithlessness and I fear you and honor you.
> SIMIA: I am skilled to give that to others. You aren't able to thrust that flattery on me.

Simia thus keeps his sentiments—his subjective self—untouched and thereby undefined to Pseudolus. From the perspective of the master, the humor could arise from watching two slaves battle each other. From the perspective of the slave, reticence becomes a mechanism of self-assertion and itself a trick that obscures an independent, resisting self.

In this chapter, I have been reading with the text, because it is a piece of literature, and against the text, because it is a historical document of a slave society. In Plautus, the trickster tale has become a public performance, and in Plautus's staging the Roman trickster emerges as a role model and an anti-model. The characteristics of the trickster find parallels in the universal myth of the trickster, in the slave trickster tale of Aesop, and in the slave culture of the American South. From the perspective of the master, the play rhetorically underscores the moral superiority of master over slave and so implicitly legitimizes slavery as a moral system. From the perspective of the slave, the trickster's behavior represents one of the solutions to the problem of survival posed by slavery. The trickster exploits the same skills of accommodation that every slave needed in order to survive. The play shows that a trick of self-assertion by the trickster stands behind the obvious trick in the interests of the master. Thus from the perspective of the historian, the trickster emerges as an analytical anti-model, for the trickster had to cloak his self-assertion. The trickster's trick obscures the knowable historical subject, the ultimate trick.

Works Cited

Abrahams, R. D., *The Man-of-Words in the West Indies: Performance and the Emergence of Creole Culture* (Baltimore 1983).

————, *Singing the Master: The Emergence of African American Culture in the Plantation South* (New York 1992).

Anderson, W., *Barbarian Play: Plautus' Roman Comedy* (Toronto 1993).

Arnott, W. G., "Calidorus' Surprise: A Scene of Plautus' *Pseudolus*, with an Appendix on Ballio's Birthday," *Wiener Studien* 16 (1982) 131–48.

Barsby, J., "Plautus' *Pseudolus* as Improvisatory Drama," in *Plautus und die Tradition des Stegreifspiels. Festgabe für Eckard Lefèvre zum 60. Geburtstag*, ed. L. Benz, E. Stärk, and G. Vogt-Spira (Tübingen 1995) 55–70.

Berlin, I., *Many Thousands Gone: The First Two Centuries of Slavery in North America* (Cambridge 1998).

Blassingame, J., "Redefining *The Slave Community*: A Response to Critics," in *Revisiting Blassingame's* The Slave Community: *The Scholars Respond*, ed. A.-T. Gilmore, Contributions in Afro-American and African Studies 37 (Westport and London 1978) 135–68.

Bontemps, A., *The Punished Self: Surviving Slavery in the Colonial South* (Ithaca 2001).

Bradley, K., *Slaves and Masters in the Roman Empire: A Study in Social Control* (Oxford 1987).

————, "Roman Slavery and Roman Law," *Historical Reflections/Reflexions Historiques* 15 (1988) 477–95.

————, "Roman Law and the Troublesome Slave," *Slavery and Abolition* 11 (1990) 135–57.

Brunt, P. A., *Italian Manpower, 225 B.C.–A.D. 14* (Oxford 1971).

Crawford, M., *Roman Statutes*, 2 vols., *Bulletin Institute of Classical Studies* Supplement 64 (London 1996).

Dover, K., ed., *Aristophanes* Frogs (Oxford 1993).

Duckworth, G., *The Nature of Roman Comedy: A Study in Popular Entertainment*, 2nd ed. (Norman 1994).

Earl, D. C., *The Moral and Political Tradition of Rome* (Cornell 1967).

Finley, M. I., *Ancient Slavery and Modern Ideology*, ed. B. Shaw, rev. ed. (Princeton 1998).

Fraenkel, E., *Elementi Plautini in Plauto*, trans. F. Munari (Florence 1960).

————, "Ein Motiv aus Euripides in einer Szene der neuen Komödie," in *Studi in onore di Ugo Enrico Paoli*, ed. L. Banti (Florence 1955). Reprinted in *Kleine Beiträge zur klassischen Philologie*, 2 vols. (Rome 1964) 1:487–93.

Frank, T., *An Economic Survey of Ancient Rome*, vol. 1: *Rome and Italy of the Republic* (Baltimore 1933).

Franko, G., "*Fides*, Aetolia, and Plautus' *Captivi*," *Transactions of the American Philological Association* 125 (1995) 155–76.

Gadimer, H.-G., *Hegel's Dialectic: Five Hermeneutical Studies*, trans. P. C. Smith (New Haven 1976).

Garnsey, P., *Ideas of Slavery from Aristotle to Augustine* (Cambridge 1996).

Gates, H. L., *The Signifying Monkey: A Theory of African-American Literary Criticism* (Oxford 1988).

Gatwick, A. S., "Drama," in *The Cambridge History of Classical Literature*, vol. 2: *Latin Literature*, ed. E. J. Kenney and W. V. Clausen (Cambridge 1982) 93–127.

Genovese, E., *Roll Jordan Role: The World the Slaves Made* (New York 1974).

Goins, S. E., "The Influence of Old Comedy on the *Vita Aesopis*," *Classical World* 83 (1989) 28–30.

Hägg, T., "A Professor and His Slave: Conventions and Values in the *Life of Aesop*," in *Conventional Values of the Hellenistic Greeks*, ed. P. Bilde, T. Engberg-Pedersen, L. Hannestad, and J. Zahle (Aarhus 1997) 180–203.

Halporn, J., "Roman Comedy and Greek Models," in *Theater and Society in the Classical World*, ed. R. Scodel (Ann Arbor 1993) 191–213.

Harris, W., *War and Imperialism in Republican Rome, 327–70 B.C.* (Oxford 1979).

————, "Roman Warfare in the Economic and Social Context," in *Staat und Staatlichkeit in der frühen römischen Republik*, ed. W. Eder (Stuttgart 1990) 498–510.

————, *Restraining Rage: The Ideology of Anger Control in Classical Antiquity* (Cambridge, Mass. 2001).

Hill, J. D., "'Made from Bone': Trickster Myths, Musicality, and Social Constructions of History in the Venezuelan Amazon," in *Myth: A New Symposium*, ed. G. Schrempp and W. Hansen (Bloomington 2002) 72–88.

Hölkeskamp, K. J., *Die Entstehung der Nobilität. Studien zur sozialen und politischen Geschichte der römischen Republik im 4. Jhdt. v. Chr.* (Stuttgart 1987).

Holzberg, N., "Der Äsop-Roman. Eine strukturanalytische Interpretation," in *Der Äsop-Roman. Motivgeschichte und Erzählstruktur*, ed. N. Holzberg (Tübingen 1992) 33–75.

Hopkins, K., *Conquerors and Slaves*, Sociological Studies in Roman History 1 (Cambridge 1978).

———, "Novel Evidence for Roman Slavery," *Past and Present* 138 (1993) 3–27.

Hyde, L., *Trickster Makes This World: Mischief, Myth, and Art* (New York 1998).

Isaac, R., *The Transformation of Virginia* (Chapel Hill 1982).

Jachmann, G., "Zum *Pseudolus* des Plautus," *Philologus* 88 (1933) 443–56.

Joyner, C., "The Trickster and the Fool: Folktales and Identity among Southern Plantation Slaves," *Plantation Society* 2 (1986) 150–56.

Konstan, D., *Roman Comedy* (Ithaca 1983).

Kwintner, M., "Plautus *Pseudolus* 782: A Fullonious Assault," *Classical Philology* 87 (1992) 232–33.

Lefèvre, E., *Plautus'* Pseudolus, Scripta Oralia 101 (Tübingen 1997).

Leo, F., *Plautinische Forschungen. Zur Kritik und Geschichte der Komödie*, 2nd ed. (Berlin 1912).

Levine, L. W., *Black Culture and Black Consciousness: Afro-American Folk Thought from Slavery to Freedom* (Oxford and New York 1977).

Lintott, A., *Violence in Republican Rome* (Oxford 1968).

Lowe, J. C. B., "Aspects of Plautus' Originality in the *Asinaria*," *Classical Quarterly* 42 (1992) 152–57.

———, "Pseudolus' 'Intrigue' against Simo," *Maia* 51 (1999) 1–15.

MacCary, W. T., "Menander's Slaves: Their Names, Roles, and Masks," *Transactions of the American Philological Association* 100 (1969) 277–94.

McCarthy, K., *Slaves, Masters, and the Art of Authority in Plautine Comedy* (Princeton 2000).

McDonnell, M., "Roman Men and Greek Virtue," in *Andreia: Studies in Manliness and Courage in Classical Antiquity*, ed. R. M. Rosen and I. Sluiter (Leiden 2003) 235–61.

Moore, T. J., *The Theater of Plautus: Playing to the Audience* (Austin 1998).

Paratore, E., "Plauto imitatore di se stesso," *Dionisio* 46 (1975) 29–70.

Parker, H., "Crucially Funny or Tranio on the Couch: The *Servus Callidus* and Jokes about Torture," *Transactions of the American Philological Association* 119 (1989) 233–46.

———, "Loyal Slaves and Loyal Wives. The Crisis of the Outsider-within and Roman *exemplum* Literature," in *Women and Slaves in Greco-Roman Culture: Differential Equations*, ed. S. Joshel and S. Murnaghan (London and New York 1998) 152–73.

Perna, R., *L'Originalita di Plauto* (Bari 1955).

Petrone, G., *Teatro antico e inganno: Finzioni Plautine* (Palermo 1983).

Pritchett, W. K., *The Greek State at War*, vol. 5 (Berkeley 1991).

Rauch, L., "Mastery and Slavery," in *Hegel's Phenomenology of Self-Consciousness*, ed. L. Rauch and D. Sherman (Albany 1999) 87–101.

Saller, R., *Patriarchy, Property and Death in the Roman Family* (Cambridge 1994).

Scott, J., *Domination and the Arts of Resistance: Hidden Transcripts* (New Haven 1990).

Segal, E., *Roman Laughter: The Comedy of Plautus* (Cambridge, Mass. 1968).

Sharrock, A., "The Art of Deceit: Pseudolus and the Nature of Reading," *Classical Quarterly* 46 (1996) 152–74.

Slater, N., *Plautus in Performance: The Theatre of the Mind* (Princeton 1985).

Stace, C., "The Slaves of Plautus," *Greece and Rome* 15 (1968) 64–77.

Stärk, E., "Plautus' *uxores dotatae* im Spannungsfeld literarischer Fiktion und gesellschaftlicher Realität," in *Theater und Gesellschaft im Imperium Romanum*, ed. J. Blänsdorf (Tübingen 1990) 69–79.

Stehle, E., "Pseudolus as Socrates, Poet and Trickster," in *Classical Texts and Their Traditions: Studies in Honor of C. R. Trahman*, ed. D. Bright and E. Ramage (Chico 1984) 239–51.

Toynbee, A., *Hannibal's Legacy*, 2 vols. (London 1965).

Vogt, J., *Ancient Slavery and the Ideal of Man* (Cambridge, Mass. 1975).

Watson, A., *Rome of the XII Tables* (Princeton and London 1975).

———, *Roman Slave Law* (Baltimore and London 1987).

Wieacker, F., *Römische Rechtsgeschichte. Quellenkunde, Rechtsbildung, Jurisprudenz, und Rechtsliteratur*, Handbuch der Altertumwissenschaft 10.3.1.1 (Munich 1988).

Willcock, M. M., ed., *Plautus* Pseudolus (Bristol 1987).

Williams, G., "Some Problems in the Construction of Plautus' *Pseudolus*," *Hermes* 84 (1956) 424–55.

Wright, J., "The Transformations of Pseudolus," *Transactions of the American Philological Association* 105 (1975) 403–16.

4 ◆ FORGING IDENTITY IN THE ROMAN REPUBLIC: TROJAN ANCESTRY AND VERISTIC PORTRAITURE

Charles Brian Rose

One of the most significant gaps in the scholarship on ancient Rome is an analysis of republican art, primarily because there are no clearly defined imperial reigns to use for structure. In most books, even those produced recently, there is one chapter on the republic and ten on the empire, in spite of the fact that the former was two hundred years longer than the latter. One of the principal problems is the size of the geographical area involved in such an assessment: during the middle and late republic, in particular, Rome's interaction with the other cities of the Mediterranean was strong, continuous, and highly influential, and tracing the development of political imagery therefore requires an examination of the material culture from both center and periphery. In keeping with the theme of this volume, I would like to treat two different models used in the construction of republican Roman identity: one mythological, and connected to Trojan ancestry; and one historical, dealing with elite male portraiture, with an emphasis on the ambiguity inherent in both categories.

Trojan Ancestry

The aristocrats of republican Rome consistently searched for ways to trace their ancestry from the gods themselves, and Rome as a people followed the same scheme in linking their history to the Trojans.[1] The date at which Troy was identified as Rome's mother city is not certain, but the literary evidence suggests that it was probably in place by the late fourth century B.C.[2] Some scholars have pointed to the paintings in the François Tomb at Vulci as one of the first signs of this newly established ancestry, and the same motive may lie behind the restoration and enlargement of an archaic tumulus at Lavinium, the city reportedly founded by Aeneas 28 kilometers south of Rome.[3] This tomb has usually been associated with the heroon of Aeneas described by Dionysius of Halicarnassus, and it looks as if the renovation was a by-product of this Trojan-Roman association.[4]

I would like to thank Andrea Berlin and Sharon Herbert for allowing me to publish several of the bullae excavated at Kedesh (Israel) in 1999 and 2000. Versions of this chapter were presented in Minneapolis, Toronto, and Rome, and I have tried to incorporate here as many of the comments from the audience as I could. Special thanks are extended to Andrea Berlin, Erich Gruen, Eve D'Ambra, Susan Walker, Tonio Hölscher, Bert Smith, Ann Kuttner, Barbara Burrell, Tom Carpenter, Harry and Margot Gotoff, and Michael Sage, as well as the organizers of the AAR/BSR Role Models conference in Rome: Inge Lyse Hansen, Sinclair Bell, and Helen Langdon.

[1] Wiseman 1974.

[2] The first section of this chapter summarizes the arguments in Rose 2002.

[3] For the François Tomb in Vulci, see Holliday 1993, 181; Coarelli 1983.

[4] Holloway 1994, 135–38; Giuliani 1981, 169–77; Torelli 1984, 11–15; Gruen 1992, 23–25, 28. Dion. Hal. *Ant. Rom.* 1.64.4–5.

Fig. 1. Bronze coin of Roma wearing a Phrygian cap (after Kent 1978, pl. 12.36).

Fig. 2. Silver plate with a bust of Attis from Hildesheim (after Vermaseren and DeBoer 1986, pl. 39, fig. 345).

The first numismatic indication of this link occurred during the war with Pyrrhus of Epirus in the early third century B.C. The Roman bronzes issued then featured the head of Roma, which was the standard numismatic image; but she was now shown wearing the Phrygian cap, and this type would continue through the third century and into the second (fig. 1).[5] That cap had developed into a sign of Trojan status during the classical period, and the Romans used it as such in their construction of a more complex symbol of civic identity.[6] There is no evidence that the Phrygian cap, or eastern attire in general, had acquired a negative significance by this point: Rome had not fought any battles east of the Aegean, and the Parthians were not yet an enemy.

In fact, the kind of eastern costume that the Trojans wore was about to acquire an even more positive significance. In 205 B.C., toward the end of the Second Punic War, the cult of Cybele and Attis was imported from Asia Minor to Rome and enshrined in a large new temple at the southwest corner of the Palatine hill, overlooking the Circus Maximus.[7] It seems likely that the primary reason for this transfer was the cult's strong association with Troy, and her formal presence in Rome would certainly have stressed the Trojan ancestry of the Romans.[8] This connection between Cybele and Troy is abundantly attested in the ancient sources, especially Ovid, Vergil, and the inscriptions of Samothrace.[9] At Ilion, the prominence of the cult of Cybele has been amply demonstrated by the recent excavations in the West Sanctuary, where the finds include an abundance of Cybele terracottas as well as the bones of lions, which appear to have been kept in the complex. In Rome, the cult's Trojan affiliation was highlighted by the temple's placement on the southwest side of the Palatine, which had more legendary associations with Troy and its descendants than any other part

[5] Roma with Phrygian cap: Di Filippo Balestrazzi 1997, 1050, no. 11; Crawford 1974, nos. 19.2, 21.1, 22.1, 24.1, 27.5, 41.1, 288, 269.1. For the iconography of the Phrygian cap, see Schneider 1986, 123–24 with n. 866; Seiterle 1985.

[6] For the developing iconography of Troy during the classical period, see Miller 1995. Pyrrhus himself reportedly commented on the Trojan ancestry of the Romans: Paus. 1.12.1; Gruen 1990, 12.

[7] Pensabene 1996; Roller 1999, 263–85; Vermaseren 1977, 41–43.

[8] Gruen 1990, 5–33; Gruen 1992, 47; Roller 1999, 269–71.

[9] *Aen.* 9.77–83, 107–22; 10.156–58; Ov. *Fast.* 4.247–76; Wiseman 1984; Lewis 1958, nos. 31, 59, 142, 144, 145.

of the city.[10] Cybele's consort Attis was regularly dressed in eastern garb, with long pants, a tiara or Phrygian cap, and eventually a low-hanging torque, and most of these attributes were also worn by the priests of the cult (fig. 2).[11]

It looks as if the garb of these priests influenced another venerable Roman institution connected to Troy—the *lusus Troiae*—although this has never been recognized. The *lusus Troiae* was an equestrian parade and mock battle staged by the patrician youths of Rome in the Circus Maximus, and it had become firmly linked to Troy in the course of the republic.[12] The two most distinctive features of the boys' costume were a twisted metal torque, worn low, and a *tonsa corona*, which is usually interpreted as a garland of cut leaves.[13] Scholars have consistently wondered why the youths wore torques since they were never a feature of Trojan costumes; but they were worn by the priests in the cult of Cybele, whose Trojan associations were strong, and the priests appear to be the most likely model. It is worth noting that the *lusus Troiae* was always staged in the Circus Maximus, directly below the temple of Cybele and the residence of her priests, which meant that the two institutions would have been linked both topographically and visually.[14]

Until the second century B.C., Roman images of men wearing long trousers and Phrygian caps had an essentially positive value since they were linked to Troy and the cult of Cybele.[15] But this would change once the east became the enemy and battle paintings of Romans fighting easterners began to be included in triumphal processions. The new iconography seems to have been visible by the first half of the second century: in the terracotta friezes from Fregellae, which appear to show scenes from the First Syrian War, there are figures of warriors in Phrygian caps.[16] The same sort of imagery was undoubtedly visible in Pompey's triumph over the Pontic king Mithridates in 63 B.C., when Roman soldiers carried battle paintings featuring Pontic and Armenian warriors.[17] In the course of the next three decades, especially following the Parthians' resounding victory over Crassus at Carrhae in 53 B.C., eastern costume would acquire an even stronger negative connotation.[18]

[10] For the Sanctuary at Ilion, see Rose 1998; for the sacred associations of the Palatine, see Wiseman 1984, 126; Coarelli 1993a; Coarelli 1993b; Coarelli 1996; Pensabene 1999; Tagliamonte 1999. For the role of Pergamon in the transfer of the cult, see Gruen, n. 8 above; Kuttner 1995b.

[11] For a description of the priest's costume, see Dion. Hal. 2.19.3–5; Polyb. 21.37.4–7; Diod. Sic. 36.13.1–3; Plut. *Mar.* 17–18; Livy 38.18.9–10; Graillot 1912, 287–319; Vermaseren 1977, 96–101; Beard 1994, 165, 173–76; Roller 1998; Roller 1999, 290–91, 297–303. On Attis in general, see Lancellotti 2002.

[12] For the *lusus Troiae*, see Schneider 1927; Mehl 1956; Daremberg and Saglio 1877–1919, 5:493–96, s.v. Troiae ludus (J. Toutain); Weinstock 1971, 88; Williams 1960, 145–57; Fuchs 1990; Junkelmann 1991, 142–51. The *lusus Troiae* was often held in conjunction with other major events: Caesar's triumph in 46 B.C., the Ludi Apollinaris in 40 B.C., the dedication of the temple of Divus Julius Caesar in 29 B.C., the dedication of the Temple of Divus Augustus in 37, the deification of Drusilla in 38, and the Saecular Games of 47.

[13] Williams (1960, 148) offers the most plausible discussion.

[14] In the *Aeneid*, Aeneas and the Trojans were actually compared with the priests of Cybele: *Aen.* 4.215, 9.617–20,

12.97–100; Roller 1999, 302–4.

[15] The priests of the Magna Mater were later consistently denigrated in Roman literature, in part because of their eastern clothing, but this did not begin until the Parthian campaigns of the first century B.C.: Lucr. *De rerum natura* 2.610–28; Ov. *Fast.* 4.179–88; Mart. *Ep.* 3.81; Juv. *Sat.* 6.511–16; Beard 1994.

[16] Coarelli 1994, 98–99, figs. 7–8; Albentiis and Furiani 1997, 42–47.

[17] App. *Mith.* 17.116–17. There is no evidence that men in eastern garb appeared in paintings carried in the Seleucid triumph of 189 B.C.: Livy 37.57.12; 37.58.3. Trousers surely formed part of the iconography of western barbarians by 101 B.C., when paintings of the Cimbri and Teutones were presumably featured in the triumphal procession of Marius: Plut. *Mar.* 27.6.

[18] The personification of Armenia in the Julio-Claudian Sebasteion at Aphrodisias wore a Phrygian cap (Erim 1986, 116), as does the subjugated Parthian on the Grand Cameo of France, but Armenia personifications on Roman coinage wear a boxlike tiara, not a Phrygian cap (Balty 1984, 613). The pointed tiara, which is similar to the Phrygian cap, was worn by the ancestors of Antiochus of Commagene on the Nemrud

*Fig. 3. Reconstruction
of the Parthian arch of
Augustus, Roman Forum
(B. Rose and J. Wallrodt).*

SENATVS
POPVLVSQVEROMANVS
IMP·CAESARI·DIVI·IVLII·F
AVGVSTO·COS·XI·TR·POT·VI

No illustrations of these catastrophes would have been featured in Rome, of course; but Parthians did appear in coinage and monuments several times after the return of the lost Roman standards in 20 B.C., usually wearing long pants and sometimes a Phrygian cap. During the Augustan period alone, images of Parthians appeared on the attic of the "Parthian arch" in the Roman forum in 19 B.C. (fig. 3); on Augustan coinage from the mint of Rome, and on the breastplate of the statue of Augustus from Primaporta.[19] There were also forty over-life-size pavonazzetto statues of Parthians within or on the facade of the Basilica Aemilia, adjacent to the Parthian arch, and these are usually dated to the Augustan period.[20] By the first century B.C., then, eastern costumes (trousers, torque, and Phrygian cap) had acquired a dual significance, in that they were simultaneously associated with

Dag hierothesion, dedicated in 62 B.C. (Sanders 1995, 394–95). Tiara-clad kings of the eastern Mediterranean in attitudes of submission also began to appear on Roman coinage in the mid-first century B.C. (Kent 1978, figs. 60, 61 [Aretas IV and Bacchius of Judaea]), but these tiaras were very different from the Phrygian caps of the Parthians and Trojans.

[19] Parthian arch: Sutherland and Carson 1984, 68, no. 359; Fuchs 1969, 40–41; Kleiner 1985, 25–28; De Maria 1988, 269–72, no. 59; Nedergaard 1993; Nedergaard 1994–95; Levi 1952, 6–9. Augustan coinage: Sutherland and Carson 1984, 62 nos. 287–88; Kent 1978, fig. 131. Primaporta breastplate: Kleiner 1992, fig. 42. The mythical Arimaspeans, in trousers and Phrygian caps, also served as symbols of the subjugated east in early imperial cuirass designs: Stemmer 1978, 96–97, pls. 64, 65; Hanfmann and Vermeule 1957, 234–36.

[20] Boni 1904, 569; Schneider 1986, 116, 123, 200. No authoritative publication of the barbarians has ever appeared, but in his study of the Basilica Aemilia, Bauer (1988, 202

and fig. 99) restored them above the cornice over the frieze, which has projections on which bases stood. If Bauer is right, and if the cornice dates to 14 B.C., as Mattern (1997) convincingly argued, then so do the statues. There would have been forty of them if one stood above each interior column. James Packer has conveyed to me in conversation his belief that the Parthians were placed on the facade of the Basilica Aemilia and served as a model for the caryatids in the Forum of Augustus and the Dacians in the Forum of Trajan (see also Kuttner 1995a, 83). Either way, there were two sets of over-life-size Parthians placed adjacent to each other in the center of the Roman Forum, probably during the Augustan period. Adjacent to the Basilica Aemilia was a monument to Gaius Caesar, son of Augustus, that may have featured Parthian standards: Rose 1997, 19. Rolf Schneider (1986, 120) has argued that there was a monumental tripod supported by kneeling Parthians at the temple of Apollo on the Palatine, but there is no solid evidence for this. For the literary tradition involving the Parthians in Augustan literature, see Wissemann 1982; Nedergaard 1994–95, 68 n. 73.

Fig. 4. Pompeian painting of Aeneas, Anchises, and
Ascanius (after Spinazzola 1953, fig. 183).

Fig. 5. Relief of Aeneas, Anchises, Ascanius, and Aphrodite
from the Aphrodisias Sebasteion (Erim 1986, 56 fig. 80).

positive concepts, such as Cybele and Attis, the *lusus Troiae*, and the Trojans, and with negative concepts, such as the Parthians and the Celts. The value of the costume depended on the context of the associated image.[21] The same distinction is apparent in Latin literature of the late republic and early empire, where different words were used to refer to the two types of easterners: Trojans were "Phryges," while Parthians were "Medes."[22]

   In light of this multifaceted attitude toward the east during the late republic, it is not surprising that the Romans proceeded cautiously with the iconography of the Trojans.[23] Although Aeneas had been represented on coins since the late second century, a fixed iconography for him and his family would not emerge until 2 B.C., when a Trojan statuary group was dedicated in one of the exedrae in the Forum of Augustus.[24] One of the best examples of this widely copied group is the painting on the facade of a first-century A.D. house in Pompeii, which was juxtaposed with an image of Romulus also copied from the Forum. Here Aeneas appears as a contemporary Roman general in full dress armor, again with a draped Anchises on his back. Little Ascanius was now introduced, but he was dressed like an easterner with trousers and a Phrygian cap, and the type was repeated all over the empire (figs. 4–5).[25] The group was therefore an intriguing mix of east and west, with the costume of the father representing the future and the costume of the son signifying the past.

[21] For the ambiguous position of Trojans in the Roman world and their association with barbarians, see Galinsky 1969, 93–102.

[22] Pani 1975; Scheider 1986, 123.

[23] For the iconography of Aeneas, see Calciani 1981; Galinsky 1969, 5–6; Evans 1992, 39–57.

[24] Calciani 1981, nos. 98, 146; Fuchs 1973; Noelke 1976; Zanker 1988, 202.

[25] Paribeni 1984, 862–63; Noelke 1976. The trousers are difficult to see in Spinazzola's (1953) reproduction of the painting, but they are clear in the Aeneas relief from Aphrodisias: Smith 1990, 98 fig. 9, 100. Ascanius appears in only two archaic vase paintings, and then not again until the end of the republic.

This is the reverse of what one would expect, but it makes sense if one reviews the cultural context, which I will try to do here. In the mid-Augustan period the decision seems to have been reached to include Asian iconography in Aeneid family groups—specifically, trousers and a Phrygian cap for Aeneas's son. This addition made it clear that the origins of Rome lay in the east, and it was undoubtedly a by-product of the increased emphasis at that time on the Trojan ancestry of the Julian *gens*. Nevertheless, the costume was confined to children in public displays, and Aeneas would not be shown in eastern garb until late antiquity.[26] If one looks at the group from the point of view of costume, the message seems to be that it was the destiny of Rome to dominate the east, from which it had originally come, although the dress of father and son has been reversed to prevent Aeneas from looking like a Parthian.

A survey of the public monuments in central Rome reveals that the ancient designers were clearly concerned about the ambiguous nature of the eastern costume. Consequently, there were no Trojan statuary groups in the center of the Roman Forum, probably because images of Parthians in the same costume adorned the Parthian arch and the Basilica Aemilia. Again, the same iconography held both positive and negative connotations depending on its context. Trojan ancestry had allowed the Romans to claim a connection to the Homeric tradition; but since Asians could be bad or good, that ancestry would be characterized by a fundamental ambiguity consistently detectable in Roman triumphal commemoration.

Veristic Portraiture

The same kind of ambiguity is perceptible in the portraiture of elite men of the Roman republic, although the layers of meaning in that genre are much more complex. When one attempts to visualize the republic, the first image that usually appears is that of a male aristocrat whose portrait bears the signs of advanced age: incised lines on or around the forehead, cheeks, mouth, and eyes, as well as short, closely cropped hair, more frequently straight than curly and often receding (figs. 6–13, 16, 17).[27] On occasion there is no hair at all, and the irregularly shaped heads frequently feature large ears, thick lips, and sharply aquiline noses. These portraits convey the impression of men who valued morals, character, and service to the state above classical ideals of beauty, and during the empire this mode of presentation became so closely associated with the republic that it was continually revived whenever the emperors (Vespasian and Trajan, in particular) announced a return to republican traditions.[28]

The portrait type was a popular one: there are nearly 350 examples in museums around the world, although unfortunately none comes from a well-dated archaeological context and few can be associated with inscriptions.[29] The type begins to appear on Roman coins in the second quarter

---

[26] The first examples include the Vergilius Romanus (Rosenthal 1972; Weitzmann 1979, 227–28, no. 204; Calciani 1981, nos. 199–202; Wright 1992, 81–124) and the fourth-century mosaic from Lowham with scenes from the *Aeneid* (Calciani 1981, no. 159; Weitzmann 1979, 201 fig. 25).

[27] The scholarship on this subject is now vast: Zadoks-Josephus Jitta 1932; Vessberg 1941, 173–231; Brommer 1953–54; Adriani 1970; Vollenweider 1972–74; Bieber 1973; Breckenridge 1973; Gazda 1973; Hiesinger 1973; Zanker 1976; Drerup 1980; R. R. R. Smith 1981; Zanker 1983; Giuliani

1986; Smith 1988, 125–32; Lahusen 1989; Smith 1991, 256; Gruen 1992, 152–82; Zanker 1995a; Tanner 2000; Croz 2002, esp. 238–50. Sehlmeyer (1999) has treated all of the literary evidence for these statues.

[28] Gross 1940; Daltrop, Hausmann, and Wegner 1966, 9–18.

[29] All of the surviving veristic portraits have been catalogued by Croz 2002, 23–104. The closest we can come to the late republican bronze statues in veristic style is the Arringatore

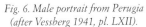

Fig. 6. Male portrait from Perugia
(after Vessberg 1941, pl. LXII).

Fig. 7. Male portrait from Delos
(after Michalowski 1932, pl. X).

of the first century B.C. and loses its dominance during the second triumvirate, when the youthful portrait of Octavian becomes the more influential type.[30] The portraits in this style, which is usually labeled "veristic," tend to be dated between 60 and 40 B.C., since nearly all of the coins with veristic portraits date within those two decades.[31] This is admittedly not a very reliable system: it was only at this time that the entire obverse field of coins featured heads of historical Romans, and the coins therefore supply only a *terminus ante quem* for the advent of the type.

Scholars have often assumed that the veristic type was used for most of the portrait statues erected in the public spaces of Rome during the second century B.C., but all of these images appear to have been of bronze, and none has survived.[32] The absence of such evidence has hindered an examination of the political and social conditions that prompted the creation of the type, and so far it has been impossible to identify with any certainty the regional styles that played a role in its development, although Etruria, Egypt, and Greece have all been cited. Fortunately, the situation has been considerably clarified by recent archaeological work at the site of Kedesh in the northern Galilee, where the type has been discovered in a sealed context dated to the first half of the second

in Florence: Dohrn 1966; Fittschen 1970. The inscribed examples come mainly from Pompeii (Bonifacio 1997, nos. 1, 3, 32, 35, 36) and the "freedmen" reliefs from the Via Appia (Zanker 1975; Kleiner 1977).

[30] Vessberg 1941, 115–72; Bieber 1973; Crawford 1974, nos. 749–50; Lahusen 1989; Sehlmeyer 1999, 178–85.

[31] The best discussion is still that of Vessberg 1941, 40–46, 71–79, 173–231. See also Poulsen 1962; Johansen 1994, 26–87.

[32] Smith 1988, 125–26; Gruen 1992, 161, 167–68.

Fig. 9. Bulla with male portrait from Kedesh (Kedesh Excavations Photo no. K99 BL0025).

Fig. 8. Bulla from the Maison des Sceaux, Delos (after Boussac 1988, 332 fig. 63).

Fig. 10. Male shoulder busts from the Maison des Sceaux, Delos (after Queyrel, Hermary, and Jockey 1996, 218, no. 99).

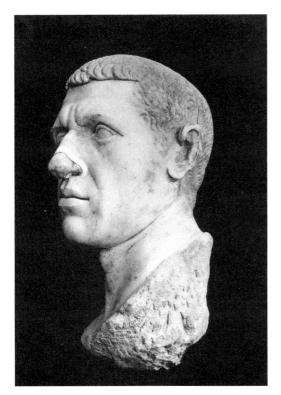

Fig. 11 (above left). Male portrait from the Agora of the
Italians, Delos (after Michalowski 1932, pl. XVII).

Fig. 12 (above). "Pseudo-athlete" from the House of the
Diadoumenos, Delos (after Queyrel, Hermary,
and Jockey 1996, 192, no. 86).

Fig. 13 (left). Bulla with male portrait from Kedesh
(Kedesh Excavations Photo no. K00 BL0264).

century B.C.[33] The Galilee initially strikes one as an unlikely place to find information concerning early veristic portraiture, and to understand the importance of the Kedesh material one needs first to examine the evidence supplied by several other excavations in the eastern Mediterranean.

Statues of Romans and their families were set up throughout Greece and Asia Minor during the second and early first century B.C., but so far only Delos has yielded stone portraits that can be securely identified as Romans.[34] Roman merchants began their involvement with the island in 166,

---

[33] Herbert and Berlin 2000; Herbert and Berlin 2003; Ariel and Noveh 2003.

[34] Payne 1984 (Greece); Tuchelt 1979 (Asia Minor); Sehlmeyer 1999, 151–52; Croz 2002, 185–224.

after it was made a free port under Athenian protection, and commercial activity thrived there until 88 B.C., when Mithridates of Pontus sacked it. During this period Delos served as one of the most important centers for the slave trade, much of which was overseen by Italian businessmen, whose headquarters (the "Agora of the Italians") was the largest complex on the island.[35] The Italian Agora and the other public spaces of Delos featured a wide variety of sculptural decoration and, since marble was less expensive to procure there than it had been in Italy, much of the sculpture was produced in that medium and therefore still survives. Nearly twenty well-preserved male portraits have been recovered on the island, the majority of which feature the same "veristic" treatment as on the later marble portraits from central Italy.[36] The formal similarities between the central Italian and Delian portraits have been doubted, but the same components (advanced age, variation in shape of face and facial features, closely cropped hair) are apparent in both if one compares representative portraits from each group (see figs. 6–7).

The question frequently asked is whether all of the Delian portraits in this group actually represent Romans, and if one examines the material carefully, it is clear that they do. Our most important evidence for this link comes from bullae on the island, of which approximately 14,000 have been uncovered. These were lumps of clay pressed into the strings or cords that bound official documents and subsequently impressed with the symbol of the authority who issued the document or those who witnessed it.[37] Although the documents sealed by these bullae rarely survive, the terracotta bullae themselves are usually found intact in archives whose destruction can be dated by the associated coins and pottery. Many of these caches of Hellenistic bullae have not been completely published, but scholarly interest in them has recently intensified, and they are now being examined for evidence regarding the development of Roman portraiture.

Within the Delian "Maison des Sceaux" nearly five thousand of these bullae have been recovered (e.g., fig. 8), a significant number of which bear the names of Roman families, including the Cornellii Dolabellae, Aufidii, Heii, Lollii (?), Shii, Naevii, Mevii, Vibii, and Arellii, among others.[38] In some cases the images on the bullae are accompanied by legends, and one can determine the ethnicity of the man portrayed. One bulla with the legend P. OCRA probably represents Publius Ocratius, whose family was active in Capua and Rome during the republic.[39] The associated portrait is distinctly veristic, with lines on the forehead and around the eyes and mouth. Another one with the legend "Q(uintus) Non(nius) Dip(ilus)" appears to show the same kind of lined face with receding hairline, and there are additional bullae from the same context that show similar aged types without identifying legends.[40]

It has often been assumed that this house belonged to a Roman, and two of the portraits found within it lend further support to this theory. These are pendants (fig. 10), and both are of veristic

[35] Hatzfeld 1912; Lapalus 1939; Marcadé 1969, 307–54, 363–66; Bruneau 1983, 166–68; Hallett 1993, 120–21; Rauh 1993, 5–22, 289–338; Croz 2002, 152–63, 203–15.

[36] Michalowski 1932; Stewart 1979, 65–98; Pollitt 1986, 73–76; Smith 1991, 255–68; Ridgway 2000, 303–4.

[37] For an overview of bullae, see Rostovtzeff 1932, esp. 22–23; McDowell 1935; Invernizzi 1996; Wallenfells 1996.

[38] Boussac 1988, 317, 322–25. For the Maison des Sceaux, see also Bruneau 1983, 185–88; Marcadé 1990, 148; Hallett 1993, 121; Rauh 1993, 215–19.

[39] Boussac 1988, 327, fig. 37a; Pauly and Wissowa 1937, 17.2:1777, s.v. Ocratius.

[40] Boussac 1988, 325, fig. 34. Judging by the name, this particular seal may have represented a Roman freedman who copied the veristic type of his patron. One of the Delian seals shows a Roman or Roman freedman with the legend T. NAEVI[US] and a petasus on his head (Boussac 1988, 324, fig. 33), and the same headgear appears on a man with a veristic portrait on one of the Kallipolis seals (Pantos 1996, pl. 38, fig. 5). The petasus was, of course, one of the principal attributes of Mercury, tutelary deity of commerce, and it may have been intended here as one of the signs of merchant status.

type, although one is more aged than the other, and they may represent two generations of one family.[41] The portraits have been presented in a shoulder bust format, which was an Italian innovation that first appeared in the third quarter of the second century B.C.[42] Aside from these two examples on Delos, the format is not otherwise attested in the Aegean during the Hellenistic period, and it seems to have been intended as an indication of Roman identity.

The material in the Maison des Sceaux dates between 166 and 69 B.C., when the building was destroyed by a fire, and so it provides us with a context for the veristic type only slightly earlier than the traditional dating of the portraits from Italy. But there are marble portraits in the same style from other Delian contexts that can be dated to an earlier period with a fair degree of certainty.[43] The first two of these come from the Agora of the Italians, which had probably begun operation shortly after the island was declared a free port, although the north and west porticoes were not built until the last quarter of the second century. Fourteen statue bases were found within the Agora, and most of the dedicators were freedmen who were now growing rich on the slave trade themselves. The images represented their patrons, usually members of the senatorial elite who would only occasionally have visited Delos from Rome.[44]

It seems likely that permission to erect the statue would have come from Rome, along with the portrait model that was to be used, and the same veristic type that appeared in late republican coinage and sculpture would consequently have been repeated in the public dedications of Romans in the eastern Mediterranean.[45] Only one base (that of Gaius Marcus Ofellius) can be linked to its associated statue, which is unfortunately headless,[46] but all of the inscribed bases originally supported statues of Italians, and the two portraits that have been recovered from the Agora can therefore be safely identified as such.[47]

The more fragmentary example includes only a part of the face and scalp, but it clearly featured a receding hairline.[48] The better-preserved example contains the same closely cropped hair found in the portraits of central Italy, although the hairline is not noticeably receding (fig. 11).[49] There are strong incisions above the bridge of the nose and framing the upper lip, and Marie Françoise Boussac, who is publishing the Delian bullae, has compared the severity of the features to those on the bullae from the Maison des Sceaux.[50]

A much less severe visage has been incorporated into the other Delian image generally regarded as the representation of a Roman: the "pseudo-athlete" from the House of the Diadoumenos (fig. 12).[51] The sense of greater age here is prompted by the total baldness of the head rather than by a profusion of lines on or around the face. The main reason for assuming that the man is Roman

[41] Queyrel, Hermary, and Jockey 1996, 218, no. 99; Croz 2002, 156–57.

[42] Kilmer 1977, 307–8, pls. 143–44, 186–89; Motz 1993, 29, 34, 35.

[43] Michalowski 1932; Tuchelt 1979, 88–89; Smith 1991, 255.

[44] Rauh 1993, 198–200, 232.

[45] This was undoubtedly the same kind of gift-exchange system that operated between the emperors and provincial cities: Price 1984, 65ff.

[46] Zanker 1983, 252–54; Queyrel 1991, esp. 429, 447; Queyrel,

Hermary, and Jockey 1996, 190, no. 85; Marcadé 2000; Ridgway 2000, 242–43, 307, 319; Croz 2002, 29–30 (B1).

[47] I. de Délos nos. 1679, 1688, 1695, 1696, 1699, 1722, 1727, 1848, 1849, 1858, 2000, 2002.

[48] Michalowski 1932, 52.

[49] Michalowski 1932, 39–41; Queyrel, Hermary, and Jockey 1996, 202, no. 91.

[50] Boussac 1988, 335. See also Marcadé 1990, 146–48.

[51] Queyrel, Hermary, and Jockey 1996, 192, no. 86; Ridgway 2002, 126–28; Croz 2002, 24 (A4); with Kreeb 1988, 156–57 on the House of the Diadoumenos.

is the uneasy link between body and head, with the former presented as youthful and the latter as middle-aged. This kind of discordant image is not a feature of Greek sculpture, wherein the age of the portrait tends to be in harmony with that of the body below. In Roman sculpture, however, the age of the two was not always aligned, and this is especially true for late republican portraits of men, with the general from Tivoli (fig. 17) serving as one of the best examples.

The Delian images listed above can be dated only approximately since they lack their associated inscriptions, but the majority of the inscribed portrait bases on Delos can be placed between ca. 124 and 88 B.C., and this holds true for most of the bases from the Agora of the Italians.[52] We can therefore probably assign the origins of the veristic type to a time earlier than 88 B.C., which is admittedly not a dramatic advance over what the central Italian material had indicated; but the Delian evidence shows that the veristic type was already in place as a badge of Roman identity by the beginning of the first century B.C. It is also worth noting that on Delos the veristic type appears to have been used only for images of Italians or Roman freedmen, judging by the material so far uncovered.

Additional evidence is supplied by bullae recovered at two other eastern Mediterranean sites. Those from Kallipolis, near Delphi, can be dated before the middle of the second century B.C., and a few contain portraits with an aged appearance and short, closely cropped hair. This had led Pantos Pantos, the publisher of the archive, to link them to the marble portraits uncovered on Delos and to propose that the Kallipolis bullae be brought into the discussion of Roman veristic portraiture.[53]

A much more important source of evidence has recently come to light at Kedesh, the southern Phoenician site ca. 10 kilometers northwest of Hazor that is being excavated by the Universities of Michigan and Minnesota. Fieldwork in 1999 and 2000 yielded a large administrative building that may have been used by the governor of the eparchy of the Gallilee or the strategos of Coele-Syria.[54] Within the building was an archive room that contained more than 2,000 clay bullae, each of which ranges between 15 and 19 mm in size.

Approximately 18 of the bullae contain veristic portraits (short, closely cropped hair, often receding, as well as facial lines), and some of the Kedesh portraits are near duplicates of the ones found on Delos (figs. 9, 13). The seal in figure 9 was excavated at Kedesh; the one in figure 8, from the Maison des Sceaux on Delos, contains a Latin legend and therefore certainly represents a Roman or Italian.[55] Common to both are the long, narrow, somewhat irregularly shaped heads that are also found on the Italian portraits of the late republic. The most important aspect of the Kedesh discovery is that it can be closely dated: the associated coins and pottery indicate that the archive was in use during the first half of the second century and destroyed ca. 146 B.C., probably in a Maccabean raid. The evidence from Kedesh, then, indicates that the veristic type had been adopted by the Romans by 150 B.C. and that documents sealed with portraits of this type had traveled as far as the Levant by that time. In other words, the veristic type must have been developed by the first half of the second century, as a number of scholars have suggested.

There were strong commercial and cultural links between Delos and the Levant during the second century B.C., and it seems likely that the seals found at Kedesh would have ultimately traveled there from Delos. The northern colonnade of the Agora of the Italians was sponsored by a businessman from Ascalon named Philostratus, who subsequently received Neapolitan citizenship,

[52] Stewart 1979, 66–73.

[53] Pantos 1985, 374–76, 516–17; Pantos 1996, 191–94.

[54] Herbert and Berlin 2000; Herbert and Berlin 2003; Ariel and Noveh 2003.

[55] For the Delian seal, see Boussac 1988, 332, no. 63.

and Phoenician Tanit images adorned some of the Delian houses.[56] Also on the island was a community of Israelites from Gerizim in Samaria, and within the temple of Delian Apollo one would have seen statues of the personifications of Tyre and Sidon, dedicated by Tyrian merchants and identified by a bilingual Punic-Greek inscription.[57] Commerce between the two areas was strong throughout the second century, but it seems likely that the Kedesh seals can be fixed to a period between 166, when Delos began operating as a free port, and 146, when the Kedesh archive building was destroyed.

It is unfortunately not possible to establish with certainty a *terminus post quem* for the development of the type, since our evidence from Italy and the eastern Mediterranean is so lacunose. Roman coinage with historical portraits from the second century B.C. features full-length figures rather than faces, and the portraits of Roman commanders in the Esquiline tomb paintings, on the terracotta friezes from Fregellae, and on the monument of Aemilius Paullus unfortunately do not survive.[58]

The only well-preserved Roman historical portrait remaining from the late third/early second century B.C. is the gold stater of Ti. Quinctius Flamininus, who defeated Philip V of Macedon and was hailed as a liberator of the Greeks. The stater featuring his portrait was struck in Greece in 196 B.C., and scholars have consistently searched for the origins of the veristic type in this issue.[59] The link between the portrait and the veristic type is not compelling: there are no discernible indications of age, and the light beard, long curly hair, bulging brow, and aquiline nose are duplicated on coin portraits of contemporary Macedonian kings.[60] The only significant differences lie in the identifying Latin legend and the lack of a royal diadem.[61] Flamininus's appearance on these coins should not necessarily be construed as an indication that the veristic style had not yet been developed, but it had apparently not yet become so closely associated with the Roman aristocracy that its use would have been considered standard practice. In summary, the limited evidence available suggests that the veristic type was developed around 200 B.C., and it subsequently circulated through the commercial channels of the eastern Mediterranean.

There has been considerable discussion concerning the exclusivity of this type to Romans in Hellenistic portraiture, and it has been argued that both Greeks and Romans used youthful, idealized types as well as the veristic format during the second century.[62] Fortunately this thesis can be checked against the Greek evidence, both royal and nonroyal, over the course of the Hellenistic period. Our best source for the latter category is the corpus of funerary reliefs from the Greek islands and Asia Minor, which have been catalogued by Ernst Pfuhl and Hans Möbius. Of the Hellenistic reliefs that they assembled, there are 133 where the faces survive in enough detail that one can assess the age of the deceased or members of his family. Only eleven show signs of age, and the majority

[56] Rauh 1993, 45, 52–53, 204, 298–99, 310–11; Bruneau 1983, 240–43.

[57] Bruneau 1982; Bruneau 1983, 206–8 (Gerizim/Synagogue); *I. Délos* 50; Millar 1983, 68 (statues of Tyre and Sidon).

[58] Fregellae: Coarelli 1994; Albentiis and Furiani 1997, 42–47; Esquiline paintings and Aemilius Paullus monument: Holliday 2002, 83–96. The same is true for the base of Marcus Antonius (also known as the altar of Domitius Ahenobarbus), where the head of the censor officiating at the altar is restored: Kähler 1966, pl. 10.

[59] Crawford 1974, 544, no. 548; Smith 1988, 126–28; Stewart 1988, 35; Gruen 1992, 161–62.

[60] Kraay 1966, pl. 175, nos. 577, 578.

[61] Flamininus was probably involved to some extent in the decision to mint the coins, as Crawford (1985, 124) notes, since both praenomen and nomen are included in the legend, which was not standard Greek practice.

[62] Cf. Zanker 1995a, esp. 476 and 480, who argues that the veristic type may have signaled social class but not necessarily ethnicity. He dates the majority of the preserved veristic portraits to the 40s and 30s B.C. and views them as imitating the type used by Julius Caesar. See also Smith 1988, 116, 132; Gruen 1992, 168–69.

of those (seven out of eleven) date to the end of the second or the first century B.C., after the Roman veristic type had been well established; two of the remaining four present the deceased in the guise of a philosopher, which entails an older type.[63] The other 122 employ youthful and generally idealized portraits, and this is true also for nearly all portraits of Greek royalty, both numismatic and sculptural, that were produced during the third and second centuries B.C.

The only exceptions appear on the royal coinage of Pontus and Bactria, two far-flung regions on either side of the Persian empire. The Pontic coins of Mithridates III (220–185/3 B.C.) and Mithridates IV (170–150 B.C.) are not so much aged as sharply individualized, with thick lips, a double chin, and a double furrow on the forehead.[64] In viewing these coins, it is important to keep in mind that the Pontic kingdom comprised a substantial Persian nobility, and sharply individualized portraiture had a long tradition in Persian iconography, especially in satrapal coinage and reliefs.[65] It seems likely that the kings were attempting to forge a link to those traditions, thereby distinguishing themselves from the Greek kingdoms farther to the west. The other example is Bactria, where the coins of Antimachus I (ca. 180 B.C.) again present a large face with a double furrow on the forehead. The kings of Bactria were Greek, but the attributes chosen for their coins—an elephant skin headdress, Macedonian kausia with diadem, and broad-rimmed helmet—are not duplicated on the coins of any other Greek kingdoms of the second century B.C. They seem to have been intended to lend a distinct identity to the kingdom, and the portly appearance of Antimachus I is probably another component of that system.[66]

It is this notion of identity and distinction that may explain why the veristic type was adopted for the Romans and why it began when it did. The evidence presented above suggests an inception date for the Roman veristic portrait of ca. 200 B.C., which was a period when the Romans were consistently attempting to define themselves against the background of many wars in many disparate regions of the empire, especially the Second Punic War and the first two Macedonian Wars. There are signs of this developing self-definition in both religion and literature: the import of the cult of Cybele from Asia Minor was a significant component in the construction of Rome's cultural identity, as Erich Gruen has shown.[67] This was also the time in which the first histories of Rome began to be written, beginning with Naevius and Fabius Pictor and continuing shortly thereafter with Cato's *Origines*, wherein Rome's Trojan ancestry and her reaction and interaction with other ethnic groups were detailed for the first time.[68]

One of the most significant by-products of these wars was Rome's inundation with bronze and marble statues seized by *triumphatores* from conquered Greek and Magna Graecian cities, and the public display of this plundered sculpture was a central feature of the aristocratic competition that flourished in Rome during the second century B.C.: M. Fulvius Nobilior's triumph over the Aetolians in 187 contained 515 bronze and marble statues, and that of Aemilius Paullus in 168 included 250 wagons, all filled with looted statues and paintings.[69] By the end of the first half of the second century, the public spaces of Rome would have been crowded with thousands of

[63] Pfuhl and Möbius 1977–79, nos. 108, 159, 161, 170, 831, 855, 868, 1505, 1968, 2034, 2321.

[64] Kraay 1966, no. 769; Davis and Kraay 1973, 264–67; Pollitt 1986, 36; Morkholm 1991, 175.

[65] Mørkholm and Zahle 1976; Bodenstedt 1982; Zahle 1982; Sevinç et al. 2001, 394.

[66] Kraay 1966, no. 778; Davis and Kraay 1973, 237–38; Pollitt 1986, 284–89; Smith 1988, 13, 113–14; Mørkholm 1991, 118–22, 180–82.

[67] Gruen 1990, 5–33.

[68] Gabba 1967; Gruen 1990, 11–33; Gruen 1992, 6–51; Sehlmeyer 1999, 27–34.

[69] Livy 39.5.13–16 (M. Fulvius Nobilior); Plut. *Aem.* 32–33. See also Vessberg 1941, 26–34, 46–56; Pape 1975; Künzl 1988a; Gruen 1992, 84–130; Aberson 1994; Kuttner 1999; Sehlmeyer 1999, 121–23; Holliday 2002, 22–62.

statues that formed part of the spoils of war. The appearance of central Rome, and of what Rome represented, was now completely altered, and the transformation was criticized as a threat to the moral fiber of the Romans as well as a magnet for degeneracy. "I fear these will make prisoners of us rather than we of them," declared Cato, and his comments were echoed by others even as the booty-laden wagons continued to arrive.[70]

This same period witnessed a dramatic rise in the number of portrait statues set up in Rome by or in honor of many of the commanders who had waged these wars, along with images of civic magistrates. The numbers of such honorific statues rose to a level where they were hindering access to public buildings, and the censors of 179 and 158 B.C. removed all portraits from the Capitoline and Forum, respectively, that had not been authorized by the senate or people.[71] These portrait statues were set up in the same public areas of Rome as the Greek images brought to Rome by conquest; and occasionally a portrait of the conqueror was set up next to the plundered spoils, such as the statue of Flamininus at the side of the image of Apollo from Carthage.[72] The loud public concerns about the potential danger of the conquered influencing the conqueror meant that the latter had to be distinguished from the former, especially if the images of both were to occupy the same spotlight.[73] The use of veristic portraiture would have established a clear distinction between the two, immediately signaling the difference in character between victor and vanquished.[74] There may, of course, have been a variety of political developments in Rome during the late third/early second century that fueled the development of the type, but changes in the commemoration of foreign triumphs and *triumphatores* were undoubtedly two of the most significant factors.

ETRURIA AND EGYPT

The veristic type was quite influential in central Italy once it had been established, and a similar style appears on the heads of some of the reclining figures above Etruscan terracotta ash urns.[75] Some scholars have, in fact, questioned whether the origins of the veristic style lay with the Etruscans rather than the Romans, but all of the ash urns with veristic portraits appear to date to the later second

[70] Livy 34.4.1–4. See also Plin. *HN* 33.148–50; Plut. *Cat. Mai./Min.* 19. See also n. 74 below. For an example of what these statues of Greek commanders would have looked like, see Queyrel, Hermary, and Jockey 1996, 194, no. 87.

[71] Plin. *HN* 34.30 (Forum, 158 B.C.); Livy 40.51.3 (Capitoline, 179 B.C.). On the abundance of public portrait statues in the early second century, see also Plut. *Cat. Mai./Min.* 19; Vessberg 1941, 40–46, 71–79; Smith 1988, 125–26; Gruen 1992, 118–23; Sehlmeyer 1999, 134–38, 142–77. For honorific statues set up on the Capitoline or in the Forum, see Lahusen 1983, 45–61; Sehlmeyer 1999, Capitol: 67–82, 110–29, 142–45, 159–61, 166, 191–96, 211–12, 227–31, Forum: 48–66, 83–108, 171–73, 204–9, 231–34, 245–53, 255–59.

[72] Plut. *Flam.* 1; Sehlmeyer 1999, 143–44 (Circus Flaminius). Fabius Maximus set up a statue of Hercules plundered from Tarentum on the Capitoline (Strabo 6.3.1), and his equestrian statue was placed next to it (Plut. *Fabius Maximus* 22.6; Sehlmeyer 1999, 125–26). Also dedicated on the Capitoline was the colossal statue of Apollo plundered by Lucullus from Apollonia on the Black Sea: Strabo 7.6.1. See also Hölscher

1978, 322–24, 340–41.

[73] Cf. the comments of Polybius (9.10.5–6): "But if, on the contrary, while leading the simplest of lives, very far removed from all such superfluous magnificence, they [the Romans] were constantly victorious over those who possessed the greatest number and finest examples of such works, must we not also consider that they committed a mistake? To abandon the habits of the victors and to imitate those of the conquered, not only appropriating the objects, but at the same time attracting that envy which is inseparable from their possession, which is the one thing most to be dreaded by superiors in power, is surely an incontestable error."

[74] Hiesinger 1973, 818; Smith 1988, 129; Flower 1996, 39; cf. Plin. *HN* 35.6.

[75] Maggiani 1976, 44; R. R. R. Smith 1981, 30–31; Gruen 1992, 156–57; Maggiani 1972; Nielsen 2002, 107 fig. 12, 109 fig. 15, 113 fig. 17, 114–19; Croz 2002, 315–23. The similarities consist primarily of lines on the forehead and mouth, which appear on both male and female heads.

or first century B.C., and there is no veristic tradition apparent in earlier Etruscan art.[76] Moreover, Etruria was subject to Rome during the middle and late republic and had its own language and culture, even though it was steadily being Romanized and colonized.[77] It seems unlikely that Etruscan funerary portraits would have been chosen as models for images of the Roman aristocracy.[78]

The origin of the veristic style has also been sought in Egypt, primarily because the marks of advanced age appear on a series of stone portraits, many of which are priests, that have often been dated to the Hellenistic period, although precise dating has proved elusive.[79] Achille Adriani argued that these portraits functioned as the primary influence on Roman republican portraits, with the rise of the Isis cult in Italy playing a prominent role in the transmission, and the same general argument has been echoed by Bernard Bothmer.[80]

Advanced age admittedly had a greater popularity in the portraiture of Egypt than of Greece and Rome, although its significance was by no means static. Completely bald heads are a standard feature of priestly portraiture from the beginning of the Old Kingdom, as an indication not of age but rather of purity.[81] Light lines on the forehead, mouth, and chin are sometimes added to their portraits, as well as to portraits of members of the royal court such as Senenmut, the chancellor of Hatshepsut.[82] But the significance of the format was not always positive: in the New Kingdom, advanced age (receding hairlines, profusion of wrinkles) was an identifying feature of the foreign enemies of Egypt, as represented most prominently by the reliefs in the Tomb of Horemheb at Memphis (ca. 1340 B.C.).[83]

We cannot be certain whether the Egyptian priest portraits with marks of age date before or after the first appearance of Roman verism, but they seem to form part of an independent tradition that reaches back as early as the third millennium B.C. Roman influence on their development is unlikely, and it seems equally implausible that the Egyptian portraits, whatever their date, were influential in the development of Roman verism. The latter was chosen as the visual demarcation of a particular set of values claimed by the Roman aristocracy, and it is hard to believe that Egyptian priests would have been selected as the model. It is not unlikely, however, that some viewers would have read in the late Hellenistic portraits of these Egyptian priests the same concepts of wisdom and ethics that were incorporated into the Roman examples.[84]

IMAGINES AND MORES

Ascertaining the date by which veristic portraits were introduced only solves part of the problem; we still need to examine why the veristic type *per se* was employed for public aristocratic

[76] M. Nielsen (2002, 118–19) has shown that these heads were in fact stock types available in the workshop rather than individualized portraits of specific persons.

[77] Harris 1971, 177.

[78] The reverse, in fact, seems to be true, as attested by the bronze Arringatore, probably made sometime shortly after 89 B.C.: Dohrn 1966; Fittschen 1970. The statue, which features a veristic portrait and an Etruscan inscription, appears to represent a man of Etruscan birth who had acquired Roman citizenship.

[79] R. R. R. Smith 1981, 32–33; Gruen 1992, 158–59; Walker and Higgs 2000, 53, 1.38; 130, 2.23; 251, 4.27.

[80] Adriani 1970; Bothmer 1969, 133–34, 164–66, 170–72,

182–84; Bothmer 1988; Croz 2002, 173–84.

[81] Hdt. 2.36–37.

[82] Lange 1968, figs. 24 (Ankh-haf, ca. 2700), 135 (Senenmut, ca. 1470), 260 (Petamenophis, ca. 660); W. S. Smith 1981, 415, 418.

[83] Lange 1968, figs. 266, 210; W. S. Smith 1981, 342–46; Martin 1989, 87–92, 94–97.

[84] Baldness as an indication of purity was also a feature of Mesopotamian religious art, such as the pious Gudea statues or the figurines from Tell Asmar and Mari, although unlike in Egypt, the bald holy men in Mesopotamia were sometimes shown with beards: Strommenger 1964, figs. 88–91, 96, 99.

commemoration in Rome. In the veristic type there are two features in particular that stand out: first, the size and shape of the head and facial features; and second, the indications of advanced age. The two issues are usually discussed as one, but there were quite different sources for each, and they require separate discussion.

The first involves the form of the facial features and, indeed, the heads themselves. The noses are often large and aquiline; the lips are unusually thick or thin; and the shape of the head frequently varies from long and narrow to short and broad. The ears are also often cited as being unusually large and protruding, and occasionally they are; but in general they seem more conspicuous because the surrounding scalp hair is either quite short or nonexistent, whereas in Greek portraits the longer curlier hair usually covers part of the ears, and size is consequently less apparent. This kind of facial configuration is not evinced in earlier Italic or Etruscan art, nor is it a standard feature of Greek portraits. A more likely potential source lies in the *imagines*, or wax masks of Roman officials that were regularly made during the middle and late republic. These are often (wrongly) confused with death masks, and the scholarly literature dealing with their production has never been as comprehensive as it should be.[85] Three aspects of the *imagines* need to be addressed if their relationship to veristic portraiture is to be understood: their significance, the methods used in their production, and the time in one's life when they would have been produced.

The wax masks were made only for family members who had at least held the office of aedile, and so their very existence indicated a significant achievement in the service of the Roman state.[86] They were, in general, intended to be a model for future generations, symbolizing a standard of excellence that boys in the family would strive to equal or surpass.[87] *Imagines* began to be produced by the third century B.C., and all were labeled and stored as a group in cabinets in the atrium, next to genealogical charts fixed to the wall.[88]

They are best known for their use in aristocratic funerals, and Polybius provides an eyewitness account of the custom. Each *imago* was worn by an actor who closely resembled the deceased in stature, and his dress and attributes commemorated the dead man's civic, military, and religious achievements.[89] The biographical data summarized in these portraits were reiterated and expanded in a public oration, and the portrait was thereby framed by visual and verbal narratives that justified its creation and public display.

Polybius stresses the extent to which the masks faithfully recorded the shape and contour (*plavsiss* and *upographen*) of a man's face, and Pliny refers to them as faces pressed in wax (*expressi cera vultus*).[90] The wax could not have been pressed directly onto the skin and must have been made from a plaster cast of the face. I outline here the steps of the process that were probably followed, since such discussion is rarely included in articles on *imagines*, and here I acknowledge the assistance of sculptor Margot Gotoff, who made a wax mask of the author as a test case.[91] The skin would first

[85] Their significance has recently been very successfully presented by Harriet Flower (1996). See also Zadoks-Josephus Jitta 1932; Hölscher 1978, 325–26; Drerup 1980; R. R. R. Smith 1981, 31–32; Jackson 1987; Dupont 1987; Gruen 1992, 153–56; Sehlmeyer 1999, 45–48; Croz 2002, 242–44.

[86] Flower 1996, 2, 10, 56, 59, 61, 288–89 (T21), 290, T24; Sehlmeyer 1999, 47–48.

[87] Flower 1996, 9–10, 62, 64, 136–39, 277, 311 (Sall. *Iug.* 4.5–6).

[88] Flower 1996, 40–47, 59, 211–17, 339–43; Rose 1997, 7.

[89] Polyb. 6.53–4; Diodorus 31.25.2; Plin. *HN* 35.6; Sen. *Ben.* 3.28.2 are the most important, but all the relevant sources have been collected by Flower 1996, 281–332.

[90] Polyb. 6.53.6; Plin. *HN* 35.6.

[91] On technique, see also Hoffmann 1939, 266–68; Drerup 1980, 82, 93–97; McDonnell 1999, 547–49. One wax mask, found in a tomb of imperial date at Cumae, has survived: Drerup 1980, 93–94, pl. 49.1.

be coated with olive oil, and strips of fabric soaked in plaster would then be gently molded onto the face.[92] Once the plaster had hardened and cured, it would be removed from the face and soaked in water.[93] A layer of melted wax would then be brushed into the inner side of the plaster mask, followed, in all likelihood, by a layer of cloth that would provide support, and then a final layer of wax.[94] Considering the emphasis on the lifelike nature of these masks, the wax was probably tinted or painted so that the final product would conform more closely to skin color.[95]

To wear these masks one would have needed string, which could not have been attached directly to the wax. The cloth therefore probably extended beyond the confines of the *imago*, near the temples, so that string could easily be threaded through it. Funerals in the Forum lasted a significant part of the day, and in the summer it is not unlikely that patches on the surface melted, thereby revealing the underlying cloth, and repairs may occasionally have been necessary.[96] This reconstruction, although hypothetical, fits beautifully with the description of the *imagines* by Polybius and Pliny. The masks would consequently have recorded faithfully the shape of the face as well as the form of the facial features, and they probably served as models for the veristic portraits of the second and first centuries B.C.[97]

The next question to be addressed is whether these masks would have contained the features of advanced age, and to answer it we need to establish the time in one's life when the masks would regularly have been made. The production of the mask was in and of itself a signal that the man in question had reached a level that brought with it the conferral of full senatorial dignity. The *imagines* were, in effect, rewards for having reached the office of aedile, or praetor if the aedileship was skipped, and it stands to reason that they were produced as soon as they possibly could be. It would be much more difficult to understand a delay in their production, especially considering the competitive political climate of the middle and late republic. There was also the danger that adverse fortune would strike the officeholder at a later date, such as death in war or a fatal accident, which would prevent the production of an accurate mask. Making it at the earliest opportunity would be the most logical and safest solution. Consequently, the age range for the aedileship, probably between 36 and 39, should be the time in which the *imagines* were produced.[98] In other words, the masks would have copied the appearance of relatively young men, whose faces, in most cases, would not have evinced the signs of advanced age.

The reconstruction presented above is bolstered by the literary sources, which make it clear that *imagines* were made while the subject was still alive.[99] The *senatus consultum* of Gn. Calpurnius Piso, governor of Syria in A.D. 19 and the alleged murderer of Germanicus, specifies that all public statues

---

[92] This was probably a fine fabric such as linen.

[93] The water is the release agent and would later ensure an easy separation of the wax and plaster.

[94] This cloth would have to have been relatively strong, and something similar to burlap was probably chosen.

[95] Plin. *HN* 35.4.

[96] Myles McDonnell has expressed doubt that a full plaster mask would have been used due to problems of ownership (McDonnell 1999, 547), but since new masks would have been made for each new generation, there must have been "master" plaster casts to produce them. The sources do not mention who controlled these masks, as McDowell notes, but

the Latin sources also say virtually nothing about the meaning of the *imagines* themselves. It seems to have been regarded as common knowledge, not worthy of extensive commentary, and without Polybius we would know comparatively little about them.

[97] This range of shapes can easily be seen on the skulls excavated in ancient Roman cemeteries, especially Herculaneum: Bisel 1987; Bisel 1988; Bisel 1991.

[98] Austin 1958, 31–45 ("What were the minimum ages for the various magistracies in the second century?").

[99] Flower 1996, 2, 4, 23–26, 38, 58, 102–3. According to Pliny (*HN* 35.153), lifetime plaster casts had been made since at least the late fourth century B.C.

of Piso were to be destroyed and that his wax mask should not be carried in funeral processions or set up with the other masks of the Calpurnian family.[100] Piso committed suicide during the trial, and his *damnatio* followed immediately thereafter, which indicates that the *imago* must have been made during his life.[101] The case of Marcus Scribonius Libo Drusus furnishes a second example. In A.D. 16, shortly before Germanicus's death, Libo was accused of attempting to assassinate Tiberius and his sons. He too committed suicide during the trial, and Tacitus notes that his *imago* was banned from any future funerals.[102] Libo was praetor or praetor-designate when he was accused, and his mask must already have been made by that point. The evidence therefore strongly suggests that the masks were produced during one's lifetime, and relatively early in one's public career.[103]

As Harriet Flower has noted, Polybius's description makes it clear that the masks were intended to convey what the deceased man looked like when he was alive.[104] There is no indication that *imagines* were death masks produced after rigor mortis had set in, nor is it surprising that they were cast from life: each *imago* was intended to celebrate the political success achieved by a man during the prime of his life, and such accomplishments would be harder to encapsulate in an image that copied a lifeless and disintegrating face of a corpse.[105]

The discussion above has shown that the *imagines* would have recorded the shape and contour of the face, just as Polybius said, but they would not, in most cases, have featured the marks of advanced age. Since age is one of the distinguishing characteristics of the veristic portrait, we need to consider additional sources of influence on its development, and this requires an investigation of what advanced age was intended to signify in antiquity. During the archaic and classical periods the hallmarks of age were not a common feature of mythological or political representations in Greek, Roman, or Etruscan areas. The age of most older male mythological figures, such as Nestor or Aegeus, was conveyed through the inclusion of a cane or white hair; balding lined faces were generally avoided, nor did they figure in the iconography of gods.[106]

But there are several characters or character types in which advanced age was a fundamental component of their iconography, namely seers and prophets, teachers and orators, and philosophers.[107] One therefore sees an aged face and balding head used for the seer on the east pediment of the temple of Zeus at Olympia (fig. 14), as well as for Teirisias and Phineus on Greek vases. The same holds true for Phoenix, tutor of Achilles, and the teacher of Chrysippus on Praenestine cists; for Demosthenes, in the famous image by Polyeuktos; and for a broad range of philosophers (fig.

---

[100] Flower 1996, 23–26, 330–31 (I16).

[101] *Damnatio* deprived an officeholder of the memory of his achievements, and his life would have been marked by a gap in his family's parade of ancestors: Flower 1996, 24–31.

[102] Flower 1996, 26; Tac. *Ann.* 2.27–32.

[103] Cf. Flower 1996, 277: "A man's *imago* marked his status and hence his worth in society. . . . An *imago* could therefore not portray an outcast, a convicted criminal, or someone subject to *damnatio memoriae*."

[104] Flower 1996, 38.

[105] For the effects of rigor mortis on the face, see Zadoks-Josephus Jitta 1932, 47–48; Gruen 1992, 155–56. There is certainly evidence that death masks were occasionally made (cf. Quint. 6.1.40), and a few of them, primarily in plaster,

have actually been found (generally in tombs), but none can be dated before the first century A.D., and nearly half of the total number recovered were found in Egypt and North Africa: Drerup 1980, 99–100. There is no literary or archaeological evidence indicating that death masks played a role in Roman funerals or that they were synonymous with or linked to the *imagines*.

[106] Kron 1981 (Aigeus); Lygouri-Tolia 1994; Sevinç 1996, 256–57, figs. 9, 10 (Nestor). For images of gods on Roman republican coins, see Böhm 1997, 27–110. Hephaestus appears aged on one Praenestine cist (Battaglia and Emiliozzi 1990, 175–79, no. 57) but otherwise is shown the same age as the other gods.

[107] For the philosopher type, see Richter 1965, 164–251; Giuliani 1986, 134–40; Pollitt 1986, 59–70; Smith 1991, 33–50; Dillon 1994, 211–16; Zanker 1995b.

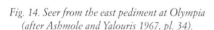

Fig. 14. Seer from the east pediment at Olympia   Fig. 15. Portrait of the Stoic philosopher Chrysippus
(after Ashmole and Yalouris 1967, pl. 34).   (after Zanker 1995b, 100 fig. 55).

15), beginning at least as early as 440 B.C. with a vase painting of Aesop.[108] In these cases, the veristic type was used to signal a preoccupation with the spiritual as opposed to the physical, especially intellectual and ethical excellence.

This link between advanced age and wisdom would have been well established in Rome by the beginning of the second century B.C. Images of orators and philosophers had been set up in Greek and Magna Graecian cities throughout the Hellenistic period, and they would have figured among the booty brought to Rome by *triumphatores*, although some, like the statue of Pythagoras in the Comitium, had long been in place in Rome.[109] The same kind of sculpture decorated the villas of Italy during the republic and empire, and Richard Neudecker found that such images accounted for nearly 75 percent of the statues that have been discovered in Italian villas.[110]

It seems likely that portraits of the man of mind served as one of the primary sources for veristic portraits of the Roman aristocracy, and the formal link is readily apparent when one compares a philosopher portrait, such as that of the Stoic Chrysippus (fig. 15), with a fairly standard veristic portrait of the first century B.C. (fig. 16): the facial lines, crow's-feet, receding hair, and sunken cheeks are the same in both. This connection has generally not been recognized because the beards, himations, and seated poses of the Greek intellectuals have been omitted from the Roman portraits,

[108] Ashmole and Yalouris 1967, figs. 31–38; Zimmerman 1997 (Teirisias); Kahil 1994 (Phineus); Kauffman-Samaras 1997 (Phoenix); Schefold 1986, 288, no. 7; Battaglia and Emiliozzi 1990, 226–32, no. 69 (teacher of Chrysippus); Zanker 1995b, 83–89 (Demosthenes), 33–34 (Aesop). The only kings who were shown bald on occasion are Priam (Neils 1994) and Tyndareus (Kahil 1997, 146–47, nos. 5, 10, 11). Once the Phrygian cap is added to Priam's iconography at the end of the fifth

century (Miller 1995), there is no further hint of baldness.

[109] For the Comitium statue of Pythagoras, see Plin. *HN* 34.26; Sehlmeyer 1999, 88–90. In Greek cities, statues of the heads of philosophical·schools were regularly set up after their death: Diog. Laert. 5.15, 31, 64, 69.

[110] Neudecker 1988, esp. 5–30; Zanker 1995b, 205–8.

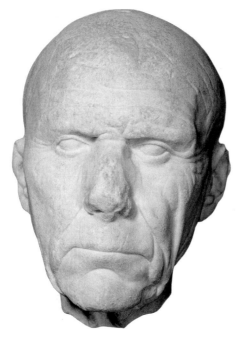

*Fig. 16. Male portrait from Scoppito, now in Chieti
(after D'Ambra 1998, 27 fig. 11).*

but if one removes Chrysippus's beard, there is no fundamental difference between his head and that of the Roman veristic portrait in figure 16.[111] Klaus Fittschen's discovery that the head of the Vatican Posidippus was recut into the portrait of a late republican man constitutes another excellent illustration of this link: both portrait types embraced the marks of advanced age used to connote probity, so the transition from one to the other was relatively easy.[112]

The appropriation of this type by the Roman aristocracy is not at all unusual: in the ancient reports on the triumphs of the late third and early second century B.C. there is a consistent emphasis of the moral superiority of the Romans vis à vis the Greeks, which increased as Greek booty began to envelop Rome. The adoption of the veristic type essentially enabled the Romans to co-opt the moral superiority associated with the features of advanced age and simultaneously distinguish themselves from the looted images of their opponents in the wars just concluded. In other words, the Romans selected a veristic type for the same reason that it was used for representations of philosophers, teachers, and orators: the format succinctly conveyed a disposition toward probity, piety, and character—in effect, *dignitas*.[113] The Romans were not presenting themselves as philosophers, orators, or seers directly but appropriating and modifying an iconography linked to wisdom and ethics.[114]

[111] See also Brommer 1953–54, 168 on the similarities between philosopher and veristic portraits. These portraits would have been made by Greeks, who came in great numbers to Italy during the first half of the second century (Plut. *Aem.* 6.5; *Flam.* 1.1; Plin. *HN* 35.115 and 135). It is likely that some, perhaps most, had already produced images of intellectuals and were familiar with the rendering of advanced age.

[112] Fittschen 1992, 236–50.

[113] Giuliani 1986, 205–38; Croz 2002, 244–49.

[114] See Gehrke 1994 on the interaction between Roman culture and Greek ethics. It is worth noting that the status of philosophers in republican Rome was, in general, quite high: following his victory over Perseus at Pydna, Aemilius Paullus brought Greek philosophers back to Rome to serve as tutors for his sons (Plin. *HN* 35.135), and the Romans thronged to the lectures of Carneades in the mid-second century (Gruen 1990, 174–76; Ferrary 1988, 602–15). This does not mean that they did not, on occasion, provoke ire from the conservative factions in Rome. The senatorial decree of 161 B.C. indicating that philosophers and orators should not live in Rome (Suet. *Rhet.* 1) is one such example. But their popularity in Rome throughout the middle and late republic was significant: Gruen 1990, 158–92; Gruen 1992, 64–83, 233, 247–48, 251–71.

In searching for the ingredients of the Roman veristic portrait, then, one has to consider at least three factors. The influx of a large quantity of booty from Greek and Punic areas created a situation whereby the development of a new portrait type for the conquerors was highly desirable—a type that allowed the viewer to distinguish more easily between conqueror and conquered. One of the sources for the new mode of display was the wax *imago*, which, like the new portrait statues, effectively symbolized the subject's achievements in political and military spheres of activity. Since most of the public statues erected in Rome during the middle and late republic represented men who had reached the position of aedile or praetor, the wax mask would already have been made and would have been available as a model. Applied to the form of the *imago* were the features of advanced age—some more advanced than others—which conferred upon the images the same kind of intelligence and moral superiority that had been employed for images of teachers, seers, and philosophers. The new formula was so successful that these non-idealized images came to be viewed as synonymous with the values linked to aristocratic Roman men by Cato, Cicero, and Vergil, among others, even though some of the sources of that iconography were Greek.[115]

STATUARY TYPES

Just as important as the portrait was the statuary type that accompanied it, and this is the final component of Roman portrait iconography that needs to be addressed here. A particularly instructive introduction to this subject is provided by the inscription on the sarcophagus of Scipio Barbatus, dated to the third century B.C., which praised his wisdom and bravery while noting that his looks were equal to his valor.[116] In other words, his exalted status in Roman society was a consequence of his intelligence and martial prowess. Conveying both of these qualities within a single portrait statue was not an easy feat: the veristic type highlighted strength of character, but the facial lines and receding hair that constituted the type conferred a distinctly aged appearance on the person being portrayed. To counterbalance this effect, body types that emphasized physical strength were employed, and we can reconstruct the types to some extent from the few full statues of republican date that have survived and from the literary references to those that have not.

The vast majority were cuirassed, equestrian, or else togate.[117] On rare occasion, beginning in the first century B.C., nude body types were appropriated from the iconographic corpus of gods, heroes, and athletes.[118] With this group of portraits, in particular, one sees the uneasy assimilation of heroic and veristic types, with the body modeled on the former and the head on the latter.[119] There

[115] Giuliani 1986, 205–38. Not all images of adult men would have featured the veristic format. More youthful/idealized types would probably have been used for younger men who had died prior to holding a public office, and a tufa head from the Tomb of the Scipios, most likely carved during the second century B.C., is a case in point. Coarelli (1972, 97–102) identified the head as a man who had triumphed, based on the laurel crown in the hair; but the face is clearly that of a youth, and during the republic laurel had a broad purificatory and apotropaic significance (Ogle 1910). It was worn by deceased men on the lids of Etruscan urns, and the same sense is probably intended by the wreath on the Scipionic head (Dohrn 1962, 89–91). See also Gazda 1973, 859, 869; Croz 2002, 37 (C1).

[116] Saladino 1970; Giuliani 1986, 197–99; Wachter 1987, 301–42; Flower 1996, 160–84, esp. 172; Zevi 1999.

[117] Lahusen 1983, 45–61; Himmelmann 1989, 116; Croz 2002, 251–90.

[118] For Roman attitudes toward nudity, see Kleiner 1977, 185; Wrede 1981, 19–30; Zanker 1983, 255; Lahusen 1983, 53–56; Himmelman 1989, 39–68; Bonfante 1989 (Etruscans and Greeks); Pollini 1990; Queyrel 1991, 440; Hallett 1993, 67–173; Stevenson 1998; Sehlmeyer 1999, 174–76; Croz 2002, 259–75.

[119] Zanker 1983, 257–60. A Praenestine cist in Providence features a seated figure with an aged face and a younger, muscular body, which would seem to be an Italic antecedent for the later heroic/veristic portraits, but Battaglia and Emiliozzi (1990, 207–10, no. 67) believe it to be a forgery.

is no indication in the literary sources that the wedding of such diverse types was considered unusual by the Romans (although it was scrupulously avoided in the statues of elite Greeks), and it allowed for the presentation of moral character and physical strength within a single unit.[120]

The rarity of nude statues of Romans during the republic is worthy of additional discussion since scholars have often assumed that nudity in elite portraiture could be employed at any time. Attitudes toward nudity in republican Rome were very different from those in Hellenistic Greece. Partial or complete nudity was not infrequent in the portraiture of Hellenistic rulers, commanders, or athletes; and statues of non-Greeks set up in Greek cities were often presented in the same fashion, the most prominent examples being the Roman statues of Ofellius Ferus and the "pseudo-athlete" on Delos (fig. 12).[121]

In contemporary Rome, however, the type was generally avoided: if one surveys the literary references to statues of elite men set up in Rome during the republic, it is clear that all were clothed, either in a cuirass or a toga. An examination of republican coin types yields an identical picture: all of the statues reproduced on the reverses are clothed, as are the images of commanders, priests, and magistrates. The most likely explanation for this is that Rome had quickly been filled with nude statues from Magna Graecian and Greek cities, and Roman commanders wanted to distinguish their portraits, both heads and bodies, from the statues that formed part of their triumphal booty. This restrained approach to heroic nudity in statuary is in direct compliance with Roman attitudes toward public nudity in daily life during the late republic, when it was considered appropriate for slaves or prisoners but unacceptable for living Roman citizens.

There is no sign of a regional change in this practice until the second quarter of the first century B.C., when the statue of a semi-nude commander was set up in the Sanctuary of Hercules at Tivoli (fig. 17), and the type is subsequently found on funerary reliefs from the Via Appia, in the tomb of M. Artorius Geminus on the Tiber, and in tomb sculpture from Aquileia.[122] There is no evidence for fully nude statues of elite Romans in Rome itself until the late first century B.C., and the type never became common there.[123]

---

[120] This is certainly an instance in which republican male portraiture departed from the Greek image of the intellectual. The age of face and body were synchronized in the latter category.

[121] For nudity in ancient Greece, see Bonfante 1989; Queyrel 1991, 440; Hallett 1993, 8–66.

[122] Tivoli General: Giuliano 1979, 267–69, no. 164; Coarelli 1987, 99; Himmelmann 1989, 219–24, no. 12; Giuliani 1970, 199; Croz 2002, 24 (A5), 265–66; Via Appia reliefs: Kleiner and Kleiner 1975; Zanker 1975; Kleiner 1977; Artorius Geminus: Silvestrini 1987, esp. 73–75; Silvestrini 1999; Aquileia: Scrinari 1972, 28, no. 81; Croz 2002, 35 (B39). It is likely that the nude male statue from Formia of Hermes Lansdowne type is also posthumous, although the function of the building in which it was found is uncertain: Aurigemma 1922; Aurigemma and de Santis 1955, 33–34, Tav. XX, XXI; Maderna 1988, 230 H7; Croz 2002, 25 (A8). The same probably applies to the Foruli general from Chieti: Krauss 1967, 252, no. 284; Maderna 1988, 197 D1; Hallett 1993, 122, 123, 226, no. 3; Croz 2002, 24–25 (A7), 272–73.

[123] The first examples are the marble funerary relief from the Via Appia and the Grimani Agrippa (Kleiner and Kleiner 1975; Hallett 1993, 123–24; Romeo 1998, 187–89, R23). There is no secure evidence that nude lifetime statues of Augustus were set up in Rome, although such statues have often been posited on the basis of numismatic evidence: Zanker 1988, 37–43; Sehlmeyer 1999, 255–59. This conservative attitude toward lifetime nudity in public statuary in and around Rome applies to non-imperial dedications as well. The statue of C. Cartilius Poplicola outside the temple of Hercules at Ostia, usually cited as a lifetime nude dedication (Calza 1955; Block 1955; Croz 2002, 34–35 [B35]), needs to be reconsidered. The name of Cartilius is in the nominative, which means that he was the dedicator of the statue, not necessarily its subject. The statue is headless, and the body type was used for the representation of a variety of heroes, including Hercules. Moreover, the self-dedication of statues seems largely to have ended with the decision in 158 B.C. to remove from the Forum all statues not authorized by the people and the senate (Plin. *HN* 34.30–31). The last self-dedicated statue during the republic was of Hostilius Mancinus in 136 B.C., which was a very special case (Rosenstein 1986; Sehlmeyer 1999, 166–67).

Fig. 17 (near right).
"Tivoli General,"
Archivio Storico
Olivetti, Ivrea, Italy
(after Himmelmann
1989, 218 fig. 12a).

Fig. 18 (far right).
"Terme Ruler,"
Archivio Storico
Olivetti, Ivrea, Italy
(after Himmelmann
1989, 144).

The only republican literary reference to a nude statue comes from the *Verrine Orations*, in which Cicero speaks disparagingly of the nude statues of Verrus's son in Syracuse.[124] One might be inclined to infer from Cicero's comments that nude statues were considered inappropriate at that time, although the appearance of the statues listed above indicates that such an interpretation is unjustified.

Cicero's comments take on new meaning, however, if we consider the contexts in which these nude statues were found. Not all of the contexts, of course, can be reconstructed, but many of them were funerary, and we should probably view the statues listed above as posthumous dedications. Artists appear to have appropriated the costume of nudity from divine iconography to signal that the person represented had passed to a different realm of existence, one that was purely spiritual. A similar situation would prevail during the Julio-Claudian period, when the portraits of deified imperial women featured attributes, such as the diadem and *infula*, previously used by gods or priests.[125]

If we now return to Cicero's comments with this interpretation in mind, then his disdain will have been caused not by the fact that a nude statue of Verrus's son had been erected but because it had been set up while he was still alive.

[124] *Verr.* 2.2.154 (above an arch); 2.4.143 (in the Bouleu-
terion). See also Sehlmeyer 1999, 213–15.

[125] Rose 1997, 76–77.

It is not surprising that the Romans treated the representation of nudity as cautiously as they did their Trojan ancestry. Inherent in the costume of nudity was the same kind of ambivalent value as in eastern costume: depending on the context, nudity could be construed as exalted (gods, personifications, heroes) or debased (defeated foes).[126] It could, in other words, have a bilingual significance. Consequently, imperial monuments in Rome never featured a nude image of the emperor if a god/personification or enemy was also included.

This discussion of nudity is relevant to the interpretation of the "Terme Ruler," an over-life-size bronze discovered near the Baths of Constantine in 1885 and usually dated to the second century B.C. (fig. 18).[127] The nude body type draws on both royal and heroic iconography, although the individualized facial features indicate that the statue is a portrait.[128] Many have assumed that the man represented is, in fact, royal, explaining the lack of a diadem as an indication that he had not yet been declared king. Others have identified the statue as a Roman republican general, and J. Ch. Balty has linked him to Flamininus.[129] As I have attempted to show above, nudity was treated very cautiously by the Romans, especially during the republic, and all of the evidence—literary, numismatic, and sculptural—speaks against the representation of a fully nude Roman general in the city of Rome prior to the late first century B.C.

It is far more likely that the statue formed part of the booty brought to Rome by a general during the second century, and this interpretation would be in complete harmony with the evidence. The thousands of bronze and marble images removed from Greek and Magna Graecian cities during the middle and late republic included a plethora of kings, soldiers, and athletes, many of whom would have been nude. Pinpointing the identity of the figure may never be possible, but the nudity alone, set against the evidentiary context, indicates that the "Terme Ruler" should not be regarded as the portrait of a Roman. It was, instead, the introduction of this kind of image to Rome that prompted the veristic style to be developed.

MATERIALS

It looks as if all of the elite male portrait statues set up in the public spaces of Rome during the second and early first century B.C. were bronze, which would explain why only the literary references to them survive.[130] Marble at that time had to be imported from the eastern Mediterranean, and it appears to have been reserved primarily for the temples of the gods, such as the Round Temple in the Forum Boarium, or the associated cult statues, like the "Fortuna" from Temple B in Largo Argentina.[131]

Ascertaining the type of marble used for the surviving Italian veristic portraits should enable us to date them with greater precision. As I mentioned at the beginning of this discussion, the portraits

[126] Picard 1957, pls. XVI, XXI; Kent 1978, pls. 21.76R, 69.238, 72.249R; Kuttner 1995a, fig. 85.

[127] Giuliano 1979, 198–201, no. 124; Smith 1988, 84–85, 164, no. 44; Zanker 1988, 5–8; Himmelmann 1989, 126–49, 205–207, no. 4; Queyrel 1990, 142, no. 315; Meyer 1996; Ridgway 2000, 305–9; Croz 2002, 23 (A1), 266–68.

[128] Ridgway 2000, 305–9.

[129] Balty 1978, followed by Croz 2002, 267. A list of articles wherein the Terme Ruler has been identified as a Roman general is provided by Smith 1988, 164, no. 44.

[130] The materials used for Roman republican portraits have

been analyzed by Croz 2002, 105–20.

[131] For marble cult statues in republican Rome, see Martin 1987, with figs. 13, 14 of the Fortuna. The earliest marble portrait in Rome seems to have been that of Ennius, which was added to the Tomb of the Scipios in the mid-second century B.C.: Livy 38.56.3–4; Cic. Arch. 9.22; Val. Max. 8.14.1; Plin. HN 7.114; Sehlmeyer 1999, 67. In the Aegean itself marble was far more affordable, although late Hellenistic inscriptions indicate that marble was considered higher in status than bronze (Tuchelt 1979, 70–90), and there too one finds evidence for far more statues in bronze than marble. The marble medium of the Delian statues is therefore quite unusual, and the images would have been construed as a sign of the esteem in which the clients held their patrons.

are dated to the mid-first century B.C. solely because the type was popular on coinage then, although many believe that the portraits were produced over a broader period of time. This period fortunately coincides with the early exploitation of the marble quarries at Luna/Carrara, in northwestern Italy.[132] The history of these quarries is not yet as clear as one would like, but it looks as if large-scale work was inaugurated by Caesar's *praefectus fabrum* Mamurra in the late 50s, after which the output steadily increased. This made marble a more inexpensive medium in which to work, and the time involved in transport was also considerably reduced. If isotopic analysis of the marble in most of the veristic portraits indicates that it is Carraran, then the change in portrait medium can be linked to the opening of the quarries. If a significant proportion has been carved from east Greek marble, then the dating of the corpus should be modified, and a different rationale for the change will have to be sought.[133] In any event, this is a theory that can and should be tested.

Concluding Remarks

During the second triumvirate, the changes that occurred in elite portraiture were just as dramatic as those related to Trojan iconography. The facial lines were removed as the hair returned, and the youthful, idealized result linked the portraits of elite Romans more closely to those of elite Greeks.[134] It would be difficult to overestimate the effect of this change, as the new youthful images, primarily members of the Julio-Claudian family, came to occupy the same spaces as the veristic portraits of earlier generations. America experienced a similarly striking change in ruler iconography in 1961, when the veristic type of Dwight Eisenhower suddenly changed to the Augustan classicism of John Kennedy with its new prospective outlook; but the juxtaposition of types in the public spaces of Rome would have been even more dramatic.

Meanwhile, the freedmen of Augustan Rome, many of whom were Greek, continued their use of the veristic type for the travertine portraits that adorned their tombs on the Via Appia.[135] These types, along with the Latin names beneath them, were still regarded as the principal hallmarks of Roman identity, even though the new ruling power had now chosen to define its identity in different visual terms. Not surprisingly, the veristic type continued to be used for men of learning outside the imperial family, as demonstrated by the portraits from the "Medical School" at Velia, as well as for the tombstones of Roman veterans, especially in northern Italy and the Rhineland.[136]

Examining Trojan ancestry and veristic portraiture together effectively highlights the ambiguous nature of both. These two features of Roman identity selectively co-opted components of the Hellenic tradition yet still stood apart from it. By the third century B.C., Trojan ancestry had emerged as one of the most conspicuous features of Roman identity, with a significant impact on the religious configuration of the city; but the rise of the Parthians as the Romans' principal eastern foe, and their common iconography with the Trojans, meant that public commemoration of ancestry and triumph had to be constructed more carefully than in the past, since the east now had a variable value.

[132] Plin. *HN* 36.14, 36.48–50; Dolci 1988, 78–79; Dolci 1989, 28, 33–34.

[133] The "Tivoli General," which is usually assumed to be one of the earliest veristic portraits, is described as "marmo Greco" in the Terme Museum catalogue (Giuliano 1979, 267, no. 164), and Susan Walker, in conversation, has expressed the same opinion.

[134] Massner 1982; Boschung 1993. The veristic format of Julius Caesar's portraits was also changed to a more youthful type during the second triumvirate and Augustan period: Zanker 1988, 33–37.

[135] Zanker 1975; Kleiner 1977, 88–117, 186–91.

[136] Boschung 2002, 112–14, pl. 89 (Velia); Pflug 1989, 68–76; Künzl 1988b, 566–68 (northern Italy; Rhineland).

In designing the portraits of the men who achieved these triumphs, the Romans selected a model that immediately distinguished them from images of the enemy and yet simultaneously associated them with the same concepts of wisdom and moral excellence that were echoed in contemporary literature. In so doing, they drew upon their own *imagines* for the framework yet conflated it with components selected from the image of the intellectual. This was a mode of presentation never compromised by changes in the iconography of the enemy, and it was altered only when Augustus's revised conception of *Romanitas* required new visual modes of expression.

Works Cited

Aberson, M., *Temples votifs et butin de guerre dans la Rome republicaine* (Rome 1994).

Adriani, A., "Ritratti dell'Egitto Greco-romano," *Mitteilungen des deutschen archäologischen Instituts, römische Abteilung* 77 (1970) 72–109.

Albentiis, E. de, and M. Furiani, *L'antica Fregellae e il museo di Ceprano: archeologia e tradizioni* (Rome 1997).

Ariel, D., and J. Noveh, "Selected Inscribed Sealings from Kedesh in the Upper Galilee," *Bulletin of the American Schools of Oriental Research* 329 (2003) 61–80.

Ashmole, B., and N. Yalouris, *Olympia: The Sculptures of the Temple of Zeus* (London 1967).

Aurigemma, S., "Recenti scoperte in Formia 1. Statue di personnaggi della prima eta imperiale," *Bollettino d'arte* 7 (1922) 309–35.

Aurigemma, S., and A. de Santis, *Gaeta-Formia-Minturno* (Rome 1955).

Austin, A. E., *The Lex Annalis before Sulla*, Collection Latomus 32 (Brussels 1958).

Balty, J. C., "La statue de bronze de T. Quintus Flamininus ad Apollonis in Circo," *Mélanges de l'École française de Rome, Antiquité* 90 (1978) 669–86.

———, "Armenia," in *Lexicon Iconographicum Mythologicae Classicae* (Zurich 1984) 2:610–13.

Battaglia, G. B., and A. Emiliozzi, *Le ciste prenestine*, vol. 1. Corpus. fasc 1. A, 1–2, numeri I–XX; B, numeri 1–56 (Rome 1990).

Bauer, H., "Basilica Aemilia," in *Kaiser Augustus und die verlorene Republik: eine Ausstellung im Martin-Gropius-Bau, Berlin, 7. Juni–14. August 1988*, ed. W. Dieter-Heilmeyer (Berlin 1988) 200–212.

Beard, M., "The Roman and the Foreign: The Cult of the 'Great Mother' in Imperial Rome," in *Shamanism, History, and the State*, ed. N. Thomas and C. Humphrey (Ann Arbor 1994) 164–90.

Bieber, M., "The Development of Portraiture on Roman Republican Coins," in *Aufstieg und Niedergang der römischen Welt*, vol. 1.4: *Von den Anfängen Roms bis zum Ausgang der Republik*, ed. H. Temporini (Berlin 1973) 871–98.

Bisel, S. C., "Human Bones at Herculaneum," *Rivista di studi pompeiani* 1 (1987) 123–29.

———, "The Skeletons of Herculaneum, Italy," in *Wet Site Archaeology*, ed. B. A. Purdy (Caldwell 1988) 207–18.

———, "The Human Skeletons of Herculaneum," *International Journal of Anthropology* 6.1 (1991) 1–20.

Bloch, H. C., "Cartilius Poplicola," in *Scavi di Ostia III.1. Le necropoli. Parte I: le tombe di eta repubblicana e augustea*, ed. M. F. Squarciapino (Rome 1955) 209–19.

Bodenstedt, F., "Vorstufen der Porträtkunst in der ostgriechischen Münzprägung des 5. und 4. Jh. v. Chr.," in *Proceedings of the 9th International Congress of Numismatics*, Berne, September 1979 (Louvain 1982) 1:95–99.

Böhm, S., *Die Münzen der römischen Republik und ihre Bildquellen* (Mainz 1997).

Bonfante, L., "Nudity as a Costume in Classical Art," *American Journal of Archaeology* 93 (1989) 543–70.

Boni, G., "Foro Romano," *Atti del congresso internazionale scienze storiche* (Rome 1904) 5.4:493–584.

Bonifacio, R., *Ritratti romani da Pompei* (Rome 1997).

Boschung, D., *Die Bildnisse des Augustus* (Berlin 1993).

———, *Gens Augusta: Untersuchungen zu Aufstellung, Wirkung und Bedeutung der Statuengruppen des julisch-claudischen Kaiserhauses* (Mainz 2002).

Bothmer, B. V., *Egyptian Sculpture of the Late Period, 700 B.C. to A.D. 100* (New York 1969).

———, "Egyptian Antecedents of Roman Republican Verism," in *Ritratto ufficiale e ritratto privato*, ed. N. Bonacasa and G. Rizza, Atti della II. Conferenza Internazionale sul Ritratto Romano (Rome 1988) 47–65.

Boussac, M. F., "Sceaux déliens," *Revue archéologique* (1988) 307–40.

Breckenridge, J. D., "Origins of Roman Republican Portraiture: Relations with the Hellenistic World," in *Aufstieg und Niedergang der römischen Welt*, vol. 1.4: *Von den Anfängen Roms bis zum Ausgang der Republik*, ed. H. Temporini (Berlin 1973) 826–54.

Brommer, F., "Zu den römischen Ahnenbildern," *Mitteilungen des deutschen archäologischen Instituts, römische Abteilung* 60–61 (1953–54) 163–71.

Bruneau, P., "'Les israélites de Délos' et la juiverie délienne," *Bulletin de correspondance hellénique* 106 (1982) 465–504.

———, *Guide de Délos* (Paris 1983).

Calciani, F., "Aeneas," in *Lexicon Iconographicum Mythologicae Classicae* (Zurich 1981) 1:381–96.

Calza, R., "La statua ritratto di C. Cartilio Poplicola," in *Scavi di Ostia III.1. Le necropoli. Parte I: le tombe di età repubblicana e augustea*, ed. M. F. Squarciapino (Rome 1955) 221–28.

Coarelli, F., "Il sepolcro degli Scipioni," *Dialoghi di archeologia* 6 (1972) 36–106.

———, "Le pitture della tomba François a Vulci: una proposta di lettura," *Dialoghi di archeologia* 3 (1983) 43–69.

———, *Santuari del Lazio in età repubblicana* (Rome 1987).

———, "Auguratorium," in *Lexicon Topographicum Urbis Romae*, ed. E. M. Steinby (Rome 1993a) 1:143.

———, "Casa Romuli (Cermalus)," in *Lexicon Topographicum Urbis Romae*, ed. E. M. Steinby (Rome 1993b) 1:241–42.

———, "Due fregi da Fregellae. Un documento storico della prima guerra siriaca?," *Ostraka* (1994) 3:93–108.

———, "Lupercal," in *Lexicon Topographicum Urbis Romae*, ed. E. M. Steinby (Rome 1996) 3:198–99.

Crawford, M. H., *Roman Republican Coinage* (London 1974).

———, *Coinage and Money under the Roman Republic: Italy and the Mediterranean Economy* (Berkeley 1985).

Croz, J.-F., *Les portraits sculptés de romains en Grèce et en Italie de Cynoscephales à Actium (197–31 av. J.C.)* (Paris 2002).

Daltrop, G., U. Haussmann, and M. Wegner, *Die Flavier* (Berlin 1966).

D'Ambra, E., *Roman Art* (Cambridge 1998).

Daremberg, C., and E. Saglio, *Dictionnaire des antiquités grecques et romaines d'après les textes et les monuments* (Paris 1877–1919).

Davis, N., and C. Kraay, *The Hellenistic Kingdoms: Portrait Coins and History* (London 1973).

De Maria, S., *Gli archi onorari di Roma e dell'Italia romana* (Rome 1988).

Di Filippo Balestrazzi, E., "Roma," in *Lexicon Iconographicum Mythologicae Classicae* Supplement (Zurich 1997) 1048–68.

Dillon, S., "Studies in the Civic and Intellectual Portraits of the Greeks" (Ph.D. diss., New York University 1994).

Dohrn, T., "Der vatikanische 'Ennius' und der Poeta laureatus," *Mitteilungen des deutschen archäologischen Instituts, römische Abteilung* 69 (1962) 76–95.

———, *Der Arringatore* (Berlin 1966).

Dolci, E., "Marmora Lunensia: Quarrying Technology and Archaeological Use," in *Classical Marble: Geochemistry, Technology, and Trade*, ed. N. Herz and M. Waelkens (Dordrecht 1988) 77–84.

———, "Il marmo nel mondo romano: note sulla produzione e il commercio," in *Il marmo nella civiltà romana. La produzione e il commercio*, ed. E. Dolci (Lucca 1989) 11–37.

Drerup, H., "Totenmaske und Ahnenbild bei den Römern," *Mitteilungen des deutschen archäologischen Instituts, römische Abteilung* 87 (1980) 81–129.

Dupont, F., "Les morts et la mémoire: le masque funèbre," in *La mort, les morts et l'au-delà dans le monde romain*, ed. F. Hinard (Caen 1987) 167–72.

Erim, K., *Aphrodisias, City of Venus Aphrodite* (New York 1986).

Evans, J., *The Art of Persuasion: Political Propaganda from Aeneas to Brutus* (Ann Arbor 1992).

Ferrary, J. L., *Philhéllenisme et impérialisme. Aspects idéologiques de la conquête romaine du monde hellénistique de la seconde guerre de Macédoine à la guerre contre Mithridates* (Rome 1988).

Fittschen, K., "Der Arringatore—ein römischer Bürger?," *Mitteilungen des deutschen archäologischen Instituts, römische Abteilung* 77 (1970) 177–84.

————, "Zur Rekonstruktion griechischer Dichterstatuen. 2. Teil: Die Statuen des Poseidippos und des Ps.-Menander," *Mitteilungen des deutschen archäologischen Instituts, athenische Abteilung* 107 (1992) 229–71.

Flower, H., *Ancestor Masks and Aristocratic Power in Roman Culture* (Oxford 1996).

Fuchs, G., *Architekturdarstellungen auf römischen Münzen der Republik und der frühen Kaiserzeit* (Berlin 1969).

Fuchs, H., "Lusus Troiae" (Inaugural dissertation, Universität zu Köln 1990).

Fuchs, W., "Die Bildgeschichte der Flucht des Aeneas," in *Aufstieg und Niedergang der römischen Welt*, vol. 1.4: *Von den Anfängen Roms bis zum Ausgang der Republik*, ed. H. Temporini (Berlin 1973) 615–32.

Gabba, E., "Considerazioni sulla tradizione letteraria sulle origini della Republica," in *Les origins de la république romaine* (Geneva 1967) 133–74.

Galinsky, K., *Aeneas, Sicily, and Rome* (Princeton 1969).

Gazda, E. K., "Etruscan Influence in the Funerary Reliefs of Late Republican Rome. A Study of Roman Vernacular Portraiture," in *Aufstieg und Niedergang der römischen Welt*, vol. 1.4: *Von den Anfängen Roms bis zum Ausgang der Republik*, ed. H. Temporini (Berlin 1973) 855–70.

Gehrke, H. J., "Römischer mos und griechische Ethik. Überlegungen zum Zusammenhang von Akkulturation und politischer Ordnung im Hellenismus," *Historische Zeitschrift* 258 (1994) 593–622.

Giuliani, C. F., *Forma Italiae* 3.1. Tibur I. (Rome 1970).

————, "Santuario delle tredici are, heroon di Enea," in *Enea nel Lazio. Archeologia e mito* (Rome 1981) 169–77.

Giuliani, L., *Bildnis und Botschaft: hermeneutische Untersuchungen zur Bildniskunst der römischen Republik* (Frankfurt am Main 1986).

Giuliano, A., ed., *Museo Nazionale Romano. Le sculture* 1.1 (Rome 1979).

Graillot, H., *Le culte de Cybele, mère des dieux, à Rome et dans l'Empire Romain* (Paris 1912).

Gross, W. H., *Bildnisse Traians* (Berlin 1940).

Gruen, E., *Studies in Greek Culture and Roman Policy* (Leiden 1990).

————, *Culture and National Identity in Republican Rome* (Ithaca 1992).

Hallett, C. H., "The Roman Heroic Portrait" (Ph.D. diss., University of California, Berkeley 1993).

Hanfmann, G., and C. Vermeule, "A New Trajan," *American Journal of Archaeology* 61 (1957) 223–53.

Harris, W. V., *Rome in Etruria and Umbria* (Oxford 1971).

Hatzfeld, J., "Les italiens residant à Delos mentionés dans les inscriptions de l'ile," *Bulletin de correspondance hellénique* 36 (1912) 5–218.

Herbert, S., and A. Berlin, "Tel Kedesh, 1997–1999," *Israel Exploration Journal* 50 (2000) 118–23.

————, "A New Administrative Center for Persian and Hellenistic Galilee: Preliminary Report of the University of Michigan/University of Minnesota Excavations at Tel Kedesh," *Bulletin of the American Schools of Oriental Research* 329 (2003) 13–59.

Hiesinger, U. W., "Portraiture in the Roman Republic," in *Aufstieg und Niedergang der römischen Welt*, vol. 1.4: *Von den Anfängen Roms bis zum Ausgang der Republik*, ed. H. Temporini (Berlin 1973) 805–25.

Himmelmann, N., *Herrscher und Athlet: die Bronzen vom Quirinal* (Milan 1989).

Hoffman, M., *Sculpture Inside and Out* (New York 1939).

Holliday, P., "Narrative Structures in the François Tomb," in *Narrative and Event in Ancient Art*, ed. P. Holliday (Cambridge 1993) 175–97.

————, *The Origins of Roman Historical Commemoration in the Visual Arts* (Cambridge 2002).

Holloway, R. R., *The Archaeology of Early Rome and Latium* (London 1994).

Hölscher, T., "Die Anfänge römischer Repräsentationskunst," *Mitteilungen des deutschen archäologischen Instituts, römische Abteilung* 85 (1978) 315–57.

Inscriptions de Délos. IG XI, 2 and 4 (Felix Durrbach) (Berlin 1926–27).

Invernizzi, A., "Gli archivi pubblici di Seleucia sul Tigri," in *Archives et sceaux du monde hellénistique/Archivi e sigilli nel mondo ellenistico*, Torino, 13–16 gennaio 1993 (Paris 1996) 131–43.

Jackson, D., "Verism and the Ancestral Portrait," *Greece and Rome* 34 (1987) 32–47.

Johansen, F., *Roman Portraits: Catalogue, Ny Carlsberg Glyptotek, Copenhagen* (Copenhagen 1994).

Junkelmann, M., *Die Reiter Roms, Teil II: Der militärische Einsatz* (Mainz 1991).

Kahil, L., "Phineus I," in *Lexicon Iconographicum Mythologiae Classicae* (Zurich 1994) 7.1:387–91.

———, "Tyndareos," in *Lexicon Iconographicum Mythologiae Classicae* (Zurich 1997) 8.1:145–47.

Kähler, H., *Seethiasos und Census. Die Reliefs aus dem Palazzo Santa Croce in Rom* (Berlin 1966).

Kauffmann-Samaras, A., "Phoinix II," in *Lexicon Iconographicum Mythologiae Classicae* (Zurich 1997) 8.1:984–87.

Kent, J. P. C., *Roman Coins* (London 1978).

Kilmer, M., *The Shoulder Bust in Sicily and South-Central Italy: A Catalogue and Materials for Dating* (Gothenburg 1977).

Kleiner, D., *Roman Group Portraiture: The Funerary Reliefs of the Late Republic and Early Empire* (New York 1977).

———, *Roman Sculpture* (New Haven 1992).

Kleiner, D., and F. Kleiner, "A Heroic Funerary Relief on the Via Appia," *Archäologischer Anzeiger* (1975) 250–65.

Kleiner, F. S., *The Arch of Nero in Rome: A Study of the Roman Honorary Arch before and under Nero* (Rome 1985).

Kraay, C., *Greek Coins* (London 1966).

Krauss, T., *Das römische Weltreich* (Berlin 1967).

Kreeb, M., *Untersuchungen zur figürlichen Ausstattung delischer Privathäuser* (Chicago 1988).

Kron, U., "Aigeus," in *Lexicon Iconographicum Mythologiae Classicae* (Zurich 1981) 1.1:359–67.

Künzl, E., *Der römische Triumph: Siegesfeiern im antiken Rom* (Munich 1988a).

———, "Romanisierung am Rhein—Germanische Fürstengräber als Dokument des römischen Einflusses nach der gescheiterten Expansionspolitik," in *Kaiser Augustus und die verlorene Republik: eine Ausstellung im Martin-Gropius-Bau, Berlin, 7. Juni–14. August 1988* (Berlin 1988b) 546–605.

Kuttner, A., *Dynasty and Empire in the Age of Augustus: The Case of the Boscoreale Cups* (Berkeley 1995a).

———, "Republican Rome Looks at Pergamon," *Harvard Studies in Classical Philology* 97 (1995b) 157–78.

———, "Hellenistic Images of Spectacle, from Alexander to Augustus," in *The Art of Ancient Spectacle*, ed. B. Bergmann and C. Kondoleon (Washington 1999) 96–123.

Lahusen, G., *Untersuchungen zur Ehrenstatue in Rom: literarische und epigraphische Zeugnisse* (Rome 1983).

———, *Die Bildnismünzen der römischen Republik* (Munich 1989).

Lancellotti, M. G., *Attis between Myth and History: King, Priest, and God* (Leiden 2002).

Lange, K., *Egypt: Architecture, Sculpture, Painting in Three Thousand Years*, 4th ed. (London 1968).

Lapalus, E., *L'agora des italiens, Exploration archéologique de Délos* 19 (Paris 1939).

Levi, A. C., *Barbarians on Roman Imperial Coins and Sculpture, American Numismatic Society Numismatic Notes and Monographs* 123 (New York 1952).

Lewis, N., *Samothrace 1. The Ancient Literary Sources* (New York 1958).

Lygouri-Tolia, E., "Nestor," in *Lexicon Iconographicum Mythologiae Classicae* (Zurich 1994) 7.1:1060–65.

Maderna, C., *Iuppiter Diomedes und Merkur als Vorbilder für römische Bildnisstatuen: Untersuchungen zum römischen statuarischen Idealporträt* (Heidelberg 1988).

Maggiani, A., "Ritrattistica tardo-ellenistica fra Etruria e Roma," *Prospettiva* 66 (1972) 36–47.

———, "Contributo alla cronologia delle urne volterrane. I coperchi," *Memorie. Atti della Accademia nazionale dei Lincei, Classe di scienza morali, storiche e filologiche* 19 (1976) 3–44.

Marcadé, J., *Au musée de Délos, étude sur la sculpture hellénistique en ronde bosse découverte dans l'île* (Paris 1969).

———, "Sur la sculpture hellénistique délienne," in *Akten des 13. internationalen Kongresses für klassische Archäologie Berlin 1988* (Mainz 1990) 145–50.

———, "De cape et d'épée. À propos de l'effigie délienne de C. Ofellius Ferus," *Ktema* 25 (2000) 47–54.

Martin, G. T., *The Memphite Tomb of Horemheb, Commander-in-chief of Tutankhamun. 1. The Reliefs, Inscriptions, and Commentary* (London 1989).

Martin, H. G., *Römische Tempelkultbilder: eine archäologische Untersuchung zur späten Republik* (Rome 1987).

Massner, A.-K., *Bildnisangleichung: Untersuchungen zur Entstehungs- und Wirkungsgeschichte der Augustusporträts (43 v. Chr.–68 n. Chr.)* (Berlin 1982).

Mattern, T., "Die Bauphasen der frühkaiserzeitlichen Basilica Aemilia," *Boreas* 20 (1997) 33–41.

McDonnell, M., "Un ballo in maschera: Processions, Portraits, and Emotions," *Journal of Roman Archaeology* 12 (1999) 541–52.

McDowell, R. H., *Stamped and Inscribed Objects from Seleucia on the Tigris* (Ann Arbor 1935).

Mehl, E., "Troiaspiel," in *Paulys Real-Encylopädie der klassischen Altertumswissenschaft* (1956) Supplement 8:888–905.

Meyer, H., "The Terme Ruler. An Understudied Masterpiece and the School of Lysippus," *Bullettino della Commissione archeologica Communale di Roma* 97 (1996) 125–48.

Michalowski, K., *Les portraits hellénistiques et romains, Exploration archéologique de Délos* 13 (Paris 1932).

Millar, F., "The Phoenician Cities: A Case-Study of Hellenisation," *Proceedings of the Cambridge Philological Society* 209 (1983) 55–71.

Miller, M., "Priam, King of Troy," in *The Ages of Homer*, ed. J. Carter and S. Morris (Austin 1995) 449–65.

Mørkholm, O., *Early Hellenistic Coinage: From the Accession of Alexander to the Peace of Apamea (336–188 B.C.)* (Cambridge 1991).

Mørkholm, O., and J. Zahle, "The Coinage of the Lycian Dynasts Kheriga, Kherêi and Erbbina. A Numismatic and Archaeological Study," *Acta archaeologica* 47 (1976) 47–90.

Motz, T., "The Roman Free-Standing Portrait Bust: Origins, Context, and Early History" (Ph.D. diss., University of Michigan 1993).

Nedergaard, E., "Arcus Augusti (a. 19 a.C.)," in *Lexicon Topographicum Urbis Romae*, ed. E. M. Steinby (Rome 1993) 1:81–85.

———, "La collocazione originaria dei Fasti Capitolini e gli archi di Augusto nel Foro Romano," *Bullettino della Commissione archeologica Communale di Roma* 96 (1994–95) 33–70.

Neils, J., "Priam," in *Lexicon Iconographicum Mythologiae Classicae* (Zurich 1994) 7.1:507–22.

Neudecker, R., *Die Skulpturenausstattung römischer Villen in Italien* (Mainz 1988).

Nielsen, M., "*. . . stemmate quod Tusco ramum millesime ducis . . .*": Family Tombs and Genealogical Memory among the Etruscans," in *Images of Ancestors*, ed. J. M. Højte (Aarhus 2002) 89–126.

Noelke, P., "Aeneasdarstellungen in der römischen Plastik der Rheinzone," *Germania* 54 (1976) 409–39.

Ogle, M. B., "Laurel in Ancient Religion and Folk-lore," *American Journal of Philology* 31 (1910) 287–311.

Pani, M., "Troia resurgens: Mito troiano e ideologia del principato," *Annali della Facoltà di lettere e filosofia, Università degli Studi, Bari* 18 (1975) 65–85.

Pantos, P. A., *Ta sphragismata tes Aitolikes Kallipoleos* (Athens 1985).

———, "Porträtsiegel in Kallipolis. Einige methodologische Bemerkungen," in *Archives et sceaux du monde hellénistique/Archivi e sigilli nel mondo ellenistico*, Torino, 13–16 gennaio 1993 (Paris 1996) 185–94.

Pape, M., *Griechische Kunstwerke aus Kriegsbeute und ihre öffentliche Aufstellung in Rom* (Hamburg 1975).

Paribeni, E., "Ascanius," in *Lexicon Iconographicum Mythologiae Classicae* (Zurich 1984) 2.1:60–863.

Pauly, A., and Wissowa, G., *Real-Encyclopädie der klassischen Altertumswissenschaft*, vol. 17 (Stuttgart 1937).

Payne, M., "Aretas Eneken: Honors to Romans and Italians in Greece from 260 to 27 B.C." (Ph.D. diss., Michigan State University 1984).

Pensabene, P., "Magna Mater Aedes," in *Lexicon Topographicum Urbis Romae*, ed. E. M. Steinby (Rome 1996) 3:206–8.

———, "Scalae Caci," in *Lexicon Topographicum Urbis Romae*, ed. E. M. Steinby (Rome 1999) 4:239–40.

Pflug, H., *Römische Porträtstelen in Oberitalien: Untersuchungen zur Chronologie, Typologie und Ikonographie* (Mainz 1989).

Pfuhl, E., and H. Möbius, *Die ostgriechischen Grabreliefs* (Mainz 1977–79).

Picard, G. C., *Les trophées romains. Contribution à l'histoire de la religion et de l'art triomphal de Rome* (Paris 1957).

Pollini, J., "Man or God. Divine Assimilation and Imitation in the Late Republic and Early Principate," in *Between Republic and Empire: Interpretations of Augustus and His Principate*, ed. K. Raaflaub and M. Toher (Berkeley 1990) 334–63.

Pollitt, J. J., *Art in the Hellenistic Age* (Cambridge 1986).

Poulsen, V., *Les portraits romains,* vol. 1: *Republique et dynastie julienne*, Ny Carlsberg Glyptotek (Copenhagen 1962).

Price, S., *Rituals and Power: The Roman Imperial Cult in Asia Minor* (Cambridge 1984).

Queyrel, F., "Portraits princiers hellénistiques. Chronique bibliographique," *Revue archéologique* (1990) 97–172.

———, "Ofellius Ferus," *Bulletin de correspondance hellénique* 115 (1991) 389–464.

Queyrel, F., A. Hermary, and P. Jockey, *Sculptures déliennes, École française d'Athènes. Sites et monuments* 17 (Paris 1996).

Rauh, N. K., *The Sacred Bonds of Commerce: Religion, Economy, and Trade Society at Hellenistic Roman Delos, 166–87 B.C.* (Amsterdam 1993).

Richter, G. M. A., *The Portraits of the Greeks*, vol. 2: *The Fourth and Third Centuries* (London 1965).

Ridgway, B., *Hellenistic Sculpture II. The Styles of ca. 200–100 B.C.* (Madison 2000).

———, *Hellenistic Sculpture III. The Styles of ca. 100–31 B.C.* (Madison 2002).

Roller, L., "The Ideology of the Eunuch Priest," in *Gender and the Body in the Ancient Mediterranean*, ed. M. Wyke (Oxford 1998) 118–35.

———, *In Search of God the Mother: The Cult of Anatolian Cybele* (Berkeley 1999).

Romeo, I., *Ingenuus Leo. L'imagine di Agrippa* (Rome 1998).

Rose, C. B., *Dynastic Commemoration and Imperial Portraiture in the Julio-Claudian Period* (Cambridge 1997).

———, "The 1997 Post-Bronze Age Excavations at Troia," *Studia Troica* 8 (1998) 71–113.

———, "Bilingual Trojan Iconography," in *Mauerschau. Festschrift für Manfred Korfmann* (Tübingen 2002) 329–50.

Rosenstein, N., "Imperatores victi. The Case of C. Hostilius Mancinus," *Classical Antiquity* 5 (1986) 230–52.

Rosenthal, E., *The Illuminations of the Vergilius Romanus (Cod. Vat. Lat. 3867). A Stylistic and Iconographical Analysis* (Zurich 1972).

Rostovtzeff, M., "Seleucid Babylonia. Bullae and Seals of Clay with Greek Inscriptions," *Yale Classical Studies* 3 (1932) 1–114.

Saladino, V., *Der Sarkophag des Lucius Cornelius Scipio Barbatus* (Würzburg 1970).

Sanders, D., ed., *Nemrud Dagi: The Hierothesion of Antiochus I of Commagene: Results of the American Excavations Directed by Theresa B. Goell* (Winona Lake, Ind. 1995).

Schefold, K., "Chrysippus I," in *Lexicon Iconographicum Mythologiae Classicae* (1986) 3.1:286–89.

Schneider, K., "Lusus Troiae," in *Paulys Real-Encylopädie der klassischen Altertumswissenschaft*, ed. A. F. Pauly and G. Wissowa (Stuttgart 1927) 13:2059–67.

Schneider, R., *Bunte Barbaren: Orientalenstatuen aus farbigem Marmor in der römischen Repräsentationskunst* (Worms 1986).

Scrinari, V. S. M., *Museo archeologico di Aquileia. Catalogo delle sculture romane* (Rome 1972).

Sehlmeyer, M., *Stadtrömische Ehrenstatuen der republikanischen Zeit. Historizität und Kontext von Symbolen nobilitären Standesbewusstseins* (Stuttgart 1999).

Seiterle, G., "Die Urform der Phrygischen Mütze," *Antike Welt* 16.3 (1985) 2–13.

Sevinç, N., "A New Sarcophagus of Polyxena from the Salvage Excavations at Gümüşçay," *Studia Troica* 6 (1996) 251–64.

Sevinç, N., R. Körpe, M. Tombul, C. B. Rose, D. Strahan, H. Kiesewetter, and J. Wallrodt, "A New Painted Graeco-Persian Sarcophagus from Çan," *Studia Troica* 11 (2001) 383–420.

Silvestrini, F., *Sepulcrum Marci Artori Gemini: la tomba detta dei Platorini nel Museo nazionale romano* (Rome 1987).

———, "Sepulcrum: M. Artorius Geminus," in *Lexicon Topographicum Urbis Romae*, ed. E. M. Steinby (Rome 1999) 4:275–76.

Smith, R. R. R., "Greeks, Foreigners, and Roman Republican Portraits," *Journal of Roman Studies* 71 (1981) 24–38.

———, *Hellenistic Royal Portraits* (Oxford 1988).

———, "Myth and Allegory in the Sebasteion," in *Aphrodisias Papers. Recent Work on Architecture and Sculpture*, ed. C. Roueché and K. Erim, *Journal of Roman Archaeology* Supplement 1 (Ann Arbor 1990).

———, *Hellenistic Sculpture: A Handbook* (London 1991).

Smith, W. S., *The Art and Architecture of Ancient Egypt* (New York 1981).

Spinazzola, V., *Pompei alla luce degli scavi nuovi di Via dell'Abbondanza* (Rome 1953).

Stemmer, K., *Untersuchungen zur Typologie, Chronologie und Ikonographie der Panzerstatuen* (Berlin 1978).

Stevenson, T., "The 'Problem' with Nude Honorific Statuary and Portraits in Late Republican and Augustan Rome," *Greece and Rome* 45 (1998) 45–69.

Stewart, A. F., *Attika: Studies in Athenian Sculpture of the Hellenistic Age* (London 1979).

———, "Hellenistic Art and the Coming of Rome," in *Hellenistic Art in the Walters Art Gallery*, ed. E. Reeder (Baltimore 1988) 35–44.

Strommenger, E., *5,000 Years of the Art of Mesopotamia* (New York 1964).

Sutherland, C. H. V., and R. A. G. Carson, *Roman Imperial Coinage I*, 2nd ed. (London 1984).

Tagliamonte, G., "Palatium, Palatinus Mons (fino alla prima età repubblicana)," in *Lexicon Topographicum Urbis Romae*, ed. E. M. Steinby (Rome 1999) 4:14–22.

Tanner, J., "Portraits, Power, and Patronage in the Late Roman Republic," *Journal of Roman Studies* 90 (2000) 18–50.

Torelli, M., *Lavinio e Roma: riti iniziatici e matrimonio tra archeologia e storia* (Rome 1984).

Tuchelt, K., *Frühe Denkmäler Roms in Kleinasien. Beiträge zur archäologischen Überlieferung aus der Zeit der Republik und des Augustus* (Tübingen 1979).

Vermaseren, M., *Cybele and Attis: The Myth and the Cult* (London 1977).

Vermaseren, M., and M. DeBoer, "Attis," in *Lexicon Iconographicum Mythologiae Classicae* (1986) 3:22–44.

Vessberg, O., *Studien zur Kunstgeschichte der römischen Republik* (Lund 1941).

Vollenweider, M.-L., *Die Porträtgemmen der römischen Republik* (Mainz 1972–74).

Wachter, R., *Altlateinische Inschriften. Sprachliche und epigraphische Untersuchungen zu den Dokumenten bis etwa 150 v. Chr.* (Bern 1987).

Walker, S., and P. Higgs, *Cleopatra, Regina d'Egitto* (Milan 2000).

Wallenfels, R., "Private Seals and Sealing Practices at Hellenistic Uruk," in *Archives et sceaux du monde hellénistique. Archivi e sigilli nel mondo ellenistico*, Torino, 13–16 gennaio 1993 (Paris 1996) 113–29.

Weinstock, S., *Divus Iulius* (Oxford 1971).

Weitzmann, K., ed., *Age of Spirituality: Late Antique and Early Christian Art, Third to Seventh Century* (New York 1979).

Williams, R. D., ed., *Virgil. Aeneis. Liber 5* (Oxford 1960).

Wiseman, T., "Legendary Genealogies in Late Republican Rome," *Greece and Rome* 21 (1974) 153–64.

———, "Cybele, Virgil, and Augustus," in *Poetry and Politics in the Age of Augustus*, ed. T. Woodman and D. West (Cambridge 1984) 117–28.

Wissemann, M., *Die Parther in der augusteischen Dichtung* (Frankfurt am Main 1982).

Wrede, H., Consecratio in formam deorum. *Vergöttlichte Privatpersonen in der römischen Kaiserzeit* (Mainz 1981).

Wright, D. H., *Codicological Notes on the Vergilius Romanus (Vat. Lat. 3867)* (Rome 1992).

Zadoks-Josephus Jitta, A. N., *Ancestral Portraiture in Rome and the Art of the Last of the Republic* (Amsterdam 1932).

Zahle, J., "Persian Satraps and Lycian Dynasts. The Evidence of the Diadems," in *Proceedings of the 9th International Congress of Numismatics*, Berne, September 1979 (Louvain 1982) 1:101–12.

Zanker, P., "Grabreliefs römischer Freigelassener," *Jahrbuch des deutschen archäologischen Instituts* 90 (1975) 267–315.

———, "Zur Rezeption des hellenistischen Individualporträts in Rom und in den italischen Städten," in *Hellenismus in Mittelitalien.* Kolloquium in Göttingen vom 5. bis 9. Juni 1974, ed. P. Zanker, *Abhandlungen der Akademie der Wissenschaften zu Göttingen* 97 (Göttingen 1976) 2:581–619.

———, "Zur Bildrepräsentation führender Männer in mittelitalischen und campanischen Städten zur Zeit der späten Republik und der julisch-claudischen Kaiser," in *Les bourgeoisies municipales italiennes aux 2e et 1er siècles av. J.C.*, Centre Jean Bérard, Institut français de Naples, 7–10 décembre 1981 (Paris 1983) 251–66.

———, *The Power of Images in the Age of Augustus*, trans. A. Shapiro (Ann Arbor 1988).

———, "Individuum und Typus. Zur Bedeutung des realistischen Individualporträts der späten Republik," *Archäologischer Anzeiger* (1995a) 473–81.

———, *The Mask of Socrates: The Image of the Intellectual in Antiquity*, trans. A. Shapiro (Berkeley 1995b).

Zevi, F., "Sepulcrum (Corneliorum) Scipinonum," in *Lexicon Topographicum Urbis Romae*, ed. E. M. Steinby (Rome 1999) 4:281–85.

Zimmerman, K., "Teirisias," in *Lexion Iconographicum Mythologiae Classicae* (1997) 8.1:1188–191.

5 ◆ ELUDING *ROMANITAS*: HEROES AND ANTIHEROES IN SILIUS ITALICUS'S ROMAN HISTORY

Efrossini Spentzou

In the late first century A.D. the Roman poet Silius Italicus produced a new epic version of the Second Punic War. This war represents one of the finest moments of resilient, old *Romanitas*, and Livy describes it as the critical period in the history of the Roman republic: *bellum maxime omnium memorabile* ("the most memorable war in history").[1] The prolonged crisis elevated the period to one of national pride, in which Romans reached the pinnacle of their heroism and persistence. But if we were to expect another eulogistic and nostalgic foray into Roman worthiness and the core values of the past from this late first-century senator, we would be disappointed.

Silius is a striking case of staid bookishness and erudition. Pliny the Younger's *Epistle* 3.7, an obituary to Silius, is a testimony to a life spent in literary salons and erudite disputes and exchanges within the literate elite circles (3.7.4). It also reveals Silius's lasting and profound appreciation of past masters, above all Vergil (3.7.8). As the empire around him grew larger and the emperor and actual power more distant, this belletristic approach to life suited a disempowered senator of the Dominianic era such as Silius. Pliny, who had reflected long and hard on the dilemmas of service in the castrated senate, also argued that literary life and, importantly, literary fame were a suitable alternative lifestyle in response to compulsory political inertia.[2] Erudite antagonism and debate were the new power games in an environment struggling to come to terms with impotence in the political arena. And next to this, Romans were increasingly perceiving themselves as (only a) part of a whole. The Flavian regeneration followed years of generalized turmoil, social, political, personal, but by the later years of the first century A.D., Rome was managing a plethora of peoples, cultures, traditions, and religions.[3] Would the original models of a small but vibrant nation's success and pride, as exemplified by Livy's account of the Punic Wars, be in the position to respond adequately to the experiences of the Roman citizens in this imperial mosaic? Silius's story provides us with an engaging counterstory, emphasizing at the same time that, rather than simply being a disengaged philological pastime, erudite antagonism can have a sharp political point.

An Epic in Search of a Hero

Considered against this sociopolitical chiatus, Silius's underdeveloped characters and flawed battle scenes have steadily gained attention and favor amongst the critics. What in old histories of Latin

I would like to thank the Leverhulme Trust for their generous funding of a project on Imperial Identities, of which this chapter is a part.

[1] Livy, *Ab urbe condita* 21.1.1. This is obviously a topos of historiography, but Livy backs his assertion with an elaborate catalogue of evidence in the rest of 21.1.

[2] See also Tac. *Dial.* and cf. Alston's chapter in this volume; Pomeroy (2000, 150–52), who also makes a strong case for the social integration of literary trends in Silius's time; and for an earlier approach to Silius's erudition, Pomeroy 1989.

[3] Edwards and Woolf (2003) explore the image of Rome within this multicultural imperial mosaic from a wide range of angles.

literature was considered contemptuously "an epic without a hero"[4] has become an object of sophisticated intertextual studies that have rightly interpreted the epic's loose ends as self-conscious
attempts at differentiation and, indeed, subversion of the (primarily Vergilian) epic code.[5] The appreciation of the poem's complexity has been slow; in fact, it is still an ongoing affair. Building on
the staunch patriotism of the Roman war effort, firmly established by Livy, criticism of the *Punica*
was bound to notice that the epic works with the *Aeneid* as a model, as it narrates the perilous
journey of Scipio Africanus toward final Roman victory. One would expect from such a poem a
paean of praise for Roman values and denigration of the moral properties of the barbarian, whatever
his martial qualities might be. Indeed, the poem offers ample servings of stereotypical barbarian
(Carthaginian) excess, including the particularly striking encounter of the Carthaginians with the
Capuans in book 11. Following the Roman defeat at Cannae, Hannibal spends the winter in Capua.
First, we are offered a long and detailed account of Capua's already notorious arrogance, luxury,
and decadence (11.28–54). Then we watch Hannibal, and eventually his whole army, as they sink
without resistance into the effeminate pleasures of music and art offered by the affluent but indolent
city (11.259–368; 11.37–482). The effects of a winter spent in unmanly sloth are only too apparent
as soon as the Carthaginians leave Capua in book 12, and the degenerate army fails in its first attacks
on nearby cities such as Neapolis, Cumae, and Puteoli (12.1–103).

Hannibal's interval in Capua inevitably recalls for us another well-known interval, namely
Aeneas's (in)famous sojourn in Carthage on his way to Italy. Following Hannibal's slothful stay in
Capua, Vergil's careful readers would easily bring to mind Aeneas clad in ornate, oriental, quasi-
effeminate robes during his interaction with Mercury, who rouses him from his idleness in *Aeneid*
4.259–76.[6] Significantly, also, both leaders receive new armor in the course of their epic journeys,
armor that features in some strikingly similar episodes. Yet Aeneas's armor was a gift of honor,
ordered from a god (Vulcan) by a goddess (Venus), while Hannibal was given his shield by the
Gallicians (2.395–456), whose generosity was aroused by fear that they may be the next target of
Carthaginian imperialism after the flattening of Saguntum.[7] It is noticeable that Aeneas's shield
is devoted to the future of Rome and therefore takes us beyond individual fears or hopes, while
Hannibal's armor focuses on the Carthaginians' past history and especially his own *gens*, depicting
glorious as well as ignominious moments in the lives of Hannibal's ancestors.[8] Through striking
juxtapositions such as the above, it becomes apparent that Hannibal may be the dominant figure
in the epic, but he is an antihero who shines through his inadequacies and lacks the endorsement
of Fate, trapped in long-gone but still simmering passions, a Turnus and a Mezentius far more than
an Aeneas.[9] Seen from this angle, Silius's story still points to a reassuringly eulogistic Roman past
and, as we know, the barbarians do get their comeuppance at the end of the poem.

---

[4] See, e.g., Owen 1909, 254; Pichon 1924, 588; Rostagni 1964, 42–54, amongst many others.

[5] Feeney (1991, 302–12) and Hardie (1993, passim) are two of the most sustained explorations of this kind.

[6] See also Pomeroy 2000, 159 with n. 43.

[7] For a detailed intertextual reading of the *Punica* in the light of the *Aeneid*, see Pomeroy (2000, esp. 153–60), who sees a systematic reversal and dispersion of the Aeneadic motifs throughout Silius's epic.

[8] These differences recall the differences between Aeneas's

and Turnus's less noticed shield in *Aeneid* 7.783–92. Cf. Gale 1997, esp. 189: "Turnus' shield refers to his noble ancestry and to his own character and fate. Aeneas' shield, by contrast, does not refer directly to the hero himself, but represents the future exploits of his distant descendants." Indeed the shields in the *Aeneid* (just like the shield in the *Punica*) represent the differences in ethos that drive the two heroes: personal glory versus impersonal duty; private desires versus public *pietas*. The similarity in motifs prompts us yet again to read the two epics "in parallel."

[9] See here von Albrecht 1964, 172–77; also Matier 1989, passim for a thorough examination of Hannibal's antiheroism in the light of Vergilian heroics.

However, Silius's patriotism is unnervingly temperate. First and foremost, the moral impact of Scipio (Aeneas's most convincing successor in this epic) on the story is delayed by an astonishing twelve books: he does not feature significantly until book 13. In the meantime, other Roman heroes—notable amongst them Regulus (book 6), Fabius Cunctator (book 7), Paulus (books 9 and 10), and Marcellus (books 12 and 14)—come to the limelight and establish their immortality through brief moments of excellence. Are these also representatives of true *Romanitas*? Attached to the epic vision of the single "great man" established by previous epics and firmly under the spell of the *Aeneid*, critics have been hesitant to embrace the values of a heroism based on *multos viros*.[10] Such reluctance has its roots in the perception that the many heroes destabilize polarities fundamental for the Roman epic. The rotating display of heroes and heroic virtue weakens the Roman ideal, which opens itself up to interpretation and gets inevitably diluted in a series of occasionally contradictory behaviors. On the one hand, *Romanitas* seems to be strengthened as it becomes a corporate value; yet it then gets undermined by the dubious behavior of the corpus, or members of this corpus, that is meant to sustain this value.

This precariousness is eloquently confirmed toward the end of book 1, as the assembly of the Roman senators is summoned by the consul to decree Rome's reaction to the siege of Saguntum. The gathering is depicted with the deepest respect:

> *Consilium vocat augustum castaque beatos*
> *paupertate patres ac nomina parta triumphis*
> *consul et aequantem superos virtute senatum.*
> *facta animosa viros et recti sacra cupido*
> *attollunt; hirtaeque togae neglectaque mensa*
> *dexteraque a curvis capulo non segnis aratris;*
> *exiguo faciles et opum non indiga corda,*
> *ad parvos curru remeabant saepe penates.*
>
> (1.609–16)

The consul summoned the worshipful assembly—the Fathers rich in unstained poverty, with names acquired by conquests—a senate rivaling the gods in virtue. Brave deeds and a sacred passion for justice exalted these men; their dress was rough and their meals simple, and the hands they brought from the crooked plough were not slow with the sword hilt; content with little, uncovetous of riches, they often went back to humble homes from the triumphal car.[11]

As soon as the credentials of the Roman senators have been asserted, the narrator proceeds with an elaborate description of the scenes portrayed on the doors and walls of the temple where the senate convened: proud memories of victorious battles and glorious spoils accumulated in the course of Rome's expansion (617–29). And yet, once the thorny issue of Saguntum is opened to debate, opinions differ. Cornelius Lentulus and Fabius Maximus see Rome's position and future in contrasting ways and hold opposite views. Nagging questions surface: who of the two is the worthy keeper of all that Rome represents? And who is most capable of leading Rome's cause to a successful resolution? The doubts expressed and the inconclusive nature of the debate contrast with the *Aeneid*'s often painful but always driving certainties. In the world of the *Aeneid*, Roman destiny may often elude the struggling mortals' comprehension, but it has always been set in stone.

[10] And they are challenged in this conviction by Feeney (1986). For recent discussions of this challenging aspect of Roman epic, see, e.g., Helzle 1996, 231–300; Wilson 1993; Hardie 1993, passim and esp. 8–10, 24–25, 38–39, 69–71, 96–97.

[11] Translations of the *Punica* are by J. D. Duff (1934), of the *Aeneid* by C. Day Lewis, occasionally adapted. Translations of Ovid's *Heroides* are mine.

In Silius, however, it seems to be a series of negotiable values, contingent on the right decision being made in debate.[12]

Roman self-representation reaches a crisis just after the Roman humiliation at the battle of Cannae with which book 10 ends. As book 11 begins, Rome is still reeling from the crushing defeat. Amidst the general panic and disillusionment, several Italian peoples decide to defect and join the Carthaginian side. Silius exposes the faithlessness of the demoralized tribes (11.1–27); fiercest of all, the Samnites are only too eager to reignite the old feuds, followed by the fickle Bruttians, the treacherous Apulians, the vain Hirpini, and so forth. A first-century A.D. poet is able to construct a list of Italian barbarians in marked contrast to the Vergilian vision of an Italian Roman Empire carefully promoted in the *Aeneid*.[13]

Alerted by these contradictions, recent criticism has indeed focused on the inadequacies and flaws in Silius's portrait of Rome. So, for example, the fate of Saguntum has been inspected as a parallel to that of Troy, whose encounter with the imminence of annihilation is a paradigmatic epic topos.[14] Similar attention has been paid to the multiple connections between Saguntum and Rome itself, not least among which is the emphatically stressed Italian blood of the Saguntines, such as Daunus. Daunus comes from Apulia but has insufficient moral and physical strength to overpower Hannibal (1.440–51), while Murrus, who is of mixed Rutulian, Spanish, and even Greek blood (1.476–79), reflecting the union of Italian, Spanish, and Greek civilization, and thus can be seen as representative of first-century A.D. *Romanitas*, is also slaughtered by Hannibal. Moreover, the Saguntines' dutiful and loyal conduct throughout the episode is a stark reminder of the legendary qualities of old *Romanitas*, which the Romans of Hannibal's time seem to have abandoned, as they dither and calculate their own interests with destructive result for their Spanish allies. In fact, Fabius's irritated and rushed declaration of war against the Carthaginians, declared peremptorily and delivered in person to the assembled Carthaginian senators (2.383–90), bears an uncanny resemblance to Hannibal's own reckless and belligerent behavior, thus rendering the Saguntines' persistent *Romanitas* yet more dramatically isolated.[15] On the other hand, decadent Capua is not just another Carthage; as critics have noticed, it is also a dark reflection of Rome itself, of the disintegration that has gripped the city, a pale shadow of its former morality and faith.[16]

This is a topsy-turvy world indeed, with the boundaries between good Romans and bad barbarians gradually eroded, often meshed with each other, and continuously redefined. In Philip Hardie's landmark study of post-Vergilian epic, this confusion, excess, and disorder are scrutinized as powerful expressions of a faltering world. Hardie has several case studies, but his exploration of Heaven and Hell merging into each other during the siege and fall of Saguntum deserves special attention.[17] As the Saguntines plunge toward their doom, buckling under the persistence of the Carthaginian siege, Juno sends along the Fury Tisiphone to urge them to their destruction; in turn, Hercules, pitying the city he once founded, asks for the presence and help of Fides. The effects of

---

[12] For an interesting counterargument to this concern, see Pomeroy (2000, 160–62), who sees in the multiplicity of individuals who uphold the Roman cause at different stages in the story a confirmation of the collective ethos of self-effacing and civic-minded senators that contributed to the prosperity of the Roman republic in old times. To Pomeroy's view, though, contrast Tipping (1999), who sees the *Punica* as exposing the transgressive, self-promoting potential behind the individuals of the late republic whose deeds are celebrated in Silius's epic.

[13] For an extensive study of Vergil's allegiance to Italy, see

Ando 2002.

[14] See, e.g., Hardie 1993, 81–82.

[15] For an extended exploration of these parallels, see Dominik 2003, passim and esp. 476–85.

[16] I am grateful to Bob Cowan for showing me unpublished work on the topic of Rome's relation to Capua.

[17] Hardie 1993, 81–83.

the two deities are disconcertingly similar (2.516–18). The hard-earned certainties of the Aeneadic world are now destroyed. The restorative power of Fides can no longer be relied upon, and we brace ourselves to face (together with the protagonists of the epic) a world where good can be as fierce and forceful as evil.

Garbled models of problematic Romans and good barbarians add to this thematized confusion.[18] Whatever their other similarities located throughout the text, Scipio and Hannibal are sent down to history together. In Scipio's greatest hour of success, it is the humiliated Hannibal that asserts poetic immortality. As he looks down at the massacre in the battlefield of Zama from a nearby hill and the size of the disaster gradually dawns upon him, he prepares to flee into exile, addressing this final warning to Rome and his principal foe:

> *decedesque prius regnis quam nomina gentes*
> *aut facta Hannibalis sileant. nec deinde relinquo*
> *securam te, Roma, mei; patriaeque superstes*
> *ad spes armorum vivam tibi. Nam modo pugna*
> *praecellis, resident hostes: mihi satque superque,*
> *ut me Dardaniae matres atque Itala tellus,*
> *dum vivam, expectent nec pacem pectore norint.*
>
> (17.609–15)

You shall step down from your throne before the world forgets the name or achievements of Hannibal. Nor do I leave you, Rome, free from my care. I shall survive my country and live in the hope of a war against you. You win just this battle, but your foes are lying low. Enough, and more than enough for me, if Roman mothers and the people of Italy dread my coming while I live, and never know peace of mind.

Indeed, the sinister shadow of a trespassing loser accompanies the victor of Zama on his return to Rome, literally as well as metaphorically, as the picture of the fleeing Hannibal is included in the processional images of Scipio's triumph. As we are told (17.643–44), it is Hannibal's picture that attracts the greatest attention by the attending crowd; one might say that Hannibal becomes a perverse sort of *triumphator*—it is *his* procession, so to speak. As Hannibal blends with Scipio in this procession, we get a grim warning that the potential for transgression lurks at the very moment of triumph of an exemplary Roman. The astute reader cannot fail to look back to the future to figures such as Lucan's Caesar, first and foremost amidst the various transgressors implicated in the numerous civil wars yet to come in Roman history.[19]

Aeneas as the Other

Building on the deliberately insecure images of *Romanitas* explored above, the rest of my study will continue to probe Silius's response to all major landmarks of Roman history and famous *exempla* of Roman leadership against which he worked.[20] The opening of the poem appears to establish familiar

[18] As explored in Tipping (1999; see n. 12 above), who deals extensively with the transgressive potential of the successful but flawed republican individual and the crippling effect of this tendency to transgression on the republic.

[19] Cf. here Tipping (1999, 274–78) with interesting remarks on the shadow cast on the exceptional Roman leader triggered by this procession.

[20] For a recent recapitulation of these models, see Dominik 2003, 474–75.

polarities of virtue and vice as they were articulated and established in Vergil's Roman national epic. Faithlessness, ferocity, and cunning are Hannibal's character traits when we are first introduced to the Carthaginian leader:

> *Ingenio motus avidus fideique sinister*
> *is fuit, exsuperans astu, sed devius aequi.*
> *armato nullus divum pudor; improba virtus*
> *et pacis despectus honos; penitusque medullis*
> *sanguinis humani flagrat sitis.*
>
> (1.56–9)

> By nature he was eager for action and faithless to his plighted word, a past master in cunning but a strayer from justice. Once armed, he had no respect for Heaven; he was brave for evil and despised the glory of peace; and a thirst for human blood burned in his inmost heart.

In the next two hundred or so lines, we witness Hannibal as a boy receiving the single most important lesson of his education: that the Romans are a hated nation, enemies of the past, awaiting punishment for the grief and destruction they caused to the Carthaginians during the First Punic War. As the years pass, Hannibal's father, Hamilcar, is killed, as is his savage son-in-law, Hasdrubal, so that young Hannibal becomes the much loved and famed leader of the Carthaginians. His first strategic decision as a commander is to break the conditions of the treaty imposed on the Carthaginians at the end of the First Punic War and attack the Saguntines, Rome's Spanish allies.[21]

As we have already seen, the heroism and endurance of the Saguntines have received much comment. Silius recalls several different heroic models during this episode, but the mapping of these by the critics is, so far, far from complete. During a fierce battle (described in the middle of the first book), young and handsome Murrus chases Hannibal with determination. But his chase is frustrated and the confrontation delayed. In Silius's own words: "Hannibal was busy somewhere else"—*parte ex alia* (1.426). This image recalls Aeneas's frustrated pursuit of Turnus in the later books of the *Aeneid*. Even though Hannibal is not preserved by a sister (as Turnus was), he still eludes Murrus rushing to another spot of the battle.

As we read on, the intertextual web thickens. When the two men finally approach each other, watching his brave enemy charging against him, Hannibal seizes a huge rock and hurls it at his enemy:

> *Haec inter cernens subeuntem comminus hostem*
> *praeruptumque loci fidum sibi, corripit ingens*
> *aggere convulso saxum et nitentis in ora*
> *devolvit, pronoque silex ruit incitus ictu.*
>
> (1.487–91)

> Meanwhile, seeing his foe come close, and that he could trust the overhanging ground where he stood, Hannibal rent the rampart and seized a huge rock and hurled it down upon the head of the climber; and the stone fell swiftly with downward force.

The above description recalls for us a strikingly similar description from the end of *Aeneid* 12, the description of Turnus's uncontrollable frenzy when he hurled a huge stone against Aeneas, as the two heroes met each other at last in a final confrontation:

---

[21] Dominik (2003, 477 n. 14), however, finds the violation story line historically dubious and refers to a long series of modern historians who see no technical violation in Hannibal's attack against Saguntum.

> *nec plura effatus saxum circumspicit ingens*
> *saxum antiquum ingens, campo quid forte iacebat,*
> *limes agro positus litem ut discerneret arvis.*
> *vix illum lecti bis sex cervice subirent,*
> *qualia nunc hominum producit corpora tellus;*
> *ille manu raptum trepida torquebat in hostem*
> *altior insurgens et cursu concitus heros.*
>
> (*Aeneid* 12.896–902)

Without a word more he looked round and his eyes lit on a huge stone. A huge old stone which for years had been lying there on the plain as a boundary mark between fields, to prevent disputes about ownership. Hardly could twelve strong men, of such physique as the earth produces nowadays, pick up and carry it on their shoulders. Well, Turnus pounced on it, lifted it, and taking a run to give it more impetus, hurled his stone from his full height at Aeneas.

Turnus missed his target. On the other hand, Hannibal in the *Punica* meets his own with devastating precision. Badly shaken, Murrus manages to pluck up courage to carry on fighting, but Hannibal's menacing figure overcomes him; his eyes grow dark, and his heart limps faint with the realization of his impending death: *. . . velut incita clausum / agmina Poenorum cingant et cuncta paventem / castra premant, lato Murrus caligat in hoste* ("It seemed as if the whole Carthaginian army were moving to close round him, and as if all the host were attacking him. The eyes of Murrus grew dark in front of his mighty foe" [1.497–99]). A single instant brings the reversal of roles, and Murrus's faint heart brings to mind Turnus's crippling fear and fatal hesitation in *Aeneid* 12.916–17, which enabled Aeneas to pierce him with his spear: *. . . Rutulos aspectat et urbem / cunctaturque metu letumque instare tremescit* ("He gazed at the city, the Rutuli; faltered with fear; trembled at the weapon menacing him"). For a moment, Murrus takes the place of Turnus, and, for that moment, Hannibal also becomes Aeneas. The sudden reversal of roles breaks the narrative and, more importantly, the ideological momentum of the battle.

The same palimpsestic duality follows Hannibal as he presses on with the siege of Saguntum. The early stages of book 2 are dominated by battle. Worthy warriors from both sides meet heroic but untimely deaths in furious encounters, recollecting the war at Latium that dominates the middle part of the *Aeneid*. Prominent amongst them, Asbyte, a maiden warrior who loved the woodland and the wild beasts, reminds us of another maiden warrior, Camilla, the Volscian ally of Turnus in the *Aeneid*. Despite her bravery, Asbyte is killed less than two hundred lines after she is first introduced into the epic, and her slaughter is described in the grotesque detail typical of silver Latin epic. Enraged by her death, Hannibal makes his presence felt in the battlefield with rattling arms and a dazzling shield:

> *namque aderat toto ore ferens iramque minasque*
> *Hannibal et caesam Asbyten fixique tropaeum*
> *infandum capitis furiata mente dolebat.*
> *ac simul aerati radiavit luminis umbo,*
> *et concussa procul membris velocibus arma*
> *letiferum intonuere, fugam perculsa repente*
> *ad muros trepido convertunt agmina cursu.*
>
> (2.208–14)

For Hannibal came up, with wrath and menace expressed in every feature; with frenzied heart he raged at the slaughter of Asbyte, and at the horrid trophy of her head borne aloft. And, as soon as his shield of glittering brass shone out, and the armour on his swift limbs, rattling afar, thundered forth doom, the enemy were suddenly stricken with fear and fled in haste towards the town.

The terror of Hannibal's sudden emergence once again recalls Aeneas: a similar terrifying light had enveloped the Trojan leader when he made his entrance into the battle on his return from Pallanteum, in book 10, a light that restored courage to his men and demoralized Turnus's army.

> *Iamque in conspectu Teucros habet et sua castra*
> *stans celsa in puppi, clipeum cum deinde sinistra*
> *extulit ardentem. clamorem ad sidera tollunt*
> *Dardanidae e muris, spes addita suscitat iras,*
> *tela manu iaciunt.*
>
> (*Aeneid* 10.260–64)

> And now, as he stood high up in the stern-sheets, Aeneas held his Trojans and their encampment in view: so he lifted his shield with his left hand and made it flash. The Dardans upon the walls raised a great shout; their fighting spirit revived at this new hope, their fire was redoubled.

Again, the two stories run on parallel planes, but, as with the episode of Murrus and Hannibal, the two stories briefly cross over. If Asbyte is the counterpart of Camilla, then Hannibal's fury at her loss really corresponds to what should be Turnus's fury at the loss of a close ally. In Silius's reading of Vergil, is Aeneas blending into Turnus at the moment of his return to battle? Is Aeneas not to be differentiated from his rash and "uncivilized" enemy?

The Other as Aeneas

This far from exhausts the similarities between Hannibal and Aeneas.[22] Hannibal has several benign interludes that also reflect Aeneas. After Hannibal's conquest of Saguntum and a subsequent massacre, the Carthaginian leader embarks on a tour of the regional tribes, early in book 3. Hannibal's transformation is a thing to marvel at. Having just flattened the faithful Saguntines, he sends for omens to the oracle of Juppiter Ammon (3.1–13) and worships at Hercules' altars, where he also spares a minute to admire the representations of the latter's twelve labors displayed at the doors of the temple (14–60). But he really has very little time for this all: his thoughts and heart are with his wife and child, and he rushes to meet them (61–62).

Youthfulness, declarations of tender love, and mingling of tears as the two lovers spend their last night together render this relationship distinctly elegiac.[23] And yet Imilce was "attached to Hannibal with an affection full of memories" (*imbuerat coniunx memorique tenebat amore* [3.65]) and "continent, married love," as she reminds him in 3.113 (*castum haud superat labor ullus amorem*: "no hardship can overcome continent love"), thus painting the image of an enduring and modest bond that relates more closely to a respectable Roman wife than to an elegiac *puella*. In many respects, Imilce, the aristocratic wife, "whose pedigree could be traced to an illustrious stock" (*atque ex sacrata repetebat stirpe parentes* [3.106]), reminds us of Dido. However, Imilce promises with

[22] Alston and Spentzou (forthcoming) incorporates an extensive discussion of the cross-fertilized representations of Aeneas and Hannibal in Silius.

[23] If we look ahead in the text, the couple's painful parting at the seashore in the end of this all-too-brief encounter (3.127–57) will also remind us of the heartrending partings of many of Ovid's *Heroides*, in this elegiac retelling of the Greek myths.

forbearance not to delay the course of fate: *sin solo aspicimur sexu, fixumque relinqui, cedo equidem nec fata moror* ("But if you judge me by sex alone, and are determined to leave me, I yield indeed and will not delay the course of destiny" [3.114–15]). On the other hand, Dido not only stops the flow of events in the Aeneid;[24] in Ovid's *Heroides*, she explicitly asks Aeneas and the master narrative for a little delay in true elegiac fashion:

> *et socii requiem poscunt, laniataque classis*
> *postulat exiguas semirefecta moras*
> *pro meritis et siqua tibi debebimus ultra,*
> *pro spe coniugii tempora parva peto.*
> (*Heroides* 7.175–78)

Your companions, too, require some rest, and your battered fleet, semi-repaired, demands a little delay. In return for my services, and if, besides that, I owe you anything, I ask for a little time, in place of my hope of marrying you.[25]

Moreover, Imilce's compliance not only jars with Dido's temper but also reminds us of Creusa, Aeneas's soft-spoken Trojan wife. Of course, in comparison with Hannibal, Aeneas has been notoriously reticent regarding his well-mannered Trojan wife. Ultimately, Hannibal has to leave Imilce behind, as Aeneas did, but Hannibal does not desert Imilce and lovingly makes provisions for the safety of his wife, a lover/warrior trapped at the intersection of epic and elegy.[26] At the same time, Hannibal is in no doubt as to what role he reserves for his son:

> *spes o Carthaginis altae,*
> *nate, nec Aeneadum levior metus, amplior, oro,*
> *sis patrio decore et factis tibi nomina condas,*
> *quis superes bellator avum; iamque aegra timoris*
> *Roma tuos numerat lacrimandos matribus annos*
> (3.69–73)

O my son, hope of high Carthage, and dread, no less, of the Aeneadae,[27] may you, I pray, be more glorious than your father and make a name for yourself by works of war which shall surpass your grandsire's. Rome, sick with fear, already reckons up your years—years that shall make mothers weep.

Hannibal's message is unambiguous: the little boy is to become strong in order to fight the enemy of his country and surpass his father in glorious deeds. As fathers' ambitions for their sons go, Hannibal and Aeneas agree on their respective sons' national mission.

As soon as his elegiac interlude with Imilce draws to a forced end, Hannibal plunges into the fever of war preparations in order to forget his grief. Ceaseless toil overcomes him, and sleep

[24] Suffice to remember Jupiter's rebuff to Aeneas via Mercury in 4.270–71: *ipse haec ferre iubet celeris mandata per auras: quid struis; aut qua spe Libycis teris otia terris?* ("The king of gods gave this message to carry express through the air: what do you aim at or hope for, idling and fiddling here in Libya?").

[25] Cf. Spentzou 2003, 174–78.

[26] In this aspect of his character, Hannibal bears an unmistakable resemblance to Pompey (another torn and misunder- stood silver epic hero from Lucan's *Civil War*) and his relationship to Cornelia; both Hannibal and Pompey ultimately "look back" to the archetypal and damned conjugal bond, that of Hector and Andromache in the *Iliad*.

[27] The specific choice of adjective, over and above several others traditionally used for the Romans, prompts me to think that Silius deliberately brings the *Aeneid* to the forefront here, thereby encouraging us to set Hannibal against Aeneas in this post-Vergilian epic.

brings rest to his warlike spirit. Mercury is once again recruited by the Father of Gods to stir the sleeping leader out of his apathy (3.162–82), upbraiding him with the same sharpness that he had previously deployed when sent to Libya for the second time in *Aeneid* 4 to wake Aeneas and drive him away from Dido for good (4.554–70). Disturbed by this dream, Hannibal mulls over Mercury's message and, like Aeneas, realizes the significance of the omen. Like the Trojan hero, he stirs his sleeping camp, and preparations for war commence overnight, just as Aeneas, startled by his dream, precipitated the flight of his fleet while Dido and the Carthaginians were still sleeping.

A Hero in Search of an Epic

Let us now attempt a last combined look at these interlaced stories. Hannibal is presented as a figure with several features in common with Aeneas, in an epic whose fundamental drive is meant to be the long-lasting division between the Carthaginians and Romans, a division meant to be not only unbridgeable but also constitutive of Roman identity. This problem is not new and has already been noticed by the critics. We cannot simply dismiss the scores of problematic Romans in the epic to focus on restorative moments, like Scipio Africanus's choice of Virtue over Pleasure in book 15, and henceforth proceed to read Silius's poem as a critique of his contemporary society and a manifesto for glorious and lost republican *Romanitas*. In the opening and programmatic books of the epic, the shameful behavior of the Romans contrasts starkly with the brave self-sacrifice of their Saguntine allies. In fact, the Saguntines increasingly resemble the Romans of a past and idealized era.[28] Naturally, then, the most recent wave of Silian scholarship elaborates perceptively on the way in which Silius's (contemporary?) Romans become increasingly more like the "Other," transgressing traditional Roman values and also the Roman epic code.

Philip Hardie has claimed that Aeneas's loneliness

> is the loneliness of the representative and original ancestor of race; in him we meet the first clearly defined example of the "synecdochic hero," the individual who stands for the totality of his people present and future, part for whole. The line of such heroes leads eventually to Adam and Christ of "Paradise Lost". . . . There is a supra-individual quality in Aeneas and Turnus.[29]

In the long line of heroes, neatly defined by Hardie, individuals jostle and clash, teasing and challenging the notional divide that separates good from evil and their countless metaphors and metonymies, on which all epics and the very idea of a Roman state itself are founded.

In contrast to Hardie's "synecdochic heroes," Silius's heroes confuse these representative qualities. That Hannibal comes so close to Aeneas is not merely a symptom of the decline of the Roman state. The continuity of "synecdochic heroes" was indeed constitutive for the Roman epic, but, by Silius's time, this continuity was also severely compromised. Lucan's Pompey, a sort of hero for want of a better one, spends most of the epic repeatedly failing to communicate to his own troops a rhetoric of historic continuity. Caesar, in the same epic, conspicuously alienates himself from Troy, despite his propaganda and pseudo-respectful visit to the site in book 9.[30] In Statius's

[28] According to Dominik 2003, 493–96.

[29] Hardie 1993, 4.

[30] For the alienation and isolation of the epic hero in Lucan and generally the post-Vergilian epic, see Alston and Spentzou forthcoming.

Thebaid, pietas—this solid, Vergilian, supra-individual quality—is replaced by impious weapons and a bold and shameless virtue, glory in battle at all costs, a distinctly individualistic quality that blocks out any concerns for the world around.

Lucan's and Statius's response in the *Civil War* and in the *Thebaid*, respectively, is unmitigated despair at the anxiety brought about by a general collapse of social unity. Silius's epic emerges from the background of this alienating culture of excess. Profane virtue—*improba virtus*—was also one of Hannibal's main character traits in *Punica* 1, as we have seen above. That is, Silius, too, worries deeply and talks about this generalized social dysfunction (not least in his unblinking portrait of the dithering Romans who abandon the heroic Saguntines in the first two books of the *Punic War*); but he does not retreat to despair. Instead of simply mourning the collapse of republican ideologies, he also seems capable of contemplating new and untried identifications for his heroes.

Silius's rewriting of Aeneas in his epic exposes the latent strains in Aeneas's supra-individual personality (to borrow once again Hardie's phrase), strains that were mostly confined within disturbing and unsettling similes and metaphors in the *Aeneid*.[31] Collective signifiers in the *Aeneid*, such as Jupiter's prophesy in book 1 and, first and foremost, Anchises' Roman prophesy in book 6 when he meets Aeneas again in the Underworld, signifiers that determined the supra-individual quality of the epic and with which Aeneas struggled to comply throughout the epic, are replaced by an overpowering sense of uncertainty and lack of commitment in Silius's poem.[32] Let us briefly recall a couple of prominent examples. The first has to do with Hercules' allegiances throughout the epic. In book 1, as Murrus braces himself to face the charging Hannibal, he prays to Hercules, the founder of his motherland, for help (505–7). Catching him in this moment of supplication, Hannibal hastens to suggest with a certain arrogance that Hercules will recognize a warrior worthy of himself in his face and will come to his assistance instead, in the name of their common hatred for the Trojans (508–14). Indeed, as Hannibal forces the overwhelmed soldiers to cross the highest peaks of Alps in book 3, he invokes Hercules' support as a fellow spirit also motivated by a compelling drive for transgression (500–515). Yet, in book 2, Hercules weeps with compassion for Saguntum's plight, pitying the city he founded, and appeals to Fides for help (475–92).[33]

The second example comes from the heart of the Carthaginian senate. When summoned to respond to Roman demands for cooperation in book 2, Hanno and Gaspar, both members of the Carthaginian senate, paint two directly opposing versions of Roman and Carthaginian history in the court of Carthage (270–390). Both cases just discussed suggest that there is a sense in this epic that traditions are malleable and that history could be different. The overall pace of the narrative itself prompts such an understanding: whereas the *Aeneid* presents a Roman universe moving irrevocably toward triumph, despite failures, worries, and frequent confusion, the *Punica* cultivates a much more sustained and complex web of insecurities with a hero and a state heading toward disaster.

---

[31] Expertly explored by Lyne 1987.

[32] Sibyl's vision of the harsh destiny awaiting the Roman state in 13.850–67 makes for a particularly bleak end to Scipio's visit to the Underworld to meet his fellow statesmen and thus forms a stark contrast to her Vergilian counterpart and to Aeneas's visit to the Underworld, which concludes with Anchises' vision of the glories of future Rome. And even Jupiter's Roman prophecy (3.570–629) is much less reassuring for Cytherea this time than in the previous encounter of the two in *Aeneid* 1: Silius's Jupiter addresses Cytherea's concerns by confirming that he plans to test the Romans'

endurance with war because they have forgotten their glorious ancient history (572–84). Rome will soon be glorious, but for its calamities rather than its triumphs (584–85). And even when Jupiter looks further into the future and predicts better days (592–629), his emphasis is distinctly on the glory and success of the future emperors, a prediction that notably omits any accolades for the glory of Rome itself.

[33] Cf. also here other similar expressions of Hercules' loyalty to the Romans later on in the *Punica*, such as 15.78–79 and 17.649–50.

Conclusion

Silius's individuals personify at the same time republican and imperial and, it might be said, post-imperial debates on self and other, subject and ethnicity. Hannibal comes both before and after Augustan Aeneas, before and after Neronian Caesar. For all of Silius's comfortable life of erudition, his "exemplary" Roman exists in the aftermath of recent traumas that are still present in the collective as well as personal memory. Silius presents us with an individual distanced, but also freed, from the social economy within which the previous exemplary Romans—Aeneas first and foremost—carved their identities. Coming in the wake of prolonged war and an age of terror, Silius's heroic models are tempted to experience the "young peace" of their times by molding an existence in the interstices of subsequent failed regimes and social orders that plagued Rome for centuries. In so doing, they can be seen to assimilate within their subjectivities a blend of identifications not previously available or even allowed to the elite individuals of earlier epics.

Loyalty to, and assimilation within, a communal destiny, with varying degrees of success and angst, has been a vital motif in the making of the Roman epic and the Roman hero. Yet, arguably, when individuals manage to conform successfully to an ideological system, a certain loss of self-realization and self-determination comes as an inevitable part of this integration. Moreover, it is the longing for the ever absent (and ever present) "excess" in one's self, which is not integrated into expressed social identities, that seems to bring the encounter with somebody's truest but ever fleeting existence.[34] In Silius's epic, especially its early stages, isolated individuals are pushed to the extreme boundaries of their expressed identities by the chaos around them. Such circumstances make them face the mismatch between their inner and social selves. In Silius's poem, there is no reassuring sense of belonging. Silius's heroes falter, and original models are no longer satisfactory. Late first-century A.D. Rome was a thriving and bewildering empire with "Others" that form a disturbing, festering but also challenging and liberating part of its hegemony. As forms of social and political order are opened to revision in Silius's Rome, there are opportunities for new identifications, such as Silius's Hannibal. Silius's Hannibal is close to Aeneas not (only) because Silius worries that Romans have come too close to the barbarians but also because he wonders how close the barbarians could actually be to the Romans. Hannibal is always the archetypal "Other" but an "Other" with whose undecided status the Romans of the first century A.D. might empathize. Silius's uncertain role within a multicultural empire and ideological order that is tempted, as well as forced, to look increasingly outward could find echoes in a Hannibal both external to and now incorporated within Roman tradition and ideology. Hannibal is problematic, but so was Silius's Aeneas. At the same time, Hannibal is capable of actions of high moral value as much as, if not more than, Aeneas. Through these disturbing and never entirely satisfactory associations, new possibilities for criticism and self-awareness seem to emerge that at once reflect and voice the concerns and ambitions of the increasingly uneasy and self-conscious individuals of the late first-century A.D. Roman elite.

---

[34] The compelling fascination with this "excess" and with moments of disrupted self-representation is a feature of recent psychoanalytical approaches, predominantly those of Jacques Lacan and Slavoj Žižek. A good introduction to their work on the "lacking subject" is Easthope 2001, 120–56. Stavrakakis (1999, passim and esp. 13–39) explores deftly the significance of this Lacanian "impossibility" of identity, and Žižek (1999, 70–124) elaborates on the "ticklish subject," the individual that is never quite content with his or her identifications.

Works Cited

Albrecht, M. von, *Silius Italicus: Freiheit und Gebundenheit römischer Epik* (Amsterdam 1964).

Alston, R., and E. Spentzou, *Reflecting Romanitas: Discourses of Subjectivity in an Imperial Age* (forthcoming).

Ando, C., "Vergil's Italy: Ethnography and Politics in First-century Rome," in *Clio and the Poets. Augustan Poetry and the Traditions of Ancient Historiography*, ed. D. S. Levene and D. P. Nelis (Leiden and Boston 2002) 123–42.

Dominik, W. J., "Hannibal at the Gates: Programmatising Rome and *Romanitas* in Silius Italicus' *Punica* 1 and 2," in *Flavian Rome: Culture, Text, Image*, ed. A. J. Boyle and W. J. Dominik (Leiden and Boston 2003) 469–97.

Duff, J. D., *Silius Italicus: Punica* (Cambridge, Mass. and London 1934).

Easthope, A., and C. Belsey, eds., *Privileging Difference* (New York 2001).

Edwards, C., and G. Woolf, eds., *Rome the Cosmopolis* (Cambridge 2003).

Feeney, D., "Epic Hero and Epic Fable," *Comparative Literature* 38 (1986) 137–58.

———, *The Gods in Epic: Poets and Critics of the Classical Tradition* (Oxford 1991).

Gale, M., "The Shield of Turnus: *Aeneid* 7.783–92," *Greece & Rome* 44 (1997) 176–96.

Hardie, P. R., *The Epic Successors of Virgil* (Cambridge 1993).

Helzle, M., *Der Stil ist der Mensch. Redner und Reden im römischen Epos* (Stuttgart 1996).

Lyne, R. O. A. M., *Further Voices in Vergil's* Aeneid (Oxford 1987).

Matier, K., "Hannibal: The Real Hero of the *Punica*," *L'Antiquité classique* 32 (1989) 3–17.

Owen, S. G., "On Silius Italicus," *Classical Quarterly* 3 (1909) 254–57.

Pichon, R., *Histoire de la littérature latine*, 12th ed. (Paris 1924).

Pomeroy, A. J., "Silius Italicus as *Doctus Poeta*," *Ramus* 18 (1989) 119–39.

———, "Silius' Rome: The Re-writing of Vergil's Vision," *Ramus* 29 (2000) 149–68.

Rostagni, A., *Storia della letteratura latina* (Turin 1964).

Spentzou, E., *Readers and Writers in Ovid's* Heroides: *Transgressions of Gender and Genre* (Oxford 2003).

Stavrakakis, Y., *Lacan and the Political* (London and New York 1999).

Tipping, B., "Exemplary Roman Heroism in Silius' *Punica*" (D.Phil. diss., Oxford University 1999).

Wilson, M., "Flavian Variant: History. Silius' *Punica*," in *Roman Epic*, ed. A. J. Boyle (London 1993) 218–36.

Žižek, S., *The Ticklish Subject. The Absent Centre of Political Ontology* (London 1999).

6 ◆ HISTORY AND MEMORY IN THE CONSTRUCTION OF IDENTITY IN EARLY SECOND-CENTURY ROME

Richard Alston

For those influenced by philosophers of the Enlightenment, it is tempting to construct a reductionist self that is distinct from identity. The self is the inner core, the *ego* brought into being by the *cogitans*. Identity, however, is rather more complex. One's identity is not divine but an achieved state that is negotiated within our social world.[1] Nevertheless, it is difficult to maintain that separation between self and identity. One's identity might not be a perfect replication of one's self. There is normally some mismatch, some part of the self that does not fit with identity, which should probably be regarded as a function of the interaction of the personal (the self) and the social world. In turn, the self can be affected by identity, shaped and reshaped by experience in the social world.[2] This is of major interest for any study of identity, for although ancient historians and archaeologists have commonly discussed identity in terms of broad social and political categorizations, such as national or ethnic groups, identity lies close to the heart of the individual and stems from that individual.[3]

We can establish identity within a particular sociological framework in relation to a series of markers.[4] We can "place" individuals sociologically, and our individual ability to manipulate social situations depends very much on that capacity to locate the individual. Our identities can be established from how we dress, talk, and walk. Our gender, race, culture, and wealth can be read from

This chapter results from a project on Imperial Identities in an Age of Monarchy funded by the Leverhulme Trust, to whom I give thanks. I also thank Philip Smith and Efi Spentzou, who read and commented on an earlier draft.

[1] Giddens 1991, 3: "the self, like the broader institutional contexts in which it exists, has to be reflexively made."

[2] Giddens 1991, 2: "The self is not a passive entity, determined by external influences: in forging their self identities, no matter how local their specific contexts of action, individuals contribute to and directly promote social influences that are global in their consequences and implications." This is partly why the topic remains so controversial. Ranger (1999) describes giving a lecture in Zambia, in which he argued that tribal identity was invented in the colonial age, and hearing the dean of arts ask a colleague, "Who were we then?" Deconstructing ethnicity problematizes identity.

[3] A kind of functionalism has dominated interpretations. For instance, the hugely influential study of Smith (1981) has shown that the rise of ethnic nationalism in the nineteenth century correlates closely to the rise of bourgeois society. Smith argues that the new bourgeois identified sources of

power in the burgeoning civil-service, educational, and professional systems and that some within these groups, not fluent in the dominant culture or somehow isolated and therefore at a disadvantage, sought to establish new "national" systems. In this model, ethnic and national groups are merely preexisting and convenient tools in conspiracies on the part of the bourgeoisie (cf. Smith 1986, 21–46). The model leaves open the issue of why particular groups of the bourgeoisie broke away from the hegemonic culture and, most importantly, why groups other than the bourgeoisie display ethnic loyalty. Millions have died over the last two centuries at least in part to defend ethnic identity, but few would benefit from an increased ability to become a civil servant. They may have been duped or have adopted the hegemonic ideology of the bourgeoisie for reasons of their own, but it seems much more likely that ethnicity had become part of their identity, which reflected or established their selfhood.

[4] Parsons 1975, 57: "Ethnicity in some cultures . . . has little to do with the home nation, rather with a series of symbols that the ethnic groups identify with home." Patterson (1975) discusses the Jamaican Chinese, whose key signifiers of ethnic identity have shifted from somatic to cultural markers.

subtle signifiers.[5] Nevertheless, sociological location is only one element in the creation of identity. We also find ourselves in a cosmological frame, which may have many aspects but commonly sets the individual in the context of parents, grandparents, and generations past. Such relationships may be regarded as largely fictive since what we know of our pasts normally relates to the stories that are told about it and that we can choose to believe or ignore.[6] Our identities are not, however, roles to be picked up or laid aside as it suits us but are formed of complex and overlapping narratives that conjoin to other narratives spun by different individuals and agencies.[7] For a new group identity to emerge, there would have to be a new narrative, or the revitalization of an old narrative, that would give the new group its identity. It is, therefore, unsurprising that the emergence of the bourgeoisie went alongside the greater availability of education and the dissemination of narratives of ethnicity to feed the politics of identity.[8]

Identities rest in the realm of narratives. Yet narratives are notoriously and obviously disputable, and the range of options as to constructible narratives and thus identities is, I think, theoretically infinite. Nevertheless, narratives of self, the claim to status inherent in those narratives, and the power/status that results, are all subject to social influence.[9] If someone wanted to assert power as a Roman elite male, he would have to develop an identity narrative that was accepted as establishing a valid claim to that identity. Every stage in the process of development and reception of the narrative is subject to dispute and social negotiation.[10] It follows inevitably that in no society or social situation will the individual be able to attain completely the desired identity, and the process of assertion and establishing of identity will always be potentially traumatic at social and psychological levels.[11] Individuals and society will always be in conflict. Nevertheless, in periods of political and social change, when the mismatching of power/status, status claim, and identity narrative becomes more prominent, the potential for social trauma (i.e., society or the political order being blamed) or psychological trauma (the claimant becoming racked by doubt) is greatly increased.[12]

---

[5] Sociological location is established by reading of the habitus (Bourdieu 1990, 52–65). Bourdieu explains the habitus in a number of ways but writes, "the practices of the members of the same group or, in a differentiated society, the same class, are always more and better harmonized than the agents know or wish, because, as Leibniz . . . says 'following only (his) own laws', each 'nonetheless agrees with the other.' The habitus is precisely this immanent law, *lex insita*, inscribed in bodies by identical histories, which is the precondition not only for the co-ordination of practices but also for the practices of co-ordination" (59). It follows that individuals will be able to recognize differences by the noncoordination of practices and ascribe social location to those who follow different practices.

[6] Gellner (1983) emphasizes the role of industrialization in undermining existing social and identity relations and establishing a social and political purpose for developing ethnic identity to unite socially and politically diverse individuals. Industrialization often coincided with significant social concern about social schisms and an idealization of a rural, unified past.

[7] For the use of complex narratives to create identities, see Hobsbawm and Ranger 1983.

[8] See Anderson (1991, 37–46) on the relation between nationalism and the rise of mass media.

[9] See Bourdieu (1990, 58–60) on the relationship between an individual habitus and that of a social group.

[10] Penrose and Jackson (1993, 207) write, "the struggle for identity is a struggle for power and always takes place within a hegemonic system of social relations. Hegemony sets the context both for the reinforcement of privilege and resistance to it. . . . This power includes the capacity to set the parameters for the negotiation within any given system."

[11] Stavrakakis (1999, 29–39) argues from Lacan that individuals (subjects) are marked by their lack: an inability to identify completely with an identity: "the fullness of identity that the subject is seeking is impossible both in the imaginary and in the symbolic level. The subject is doomed to symbolise in order to constitute her- or himself as such, but this symbolisation cannot capture the totality and singularity of the real body. . . . Symbolisation, that is to say the pursuit of identity itself, introduces lack and makes identity ultimately impossible" (Stavrakakis 1999, 29).

[12] See, e.g., the individual and general traumas in a Javanese village caused by progressive Islamicization and related social changes as described in Geertz (1975, 142–69).

The traditional identity narrative of the Roman elite drew on the traditions of the Roman republic. The first emperors had emphasized the power of this tradition and associated their rule with republican forms of governance.[13] By the end of the first century, however, senators had enough collective experience of imperial power to know that whatever their narratives (and the imperial period saw alternative claims to status that potentially usurped senatorial power), their status and power were vulnerable to imperial pressure. In such circumstances, the elite could choose to use the rhetoric of their narrative to enforce change in society (creating a political clash), withdraw the claim to social status (effectively withdrawing from political life), or alter the narrative and thereby modify the particular status claims being made. Almost inevitably, given the nature of our sources, it is those who take the first option who make the most noise: Helvidius Priscus lambasting the emperor before the senate, Thrasea Paetus fleeing the senate rather than tainting his person with praise of Nero's matricide, Petronius writing a last account of Nero's sexual perversions instead of a note begging forgiveness, and the biographies of Helvidius Priscus and Thrasea Paetus by Arulenus Rusticus and Herennius Senecio all displayed republican freedoms of speech.[14]

Tacitus, however, was engaged in the third available option, crucially shifting the narratives of imperial elite identity by examining and establishing the relationship of that elite to the Roman past.[15] I argue that this is a fundamental theme of Tacitean historiography and that Tacitus makes explicit that purpose both in the structure of his works and, most clearly, in various comments on his historiographical purpose. Furthermore, the Tacitean mission was controversial, as can be seen both from the ideological context that Tacitus constructs for his historiographical excursions and in comparison with the very different construction of the past that we see in the writings of the younger Pliny.

Tacitus and the Past

Reconstructing Tacitus's political ideology is deeply contentious, partly because Tacitus was not prone to open theorizing. Furthermore, Tacitus is notoriously ironic, and that irony is used both to undermine the characters portrayed but also to force the reader to stand outside the text, to take a critical and analytical position on what he or she is being told and continuously question the obvious meanings of words and events.[16] Luce argues that Tacitus is a particularist and not a theorist and hence what we think of as the overarching ideologies of a work, which we expect modern historians to at least acknowledge, are obscured.[17] Henderson points out that the annalistic form had the potential endlessly to defer closure, the *telos* so important for giving the historical work its meaning, and that modern readings of Livy especially tend to strive for a meaning in the work as a whole that simply cannot be convincingly reconstructed.[18] Literary meaning, such as it is, is fragmented in the

[13] See, most recently, the discussion in Rich and Williams 1999.

[14] Dio Cass. 66.12; Tac. *Dial.* 2; Suet. *Vesp.* 15; Tac. *Ann.* 14.12, 16.18–21; Tac. *Agr.* 2.

[15] The close connection of the argument here to that of Spentzou (this volume) should be noted.

[16] O'Gorman (2000, 17) writes that "it could be argued that irony in particular is mobilised in relation not only to the principate but also to its critics, suggesting that they examine closely the nature of the principate they criticise *and* the nature of their criticism. The ironical statement therefore not only embodies a particular sceptical attitude on the part of the writer, but also compels the reader to take her political stance in relation to the past."

[17] Luce 1986.

[18] Henderson 1989.

annalistic episodes. Henderson offers a radical and different way of reading works without closure, and it must be possible that the conventions of reading Roman histories were radically different from our own historiological practice. Yet, although we do not have closures in Tacitus, we do have openings, and starting is at least as important as finishing.

Tacitus's openings, both of the *Histories* and *Annales*, raise problems. In both cases, the start date seems problematic. The *Histories* opens not with the death of Nero but with the first January of Galba's principate. Tacitus appears to have chosen that point in order to maintain a rigid annalistic structure. The realities of political power, however, would make the accession of an emperor or the end of a dynasty the key political opening. Clarke argues that the annalistic structure is maintained for the *Annales* (and thus for the *Histories*) because Tacitus wishes to recall the conventions of republican historiography.[19] His purpose is to demonstrate that even in the imperial period, it is possible for history to fulfill its traditional vocation (which is providing moral *exempla*), though the stage for this proper Roman behavior was the provinces and not Rome itself. For Clarke, Tacitus is a Francis Fukuyama for his day, declaring conventional history to be over but then finding a new stage in which to set history.[20] Ginsburg also suggests that the annalistic form was used to evoke a past age, and its very incongruity was a demonstration of change.[21] The annalistic form becomes a deliberate archaism, though it did provide Tacitus with a ready-made structure for his narrative that has considerable benefits, given the overlapping complexities of his stories. This may be enough to explain the starting of the *Histories*, but the *Annales*, commencing in A.D. 14, poses more problems. Tacitus suggests in 3.24 that he would return to the theme of the Augustan principate in a later work, should he live that long. The presentation of this intention (in the context of a discussion of Augustus's purge of the elder Julia and her circle) does not suggest that Tacitus was having "second thoughts" about the start date of the *Annales*.[22] If this had been the case, it is quite difficult to believe, given the practice of partial prepublication of literary work, that Tacitus was unable to revisit the structure of his work. Starting in A.D. 14 suggests that he viewed that date as being of greater significance than others, and such an opening provides at least some clue to the purpose of the work.[23] Tacitus himself presents the decision as a literary one, the Augustan age having had historians of merit, but this is also difficult to take at face value.[24] After all, as we shall see below, one of the claims repeated in the historiographic introductions to the *Annales* and *Histories,* and in *Agricola* 1, is that the times produced the historians. A change in historiographic practice between Augustus and Tiberius was thus historically significant.

The brief treatment of the Augustan period in the *Annales* differs very considerably from Dio's much later treatment of the same events. For Dio, the principate comes into being with the settlements following the battle of Actium, and the long constitutional speeches attributed to Maecenas and Agrippa are ways of marking that transition. From the ending of the senatorial debates of 27 B.C., the imperial system is in place. Tacitus, by contrast, places very little emphasis on Actium or

---

[19] Clarke 2002.

[20] Fukuyama 1992.

[21] Ginsburg (1981, 100) suggests that the breaches from annalistic discipline were meant to reflect on the disciplined regularity of the Livian structure and establish a contrast.

[22] See Syme (1958, 364–73) on the reasons for Tacitus starting in A.D. 14, which Tacitus describes as literary and Syme accepts. Syme also accepts that the "second thoughts" in book

3 were recognition of a genuine mistake and that he came to recognize the importance of the fall of the republic and the emergence of *dominatio* under Augustus.

[23] The alternative is to take Henderson's (1989) suggestion on closure seriously for openings and argue that Tacitus was not very concerned when he started. Thus the *Annales* becomes merely the successor work to the *Histories.*

[24] *Ann.* 1.1.

28–27 B.C., racing through the Augustan period. The Augustan principate is thus a transitional phase in which the republic passed from a living political entity to become the stuff of history. In this, Tacitus appears close to the depiction of imperial power that we see in the *Res Gestae Divi Augusti*, a text that shows little shyness about Augustan accumulation of influence but that denies any dated transformation of the constitutional situation. With the transition of imperial authority, A.D. 14 becomes an ideal date from which to start the analysis, not because the Augustan period was not monarchic but because the debate about the Augustan period, and the relationship between the present and the republic, became a significant issue.

Tacitus opens the *Annales* by dealing with all Roman history from the foundation to Octavian in fewer than fifty words. Taking only slightly longer with the defeat of Pompey and Lepidus, the killing of Antony, Augustus's seizure of the Julian faction and the offices of consul, triumvir and tribunician power, he summarizes the career of Augustus:

> *ubi militem donis, populum annona, cunctos dulcedine otii pellexit, insurgere paulatim, munia senatus magistratuum legum in se trahere, nullo adversante, cum ferocissimi per acies aut proscriptione cecidissent, ceteri nobilium, quanto quis servitio promptior, opibus et honoribus extollerentur ac novis ex rebus aucti tuta et praesentia quam vetera et periculosa mallent.* (*Annales* 1.2)

> He seduced the soldiers with gifts, the people with food, and rest with the sweetness of leisure. Little by little he pressed on, dragging to himself the duties of the senate, the magistrates and the law, without opposition, since the most fierce had been slaughtered in battle or through proscription, and the rest of the nobles, somewhat more eager for slavery, were raised up by wealth and honors, and, having gained from the revolution, preferred safety and the present to the old and dangerous.

Tacitus provides us with a model of gradual but fundamental change that, as in *Annales* 3.65, is connected to a decline in individual character: nobles "are eager" for slavery, a servitude that marks a fundamental break with the traditions of republicanism.

Tacitus sums up the Augustan period:

> *Domi res tranquillae. eadem magistratuum vocabula. iuniores post Actiacam victoriam, etiam senes plerique inter bella civium nati. quotus quisque reliquus qui rem publicam vidisset? igitur verso civitatis statu nihil usquam prisci et integri moris. omnes exuta aequalitate iussa principis aspectare.* (*Annales* 1.3–4)

> At home, things were quiet. The magistrates had the same names. The younger men were born after the Actian victory. Even most of the old had been born during the civil wars. How many were there remaining who had seen the republic? The state had, therefore, been transformed and there was nothing of the original and pure customs. Equality had gone and all looked to the orders of the *princeps*.

The transition between republic and empire is not dated or associated with a single event. Instead, it is described as a process in which Augustus gradually accumulated authority and influence and in which the traditions of republicanism were eroded. Indeed, the process only seems complete when the politics of the republic had become a purely historical phenomenon, not something about which living Romans had experience. Tacitus may have been thinking of the practice of identifying a new *saeculum*, which dawned when all were now dead who had been alive at the point when the previous *saeculum* had started; A.D. 14 can be seen as marking an imperial *saeculum*. This gap in understanding can be seen as being one of the great themes of the Tiberian books, and especially of books 1–3, the conflict between the more monarchic style of Germanicus and the republican style of Tiberius, which could be represented as a dispute as to whether that fundamental change had occurred: the official Tiberian line being denial.[25]

Annales 1–3 offers little historical theory, but in Annales 4 Tacitus explains his mission.

> Pleraque eorum quae rettuli quaeque referam parva forsitan et levia memoratu videri non nescius sum: sed nemo annalis nostros cum scriptura eorum contenderit qui veteres populi Romani res composuere. ingentia illi bella, expugnationes urbium, fusos captosque reges, aut si quando ad interna praeverterent, discordias consulum adversum tribunos, agrarias frumentariasque leges, plebis et optimatium certamina libero egressu memorabant: nobis in arto et inglorius labor. (Annales 4.32)

> I am not unaware that much of what I retold and what I will tell may seem perhaps minor and of little importance but no one could oppose the annals of our times with the writings of those ancients who concerned themselves with the state of the Roman people for they had great wars, the assault on cities and the flight and capture of kings or, if they turned to internal matters, they could freely recount the disputes between consuls and tribunes, agrarian and corn laws, the contests between plebs and optimates, while I have an inglorious and strictly limited labor . . .

Tacitus argues the history of the period of autocracy has its uses in teaching men to distinguish "honorable from lesser behavior, practicality from wrongdoing" (Annales 4.33). Tacitus is explicit about the moral purpose of history in providing exempla for his audience. Exempla can be understood as providing a route map to a collective identity: strongly normative narratives that construct both "good" and "bad" model identities.[26] In this moral purpose, Tacitus is firmly within the traditions of Roman historiography.[27]

This editorial digression is immediately followed by the prosecution of Aulus Cremutius Cordus for his praise of Brutus and Cassius.[28] Tacitus gives Cordus a long justificatory speech in which he notes the achievements of writers and historians of the past—Livy, Asinius Pollio, and Messala Corvinus (4.34)—and claims that, as they could praise republican heroes, so he too should be able without constraint to "speak of those whom death has put beyond hatred or thanks" (prodere de

---

[25] Pelling 1993.

[26] Luce (1991, 2911) argues that Tacitus writes because "the moral excellence of men of the past must be brought to light and receive a place of honor in a memorial whose high qualities will ensure its survival in future ages." Luce downplays the role of history as providing exempla for imitation. Instead, history is seen as a deterrent as it shows misbehavior. This moral encouragement is designed to create anxiety in Tacitus's senatorial audience. Fama is thus crucial as a moral concept for the historian, which Luce relates to Pliny's obsession with his reputation. My argument widens the audience for Tacitean history from an exclusively senatorial audience.

[27] Annales 3.65 seems on some translations to claim that the "highest purpose of history" was to provide moral judgments. Woodman (1995) shows that the passage should rather be interpreted as a technical claim that his report edits the record, which is an obligation placed on the historian.

[28] The juxtaposition of the digression and Cordus episode has attracted considerable comment. McCulloch (1991) argues that Tacitus sees himself in Cordus, the historian who will be remembered, recording the vices of the age. This becomes a key passage for interpreting the Annales since it dramatizes for McCulloch the difference between the historian (who can observe impartially) and the actor (who must soften his language), with Cordus and M. Lepidus paralleling Agricola and Tacitus. See also Ginsburg (1981, 48–50), who suggests that the epitaph of Cordus is meant for Tacitus. Sage (1991, 3387) argues that "The Cordus episode emphasizes the close links in Tacitus' mind between the values of the Republic and the new constraints placed upon senatorial libertas and the writing of history that the Principate enjoined. It serves as a striking example of the continuity of Tacitus' attitude with that of writers of the Julio-Claudian period and illustrates in a concrete manner the ideas expressed in the preceding digression and the problems faced by a writer of imperial history for whom the Republic was still a living issue." My argument is directly contrary to Sage, and I agree with Martin and Woodman (1989, 169), who note that 4.32 is preparing us for 4.34–35 and argue that Cordus's argument is flawed (183).

iis quos mors odio aut gratiae exemisset [4.35]). Yet this was disingenuous. By calling C. Cassius *ultimus Romanorum* ("the last of the Romans" [4.34]), Cordus asserted that *Romanitas* existed in republicanism and could not have been unaware of the political implications for his contemporary audience. The speech concludes, "Should I be condemned, they will remember not just Brutus and Cassius, but also me" (*si damnatio ingruit, qui non modo Cassii et Bruti set etiam mei meminerint* [4.35]). Cremutius Cordus then left the court and killed himself. By facing down the tyrant and claiming his freedom, if only through his ultimate sacrifice, Cordus claimed an association with that "last Roman." We are invited by Tacitus to read Cordus as an *exemplum*, but Cordus fails to learn the lessons of his own history, presenting Cassius in his final oration as the penultimate Roman, Cordus following the same tradition. Tacitus has already told us that the age of the republic was killed off by Augustus, dismissed by Tacitus in fewer than fifty words.[29] By calling Cassius "the last of the Romans," Cordus broke the connection with the past, setting the Roman elite on a search for a new narrative identity. That Cordus promptly forgot that, or chose not to abide by his own history, or simply lived too long, is only one of the many ironies of the Tacitean account. Tacitus does not teach his reader to be Brutus, Cassius, or Cordus, for their history has passed. Instead, the imperial age calls for different *exempla*, different narratives of identity.

The *Histories* opens with a pessimistic contrast of Tacitus's achievements with those of his predecessors,

> *nam post conditam urbem octigentos et viginti prioris aevi annos multi auctores rettulerunt, dum res populi Romani memorabantur pari eloquentia ac libertate: postquam bellatum apud Actium atque omnem potentiam ad unum conferri pacis interfuit, magna illa ingenia cessere.* (*Histories* 1.1)

> For the age of the 820 years after the foundation of the city, many authors have written with both eloquence and freedom, while they recalled the events of the Roman republic, but after the war of Actium was fought for peace and all power was concentrated on one, such great talent ended.

Nevertheless, even these Flavian times can provide *bona exempla*

> *comitatae profugos liberos matres, secutae maritos in exilia coniuges: propinqui audentes, constantes generi, contumax etiam adversus tormenta servorum fides; supremae clarorum virorum necessitates fortiter toleratae et laudatis antiquorum mortibus pares exitus.* (*Histories* 1.3)

> mothers accompanying their children in flight, wives who followed their husbands into exile, courageous kinsmen, resolute sons-in-law, the loyalty of slaves defiant even in the face of torture, the courage of famous men suffering the ultimate inevitability and partings equal to the deaths praised of old.

This contrast allows Woodman to argue that the preface is, in fact, optimistic, the language echoing Cicero rather than the pessimistic Sallust, and the contrast becomes one between the talents of the ages (republic and post-69 empire) and not between the availability of moral *exempla* for the historian.[30] There is thus fundamental change between republic and empire, but the possibility of moral excellence is not thereby lost, though possibly diminished.

---

[29] There is considerable disagreement as to the force of Tacitean republicanism. Classen (1988, 114) concludes a study of political language in Tacitus by arguing that "Whatever Tacitus thought of the collapse of the republic and the disappearance both of its institutions and the qualities on which it

had been built, he was realistic enough to see that times had changed and that . . . he could [not] revive and advocate the qualities for which there was no longer room."

[30] Woodman 1988.

Nostalgia for the republic becomes something of a theme in *Histories* 1, the first half of which concentrates on Galba and his overthrow. One of the more problematic aspects of Galba's portrayal is his adoption of Piso and the speech that goes with it (15–16). In adopting a seemingly admirable, aristocratic young man, Galba gives a long address in which he laments the necessity of imperial rule and yet claims that the best possible means of discovering the next emperor is adoption, a measure taken by Augustus, who looked only to his own family for suitable adoptees. Galba supposedly searched through the whole of the available aristocracy before alighting on Piso. It is difficult to read this speech without seeing in it a comment on Nerva's adoption of Trajan, a commentary that might at first sight appear to border on the panegyrical. Nevertheless, as ever with Tacitus, the speech is not quite as simple as it seems. The alert may notice that Galba condemns the hereditary principles that made the Roman people "almost the heirloom of a single family under Tiberius, Gaius, and Claudius" (*sub Tiberio et Gaio et Claudio unius familiae quasi hereditas fuimus* [16]) and asked this audience "to call to mind Nero, who was made proud by a long line of Caesars" (*sit ante oculos Nero quem longa Caesarum serie tumentum* [16]), seemingly failing to remember that Nero, though indeed descended from a long line of Caesars, was adopted over and above the emperor's natural son. Furthermore, although we might appreciate the sentiments, Galba's complete failure to understand the principate and the political events of which he was a part undercuts our judgment of the speech. Already by the time Piso was adopted, Vitellius was gathering his forces in Germany, and Otho was conspiring in Rome. The adoption of Piso had no effect on his enemies. In 1.5, Tacitus tells us that the urban soldiery were lost through Galba's meanness. He is supposed to have declared, *legi a se militem, non emi* ("I choose troops, not buy them"), a policy out of keeping with his other dealings during his brief rule. When Piso was presented to the troops (1.18), Galba again refused a donative, and Tacitus remarks that he might have maintained the peace even at this stage by a show of liberality. However, *nocuit antiquus rigor et nimia severitas, cui iam pares non sumus* ("Such antique discipline and great austerity was injurious, for now we are not up to it").

Galba's reign ended in farce. Prematurely believing that Otho's revolt was over, he entered the Forum, where he was caught by Otho's troops. As his slaves fled, Galba was thrown from his chair. Tacitus preserves two traditions of the tenor of his last words: either begging for a few extra days to meet the donative or offering his throat to the soldiers (1.41). From beginning to end, Galba used the rhetoric of republican severity but was undermined by imperial brutality.[31] He was unable to manipulate the situation, a case study of someone who did not understand the *arcana imperii* and that the old ways of the republic were dead. His adoption of Piso becomes yet another example of admirable sentiment and political foolishness.

The examples of historical misunderstandings could be multiplied: one could consider the reign of Claudius at some length, for example. Tacitus's attitude toward the republican past is in some ways very clear.[32] The past was gone. Nevertheless, it would seem that the conservatism of form in the *Annales* and *Histories* could be read not as ironic comment on the decease of history but as a claim to historiographical continuity. The historian retained value by providing understanding and *exempla* for the new age. It was only through the correct understanding of the Roman past that the present could be understood. Although times had changed, the function of history had not. Tacitus provided his audience with a new history for the new age, new role models, and a new way of constructing their identity in relation to imperial power and the Roman past.

---

[31] Galba had already removed some of his enemies from their posts, struck financially at Nero's supporters (*Histories* 1.20), and killed some of his enemies in his march on Rome (*Histories* 1.6–7). He appears to have been uninterested in building his political support.

[32] See also Ginsburg 1993.

Pliny and the Memory of History

Pliny's relation to history is less radical. Book 9 of the letters contains much that concentrates on *fama*. In 9.3, Pliny claims always to have immortality before his eyes, though, notably, for Pliny it is literature that ensures *fama* and not politics. In the previous letter, he had compared his own epistolary output with that of Cicero.[33]

> *neque enim eadem nostra condicio quae M. Tulli, ad cuius exemplum nos vocas. Illi enim et copiosissimum ingenium, et par ingenio qua varietas rerum qua magnitudo largissime suppetebat; nos quam angustis terminis claudamur etiam tacente me perspicis. (Ep. 9.2)*

> our condition is not the same as that of Marcus Tullius, to whose example you call me. For he had both a great talent and supplied that talent with a great variety of important matters, but you know without my mentioning it how we are confined with narrow boundaries.

As ever, Pliny's letter is densely written. The "narrow boundaries" (*angustis terminis*) recall the conventional poetic distinction between the broad canvas of epic and the narrower remit of neoteric, in which pure waters Pliny, from time to time, dabbled, and points up a further comparison between his life and that of Sabinus, his correspondent, who served in the legions. Pliny falls short of Ciceronian epic, not because of any lapse on Pliny's part but because of the different times in which the two authors operated. Nevertheless, Pliny presents us with numerous accounts of individuals achieving *fama*. I take only the most obvious examples.

The death of Verginius Rufus leads Pliny to wonder

> *si tamen fas est aut flere aut omnino mortem vocare qua tanti viri mortalitas magis finita quam vita est. Vivit enim vivetque semper atque etiam latius in memoria hominum et sermone versabitur, postquam ab oculis recessit. (Ep. 2.1)*

> if it is right to weep or even to call death what is more the end of the mortality of so great a man than the end of his life. For he lives and will always live and will appear even more widely in the memory of men and in our conversations once he has left our view.

Rufus is history, but is his *fama* Tacitean and imperial or Ciceronian and republican? In response to a criticism of Rufus's self-publicity, Pliny writes

> *Omnes ego qui magnum aliquid memorandumque fecerunt, non modo venia verum etiam laude dignissimos iudico, si immortalitatem quam meruere sectantur, victurique nominis famam supremis etiam titulis prorogare nituntur. (Ep. 9.19)*

> I think all who have performed something great and memorable are most worthy not just of forgiveness but even of praise if they seek the immortality which they deserve and labor to increase the fame of their glorious name even by their final epitaph.

Pliny's defense is that Rufus was due this honor. It had been hard won, and such epitaphs are in themselves virtuous, presumably as they established *exempla* to be followed. This is glossed by an

---

[33] The letter parallels 1.2, which acts as an introductory letter to the collection, and Cicero is an ever-present ghost at Pliny's literary table.

anecdote. Rufus had received a prepublication copy of a history by Cluvius Rufus with the request to emend any passage of which he disapproved. Rufus declined the opportunity since

Tune ignoras, Cluvi, ideo me fecisse quod feci, ut esset liberum vobis scribere quae libuisset. (Plin. *Ep.* 9.19)

Do you not know, Cluvius, that I did what I did so that there is freedom for you to write what you wish.

In some ways, this is a perverse boast since Rufus's actions led indirectly to the Domitianic period, but the defense of *libertas*, a republican watchword, becomes Rufus's claim to *fama*.

Titinius Capito (*Ep.* 1.17; 8.12) is known to us from *ILS* 1448. He served as *ab epistulis* and *a patrimonio* in Domitian's household. He survived Domitian's fall and prospered under Trajan. Pliny praises him for gaining permission to erect a statue to Lucius Silanus, probably the Lucius Silanus who fell victim to Nero. According to Pliny, Capito was known for his reverence of the famous (*claros viros*), but even more remarkable was his domestic reverence for statues of Brutus, Cassius, and Cato. In 8.12, Pliny describes Capito as "the best of men, numbered among the shining ornaments of our age," who writes on "the deaths of outstanding men, some of whom were very dear to me." For Capito, martyrologist for the republican opposition, such values were compatible with imperial service.

There can be no doubt that Pliny recognized fundamental differences between the ages of Cicero and Trajan and that these differences caused him and his contemporaries difficulties.[34] The narratives of elite identity were in flux, and such flux generated uncertainties. The tensions that animated the lives of the elite, the balance between the public life (*negotium*) and the leisure (*otium*) so visible in Pliny, Seneca, and Tacitus's *Dialogus*, reflect uncertainty as to the value of public life, the traditional sphere of the male elite. The clash of narratives underlies the political chaos of the Domitianic period, and Pliny's own desperate attempt to reconcile the traditional senatorial narrative and imperial rule in the *Panegyricus*. In his attitude to history, Pliny demonstrates a consciousness of change (he was not like Cicero in spite of being his literary heir), yet he adheres self-consciously to republican values and either does not see or diminishes the historical break between republican and imperial systems. His imperial heroes are to be compared with republican heroes and even defenders of republican *libertas*. In contrast to the views of Tacitus, Pliny presents republican history and *exempla* as powerful in contemporary society and sees a fundamental historical continuity between the elite of his own day and that of the republic.

Bourdieu writes that "The *habitus*—embodied history, internalized as a second nature and so forgotten as history—is the active presence of the whole past of which it is the product."[35] Another way to think of the habitus is as a "thick history," a way of talking about all the traditions and customs that go into creating a society. It is more immediate than conventional history for it is a living part of the ideological framework in which individuals operate at an everyday level. For the Romans, being a historical society (a society that sought meaning in history), conventional history (meaning the story of the past) was a crucial part of the habitus (the ideological world in which they grew up). Disputes about the relation of the Romans of the first century to their history, and

[34] To Pliny's conservative heroes, we can add Pompeius Saturninus, a historian and poet (1.16) whose poems deliberately lacked the polish of the Augustan age, while his wife supposedly composed letters in the archaic style of Plautus and Terence (their loss is an ever-present sorrow).

[35] Bourdieu 1990, 56. See n. 5 above for a discussion of habitus.

Tacitean attempts to impose a hiatus between republic and empire, go to the heart of individual identity. For Pliny, republicanism was a rock, a historical certainty that affirmed identity. Whatever was happening in contemporary politics and society, the Roman elite could always look back to a glorious past, to the achievements of their ancestors, of whom they were the direct continuators. The past was firm and unchangeable, and from the certainties of the past, the Roman elite could affirm their identity in the dangerous and fluid present.

Conclusion

The parallels between the modern discourse on ethnic identity and the ancient debate on the past are here remarkable. So often ethnic identities depend on a fixed view of the past and a perception both of a uniform experience of that past and that the past continues to have a determining and vital force in building identities and social relations in the contemporary world, in spite of all the social and political change since the "foundation period" of the identity myth to which contemporary identities continuously refer. Stuart Hall writes about such identities that

> there is something guaranteed about [such a] . . . discourse of identity. It gives us a sense of depth, out there and in here. . . . Increasingly I think one of the main functions of [such] concepts is that they give us a good night's rest. Because what they tell us is that there is a kind of stable, only very slowly-changing ground inside the hectic upsets, discontinuities and ruptures of history. Around us history is constantly breaking in unpredictable ways but we, somehow, go on being the same.[36]

Tacitus and Pliny may have lost sleep due to the buffeting of historical changes, but whereas Pliny tends to lull his contemporary audience back to tranquility by announcing that the rupture was incomplete, that the republic still lived in the spirits of his friends and associates, Tacitus assures his audience that their nightmares are true, that the republic has gone, and that republican behaviors are both false and anachronistic. Individual behavior that manifests identity is intensely political. Tacitus does not, however, despair. If the old myths that assured somnolence no longer work, and, indeed, are much more likely to result in insomnia, he provides new *exempla*, which offered guides to behavior and identity in the changed circumstances of the empire. Those reading and understanding Tacitus's history are assured of a (relatively) good night's sleep.

---

[36] Hall 1991, 43. Hall is theorizing shifting identities in relation to "Black" identity in late twentieth-century Britain, but the sense of shifting paradigms of identity, and also the oppressiveness of certain elements of the paradigm, would seem an appropriate parallel to the debates of the late first century.

Works Cited

Anderson, B., *Imagined Communities: Reflections on the Origin and Spread of Nationalism* (London and New York 1991).

Bourdieu, P., *The Logic of Practice* (Cambridge and Oxford 1990).

Clarke, K., "*In arto et inglorious labor*: Tacitus's Anti-history," in *Representations of Empire: Rome and the Mediterranean World*, ed. A. K. Bowman, H. M. Cotton, M. Goodman, and S. Price, *Proceedings of the British Academy* 114 (Oxford 2002) 83–103.

Classen, C. J., "Tacitus—Historian between Republic and Principate," *Mnemosyne* 41 (1988) 42–116.

Fukuyama, F., *The End of History and the Last Man* (London 1992).

Geertz, C., *The Interpretation of Cultures* (London 1975).

Gellner, E., *Nations and Nationalism* (Oxford 1983).

Giddens, A., *Modernity and Self-identity: Self and Society in the Late Modern Age* (Cambridge and Oxford 1991).

Ginsburg, J., *Tradition and Theme in the Annals of Tacitus* (New York 1981).

———, "*In maiores certamina*: Past and Present in the *Annals*," in *Tacitus and the Tacitean Tradition*, ed. T. J. Luce and A. J. Woodman (Princeton 1993) 86–103.

Hall, S., "Old and New Identities, Old and New Ethnicities," in *Culture, Globalization and the World System: Contemporary Conditions for the Representation of Identity*, ed. A. D. King (Basingstoke 1991) 41–68.

Henderson, J., "Livy and the Invention of History," in *History as Text: The Writing of Ancient History*, ed. A. Cameron (London 1989) 66–85.

Hobsbawm, E., and T. Ranger, eds., *The Invention of Tradition* (Cambridge 1983).

Luce, T. J., "Tacitus' Conception of Historical Change: The Problem of Discovering the Historian's Opinions," in *Past Perspectives in Greek and Roman Historical Writing*, ed. I. S. Moxon and A. Woodman (Cambridge 1986) 143–55.

———, "Tacitus on 'History's Highest Function': *praecipuum munus annalium* (Ann. 3.65)," *Aufstieg und Niedergang der römischen Welt*, ed. H. Temporini (1991) 2.33.4:2904–27.

Martin, R. H., and A. J. Woodman, *Tacitus Annals Book IV* (Cambridge 1989).

McCulloch, H. Y., "The Historical Process and Theories of History in the 'Annals' and 'Histories' of Tacitus," in *Aufstieg und Niedergang der römischen Welt*, ed. H. Temporini (1991) 2.33.4:2928–48.

O'Gorman, E., *Irony and Misreading in the Annales of Tacitus* (Cambridge 2000).

Parsons, T., "Some Theoretical Considerations of the Nature and Trends of Ethnicity," in *Ethnicity: Theory and Experience*, ed. N. Glazer and D. P. Moynihan (Cambridge, Mass. 1975) 53–83.

Patterson, O., "Context and Choice in Ethnic Allegiance: A Theoretical Framework and a Caribbean Case Study," in *Ethnicity: Theory and Experience*, ed. N. Glazer and D. P. Moynihan (Cambridge, Mass. 1975) 305–49.

Pelling, C., "Tacitus and Germanicus," in *Tacitus and the Tacitean Tradition*, ed. T. J. Luce and A. J. Woodman (Princeton 1993) 59–85.

Penrose, J., and P. Jackson, "Conclusion: Identity and the Politics of Difference," in *Constructions of Race, Place and Nation*, ed. P. Jackson and J. Penrose (London 1993) 202–9.

Ranger, T., "The Nature of Ethnicity: Lessons from Africa," in *People, Nation and State: The Meaning of Ethnicity and Nationalism*, ed. E. Mortimer (London and New York 1999) 12–27.

Rich, J. W., and J. H. C. Williams, "*Leges et iura P. R. Restitvit*: A New Aureus of Octavian and the Settlement of 28–27 B.C.," *Numismatic Chronicle* 159 (1999) 169–213.

Sage, M. M., "The Treatment in Tacitus of Roman Republican History and Antiquarian Matters," in *Aufstieg und Niedergang der römischen Welt*, ed. H. Temporini (1991) 2.33.5:3385–3419.

Smith, A. D., *The Ethnic Revival*, Themes in the Social Sciences (Cambridge 1981).

———, *The Ethnic Origins of Nations* (Oxford 1986).

Stavrakakis, Y., *Lacan and the Political* (London 1999).

Syme, R., *Tacitus* (London 1958).

Woodman, A. J., "History and Alternative Histories: Tacitus," in *Rhetoric in Classical Historiography* (London and New York 1988) 160–96. Reprinted as "History and Alternative Histories" in Woodman 1998, 104–41.

———, "*Praecipium munus annalium*: The Construction, Convention and Context of Tacitus, *Annales* 3.65.1," *Museum Helveticum* 52 (1995) 111–26. Reprinted in Woodman 1998, 86–103.

———, *Tacitus Reviewed* (Oxford 1998).

7 ◆ LIFE WITHOUT FATHER: DECLAMATION AND THE CONSTRUCTION OF PATERNITY IN THE ROMAN EMPIRE

Margaret Imber

I begin by considering two propositions about Roman society and the question that their juxtaposition raises. First, Roman society was patriarchal. Second, at least among the male elite, Roman fathers frequently were absent from the daily lives of their sons. If these two assertions are correct, we should wonder, how, if not from their absent fathers, did the sons of the Roman political and economic elite learn to be *patres*? The answer, in some part, I believe may be found in the Roman pedagogical practice of declamation. Roman *rhetores* routinely assigned their students the task of composing mock courtroom speeches arising out of conflicts that imagined the gamut of possible crises a Roman man in his public and private life might possibly confront. The practice of declaiming, therefore, allowed Roman sons to rehearse their future roles as *patres* and *cives*. I argue that Roman sons learned to be Roman fathers, in part, by declaiming. In so doing, I hope to illuminate the complex nature of the patriarchal ideology that declamation served and perpetuated.

The Problem of Absent Fathers in a Patriarchal Society

To begin with the first proposition—the patriarchal nature of Roman society. Only Roman male citizens exercised political power throughout the history of the republic and empire. It is true that female citizens gradually obtained a relatively high degree of economic autonomy and that Roman history is replete with anecdotes about the meteoric rise of imperial slaves and freedmen to places of extraordinary social, economic, and political power. It is equally true that the political significance of citizen identity declined over time. Rome, nevertheless, was a man's world, a male citizen's world.

The male citizen as *pater* linked the *domus* to the *res publica*. The legitimate son, whom only a *pater* could produce, guaranteed the preservation of a family's identity from generation to generation. This son was also a potential soldier and citizen who guaranteed the security of Rome into the next generation. The *pater*, then, was the nexus between family and state, and each social institution depended on him.

Commensurate with his burdens were the privileges enjoyed by the Roman father, especially within his family. The *pater*'s children possessed no greater legal and economic rights than his slaves. The *pater familiae* enjoyed the legendary *ius necandi*. Romans, in law, termed this bundle of paternal rights *patria potestas*, and they considered its scope extraordinary. Gaius, for example, wrote, "there are scarcely any other men who have as much power over their sons as we do" (*Digest* 1.55). Turnus was reputed to have said that no case "could take up less time than one between a father and a son, it could be settled in a few words; if the son did not comply with the father's wishes he would get into trouble" (*Digest* 1.50.9).

As scholars are well aware, however, precisely what we mean by "patriarchal" in any context, but especially in the Roman context, is not self-evident.[1] As Saller has demonstrated, there is precious little evidence that Roman fathers routinely resorted to the exercise of legally articulated paternal rights like the *ius necandi* to discipline grown sons.[2] To the contrary, there is much compelling evidence that cultural norms of affection and self-restraint effectively checked a Roman father in his exercise of *patria potestas*.[3] Livy's legendary stories of Rome's famous fathers, nevertheless, suggest that Romans were keenly aware that managing both *patria potestas* and the heavy burdens of civic obligation was no easy task.

Livy, for example, gives us a disturbing representation of the Roman *pater* exercising the fullest extent of his powers. Manlius Torquatus, consul and general of Rome's army in 340 B.C., gave orders that no soldier should engage the enemy. His son, a cavalry scout, egged on by the taunts of the enemy, forgot his father's commands and doughtily engaged in single combat with the enemy's champion. He returned a victor to camp and submitted himself to his father's authority. Torquatus ordered that he be executed for his disobedience.[4]

Did Torquatus act as consul, general, or father when ordering the execution of his son? We cannot know, and that, for Livy, is precisely the problem. Livy's tale does not emblematize the extent of *patria potestas* as much as it identifies the disastrous consequences of simultaneously performing the parts of father, general, and consul. Manlius Torquatus represents here not the assertion of unambiguous patriarchal authority but rather the contradictions and tensions of that authority. Torquatus, indeed, provided a complicated cautionary tale, not to Roman sons who might contemplate rebellion but to Roman fathers who confronted the social and psychological reality of their sons' desire for an independent identity. As Miles notes, the son in this tale emulates, perhaps rivals, both his father's own heroic exploits on behalf of Rome and his father's own famed pietas in submitting to the harsh discipline of his father, Lucius Manlius Imperiosus.[5] Good fathers endeavored mightily to avoid the conflict Torquatus faced. They succeeded in this endeavor by refusing the literal power offered to them by the law.[6] Cicero's exasperation with his own son, an exasperation that most of us would easily recognize, was the norm, not the exercise or even the threat of the *ius necandi*.

Roman patriarchal ideology, accordingly, offers at least two points worth considering here. First, the *pater*, as Romans theorized and idealized him, was the embodiment of the connection between the *res publica* and the *domus* and as such could face impossible and contradictory obligations. Romans were well aware of these tensions, as the story of Torquatus suggests. Second, the gap between paternal practice and patriarchal ideology could be vast. Indeed, one indication of the discontinuity between Roman ideological assertions of paternal authority in law codes and the day-to-day experience of Roman fathers and sons is suggested by my second proposition. At least

---

[1] Harlow 1998, 155.

[2] See Dixon (1992, 44) on the difference between the stereotype and reality of *paterfamilias*.

[3] Saller 1994, 2.

[4] *nos potius nostro delicto plectemur quam res publica tanto suo damno nostra peccata luat; triste exemplum sed in posterum salubre iuuentuti erimus. me quidem cum ingenita caritas liberum tum specimen istud uirtutis deceptum uana imagine decoris in te mouet; sed cum aut morte tua sancienda sint consulum imperia aut impunitate in perpetuum abroganda,*

nec te quidem, si quid in te nostri sanguinis est, recusare censeam, quin disciplinam militarem culpa tua prolapsam poena restituas—i, lictor, deliga ad palum (Livy, *Ab urbe condita* 8.7.17–20).

[5] Livy 7.4–5. See Miles 1995, 67, 70–73.

[6] Indeed, as Thomas (1984) and Saller (1994, 115–17) have demonstrated, the power of life and death was not meant by the jurists to describe a sociological reality but rather to articulate the complete ambit of the *pater*'s authority within the *familia*.

among the political and economic elite, Roman fathers frequently, perhaps even typically, did not play an active role in their sons' daily lives. Saller's analysis of marriage, birth, and death patterns in the Roman Empire suggests that the elite Roman family's period of greatest fragility occurred during a man's adolescence. According to his demographic model, between a quarter and a third of Roman boys of elite status would have lost their father by the age of fifteen.[7]

Even when a father survived until his son's adulthood, he may still have been frequently absent for lengthy periods of time from his son's life. Overseas military and political or diplomatic duties imposed upon the senatorial class grew exponentially during the late republic and early empire as the geographic scope of Rome's dominion expanded. As the empire grew, moreover, commercial interests more frequently would have called further from home members of the economic elite who did not participate in political life. I don't believe the numbers of absent fathers who would have fallen under these rubrics can be estimated with any certainty. Moreover, some of these fathers could well have taken their sons with them on their journeys of imperial service and financial business.[8] Nevertheless, I think it is fair to conclude that one consequence of membership in the Roman political and economic elite was the increased likelihood that sons were as accustomed to a father's absence as his presence in their lives.

Declamation and the Ideology of Roman Patriarchy

Declamation was a schoolboy's exercise in the composition and delivery of public, usually forensic, speeches. Only Roman boys, usually teenagers, from the wealthier classes studied declamation.[9] Students composed declamations based on a homework assignment called a *controversia*. The *controversia* usually had a title, a brief narrative description of a conflict that has reached a point of public adjudication and, on occasion, a statement of one or more laws related to the conflict. Most of the time, the student was assigned the job of writing the speech that a male character in the declamation would himself give at trial. Declamation, in other words, inherently involved imagining and playing the roles a student would inhabit as an adult.

The overwhelming majority of *controversiae* center on a conflict of allegiances between two social roles inhabited by one character in a *controversia*—a son's love for his mother threatens his loyalty to his father, for example. The conflicts that the *controversiae* contemplate, moreover, are irresolvable. Declamation, despite its similarity in plots and characters to comedy, insists on a choice with tragic consequences. If a son values his father over his mother, his mother must die. If he values his mother over his father, his family's honor is lost. In composing his declamation, accordingly, a Roman boy would have to consider carefully the different values that the *controversia* put into competition and the cost of preferring one value over another.

It is not unreasonable to question how declamations like these prepared Roman boys for anything. Indeed, scholars of education since Quintilian have deplored the pedagogy. How could this exercise possibly prepare a Roman boy to become an *advocatus* or *orator*—the nominal general

---

[7] Assuming an age of first marriage between sixteen and twenty for women of the elite class, and an age of twenty to twenty-five for men, as well as a practice of remarriage upon the spouse's death. See Saller 1994, 26, 37 (women); 38–39 (men); 46 (elite remarriage); 121 (death of fathers by adolescence).

[8] Indeed, Suetonius provides a number of striking examples of teachers who accompanied their students and patrons on trips abroad: Suet. *Gram.* 10 (Lucius Ateius Philologus and the Claudii), 15 (Pompeius Lenaeus and Pompey).

[9] See Imber 2001 for a more comprehensive discussion of declamatory pedagogy.

purpose of the practice—or *pater* and *civis*, as I argue here? The answer can be found by examining the steps a Roman boy would have taken to compose a declamation.

The *controversiae* the *rhetores* assigned their students offer no hints to the proper answer. In fact, they carefully avoid articulating the causal relationship between events in any plot or the liability of any character. The declaimer had to imagine the causal relationship between events detailed in the *controversiae* and then argue for them. The most potent tool of argument was the social stereotype. Stereotypes of the wicked stepmother flourish in the declamations students gave, although they never appear in the *controversiae*. Thus, declaimers appealed to archetypal figures that existed in popular imagination for the logic of their arguments. Romans associated a set of values and expectations with each of the stereotypical figures that declaimers used in their arguments. The wicked stepmother, rapacious tyrant, greedy pirate, and dissolute son embody a complex set of social valuations determined by gender, class, and status. The links between the stereotypes and the values associated with them are, moreover, to our point of view, stunningly unexamined in rhetorical treatises. Quintilian had no need to examine or explain them. Such associations were part of the stock of cultural knowledge that every Roman possessed. As St. Jerome observed, "all the comedies and mimes and common places declaimed against the wicked stepmother."[10] Roman boys acquired this knowledge, in part, at school.

Because of the stock nature of the plots, a student could concentrate on the motives of the stock characters and on crafting clever *sententiae* in which he neatly linked the banal fact of a particular *controversia* to the celebrated archetypes of declamation. Practicing declamation at school, the young student of rhetoric mastered not merely the association of status and gender traits to archetypes; he enhanced the imaginative power of these archetypes with his own *sententiae*. Teachers rewarded students for finding the wittiest way to say that good women devoted their lives to their husbands and sons; that sons happily and absolutely obeyed fathers; that good fathers exercised their authority benevolently. In declaiming, young Roman boys learned that these Roman categories of gender, class, and status naturally and absolutely divided society into a hierarchy of power. At the top of the ladder stood the *vir bonus*, the *civis* and *pater* the student would one day become.[11] The student of declamation, accordingly, did not simply passively learn the ins and outs of Roman social values, their complexities and contradictions, at school. His education instead was dynamic and interactive. Student declaimers actively contributed to the ideological tradition that was itself shaping their own identities.

If we explore the declamations that treat fathers in general, and absent fathers in particular, therefore, we should discover how Romans considered the problem of paternal identity and patriarchal authority and how they taught their sons to consider it.

Declamatory Fathers

Many of the declamations in the corpus consider the Roman social roles of *civis* and *pater*. And it is here that I would offer a footnote to Saller's observations about Roman literary representations of the exercises of *patria potestas* by a character identified as a *paterfamilias*. Saller, indeed, suggests

[10] St. Jer. *Ep.* 54.15.4.

[11] Cf. Brown 1992, 48–58 and Kaster 1984, 19 on rhetorical education as a means of inculcating moral and social values in the sons of the Roman elite, who were otherwise quite unconstrained in their exercise of considerable personal power. See also Kevin Robb's discussion of the didactic function of Homeric poetry in Greek culture: "In a word, Homeric speech conveyed the proper mores of class behavior, especially as those classes related to each other" (Robb 1994, 165).

that for the Romans, the term *paterfamilias* had connotations largely limited to property possession. In a nonlegal context the term would have been understood by Romans to mean something like "proper gentleman," with its associations of competent estate management and social reliability. Indeed, the word *paterfamilias* occurs infrequently outside the corpus of legal literature. Moreover, as Saller notes, apart from a fable in Aesop, there are no literary representations of a father's assertion of his authority over his children that use the term *paterfamilias*.[12] Saller's general point is that the tyrannical patriarch is a character of more interest to modern social historians than ancient Romans. This modern fascination, he warns, runs the risks of obscuring the actual power relations of the Roman household.[13] In general, I agree. But declamation, a genre that is simultaneously sublegal and subliterary, if not quite sub rosa, offers evidence of a more complicated reality. While the *controversiae* do not use the term *paterfamilias*, they are obsessed with the social consequences of the exercise of the legal powers of *patria potestas.*

Some examples: In *Declamationes Minores* 291, a father instructs one of his two sons to divorce his wife so that his brother may marry her. In *Declamationes Minores* 300, a father repudiates his son after he fails to convict his mother of adultery in a family *consilium*. In *Declamationes Minores* 306 a husband orders his wife to expose their son. In *Declamationes Maiores* 18 and 19 a father, who comes to believe the son is having an incestuous relationship with his mother, tortures his son to death.

Not all declamations drip with so much gore. Fathers who actually kill their sons are not all that frequent in declamation. Fathers who repudiate their sons, however, loom large in the declamatory corpus. Repudiation was declamation's version of disinheritance. Declaimers conceived of it as a formal lawsuit to end the relationship of father and son. Repudiation in declamation, I think, served as a way to routinely imagine what Romans, as Saller and others have demonstrated, found unimaginable—the exercise of *ius necandi*. Repudiation created for the declaimer's imagination the possibility of social death—of a man who had no father and thus who could have no sons. In so exercising their imaginations, young Roman declaimers had to explore the relationship between the legal construction of *patria potestas* on the one hand and the social experience of citizenship and paternity on the other.

About one in ten *controversiae* proposes factual situations in which a Roman has left his city. A subset of these involve the topos of exile.[14] These *controversiae*, however, are concerned not with particular political crisis and conflicts that might have caused the exile but rather with the relationship of the exiled *civis* to his *civitas*. Consider *Declamationes Minores* 248, which treats the fate of an accidental murder. The *controversia* is entitled *Octo anni duplicis inprudentiae* ("Eight years for a double manslaughter"). Two laws are included for the declaimer's consideration. The first provides that the penalty for manslaughter is exile for a term of five years. The second outlaws a person who has been exiled; that is, it provides that an exile has *no* civil or legal rights if he returns to his city before the term of his exile: "Let it be permitted to kill an exile [found] within the borders." Given the title and the laws, it is not hard to imagine what the *controversia* will say:

> A man who had committed manslaughter went into exile. While in exile, he committed another manslaughter. He served a five-year term of exile from the time of the second killing. Someone killed him within the borders when he was returning after eight years. This person is charged with murder.

---

[12] Saller 1994, 191.

[13] Saller 1994, 197.

[14] See also *DM* 266, 269, 285; *ES* C.7.6.

The student declaimer must play the role of the man who murdered the exile and defend himself on a charge of murder. The model declamation offered treats the technical legal issue of the length of the exile. It is peppered, however, with observations about the kind of person who would return to his country before his term was up: One example is a general, moralizing statement: "But he who knowingly returns against the law tries to conquer the law, and he will persevere in his lack of respect [for the law]." A second directly blackens the victim's character: "I can't even marvel enough at this man's lack of respect for the laws or at this, that he hurried to return so quickly to his country." This declamation, accordingly, requires the student to develop *sententiae* that approve the social death that exile implies. These *sententiae* are grounded in an ideological premise that enshrines law as the guarantor of civic order, and hence civic identity.

Mary Beard has suggested that declamation is a site of Roman myth-making and that the law in declamatory texts plays a role comparable to that of gods in Greek myths:

> [T]hey [*controversiae*] construct a fictional world of "traditional tales" for negotiating, and re-negotiating, the fundamental rules of Roman society; they "naturalize the arbitrariness" of those rules by setting them in the context of *legal* sanction; they offer a vision of *higher* authority—defined not in terms of divine intervention, but in terms of the social sanction of Roman *law;* they provide a focus for the re-presentation and constant re-resolution of central Roman/human conflicts that everyday social regulations do not (and *can* not) solve; they offer an arena for learning, practising and recollecting what it is *to be and think Roman*.[15]

I would characterize the effects Beard describes in ideological, rather than mythopoetic, terms. By naturalizing the arbitrariness of Roman laws as well as Roman social customs and institutions, Roman declamation played a critical role in the formation of elite Roman identity. The boys who declaimed would grow up to command legions and provinces. As both Peter Brown and Robert Kaster have observed, moreover, male members of the Roman elite in their public and private lives suffered few practical constraints upon the authority they derived from their status, office, and wealth.[16] The most effective of those constraints, Nero's fondness for declamation notwithstanding, were values Romans internalized in their youth. The *controversiae* that contemplated exile taught the student declaimer that a metaphorical journey outside the bounds of Roman law was death and deservedly so.

In addition to such metaphorical journeys, there are a number of declamations that consider what happens to the family and *domus* when a son or father goes on a more literal voyage.[17] The short answer is death and destruction, occasionally dishonor, always disaster. In one declamation, *Declamationes Minores* 259, a rich man and his daughter and his friend, a poor man, go sailing. A storm arises, and the rich man is forced to suffer the indignity of having his daughter saved by the poor man and coping with the romance between them that inevitably ensues. In a declamation in Pseudo-Quintilian's school collection (*DM* 257), a variation of which is offered in the Elder Seneca's selection of adult declamations (*ES* C.5.2), a man is captured by pirates while traveling. His son is compelled to marry the daughter of a rich man (by definition his father's enemy) in order to raise

---

[15] Beard (1993, 56; emphases in original). Beard thus particularizes for the Roman practice of declamation Bourdieu's observation (1977, 164) that established orders tend to reproduce the naturalization of their own arbitrariness.

[16] As Peter Brown has noted (1992, 48–58), rhetorical education was one of the few means by which the extraordinary

power the Roman *pater* enjoyed in his daily life was tempered. Cf. Robert Kaster's description of the freedom students obtained by embracing the discipline of grammatical instruction: Kaster 1984, 19.

[17] *DM* 259, 286, 306, 335, 347; *CF* 23; *ES* C.5.2; *DMaj* 16.

the ransom. Our ransomed hero finds he has no choice but to disinherit his son for such disloyalty (once he is safely home). An earnest young hero in *Declamationes Minores* 286 is saddled with a treacherous brother who rapes his fiancée while he is traveling abroad. The girl and her rapist marry, but it is not, as we can imagine, a match made in heaven. When her errant former fiancée returns, she begins an affair with him. They are discovered by her husband, who quite lawfully kills his adulterous brother. The father of the two boys elects his only legal option—repudiating his surviving son.

The topos of the traveling youth is repeated in the professional declamation *Declamationes Maiores* 16. There a young man and his friend decide to go traveling. A tyrant captures them, and our hero's widowed mother goes blind weeping for her son. The captured youths make a bargain with the tyrant under which our hero can return home to attend to his mother. In turn he swears a solemn oath to the tyrant to return, and his companion offers his own life as surety for the pledge. No sooner does the blind mother hear of her son's plans to keep his vow than she sues to prevent his return (under a law preventing children from abandoning disabled parents).

The risk travel poses to the family left behind is also contemplated by the *controversiae* in a school declamation (*DM* 347) and a declamation in a collection (*CF* 23) attributed to the Calpunius Flaccus. In the former, a traveling man's wife hears false rumors of her husband's death and remarries. The husband, returning home late at night, finds her in bed with her new husband, whom he assumes is an adulterer and kills. Murder charges ensue. In the latter, the son of a traveling man finds his mother in bed with her paramour and pursues her with his sword, attempting to kill her, as his apparent legal right and moral duty. His mother, apparently well versed in the law, shouts, "you are not my legal son!," thereby clouding his claim to legitimacy, citizenship, and the right to kill her. Unmoved, he kills her, whereupon his maternal grandfather sues to have him declared a foreigner pretending to citizenship. The boy loses the suit and is declared a slave of the city. The grandfather then purchases our hero from the city with the intention of having him crucified. It is only at this point that his father returns home.

How then might we say that the declamations imagined the absence of the citizen-father from his home? The *controversiae*, even those populated by tyrants and pirates, are concerned with the perilous state a *domus* is left in when a *pater* goes traveling. Yet a significant number of the boys who declaimed on these *controversiae* had significant travel in their future, particularly those who planned a public life. I don't believe the teachers of declamation intended to turn their students into neurotics, obsessed with fears about treacherous, lecherous brothers, the imperious demands of aging parents, and the uncertain affections of their brides. So why were foreign destinations so dangerous in declamation?

Precisely, I think, because student declaimers would travel so much as adults. They would leave young wives and sons and aged parents behind. The realities of their lives would frequently take them far from home. And in reality their wives and sons and aged parents would by and large manage without them. Declamation constructs an imaginary *pater* whose presence is critical to the survival of his family. In effect, declamation inscribes and justifies the *pater*'s place in his *domus*, the extraordinary theoretical power Roman law and imagination granted to the *paterfamilias*, despite the fact that Roman fathers frequently were not home to fill that place or exercise that power.

This imaginary *pater* served several purposes. First of all, everyone likes to be needed. A Roman who had studied declamation in his youth knew he was needed at home. To be a *civis*, he needed to be a *pater* with a home that depended on his return, whatever the attractions of Alexandria or Athens or Marseilles. Rome wanted her leaders to be more in the mold of Ovid, who pined to return, than Antony, who could enjoy a world beyond Rome and found the city's geographical and imaginative confines rather limiting.

More importantly, however, the practice of declamation allowed Rome's future leaders to master the complexities and contradictions of Roman ideology and Roman practice. The demands of the citizen's public life could well risk the security of his private relationships. The ideal citizen could decline neither role to secure the other. The ideal Roman man, the *vir bonus*, was both *pater* and *civis*. The sons of the Roman elite, especially those with absent fathers, needed to understand the tensions between their public and private duties in order to fulfill both successfully. There might well be dragons in the dangerous destinations that awaited the student declaimer. He had, at least, however, slain a few at school.

Works Cited

Beard, M., *Looking (Harder) for Roman Myth: Dumezil, Declamation, and the Problems of Definition* (Stuttgart and Leipzig 1993).

Bourdieu, P., *Outline of a Theory of Practice* (Cambridge 1977).

Brown, P., *Power and Persuasion in Late Antiquity: Towards a Christian Empire* (Madison 1992).

Dixon, S., *The Roman Family* (Baltimore 1992).

Harlow, M., "In the Name of the Father: Procreation, Paternity and Patriarchy," in *Thinking Men: Masculinity and Its Self-representation in the Classical Tradition*, ed. L. Foxhall and J. Salmon (London and New York 1998) 155–69.

Imber, M., "Practised Speech: Oral and Written Conventions in Roman Declamation," in *Speaking Volumes: Orality and Literacy in the Greek and Roman World*, ed. J. Watson, *Mnemosyne* Supplement 218 (Leiden 2001) 201–16.

Kaster, R., *Guardians of the Language: The Grammarian and Society in Late Antiquity* (Berkeley 1984).

Livy, *Ab urbe condita*, *History of Rome / Livy*, trans. Rev. Canon Roberts (New York 1912).

Miles, G., *Livy: Reconstructing Early Rome* (Cornell 1995).

Robb, K., *Literacy and Paideia in Ancient Greece* (New York and Oxford 1994).

Saller, R., *Patriarchy, Property and Death in the Roman Family* (Cambridge 1994).

Thomas, Y., "*Vitae necisque potestas.* La père, la cité, la mort," in *Du châtiment dans la cité. Supplices corporels et peine de mort dans le monde antique*, *Collection de l'École française de Rome* 79 (Rome 1984) 499–548.

8 ◆ DAUGHTERS AS DIANA:
MYTHOLOGICAL MODELS IN ROMAN PORTRAITURE

Eve D'Ambra

A group of Roman funerary portraits, statues and reliefs, from the first through third centuries A.D. represents girls and young women as the goddess Diana. Although a limited phenomenon with eleven portraits in sculpture and seven reliefs,[1] the corpus originally must have been larger, with the addition of works that have gone unrecognized due to portrait features obscured by damage and, no doubt, with many others misidentified as statues of the goddess due to reworking and reuse.[2] The Diana portraits allow us to consider the commemoration of a cherished and mourned group in Roman society, girls denied the culminating experiences of marriage and motherhood, who were honored by the mythological identification. The maiden goddess, as I will argue, is an entirely appropriate choice for their stage of life but also one that exemplified antisocial or transgressive behavior with the goddess's fierce and permanent virginity, her habitat in the wilds, and her predatory behavior in the hunt. The problematic nature of the identification has significance for the social perceptions of daughters and habits of commemoration. Furthermore, the scholarship's compartmentalization of the sculptures into *idealized* bodies and *realistic* heads, the former only of interest for their reflection of Greek statuary types and the latter considered as faithful likenesses of individual subjects at their time of death—that is, the bodies are works of art, while the portrait heads are mere documents—has hampered our appreciation of the works.[3]

The mythological portrait has been understood as a hybrid, with its portrait head and generic body in the form of a Greek statue type. The latter connoted the high classical culture of imperial Rome, its Hellenic repertoire of immortals, and the urbanity of its cities with porticoes and temples animated by statues of divinities that inspired imitation. Henning Wrede has proposed that freedmen, especially imperial freedmen, commissioned mythological portraits.[4] We assume that statues of members of the imperial family served as models (the range of which is better reflected in the imagery of gems and coins).

What has been missing from the discussion is an awareness of the sculptures' role in the conventions of commemoration, which include the social milieu and the etiquette of display because the erection and outfitting of a tomb, the funeral, and subsequent rituals for the dead were public acts.[5] These actions connoted the value of the deceased, coinciding with, we would like to think,

---

[1] Wrede 1981, 227–30, nos. 94, 95, 96, 97. I omit the third-century hunt sarcophagi from this chapter because they comprise a separate body of material with their own problems and methods of analysis, especially for questions of the representation of narrative, the meanings of myth, and social identity.

[2] Wrede 1981, 222–30; of course, it is impossible to speculate on the numbers of portrait statues now lost, defaced, or reworked, but the likelihood that our evidence is woefully incomplete should be kept in mind.

[3] See Smith 1998, 57–61 for a discussion of the unquestioned assumptions of the traditional approaches to portraiture.

[4] Wrede 1981, 93–105, 159–70.

[5] Koortbojian 1996.

feelings of grief and loss, although the disposal of the deceased in the tomb required highly codified ceremonies and the formulaic phrases of epitaphs. Emotions are rather hard to come by in the
protocols of funerary rites and the archaeological record, but literary accounts of mourning parents
give vent to their sadness despite claims that parents remained aloof from the lives of their infants
and young children.[6] Most interesting in relation to the sculpture are descriptions of exemplary
girls bearing notably masculine virtues. The selection of attributes for girls stems from both the
public and private spheres rather than being confined to typically feminine virtues. The refusal to
characterize daughters in rigid categories of gender brings Diana's proclivities to mind. As a goddess who staunchly resists marriage and motherhood, Diana nonetheless takes responsibility for
bringing youths to adulthood and assists in rites of passage.

The following discussion of select portraits begins with reliefs on funerary altars because of
the accompanying inscriptions, some of which indicate the age of the deceased, her relationship to
the dedicant, or the family's social status. The latter half of the chapter turns to portrait sculpture
in the form of statues and busts, and then to myth and rituals of passage, in order to consider the
meaning of Diana as a model for Roman girls.

Reliefs on Altars

A funerary altar, now in the Louvre, was erected by the parents of Aelia Procula to their deceased
daughter, described, characteristically, in the rather laconic style of epitaphs as *dulcissima* (*CIL* 6
10958) (fig. 1).[7] The date is usually given as A.D. 140 because of the relief's style and the father's
identification as an imperial freedman of Hadrian; his cognomen, Asclepiacus, suggests the occupation of a physician, while the mother's name, Ulpia Priscilla, suggests descent from a freedman of
Trajan. The status of imperial freedmen, the emperor's ex-slaves who often held highly responsible
positions in the court, was proudly displayed with bigger and more prominently placed letters of
the abbreviation *Aug. Lib.* Of particular interest is the phrase above, *sacrum Deanae* (*sic*), taken to
indicate that the altar is also dedicated to Diana, a rather unusual tactic in the corpus. The disposition of text and image is striking, with the top part of the epitaph divided into two columns by the
relief of Aelia Procula in the guise of Diana. That the phrases *sacrum Deanae et memoriae Aeliae
Proculae* are interrupted by a representation of an architectural structure, a pair of pilasters sur-
mounted by an arch that frames the figure of the deceased, gives the image prominence. A shrine
would have a niche adorned with a statue of the goddess. Instead, here a well-known statue type
has been supplied with a portrait head of the young girl; the wrap-around text states that this is in
memory of Aelia Procula.

It may be no coincidence that imperial freedmen erected tombs with statue galleries of their dearly
departed wives in the guise of the immortals: Statius praises Abascantus for erecting a sumptuously
appointed tomb for his wife Priscilla that seems to have had niches for mythological portraits (*Silvae*
5.1.231–33; A.D. 90s, including one in the guise of Diana), and the fragments of the tomb of Claudia
Semne on the Via Appia (A.D. 120–30) included garden *aediculae* for mythological portrait statues that
recall the representation of Aelia Procula on her altar, as Henning Wrede has observed.[8] The literary
and archaeological evidence points to commemorations of wives and mothers with portrait galleries;

---

[6] King 2002.

pl. 12.2.

[7] Altmann 1905, 282; Picard 1939, 124, no. 2; Kleiner
1987, 241–42, no. 104, pl. 60.1; Wrede 1981, 226, no. 91,

[8] Wrede 1971.

Fig. 1. Funerary altar of Aelia Procula. Paris, Musée du Louvre, inv. no. MA 1633 (photo courtesy Musée du Louvre).

it is, of course, likely that the practice was extended to daughters and that P. Aelius Asclepiacus was alluding to the portrait galleries in the abbreviated format of the altar. Scholars have long noted the depiction of Aelia Procula in the form of a well-known Greek statuary type, yet it is easy to overlook that the simple and understated architectural form of the statue niche stands for the prestige of public monuments and sacred sites in Rome adapted for citizens' tombs.

The allusion to the portrait gallery informs the viewer that the deceased girl was commemorated in the high style to which imperial freedmen and their dependents were accustomed. The altar's findspot in the vicinity of the Via Appia near S. Sebastiano suggests that it came from the family tomb; whether Aelia Procula was graced with a statue gallery in the tomb is difficult to ascertain and not important—her parents' aspirations are telling in their representation of a commemorative practice associated with the staff of the imperial court and followed by other well-to-do freedmen in trade or professions.

Although the figure of Aelia Procula imitates a distinguished Hellenic statue, the portrait head is turned out toward the viewer to show a childish, round face with full cheeks and lips that pout. The girl's hair is rather severely parted so that ringlets fall at the temples, while the hair in the center of the forehead is pulled back into a knot. The combination of a petulant expression, pronounced physiognomy, and well-dressed hair recalls another portrait in the corpus, a bust in the Museo Torlonia (fig. 2).[9] The mid-second-century bust depicting another maiden as Diana with

[9] Wrede 1981, no. 86, pl. 10.1; Gercke 1968, 77, FM 38.

Fig. 2. Bust of girl in the guise of Diana.
Rome, Museo Torlonia, inv. no. 103
(photo Felbermeyer, DAIR, neg. no. 35.697).

Fig. 3. Altar of Aebutia Amerina. Rome,
Museo Nazionale Romano, inv. no. 108611
(photo Kolbe, DAIR, neg. no. 67.147).

the attribute of the quiver also portrays a little girl ranging, perhaps, from six to eight years old. Both portraits' features exhibit a striking juxtaposition of typical childish characteristics, such as the broad faces, pouty cheeks, and wide-open eyes, with marks of strong character or willfulness, as seen in the bold stares and thin lips firmly set; other funerary portraits of children show characteristically bland and inexpressive features. The portraits of Aelia Procula and the anonymous girl in the Museo Torlonia bust represent a type in which the features of girlhood are inflected with markers of a sullen or headstrong character, which registers with greater poignancy than the sweetness often attributed to them.

The representation of Aelia Procula has a classical pedigree in its borrowing of the Artemis of Versailles (Leptis Magna) type originating in the fourth century B.C. but popular through the early and high empire, as attested by the Hadrianic copy from which it takes its name.[10] The statuary type, depicting the goddess in a running pose and brandishing her bow with a hunting dog by her side, portrays the huntress in action. Aelia Procula, thus, embodies the goddess's grace, her swiftness, agility, and fierce pursuit of her prey, demonstrating her prowess in the hunt. Such qualities resonated with Romans, providing a model of bravery and efficient killing. These accomplishments, of course, were not expected of daughters, but Diana's status as a maiden with exceptional powers as expressed by her unfettered movement and uncompromising purity proved auspicious for parents mourning young girls.

[10] Bieber 1977, 73, fig. 268; the sculpture is usually attributed to Leochares, but see Pfrommer 1984 for a Hellenistic date.

The figure on the relief, however, is modified by the exposure of the right breast, a motif that emphasizes the incongruity of the developed body and the childish face. The depiction of the huntress with the bared breast derives from Hellenic traditions, and the Amazons, in particular, provide a model for the costume.[11] Both Artemis and Amazons share mythological attributes as females who hunt in the wilds, beyond the confines of civilization and without the protection of husbands. Their classification as untamed virgins allows them to be thought of as mythological *sisters*, and some Amazonian features, no doubt, were suitable for Artemis's powers and domain.

In an imperial context, the image of the Amazonian Diana should be seen alongside the other figures that make use of the iconography of the eastern women warriors, the personification of the city and empire, Roma, and her double, Virtus, who are represented with one bare breast.[12] Although more frequently depicted with breast covered, Diana comes of age and plays her part as goddess of the Latin League in the republic and, then as an attendant to emperors, a comrade in arms.[13] A reflection of her civic role may be seen in an altar dedicated to Diana Victrix by a citizen, Aebutia Amerina, for a shrine near Rome in the late first or early second centuries A.D. (fig. 3).[14] In this altar the goddess, lacking an individualized portrait head, displays the idealized appearance of the immortals.

Aelia Procula is not the only girl to be commemorated as Diana in Amazon mode. There is another funerary altar, which had been considered lost but has reappeared recently in Diana's sanctuary in Nemi (fig. 4). Although its current location in Nemi is fitting, the altar originally adorned a tomb on the Via Latina in Rome. It depicts a girl in the same pose and costume, differing only in the footwear and the pose of the dog, turning back toward its mistress in the Nemi relief.[15] The quiver also crosses the chest and juxtaposes the naked with the draped breast. The portrait of the girl conforms to a mid-second-century type (A.D. 140–50), with a coiffure of braids wound tightly on the top of the head in a coil; the face is characterized with strong features, deep-set eyes set close together, sharp cheekbones, narrow jaw, and protruding ears, which provide a girl of, perhaps, ten through fourteen years with what seems to be an uncompromising character. Comparisons with other second-century portraits of girls suggest that the type employed a repertoire of stock features evoking character rather than charm or beauty to cast a likeness.[16]

This altar has an inscription (*CIL* 6 6826) stating that it was erected by Aelia Tyche's parents and sister for their most dutiful daughter and best sister.[17] It was reported to have come

[11] Pausanius (1.40.2 and 10.37.1) on statues of Artemis; Pliny (*HN* 36.4.24) on Praxiteles' Diana in the Temple of Juno in the Porticus Octavia; *LIMC* 2.2, 808, no. 32 and no. 32a; Sestieri (1941, figs. 3–6) argues that Praxiteles' son, Kephisodotos, developed the type that became a cult statue in Rome, as reflected by statuettes and the relief of Aelia Procula. Little is made of the significance of the bare right breast, but see Lindner 1982, 357–63 on this motif in the statuary of Artemis, as well as in Roman sculptures and reliefs.

[12] Vermeule 1959; Mellor 1981.

[13] Hänninen 2000; for the empire, see, e.g., the inclusion of Diana with the deities depicted in the attic relief on the country side of the Arch of Trajan in Benevento (Fittschen 1992, pl. 83.2, with bibliography).

[14] Helbig 1972, 4, 3, 366–67, no. 2429 (E. Simon); Hermann

1961, 122, no. 52, fig. 10; Candida 1979, 122–26, no. 55, fig. 42, 43.1; Schraudolph 1993, 128–29, no. D9 on the Artemis Rospigliosi type as the model.

[15] Museo della Navi; the Nemi relief also depicts a tree stump on the left edge. I thank Giuseppina Ghini, Director of the Museum, who also supplied information about the findspot and previous collections of the altar in a letter written on 23 July 2002; see Granino Cecere 2003. For the previously published sculptural finds from Nemi, see Guldager Bilde 2000; Guldager Bilde 1998; Guldager Bilde 1995; Moltesen 2000.

[16] See the portraits of girls represented as Diana in Wrede 1981, 222–27, cat. nos. 82–93.

[17] Altmann 1905, 282; Wrede 1971, 139; Wrede 1981, 226 n. 92.

Fig. 4. Funerary altar of Aelia Tyche. Nemi, Museo delle Navi (photo Granino, DAIR, neg. no. 94.736).

from the columbarium of the freedmen of the *gens* Allidia on the Via Latina in Rome and, thus, provides evidence of a social context. The altar of Aelia Tyche provides further evidence of the commemorative practices of freedmen in the mid-second century who chose to honor their daughters with the imagery of the Amazonian Diana. In the reliefs on their altars, Aelia Procula and Aelia Tyche turn the tables on death, so to speak, by initiating the hunt with full speed as demonstrated by the flying drapery and active poses. That the prey is not represented or the end depicted shifts the focus to the hunter and her promise, clearly an appropriate aspect in the case of those who lost their lives so young. The subjects of the Diana portraits are, after all, girls and young women who, being neither fully mature nor domesticated, can aspire to the male world of risk and adventure.

Statues

The statues of girls and young women represented as Diana conform to the well-known types from the Greek canon: the Artemis of Versailles as mentioned above, the Artemis of Dresden, and the Artemis Colonna, etc. As in the case of other works of *Idealplastik*, the sculptures often wear their celebrated pedigrees lightly; that is, they combine features from several Greek types and adapt them into Roman creations that are rather more than the sum of their Hellenic parts.[18] The statues and busts range in date from the late first through the early third centuries and usually have only general or sketchy provenances. A documented archaeological context is rare among the group;

[18] Gazda 2002; Perry 2002.

there are no extant inscriptions accompanying the statues. In this brief discussion I focus on one characteristic statue that exhibits features representative of the group.

One of the better-preserved works is a statue now on display in the Palazzo Massimo of the Museo Nazionale Romano (fig. 5).[19] This statue was discovered in 1922 in Ostia, and its findspot in a lime kiln in the Terme dei Cisiarii suggests that it had been taken from a tomb located nearby on one of the streets leading to the city, perhaps the Via Ostiensis or the later developed Via dei Sepolcri. Although it lacks an archaeological context and inscription, the circumstantial evidence points to its function as a funerary portrait for a girl commemorated as the goddess. The work of Greek marble, standing 1.49 m tall despite damage to the extremities and head, displays a high degree of craftsmanship, apparent in the carving of the tunic in paper-thin folds and also in the delicacy of the facial features, which convey the girl's youth and beauty. The quality of this statue has led some scholars to the conclusion that the subject of the portrait must be a member of the Julio-Claudian dynasty, yet comparisons with portraits of imperial maidens are not telling.[20] Art historians and archaeologists have dated the work from A.D. 25–30 to 70–90, although probably a date of ca. 55–75 should be preferred because of the style of the carving.[21]

The figure is posed preparing to take action, with her right arm reaching back to pluck an arrow from the quiver on her back and her left probably holding a bow next to her thigh (traces of the hand's support remain on the tunic). The hunting gear is complete with a crouching dog at her right side (the remains of the dog are visible by the right calf, in front of a tree trunk providing support for the weight-bearing leg). The composition balances repose and effort, with the raised right arm reaching behind balanced by the left leg flexed forward, and the supporting right leg opposed to the resting left arm.[22] Sources for the statue are found in the late classical and Hellenistic repertoire: the pose of the upper torso and arms, as well as the coiffure, reflects that of the type of the Artemis of Dresden from the fourth century B.C., while aspects of the short costume and lower body recall those of the Seville-Palatine ("Laphria") type, originating early in the second century B.C. and replicated frequently during the imperial period, especially in the second century A.D.[23]

The Palazzo Massimo statue, however, may evoke the domain of the uncivilized, the realm of both the Amazons and Diana, in details of the costume. The lower calves are encased in hunting boots decorated with small panthers' heads, a motif of the untamed and wild as worn by both Amazons and maenads—here the point of contact for the shared Dionysian iconography is the status of both groups as *other*, females beyond social control.[24] The infiltration of a highly charged motif serves to inflect the Diana imagery with a more extreme or exotic brand of adventure, although

[19] Calza 1921; Calza 1922; Paribeni 1928, 87, no. 109; Becatti 1950, 490; Felletti-Maj 1953, 70–71, no. 119; Calza 1965, 38, no. 46, pls. 27–28; Traversari 1968, 16, pl. 7; Gercke 1968, 66–68, FM 26; Helbig 1972, no. 2195 (H. v. Heintze); Giuliano 1979, 23–24, no. 24, inv. 108518 (V. Picciotti Giornetti); Wrede 1981, 223, no. 83, pl. 10.2, 4; *LIMC* 2.1, 802, no. 18; Tittoni and Guarino 1992, 115 (L. Nista). The statue is now on display in a gallery on the first floor of the Palazzo Massimo. I thank Dottoressa Marina Sapelli for allowing me to see the statue before the Palazzo Massimo was open to the public and Dottoressa Rosanna Friggeri for help in securing photographs.

[20] Felletti-Maj 1953, 71; Helbig 1972, no. 2195 (H. v. Heintze).

[21] Calza 1921: first half of first century A.D., perhaps Claudian;

Calza 1965: A.D. 25–30; Muthmann 1950: statue is Claudian, but the support is later, perhaps Hadrianic or Antonine in date; Helbig 1972: A.D. 25–30 (H. v. Heintze); Gercke 1968: late Neronian or early Flavian; Giuliano 1979: late Neronian or early Flavian (V. Picciotti Giornetti); Wrede 1981: Flavian; Tittoni and Guarino 1992: Julio-Claudian; the hairstyle is the idealized type seen in the portraits of women of the Julio-Claudian dynasty that is also similar to the coiffures of well-known statuary types of the goddess.

[22] Stewart 1990, 160–63 for a discussion of the effects and meaning of Polykleitan contrapposto.

[23] *LIMC* 2.1, 803–4, no. 22, on the Seville-Palatine ("Laphria") type.

[24] Stewart 1997, 196–99; Parisinou 2002.

Fig. 6. Detail: Head of portrait statue of girl as Diana. Rome, Museo Nazionale Romano, Palazzo Massimo, inv. no. 108518 (photo F. Palaia).

Fig. 5. Portrait statue of girl as Diana. Rome, Museo Nazionale Romano, Palazzo Massimo, inv. no. 108518 (photo F. Palaia).

it is in a minor key. The rest of the clothing and gear is functional (*contra* Calza) and allows for movement, as seen in the short belted tunic, which falls from the shoulders in fabric gathered in crinkly folds like strands of knotted or twisted fibers on the upper torso, except for the sheathlike treatment over the breasts.

The portrait head of the Palazzo Massimo statue (fig. 6) conveys an expression of alertness, as if the figure is ready to raise the bow and take aim as the head turns slightly to the left (the head has been reattached but belongs to the statue). The cast of the head, the wide-open eyes, the parted lips, and the slightly raised chin may even suggest an attitude of vigilance appropriate for the hunt. The facial features are idealized to emphasize conventions of beauty to some extent: the oval face with high cheekbones gives definition to the broad and clear features, as well as to the smooth planes of the forehead, the gently rounded cheeks, and large chin. Yet the beauty of the portrait marks the immaturity of the subject in the overly large almond-shaped eyes and the soft under-chin to suggest the stage of adolescence in which grace and awkwardness meet and in which the incipient signs of growing up, the long neck with Venus rings and shapely lips, are combined with more childish features.

The hairstyle, like the facial features, also shows a mixture of idealization and specificity: the style of wavy locks combed from a center part and gathered in a large, loose bunch of locks in the back is represented on the statue type of the Artemis of Dresden. A similar type of coiffure is also worn by Roman women in the first century but with corkscrew curls framing the face and a queue in the back.[25] The grooming of the Palazzo Massimo statue, however, imparts the modesty of a girl

[25] See Calza 1922, 398 on the ideal hairstyle of the goddess represented here. Fittschen and Zanker 1983, 5–7, nos. 4–5, pls. 4–6.

uncorrupted by excess and *luxuria*. For the Ostian family who commissioned this portrait, appearances counted or, perhaps, a demure and reserved appearance mattered. The coiffure frames the youthful features in a style that suits both the goddess and a girl, with or without the influences of fashionable society.

The high quality of the statue does not necessarily predicate an elite patron, as earlier generations of scholars had assumed. That the altars are rather substantial dedications by patrons with modest means should provoke us to consider the social background of the dedicant of the Palazzo Massimo statue in Ostia. As the port of Rome, Ostia had shops and services that catered to the needs of the sea-going commerce and its traders, sailors, and suppliers. One could imagine that the parents of the girl represented by the statue were as likely to be merchants or artisans as members of the city's elite, who also came to be culled from the most successful members of the mercantile class in the second century.[26]

Most scholars refer to the subject as a girl or a maiden, and I hazard a guess that the portrait depicts a preadolescent girl in the range of ten to thirteen years old.[27] As the chronological span of matronhood is extended for Roman women, we may also consider whether maidenhood was compressed, given the high childhood mortality rates, the relatively early age of first marriage, and high rates of fertility thereafter. The state of childhood was quantitatively and qualitatively different in ancient Rome, with its elaborate rites of passage (discussed below) marking the transitions to adulthood. The other Diana statues also depict maidens on the cusp of maturity with ambivalent combinations of facial features, yet the bodies tend to conform to statuary types of the huntress, a significant factor for both the worship of Diana and her supervision of girls' coming of age.

Rites of Passage

Although the evidence for Roman rites of passage is fragmentary and derives from early republican sources (or later authors' glosses on them), the protocols indicate the milestones of young lives and the expectations for them.[28] For our purposes, the most important set of rites focused on the adolescent's entry into society. For elite Roman boys, training in rhetoric and oratory, the shaving of the first beard, and the presentation in the Forum with their fathers for military assignments mark the induction into public life; for Roman girls marriage and motherhood were the goals of their preparations and instruction, and they were to put aside childish things, such as dolls, before leaving home (though some brides of the upper social orders would have been barely older than children from our point of view).[29]

It is thought that Diana aided young women on the verge of marriage and motherhood, just as the Greek rites of Artemis at Brauron tempered girls' raucous spirits so that they might acquire the modesty and reserve of brides.[30] In the Augustan period, Propertius and Ovid tell of torch-

[26] Meiggs 1973, 214–34.

[27] See Kleiner (1987, 29) on the phenomenon of funerary portraits appearing older than the deceased at the age of death. She suggests the use of stock portraits for funerary monuments that may not have had much to do with the likeness of the deceased at all; if deceased boys are shown to be older, i.e., in their roles as citizens, then would deceased girls also be depicted as wives or mothers? The Diana portraits speak against this in some aspects: the girls appear to be

young, but several have mature features.

[28] Dixon 1992, 101–2; Boëls-Janssen 1993, 19–95; *contra* Boëls-Janssen, see Scheid 1992, 385.

[29] Dixon 1992, 101–2; Harlow and Laurence 2002, 54–64; Plin. *Ep.* 1.9 on his daily activities: "I was present at a coming-of-age ceremony."

[30] Cole 1984, 233–44; Faraone 2003.

lit processions to Diana's temple at Aricia overlooking Lake Nemi: women worshipers washed their hair and left terracotta votives of reproductive organs and other offerings, such as clothing.[31] Women in labor appealed to Diana (the newly born, closer to the category of the untamed than that of the civilized, fall under the goddess's influence).[32] In early Italic religion, Diana was a goddess who brought the nocturnal light of the moon, but her domain of the woods and water allowed her to be assimilated into the Greek Artemis, at least by the later republican and Augustan periods, if not earlier.[33]

Recent research, however, has called into question the notion of Diana as a woman's goddess: it has been pointed out that terracotta votives of female body parts appear in sanctuaries of gods as well as goddesses and that, since many of the votives left at Nemi do not represent female anatomy, the healing powers of the goddess had a wider range.[34] Furthermore, the inscriptions show that the overwhelming majority of the dedicants at Diana's shrine at Nemi were male.[35] Male worshipers are also attested in literary sources, including Ovid, who participated in rites at Nemi, and Horace, who honored the goddess at his villa.[36]

It is now apparent that the evidence for Diana's worship has been analyzed only selectively, while other sources have been distorted or ignored since Wissowa cast the goddess as a protector of women rather than the hunt.[37] Diana's primary role was as a hunting goddess (although during the period of the empire she acquired a wider portfolio of related activities, as did the other major deities), and, in fact, Alföldi cast her as a warrior goddess with little to do with women's lives.[38] Vergil in the *Aeneid* has the goddess involved in military and political affairs, and he also evokes the *rex Nemorensis,* the fugitive slave who held the honorary title at the grove at Lake Nemi (another male involved in the worship of Diana).[39] It also appears that Diana was in charge of a male rite of passage: a minor Augustan poet, Grattius, tells of ephebic rites in Diana's grove at Nemi.[40] These annual rites brought groups of elite youths together for exercises that were part military training and part social orientation to their responsibilities and privileges as adults, the leading citizens of Rome. Diana's supervision of ephebes is significant for our purposes, as inscriptions at the shrine attest through the first century A.D.

Artemis/Diana has two faces: she is a guardian of youths undergoing rites of passage, and she presides over the hunt and slaughter.[41] The mythology of Artemis recounts a world of conflict and aggression in which the goddess participates in traditionally male pursuits: protecting her mother's reputation at the side of her brother Apollo, demanding a father's sacrifice of his daughter in retribution for the killing of a deer, etc. Artemis's domains converge on the location of the frontier, where hunting takes place, and on the notion of the boundary, which demarcates beast from human and civilization from savagery. Artemis escorts the young to the threshold of

[31] Ov. *Fast.* 3.259–70; Prop. 2.32.8–10; Hor. *Carm. Saec.* 2.12.17–21; Stat. *Silv.* 3.1.55–60, 69–75; Plut. *Quaest. Rom.* 100, 278e–f.

[32] Gordon 1934; Pairault 1969.

[33] Gordon 1934, 10–12 on the Hellenization of Diana by 399 B.C.

[34] Holland 2002, 164; Green 2002 on Diana's healing of mental illness.

[35] Holland 2002, 164.

[36] Holland 2002, 163.

[37] Green 2002; Wissowa 1912, 247–48; also Frazer 1911.

[38] Alföldi 1963, 48.

[39] Verg. *Aen.* 1.499, 3.681, 4.511, 7.306, 7.769, 11.537, 11.582, 11.652, 11.843, 11.857. Holland 2002, 163–64.

[40] Holland 2002, 163; Green 2002; Grattius 483–96; also Hor. *Carm.* 4.6 on the goddess's wildness and relationship to children.

[41] Vernant 1991, 195–260.

adolescence and then leaves her charges as they grow up and take on social identities as citizens and matrons.

Girls commemorated as Diana in imperial Rome assume the form of the huntress. Diana as huntress holds sway over the uncultivated open spaces and rules her domain, alternately killing or caring for wild creatures, without any of the encumbrances that accompany domesticity, the lot of mortal women.[42] Rather than as a guide for brides-to-be, the goddess represented in the commemorative statues and reliefs assumes her most aggressive, brutal aspect. As the activity that best prepared Greek youth to become warriors and served as a fitting leisure pursuit for Roman emperors and aristocrats, hunting has a long history as a viable survival tactic or economic endeavor, a training ground for manhood, and a pastime symbolic of nobility in the ancient world.[43] The imagery of the huntress summons the male world of conflict and aggression, a field from which women and girls, of course, were excluded. I make a point of this because the association of girls with the virgin goddess seems natural and so, too, does the goddess's identity as a huntress; this line of reasoning leads us to interpret the statues of girls with quivers strapped to their backs and bows in their hands as nothing more than charming masquerades. Yet the mythological sources and cult tradition portray a remote, strange, and often lethal goddess.

Girls were depicted as Diana in Roman funerary sculpture not only because the goddess's status as chaste maiden reflected the girls' stage of life but also because the huntress could signify the heroic mode of representation or even *virtus*, the premier male virtue of courage and valor (recall the bare right breast on some of the figures, an attribute shared with depictions of Amazons and the manly personifications Virtus and Roma). Diana was chosen not because she protects women; rather, it is the ambivalence of Diana, her resistance to categories of gender and of mature sexuality, that appealed to parents mourning their daughters. Dying young, these girls lacked the traditional repertoire of feminine accomplishments (fidelity to a husband and tireless devotion to domestic tasks) that served to praise women in epitaphs; more importantly, they lacked the defining characteristics of the female, that is, the sexual development that begins with marriage and culminates in motherhood. Precisely because they are without this experience, they can be seen as being more like the male, as evidenced in the aggression and vigilance of the huntress in the portrait statues and reliefs. I suggest that the deceased girls were endowed with *virtus* in compensation for the loss of their lives or for their unfulfilled state as virgins and that their assumption of the goddess's identity brings them glory. The deceased girls depicted as Diana have bypassed the usual accolades accorded to exemplary women and, despite their gender, have been accorded a heroic portrait reserved for daughters who didn't get a chance to live up to their parents' expectations.

[42] Vernant 1991, 197–202.   [43] Barringer 2001, 10–59.

Works Cited

Alföldi, A., "Diana Nemorensis," *American Journal of Archaeology* 64 (1960) 137–44.

———, *Early Rome and the Latins* (Ann Arbor 1963).

Altmann, W., *Die römischen Grabaltäre der Kaiserzeit* (Berlin 1905).

Barringer, J., *The Hunt in Ancient Greece* (Baltimore and London 2001).

Becatti, G., *Arte e gusto negli scrittori latini* (Rome 1950).

Bieber, M., *Ancient Copies* (New York 1977).

Boëls-Janssen, N., *La vie religieuse des matrones dans la Rome archaïque, Collection de l'École française de Rome* 176 (Rome 1993).

Calza, G., "Il tipo di Artemide Amazzone," *Ausonia* 10 (1921) 160–68.

———, "L'Artemide di Ostia," *Bollettino d'arte* 9 (1922) 394–402.

Calza, R., *Scavi di Ostia*, vol. 5.1: *I Ritratti.* (Rome 1965).

Candida, B., *Altari e cippi nel Museo Nazionale Romano* (Rome 1979)

Cole, S. G., "The Social Functions of Rituals of Maturation: The Koureion and the Arkteia," *Zeitschrift für Papyrologie und Epigraphik* 55 (1984) 233–44.

Dixon, S., *The Roman Family* (Baltimore and London 1992).

Faraone, C., "Playing the Bear and Fawn for Artemis: Female Initiation or Substitute Sacrifice?," in *Initiation in Ancient Greek Rituals and Narratives: New Perspectives*, ed. D. B. Dodd and C. A. Faraone (London 2003) 43–68.

Felletti-Maj, B. M., *Museo Nazionale Romano: I Ritratti* (Rome 1953).

Fittschen, K., "Mädchen, nicht Knaben," *Mitteilungen des deutschen archäologischen Instituts, römische Abteilung* 99 (1992) 301–5.

Fittschen, K., and P. Zanker, *Katalog der römischen Porträts in den Capitolinischen Museen und den anderen kommunalen Sammlungen der Stadt Rom*, Band 3: *Kaiserinnen- und Prinzessinnenbildnisse Frauenporträts* (Mainz 1983).

Frazer, J. G., *The Golden Bough: A Study in Magic and Religion*, 3rd ed. (London 1911).

Gazda, E., "Beyond Copying: Artistic Originality and Tradition," in *The Ancient Art of Emulation: Studies in Artistic Originality and Tradition from the Present to Classical Antiquity*, ed. E. Gazda (Ann Arbor 2002) 1–24.

Gercke, W., "Untersuchungen zum römischen Kinderporträt von den Anfängen bis in hadrianische Zeit" (D.Phil. diss., Universität Hamburg 1968).

Giuliano, A., ed., *Museo Nazionale Romano*, vol. 1.1: *Le sculture* (Rome 1979).

Gordon, A. E., "The Cults at Aricia," *University of California Publications in Classical Archaeology* 2.1 (1934) 1–20.

Granino Cecere, M. G., "A Nemi una Diana non nemorense," *Mitteilungen des deutschen archäologischen Instituts, römische Abteilung* 108 (2003) 287–92.

Green, C., "The Wounds of Diana," paper read at the 2002 Annual Meeting of the Classical Association of the United Kingdom and Scotland, Edinburgh, 4–7 April 2002.

Guldager Bilde, P., "The Sanctuary of Diana Nemorensis: The Late Republican Acrolithic Sculptures," *Acta archaeologica* 66 (1995) 191–217.

———, "'Those Nemi Sculptures . . .' Marbles from a Roman Sanctuary in the University of Pennsylvania Museum," *Expedition* 40 (1998) 36–47.

———, "The Sculptures from the Sanctuary of Diana Nemorensis, Types and Contextualization: An Overview," in *Nemi-Status Quo*, ed. J. Rasmus Brandt, A.-M. Leander Touati, and J. Zahle (Rome 2000) 93–109.

Hänninen, M.-L., "Traces of Women's Devotion in the Sanctuary of Diana at Nemi," in *Nemi-Status Quo*, ed. J. Rasmus Brandt, A.-M. Leander Touati, and J. Zahle (Rome 2000) 45–50.

Harlow, M., and R. Laurence, *Growing Up and Growing Old in Ancient Rome: A Life Course Approach* (London and New York 2002).

Helbig, W., ed., *Führer durch die öffentlichen Sammlungen klassischer Altertümer in Rom*, vol. 4, 4th ed. (Tübingen 1972).

Hermann, W., *Römische Götteraltäre* (Kallmünz 1961).

Holland, L., "Worshiping Diana: The Cult of a Roman Goddess in Republican Italy" (Ph.D. diss., University of North Carolina, Chapel Hill 2002).

King, M., "'A Son, a Little Child of Unknown Promise is Dead: A Fragment of Time Has Been Lost': The Perception of Infant Mortality in Roman Consolation Literature," paper read at the Annual Meeting of the Classical Association of the United Kingdom and Scotland, Edinburgh, 4–7 April 2002.

Kleiner, D. E. E., *Roman Imperial Funerary Altars with Portraits* (Rome 1987).

Koortbojian, M., "*In Commemorationem Mortuorum*: Text and Image along the 'Street of Tombs'," in *Art and Text in Roman Culture*, ed. J. Elsner (Cambridge and New York 1996) 210–33.

Lindner, R., "Die Giebelgruppe von Eleusis mit Raub der Persephone," *Jahrbuch des deutschen archäologischen Instituts* 97 (1982) 303–400.

Meiggs, R., *Roman Ostia* (Oxford 1973).

Mellor, R. "The Goddess Roma," *Aufstieg und Niedergang der römischen Welt*, ed. H. Temporini (Berlin and New York 1981) 2.17.2:950–1030.

Moltesen, M., "The Marbles from Nemi in Exile: Sculpture in Copenhagen, Nottingham, and Philadelphia," in *Nemi-Status Quo*, ed. J. Rasmus Brandt, A.-M. Leander Touati, and J. Zahle (Rome 2000) 111–19.

Muthmann, F., *Statuenstützen und dekoratives Beiwerk an griechischen und römischen Bildwerken*, Abhandlungen der Heidelberger Akademie der Wissenschaften, Philosophisch-Historische Klasse 3 (1950).

Pairault, F.-H., "Diana Nemorensis: déesse latine, déesse hellénisée," *Mélanges de l'École française de Rome, Antiquité* 81 (1969) 425–71.

Paribeni, R., *Le Terme di Diocleziano e il Museo Nazionale Romano* (Rome 1928).

Parisinou, E., "The 'Language' of Female Hunting Outfits in Ancient Greece," in *Women's Dress in the Ancient Greek World*, ed. L. Llewellyn-Jones (London 2002) 55–72.

Perry, E., "Rhetoric, Literary Criticism, and the Roman Aesthetics of Artistic Imitation," in *The Ancient Art of Emulation: Studies in Artistic Originality and Tradition from the Present to Classical Antiquity*, ed. E. Gazda (Ann Arbor 2002) 153–72.

Pfrommer, M., "Leochares? Die hellenistischen Schulen der Artemis Versailles," *Istanbuler Mitteilungen* 34 (1984) 171–82.

Picard, G.-C., "La Vénus funéraire des romaines," *Mélanges de l'École française de Rome, Antiquité* 56 (1939) 121–35.

Scheid, J., "The Religious Roles of Roman Women," in *A History of Women in the West*, vol. 1: *From Ancient Goddesses to Christian Saints*, ed. P. Schmitt Pantel (Cambridge, Mass. and London 1992) 377–408.

Schraudolph, E., *Römische Götterweihungen mit Reliefschmuck aus Italien. Altäre, Basen und Reliefs*, Archäologie und Geschichte Band 2 (Heidelberg 1993).

Sestieri, P. C., "Diana Venatrix," *Rivista del Reale Istituto d'Archeologia e Storia dell'Arte* 8 (1941) 107–28.

Smith, R. R. R., "Cultural Choice and Political Identity in Honorific Portrait Statues in the Greek East in the Second Century A.D.," *Journal of Roman Studies* 88 (1998) 56–93.

Stewart, A., *Art, Desire, and the Body in Ancient Greece* (Cambridge 1997).

———, *Greek Sculpture* (New Haven and London 1990).

Tittoni, M. E., and S. Guarino, eds., *Invisibilia* (Rome 1992).

Traversari, G., *Aspetti formali della scultura neoclassica a Roma dal I al III sec. d.C.* (Rome 1968).

Vermeule, C. C., *The Goddess Roma in the Art of the Roman Empire* (Cambridge 1959).

Vernant, J.-P., *Mortals and Immortals: Collected Essays*, ed. F. I. Zeitlin (Princeton 1991).

Wissowa, G., *Religion und Kultus der Römer*, 2nd ed. (Munich 1912).

Wrede, H., "Das Mausoleum der Claudia Semne und die bürgerliche Plastik der Kaiserzeit," *Mitteilungen des deutschen archäologischen Instituts, römische Abteilung* 78 (1971) 125–66.

———, Consecratio in Formam Deorum. *Vergöttliche Privatpersonen in der römischen Kaiserzeit* (Mainz 1981).

9 ◆ TRANSCENDING GENDER: ASSIMILATION, IDENTITY, AND ROMAN IMPERIAL PORTRAITS

Eric R. Varner

Romans had a richly allusive array of visual models from which to choose in fashioning their artistic identities in portraiture. Assimilation through attributes, costumes, and body types confirmed the social positions and civic, heroic, or divine aspirations of Roman patrons, both men and women. While male and female societal roles were more diachronically defined, portrait identities and the concomitant role models they established were not conceived around binary opposition of gender. Indeed, the resulting images could in fact be quite fluid and confidently transgendered, consciously hybridizing elements of traditional male and female categorizations.

Assimilation required that visually literate Roman audiences recognize a complex system of reference and counterreference that lies at the heart of Roman portrait production. Recent assessments, however, by Marianne Bergmann, R. R. R. Smith, and Fred Albertson, of the Colossus of Nero have called into serious question long-held assumptions about theomorphic assimilation and imperial identity.[1] Often interpreted as an intended representation of Nero in the guise of Sol Apollo, the Colossus may have been precisely the conceptual reverse, an image of the sun god with Neronian attributes. Thus, the Colossus can be read as a particularly imperial incarnation of the deity Sol Augustus.[2]

Gender Blending: Emperors and Goddesses

While such public linkages of gods and emperors are not surprising, assimilative images of deities imbued with individualized imperial physiognomy are not gender specific. Ultimately, the mixture of human and divine, male and female, in assimilative imperial portraits intentionally blurs traditional taxonomic categories and unequivocally asserts the transcendence of imperial authority over prescribed gender roles. Beginning with Augustus, male rulers and goddesses were also visually conjoined. A reverse of a *denarius*, minted by C. Marius in 13 B.C., depicts the goddess Diana with Augustus's masculine physiognomy; Augustus's own profile appears for ready comparison on the obverse.[3]

[1] Bergmann 1998, 189–201, fig. 3; Smith 2000, 532–38; Albertson 2001.

[2] An altar commissioned by Eumolpus, who was slave in charge of furnishings at the Domus Aurea, presents important visual evidence for the contemporary reception of this concept (Florence, Museo Archeologico, inv. 86025; *CIL* 6 3719 = 31033; *ILS* 1774; Bergmann 1994, 9, pl. 5.3; Bergmann 1998, 194–201, pl. 38; Smith 2000, 539). The altar is dedicated to Sol, who appears as a radiate bust with facial features and elaborate coiffure derived from

Nero's fourth and final portrait type, in use between A.D. 64 and 68.

Unfinished at the time of Nero's suicide on 9 June A.D. 68, the Colossus was finally dedicated in A.D. 75 under Vespasian, minus any of the intended Neronian references. The Colossus continued to be an enduring symbol of the *aeternitas* of Rome and imperial authority. An intaglio in the Pergamon museum in Berlin appears to reflect its Vespasianic appearance; Bergmann 1994, 11, pl. 2.3.

[3] *BMCRE* 1, 21, nos. 104–5, pl. 42.2.

Fig. 1. *Diana Augusta*, denarius, *Rome, 13 B.C.,*
Bibliothèque Nationale de France
(after Girard 1976, pl. XXV.524).

Fig. 2. *Domitian/Minerva, Paris, Bibliothèque*
Nationale de France, Cabinet des Médailles 26, ca. A.D.
81–96 (after Megow 1987, pl. 37.5).

Although sometimes identified as Augustus's daughter Julia assimilated to Diana (the argument is that she looks like her father), the numismatic image, as more plausibly suggested by both John Pollini and Susan Wood, is likely an evocation of Diana Augusta, in which the goddess is subtly assimilated to the emperor (fig. 1).[4] Associations of Augustus with Diana may have been partially motivated by the emperor's prominently vaunted connections to Apollo, the brother and masculine complement to Diana. For example, a cameo in Florence endows Augustus with a long Apolline (and more feminine) coiffure.[5] Venus, the ancestress of the *gens Iulia*, also appears on a *denarius* ca. 16 B.C. with a masculinized Augustan profile, as does the goddess Feronia on a *denarius* ca. 19–18 B.C.[6]

The Augustus-Diana imagery may also be intended to allude to the all-important imperial virtue of *virtus* (strength) as well. Eve D'Ambra has explored the goddess's masculine inflections of *virtus* and the surprisingly active and long-lived male and ephebic involvement in the goddess's cult at Nemi.[7] Indeed, as early as 18 B.C., the goddess Virtus was also represented with a recognizably Augustan profile in a series of *denarii* minted by L. Aquillius Florus.[8] Ultimately, Augustus's visual promotion of his own *virtus* in the Diana and Virtus coins must be derived from the *Clupeus*

[4] Fullerton 1985, 476, 480, pl. 55.10; Pollini 1990, 353–55, fig. 29b; Wood 1999, 64, 67–68.

[5] Museo Archeologico, inv. 14521, 8.4 × 4.9 cm (formerly in the Medici collection); Giuliano 1989, 228, no. 152, with figs.

[6] Paris, Bibliothèque Nationale, H 37332 (Venus); Paris,

Bibliothèque Nationale, 89 A 61678 (Feronia); Pollini 1990, 355–56, figs. 32–33.

[7] See her contribution in this volume.

[8] *BMCRE* 7, no. 36, pl. 1.19, 8, nos. 43–44, pl. 2.3–4; Palazzo Massimo, no. 46.

Virtutis set up in the Curia Julia in 27 B.C., which codified Augustus's virtues as *virtus, clementia, pietas,* and *iustitia.* These virtues in turn became canonical for all subsequent emperors.

Later in the first century A.D., Claudius permitted the citizens of Alexandria to dedicate a golden statue of the goddess, *Pax Augustana Claudiana,* at Rome.[9] This representation is mentioned in a letter written by Claudius to the Alexandrians on 10 November A.D. 41 that primarily discusses the erection of various portraits of the emperor and other members of the imperial family. Somewhat surprisingly, Claudius feared that the statue might appear "offensive" (φορτικότερος), and this may have been the result of its investiture with elements of Claudius's own male physiognomy.

Similar striking marriages of masculine physiognomy with divine female iconography occur under Domitian, helping to foster an identity for the emperor that is not beholden to traditional gender categories. In three gems in the Cabinet des Médailles, the emperor's patron goddess Minerva is imbued with the emperor's distinctive (and masculine) facial features.[10] In two of the gems, Minerva appears in bust form wearing the helmet and aegis, while a third (fig. 2) is a full-length presentation of the goddess with her recognizably female body but whose Domitianic facial features are again clearly discernible. The body type used for the goddess also appears on Domitianic coin reverses, as for instance a *sestertius* from Rome issued in 81.[11] All three gems appropriate the emperor's physiognomy as visual embodiments of Domitian's close association with Minerva and furthermore incarnate the goddess as Minerva Augusta.

The Paris gems are expensive works of art, likely commissioned either by Domitian himself as distribution pieces or by one of his partisans. As such, they must reflect contemporary court ideology concerning the emperor's identification with Minerva, which endowed him with all of her virtues including wisdom and military strength. Domitian's conceptual identification with the goddess found monumental expression in the Forum Transitorium, whose surviving imagery is predominantly female and represents various women and goddesses and the story of Arachne's punishment by Minerva.[12] The imagery functions as visual *exempla* of correct moral behavior for Roman women and corresponds to Domitian's revival of Augustus's earlier legislation regarding adultery, divorce, and procreation. One of the principal audiences for whom the forum was designed was clearly Roman elite women, whose behavior was the target of Domitian's legislation, perhaps suggesting that the designers of the cameos also had female viewers in mind as at least one of their target audiences.

The agglomerative strategy adopted in the Domitianic gems for creating a recognizably Augustan identity for Minerva was not limited to the more restricted realm of glyptic sculpture for it was also employed in a colossal head from Rome and now in Budapest (fig. 3).[13] The combination of masculine facial features and female coiffure has problematized the identification of this portrait, and it has been assigned to Livia, identified as a reworked private Julio-Claudian woman, or described as Domitian refashioned into an ideal likeness.[14] Nevertheless, the hairstyle itself is clearly that of

[9] London Papyrus 1912.35–38; Rose 1997, 186–88.

[10] Bibliothèque Nationale, Cabinet des Médailles 22, inv. 71.A 234431, 9.9 × 7.0 cm, Megow 1987, 223–24, no. A 113, pl. 37; Bibliothèque Nationale, Cabinet des Médailles 26, 12.0 × 5.5 cm; Bibliothèque Nationale, Cabinet des Médailles 128, 13.4 × 8.1 cm ; Megow 1987, 108, 124 138, 143, 221–22, nos. A 110–11, pl. 37.1–2 (with earlier literature); Guiraud 1996, 94, fig. 2.

[11] ANS 1944.100.42561; Varner 2000, 154–56, no. 33, with figs.

[12] D'Ambra 1993; Bauer and Morselli 1995.

[13] Museum, inv. 347016. Kreikenbom 1992, 107–8, pl. 35. The head is from the Palazzo Brancaccio in Rome and is worked for insertion (likely into an acrolithic statue).

[14] Matheson 2000, 72, figs. 2a–b.

Fig. 4. "Galliena Augusta," aureus, Rome, ca. A.D. 267 (after Kent 1978, fig. 496).

Fig. 3. Domitian/Minerva, Budapest, Museum, inv. 347016, ca. A.D. 81–96 (after Varner 2000, 72 fig. 2a).

Minerva, comparable to the Minerva Giustianiani, while the physiognomy is that of Domitian.[15] The Parisian gems provide important parallels for the correct identification of the colossal head. The cuttings along the side and back of the head were intended to anchor a helmet, probably in metal. The colossal scale of the head would have made this one of the most visually emphatic expressions of the Domitian-Minerva axis in Rome. There may also be intimations of a kind of divine transvestitism in reports by both Martial and Quintillian that Domitian wore the *aegis*.[16]

Minerva was not the only goddess to be represented with the emperor's likeness, as attested by a *dupondius* of Julia Titi likely minted at the outset of Domitian's principate in 81 that depicts Vesta on the reverse, masculinized with a recognizably Domitianic physiognomy.[17] As with the Domitianized representations of Minerva, the coin image allows the emperor to align himself visually with the goddess and appropriate all the virtues she embodies. Indeed, Domitian's connections with the Vestals and Vesta are well attested in ancient sources.[18] Similarly, Domitian can be aligned with Ceres through his adoption of the *corona spiccea* on coins from Alexandria.[19] These Domitianic representations dramatically demonstrate the surprisingly pervasive (perhaps even invasive) nature of the emperor's image and that the emperor's identification with female divinities is not restricted by his masculinity or impeded by their femininity.[20] Furthermore, the amorphous conceptions of sex and gender embedded in the Domitianic Minervas, Vesta, and Ceres may have additional heroic reverberations especially appealing to first-century A.D. audiences, as witnessed by the popularity

---

[15] Rome, Musei Vaticani, Braccio Nuovo, inv. 2223; Canciani 1984, 1086, no. 154.

[16] Earlier, both Alexander and Demetrios Poliorcetes had aligned themselves with Athena; for Alexander, see Stewart 1993, 44. For Demetrios and his coins that may conflate his own features with those of the goddess, see Head, Hill, and Walker 1959, 54, pl. 29, nos. 8–10; Green 1990, 44.

[17] *BMCRE* 279, nos. 256–58, pl. 53.8; Kent 1978, 240.

[18] Suet. *Dom.* 8.3–4; *Ep.* 4.11; Dio 67.3.3–4; Stat. *Silv.* 1.1.35–36; Plut. *Num.* 10.8; Philostr. *VA* 7.6.

[19] *RPC* nos. 2574, 2597, 2613, 2628–29, 2632, 2651, 2656; Lichoka, 1997, 88.

[20] As suggested by Bartman was earlier the case with Augustus and Vesta or Cybele: Bartman 1999, 94–95.

of the Achilles on Skyros motif in painting and literature.[21] The story, which documents Achilles' transfiguration from male to female and back again to male, occurs in nearly contemporary private and imperial contexts, as for instance the House of Castor and Pollux in Pompeii[22] and in Nero's Domus Aurea,[23] as well as in book 1 of Statius's *Achilleid*, written under Domitian.[24]

By the mid-third century, the emperor's ability to construct compound male and female personae finds visual expression on *aurei* of Gallienus minted in Rome ca. 267 that amalgamate a pronounced male bearded profile with a female epigraphic identity as Galliena Augusta (fig. 4).[25] Gallienus's own initiation at Eleusis and his subsequent close association with Demeter may have provided the impetus for this particular numismatic evocation of imperial gender transcendence.[26] A Gallienic *sestertius* is equally sexually ambiguous and depicts a radiate Genius of the Roman people with long flowing feminine locks, Gallienus's beardless profile, and a turreted crown usually associated with female divinities like Cybele and Fortuna or Tyche.[27] The deliberate ambivalence of gender in these images again creates a fluid visual persona for the emperor that eclipses standard definitions of masculine and feminine.

Assimilated Identities: Imperial Husbands and Wives

The admixture of political power, gender, and transcendence is also present in the numerous images of imperial women that have been intentionally masculinized or assimilated to their male counterparts. This phenomenon has Ptolemaic precedents, especially in the representations of Cleopatra I, II, and III that combine heavy masculine facial features with the queens' characteristic Isis coiffures. Sculpted portraits of Cleopatra II or III in Vienna[28] and the Louvre[29] are emblematic of these images, as is a bronze head from the Villa of the Papyri.[30] Masculinized presentations of these Ptolemaic queens even pervaded the normally more idealizing and classicizing realm of royal gem production. The heavier, more masculine facial features of an agate cameo in Florence were identified in the Renaissance as those of Ptolemy Apion, the last king of Cyrene.[31] A similar cameo in Naples was also identified as the Cyrenaican king, although both gem portraits should rather be associated with Cleopatra II or III.[32] Modern and early modern expectations about gender have impacted the misidentification of these images.

[21] Trimble 2002, 231–38.

[22] Pompeii VI, 9, 6; Naples, Museo Nazionale Archeologico, inv. 9110; Cantilena et al. 1986, 152, no. 205.

[23] Domus Aurea room 119; Iacopi 1999, 51–71; Segala and Sciortino 1999, 86–90 (with figs.).

[24] Stat. *Achil.* 325–857.

[25] *RIC* 229; Kent 1978, 314, no. 496.

[26] Matthew 1943, 68; Alföldi 1979, 585–606; Spaeth 1996, 27–60; Lichoka 1997, 91. Kent (1973) suggests that the form of the emperor's name is actually a hypercorrected vocative but acknowledges its ambivalent and unconventional nature.

[27] Bastien 1994, pl. 100.5.

[28] Kunsthistorisches Museum, inv. AS I 406; h. 0.31 m; Walker and Higgs 2001, 60, no. 26 (A. Bernhard-Walcher

and S. A. Ashton), with fig. and earlier literature.

[29] MA 3546, h. 0.022 m; Walker and Higgs 2001, 59, no. 25 (S. A. Ashton), with figures and earlier literature.

[30] Inv. 5598, h. 0.405 m; Smith 1988, 160, no. 24, pl. 19 (with earlier literature); Cantilena et al. 1989, 136, no. 201, with fig. Although they lack the masculinized physiognomies of the Cleopatra portraits, paired mosaic representations of two Ptolemaic queens (likely Arsinoe II and Berenike II) from Thumis do include male military costume and armor; see Kuttner 1999, 112.

[31] Museo Archeologico, inv. 14650, 2 × 1.8 cm (formerly in the Medici Collection); Giuliano 1989, 222, no. 143, with earlier literature; Borea and Gasparri 2000, 550–51, no. 11 (M. E. Micheli).

[32] Naples, Museo Nazionale Archeologico, inv. 25856, 1.2 × 1.1 cm (formerly belonging to Fulvio Orsini and then the Farnese); Gasparri 1994, 142, no. 120, fig. 115.

In the late republic, numismatic images of both Octavia and Cleopatra VII are rendered more male and assimilated to those of their consort Antonius. A *cistophorus*, minted in 39 B.C., probably at Ephesus, represents Antonius and Octavia with nearly identical jugate profiles.[33] The visual *similitudo* expressed on the Ephesian coin is striking and underscores their union and marriage. Seven years later, in 32 B.C., a similar method is adopted on a *denarius* featuring Cleopatra.[34] Cleopatra's facial features have been made to resemble Antonius's, and even her characteristic melon hairstyle (*melonenfrisur*) has been redesigned to make it more like the textured coiffure of her consort. As in her other numismatic images and her three surviving sculpted portraits in Berlin,[35] the Vatican,[36] and Cherchel,[37] Cleopatra wears the flat royal diadem, traditionally a symbol of male royal authority that had been featured by several of her Ptolemaic ancestresses. Again, the emphatic *similitudo* on the coins celebrates the sexual, marital, and political alliance of the pair. The more masculine, Antonian appearance of the queen may also have been designed to appeal to Antonius's Roman soldiers, who were undoubtedly a primary audience of this carefully contrived numismatic imagery. Many modern observers have taken these coins literally *at face value* and have been unable to reconcile the heavy masculine facial features and prominent hooked nose with the literary accounts of Cleopatra's charm and beauty. The identity that the coins construct for Cleopatra as Antonius's twin and equal, however, had little to do with Cleopatra's actual physical appearance. These numismatic representations have been consciously manipulated, as is underscored when they are compared to her three surviving sculpted images, which are classicizing and idealizing representations of the queen.

In view of modern feminist approaches, these numismatic images raise the additional question of whether Cleopatra's female identity is being subsumed by and intentionally subordinated to Antonius's male identity. The initial answer would seem to be yes, as Cleopatra's image is adjusted to conform to that of Antonius. However, an alternative reading is possible for it seems equally likely that Cleopatra is proactively expropriating the positive aspects of Antonius's masculinity as she fashions an image of a powerful ruler capable of opposing Octavian in the east.

Quite the opposite can also occur in the case of Antonius's visual dialogue with Octavia. Her own individual feminine facial features are not always suppressed in order to facilitate her assimilation to Antony, and, in fact, on certain issues, it is Antony's features that are massaged and softened to conform more closely to those of Octavia, as in an *aureus* of 38 B.C. from an unspecified eastern mint (fig. 5).[38] These images are likely designed to stress Antony's *similitudo* with Octavian, through the figure of Octavia, during the period of their reconciliation. Negative aspects of femininity, including softness and passivity, were also used to discredit Antonius during his alliance with Cleopatra. A series of Arretine bowls depict Hercules and Omphale in their exchanged clothing and gender roles, and they use the allusive language of mythology as negative comments on Antonius's perceived enslavement to the foreign queen Cleopatra during his conflict with Octavian.[39]

Although Livia's images are not overtly masculinized, they are assimilated stylistically to those

[33] Kent 1978, 110.

[34] *BMCR* 2.525.179; Kent 1978, 111; Pollini 2002, 32–33 n. 59.

[35] Berlin, Staatliche Museen, inv. 1976.10; h. 0.27 m; Smith 1988, 169, no. 68, pl. 45.4–6; Walker and Higgs 2001, 220, no. 198 (P. Higgs).

[36] Museo Gregoriano Profano, inv. 38511, h. 0.39 m; Smith 1988, 35, 97–98, 133, 169, no. 67, pl. 44; Walker and Higgs

2001, 218–19, no. 196 (P. Higgs).

[37] Cherchel, Museum, inv. S66 (31), h. 0.31 m; Smith 1988, 169, no. 69, pl. 45.1–3; Walker and Higgs 2001, 219, no. 197 (M. Ferroukhi).

[38] *RRC* no. 533/3a; Wood 1999, 46–50, esp. 49; Walker and Higgs 2001, 240, no. 259 (J. Williams); Pollini 2002, 32–33, fig. 26.

[39] Kampen 1996, 235.

Fig. 5. Antonius and Octavia, aureus, unspecified eastern mint, 38 B.C., London, British Museum, BMCRR East 144 (© Copyright the Trustees of The British Museum).

of Augustus, as in the dynastic group that also included Tiberius from Arsinoe in Egypt.[40] Nevertheless, Livia's portraits can be endowed with masculine attributes, including the laurel crown of the triumphing Roman general that became a standard imperial insignia in male likenesses. Livia wears the *corona triumphalis* on four cameos in Florence[41] and St. Petersburg.[42] Not surprisingly, Livia's close association with laurel and triumph is not coincidental and is linked to the revered laurel grove of her villa at Prima Porta, which was created by rooting the sprigs of laurel that the male members of her family had carried in their own triumphal processions in Rome.[43] A headless statue of Livia in Munich deemphasizes the female aspects of her body, especially in the rather flat hips and abdomen, and the draping of the palla exhibits similarities to the toga.[44] Livia's adoption of male attributes, characteristics, or behavior is also reflected in Caligula's epithet for her, *Ulixes stolatus* (Ulysses wearing a *stola*).[45] Livia's female descendants also wear the laurel crown, especially her great granddaughter Agrippina Minor, as in a sardonyx cameo in the British Museum.[46] In a Claudian context, Agrippina's *corona triumphalis* would have additionally proclaimed her position as the only surviving child and legitimate heir of the popular and charismatic general Germanicus. Indeed, in Tacitus, Agrippina Minor, like her mother before her, is cast in the role of *dux femina*, a woman who transgressed her proper female roles and dared to act as a leader in her own right.[47]

More aggressive assimilative strategies for representing ruling couples become commonplace during the imperial period. Agrippina Minor's physical resemblance to her uncle and husband Claudius is stressed on coins like a *cistophorus* from Ephesus minted ca. 50–51,[48] just as earlier provincial coinage had presented Claudius's previous wife Messalina with facial features modeled on those of the emperor.[49] Agrippina's heavier masculine facial features on the Claudian *cistophorus* stand in stark contrast to her more feminine presentations in sculpted replicas of her first portrait

[40] Ny Carlsberg Glyptotek: Livia: inv. 1444, h. 0.34 m; Johansen 1994, 96–97, no. 36; Augustus: inv. 1443; h. 0.55 m; Johansen 1994, 90–91, no. 33, with figs.; Tiberius: inv. 1445, h. 0.47 m; Johansen 1994, 114–15, no. 45.

[41] Museo Archeologico, inv. 14528, 4.7 × 3.7 cm; Giuliano 1989, 229, no. 153, with figs.

[42] Hermitage, inv. Ž154, 2.1 × 1.8 cm; Bartman 1999, 192–93, no. 106, fig. 94; Hermitage Ž267, 4 × 3.1 cm; Bartman 1999, 193, no. 107; Hermitage Ž268, 3.1 × 2.5 cm; Bartman 1999, 193, no. 108.

[43] The site of the villa was determined by a *miraculum* in which a white hen holding a laurel branch in its beak was dropped by an eagle into Livia's lap. The branch was rooted, and the later sprigs were taken from this tree: Kellum 1994, 222–23.

[44] Munich, Staatliche Antikensammlungen und Glyptotek 367, h. 1.67 m; Bartman 1999, 41, 154, no. 18, fig. 39.

[45] Suet. *Calig.* 23.2.

[46] 3593, inv. 99.7-22.3; Megow 1987, 292, no. D14, pl. 18.6.

[47] Santoro L'Hoir 1984.

[48] *BMCRE* 197, no. 231; Kent 1978, 187, no. 284; Bastien 1994, pl. 30.3.

[49] *BMCRE* 199, no. 242, pl. 34.8; *BMC Cappodocia* 46, pls. 58–59; Mickoki 1995, 45, 187, no. 245; Wood 1999, 275–76.

Fig. 6. Claudius and Agrippina Minor, Gemma Claudia, Vienna Kunsthistorisches Museum, inv. IX a 63, ca. A.D. 41–54 (after Megow 1987, pl. 32.4).

type created under her brother Caligula, such as those in the Schloss Fasanerie and the Rhode Island School of Design.[50] The physical resemblance between Agrippina and Claudius is especially evident in the Gemma Claudia, in which their jugate profiles are juxtaposed with those of Agrippina's mother and father, Germanicus and Agrippina Maior (fig. 6).[51] Indeed, the stressed resemblance between Agrippina and Claudius is striking, and perhaps even shocking, in the cameo as it broadcasts not just the *similitudo* and *concordia* between the reigning *princeps* and his wife; this familial composition draws attention to cosanguinity connecting all four and the uncle-niece ties between Claudius and Agrippina that many of their opponents claimed made their union incestuous.

Later, Domitian and Domitia are often depicted with similar facial features in their sculpted and numismatic likenesses, including a *tetradrachm* likely minted at Ephesus ca. A.D. 82.[52] The palpable *similitudo* of these couples is another example of the visual rhetoric employed to communicate concepts of imperial *concordia* and is continued in the second century, as for instance in representations of Marcus Aurelius and Faustina Minor. Their heavy-lidded and bulging eyes visually conjoin their portraits, as in images created for them at the time of their betrothal and marriage.[53] Similarly, likenesses of female relatives of Marcus's co-emperor, Lucius Verus, stress their demonstrably different and elongated eyes in order to link them to the (other) emperor, as is evident in images of one of his sisters, either Ceionia Fabia or Ceionia Plautia.[54]

The notion of imperial *concordia* was even more politically charged and entrenched in the middle years of the third century as the empire was engulfed in a fifty-year period of military,

[50] Schloss Fasanerie, cat. no. 22, h. 0.322 m; Wood 1999, 238, 240, 295–96, figs. 109–10; Rhode Island School of Design, inv. 56.097, h. 0.305 m; Wood 1999, 238, 240, 295–96, figs. 107–8.

[51] Vienna, Kunsthistorisches Museum, inv. IX a 63; Megow 1987, 200–201, no. A 81, pls. 31, 32.1, 2–4.

[52] *BMCRE* 353, no. 252, pl. 68.1.

[53] Marcus: Museo Palatino, inv. 3683; Tomei 1997, 93, no. 66.

Faustina: Museo Capitolino, Stanza degli Imperatori 2, inv. 449; Fittschen and Zanker 1983, 20–21, no. 19, pls. 24–26.

[54] Rome, Museo Capitolino, Sala delle Colombe 62, inv. 336; Fittschen and Zanker 1983, 26–27, no. 26, pls. 35–36; Rome, Museo Capitolino, Magazzini, Antiquario, inv. 6269; Fittschen and Zanker 1983, 27, no. 27, pl. 37; Rome, Palazzo Spada, inv. 74; Fittschen and Zanker 1983, 26, Beil. 14a–c; Aquileia, Museo Nazionale, inv. 401; Fittschen and Zanker 1983, 26, 14d.

political, economic, social, and cultural instability. The coinage of the first of the soldier-emperors, Maximinus Thrax, prominently celebrates his deceased wife, Paulina, as *diva*. *Denarii* minted for both of them in Rome in 237 clearly demonstrate the way in which Paulina is endowed with the rugged and masculine visage of her husband, although beardless.[55] Slightly later, certain numismatic representations of Otacilia Severa, including bronze medallions from Rome, depict her with profiles very similar to those of her husband, Philip the Arab.[56] In both instances, assimilated images of the imperial women are intended to project expected imperial concepts of *similitudo*, and *concordia*, necessary to the stability of the dynasty and empire. Indeed, the legend of the medallion with Otacilia makes the allusion explicit: *Concordia Augustorum* (harmony of the two augusti and the augusta). Nearly identical concepts and assimilations are at play in a medallion of Gallienus and Salonina from Rome issued ca. 257.[57]

Striking masculinized assimilations of imperial wives to their husbands continued to encode and reinforce imperial notions of *concordia* into the fourth century, as attested by numismatic representations of Galeria Valeria, the daughter of Diocletian (founder of the tetrarchy) and wife of Galerius (first Diocletian's junior colleague, then senior tetrarch in the east).[58] As the tetrarchy began to disintegrate, marble portraits of Maxentius[59] and his wife Valeria Maximilla insisted on a fictive physical resemblance between husband and wife intended to visually manifest an equally fictive political and dynastic *concordia*.[60] In actuality, Valeria Maximilla's father, Galerius, vigorously opposed Maxentius during his six-year reign from 306 to 312. As imperial images became less individualized and more abstracted later in the fourth century, it is perhaps not stylistically surprising that wives and husbands continued to resemble each other, as for instance on *solidi* minted at Constantinople in 383 depicting Aelia Flacilla and her husband Theodosius.[61]

Private Transgressions: Feminine Men and Masculine Women

The permeability of gender clearly demonstrated in the imperial images that defy strict taxonomic or diachronic categorization also manifests itself in a number of private likenesses. Reconfigured images can quite literally amalgamate male and female. A male portrait from the later third century in the Bardo in Tunis has unequivocally been altered from a representation of a female deity, and what is perhaps even more startling is that its transformation has also transgressed boundaries of gender.[62] Much of the drapery, the breasts, and the wheat stalks and poppies held in the right hand are derived from the front half of an image of Ceres. However, the face has been recut into an older, bearded male, and a lion skin has been refashioned from the veil that originally covered the head of the goddess. In its current iteration the portrait represents a follower of the cult of Hercules, cross-dressed as Omphale. Male adoption of female clothing is a

---

[55] Maximinus: Kent 1978, 309, no. 435; *BMCRE* 236, no. 161, pl. 38; Paulina: Kent 1978, 309, no. 436; *BMCRE* 233, nos. 126–36, pl. 37.

[56] Kent 1978, 311, no. 457; Gnecchi 1912, 97–99, nos. 1–17, pl. 109.1–9.

[57] Kent 1978, 313, no. 480; Gnecchi 1912, 110, nos. 51–54, pl. 115.4–6.

[58] Bastien 1994, 30–31, pls. 154–56.

[59] Stockholm, Nationalmuseum, inv. 106; Varner 2004, 216–17, 220, 286, no. 9.1, figs. 208a–b (with earlier literature).

[60] Museo Capitolino, Magazzini, inv. 106, h. 0.26 m; Varner 2004, 215, 219–20, 288, no. 96, fig. 214 (with earlier literature).

[61] Theodosius: Kent 1978, 339, no. 717, pl. 181; Aelia Flacilla: Kent 1978, 339, nos. 717–20, pls. 181–82.

[62] Inv. 3047; Yacoub 1982, 30, fig. 32.

Fig. 7. Relief of C. Rabirius Postumus Hermodorus, Rabiria Demaris, and Usia Prima, Museo Nazionale Romano, Palazzo Massimo alle Terme, inv. 196633, ca. 13 B.C.–A.D. 5, recut ca. A.D. 81–117 (after Kleiner 1977, fig. 63a).

well-attested aspect of Hercules' cult, and at Rome it was particularly associated with Hercules Victor.[63]

Similar cultic transvestism is also celebrated on the sarcophagus of Titus Flavius Trophimas from Ostia in the collections of the Terme.[64] Commissioned by Lucius Atilius Artemas and Claudia Apphias, for themselves and their friend, the "incomparable" Trophimas, the sarcophagus depicts two male shoemakers, presumably Trophimas and Artemas. The pair appears again to the left of the inscription plaque, this time in an Isiac ritual scene in which one is dressed in female costume. The deliberate juxtaposition of the deceased's masculine work roles and their female role-playing as initiates of Isis makes the traversal of gendered categories unmistakable and, as John Clarke has elucidated, may explicitly allude to a sexual relationship between the two men.[65] Furthermore, the transvestism and transgression of sexual categories likely held eschatological implications for the deceased's transition from life to death.

Isiac and eschatological nuances may also underlie the reconfiguration of a relief honoring Usia Prima in the Palazzo Massimo (fig. 7).[66] The inscription identifies Usia Prima as a priestess of Isis (SAC. ISIDIS); the goddess's *cistrum* has been incised into the background of the relief to the right of Usia's head and a *patera* to her left.[67] Her coiffure suggests a Flavian or early Trajanic date for the portrait. Nevertheless, the relief includes two other figures of C. Rabirius Postumus Hermodorus and Rabiria Demaris whose hairstyles and veristic portraits indicate that the relief was initially commissioned by freedmen ca. 13 B.C.–A.D. 5.[68] Usia Prima's likeness has been recut from

[63] Matthews 1993, 135; Delcourt 1961, 21–22. See also Kampen 1996, 243. Lydus, *Mens.* 4.8.

[64] Museo Nazionale Romano, inv. 184, h. 0.50 m, w. 1.86 m, d. 0.55 m; Giuliano 1981, 148–50 (S. Dyan, L. Musso, and P. Lombardi).

[65] Clarke 2003, 215–19.

[66] Palazzo Massimo alle Terme, inv. 196633; Kleiner 1977, 231, no. 63, figs. 63a–c; La Regina 1998, 40 (B. Germini).

[67] *CIL* 6 2246; the full text of the inscription reads: C. RABRIVS.POST.L RABIRIA VSIA .PRIMA .SAC. / HERMODORVS DEMARIS ISIDIS.

[68] Kleiner 1977, 231. The right half of Usia Prima's upper

a preexisting male portrait. Significantly, the body has not been substantially reworked, and she retains much of the (original) male togate body. Usia Prima pointedly lacks the breast visible in the adjacent figure of Rabiria Demaris. Rabiria turns toward Usia Prima, which would conventionally suggest that the original male figure was her husband. The blank space to Usia Prima's left may also indicate that originally there was a fourth figure in the relief.[69] In its current state, the relief asserts its transformative state with its juxtaposition of two distinct portrait styles and the combination of female likeness and male body. Given the transvestism present in the sarcophagus of Trophimas, these appositions are unlikely to be coincidental. Indeed, Plutarch clearly elucidates the hybridic nature of Isis and Isiac beliefs for nearly contemporary second-century audiences.[70]

Other reconfigured private images have also crossed gender divisions. A portrait of a Severan woman in Copenhagen has been refashioned from a representation of Antinous.[71] As Hugo Meyer has shown, the original likeness reflects Antinous's main portrait type, whose coiffure is still readily visible at the back of the head.[72] A portrait on the art market in the 1960s is an even stranger mutation.[73] The image currently depicts a bearded male from the later third century, but a prominent bun of wrapped braids from a Trajanic female likeness still crowns the back of the head. Its ambiguous commingling of masculine and feminine suggests that the unstable political and social climate of the third century may have allowed more insistent mergings of established gender-specific attributes.

Portraits of young children can raise doubts about their own gender, as for instance two bust-length images at Wellesley[74] and Cleveland.[75] Both of these likenesses, almost certainly funerary in context, combine extremely short hairstyles similar to male third-century *a penna* coiffures with a patently female costume of belted chiton and quiver strap derived from representations of Diana. An ambivalence of gender is also present in an under-life-sized statue in Fondi.[76] Like the Wellesley and Cleveland busts, the Fondi image juxtaposes the female body of Diana with a portrait that includes a more masculine Trajanic coiffure and boyish facial features. In light of D'Ambra's investigations of the Diana and *virtus* connections and the deliberate transgression of gendered categories in representations of young girls as the goddess, the female costume of these examples may, in fact, be appropriate for males, or at least very young boys whose age renders them pregendered, or at least presexual.[77] In addition, it has also been suggested that, as at Nemi, male children may have participated in the cult of Artemis at Brauron, perhaps dressed like the goddess. Alternatively, these deliberately ambiguous likenesses may be highly masculinized depictions of young girls.

---

torso has been recut, but the short "sling" fold of the toga is untouched at the left side, and Usia Prima's right arm has been carved from the elbow of the original male figure. Because of its reconfiguration, Usia Prima's head is smaller than that of Rabirius and Rabiria. Usia Prima's inscription stands *in rasura* over the earlier inscription, although great care was taken in matching the original letter forms. The backgrounds of the inscriptions, however, have different treatments, with that of Rabirius and Rabiria smoothed with a flat chisel, while that of Usia Prima has been left more textured with the claw chisel.

[69] This area has been heavily worked over with a claw chisel.

[70] Plut. *De Is. et Os.* 77; on the hybrid nature and names of Osiris and Hermanubis, see also Plut. *De Is. et Os.* 61.

[71] Ny Carlsberg Glyptotek 718, inv. 3286, h. 0.32 m; Johansen 1996, 200–201, no. 88, with figs. and earlier literature.

[72] Meyer 1991, 49, no. I 26, pl. 29.5–6.

[73] Matheson 2000, 77, fig. 10a–d.

[74] Wellesley College, Davis Museum and Cultural Center, inv. 1924.22, h. 0.457 m; Kleiner and Matheson 1996, 198, no. 147 (J. Allen).

[75] Cleveland Museum of Art, inv. 51.288, h. 0.522 m; Kleiner and Matheson 1996, 198, no. 148 (J. Allen). Fittschen (1992) suggests that the female costumes of both busts mandate a female identity for the sitters.

[76] Antiquario, Chiostro di S. Francesco, h. 1.06 m; Wrede 1981, 223, no. 84, pl. 11.1–2.

[77] For Nemi, see Eve D'Ambra's contribution in this volume.

The appearance of males as the goddess, however, is not limited to presexual children, as evidenced by the late Antonine or early Severan funerary stela of Artemidoros in Athens.[78] Artemidoros is shown as a mature youth with the fully articulated female body of the goddess, including breasts, dressed in the short chiton. Artemis's more masculine pastime of hunting, itself another evocation of *virtus* in the Roman period, may have facilitated the intermingling of gender expressed on the monument. Like Minerva, Diana-Artemis is also a divinity of ambiguous sexuality or even asexual, and this aspect may have additionally made these two goddesses particularly appropriate for identification with males (as in the Domitian-Minerva pairings).[79] In the case of Artemidoros, his identification with Artemis likely has etymological motivations as well, acting as a visual pun on his name. Such visual puns are not uncommon in Roman funerary art.[80]

Private female portraits can also employ assimilative and agglomerative methodologies similar to the imperial images. A Flavian relief honoring Claudius Agathemerus and his wife, Myrtale, in the Ashmolean[81] is remarkable for the degree of masculinized verism with which Myrtale's likeness is endowed, while a slightly later relief portrait of Catilia Moschis in the Palazzo Mattei combines a thoroughly feminine and elaborate Trajanic coiffure and the slipping drapery of Venus with strongly masculinized portrait features designed to resemble those of her male relatives in the same series.[82] Indeed, her portrait in the relief is made much more legibly masculine than a corresponding portrait on her funerary altar that depicts Catilia with nearly identical coiffure combined with a much softer and more feminine physiognomy.[83] Although the inscription of the Mattei relief refers to Catlilia's female role as mother (Catliae Moschidi MATR IND), the retrospective revival of republican verism in these portraits also allows Myrtale and Catilia Moschis to access the archetypally male virtues associated with strongly realistic representations, namely *gravitas*, *dignitas*, *auctoritas*, and *sapientia*.

Gender Politics: Power and Sex

Masculinity itself appears to be an inherent visual prerequisite for Roman ruler imagery. Ulpia Severina is unique among Roman empresses, as she may actually have wielded imperial authority in her own right during a brief interregnum in A.D. 275 between the death of her husband, Aurelian, and the accession of his immediate successors, Tacitus and Florian.[84] Severina carefully constructs a visual identity on her coins by juxtaposing her elaborate female *Scheitelzopf* (skull braid) hairstyle with her husband's hypermasculine facial features. Although certain of Severina's numismatic portraits can be slightly softer and more feminine, as in two *aurelianiani* from 275, Severina's likenesses are among the most masculinized in the repertoire of female imperial portraits.[85] Indeed an *aureus* from 275, thought to be minted after the death of her husband, carefully expropriates her husband's

[78] Athens, National Museum, inv. 1192; Rhomiopoulou n.d., 65, no. 95, with fig.

[79] Alexander is also reported to have dressed as Artemis, often riding in his chariot in her costume; Athenaios 12.537e; Stewart 1993, 13, 356–57.

[80] See, for instance, the altar of Tiberius Octavius Didumenus, which depicts a recognizable work of art, the Diadumenos of Polykleitos, in order to pun visually on the deceased's Greek cognomen; Kleiner 1987, 97–98, no. 1, pl. 1.1–4; Spinola 1996, 43–44, no. PE 29.

[81] Michaelis 1882, 155.

[82] Calza 1978, 83–84, no. 110, pl. 73; Guerrini 1982, 173–74, no. 37, pl. 51 (A. Licordari).

[83] Los Angeles, J. Paul Getty Museum, inv. 83.AA.209; Koch 1988, 76–79, no. 27.

[84] HA Aur. 36–37; HA Tac. 1–2; Aur. Vict. Caes. 36.

[85] Bastien 1994, 25, pls. 116.1, 3–5.

Fig. 8. *Severina*, aureus, *Rome*, A.D. 275
(after Kent 1978, fig. 536).

Fig. 9. *Aurelian*, antoninianus, *Rome*, A.D. 274
(after Kent 1978, fig. 534).

numismatic identity by directly quoting the forehead and profile from an *antoninianus* from one year earlier (figs. 8–9).[86] Severina's coiffure is less elaborate than in other examples, and it is made to resemble the close-cropped military hairstyle of her husband, which reveals the contours of the skull. The modified coiffure, the slight bits of drapery around her shoulders, and the crescent of Diana-Luna, which are the female analogue to Aurelian's emphasis on solar imagery, are all that remain of her visual identity as a woman.[87] Nevertheless, the defeminized portrait is combined with a prominent inscription that is clearly feminine and proclaims her identity as Severina Augusta. Again, the all-important concept of *concordia* literally lurks behind Severina's numismatic presentation, as the reverse depicts *concordia militum*. It is also intriguing to consider an account in the *Historia Augusta* of Aurelian's proposed restoration of the all-female senate within the heightened atmosphere of real or perceived female political power and masculinized images of female rulers, like his wife Severina and the Palmyrene queen Zenobia.[88]

In fact, Severina's more masculine numismatic identity may also in part be a conscious response to the representations of Zenobia, whom her husband had eventually defeated and led in his triumphal procession.[89] Zenobia is actually singled out as fairly praiseworthy in the *Historia Augusta*, and she is consistently described in masculine terms. The *Historia Augusta* constructs her as a female foil to Gallienus, who is represented as an unworthy and weak tyrant. Zenobia is said to have been a superior leader, and she wields *imperium* in a superlative manner.[90] Furthermore, she

---

[86] Aurelian: Kent 1978, 318, no. 534, pl. 139; *RIC* 281, no. 151, pl. 8.127; Severina: Kent 1978, 319, no. 536, pl. 139; *RIC* 317, no. 13, pl. 9.138.

[87] A marble portrait in the Galleria Borghese has been associated with Severina on the basis of the hairstyle; Sala V (Ermafrodito), inv. 240; Moreno and Viacava 2003, 210–12, no. 192, with fig. However, the *Sheitelzopf* of the Borghese portrait is much more massive on the top of the head than in Severina's numismatic portraits. The numismatic portraits also lack the curls escaping out of the *Sheitelzopf* below the ears in the Borghese head, which more likely represents a

contemporary private woman.

[88] Earlier in the *Historia Augusta*, the *Senaculum* is negatively associated with the inappropriately masculine behavior of Julia Soemias and the correspondingly weak and effeminate attitude of her son, Elagabalus; SHA *Elag.* 4.3–4.

[89] Alexandrian *tetradrachm*: Kent 1978, 318, no. 530, pl. 138.

[90] *Tyr. Trig.* 30.1.

wears an imperial cloak like a man, and she appears in public in the manner of Roman emperors (*imperatorum more romanorum*).[91] The account also purports to quote a letter written by Aurelian praising his captive in typically male terms.[92] The discussion of Zenobia in the *Historia Augusta* may be largely fabricated, but its author certainly expected that his late fourth- or early fifth-century audiences might believe it, and her coins do depict her with heavier, masculinized facial features. The section of the *Historia Augusta* on the thirty tyrants, which contains the portrayal of Zenobia, concludes with another female ruler, Victoria or Vitruvia, the mother of the (usurper) Victorinus, who is credited with seizing sole power (*imperium*) and daring to act like a man (*ut virile semper facinus auderet*).[93] Slightly earlier, in 261, but still within the same general cultural and chronological nexus, coins are issued at Carnuntum for Dryantilla, the wife of the usurper Regalian, which give her only the most proximate female identity entirely localized in her schematized *Scheitelzopf*.[94] J. Kent has even gone so far as to say that "Dryantilla has been unfortunate enough to have the least flattering portrait in the entire Roman coinage."[95]

The visual and cultural dialogue, however, did not always privilege the masculine over the feminine. The feminized behavior or imagery of more transgressive rulers such as Julius Caesar, Caligula, Nero, Domitian, Commodus, and Elagabalus challenged traditional notions of power and expressed evolving constructs of imperial identity and concepts of empire. Julius Caesar's excessive interest in grooming is noted by Suetonius, as is his mode of dress, which included the addition of fringed sleeves and a loose girdle to the purple-striped senatorial tunic.[96] Invective instigated by accounts of Caesar's sexual liaison with Nicomedes IV, the king of Bithynia, assigned to Caesar a more feminine role and included not so veiled references to Caesar as "queen of Bithynia."[97] Ribald verses referred explicitly to Caesar's position as receptive partner in his relationship with Nicomedes: "Caesar screwed the whole of Gaul, Nicomedes screwed Caesar. / See now, Caesar rides in triumph, after screwing Gaul. / Nicomedes does not triumph, though he screwed our Caesar." Tony Corbeill has demonstrated that Caesar may have embraced and encouraged these charges of effeminacy in an effort to forge an effective oppositional political stance.[98] Caesar's foppish sartorial inclinations and transgressive sexuality, however, are somewhat contradicted by his sculpted representations, which are more traditionally veristic and masculine.

Later, Caligula's predilection for divine transvestism is criticized in Suetonius, Dio, and Aurelius Victor, who mention the emperor's appearance as the goddesses Juno, Diana, and Venus and allegations that one of the Venus drag shows occurred during his British campaign.[99] Caligula's appearance as the goddesses, however, may be the performative analogue of the Augustan evocations of Diana and Virtus made that much more challenging in that one occurred in the ostensibly hypermasculine realm of the military campaign. Josephus also describes Caligula's wearing of women's attire and wigs, as well as other costumes, in order to make himself look female in the context of cultic transvestism.[100] Like Caesar, Caligula is also censured for receptive (and hence more feminine) sexual behavior. Also like Caesar, Caligula's visual images present him in a more traditional and masculine

---

[91] *Tyr. Trig.* 30.2, 14.

[92] *Tyr. Trig.* 30.5–12.

[93] *Tyr. Trig.* 31.2.

[94] Kent 1978, 315, no. 500, pl. 133.

[95] Kent 1978, 315, no. 500.

[96] *Iul.* 45.2–3.

[97] *Iul.* 49.

[98] Corbeill 2002, 205–7.

[99] Suet. *Calig.* 52; Aur. Vict. *Caes.* 3 (*cum ipse nucn fluxo cultu Venerioque*).

[100] *AJ* 19.30.

manner, in this case derived from the classicizing repertoire of Julio-Claudian images established by his great-grandfather, Augustus. Prior to Caligula, a public appearance by Drusus Minor in the guise of Venus is also recorded.[101]

Echoing the earlier ironic invectives against Caesar, the British ruler Buduica taunts Nero for ruling like a queen, and she further refers to him in the feminine as Domitia and explicitly calls him a woman.[102] Nero's marriage ceremony to Doryphorus, in which the emperor imitated the cries of a virgin being deflowered, is also a crucial element of the *invectio* employed against him by Suetonius, as is his penchant for playing tragic female roles on the stage, including Canace in labor, Antigone and Melanippe, mentioned also by Juvenal.[103] Tacitus relates a similar episode and underscores the emperor's shocking feminine proclivities, when Nero, dressed as a bride, was wedded to Pythagoras with all the solemn rites of legitimate marriage (*in modum solemnium coniugiorum denupsisset*).[104] In Tacitus's carefully orchestrated and moralizing account, the Pythagoras incident directly precedes, and thus presages, the greatest disaster of the reign, the fire of A.D. 64. The implications are clear: Nero's violation of established sexual roles and gender categories has itself violated nature and resulted in the devastating natural disaster. The hermaphroditic, dual-sexed nature of Nero's episodes with Pythagoras and Doryphorus may have been intended to exploit positive and transcendent interpretations of hermaphroditism in cosmological, theological, and anthropological terms.[105] In fact, Nero is also reported to have hermaphroditic mares from Trier harnessed to his chariot, "deeming it a remarkable spectacle to see the emperor of the world riding in a miraculous chariot."[106]

The elaborate coiffures of Nero's last two portrait types in use from A.D. 69–68 are expressions of *luxuria* and *elegantia*, which with their carefully constructed and artificial arrangements had more in common with contemporary female approaches to hair care than the seemingly casual arrangements made popular by Augustus and may be analogous to Nero's effeminate attire noted by both Suetonius and Dio.[107] Surviving replicas of Nero's third and fourth types are diametrically (and perhaps purposefully) opposed to traditional Roman notions of masculinity, especially as formulated by nearly contemporary stoics like the elder Seneca.[108] Nero's controversial coiffures inspired other elaborately conceived male hairstyles, which may have been intended as the (sartorial) antithesis to stoic emphasis on the importance of unaffected naturalness.[109] Indeed, several of these images have generated gender confusion and have been variously identified as both male and female.[110] These

[101] Wardle 1994, 339–40.

[102] Dio 65.6.3–5.

[103] Suet. 21.3; Juv. 8.228–29.

[104] *Ann.* 15.37. Martial also mentions Pythagoras as one of Nero's lovers: 11.6.10, and his marriages also appear in Aur. Vict. *Caes.* 5; Treggari 1991, 169. Champlin (2003, 154, 167) has suggested that Pythagoras and Doryphorus are one and the same, and Doryphorus may be an epithet or a priesthood in the cult of Cybele, giving the marriage a cultic aspect. Allen (1962, 104–7) and Higgens (1985) also supply cultic explanations for the marriage, possibly related to the Floralia.

[105] Brisson 2002, 77–78. Nero's engagement with concepts of sexual duality is clearly evident in his later "marriage" to Sporus, who was castrated and costumed to resemble Nero's dead wife, Poppaea; see also Champlin 2003, 148–50.

[106] Plin. *HN* 11.262.

[107] Suet. *Nero* 51; Dio 63.13.3.

[108] Sen. *Controv.* 2, preface 2.

[109] Smith 2003.

[110] See, for instance, a portrait in the Uffizi, inv. 1914.57; Mansuelli 1961, 69, no. 63, fig. 63; Cain 1993. John Pollini has identified the Uffizi portrait and related images as representations of a *pueri delicati* whose hairstyles are modeled partially on those of imperial women in order to mark out their servile status as sex objects; see Pollini 1999, 29–31; Pollini 2001. The coiffures of the Neronian portraits are also modeled on those of the emperor's last two portrait types, and many of these clearly represent private individuals rather than *pueri delicati*. If Nero's coiffures were intended consciously to evoke images of *pueri delicati*, it would make them that much more transgressive and challenging.

Neronian portraits are in some ways the equivalent of a group of sexually transgressive statues of figures like Ganymede, Eros, and Apollo, described by Elizabeth Bartman as "sexy boys" and which similarly fuse masculine and feminine types in terms of body language, coiffure, and pose.[111]

Nero is also the first emperor to wear the *corona spicea* in sculpted portraits, as evidenced by a likeness reconfigured as Augustus in the Sala dei Busti of the Vatican.[112] Prior to Nero, this kind of crown had been chiefly associated with goddesses such as Ceres and women of the imperial house, including Livia, as in a sardonyx cameo in Florence,[113] and Nero's mother Agrippina Minor in an *aureus* (from Rome). In addition to the associations with Ceres, the *corona spicea* also stressed Nero's connections with the *Fratres Arvales*,[114] and future emperors, such as Antoninus Pius,[115] Marcus Aurelius,[116] and Lucius Verus,[117] would also be depicted with it.

After Nero and Caligula, condemned emperors like Domitian, Commodus, and Elagabalus are all criticized for receptive homosexual behavior, prostitution, feminine interest in exotic clothing, and excessive attention to hair care. Domitian's third portrait type, conceived at his accession in 81 and in use for the duration of his principate, is elaborately coiffed. Domitian is accused of prostituting himself to his future successor Nerva as a boy and having written a manual entitled "On Hair Care" (*De cura capillorum*).[118] Commodus is alleged to have been both an active and passive sexual partner with many other men while still an adolescent and is said to have ridden with his partner, Saoterus, in the triumphal chariot in his triumph of 180, afterwards kissing him in public.[119] The *Historia Augusta* further purports that he participated in (presumably) public combats with men and beasts dressed as a woman,[120] that he attended spectacles in theaters and amphitheaters in women's clothes,[121] that he dyed his hair and regularly sprinkled it with gold dust,[122] and that he added an inscription to his remodeled version of the Colossus that proudly included the epithet *Effeminatus*.[123] Herodian also derides Commodus for the feminine extravagance of his Hercules costumes, which made him appear ridiculous.[124]

Like Caligula before him, Elagabalus is also alleged to have appeared as Venus and to have depilated his entire body.[125] Recurrent charges of effeminacy were leveled against him, and a painted portrait was sent to the capital prior to the young emperor's arrival in order to accustom the inhabitants of Rome to his exotic appearance.[126] Dio recounts an exchange between Elagabalus and the well-endowed Aurelius Zoticus: when Zoticus addressed the emperor as "my lord" (κύριε

[111] Bartman 2002.

[112] Varner 2004, 11 n. 63, 61–62, 239, no. 2.10, fig. 72a–b.

[113] Museo Archeologico, inv. 14549, 4.7 × 4.4 cm; Megow 1987, no. B 17, pl. 13.9; Giuliano 1989, 231, no. 155, with figs.

[114] Chirasi-Colombo 1981, 423–25; Scheid 1990, 572 n. 36.; Liverani 1990–91, 165.

[115] Paris, Musée du Louvre, MA 1180; de Kersauson 1996, 198–200, no. 84.

[116] London, British Museum; Alföldi 1979, 581–82.

[117] Musée du Louvre, MA 1169; de Kersauson 1996, 270, no. 121.

[118] He is also alleged to have offered himself to Claudius

Pollio: Suet. *Dom.* 1.1; for the hair-care manual, see Suet. *Dom.* 18.2.

[119] SHA *Comm.* 10.1; 3.6.

[120] SHA *Comm.* 9.6.

[121] SHA *Comm.* 13.4.

[122] SHA *Comm.* 17.3. Dio also records his elaborate dress for appearances in the amphitheater: Dio 72 (73) 17.3.

[123] SHA *Comm.* 17.10. See also Dio 22.3.

[124] Hdn. 1.14.8.

[125] SHA *Elag.* 5.4–5. On the depilation of *pueri delicati*, see Sen. *Ep.* 47.7 and Pollini 1999.

[126] Herod. 5.5.6; 5.6.1–2.

Fig. 10. Portrait of Marcus Aurelius, London, British Museum, refashioned in the third century (after Blanck 1969, pl. 11).

αὐτοκράτορ χαῖρε), Elagabalus responded, "don't call me lord, I am a lady" (μή με λέγε κύριον. ἐγώ γὰρ κυρία εἰμί).[127] Dio concludes his anecdote about the emperor and Zoticus with Elagabalus's request to his physicians to give him the literal equivalent of a woman's vagina through means of a surgical incision. Significantly, these allegations of sexual transgression and the emperor's violation of gender taxonomies directly precede the account of his assassination in Dio's narrative. Mary Beard has recently located Elagabalus's attempt to endow himself with female genitalia as a response to the ambivalence concerning gender embedded in the eastern cult of the sun god Elagabal, of which he was the chief priest, and further construes his behavior as emblematic of a kind of despotic literalism that characterizes Rome's "bad" emperors.[128] In the hostile and rancorous historical discourse surrounding these condemned emperors, however, it is often difficult to discern the original context or reception of these alleged behaviors. Indeed, these emperors are historical losers and have lost (or really been robbed of) their ability to speak in much the same way as other disenfranchised, non-elite members of Roman society. The transgressive behavior of these emperors, especially in terms of sexuality and gender, may have been carefully calculated to communicate to Roman audiences the transcendent position and power of the emperor.

Even a "good" emperor, such as Marcus Aurelius, could be represented with a female body, as in a recycled portrait from Cyrene now in the British Museum (fig. 10). In the third century, the clearly male portrait head of Marcus Aurelius, now *divus*, was added to a draped female body.[129] This disjunctive image is very different from the emperor's traditional masculine iconography as

---

[127] Cass. Dio 80.16.4.

[128] Beard 2003, 39.

[129] British Museum; Blanck 1969, 41, pl. 11.

expressed in military images like the gilded bronze equestrian statue in the Palazzo dei Conserva-tori.[130] Constantine, the first Christian emperor of Rome, is also represented with female breasts in a small steel weight in the Art Museum at Princeton.[131] The quasi-official nature of this kind of object suggests that its gender-bending imagery may have been authorized. Although it is easy to discount the Cyrenaican pastiche as a misguided attempt at sculptural recycling perhaps brought on by economic necessity (or the Princeton weight as an iconographic aberration), Roman audiences had been conditioned for centuries to such agglomerative portrait constructions and their fluid iterations of identity in both imperial and private likenesses. Ultimately, the intentional slippage between fixed gender classifications often encoded in imperial images reinforces the transcendent nature of the emperor's power and position within Roman society.

[130] Museo Capitolino, without inv.; Fittschen and Zanker 1985, 72–74, no. 67, pls. 76–77.

[131] Inv. 55-3257, h. 0.125 m; Weitzmann 1979, 20–21, no. 13, with fig. (with earlier literature) (J. D. Breckenridge).

Works Cited

Albertson, F., "Zenodorus's Colossus of Nero," *Memoirs of the American Academy in Rome* 46 (2001) 95–118.

Alföldi, A., "*Redeunt Saturnia regna*, VII; Frugifer-Triptolemos im ptolemäisch-römischen Herrscherkult," *Chiron* 9 (1979) 533–606.

Allen, W., "Nero's Eccentricities before the Fire (Tac. *Ann.* XV.37)," *Numen* 9 (1962) 99–109.

Bartman, E., *Portraits of Livia: Imaging the Imperial Woman in Augustan Rome* (Cambridge 1999).

———, "Eros's Flame: Images of Sexy Boys in Roman Ideal Sculpture," in *The Ancient Art of Emulation: Studies in Artistic Originality and Tradition from the Present to Classical Antiquity*, ed. E. Gazda (Ann Arbor 2002) 249–72.

Bastien, P., *Le buste monétaire des empereurs romains*, vol. 3 (Wetteren 1994).

Bauer, H., and C. Morselli, "Forum Nervae," in *Lexicon Topographicum Urbis Romae*, ed. E. M. Steinby (Rome 1995) 2:307–11.

Beard, M., "The Triumph of the Absurd: Roman Street Theater," in *Rome the Cosmopolis*, ed. C. Edwards and G. Woolf (Cambridge 2003) 21–43.

Bergmann, M., *Der Koloss Neros: Die Domus Aurea und der Mentalitätswandel im Rom der frühen Kaiserzeit*, Trierer Winckelmannsprogramme 13 (Mainz 1994).

———, *Die Strahlen der Herrscher. Theomorphes Herrscherbild und politische Symbolik in Hellenismus und in der römischen Kaiserzeit* (Mainz 1998).

Blanck, H., *Wiederverwendung alter Statuen als Ehrendenkmäler bei Griechen und Römern*, Studia Archaeologica 11 (Rome 1969).

Borea, E., and C. Gasparri, eds., *L'Idea del Bello. Viaggio per Roma nel Seicento con Giovan Pietro Bellori* (Rome 2000).

Brisson, L., *Sexual Ambivalence: Androgyny and Hermaphroditism in Graeco-Roman Antiquity*, trans. J. Lloyd (Berkeley 2002).

Cain, P., *Männerbildnisse neronisch-flavischer Zeit* (Munich 1993).

Calza, R., *Scavi di Ostia*, vol. 9.1: *I Ritratti*, parte II (Rome 1978).

Canciani, F., "Minerva," in *Lexicon Iconographicum Mythologiae Classicae*, ed. H. C. Ackermann and J.-R. Gisler, vol. 2.1 (Zurich and Munich 1984) 1074–1109.

Cantilena, R., E. La Rocca, U. Pannuti, E. Pozzi, and L. Scatozza, *Le Collezioni del Museo Nazionale di Napoli 1.1. I Mosaici, Le Pitture, Gli Ogetti del Uso Quotidiano, gli Argenti, Le Terrecotte Invetriate, I Vetri, I Cristallo, Gli Avori* (Rome 1986).

———, *Le Collezioni del Museo Nazionale di Napoli 1.2. La Scultura Greca-Romana, Le Sculture Antiche della Collezione Farnese, Le Collezioni Monetali, Le Oreficerie, La Collezione Glittica* (Rome 1989).

Champlin, E., *Nero* (Cambridge, Mass. 2003).

Chirasi-Colombo, C., "Funzioni politiche ed implicazioni culturali nell'ideologia religiosa di Ceres nell'impero romano," in *Aufstieg und Niedergang der römischen Welt*, ed. H. Temporini (Berlin 1981) 2.17.1:403–28.

Clarke, J. R., *Art in the Lives of Ordinary Romans: Visual Representation and Non-elite Viewers in Italy, 100 B.C.–A.D. 315* (Berkeley 2003).

Corbeill, A., "Political Movement: Walking and Ideology in Republican Rome," in *The Roman Gaze: Vision, Power and the Body*, ed. D. Fredrick (Baltimore and London 2002) 182–215.

D'Ambra, E., *Private Lives, Imperial Virtues: The Frieze of the Forum Transitorium in Rome* (Princeton 1993).

Delcourt, M., *Hermaphrodite: Myths and Rites of the Bisexual Figure in Classical Antiquity*, trans. J. Nicolson (London 1961).

Fittschen, K., "Mädchen, nicht Knaben. Zwei Kinderbüsten in Cleveland und Wellesley," *Mitteilungen des deutschen archäologischen Instituts, römische Abteilung* 99 (1992) 301–5.

Fittschen, K., and P. Zanker, *Katalog der römischen Porträts in den Capitolinischen Museen und den anderen kommunalen Sammlungen der Stadt Rom*, Band 3: *Kaiserinnen- und Prinzessinnenbildnisse Frauenporträts* (Mainz 1983).

———, *Katalog der römischen Porträts in den Capitolinischen Museen und den anderen kommunalen Sammlungen der Stadt Rom 1. Kaiser- und Prinzenbildnisse* (Mainz 1985).

Fullerton, M. D., "*Domus Augusti* in Imperial Iconography of 13–12 B.C.," *American Journal of Archaeology* 89 (1985) 473–83.

Gasparri, C., ed., *Le Gemme Farnese* (Naples 1994).

Girard, J.-B., *Bibliothèque nationale, Catalogue des monnaies de l'empire romain I* (Paris 1976).

Giuliano, A., ed., *Museo Nazionale Romano. Le Sculture*, vol. 1.2 (Rome 1981).

———, *I Cammei della Collezione Medicea del Museo Archeologico di Firenze* (Rome 1989).

Gnecchi, F., *I Medaglioni Romani*, vol. 2 (Milan 1912).

Green, P., *Alexander to Actium* (Berkeley 1990).

Guerrini, L., ed., *Palazzo Mattei di Giove. Le Antichità* (Rome 1982).

Guiraud, H., *Intailles et camées romains* (Paris 1996).

Head, B. V. G., F. Hill, and J. Walker, *A Guide to the Principal Coins of the Greeks from circa 700 B.C. to A.D. 270* (London 1959).

Higgens, J. M., "Cena Rosaria, Cena Mitellita: A Note on Suetonius, *Nero* 27.3," *American Journal of Philology* 106 (1985) 116–18.

Iacopi, I., *Domus Aurea* (Milan 1999).

Johansen, F., *Roman Portraits I: Ny Carlsberg Glyptotek* (Copenhagen 1994).

———, *Roman Portraits III: Ny Carlsberg Glyptotek* (Copenhagen 1996).

Kampen, N. B., "Omphale and the Instability of Gender," in *Sexuality in Ancient Art*, ed. N. B. Kampen (Cambridge 1996) 233–46.

Kellum, B., "The Construction of Landscape in Augustan Rome: The Garden Room of the Villa *ad Gallinas*," *Art Bulletin* 76 (1994) 211–24.

Kent, J. P. C., "Gallienae Augustae," *Numismatic Chronicle* 13 (1973) 64–68.

———, *Roman Coins* (London 1978).

Kersauson, K. de, *Musée du Louvre. Catalogue des portraits romains*, vol. 2 (Paris 1996).

Kleiner, D. E. E., *Roman Group Portraiture: The Funerary Reliefs of the Late Republic and Early Empire* (New York 1977).

———, *Roman Funerary Altars with Portraits* (Rome 1987).

Kleiner, D. E. E., and S. B. Matheson, eds., *I Claudia: Women in Ancient Rome* (New Haven 1996).

Koch, G., *Roman Funerary Sculpture: Catalogue of the Collections. The J. Paul Getty Museum* (Malibu 1988).

Kreikenbom, D., *Griechische und römische Kolossalporträts bis zum späten ersten Jahrhundert nach Christus*, *Jahrbuch des deutschen archäologischen Instituts* Ergänzungsheft 27 (Berlin 1992).

Kuttner, A., "Hellenistic Images of Spectacle from Alexander to Augustus," in *The Art of Ancient Spectacle*, ed. B. Bergmann and C. Kondoleon, Studies in the History of Art Series 56, National Gallery of Art, Washington, D.C. (New Haven 1999) 97–123.

La Regina, A., ed., *Museo Nazionale Romano. Le Sculture* 1.2 (Rome 1981).

———, *Museo Nazionale Romano. Palazzo Massimo alle Terme* (Rome 1998).

Lichoka, B., "Le portrait d'empereur romain en couronne d'épis," in *Ancient Portraits: Artistic and Literary*, ed. J. Bouzek and I. Ondřejová (Mainz 1997) 88–92.

Liverani, P., "Rilavorazioni antiche e moderne su sculture dei Musei Vaticani," *Atti della Pontificia Accademia romana di archeologia. Rendiconti* 63 (1990–91) 163–92.

Mansuelli, G. A., *Galleria degli Uffizi: le sculture*, vol. 2 (Rome 1961).

Matheson, S., "The Private Sector: Reworked Portraits outside the Imperial Circle," in *From Caligula to Constantine: Tyranny and Transformation in Roman Portraiture*, ed. E. R. Varner (Atlanta 2000) 70–80.

Matthew, G., "The Character of the Gallienic Renaissance," *Journal of Roman Studies* 33 (1943) 65–70.

Matthews, T., *The Clash of Gods: A Reinterpretation of Early Christian Art* (Princeton 1993).

Megow, W. R., *Kameen von Augustus bis Alexander Severus*, Antike Münzen und geschnittene Steine 11 (Berlin 1987).

Meyer, H., *Antinoos* (Munich 1991).

Michaelis, A., *Ancient Marbles in Great Britain* (Cambridge 1882).

Mickoki, T., *Sub specie deae. Les impératrices et princesses romaines assimilées à des déesses: étude iconologique*, *Rivista di archeologia* Supplement 14 (Rome 1995).

Moreno, P., and A. Viacava, *I Marmi Antichi della Galleria Borghese. La collezione di Camillo e Francesco Borghese* (Rome 2003).

Pollini, J., "Man or God: Divine Assimilation and Imitation in the Late Republic and Early Empire," in *Between Republic and Empire: Interpretations of Augustus and His Principate*, ed. K. Raaflaub and M. Toher (Berkeley 1990) 334–63.

———, "The Warren Cup: Homoerotic Love and Symposial Rhetoric in Silver," *Art Bulletin* 81 (1999) 21–52.

———, "Two Bronze Portrait Busts of Slave Boys from a Shrine of Cobannus in Gaul," in *Studia Varia II: Occasional Papers on Antiquities of the J. Paul Getty Museum* 10 (2001) 115–20.

———, "A New Portrait of Octavia and the Iconography of Octavia Minor and Julia Maior," *Mitteilungen des deutschen archäologischen Instituts, römische Abteilung* 109 (2002) 11–42.

Rhomiopoulou, K., *National Archaeological Museum: Collection of Roman Sculpture* (Athens n.d.).

Rose, C. B., *Dynastic Commemoration and Imperial Portraiture in the Julio-Claudian Period* (Cambridge 1997).

Santoro L'Hoir, F., "Tacitus and Women's Usurpation of Power," *Classical World* 88 (1984) 5–25.

Scheid, J., *Romulus et ses frères: le collège des Frères Arvales, modèle du culte public dans la Rome des empereurs*, Bibliothèque des Écoles françaises d'Athènes et de Rome fasc. 275 (Rome 1990).

Segala, E., and I. Sciortino, *Domus Aurea* (Rome 1999).

Smith, R. R. R., *Hellenistic Royal Portraits* (Oxford 1988).

———, "Nero and the Sun-god: Divine Accessories and Political Symbolism in Roman Imperial Images," *Journal of Roman Archaeology* 13 (2000) 532–42.

———, "Nero and the Cult of Elegance," paper read at the Michael C. Carlos Museum, Atlanta, November 2003.

Spaeth, B., *The Roman Goddess Ceres* (Austin 1996).

Spinola, G., *Il Museo Pio Clementino 1* (Rome 1996).

Stewart, A., *Faces of Power* (Berkeley 1993).

Tomei, M. A., *Museo Palatino* (Rome 1997).

Treggiari, S., *Roman Marriage* (Oxford 1991).

Trimble, J. F., "Greek Myth, Gender, and Social Structure in a Roman House: Two Paintings of Achilles at Pompeii," in *The Art of Emulation: Studies in Artistic Originality and Tradition from the Present to Classical Antiquity*, ed. E. Gazda (Ann Arbor 2002) 225–48.

Varner, E. R., ed., *From Caligula to Constantine: Tyranny and Transformation in Roman Portraiture* (Atlanta 2000).

———, *Mutilation and Transformation:* Damnatio Memoriae *and Roman Imperial Portraiture* (Leiden 2004).

Walker, S., and P. Higgs, eds., *Cleopatra of Egypt from History to Myth* (Princeton 2001).

Wardle, D., *Suetonius' Life of Caligula: A Commentary*, Collection Latomus 225 (Brussels 1994).

Weitzmann, K., ed., *The Age of Spirituality: Late Antique and Early Christian Art, Third to Seventh Century* (New York 1979).

Wood, S., *Imperial Women: A Study in Public Images, 40 B.C.–A.D. 68* (Leiden 1999).

Wrede, H., Consecratio in Formam Deorum. *Vergöttliche Privatpersonen in der römischen Kaiserzeit* (Mainz 1981).

Yacoub, M., *Musée du Bardo. Musée Antique* (Tunis 1982).

10 ◆ PORTRAIT STATUES AS MODELS FOR GENDER ROLES IN ROMAN SOCIETY

Glenys Davies

Portrait statues are characteristic products of Roman imperial society: they have been found in large numbers all over the Roman world and would have been displayed in a range of urban civic and sacred spaces, including cemeteries, from the late republic to the late empire. Such statues were honorific and/or commemorative and by definition represented people who might be considered worthy of emulation. As such they can be seen as role models for contemporary society. They expressed the salient characteristics of exemplary residents of the Roman empire, both male and female: inevitably those commemorated were overwhelmingly the rich and powerful, members of elite circles in towns throughout the Roman world.

What might seem surprising is quite how many portrait statues of women there are: visit any major museum with a display of Roman sculpture, and the chances are that you will see as many female as male statues. The four pieces illustrated here from the Munich Glyptothek are fairly representative: a man in a toga dating to ca. A.D. 20–30 (fig. 1);[1] a nude statue of Domitian dating to A.D. 70–80 (fig. 2); two draped statues of women, one dated ca. A.D. 170 (fig. 3), the other in the "Ceres" type dated ca. A.D. 110–30 (fig. 4).[2] The number of statues of women is perhaps unexpected, given that women played only a very minor role in the public life of Roman society—they did not vote or hold magistracies and had a lesser role than men in religious affairs. Their position was socially and legally subordinate to that of men, yet they appear on an almost equal footing when it comes to commemoration in marble and the visibility of their images. For most statues we do not know the precise individual reason why they were erected, where they stood, or how they were displayed, but sufficient numbers have been found in a context or with an inscription to provide a general idea of how they were used. Many are portraits of emperors and empresses, which might be displayed in dynastic groups,[3] and non-imperial families might also appear in this way: in the case of the family of Herodes Atticus, for example, portrait statues of his extended family appear alongside the imperial family in a display on the Nymphaeum at Olympia.[4] Individuals might be granted the honor of a statue by the people in a public place in their city, and this applied to women as well as men. Such women were likely to have been patrons or benefactors, such as Plancia Magna in Perge or Eumachia in Pompeii.[5] Statues were also commissioned to decorate the tombs and grave plots of

---

[1] Goette 1990, 117 Ba73.

[2] Bieber 1977, 165 and n. 12, figs. 728–29.

[3] Rose 1997; Boatwright 2000.

[4] Bol 1984.

[5] Plancia Magna's statue (of large Herculaneum woman type) stood outside the gate she dedicated, which was itself decorated with portrait statues—including a statue of Sabina, also of large Herculaneum woman type: see Boatwright 1991; Boatwright 2000, 64–66, figs. 4.5 (Sabina) and 4.6 (Plancia Magna); D'Ambra 1998, 52–53, fig. 28. Eumachia's statue, dedicated by the fullers of Pompeii, stood in the building she dedicated in the forum of the town. The relevant inscriptions are recorded in *CIL* 10 810 and 813. See Kleiner 1996, 33–34; Dixon 2001, 107, figs. 5 and 6; and Dixon in this volume.

*Fig. 1 (near right).
Youthful man in a toga,
ca. A.D. 20–30. Munich,
Glyptothek, inv. no. 540
(photo author).*

*Fig. 2 (far right). Nude
statue of Domitian, ca.
A.D. 70–80. Munich,
Glyptothek, inv. no. 394
(photo author).*

those who could afford them: although these might be visible to those passing by, they were seen as essentially private, unlike the "public" statues displayed in spaces within the town.

Men might be represented in one of several different ways, reflecting their varied roles in society: as a togate figure (see fig. 1), wearing the pallium, in military dress, or in total or (more often) partial heroic nudity (fig. 2). By choosing to appear in a toga, a man emphasized his civic role and, in the provinces, his allegiance to Rome.[6] The toga was required for orators[7] as well as magistrates and indeed (in theory) all Roman citizens. The pallium suggested a more Greek orientation, a preference for the intellectual life involving the arts and philosophy. Military dress and heroic nudity are particularly associated with emperors (see the statue of Domitian illustrated in fig. 2), but both were also used for other elite males.

The range of social roles represented by statues of women appears to be rather more limited: to a large extent, this mirrors their actual role in society as well as the ideal of womanly behavior (for the elite at least).[8] Parading their women in public in the form of portrait statues seems to have created something of a dilemma for the Romans: the ideal of the sexually faithful, domestically oriented, heir-producing matron who was reluctant to be seen in the public arena vied with the reality of the politically active women of the imperial court and the financially significant female municipal patrons

[6] For togate statues, see Goette 1990 and Hölscher in this volume; for the significance of the toga, see Stone 1994; Christ 1997; Davies 2005.

[7] This may be the significance of the scroll box at the foot of the statue in Munich.

[8] Treggiari 1996.

Fig. 3 (far left). Draped statue of an unknown woman, ca. A.D. 170. Munich, Glyptothek, inv. no. 427 (photo author).

Fig. 4 (near left). Draped statue of an unknown woman, possibly Plotina or Marciana, ca. A.D. 110–30. "Ceres" type. Munich, Glyptothek, inv. no. 377 (photo author).

in towns all over the empire.[9] Livia has been seen as the empress who juggled these two roles most successfully,[10] and she appears to have been a role model for other women acting as patrons, and their statues (e.g., Eumachia).[11] It would seem that although statues of women were put up in funerary contexts in Rome in the late republic, there is less evidence for them in public contexts: Pliny records Cato's outburst in his censorship of 184 B.C. against the setting up of statues of women in the provinces but points out that he was not able to prevent them from being erected even in Rome. He cites the one certain public statue of a woman in republican Rome, to Cornelia, described as mother of the Gracchi and daughter of Scipio Africanus: it seems that by the time of Augustus at least it was her exemplary motherhood that was seen to be the justification for the statue.[12]

Funerary inscriptions emphasize the domestic and family virtues for which women were valued: chastity, marital fidelity, wifely and motherly devotion, and dedication to domestic duties.[13]

[9] Dixon 2001, 33 notes that some epitaphs (such as *CIL* 6 9499) praised a wife's lack of interest in social life outside the home. For the question of the visibility of women in public, and the related issue of veiling, in the Roman Empire, see MacMullen 1980. For the tension between this ideal and the forms of power women did in fact have, see Kleiner 1996 and Fischler 1994, 116: "[W]omen who are perceived as having gained access to power are seen as having failed to conform to the accepted social construct for their gender in their given society." Barton (2002, 220) further suggests that the *casta matrona* had to be prepared to be seen at any moment,

while at the same time being seen was the greatest test of a Roman woman's honor.

[10] Kleiner 1996.

[11] Kleiner 1996, 33–34.

[12] Plin. *HN* 34.30–31; Boatwright 2000, 62.

[13] Forbis 1990, 493; Fischler 1994, 117; see esp. *CIL* 6 10250.

But Forbis has shown there was an interesting divergence in *public* inscriptions honoring women: although in the Greek east the same epithets praising private virtues are used in both funerary and public inscriptions, in Italy women are instead praised in the public inscriptions using a vocabulary that emphasizes status in the community and public roles (e.g., as priestess), as well as the woman's generosity and wealth, which is closer to the information included in the inscriptions honoring male patrons.[14]

Fischler has pointed to the tension and anxiety created by the Roman construct of Woman, as "access to power [was] contrary to the social construct of the Roman Matron"—but was not unknown in reality.[15] Wyke sees the Roman woman as portrayed as "*essentially* a bodily being," while concern for the body was seen as womanish and beneath the dignity of a man.[16] Woman is "constrained within the domain of the body, her self-image is constructed as the object of male sexual desire": the female gender is "time-wasting, frivolous, unconcerned with true civic life, an inherently sexual being."[17] Wyke points to the passage in Livy where the repeal of the sumptuary *lex Oppia* is discussed: elegance, adornment, and finery are seen as women's badges of honor, the equivalent for them of public office for men (Livy 34.1–8). Neither Fischler nor Wyke directly addresses the visual images presented by Roman portraits of women, but their analyses of Roman values and attitudes are highly relevant to them. More recently, Kleiner has pointed to the ultimate punishment for imperial women who transgress the range of acceptable behavior (whether politically or sexually defined)—artistic exclusion.[18] The less seriously transgressive, she suggests, are portrayed in ways designed to neutralize their power:

> Even though women were engaged in acts as subversive as trying to overthrow their government, they were portrayed in art as domesticated players in the family narrative, serving as supportive helpmates to their spouses and as producers and nurturers of their children.

and:

> empresses and princesses are depicted in intricately wrapped and voluminous robes and tightly bound hair that suggest that every conceivable feminine virtue—modesty, chastity, maternal love—are woven into this perfect image.[19]

Livia, seen by Kleiner as the woman all others should emulate, is described as "fully wrapped in the garment of her Roman domesticity," although she is also given the hairstyle of a great goddess and so is portrayed as semi-divine.[20]

In this chapter I reconsider the images presented by Roman portrait statues of women from the particular viewpoint of their body language: this (including the way clothes are worn) is used to express many of the values (but not all) mentioned above. It can be a very subtle language, designed to express the tensions and contradictions inherent in the subject matter, which I would suggest is not so much an expression of the values of the particular woman portrayed as of the ideals Roman

---

[14] Forbis 1990.

[15] Fischler 1994, 127.

[16] Wyke 1994, 135.

[17] Wyke 1994, 135, 136. For an analysis of the elite male ideal of balance, restraint, and self-control, and of the concern of Roman men not to betray themselves as in any way effeminate

by their behavior, see Gleason 1999.

[18] Trimalchio makes much the same threat with regard to the statue of Fortunata on his tomb (Petron. *Sat.* 74)—*damnatio memoriae* can also occur in non-imperial circles!

[19] Kleiner 2000, 48.

[20] Kleiner 2000, 51–52.

(male) society thought all elite women (and those aspiring to that status) should espouse. Such statues are role models in that they show exemplary behavior.

Body and Identity in Portrait Statues of Women

Although some girls and young women were represented in the active poses and scanty clothing of Artemis,[21] and some mature women were represented as naked or scantily clad Venuses,[22] the vast majority were depicted heavily draped in a long dress and palla, in a variety of basically similar poses. Women may be assimilated with deities, and on occasion they may be represented as priestesses, but they do not have available to them the range of roles available for men.[23] When discussing the body types used for such statues in the Augustan and Julio-Claudian period, Bieber somewhat surprisingly claims that there was more variety for women than for men,[24] but this is because her different "types" are all variations on the same theme. As figures 3–10 show, the different types (large and small Herculaneum women, "Pudicitia," "Ceres," etc.) all share the same basic concept, unlike the different types available for men, which express the idea that men might play a variety of different roles in society (and this was especially true of the emperor).

Roman sculptors adapted a number of statue types inherited from the late classical and Hellenistic Greek world for their portraits, especially those of women.[25] The main differences between them are formed by the ways in which the body is posed and the way the copious folds of the drapery are arranged. Some of the most often used types are illustrated here: the large and small Herculaneum women (represented respectively by a statue of Crispina in Copenhagen, fig. 5, and a portrait statue of an unknown Trajanic woman in Naples, fig. 6),[26] the so-called Pudicitia (figs. 7 and 8), which was especially popular early on,[27] and the type that Bieber thought was used especially for priestesses of Ceres because they are often shown carrying a bunch of poppy heads and corn ears, the attributes of Ceres (figs. 4, 9, and 10).[28] The Roman sculptors who made these statues added a

[21] See D'Ambra in this volume.

[22] D'Ambra 1996; D'Ambra 2000.

[23] There has been much discussion of the representation of Roman women in the guise of deities following on from Wrede's seminal study (Wrede 1981), but it can be difficult to tell whether an attribute carried by a portrait statue is designed to assimilate the woman concerned with a deity, represent her as a priestess or follower of the deity, or in fact neither. Thus it has been debated whether the large and small Herculaneum woman types were thought by the Romans to represent Demeter and Persephone (as Bieber thought: Bieber 1977, 157; see Davies 2002, 230–31). Bieber also suggests that the "Ceres" type was used for women who were priestesses of Ceres mainly because they sometimes carry ears of corn and poppy capsules (Bieber 1977, 163–64; see, e.g., fig. 4: the same attribute is carried by the woman in the large Herculaneum woman type in fig. 5). I am not convinced that these types always carried such meanings, even when the attributes are present. For this reason in this chapter the type designated "priestess of Ceres" is given the convenient short-hand title "Ceres" type, but this is not meant to imply that it represents these women *as* Ceres.

[24] Bieber 1977, 195.

[25] Bieber 1977.

[26] Crispina: Poulsen 1974, 111–12, no. 101, pls. CLXIX–CLXX; Trajanic woman: Bieber 1977, 150, fig. 691. For the two types in general, see Bieber 1977, 148–62, pls. 112–22; Trimble 1999; Trimble 2000; Davies 2002.

[27] Statue in the Braccio Nuovo: Amelung 1903, 33, no. 23, pl. 4; Helbig 1963, 321–22, no. 415; Haskell and Penny 1981, 300–301, no. 74, fig. 157; statue in the Belvedere: Amelung 1908, 213–14, no. 78, pl. 8. For the type, see Bieber 1977, 132–33, pls. 100, 102–3.

[28] For the statue illustrated in figure 4, see n. 2; for the statue in Copenhagen (fig. 9): Poulsen 1974, 204–5, no. 211, pls. CCCXLIV–CCCXLVI—the Greek inscription naming the subject as the dedicator's mother-in-law, Euboulion, belongs to the later reuse of the statue; for the sarcophagus fragment in the British Museum (fig. 10) where the bride appears in the "Ceres" type: Walker 1990, 16–17, no. 4, pl. 2. For the term "Ceres" type, see n. 23.

Fig. 5 (near right). Portrait statue of Crispina, wife of Commodus, in the type of the large Herculaneum woman. Copenhagen, Ny Carlsberg Glyptothek, inv. no. 552B (photo Ny Carlsberg Glyptotek, Copenhagen).

Fig. 6 (far right). Portrait statue of an unknown woman with a Trajanic hairstyle in the type of the small Herculaneum woman. Naples, Archaeological Museum, inv. no. 6057 (photo Singer, DAIR, inst. neg. 67.558).

portrait head, often with an elaborate and fashionable contemporary hairstyle, but they also varied the angle of the head (and therefore the gaze) and might make various other changes to the model they were using—by adding or removing a veil, for example (compare figs. 7 and 8) or varying the gestures of the arms (compare figs. 4 and 9). This and their individual style can result in figures that, although using the same body type, give very different impressions of the woman portrayed, and they may therefore seem to possess a degree of individuality. Nevertheless, these bodies are clearly not individualized or personal to the sitter: they are, in a sense, not part of the portrait but rather a support for it. This is backed up by the fact that bodies could be reused and heads made separately and changed—the statue of Euboulion in Copenhagen is an example of this (see fig. 9: a body made in the Antonine period has had its head replaced in the fourth century, with the addition of a new inscription changing the identity of the subject). Nevertheless, the bodies are an integral and important part of the statue, and they have a strong impact on the viewer: the person who commissioned the statue presumably would have had some choice over which body type was to be used.

The bodies should not be dismissed as standardized and stereotypical and therefore of no interest. Bieber recognized their value as documents in the study of Roman art, arguing that they should not just be seen as evidence for the Greek originals. I suggest that they should also be treated as valuable evidence for Roman social history, and in particular gender relations in the Roman world. The bodies constitute a significant element in the visual impact of these statues, and they provide important information to the viewer, not about the appearance of this individual woman but about the societal values she held (or rather that the purchaser of the statue wished to suggest she had).

Fig. 7 (far left). Portrait statue of an unknown woman in the "Pudicitia" type (head restored). Vatican City, Vatican Museums (Braccio Nuovo), inv. no. 23 (photo Vatican Museums photographic archive XXXIX-15-19).

Fig. 8 (near left). Portrait statue in the "Pudicitia" type of an unknown Antonine woman. Vatican City, Vatican Museums (Belvedere), inv. no. 78 (photo Rossa, DAIR, inst. neg. 76.2123).

Collectively the statues present a strong and consistent picture of what Roman society thought was an exemplary appearance for a woman, how she ought to dress and behave. By analyzing them from the point of view of their body language and the way they use their drapery, we can get a clearer and deeper idea of what Roman society thought about male and female roles and the place of women in an ideal world; by comparing them with portrait statues of men, one can also see that the apparent equality suggested by the sheer numbers of statues of women (and therefore their visibility) was undermined by the many subtle differences in body language between statues of men and women.[29] Portrait statues made visibly manifest the different roles men and women were expected to play in society and that the dominant role was that of the male: the female statues also served to reinforce a particular vision of perfect womanhood by acting as role models to contemporary society. What is also interesting is that to a large extent this ideal was created in the late fourth century and early Hellenistic times in a Greek setting—yet it still seemed appropriate in the west as well as the eastern provinces, in the mid and even late empire.

Gender and Body Language

Gendered differences in body language are a feature of modern society, and it is my contention that these statues show that it was also a feature of Roman society. Body language in modern society

---

[29] Davies 1997; Davies 2002.

Fig. 9. Portrait statue of an unknown woman in the "Ceres" type: second-century body with head replaced in the mid-fourth century. Copenhagen, Ny Carlsberg Glyptothek, inv. no 552 (photo Ny Carlsberg Glyptotek, Copenhagen).

Fig. 10. Fragment of the front of a sarcophagus: the bride appears in the "Ceres" type. London, British Museum, Townley collection, inv. no. GR 1805.7-3.143 (© Copyright the Trustees of The British Museum).

can be taught as a social skill (in the recent past at classes in deportment and etiquette), and it has reemerged as a tool in business, especially selling oneself and one's ideas.[30] Boys (still) are more likely to sprawl around, taking up space and using broad gestures, whereas girls are encouraged to sit demurely with legs together or crossed, taking up as little space as possible and using small "ladylike" gestures. The "macho sprawl" is a defiant gesture of superiority and not appropriate for a female. Such gendered differences in body language were tellingly documented for modern society by Marianne Wex in a series of photographs taken in Hamburg in the 1970s.[31] Wex had an overtly feminist agenda: the point she was making was not just that male and female body language is different but that it is designed to ensure that women behave as subordinates: men assert the male sex's dominant position in society by their body language.

The bodies of Roman male portrait statues, like the men in Wex's photographs, "stress width": with the exception of some men wearing the pallium (which I have suggested elsewhere was seen as

---

[30] Pease 1990; Wainwright 1985.   [31] Wex 1979.

a relatively feminized mode of dress),[32] they hold their arms away from their bodies, often gesturing with their hands, and their heads are held erect with a level and direct gaze. A "macho" appearance is (unsurprisingly) at its most exaggerated in portraits in military dress (such as the Prima Porta Augustus) and statues of men in heroic nudity (see fig. 2, where Domitian's air of swaggering dominance is enhanced by the hand on the hip). Togate statues, understandably, tend to tone down the aggressive posture: figure 1, a statue of an unknown young man, is fairly typical. Yet in these statues the toga itself serves to enhance the width of the figure, and the arms are usually held away from the body and out to the sides, as if the subject of the statue is declaiming. He is always shown in confident control of his toga (and by extension the situation), even though in reality togas must have been difficult garments to wear with such assurance.[33]

Women in their portrait statues are far more commonly represented with their arms held close in to or across their body, forming a narrower figure that does not seem to stress width—though the legs are often quite widely spaced, with the bent knee turned out. The arms are not only held in to the body but are actually bound to it, on occasion tightly, by the voluminous drapery of the palla, which may also cover the hands partially or entirely. This is a feature of both the large and small Herculaneum women and the "Pudicitia" types (figs. 5–8). Even when the arms are allowed to be more mobile, the movement may still be hampered by the drapery: compare the two variations on the "Ceres" type, figs. 4 and 9, where the elbow and forearm of the raised arm are enclosed in a sling of drapery. Where the "Ceres" type is adapted to represent a bride in a marriage scene (fig. 10), this arm, used for the gesture of *dextrarum iunctio*, is freed from the encumbering drapery. Female drapery seems to be designed to restrict movement—not only are the arms constrained, but also in all the examples illustrated the dress falls over the feet and spills onto the ground, even when high platform soles are worn, as in figure 7. Whereas men wear the toga with an assurance that can hardly bear much relation to reality, women are usually holding or fingering the folds of their drapery, and their statues are characterized by large swathes of emphatic folds that cut across their bodies, often from arm to arm, forming a series of barriers. Whereas the male body is openly presented to our gaze, the female is protected by a series of barriers formed by the woman's arms and the drapery: in modern body language terminology these are "disguised barrier gestures."[34]

The stance adopted by women in these statues, especially the "Pudicitia" type, appears defensive: the arms and drapery are used as a way of protecting the body and warding off the outside world.[35] Such an appearance might be considered appropriate for women who are being displayed in a public arena, which is not their natural milieu. Posing these female bodies in this way creates subtle differences between them and their male counterparts: the men appear active and dominant, the women passive and hesitant. The women's body language goes some way to neutralize their display in public by signaling their subordinate position in relation to the men. And yet their legs do *not* suggest such obvious defensiveness;[36] rather they stand in a relaxed pose with one leg straight, the other bent. In most cases the bent knee is swung inward, in contrast to the stance usually adopted in statues of men (where the knee is bent outward, and the figure is shown stepping forward more actively). Even so, the position of the legs of the female statues does give them an air of assurance that is belied by the pose of the arms.

[32] Davies 2005, 125.

[33] For photographs of numerous statues of Romans in togas, see Goette 1990.

[34] Pease 1990, 63–65.

[35] Pease 1990, chap. 6 on "Arm barriers" 59–65: see in particular figs. 76–78 and 83.

[36] As illustrated in Pease 1990, figs. 83 and 84, where the legs are crossed.

Negotiating Ideal Femininity

These are far from being downtrodden little wives. The pose and the dress are also used to give out other signals. The arms may add to the elegance and allure of the figure (see particularly figs. 5–8). Wex talks about "another frequently observed position in women: the hand used as an ornament, almost like a brooch," and she sees this as "a position of humility that strongly signals the lower part of the sex-oriented hierarchy."[37] Pease perhaps is closer to the mark in describing them as "preening gestures" used in courtship display.[38] The vast amount of drapery covering the body—especially the palla draped over the head as a veil seen in figures 3, 4, 5, 7, 9, and 10, and the extra layer of the stola worn in figure 3—indicates modesty and chastity, as does a lowered gaze. But in a world where clothing was expensive this amount of drapery also signals extreme opulence.[39] The quality of the material implied by the sculptor's carving is also the best: see figure 8, where the palla is represented as so thin that the folds of the dress worn below can be seen through it, or figure 3, where the woman's breasts appear clearly modeled even under the two layers of her chiton and stola. The drapery itself is designed to be attractive and to enhance the figure in ways not seen even in the togate statues: there the sweeping curves formed by the toga conceal rather than reveal the shape of the body beneath.

This reminds us that the relationship to be negotiated between the statue and its viewer is not simply one of power: it can also be sexual. In portraits of Roman men the sexual element is usually subordinated to the expression of power, but for women it plays a much more important role, and this can create a problem for the artist, who had to express his female subject's sexuality without compromising her modesty. The popular statue types illustrated here manage a good balance: they represent a woman at ease with her sexual role, who appears elegantly feminine but not improperly flirtatious (though the "Ceres" type can perhaps flash rather a lot of thigh); these women appear neither timid nor aggressive but assured. Although they are covered in several layers of drapery, they stand in a more or less exaggerated contrapposto pose, with hips displaced to one side and the folds of the drapery smoothed so as to reveal one thigh and knee. The breasts too may be clearly indicated (even when wearing the stola), and the drapery folds may also serve to emphasize the pubic triangle, a feature particularly noticeable on the large and small Herculaneum women types (see figs. 5 and 6).

The idea that statues of elite women should show them richly decked, sexually attractive, yet modest and chaste—that is, faithful to their husbands—predates their use in the Roman Empire. Discussing a series of Hellenistic Greek statues, Smith refers to the "massively constructed, matronly figures, that express the temperate values of the married bourgeois woman," and "the fine mantle is usually pulled or wrapped tightly around the body to reveal prominent curves at hips and breasts."[40] He concludes that:

> The combination of a young beautiful head, modesty gestures, body-revealing drapery, and massive proportions creates a highly interesting mixture of signals about the propriety versus the erotic potential (held in check) of the desirable Hellenistic wife.[41]

[37] Wex 1979, 71.

[38] Pease 1990, 93.

[39] See Henner von Hesberg's contribution in this volume on

female adornment (clothing and jewelry).

[40] Smith 1991, 84.

[41] Smith 1991, 84.

This combination creates a dynamic tension that ensured this type of statue remained popular into and indeed throughout the period of the Roman Empire:[42] Hellenistic Greeks in effect provided an artistic role model for Roman sculptors to follow. The ingredient the Romans added was the portrait head, often quite realistically individualized, with its contemporary hairstyle, which was the one element that brought the statues up to date. The clothing (except when the stola was added) remained that of the Hellenistic Greek world, as were the attitudes and values the statues represented.

Honorific statues of women, because displayed in public, would have acted as role models for those aspiring to a place in the elite, so what was the role that these statues ascribe to women? Diana Kleiner has described these as domesticated women, quoting Hillary Clinton's claim that she could "make a good salad and whip up a mean omelette."[43] Yet it is hard to imagine these women in the kitchen wielding a frying pan or indeed even spinning or weaving: they are not represented with their work baskets at their feet, as the men have their scroll boxes, and only very rarely do they appear with children. Despite Kampen's suggestion that their body types are designed to allude to their fertility and their role or potential as mothers, there is little here to suggest that their primary role is maternal.[44] The closest the statues get to suggesting that women played a role in life in the same way as men is the attribute of the poppies and corn ears held by some figures, which *may* indicate that the woman concerned was a priestess of Ceres—but which might rather suggest assimilation with the goddess. The woman on the sarcophagus relief illustrated in figure 10 is also presented as a bride, and the stola represented on the statue in Munich (fig. 3) characterizes the matron.[45] But generally speaking it is the *absence* of a specific role that is noticeable in these images of women. Accompanying inscriptions and find contexts suggest that many of these women were presented as counterparts and appendages to their menfolk. The statues might be displayed in groups with them, or they were dedicated by them, and these women are commemorated because of their relationship with men. They represent an ideal: a woman who is beautiful and elegant, who shows off the expensive clothing and fancy hairdressing her family can afford for her; she is a woman of leisure who does not meddle in things that are not her concern (that is, men's public affairs); and she is modest, faithful, and chaste. Her apprehension at being seen in public (where she does not really belong) is expressed through her defensive body language. To quote Diana Kleiner:

> A woman wrapped in the pose of *pudicitia* (modesty) was not a woman of action. A woman enrobed in her domesticity was not a woman prepared for public life. Women wrapped in voluminous garments with their hair bound up were not liberated women.[46]

It was therefore all the more important that women who *did* play a public role (such as Plancia Magna in Perge or Eumachia in Pompeii—and indeed Livia herself) should appear in this way: the

---

[42] The "Pudicitia" type appears to have been most popular in the late republic (from ca. 100 B.C.) and early empire ("at least into the 2nd century": Bieber 1977, 133); the large and small Herculaneum women were used over a long period (ca. 300 B.C.–A.D. 300: Bieber 1977, 149; see also Trimble 1999), but the "Ceres" type, although it may have been based on earlier types (see statues of Antonia in Naples: Bieber 1977, fig. 726), seems to have come into vogue in the second century A.D. (Bieber 1977, 164–67).

[43] Kleiner 2000, 48.

[44] Kampen 1994, 119.

[45] This is an unusually late occurrence of the stola, which is most often represented on statues of Augustan and Julio-Claudian date.

[46] Kleiner 2000, 48.

dress and body language of their statues, ostensibly erected to honor them, made clear that they did not pose a threat to the public world of men.[47]

The draped statues of women discussed in this chapter represent traditional values, but the adoption of Hellenistic body types for statues of Roman women suggests that they are the values of the urbane Greek world rather than old Rome, where a senator reputedly divorced his wife for going out of doors unveiled.[48] Even in the imperial period veiling in public may still have been expected of women in some parts of the Roman world, and "traditional values" were always held in high esteem.[49] Now women can be seen in public, provided they dress and behave appropriately, and statues can be erected of those who deserve to be honored, but this created some anxiety and tension with regard to the proper role of women in society. The messages these statues convey are subtle and seductive: they suggest that a woman who conforms will be rewarded—not only by fine clothes and access to hairstylists but also by commemoration in a marble portrait. But by various means they also make clear that conforming means not behaving like a man, not aspiring to male roles, and knowing what a woman's place is.

[47] According to Suetonius, Caligula often called his grandmother, Livia, a "Ulysses stolata" as a way of belittling her (Suet. *Calig.* 23.2)—presumably because he did feel threatened by her.

[48] Val. Max. 6.3.10: the senator was Sulpicius Gallus, and the incident supposedly took place in the mid-second century B.C.

[49] MacMullen 1980.

Works Cited

Amelung, W., *Die Sculpturen des Vaticanischen Museums*, 2 vols. (Berlin 1903; 1908).

Barton, C., "Being in the Eyes: Shame and Sight in Ancient Rome," in *The Roman Gaze: Vision, Power and the Body*, ed. D. Frederick (Baltimore and London 2002) 216–35.

Bieber, M., *Ancient Copies: Contributions to the History of Greek and Roman Art* (New York 1977).

Boatwright, M. T., "Plancia Magna of Perge: Women's Roles and Status in Roman Asia Minor," in *Women's History and Ancient History*, ed. S. B. Pomeroy (Chapel Hill and London 1991) 249–72.

———, "Just Window Dressing? Imperial Women as Architectural Sculpture," in *I Claudia II: Women in Ancient Rome*, ed. D. E. E. Kleiner and S. B. Matheson (New Haven 2000) 61–76.

Bol, R., *Das Statuenprogramm des Herodes-Atticus-Nymphäums*, *Olympische Forschungen* 15 (Berlin 1984).

Christ, A. T., "The Masculine Ideal of 'the Race that Wears the Toga'," *Art Journal* 56.2 (1997) 24–30.

D'Ambra, E., "The Calculus of Venus: Nude Portraits of Roman Matrons," in *Sexuality in Ancient Art*, ed. N. B. Kampen (Cambridge 1996) 219–32.

———, *Art and Identity in the Roman World*, Everyman Art Library (London 1998).

———, "Nudity and Adornment in Female Portrait Sculpture of the Second Century A.D.," in *I Claudia II: Women in Ancient Rome*, ed. D. E. E. Kleiner and S. B. Matheson (New Haven 2000) 101–14.

Davies, G., "Gender and Body Language in Roman Art," in *Gender and Ethnicity in Ancient Italy*, ed. T. Cornell and K. Lomas, Accordia Specialist Studies on Italy 6 (London 1997) 97–108.

———, "Clothes as Sign: The Case of the Large and Small Herculaneum Women," in *Women's Dress in the Ancient Greek World*, ed. L. Llewellyn-Jones (London and Swansea 2002) 227–42.

———, "What Made the Roman Toga *virilis*?," in *The Clothed Body in the Ancient World*, ed. L. Cleland, M. Harlow, and L. Llewellyn-Jones (Oxford 2005) 121–30.

Dixon, S., *Reading Roman Women* (London 2001).

Fischler, S., "Social Stereotypes and Historical Analysis: The Case of the Imperial Women at Rome," in *Women in Ancient Societies: An Illusion of the Night*, ed. L. Archer, S. Fischler, and M. Wyke (Basingstoke and London 1994) 115–33.

Forbis, E. P., "Women's Public Image in Italian Honorary Inscriptions," *American Journal of Philology* 111 (1990) 493–512.

Gleason, M. W., "Elite Male Identity in the Roman Empire," in *Life, Death, and Entertainment in the Roman Empire*, ed. D. S. Potter and D. J. Mattingly (Ann Arbor 1999) 67–84.

Goette, H. R., *Studien zur römischen Togadarstellungen* (Mainz 1990).

Haskell, F., and N. Penny, *Taste and the Antique* (New Haven and London 1981).

Helbig, W., ed., *Führer durch die öffentlichen Sammlungen klassischer Altertümer in Rom*, Band 1: *Die päpstlichen Sammlungen im Vatikan und Lateran* (Tübingen 1963).

Kampen, N. B., "Material Girl: Feminist Confrontations with Roman Art," *Arethusa* 27 (1994) 111–37.

Kleiner, D. E. E., "Imperial Women as Patrons of the Arts in the Early Empire," in *I Claudia: Women in Ancient Rome*, ed. D. E. E. Kleiner and S. B. Matheson (New Haven 1996) 28–41.

———, "Now You See Them, Now You Don't: The Presence and Absence of Women in Roman Art," in *From Caligula to Constantine: Tyranny and Transformation in Roman Portraiture*, ed. E. R. Varner (Atlanta 2000) 45–57.

MacMullen, R., "Women in Public in the Roman Empire," *Historia* 29 (1980) 208–18.

Pease, A., *Body Language: How to Read Others' Thoughts by Their Gestures* (London 1990; first published 1981).

Poulsen, V., *Les portraits romains*, vol. 2, Ny Carlsberg Publication no. 8 (Copenhagen 1974).

Rose, C. B., *Dynastic Commemoration and Imperial Portraiture in the Julio-Claudian Period* (Cambridge 1997).

Smith, R. R. R., *Hellenistic Sculpture: A Handbook* (London 1991).

Stone, S., "The Toga: From National to Ceremonial Costume," in *The World of Roman Costume*, ed. J. L. Sebesta and L. Bonfante (Madison and London 1994).

Treggiari, S., "Women in Roman Society," in *I Claudia: Women in Ancient Rome* (New Haven 1996) 116–21.

Trimble, J. F., "The Aesthetics of Sameness: A Contextual Analysis of the Large and Small Herculaneum Women Statue Types in the Roman Empire" (Ph.D. diss., University of Michigan 1999).

———, "Replicating the Body Politic: The Herculaneum Women Statue Types in Early Imperial Italy," *Journal of Roman Archaeology* 13 (2000) 41–68.

Wainwright, G. R., *Body Language*, Teach Yourself Books (Sevenoaks 1985).

Walker, S., *Catalogue of Roman Sarcophagi in the British Museum* (London 1990).

Wex, M., *Let's Take Back Our Space: "Female" and "Male" Body Language as a Result of Patriarchal Structures* (Munich 1979).

Wrede, H., Consecratio in Formam Deorum. *Vergöttlichte Privatpersonen in der römische Kaiserzeit* (Mainz 1981).

Wyke, M., "Woman in the Mirror: The Rhetoric of Adornment in the Roman World," in *Women in Ancient Societies: An Illusion of the Night*, ed. L. Archer, S. Fischler, and M. Wyke (Basingstoke and London 1994) 134–51.

11 ◆ SPARTAN WOMEN AMONG THE ROMANS: ADAPTING MODELS, FORGING IDENTITIES

Sarah B. Pomeroy

How did the Romans distinguish respectable Greek women from Romans? Why did they consider Spartans different from the others? In this chapter I will discuss the complex and changing relationship between gender and ethnic identity. I selected the Spartans for this investigation because they were the most distinctive and ethnically identifiable of Greek women. "Ethnic identity" refers to inherited cultural traits that are often observable only by comparison with people who do not exhibit these traits. Ethnic identities can be carved out by members of the group being defined, by establishing similarities among them, or may be conferred by outsiders.

For this study I use postcolonial theory as currently applied by ancient historians and feminist theory that has become traditional among historians of women. I first combined these approaches in *Women in Hellenistic Egypt*, looking at the interaction between Greek settlers and Egyptians and their eclectic participation in the mixed culture of Ptolemaic Egypt.[1] In that work I showed that the rate and quality of Hellenization varied according to gender and that conquest did not result in the imperial power overwhelming and eradicating the indigenous contribution to the relationship. In the following chapter I apply this model to Spartan women under Roman domination.

Literary Models

We will look first at the west, then east across the Adriatic, beginning with images of Spartan women in Roman literature. Of course all Romans with any education would be familiar with Helen as she is depicted in epic. The first Spartan woman described in literature was beautiful, wealthy, daring, deceitful, and, as a mature woman, chose her own husband; she was the archetypal "power blonde." Doubtless Homer's Helen was the ultimate model for allusions to Spartan women in Latin poetry. Cicero (*Tusc.* 2.36) quotes a verse about Spartan maidens engaging in wrestling and military exercise. Propertius (3.14) describes a Spartan woman wrestling nude with men, boxing, throwing the discus, hunting, riding, girding on a sword, wearing her hair in a simple style, and walking openly with her lover without fear of some husband. The poet wishes his mistress Cynthia would choose to live with him thus. Ovid (*Her.* 16.151–52) depicts Helen wrestling nude. Vergil (*Georg.* 2.487–88) refers to the loud voices of Spartan girls celebrating Bacchus in the mountains.

It was in prose, however, that intellectuals in the Roman world considered Spartan women as a group that had evolved in a specific social context. Romans thought that the Spartan political system—with its mixed constitution, checks and balances, and government by the elite—was comparable to their own and far more congenial than the democracy of Athens.[2] If to the Romans

---

[1] Pomeroy 1984, 121, 124, 130, 135–36, 152–53.

[2] For affinities between Rome and Sparta: Baladié 1980, 293–95.

Greece was "the other," it was the Greece of Athens. In Greek thought, on the other hand, most of which emanated from Athens, Sparta functioned as "the other." It follows that both Rome and Sparta were similar to each other in being different from Athens. Discussions of differences between Roman and Greek mores focused on subtle distinctions between the laws of Numa and Romulus, on the one hand, and of Lycurgus on the other. Prose writers variously praised and criticized provisions for women and marriage in archaic Rome and Sparta. Referring to Spartans, Cicero (*Rep.* 4.6) prefers Roman to Greek rules about women, advocating that a censor teach men to govern their wives rather than, as the Greeks do, allow women to be supervised by a *gynaikonomos* ("praefectus," a magistrate in charge of women), a post that was common in Hellenistic Greek states.[3] Certainly Aristotle's critique of the Spartan constitution and his condemnation of women not only for licentiousness but also for the failure of the state would have inevitably constituted part of the discussion, as it does explicitly in Plutarch's *Life of Lycurgus* (14.1), where he states plainly that Aristotle was incorrect. Nevertheless, in his *Comparison of Lycurgus and Numa* (3.5) Plutarch, in agreement with Cicero, praises the demeanor of Roman women as they were said to be in the archaic period, when they were under their husband's control, and he criticizes the laws of Lycurgus that allowed Spartan women to dominate their husbands.

Plutarch's views were influenced by Plato and Xenophon, both of whom were also popular among the Romans. Plato's *Republic* was a utopia that incorporated elements of an idealized Sparta, not a blueprint for any actual society. Yet some Romans considered the *Republic* a "how-to" manual presenting role models for them rather than a work of social criticism. Epictetus reported that at Rome women were carrying copies of Plato's *Republic* because they supposed that he advocated communities of wives. They were quoting Plato to justify their own licentiousness, he alleged, but they misinterpreted him in supposing that his advice was to enter monogamous marriage and then practice promiscuous intercourse.[4] Xenophon's picture of Sparta was closer to the truth than the reflection in Plato's *Republic*,[5] but although Roman authors cite some works of Xenophon specifically, there are no clear references in Latin to his treatise on the *Spartan Constitution*.[6] In any case, if the Romans did not actually read Xenophon's monograph, they nevertheless will have gotten the information at second hand through Plutarch, an admirer of Xenophon.[7] Xenophon will have been one of his informants about the daily life of Spartan girls, including their excellent nutrition, drinking wine, physical training, and freedom from weaving (which was the usual job of Greek women). Plutarch had been to Rome and Sparta and wrote for both Greek and Roman audiences.[8] He participated to the fullest in the debate on Spartan and Roman women. Though Plutarch's avowed subject is the women of the remote past, there is no doubt that he is influenced by his contemporaries. Plutarch largely approves of the healthy regimen Lycurgus designed for Spartan girls and, as I have mentioned, asserts that Aristotle was wrong to accuse Spartan women of licentiousness: but his ideas and ideals concerning the appropriate behavior of Greek women, except Spartans, are essentially conservative and traditional in the Greek world, and barely reflect the changes of the Hellenistic period.[9]

---

[3] Since Cicero mentions drinking, and was discussing Sparta in the previous paragraph, he is probably referring to Spartan women.

[4] Arr. *Epict. diss.* Fr. 15 = Stobaeus 3.6.58 and see Schenkl 1965, 455–60, 462–75.

[5] See further Münscher 1920, 51, 63, 107, 114 and Pomeroy 2002, 148–49.

[6] Münscher 1920, 63, 106.

[7] On Plutarch and Xenophon, see Pomeroy 1999b, 36, and passim.

[8] See most recently Stadter 2002.

[9] See further Pomeroy 1999b and Nevett 2002, esp. 84, 87–88, 95.

The Influence of Ethnic Identity on Gender Roles

Like the Spartan women Aristotle had criticized (but unlike other Greek women), Romans were neither silent nor secluded.[10] Both Sparta and Rome were warrior societies ruling alien territories, with the result that long absences of men left women in charge. Aristotle did not approve of women exercising such power in default of men. In both Sparta and Rome some women controlled vast amounts of wealth that had come into their hands through dowry and inheritance. Since the fourth century B.C. Spartan women were conspicuous in their ownership and management of real property and other forms of wealth. In imperial Sparta economic status was still based on landholding, and Romans respected that indication of old wealth. Aristotle (*Pol.* 1269b12–1270a34) had criticized the Spartans for allowing women to own so much property that some men could no longer contribute to their *syssitia* and lost their status as full citizens. The Romans, on the other hand, beginning with the *lex Voconia* (169 B.C.), repeatedly tried to prevent women from obtaining large fortunes, fearing lest men might lose their rank in the higher property classes in the census and thus become exempt from heavy military obligations.[11]

In both Sparta and Rome one of the reasons women acquired wealth was that families were smaller, and women were often the sole survivors. Although there was a general decrease in the population of Greece in the late Hellenistic and early Roman periods,[12] and a particularly lamented decrease among the upper class, both Spartan and Roman women were singled out for blame. Cicero (*Tusc.* 2.36) declared that the Spartans rejected *fertilitas barbara* and that Roman women repeatedly procured abortions was a cliché among Augustan writers.[13] Thus moralists agreed that women, whose conscious goal was not only keeping their bodies unmarred but also maintaining economic and social status by securing large estates for themselves and transmitting them to their offspring, selfishly created *oliganthropia*. One unusual solution to this problem was adopted. A Spartan woman who was already married and had borne children could produce children for another man while remaining married to her original husband. Wife-lending or husband-sharing that had been unique to Spartans (among Greeks) can also be found among the Romans. The younger Cato, paragon of Stoic virtue, divorced his wife Marcia after she had borne three children to him and gave her to his friend Hortensius Hortalus, with whom she produced two more children.[14] After Hortensius died, Cato remarried Marcia (she must have been a Stoic too, unless she was simply docile and devoted to Cato). Plutarch (*Comparison of Lycurgus and Numa* 3.1–2) prefers the serial monogamy of the Romans to the concurrent husbands of the Spartans.

Symbolic similarities were obvious in the respected and powerful position of Roman and Spartan mothers. For Roman moralists, including Valerius Maximus, Aelian, Sextus Empiricus, and others, the famous mothers of Sparta as well as those of their own early and middle republic served as exemplars to "new-style" Roman women, who left the rearing of their children to outsiders or rejected motherhood completely.[15] Furthermore, at least in the ideal past, Spartan and Roman women were actively patriotic, heroic, and expected to uphold civic ideals. Spartan mothers like the mother of

---

[10] Pomeroy 1975, 181.

[11] See further Pomeroy 1975, 177–82 and Gardner 1986, 170–78.

[12] Polyb. 36.16.5–9; Alcock 1989a, esp. 105–7.

[13] References in Riddle 1992, 64–65.

[14] Luc. *Phars.* 2.326–71; Plut. *Cat. Min.* 25.4–5.

[15] Pomeroy 2002, 156.

Coriolanus reminded their sons of their patriotic duties.[16] They hectored and supported men, includ-ing not only their sons but candidates seeking political office. In Sparta and Rome wealthy widows were especially prominent among women engaged in these strategies. Patriotism and Stoicism are themes in the stories told of both, mainly by Plutarch and Livy. Plutarch paints vivid pictures of Spartan women digging trenches as a defense against Pyrrhus and of female relatives and associates of the kings Agis IV and Cleomenes III like the wife of Pantheus in the saga of Cleomenes, who is a valiant heroine on horseback and who could be compared to Cloelia, immortalized by an equestrian statue in Rome.[17] The rest of the Greek world had no stories to rival those of Spartan women.

Stoicism found adherents among both Spartan women and Romans. The Stoicism of Agiatis, wife first of Agis and then of Cleomenes, and of Cratesicleia, Cleomenes' mother, influenced Spartan domestic and foreign policy. Cratesicleia and the wife of Pantheus died dignified Stoic deaths upon the order of Ptolemy IV (Plut. *Cleom.* 37–39). Similarly, several Roman matrons in the early empire chose to die in Stoic fashion as a rebuff to emperors who had sentenced their husbands to death. Just as the wife of Panteus had encouraged Cratesicleia, so did the Roman women set examples for their husbands. The virtuous Arria chose to die with her husband, valiantly preceding him: handing to Paetus the sword she had drawn from her own breast, she said, "*Paete, non dolet.*"[18]

As part of their identity, people station themselves in a hierarchy of social status that provides an avenue to rights and disabilities. Thus Spartans were taught that they were superior to their helots, and the helots, in turn, were encouraged to feel themselves inferior, by being treated as subhuman and forced to wear primitive clothing. Spartan women were also smugly secure in their feelings of superiority over other Greek women. Plutarch quotes many of them, including an anonymous Spartan woman who was conscious of her ethnic distinctiveness and articulated it: When an Ionian woman was proud of something she had woven, a Spartan showed off her four well-behaved sons and said: "these should be the work of a noble and honorable woman, and she should swell with pride and boast of them" (*Sayings of Spartan Women* 241.9). We observe, in passing, the competi-tive nature of the Spartan's retort and are reminded of a similar statement attributed to Cornelia, mother of the Gracchi, who, when asked why she did not wear fine pearls, replied that her children were her "jewels."[19]

Contemporary Models

Not only literature but eyewitness reports from influential sources helped to shape Roman ideas about Spartan women. In 40 B.C. during the civil wars Livia and her family, including the infant Tiberius, enjoyed refuge at Sparta. One night she had to race through a forest fire that scorched her dress and hair.[20] This perilous incident shows that Sparta was still forested, as the allusions in Propertius and Vergil to women in the wilderness attest (see above). Sparta and Mantinea were the only Greek cities to back Octavian. In gratitude for their support, later while visiting Greece in 21 B.C., Augustus awarded Cythera to Sparta and honored the Spartans with the right to share Roman

---

[16] Plutarch, *Sayings of Spartan Women*, 240f2, 241.1–6; Livy 2.40.1–12.

[17] Plut. *Pyrrh.* 27.2–5; *Cleom.* 38.5; and Plin. *HN* 34.29.

[18] Death of Arria: Plin. *Ep.* 3.16.6; Mart. 1.13; for others: Tac. *Ann.* 16.10–11; Plin. *Ep.* 6.24; Stoic behavior: Sen. *Constant.* 16.

[19] Valerius Maximus 4.4, quoting Pomponius Rufus, and see further Dixon 1988.

[20] Suet. *Tib.* 6.2; Vell. Pat. 2.75.3; and see further Cartledge and Spawforth 1989, 98–99, 102.

banquets (Dio 54.7.2). After Livia's death in 29 or deification in 42, annual games were established in her honor at Sparta. All we know about these celebrations is that they included races for women requiring running a double course.[21] Thus although Roman imperial cult was the inspiration for the games, and doubtless a portrait of Livia would have been brought out to observe the events, the focus on competitions for female athletes seems peculiarly Spartan.[22]

Sparta continued to be a destination for Roman tourists. Although the small size of the Spartan population could have led them to assimilate, this attention from outsiders was one of the factors that encouraged them to preserve their ethnic distinctiveness. Women played a part in the show the Spartans put on to attract visitors, perhaps because of their costume. The Spartans were the most visible among the ethnic group of Dorians, and *Doriazein* is defined as "to dress like a Dorian girl, that is in a single garment open at the side," and "to imitate the Dorians in life."[23] Thus the wearing of revealing clothing, as well as the lack of it, for athletic and ritual purposes marked differences between Spartans and other Greek women and contributed to the racy reputation of the former, reflected in both Aristotle's accusation of licentiousness and in Roman literature.

Reviving Traditional Identities

Literary and historical models influenced the Spartans themselves, for they were pedantic students of their own traditions, which they manipulated often without distinguishing between their idealized and historical past. Visitors to Roman Sparta would have seen the unique educational system of boys and girls called the "agoge" and have been told that Lycurgus had created it nearly a thousand years ago. The agoge was terminated in 188 B.C., but a new version was revived under Roman domination in 146 B.C. and survived until the fourth century.[24] The most memorable feature of the final agoge was the whipping contest in honor of Artemis Orthia in which boys were whipped so severely that some of them died. The priestess of Artemis Orthia monitored the relationship between the male adults wielding the whips and the youths, making certain that the adults did not play favorites or accept bribes and that all boys were whipped equally (Paus. 3.16.10, Plut. *Lyc.* 18). This display may have been redesigned in imperial Greece with more gore than in the past to satisfy the taste of the period for bloody spectacle. Accounts of this ordeal mention that fathers and mothers cheered for their offspring in this competition, like the proverbial Spartans, preferring their son to be a dead hero rather than a defeated coward.[25]

The education of Spartan girls was similar to that of boys without its extreme survival tests. Spartan women will have found much that was enjoyable and that they would have been reluctant to relinquish through assimilation. Plutarch (*Inst. Lac.* 35 [239b], *Lyc.* 14.2) corroborates the reports of the Roman poets, stating that the curriculum consisted of running, wrestling, discus throwing, and hurling the javelin. Although the education of girls in Hellenistic Greece was more widespread than it had been in the classical period, and included physical training (Arist. *Pol.* 1337b), athletic prowess, competitiveness, and athletic nudity were still a distinguishing feature and source of Spartan pride. Imperial writers associated Dorians with athletics. For example, Agrippa called the

---

[21] In *SEG* 11 830 the city commemorates a woman's victory in the *diaulos*. On *ludi* celebrated in honor of both Livia and Augustus: *PIR* 1970, 5.1:77–78 s.v. Livia.

[22] For the imperial cult of Livia in Sparta, see Bartman 1999, esp. 73.

[23] *LSJ* s.v. *Doriazo* II = *dorizo*.

[24] Kennell 1995, 13–14.

[25] Stat. *Theb.* 8436–37; Lucian *Anach.* 38–39; and see further Kennell 1995, appendix 1.

gymnasium he constructed at Rome "Laconian."[26] The establishment of the women's race at the Livian games indicates that the Romans were well aware that the Spartan women of their own day were still an essential part of the Spartan ethnic identity.

Pausanias (3.13.7) mentions Dionysiades, girls who participated in races at Sparta organized by magistrates called "bideoi." The involvement of magistrates shows that in the Roman period the state was concerned with girls' physical education as it had been even a thousand years earlier. Thus this involvement was part of the recreation of the past; but it can also be seen as part of a calculated campaign to deploy both genders in a small population with a goal of preserving its unique identity. Girls also continued to perform traditional dances at the sanctuary of Artemis at Caryae near the northeast border of Spartan territory.[27] Since these dances were said to have been taught to the girls by Castor and Pollux, the movements must have been quite athletic. Roman writers' references to nude women engaging in coed contact sports, however, are not impeccable evidence, for their purpose was to titillate. Coed athletics were probably not part of the first two versions of the agoge but may have been a feature in the imperial phase. Exploiting this caricature, in the time of Nero a Spartan woman wrestled at Rome with a Roman senator.[28] Of course there must have been less notorious and more humble Spartan women to be seen at Rome too. For example, an inscription from a columbarium near San Laurentii extra muros commemorates Artemo from Laconia, wife of Sabinus, dead at 14.[29]

Thucydides (1.10) had observed that future generations could not have deduced the power of Sparta from its paltry architectural remains. Sparta, however, was not desolate: the few pre-Roman monuments in the city and at pan-Hellenic sanctuaries were well chosen to remind the viewer that Spartans—women no less than men—were notably brave, pious, and habitually victorious. Pausanias describes some of the material remains of Sparta's glorious past that survived in his day. Visitors to the temple of Hera at Elis would have seen many bronze statues dedicated by girl runners who had won victories there.[30] Most, if not all of them, were probably Spartans. Trophies at Olympia itself relevant to women's history included two equestrian monuments erected early in the fourth century B.C. by Cynisca, daughter and sister of Spartan kings, who was the first woman whose horses were victorious at Olympia.[31]

In the city of Sparta Cynisca was also celebrated with a heroön prominently located near the youths' exercise grounds. The most magnificent structure in the Spartan agora was the Persian stoa. This building, described by Vitruvius and Pausanias, was constructed with spoils of the Persian War and commemorated the city's greatest victory.[32] It housed statues of the vanquished in barbaric dress. The figure of Artemisia, queen of Halicarnassus, placed within might have brought to mind the dreaded Cleopatra VII, a more recent admiral-queen from the east. Xerxes had admired Artemisia's maneuvers at Salamis, ramming the ship of a Persian ally in order to confuse the Greeks as to which side she was on, but only a madman would have been pleased with such selfish behavior (Herod. 8.87). Romans might have compared the strategy of Cleopatra at Actium. Her desire to

---

[26] Plut. *Lyc.* 20.5; Dio Chrys. *Or.* 37.26–27; Cass. Dio 53.27; and see further Spawforth and Walker 1986, esp. 100.

[27] Lucian *Salt.* 10; Paus. 3.10.7; Poll. 4.104; Stat. *Theb.* 4.225; Diom., book 3, p. 486 (H. Keil, *Gramm. Lat.* 1). Clearchus gave Tissaphernes a ring showing the maidens dancing at Caryae (Plut. *Artax.* 18).

[28] Schol. Juv. 4.53; *IAG*, 168, for the Neronian date.

[29] *LGPN* s.v. Artemo (4) second/third century A.D.

[30] See further Pomeroy 2002, x–xi, 24–25.

[31] Paus. 6.1.6 = *Anth. Pal.* 13.16 = *IG* v.1 1564a = *I. Olympia*, no. 160 = *IAG*, no. 17, and *I. Olympia*, nos. 373, 381. On the commemorative monuments, see Frazer 1913, vols. 3, 4, ad loc.

[32] Paus. 3.11.3; Vitr. 1.1.6; and see further Plommer 1979, esp. 100.

save herself and her ships above all tilted an equivocal situation in favor of Octavian (Plut. *Ant.* 63.5, 66.3). The Spartans supported Roman campaigns in the east because they equated the Parthians with the Persians, whom they had defeated in the fifth century B.C. (Herodian 4.8.3, 4.9.4). Inscriptions in the Persian Stoa attest to the cult of Elagabalus there, and later additions include a statue of his wife, the Vestal Julia Aquilia Severa.[33] Elagabalus considered himself a descendant of Caracalla and heir to the earlier emperor's eastern campaigns. Julia Domna was another Severan honored by a huge monument.[34]

Greek Identity: Adapting Models

Spartan women were Spartans first and foremost among the Greeks, but they were also Greeks in the Roman Empire. If the Spartans had not identified their interests with those of the rest of the Greeks, their small numbers could have led them to be ignored. Pausanias (3.22.1) points out that just off the Peloponnese is the place where Helen and Paris first had intercourse, and he describes several shrines where Helen was worshiped as divine. Nevertheless, while Spartan women were reenacting and reviving the unique practices of their past, they simultaneously conformed to pan-Hellenic mores, rejecting Helen as a role model for married women and adopting Penelope. Pan-Hellenism was a reaction against Roman domination and stressed similarities among Greek women, according to the traditional paradigm known best in Athens and preferred by Plutarch.[35] Thus, in conformity with the rest of the Greek world, Spartans emphasized women's modesty and chastity. Even in the imperial period, however, Spartans drew attention to their distinctive dialect in their inscriptions, using a long alpha where other Greeks used an eta: accordingly the women are praised for virtue, *areta*, rather than *arête*. The shrine of Aidos ("Modesty"), where Penelope's father Icarius in sadness had dedicated an image of Aidos after his daughter resolutely put on her veil and left him to marry Odysseus, was a public declaration of their assimilation (Paus. 3.20.10–11). The statue probably depicted a veiled woman since Spartan women covered their hair when they became wives.[36] Aidos was a psychological abstraction that lent support to Spartan brides and their fathers, who were separated upon marriage.[37] Pausanias mentions that mothers of brides sacrificed to an ancient wooden image of Aphrodite Hera, an unusual hybrid apparently confirming an exclusive link between love and marriage.[38] He also explains a seated figure of Aphrodite Morpho, wearing a veil with chains on her feet, stating that Tyndareus, the father of Helen and Clytemnestra, dedicated it to demonstrate that wives were faithful to their husbands (Paus. 3.15.10). Probably he was tacitly defending his own daughters' virtue. This *aition* seems to have been invented as yet another defense against the charge that Spartan women were promiscuous. Plutarch (*Lyc.* 4.4), perhaps also defensively, states unequivocally that despite their nudity the girls were virtuous.

As I have mentioned, there were *gynaikonomoi* ("magistrates in charge of women") at Sparta. This magistracy was said to be *kata ta archaia ethe kai tous nomous* ("in accordance with ancient custom and laws").[39] Cicero alludes to it, but *gynaikonomoi* are first attested at Sparta in an early

---

[33] Pikoula 2001, esp. 428–29.

[34] Spawforth 1986.

[35] See further Pomeroy 1999b, esp. 40–42.

[36] Pomeroy 2002, 42.

[37] Richer 1999, esp. 93–100.

[38] Paus. 3.13.9, and see further Pirenne-Delforge 1994, 197–98.

[39] Woodward 1923–25, 165, no. B1= *SEG* 11 (1950), no. 626.

first-century A.D. inscription.[40] They must have had a full agenda since each official was assisted by five subordinates called *syngynaikonomoi*. *Gynaikonomoi* not only supervised women but also enforced sumptuary legislation. In religion, elite women enjoyed an approved avenue for conspicuous consumption. The obligation to pay for the annual feast in honor of Demeter and Core at the Eleusinion was assigned as a liturgy to female officials known as the *thoinarmostria* and *polos*, who also supervised and participated in the rituals. Some inscriptions praise women for their lavish expenditures on this banquet, which was served to all the women of the city.[41]

In Roman Sparta there is no indication of a restoration of even a pretense of the old austerity. Excavators have found large and comfortable houses typical of those in imperial Greece.[42] In Sparta, as elsewhere, the differentiation between wealthy and poor was highly visible. The population of the Roman city of Sparta was no more than 12,000,[43] and the elite, of course, comprised a very small proportion of this total. Though few in number, this elite was highly visible. Under Roman domination their activities increased, for adults and children now were responsible for sacerdotal duties previously performed by the kings.[44] The wealth and aspirations of this group produced a relative abundance of dedications to and by women.

Approximately thirty inscriptions that were dedicated mostly in the second and third centuries A.D. delineate the professional identities of priestesses at the Spartan Eleusinion alone. The dedication of a statue with accompanying inscription required the construction of a persona through image and text: with a few exceptions, only examples of the latter are extant. The purpose of the inscription is didactic: to identify the dedicatee and dedicator, to honor the dedicatee, and to instruct the viewer about the kinswoman portrayed. The dedicators not only bask in the glory reflected upon them by their honoree, for example describing her as *ton eugenestaton*[45] or her father as *philosophotatou*,[46] but also are commemorated through their indulgence in conspicuous consumption: they had the wealth to pay for the sculptures, including some in bronze.[47] Although the dedicators' goal was individuality and self-expression, the scholar surveying the remains nearly two thousand years later is impressed by the formulaic eulogies and the conformity to contemporary provincial style found elsewhere in the eastern Mediterranean.

The honorary inscriptions assert that in the Roman period Spartans valued the same virtues in women as were traditional elsewhere in the Greek world. (We observe, in passing, that this ideology was not the same as that found among the Spartans' classical predecessors.)[48] We have mentioned the shrine of Aidos and the place where Penelope had left her father. The inscriptions refer to two women as "new Penelopes." Charision, who calls herself "Sparta's leading maiden, the new Penelope," together with her father Spartiaticus dedicated a portrait herm of a certain Hegemoneus (225–50).[49]

---

[40] *IG* 5.1 209 + *SGDI* 3.2 4440 = Tod and Wace 1906, no. 203. For the date, see *LGPN* 3A s.v. Nikokles (29): *IG* 5.1 209 for the cult of Helen and the Dioscuri at Phoebaeum.

[41] *IG* 5.1 583, 584 + 604 (= *SEG* 11 812a), 594, 595.

[42] Raftopoulou 1998.

[43] Cartledge and Spawforth 1989, 133.

[44] Spawforth 1992, esp. 229.

[45] *IG* 5.1 591, also used to refer to a husband in *IG* 5.1 598.

[46] *IG* 5.1 598.

[47] Bronze: *IG* 5.1 592.

[48] See further Pomeroy 2002, 127–28.

[49] *IG* 5.1 540 = *SEG* 11 797, and see further Spawforth 1984, esp. 276–77. In the third century Aurelia Oppia is mother of Heraclia, "a new Penelope": *IG* 5.1 598.9–10, and *LGPN* 3A s.v. Teisamenos (14).

τὸν κλυτὸν ἡγε-
μονῆα Χαρείσιον
ἄνθετο κούρα
Σπάρτας ἁ πρώτα,
5   Πηνελόπεια νέα,
[ἅ]ν μέγα χάρμα πάτρᾳ
[Σ]παρτιατικὸς ἠέξη-
σεν, κυδάλιμος
[γ]ενέτωρ κυδαλίμα[ν]
10 θύγατρα.

Δημητρίου τοῦ (Δημητρίου) γλυφή.

Charision adopts a combination of incongruous attributes to describe herself. Perhaps the new Penelope meant to allude to the mythical wife's *sophrosyne*, though she herself is a *koura* who has not yet left her father. She may well have written the elegiac couplets herself, showing off her skill at *synchysis* and *homoioteleuton*. She may also be responsible for the decision to dedicate a portrait herm, a new style at Sparta, rather than (as was traditional) dedicating a freestanding statue of the honoree.[50] Without subtlety Charision exploits the occasion for honoring another person by using the inscription as a platform for her own glorification. The age minimum for the marriage of girls with Roman citizenship was twelve. Charision was probably a Roman citizen,[51] but even if she was not, she was doubtless influenced by the marriage practices of her elite peers who were citizens.[52] Thus she was probably in her early teens at the time of the dedication. Certainly in Charision's inscription it is possible to see an adolescent's view of the world where she may still choose among a cornucopia of possible identities: the self-assertion and awkward individualism of her own self-portrait stand out in comparison with the clichéd descriptions of the mature women whose virtues are lauded by their kin. A typical example is the Augustan Alcibia who was honored for her domestic virtue, the euergetism of her ancestors who were famed prophets, and the blameless life she had led for sixty years as a wife.[53]

Merely possessing *philandria*[54] and *sophrosyne*[55] or being *semnotes*[56] and *kosmiotes*[57] often are not deemed sufficient. Superlatives (even where the quality praised would not seem to allow degrees of comparison) are reminiscent of the traditional competitiveness of Spartan women. Julia Etearchis was Hestia Poleos and the city's most chaste and most decorous (*kosmiotaten*) daughter.[58] Claudia Polla was *axiologo[ta]te* and *sophronestate*.[59] Several women are singled out for their *pases arêtes en*

---

[50] Spawforth 1984, 277.

[51] Spawforth (1984, 277) suggests that the Spartiaticus who is Charision's father is P. Memmius Spartiaticus (IV), but in Spawforth (1985, 194, 211) he does not include her in the stemma or discussion. *LGPN* 3A, s.v. Spartiatikos (8) identifies him as father of Charision and perhaps the same as (9) a Memmius.

[52] The age of marriage of upper-class girls was early to mid-teens: Shaw 1987, esp. 43–44.

[53] *IG* 5.1 578.

[54] *IG* 5.1 581, 600–601, 605.

[55] *IG* 5.1 581, 586–87, 596–97, 600–601, 605.

[56] *IG* 5.1 586–87.

[57] *IG* 5.1 600.

[58] *IG* 5.1 593 (1258 is not the same person): Spawforth 1985, 225, 243.

[59] *IG* 5.1 602; *sophronestate* also *IG* 5.1 590, 608; and see further Spawforth 1985, 225, 239, 242.

tais gynaizin heneken ("virtue among women").[60] Confining their zealous ambition to the women's arena was characteristic of good women.

Despite women's protestations of modesty, the sightseer in Sparta could look at their portrayals in inscriptions and statues and witness rituals like the whipping ceremony, where the priestess held the ancient wooden image of Artemis that was said to have been brought back from Taurus by Iphigenia and Orestes.[61] Like the rituals themselves, the archaic images of Artemis Orthia and Aphrodite Hera connected the women in the Roman period directly with their remote ancestors. In some families the self-important naming patterns of women recall the glorious past. Thus among the attested descendants of Ageta whose name is reminiscent of Agido and Agesistrata, for instance, appear another Ageta, as well as women named Damostheneia, Tyrannis, Philocratia, Callicrateia, and Callistonice.

As a result of the small population, the economic and social pyramid, and the small number of families responsible for maintaining hereditary priesthoods, many women held multiple priesthoods, often simultaneously and for life. For example, Pompeia Polla and Memmia Xenocratia[62] presided over the Hyacinthia for life as *archeis* and *theoros*[63] and priestess of the Dioscureia.[64] Claudia Damostheneia held hereditary priesthoods of Carneius Boecetas, Carneius Dromaeus, Poseidon Domateitas, Heracles Genarchas, and Core and Temenius in Helos. Dedications by and in honor of Spartan women follow the general pattern in the Greek world: they are either connected with female divinities or with cults in which other family members are involved.[65] The succession to priesthoods could be matrilineal,[66] and women even served as priestesses for male divinities.[67] The duties devolving upon those filling offices connected with cults often involved spending personal funds. Some are praised in their inscriptions for their "generous souls" and for fulfilling their obligations "magnificently."[68] The Hyacinthia, the festival of Artemis Orthia, and the Gymnopaediae (the festival of naked youth) were three of the most prestigious of Spartan festivals and were well attended by visitors from the rest of Greece and Rome. Women played principal roles at these festivals: as girls, for example, some rode in elaborately decorated wicker carts, and others raced in chariots at the Hyacinthia.[69] As women they presided as priestesses over events in which not only girls and women but boys and men as well participated. The priestess of Artemis Orthia in fact is the only Spartan sacerdotal official to appear in a literary text.[70]

A new title emerged in the Roman period: "Hestia Poleos."[71] This exalted woman was in charge of the common hearth and at times even permitted to attend meetings of the Boule. Grants of honorific titles such as Hestia of the City incorporated women into the civic family. Claudia Tyrannis was titled "daughter of the city," and Claudia Damostheneia "Mother of Piety, of the Demos, and

[60] *IG* 5.1 586, 587, 590, 597.

[61] Paus. 3.16.7, 9, and see above on Aphrodite Hera.

[62] She was also Hestia Poleos, Mother of Piety, of the Demos and of the Boule: *IG* 5.1 589, second/third century, and see below. See further Alcock 1989b, 30–31.

[63] Spawforth 1985, 244.

[64] Archeis: *IG* 5.1 602, and see Robert (1974), who compares this office to the prestigious priesthood of Demeter Chamyne at Olympia, and Spawforth 1984, 286 n. 128.

[65] See further Kron 1996, esp. 158, and Turner 1983, 391.

[66] Spawforth (1985, 203–4) cites the descendants of Memmia Eurybanassa.

[67] For Damostheneia, see further Spawforth 1985, 235.

[68] See n. 41 above.

[69] Athen. 1.317, and see further Pomeroy 2002, 20.

[70] Paus. 3.16.10–11, noted by Spawforth 1992, 232.

[71] *IG* 5.1 584, 586, 604.

of the Boule."[72] Such titles imply that the Assembly and Council had adopted these women.[73] These honors may also be viewed in terms of grants of citizenship and other civic honors to Greek women in the Hellenistic period, which admitted them into the political world of men. It is also relevant to compare the Spartan titles with the familial terminology employed in honors awarded to Julia Domna, Julia Maesa, and other imperial women, including the titles of Mater Augustorum, Mater Castrorum, Mater Patriae, and Mater Senatus.

Roman Civic Identity

The final ethnic identity assumed by some elite women was juridical.[74] As their names indicate, some Spartan women were granted the status of Roman citizens. Greek marriage patterns were endogamous, mirroring the privacy of the city-state, but Roman law forbade marriage between close relatives: marrying out was a reflection of the expanding empire. In *Roman Questions* (108) Plutarch decides that the Roman way is preferable for women, for if their husbands abuse them, their kinsmen will defend them, while among the Greeks the husband is a kinsman. Among the Spartan elite with Roman citizenship it is still possible to find some marriages between cousins.[75] Other families abided by the letter of the law (if not the spirit) with multiple marriage ties with the same family, such as the Claudii with the Memmii.[76] Enforced exogamy sometimes made it necessary to claim descent from Spartan heroes or from revered prophets through the mother alone.[77] This desire to assert descent is responsible in part for the relative abundance of women's names in inscriptions. Through the *ius trium liberorum* Augustus promoted fertility with rewards and punishments. Some Spartans enjoyed the privileges bestowed on mothers of three children, including the right to make a will and to manage property without a male guardian.[78] Memmia Ageta, the divorced wife of Brasidas, a Spartan of praetorian status, bequeathed a trust to her sons, to be distributed only after their father's death because they were not emancipated and she did not believe her ex-husband would do so.[79] The case is discussed in the *Digest* (36.1.23): for Brasidas did emancipate them and Ageta's intention, rather than the letter of the law, prevailed.[80]

Though in earlier times Spartan women had managed property themselves, what their legal status had become by the first century B.C. is unclear.[81] In the Hellenistic period the legal capacity of women throughout the Greek world increased, and it is unlikely that it decreased in Sparta. For

[72] *IG* 5.1 608, and see further Spawforth 1985, 206–8, 233–35.

[73] See further Robert 1969, 316–22. For the state as a fictitious brotherhood, see Pomeroy 1997, 18, 38, 77–78, 80–81, et passim.

[74] Spawforth (1985, 218) suggests that if the women were married, they were probably granted citizenship as individuals along with their husbands. For general considerations about the effects of Roman law, see Foxhall 1999, esp. 144–45.

[75] E.g., Eudamus and Claudia Damostheneia (*IG* 5.1 589); Spawforth 1985, 234, 238.

[76] Spawforth 1985, 238.

[77] *IG* 5.1 599, and see further Spawforth 1992, 234.

[78] *IG* 5.1 168 + 603 (anonymous [fragmentary]), *IG* 5.1 586, 589, 596, 608. Hupfloher (2000, 39) notes that three of the known *thoinomostriai* held the *ius liberorum*.

[79] *IG* 5.1 581; Spawforth 1985, 215, 220–21.

[80] *LGPN* 3A s.v. Brasidas (5) lists four sons (Antipater, Pratolaus, Spartiaticus, and Brasidas), but Spawforth (1985, 228–30) argues that only the first two were children by Memmia Ageta.

[81] Foxhall 1999, 144–45, 150.

the imperial period, however, it may be useful to compare the legal status of Jewish women in Ptolemaic Egypt. Seeking upward social mobility, they used the Greek legal system: thus they began to employ a guardian for business transactions, though they would have been able to use Jewish law according to which they would not need the assistance of a *kyrios*.[82]

Shifting Identities

It is clear that ethnic identities are contingent and change over time. Furthermore, Spartan history itself was a dialogue between the present and the past that under Roman domination became a conversation with the rest of Greece and with Rome. Spartan, Greek, and Roman simultaneously, or exploiting one facet of ethnicity to suit the context, Spartan women were a microcosm of the mosaic that constituted the Roman Empire. In the final chapter, however, the image of Helen prevailed. Gibbon writes that with the Gothic invasion: "the female captives submitted to the laws of war; the enjoyment of beauty was the reward of valour."[83]

[82] Pomeroy 1984, 121.   [83] Gibbon 1776–88 [1974], 3:257.

Works Cited

Alcock, S. E., "Archaeology and Imperialism: Roman Expansion and the Greek City," *Journal of Mediterranean Archaeology* 2 (1989a) 87–135.

———, "Roman Imperialism in the Greek Landscape," *Journal of Roman Archaeology* 2 (1989b) 5–34.

Baladié, R., *Le Péloponnèse de Strabon. Étude de géographie historique* (Paris 1980).

Bartman, E., *Portraits of Livia: Imaging the Imperial Woman in Augustan Rome* (Cambridge 1999).

Cartledge, P. A., and Spawforth, A. J. S., *Hellenistic and Roman Sparta: A Tale of Two Cities* (London 1989).

Dixon, S., *The Roman Mother* (Norman 1988).

Foxhall, L., "'Foreign Powers: Plutarch and Discourses of Domination in Roman Greece," in *Plutarch's Advice to the Bride and Groom and A Consolation to His Wife*, ed. S. B. Pomeroy (New York 1999) 138–50.

Frazer, J. G., *Pausanias's Description of Greece*, 6 vols. (London 1913)

Gardner, J. F., *Women in Roman Law and Society* (London 1986).

Gibbon, E., *The History of the Decline and Fall of the Roman Empire*, ed. J. B. Bury, 7 vols. (London 1776–88; repr. New York 1974).

Hupfloher, A., *Kulte im kaiserzeitlichen Sparta. Eine Rekonstruktion anhand der Priesterämter* (Berlin 2000).

Kennell, N. M., *The Gymnasium of Virtue: Education and Culture in Ancient Sparta* (Chapel Hill 1995).

Kron, U., "Priesthoods, Dedications, and Euergetism: What Part Did Religion Play in the Political and Social Status of Greek Women?," in *Religion and Power in the Ancient Greek World: Proceedings of the Uppsala Symposiuim 1993*, ed. P. Hellström and B. Alroth, Uppsala Studies in Ancient Mediterranean and Near Eastern Civilizations Supplement 24 (Uppsala 1996) 139–82.

Münscher, K., *Xenophon in der griechisch-römischen Literatur*, *Philologus* Supplement 13.2 (Leipzig 1920).

Nevett, L., "Continuity and Change in Greek Households under Roman Rule: The Role of Women in the Domestic Context," in *Greek Romans and Roman Greeks. Studies in Cultural Interaction*, ed. E. N. Ostenfeld (Aarhus 2002) 81–97.

Pikoula, E. K., "The Bronze Portrait Statue NM 23321 from Sparta," *Annual of the British School at Athens* 96 (2001) 424–29.

Pirenne-Delforge, V., *L'Aphrodite Grecque. Contribution à l'étude de ses cultes et de sa personnalité dans le panthéon archaïque et classique*, *Kernos* Supplement 4 (Athens and Liège 1994).

Plommer, H., "Vitruvius and the Origin of Caryatids," *Journal of Hellenic Studies* 99 (1979) 97–102.

Pomeroy, S. B., *Goddesses, Whores, Wives, and Slaves: Women in Classical Antiquity* (New York 1975; with a new preface New York 1995).

———, *Women in Hellenistic Egypt* (New York 1984; with a new foreword and addenda Detroit 1990).

———, *Families in Classical and Hellenistic Greece* (Oxford 1997).

———, ed., *Plutarch's Advice to the Bride and Groom and A Consolation to His Wife* (New York 1999a).

———, "Reflections on Plutarch's *Advice to the Bride and Groom*," in *Plutarch's Advice to the Bride and Groom and A Consolation to His Wife*, ed. S. B. Pomeroy (New York 1999b) 33–42.

———, *Spartan Women* (New York 2002).

Raftopoulou, S., "New Finds from Sparta," in *Sparta in Laconia: Proceedings of the 19th British Museum Classical Colloquium*, ed. W. G. Cavanagh and S. E. C. Walker, British School at Athens Studies Supplement 4 (London 1998) 125–40.

Richer, N., "Aidos at Sparta," in *Sparta: New Perspectives*, ed. S. Hodkinson and A. Powell (London 1999) 91–115.

Riddle, J. M., *Contraception and Abortion from the Ancient World to the Renaissance* (Cambridge, Mass. 1992).

Robert, L., "Laodicée du Lycos. Les Inscriptions," in *Laodicée du Lycos, Le Nymphée, Campagnes 1961–1963*, ed. J. des Gagniers et al. (Québec and Paris 1969) 247–387.

———, "Les femmes théores à Éphèse," *Comptes rendus des séances de l'Académie des inscriptions et belles-lettres* (1974) 176–81.

Schenkl, H., *Epicteti dissertationes ab Arriano digestae* (repr. Stuttgart 1965). Original edition (Leipzig 1916).

Shaw, B. D., "The Age of Roman Girls at Marriage: Some Reconsiderations," *Journal of Roman Studies* 77 (1987) 30–45.

Spawforth, A. J. S., "Notes on the Third Century A.D. in Spartan Epigraphy," *Annual of the British School at Athens* 79 (1984) 263–88.

———, "Families at Roman Sparta and Epidaurus: Some Prosopographical Notes," *Annual of the British School at Athens* 80 (1985) 191–258.

———, "A Severan Statue-Group and an Olympic Festival at Sparta," *Annual of the British School at Athens* 81 (1986) 313–32.

———, "Spartan Cults under the Roman Empire: Some Notes," in *Filolakon: Lakonian Studies in Honour of Hector Catling*, ed. J. M. Sanders (London 1992) 227–38.

Spawforth, A. J. S., and S. Walker, "The World of the Panhellion II," *Journal of Roman Studies* 76 (1986) 88–105.

Stadter, P. A., "Plutarch's Lives and Their Roman Readers," in *Greeks, Romans, and Roman Greeks: Studies in Cultural Interaction*, ed. E. N. Ostenfeld (Aarhus 2002) 123–35.

Tod, M. N., and A. J. B. Wace, *A Catalogue of the Sparta Museum* (Oxford 1906).

Turner, J., "Hiereiai: Acquisition of Feminine Priesthoods in Ancient Greece" (Ph.D. diss., University of California, Santa Barbara 1983).

Woodward, A., "Excavations at Sparta, 1924–5," *Annual of the British School at Athens* 26 (1923–25) 116–276.

12 ◆ APHRODITE AND DIONYSUS: GREEK ROLE MODELS FOR ROMAN HOMES?

Shelley Hales

As recent studies into Roman domestic decoration have increasingly tied iconographical choices to social competition, those choices have come to be regarded as significant clues to the self-presentation of their owners.[1] Much might be made, then, of the observation that domestic art appears to have been ruled by Aphrodite and Dionysus.[2] They dominate the iconography of domestic wall paintings, mosaics, and sculpture from the beginning to the end of the Roman Empire, from Rome and Italy to the farthest western and eastern provinces. However, the reasons for their ongoing popularity in Roman domestic art have never specifically been addressed. Discussions of their popularity tend to observe their association with sentiments of the "good life," a prosperous paradise brought about by Aphrodite's sex and beauty and the gift of Dionysian wine and release.[3]

The idea that Aphrodite and Dionysus are not simply two discrete motifs sharing popularity by accident, but that they should be considered together as a cultural package, has already been demonstrated by Paul Zanker, who, in 1998, addressed the centrality of these two figures and their worlds to the art of the Hellenistic kingdoms, tracing the development of their iconography from the late classical innovations of Praxiteles. That artist's creation of the Resting Faun and the Aphrodite of Knidos reimagined the worlds of Dionysus and Aphrodite and foresaw a Hellenistic aesthetic.[4] For Zanker, the erotic, drunken worlds of the two deities fulfilled an escapist ideology of *tryphe*, which saturated Hellenistic life and was perpetuated by many Hellenistic monarchs, particularly the Ptolemies. The final pages of the book turn attention precisely to the continued centrality of these images in the Roman world, where Aphrodite and Dionysus serve as role models to their Roman audience. Their popularity demonstrates the continuation of a love of *tryphe* as a living ideology in Roman domestic life, providing a long-running theme that, through the iconography of the putto and the vine, even manages to reinvent itself for a Christian audience.[5] The *tablinum* of the House of Lucretius Fronto in Pompeii demonstrates just such a Hellenizing image of the triumph of Dionysus, an image that might well recall the Ptolemies' notorious festival processions as much as literary myth (fig. 1).[6] Meanwhile, the display of a Praxitelean Aphrodite in her Knidian temple at Hadrian's villa at Tivoli demonstrates a Roman emperor's own recall of Hellenistic public cult, sculptural aesthetic, and scandal (fig. 2).[7]

---

[1] The seminal work in this area was done by Wallace-Hadrill 1994. See also Thébert 1997 and Hales 2003.

[2] Thompson 1960, 90–123, 221; Jashemski 1979, 123–24; Dunbabin 1978, 154–58, 173–87.

[3] Grimal 1969, 317–30; Ling 1991, 135. Other possibilities for their presence, running from their cultic significance to their role as functional signposts to their iconic cultural appeal, can be found in Horn 1972; Kondoleon 1995;

Dunbabin 1999, 18–37; Havelock 1995, 55–68, 103–32; Smith 1993, 127.

[4] Zanker 1998.

[5] Zanker 1998, 111–17.

[6] *Ath.* 5.196–206. See also Plut. *Vit. Ant.* 24.

[7] Beard and Henderson 2001, 123–32.

Fig. 1. Wall painting from the tablinum, *House of Lucretius Fronto, Pompeii (photo author).*

Fig. 2. Round temple with copy of the Aphrodite of Knidos, Hadrian's villa at Tivoli (photo author).

However, the *tryphe* recalled by these examples was certainly not unproblematic in its new home. It did not escape the attention of moralists back at Rome who remodeled it as Roman *luxuria*. Domestic display was subject to a never-ending flow of invective throughout the Roman period, calling on well-established tropes of luxury: it was non-useful, self-indulgent, self-distracting, and, above all, unnatural.[8] Horace and Vitruvius both attacked fantastic, unnatural creatures and frameworks in wall painting.[9] Above all, however, these domestic luxuries were contests in visibility. The Senecas and others complained about ever bigger villas, higher houses, terraced gardens, farther-reaching

[8] The sociological and moral nature of Roman luxury is explored by Wallace-Hadrill. See Wallace-Hadrill 1990 and Wallace-Hadrill 1994, 143–74.

[9] Hor. *Ars P.* 1–5; Vitr. *De arch.* 7.5.3–4.

views; all target strategies aimed at making their owners more visible in the landscape.[10] But even as they railed, men made a name for themselves, indeed made themselves, through resort to precisely these means.

It is into this contest for visibility and manipulation of the visual world that we must drop Aphrodite and Dionysus in order to explore further what kind of role model they might provide for their Roman audiences and what kind of reaction they provoked from Roman moralists.[11] In order to demonstrate in broad terms how such models might work, we will concentrate on two particular accessories of these characters that played a crucial role in the realm of the visual: Dionysus's mask and Aphrodite's mirror.

Dionysus's Mask

The central myth panel on one of the *tablinum* walls in the House of Lucretius Fronto (fig. 1), as we have noted, might be considered typical of the Hellenistic images of Dionysus that were adopted and adapted in the Roman world. But the myth panel is only one element of the Dionysiac *tryphe* exuded throughout the wall. The panel itself is set in a luxuriant framework of garlands and vegetal columns. Gardens appear in the dado, and in the upper fields, elegant architecture. Throughout the wall, intricate objects remind us of Dionysus: panthers, tympana, kraters, and masks intersperse the decoration. Although Dionysus himself is incarcerated in the heavily framed panel, his imagery saturates the painting.[12]

One of the most popular elements of that associative imagery is the mask. Images of Dionysus's masks are found everywhere in Roman domestic art. In Pompeii, they appear in media of every scale from megalographic wall paintings to tiny plaques and *oscilla*.[13] Sometimes they appear to have explicitly grand, civic theatrical connotations; other times their presence in gardens suggests the more rustic setting of the *thiasos* or satyr play. Many times, they appear apparently out of context, in splendid isolation, or as decorative devices in mosaic borders. Sometimes they are masks of Dionysus himself or of his entourage and other times theater masks evoking comedy or tragedy. They appear in various stages of animation as demonstrated in the painting from the Theater Room in one of the terraced houses in Ephesus (fig. 3).[14] In the main field they appear in full animation worn by actors in carefully labeled scenes from Euripidean tragedy and New Comedy, while they hang empty, suspended from the schematic architectural framework of the upper fields. The popular motif of the empty mask is promoted to principal iconography in a wall painting from a townhouse in Solunto in Sicily (fig. 4). The wall is divided into large fields divided by columns, between which are suspended garlands and fillets. And from those garlands hangs down into the middle of each

---

[10] Plutarch (*Vit. Luc.* 39) recounts the extensive villas of Lucullus. Velleius Paterculus (2.14) tells us of the attempts of M. Livius Drusus to build an imposing home high on the Palatine. Nero watched the fire of Rome from the tower in the Horti of Maecenas (Suet. *Ner.* 38.2), and Seneca (*Ep.* 122.8) rants against rooftop gardens. Wiseman (1987) offers an excellent introduction to this phenomenon, explaining how the public perceptions of homeowners were closely entwined with their domestic displays. See also Wallace-Hadrill 1994 and Hales 2003, 11–60.

[11] On the qualities of Dionysus, see, e.g., Otto 1965. Grigson

(1978) provides a basic introduction to Aphrodite, while Arscott and Scott (2000) concentrate on her visual properties. Schilling (1982) and Bruhl (1953) analyze the roles of Aphrodite and Dionysus respectively in the Roman world. Otto (1965, 175–85) and Schilling (1982, 220–22) chart the perceived interaction between the two.

[12] Ling 1991, 60–61; Clarke 1991, 146–58.

[13] Bruhl (1953, 145–59) provides a most basic overview.

[14] Strocka 1977, 45–56.

*Fig. 3. Wall
painting from the
Theater Room,
Hanghaus
2, Ephesus
(Copyright:
Österreichisches
Archäologisches
Institut, Vienna;
photo Norbert
Zimmerman).*

*Fig. 4. Wall
painting from
Solunto, Museo
Archeologico
Regionale di
Palermo (photo
Museum, N.I.
2298).*

field a mask, the two outer, bearded male faces flanking a central female face.[15] The ivy wreaths of the first two masks and the grapes that hang from the garlands recall the masks' patron, reinforcing the presence of an absent Dionysus.

The mask was Dionysus's favorite attribute, not only an accessory that recalled his involvement with and patronage of the theater but a metaphor for his own character, so much so that he was often worshiped in the form of a mask.[16] The mask was a symbol of his slippery character—his ability to change his shape, to appear and disappear. It commemorated his many epiphanies and disguises, his ever presence, while simultaneously making clear his equally numerous departures

[15] Beyen 1938, 44–46.

[16] Henrichs (1993) and Otto (1965, 86–91) provide an insight

into Dionysus's relationship with the mask. Carpenter and Faraone (1993) explore this same relationship in its widest terms.

and absences.[17] Its simultaneous promise of absence and presence is well demonstrated by the Sicilian masks. Their suspension and disembodiment reveal them to be empty, but their ability to stare out of the painting marks them as an unnerving presence. Masks were also symbolic of the way Dionysus might entrance humans and how they might encounter his power. Henrichs talks of masks as a reflection of the changing identities that take shape and disintegrate under the influence of Dionysus.[18] Could this power of the mask provide a cue for considering the role masking might play in the construction of the identities of the homeowners who adopted the motif?

The masks of Roman art owe a large debt to the Hellenistic period. Masking underwent something of a revolution in the Hellenistic era with the invention of new masks for New Comedy.[19] The masks of these paintings from Italy, Asia Minor, and Africa, then, might be understood to have served as notice of the culturally informed nature of their patrons. In advertising such *urbanitas*, players from around the globe found themselves wearing the same mask of the Hellenophile connoisseur. In reinventing this ambience of Hellenistic *tryphe* in their houses, they might also be seen to recall the indulgent theatricality of the Hellenistic courts, in which the dynasts performed their dominance in a never-ending luxurious show.[20]

The popularity of other theatrical motifs in Roman decor would tend to support such a preoccupation with the theatrical symbolism of Dionysus's masks. In 58 B.C., M. Aemilius Scaurus translated a selection of the 360 marble columns and 3,000 bronze statues that had adorned his fantastic temporary theater to his own home.[21] Even the views from houses, framed by picture windows, might be compared to stage sets. Cicero compared his friend, Marcus Marius, gazing through his villa window to himself trapped as spectator of a hubristic theatrical and political performance.[22] And if such a preoccupation emerges in the rhetoric of a decadent republic, it is a familiar enough trope to allow Plutarch to assure us that Alcibiades, who kidnapped the world's first scene painter, Agatharchus, and put him to work to decorate his own house, was the founder of the lust for theatrical designs in mosaics and wall painting.[23]

The full-scale evocation of the stage set in the famous Second Style Campanian wall paintings or the notorious paintings from Nero's Domus Aurea have traditionally formed the center of studies of the theatricality of Roman art.[24] However, the motif lives on far beyond these examples. A wall painting from the House of the Tragic Actor at Sabratha (fig. 5), dated to the second century, features the typical tripartite scheme of projecting wings and a central *aedicula* behind which colonnades recede into the distance.[25] The structure and the apparent population of the set show that the stage was felt to have ongoing relevance in painting.

The Sabratha scene, however "theatrical" an impression it gives, particularly when seen in the context of the other theatrical images in the house, could not really be mistaken as a working stage set. Even more attenuated and vague references to the tripartite architecture of the theater

[17] Otto 1965, 79–95; Vernant 1990, 208–47.

[18] Henrichs 1993, 39. Osborne (1997, 204–10) discusses the interaction between maenad and Dionysus mask.

[19] Wiles 1991, 24.

[20] Chaniotis 1997. One of these dynasts' favorite performances, of course, was as Dionysus. See Plut. *Vit. Ant.* 26.

[21] Plin. *HN* 36.5.6.

[22] Cic. *Fam.* 7.1.1.

[23] Plut. *Alc.* 16. For the extent of interest in theater motifs, see, e.g., Webster 1995.

[24] Ling (1991, 23–51) lays out the development of Second Style in Pompeii. Peters and Meyboom (1982) discuss the Neronian influence behind Fourth Style theatrical painting in the Domus Aurea and beyond. Little (1971) judges these scenes in terms of illusionistic references to real theaters.

[25] Aurigemma 1962, 104–5. The painting is not the only one from house 3.5, and it is recorded as part of a longer description of the painted remains (100–111). See also Johnston 1982.

Fig. 5. Wall painting from House of the Tragic Actor, Sabratha (drawing Sue Grice).

can be glimpsed in the elegant, flimsy framework of the upper fields of the wall from the House of Lucretius Fronto (fig. 1). As Ling noted, even at the height of Second Style, rarely can painted schemes be specified as full evocations of actual theaters.[26] Mostly they are only vaguely theatrical—a jumble of influences and effects, having borrowed elements from all manner of real and imagined sources: palaces, theaters, villas, museums.[27] To privilege any one model is to miss their deliberate conflation and their recycling into painting's own fantastic language. The invocation of fantasy and subversion by wall painting, expressed by Elsner and Bryson, is further displayed in the tendencies of these paintings, through their apparent projection into the room, to create a parergonal space, a definitional no-man's land, neither painted theater nor domestic space.[28] This creation of fluid boundaries concurs well with Dionysus's saturating presence in the Lucretius

[26] Ling 1991, 30–31, 77–78.

[27] The determination to identify a "real" model for the famous frescoes of the Boscoreale bedroom demonstrates this conviction that such paintings are illusions of something attainable in that "real" world. See Lehmann 1953, 82–131.

[28] Bryson 1990, 17–59; Elsner 1995, 49–87; Hales 2003, 97–163. The idea of frames as perergonal space comes from Derrida (1987, 15–147). In fact, recognition of this blurring of boundaries takes us deeper into Greek and Roman theater traditions, which likewise deliberately blurred spatial boundaries between theater and civic space, performer and audience. See Rehm 2002, 1–34 and Wiles 1991, 36–67.

Fronto wall—apparently breaking the confines of his Hellenizing, mythic panel to infuse himself in every tiny detail of the wall.

These qualities imply that the importance of these paintings must lie in a metaphorical, rather than literal, visual allusion. They are perhaps signs not of the theater but of theatricality. Theatricality, as a mode of social performance, has been primarily discussed in terms of the *cena*, in which the entertainment and the formal conventions dictating social behavior at the event might both be described as "theatrical."[29] Janet Huskinson's excellent discussion of the mosaics of third-century Antioch sees theatricality as precisely the reason for the ambivalent framing of theatrical scenes, in which the gap between different categories of space and representation is never made clear. This ambivalence reflects a Roman theatricality, which, unlike Chaniotis's vision of the performance of Hellenistic kings, is crucial to social interaction but is never exposed purely and simply as "pretend."[30]

Huskinson's study, in opening up the possibility of theatrical motifs to a more sophisticated "play of ambivalence" borrowed from Theater Studies, in which theatricality is often as dangerous and unsettling as affirmative, discloses fresh possibilities for the specific role of masks and their relationship to personal identity.[31] Recent studies of masking have likewise drawn on anthropological studies to propose explanations of the power of the mask that stretch far beyond the notion of disguise. Stemming from the work of Lévi Strauss on the masking traditions of native North American communities, they all have the common tendency to see masks as media of revelation rather than disguise and as tools for effecting transition and metamorphosis.[32] When we consider the mask in this way, its relevance to notions of social identity might become more immediate, as its role might be seen to extend beyond the narrowly theatrical to the performative sphere—that is, beyond the confines of the specific ceremonial of the *cena* to wider social interactions.[33] As the suspension of the Solunto masks against their plain architectural background suggests, masks could stand clear of the theater.

That masking was a prevalent literal and metaphorical activity in Roman society beyond the theater might be demonstrated by turning to the ancestor mask. These masks, which commemorated the absence of the dead by keeping their empty presence in the halls of Roman houses, were brought into the public realm to be animated in performance on the occasion of the funerals of their descendents. Flower's study of these masks suggests that they were not altogether unlike the masks used in the theater.[34] Both were designed to express the aura of certain set character types, reflecting tendencies to group social beings in tropes of performance and character. As the theater masks evoked the stock characters of the stage, from the rascally slave to the young hero, so the masks of ancestors relayed the memories of successful generals, promising youths, and aged senators. Both mask types, too, challenge the boundaries of presentation and representation, bringing their

[29] See, e.g., Edwards 1994; D'Arms 1999; Huskinson 2002–2003; Leach 2004, 93–122.

[30] Huskinson (2002–2003, 145–51) discusses these ambivalent frames. Chaniotis (1997, 222) defines theatricality as deliberately dissimulating or exaggerating.

[31] Davis and Postlewait 2003, 1–39.

[32] Lévi Strauss 1983. See also Pernet (1992, 72–74, 117–35), who investigates how Kwakiutl masks can reveal several faces. See also the foreword to Napier 1986, xv–xvii and Emigh 1996, 3–7. The flexibility of masks in this model causes both Napier (1986, 27) and Wiles (1991, 95–98) to reject a psy-

choanalytical view of masking. Emigh (1996, 1–34) embraces psychoanalysis to explain masking practices.

[33] On the distinction between theatricality and performativity, see Parker and Sedgwick 1995, 1–18. Bergmann (1999, 9–35) discusses the performative nature of Roman identities.

[34] Flower 1996, 114–15, building on but disagreeing with Wiles 1991, 68–99. S. Bartsch, *The Mirror of the Self: Sexuality, Self-knowledge and the Gaze in the Early Roman Empire* (Chicago 2006) appeared too late to be included in this chapter.

characters temporarily to life through the masked performance. Even here, that performance was firmly bound back to Dionysus via the satyr actors who also frolicked in the procession.[35]

While the practice of ancestor masks might allude to a very specifically located practice, peculiar to the city of Rome, the metaphor of masking as a way of inventing a *persona* is well demonstrated on a wider scale by portrait conventions, such as verism, which presented their subjects as generic types precisely while professing to be a true likeness.[36] Similarly, it is possible to see that the ancient concept of the close relationship between action/character/status and the presented face or mask of the tragic or comic character has relevance beyond the theater. Physiognomics, a practice popular among Greek writers at the height of empire, preached the closeness of that relationship and legitimated it as natural and personal.[37] At the same time, the fact that in Greek *prosopon* might be used for both face and mask, and that in Latin *persona* can mean mask, assumed character, or a "real" person, allowed for the legitimate manipulation of generic masks/portrait faces as "natural" expressions of personal character and identity.[38]

The reaction of Roman moralists against theater and theatrical behavior is well known. The charge of effeminacy leveled at actors themselves was widened to include anybody the accusers wished to "unmask" as fraudulent and unnatural, including, in the republic, most leading *populares* and, in the empire, a sequence of "bad" emperors. Nero, the ultimate symbol of theatricality gone mad, performed in the theater, wearing masks modeled on his own face or on those of his mistresses.[39] The act is so uncomfortable precisely because it collapses already tenuous boundaries between being and performing. Likewise, men like Scaurus who depended too much on theatrical props were presented as deserving victims after their inevitable downfall.

Ancient theatricality, particularly where it is associated with Neronian behavior, has sometimes been assessed in similarly negative terms by modern accounts, which equate excessive theatricality with the enforced performance of viewers.[40] This is a tactic of domination well theorized in modern terms, where the metaphor of the enforced mask has been used to describe the colonial experience. The Martinican-born French psychologist Frantz Fanon's famous work, *Peau noires, masques blancs* explored how the French colonists foisted white language, culture, and ways of behavior onto the colonized, only constantly to remind those "acculturalized" colonials that their "blackness" stopped them from being white. The mask metaphor worked both to explain the imposition of an alien identity and constantly to expose that identity as artificial and unnatural. Later in his career, however, serving in a hospital in French Algeria, Fanon offered colonized peoples a more enabling role for the mask, exhorting the colonized to liberate themselves from the identities imposed on them precisely by manipulating them for their own ends.[41] By adopting the white mask, female insurgents were able to infiltrate the French quarter of Algiers. This example is particularly intriguing since, in the case of Arab women, the apparent acquiescence to European culture meant removing the veil, a revelation that in French eyes meant the liberation of the woman from Islamic constraints

---

[35] Dion. Hal. *Ant. Rom.* 7.72.12.

[36] Plin. *Ep.* 3.10.6 gives an insight into Roman manipulation of portraits.

[37] Gleason (1995, 21–81) offers the best discussion of physiognomy in the context of the Second Sophistic.

[38] Napier 1986, 8.

[39] Suet. *Ner.* 21. On Nero, see Bartsch 1994 and Edwards

1994. Corbeill (2002) considers charges made against leading *populares*.

[40] Chaniotis 1997, 247–53; Bartsch 1994; Koloski-Ostrow 1997; Leach 2004, 114–21.

[41] Fanon 1952, analyzed by Goldman 1995. Interesting discussions of the later application of the principles of *Peau noire, masques blancs* in Algeria can be found in Bhahba 1994 and Fuss 1994.

and her exposure to the western gaze. Masks, then, can be manipulated by the wearer and misread or, indeed, unnoticed by the viewer and can reveal as well as obscure. If the manipulation of the mask can be successful where there is only one mask, the black, then how much more effective and nuanced might the mask be, as a tool to provide *personae* through which to experience society, in an empire of multiple masks?[42]

While Roman moralist attacks all seemingly condemned a tendency we might understand as performative, their continued preoccupation, along with the incredible popularity of masks and theatrical motifs in domestic art, would seem to reinforce contentions that it was central to the successful operation of Roman society.[43] The ability to adopt, swap, and react to conventional masks might be seen as a perfectly acceptable way, indeed an imperative way, of acting on the public stage. In this model, the promise of Dionysus and the suspended masks of Solunto (fig. 4) is not simply to provide disguises of a set identity or end product, their faces a role model for our own beneath, but, through their ambiguity, to act as conduits through which identities might be imagined and created in the course of adoption and interaction with other social masks. The mediatory and transformative role of masks might help to understand why the attitude toward the theater was so ambivalent in Roman society and why domestic displays, which always threatened to dissolve into theatricality, were likewise so ambivalently regarded. Theatrical domestic art and its central symbol, the mask, simultaneously enabled and threatened to "unmask" the nature of expected social behavior.

Aphrodite's Mirror

In order to observe their own masked performances, actors needed a mirror. Actors and orators alike were well known to spend their time gazing into mirrors, inventing their *personae*.[44] The mirror appears to have allowed them to convince themselves of their transformation before attempting to convince their audiences. In using the mirror, they were adopting the favorite tool of Aphrodite, who is shown time and again wielding a mirror, as in a magnificent fifth-century mosaic from Djemila (fig. 6).[45] As a relic from Algeria, the mosaic offers a double insight into colonial life, as a relic of the Roman Empire and as an object excavated and reported under the occupation of the French experienced by Fanon.

Aphrodite's long association with mirrors is attested in cultic contexts, where mirrors were an appropriate votive to the goddess.[46] Indeed, Aphrodite frequently *is* a mirror: her doves and Erotes accompanied the female figures serving as handles on early Greek mirrors, and she and her son were often engraved on the backs of Etruscan and Roman mirrors.[47] However, the literary conceit of imagining an Aphrodite obsessed with her own reflection stems largely from the Hellenistic period. Apollonius of Rhodes has Aphrodite doing her hair in the shield of Ares.[48] The trope continues

---

[42] In fact, Corbeill's (2002) discussion of how the *populares* manipulated the attacks on them by adopting the characteristics they were charged with offers one instance of such resistance.

[43] I would here reinforce the closing remarks of Bartsch (1994, 189–90) that the upper classes perhaps chose to insist on sincerity and natural behavior despite being well aware of their own "performance."

[44] See, e.g., Plut. *Vit. Dem.* 11.850e; Wiles 1991, 36.

[45] For a full description, see Blanchard-Lemée 1975, 61–84.

[46] *Anth. Pal.* 6.1, 6.18–20, e.g., feature dedications of mirrors to Aphrodite.

[47] Keene Congdon 1981; Vernant and Frontisi-Ducroux 1997, 55; Schilling 1982, 160–73.

[48] Ap. Rhod. *Argon.* 1.742–46. See also Callim. *Hymn* 5.13–22.

Fig. 6. Mosaic of marine Venus from Cuicul (photo G. Réveillac, CNRS, Centre Camille Jullian).

via Apuleius to culminate in Claudian's vision of a goddess who lives in a hall of mirrors, so that she might see herself from all angles.[49] From the Hellenistic period onward, painted and sculpted images of Aphrodite were increasingly associated with reflection, either by situating her in or near water or giving her a mirror. Her growing self-preoccupation is demonstrated by the tendency for Aphrodite to begin to take over the iconographies of other mythic mirror users, particularly nereids, leading to her ultimate epiphany as the triumphant marine Venus from Cuicul (fig. 6).[50]

The mosaic comes from the Maison de l'Âne in the heart of the town, where it decorated a major reception room built as the owner extended his property over what had once been the sanctuary of Venus Genetrix. Naked except for her jewels and the drapery billowing behind her and crossing her thigh, she looks out toward the viewer. She holds in her right hand a mirror in which her reflection is recorded, also staring out at the audience. The viewer is allowed to do the apparently impossible, to come between the image and its reflection. The example is not isolated; the image of the marine Venus, who can recline elegantly in triumph and do her hair at the same time, becomes increasingly popular in the later empire, with other examples found in Sidi Ghrib, Sétif, and Bulla Regia.[51] Nor is the image confined to Africa—a very similar scene graces houses in Halicarnassus and Shahba-Philippopolis, in the farthest eastern stretches of empire.[52] She even came as far as the northern limits of empire, to Rudston in Yorkshire (fig. 7).[53]

At first glance, as with the mask, it might appear easy to see how Aphrodite with her mirror functions as a role model for the Roman world. Aphrodite's mirror holds up to the Roman world an image of itself as Hellenistic elegance. Aphrodite's naked form was iconic enough as a personification of the Hellenistic aesthetic that she could well be said to have served to unite an empire through appreciation of her body.[54] Indeed, in terms of the North African images in particular, it

[49] Apul. *Met.* 4.31; Claudian *Nupt. Hon.* 106–8.

[50] For the mirror as accouterment of Hellenistic Aphrodite statues, see Zanker 2003, 55–70. Dunbabin (1978, 154–55) shows how an iconography of mirror-wielding nereids increasingly became associated with Aphrodite.

[51] For a full list and discussion of the type, see Blanchard-

Lemée 1975, 73–75; Picard 1940–46; Lassus 1965.

[52] Halicarnassus (Hinks 1933, 131–32); Shahba (Balty 1977, 16–19); Balensiefen 1990, 72–81.

[53] Neal 1981, 92–93.

[54] Havelock 1995, 39–54; Hales 2002.

*Fig. 7. Mosaic of Venus
from villa at Rudston
(photo Hull Museums and
Art Gallery: Hull and East
Riding Museum).*

has been suggested that the marine Aphrodite type transmits long-standing Syrian and Phoenician traditions of the goddess Astarte through a new, imperial vision.[55] Adoption of Aphrodite's mirror allowed local cults and feminine ideals to be transformed and to communicate with the rest of the empire as Aphrodite. In the case of the Yorkshire mosaic, it is precisely the presence of a mirror that appears to transport the silhouetted figure of the large-bottomed, straw-haired female figure into the Rudston Venus (fig. 7). We find ourselves still casting identities on the basis of (however faint) reflections of the Hellenistic ideal.

But perhaps this reflection isn't quite so straightforward. Look carefully at the face of the Cuicul Aphrodite in her mirror, and it is clear that it is not a reflection of the goddess herself but a duplication. The only way this image would work would be through mirror trickery, in which a second mirror (or indeed a second Aphrodite) outside the frame (presumably the viewer) bounced the reflection back onto the mirror in the mosaic, thus flipping it for a second time.[56] This quirk, whether attributed to stupidity or ingenuity on the part of the artist, might prompt us to look harder at the appeal of mirror and reflection to Roman homeowners. It might well imply that, as with those theatrical painting schemes, illusionistic reference is not necessarily the primary drive behind the creation of these images.[57]

Understanding of the mirror's appeal can perhaps be gained by considering the numerous other ways in which reflection was effected in imperial houses. The room in which the Cuicul Aphrodite was located was equipped with at least three fountain features.[58] In many other cases,

[55] Picard 1940–46, 69–73, 102–3. See also Blanchard-Lemée 1975, 75, on the Shahba-Philippopolis Aphrodite.

[56] Lucr. 4.269–323.

[57] Balensiefen (1990, 18) suggests that the Roman artist's love of the reflection is a symptom of the desire for the

challenge of illusionism. Interestingly, she compares these mirror images directly to what she sees as the *trompe l'oeil* effects of Second Style wall painting, such as the stage sets discussed earlier.

[58] Blanchard-Lemée 1975, 27–28.

too, the marine themes of these mosaics were reflected in the wider setting.[59] Fountains, pools, and basins were essential components of the luxury home and were particularly popular in North Africa, where such features were deliberately oriented toward major reception rooms and could be decorated with mosaics of appropriate watery themes.[60] The reflective properties of water were certainly one of the attractions of these features, and Aphrodite again hogged the reflection. The proliferation of Aphrodites found in public and private baths throughout the empire suggests the continued appeal of such arrangements.[61] The Crouching Aphrodite type lent itself very well to poolside locations, such as the baths at Hadrian's villa, presumably spots where she might be reflected in the waters.[62] Back in Rome, the bath waters of Claudius Etruscus prompt Statius to imagine both Aphrodite and Narcissus enjoying its waters, a clear reference to the water's reflective properties.[63]

The aesthetic principle of reflection was also effected sculpturally by the practice of duplication and of mirror reversal, a technique that is well documented in the Roman copying trade, by which Greek prototypes could be reconfigured to fit very Roman viewing practices.[64] When combined with the presence of water, the effect might become somewhat kaleidoscopic, with an image duplicated upside down and side to side. Several Italian villas, such as the villa of the Papyri, took advantage of just such an arrangement. In the baths at Cherchel, four satyr and hermaphrodite groups reflect each other in the corners of one of the rooms.[65]

Finally, the overwhelming interest in reflection is revealed in the iconographic motifs repeated in houses across the empire, from Pompeian paintings to Syrian mosaics: Perseus and Andromeda looking at the reflection of Medusa's head, Thetis looking at herself in the shield of Achilles, and, most popular of all, Narcissus gazing at himself in the pool.[66] Like our Aphrodites, both Narcissus and his reflection often stare out at the viewer, with further reflections sometimes provided by real water features.[67] Just as the image of the reflected Aphrodite became more popular, so was reflection increasingly incorporated into other iconographies, such as that of the story of Artemis and Actaeon. Mosaic images increasingly exposed Actaeon by revealing his reflection in the goddess's bath, a technique also used by the North African novelist Apuleius in inventing his famous sculptural rendition of the myth.[68]

While these incidences all reveal a preoccupation with reflection, it is perhaps more accurate to say that they revel in the problematics of reflection. They both celebrate the illusionistic effects of the phenomenon and the triumph of artist, viewer, and homeowner over it while also parading

[59] Hinks 1933, 131.

[60] The Maison de la Cascade at Utica has a particularly impressive fountain in its peristyle: Alexander and Ennaifer 1973, 19–56. In the sumptuous Maison des Nereides in Volubilis, meanwhile, the *oecus* looks straight onto a basin decorated with a mosaic of the nereids: Etienne 1960, 69.

[61] Manderscheid 1981, 32–33.

[62] Brinkerhoff 1978, 35–55.

[63] Stat. *Silv.* 1.5.54–56. See also 1.3.17–19, where he deliberately praises the effect of watching trees reflected in a stream at the villa of Manilius Vopiscus.

[64] Vermeule 1977, 27–40.

[65] Vermeule 1977, 34.

[66] Balensiefen (1990, 98–105, 113–30) discusses Thetis and Perseus. On Narcissus, see Elsner 2000; Stewart 1996; Balensiefen 1990, 130–63; Vernant and Frontisi-Ducroux 1997, 200–221.

[67] The Narcissus painting in the House of Octavius Quartio at Pompeii offers an obvious example. Platt (2002) provides an excellent analysis of the art program at the rear of the house with particular attention to the themes of reflection and the gaze.

[68] Balensiefen 1990, 105–12. Platt (2002, 100), in recognizing that in these scenes Artemis often takes the form of the Crouching Aphrodite, further demonstrates the latter goddess's grip on reflection and water scenes. For Apuleius's Actaeon, see Apul. *Met.* 2.4–5, analyzed by Slater (1998).

the dangers of reflection and the misrecognition and exposure of the viewer.[69] Similarly, in analyzing the pendant displays of sculpture, Bartman emphasizes not simply the decorative and aesthetic effect of these arrangements but their deliberately distortive effects, which appear to be aimed at making viewers question their role in the arrangement and the status of the space around them.[70] She evokes a strategy of subversion we have already seen played out in those painted theaters.

We should here remind ourselves that ancient mirrors themselves were not sheer, reliable devices. Nearly all ancient mirrors were made of burnished metal and of small enough dimension to be held in the hand, either by a handle or mounted in a box. Being slightly convex, they would enlarge the reflection, the clarity of which would depend on the surface quality of the polish.[71] Natural mirrors of water and manmade polished metal mirrors alike were liable sometimes to give hazy and rippled reflections, offering a rather worrying distortion as easily as a reliable reflection.

This ambivalence of mirrors is reflected in their wider use in society. On the one hand, the chance of distortion and the fear that they inspired made them integral tools of magic and prophecy.[72] The magic charges against Apuleius himself included his ownership of a mirror.[73] Mirrors might literally allow you to see the impossible or the invisible, acting as a bridge between worlds. Philosophies also used the mirror as a metaphor for crossing states.[74] At the same time, mirrors were praised for their clarity and mimetic values. Historians might describe their art as that of a mirror or a sculptor, providing an accurate reflection of the past.[75] The manipulative possibilities of pleading the veracity of mirrors while presumably relying on their distortive powers perhaps led Seneca to promote his *De Clementia* as a mirror of the reasonable character of his tutee, Nero (whose link with mirrors, as with the theatrical in the previous section, has often been seen as reason enough to condemn the objects).[76]

The distrust of mirrors is most obviously seen by turning once again to the Roman moralists. To gaze in a mirror is, like Narcissus, to be enervated and entrapped. Mirrors were the property of women and imperial boyfriends, whose job was to look pretty for others.[77] Men who looked into them were seen as fops and degenerates, deviants like the short-lived emperor Otho, who gazed in mirrors to invent their beauty.[78] Seneca's line of attack on the mirror uses all the familiar tropes to demonstrate its luxury. Its inversion of nature is demonstrated by both its material, which has to be mined from the ground, and its ability to produce a reflection that allows us to see ourselves. More dangerously, though, it provides an altered presentation, a deceptive image of the viewer (a rather ironic objection, given that he had relied on precisely this aspect in his reflection of Nero

[69] In addition to the exploration of this apparent dichotomy by Elsner (2000) with regard to Narcissus, see Mack (2002) for a revision of the role of Medusa.

[70] Bartman 1988, 219–25. The whole idea of the mirror reversal is typical of Roman practice. As Vermeule points out (1977, 38), they did not invent the mirror reversal but, in adopting the Greek practice of symmetry, distorted it in new ways.

[71] Plin. *HN* 33.45.128. Balensiefen (1990) and Vernant and Frontisi-Ducroux (1997) offer the most recent, extensive accounts of ancient mirrors.

[72] Balensiefen 1990, 174–208; McCarty 1989, 168–70.

[73] Apul. *Apol.* 13–16. Too (1996) discusses the ways in

which Apuleius manipulates the idea of the mirror in his writings.

[74] The best discussions of the range of metaphorical uses of mirrors can be found in Vernant and Frontisi-Ducroux 1997, 112–32; McCarty 1989.

[75] Lucian *Hist. Conscr.* 50–51; Plut. *Vit. Tim.* 1.

[76] Sen. *Clem.* 1.1.

[77] See, e.g., Stat. *Silv.* 3.4.93–98.

[78] Aul. Gell. *NA* 6.12.5; Juv. 2.99–100; Sen. *Q Nat.* 1.12.2–5; Richlin 1995, 201–5. An excellent, wider discussion of the effeminacy of certain public figures can be found in Corbeill 2002.

as clement emperor).[79] He uses as his illustration Hostius Quadra, who derived great pleasure from the bedroom he lined with distorting mirrors, which enabled him not only to watch himself in his various contorted sexual positions but also to enjoy the fantasy, through optical illusion, of the enlarged size of his male lovers.[80] An analogous story is also told of Horace, who is depicted as entertaining his mistresses in a similarly Hugh Hefner style bedroom.[81] Just as they despised the fantasies of wall painting, the moralists' instincts in recording these stories seems to be to try to control the extent to which individuals can use their domestic decor to create new worlds and *personae* for themselves and their audiences.

The story of Hostius Quadra has also acted as a prompt to modern commentators who have understood the mirror as a sign of the decadence of a creaking empire. The conceit of seeing art as mirror offers the temptation not to look beyond the reflected image. Aphrodite's mirror traps us at surface level, swallowing us up in an eternal triangle. The same trick, most often recognized in visions of Narcissus, is also understood as the reflexive nature of a decadent, voyeuristic empire that can do nothing but gaze at its own image as it collapses in on itself.[82]

However, perhaps there is another way to explain the metaphor of Hostius's bedroom and Aphrodite's mirror. Just as masks have been used to explain the modern colonial experience, so mirrors have been used as a metaphor for the experience of diaspora in the modern world. Specifically, exile has been understood as a crooked and fluid mirror in which it becomes impossible to locate the predisplacement self.[83] On the other hand, just as Fanon inverted the colonial mask, modern thought also affords the chance to manipulate the mirror. Eco perhaps gets somewhere nearer the worth of the mirror in identity-building when he reminds us that the property of the mirror is not in providing images—after all, it cannot hold them—but in providing a frame for the images we bring to and construct within it.[84] His explanation rather affords the opportunity (or perhaps, less romantically, the necessity) to seek new identities in the shattered and distorting mirror cast back at you.

The moral bluster and complete absence of positive visual images of men with mirrors in antiquity might be understood as symptoms of the anxiety that such image-making engendered in a competitive society. In looking in the mirror, Roman viewers were able to transform themselves while acknowledging they were also in danger of being transformed. The real power (and indeed danger) of the mirror was precisely the opportunity it afforded to change the image of whoever stepped in its sights under the protest that it merely offered a true reflection. Aphrodite's crooked mirror reminded her viewers that it offered rather more than a reflection of a Greek goddess.

Epilogue

Both mirrors and masks appear to have played a major imaginative role in inventing social identities. The close links between them are made manifest at the level of terminology where, in Latin, the

---

[79] Sen. *Q Nat.* 1.15.7–8, 1.16.8, 1.17.4–10.

[80] Sen. *Q Nat.* 1.16.

[81] Suet. *Vita Hor.*

[82] Michel (1982) and Koloski-Ostrow (1997, 255) detect

Neronian voyeurism in the Fourth Style paintings of Pompeii. They are joined by Leach 2004. Sharrock (2002, 265–67) reminds us to consider these images in more flexible ways.

[83] Hallesten 1995, 76.

[84] Eco 1986, 228–30.

term *imago* might apply equally to mask or reflection.[85] We have already mentioned actors looking at their character masks in the mirror. We might also point to Augustus, who, having consulted his mirror to adjust his metaphorical mask, asked his death-bed audience to applaud him from the stage.[86] At the less heroic end of Roman society, Hostius Quadra's far too intimate relationship with his mirrors was reconfigured as a far too literal immersion of his character into the theatrical, when his exploits became the subject of a theatrical performance.[87] While Hostius is clearly a perversion of Augustus's model control over his mirror and ironic comment on the theatricality of his life, both stories might be taken to stress a realization that in a society where beauty is not even skin deep, where (re)presentation *is* identity, devices such as mirrors and masks are crucial apparatus.[88] Mirrors and reflections, like masks, helped to form new faces and construct social *personae*. Such a necessity faced not only the North African provincial or the Roman pervert but even (and perhaps above all others) the emperor himself.[89]

Roman moralists like Seneca who were vocal opponents of such a system often framed their response through their Stoicism, which also prompted belief in the unity of the individual and in fixed identity. Of course, on a more immediate, practical level, they were usually men of privileged economic and social status who had a vested interest in hanging on to a very precise ideal of Romanness, which they were able to naturalize by contrasting it constantly with eastern and barbaric luxury. Nearly all accusations of domestic luxury were voiced by Roman elites scared of losing out to their flashier peers or, worse, to flashier social or ethnic inferiors. They were ongoing opponents of this flexibility, though as we have seen, they did not necessarily live up to their professed standards and were happy to exploit the devices they deplored.[90]

As the preoccupation with forging identities is often associated with loss or crisis of old identifications, it is perhaps not surprising that mirrors and masks have played a role in discourses of surviving empire in the twentieth and twenty-first centuries.[91] In a modern context, globalization has produced fractured, pluralistic identities the world over. Where people might have once been able to define themselves by ethnicity, language, or religion, the migration of peoples, the devolution of empires, and the coming together of new communities predicated on new impulses, such as the urge to create economic alliances, find individuals on a world stage, acting up to a bewildering set of identities through which they have to face the world. One response has been to deplore such upheavals that threaten to destabilize the sense of self, particularly a sense of self commonly understood as a complete unity defined by polarity to an identified other. Other responses, far from understanding these processes in negative terms as the enforced dissolution of old identities or the imposition of new, have seen the resultant "hybridity" and fluidity as providing a creative impulse and an opportunity, however difficult, to move beyond traditional polarities.[92] What is

[85] Flower 1996, 32–59. Lucretius (4.269–323) explains our reflection as the film of our face flung back at us in reverse like a mask whacked against a hard surface.

[86] Suet. *Aug.* 99.1.

[87] Sen. *Q Nat.* 1.16.1.

[88] The conviction that presentation is identity is most strongly argued in Henderson 2002.

[89] Suet. *Aug.* 99.1. The moment should be contrasted with

Ner. 49.4, where, despite a life spent in self-invention, Nero leaves a horrific death grimace to future memory.

[90] Cic. *Leg.* 3.13.30.

[91] Hall 1992, 275; Porter (2001, 84–85) recognizes this in the case of Pausanias.

[92] Hall 1992; Steyn 1997, 1–6; Henderson 1995, 2–5; Suleri 1995, 174–75. Pajaczkowski (1997) discusses how Europeans are having to reinvent their old viewpoints of self and others. Said (1978) provides the classic account of Europe's great

certain, however, is that these new identities are often tested in the sphere of the visual. In order
to function on that world stage, individuals have to learn to articulate and mobilize many different
identities as the occasion demands—identities that have to be demonstrated through performance
and (re)presentation.[93]

These observations might serve as a useful analogy for the experience of living within the Roman Empire. The inhabitants of that empire, too, were affected by their part in a Roman world
bigger than they could ever experience and found themselves moving in new circles and facing new
experiences, which all commanded different identities.[94] The adoption of Hellenistic culture, of the
motifs of Aphrodite and Dionysus, throughout the empire reinforces the notion of a visual language
that, although not of Rome's invention, became the accepted visual currency of empire. That is not
to say that the repeated motifs were intended to solve the empire's identity crisis by providing a
full, convincing disguise.[95] They did, however, provide a medium through which to express difference and community. Dionysus's mask and Aphrodite's mirror provided models for an ambiguous
visuality, predicated simultaneously on the claims of truth and revelation, disguise and distortion.
The ongoing rhetorical resistance to these devices implied that this ambiguity was eagerly sought,
providing audiences with an opportunity to explore and create identities for themselves. At the
same time, it remained the prerogative of those who could command the rhetorical skills to expose
and attack those identities should they wish and to do so in the name of Romanness by reflecting
Hellenistic *tryphe* as Roman *luxuria*. In this way, some players were able to retain control, at critical
moments, over the inventions of others.

Although some fears have been expressed in the classics community that such notions of hybrid
and contingent identities smack far too much of a liberal postmodernism, in which anything goes,
the ceding of visual and identificational opportunities to imperial audiences is not to repackage
Roman imperialism as attractive and utopian. It is to suggest that this audience was operating in
an empire that, however brutal in the acquisition and maintenance of empire, had never imposed
one model solution for being Roman, that instead might be understood to thrive on a model in
which identities were plural and shifting, contingent and fragmentary, to both the advantage and
disadvantage of its people. As individuals found themselves bearing several different, and sometimes
conflicting, identities, their grasp of the literal and metaphorical effects of the mirror and the mask
might prove crucial in ensuring successful social participation in empire.[96]

For any group wanting to make imperial audiences aware of their attempts to distance themselves from or to act upon the floating identities of empire, it would be crucial to exert control
over the established visual language and traditions of (re)presentation.[97] So it is the Venus bedroom
pinup through which Clement of Alexandria attacks pagan ways of viewing and the self-indulgence
of the viewer who, as he embraces his lover on his bed, looks up to watch his acts reflected in his
painting of Aphrodite, ensnared in the arms of Ares.[98] Elsewhere he challenged the devices by which

---

other, Islam. Recent political events, of course, have been
fueled by a way of thinking that rejects pluralism in favor of
polarization. Sardar (1997) writes as someone whose identity
as British Muslim straddles these imposed poles.

[93] Hall 1992, 278–79; Diawara 1995.

[94] Goldhill 2001, 19–20; Whitmarsh 2001.

[95] For the difficulties of discussing hybridity through the
constraints of the language of Hellenism, see Porter 2001,

esp. 90–91.

[96] Dench (2005) provides an assessment of recent approaches
to imperial identities. Goldhill (2001), Barton (2002), and
Henderson (2002) provide strategies for imperial survival.

[97] Gleason (2001, 53) talks about the fear of identities that are
not clear-cut and the impulse to demonstrate difference.

[98] Clem. Al. *Cohortatio ad Graecos* 4.

viewers made their own faces, claiming that mirrors offered only deceptions, which deflected the viewer from seeing inner beauty, and that women embellishing their looks do nothing but change their faces into masks.[99] The exploitation of the connection between house and theater was also attacked, invoking the disdain of John Chrysostum, while Augustine railed against theatrical *personae* as antithetical to true identities.[100] But, of course, even as he wrote, the owner of the Maison de l'Âne was still gazing into Aphrodite's mirror, enjoying the transformations her reflection offered. Along with Dionysus's mask, it survives even today as a medium through which we endeavor to experience and to see ourselves in the Roman Empire.

---

[99] Clem. Al. *Paedogogus* 3.2.

[100] John Chrys. *Homily 83 on Matthew*. See Huskinson 2002–2003, 133. August. *De civ. D.* 2.8–14.

Works Cited

Alexander, M., and M. Ennaifer, *Corpus des mosaïques de Tunisie* (Tunis 1973).

Arscott, C., and K. Scott, eds., *Manifestations of Venus: Art and Sexuality* (Manchester 2000).

Aurigemma, S., *L'Italia in Africa. Tripolitania*, vol. 1.2 (Rome 1962).

Balensiefen, L., *Die Bedeutung des Spiegelbildes als ikonographisches Motiv in der antiken Kunst* (Tübingen 1990).

Balty, J., *Mosaïques antiques de Syrie* (Brussels 1977).

Bartman, E., "Décor et Duplicatio: Pendants in Roman Sculptural Display," *American Journal of Archaeology* 92 (1988) 211–25.

Barton, C., "Being in the Eyes: Shame and Sight in Ancient Rome," in *The Roman Gaze: Vision, Power and the Body*, ed. D. Fredrick (Baltimore 2002) 216–36.

Bartsch, S., *Actors in the Audience: Theatricality and Doublespeak from Nero to Hadrian* (Cambridge, Mass. 1994).

Beard, M., and J. Henderson, *Classical Art* (Oxford 2001).

Bergmann, B., "Introduction," in *The Art of Ancient Spectacle*, ed. B. Bergmann and C. Kondoleon (Washington 1999) 9–35.

Beyen, H. G., *Die Pompejanische Wanddekoration vom zweiten bis zum vierten Stil* (The Hague 1938).

Bhahba, H. K., *The Location of Culture* (London and New York 1994).

Blanchard-Lemée, M., *Maisons à Mosaïques du Quartier Central de Djemila (Cuicul)* (Paris 1975).

Brinkerhoff, D. M., *Hellenistic Statues of Aphrodite* (New York 1978).

Bruhl, A., *Liber Pater. Origine et expansion du culte dionysiaque à Rome dans le monde romain* (Paris 1953).

Bryson, N., *Looking at the Overlooked* (London 1990).

Carpenter, T., and C. Faraone, eds., *Masks of Dionysus* (Ithaca 1993).

Chaniotis, A., "Theatricality beyond the Theatre: Staging Public Life in the Hellenistic World," *Pallas* 47 (1997) 219–59.

Clarke, J. R., *The Houses of Roman Italy, 100 B.C.–A.D. 250* (Berkeley 1991).

Corbeill, A., "Political Movement: Walking and Ideology in Republican Rome," in *The Roman Gaze: Vision, Power and the Body*, ed. D. Frederick (Baltimore 2002) 182–215.

D'Arms, J., "Performing Culture: Roman Spectacle and the Banquets of the Powerful," in *The Art of Ancient Spectacle*, ed. B. Bergmann and C. Kondoleon (Washington 1999) 301–19.

Davis, T. C., and T. Postlewait, eds., *Theatricality* (Cambridge 2003).

Dench, E., *Romulus' Asylum: Roman Identities from the Age of Alexander to the Age of Hadrian* (Oxford 2005).

Derrida, J., *The Truth in Painting* (Chicago 1987).

Diawara, M., "Cultural Studies/Black Studies," in *Borders, Boundaries and Frames*, ed. M. Henderson (New York and London 1995) 202–11.

Dunbabin, K., *The Mosaics of Roman North Africa: Studies in Iconography and Patronage* (Oxford 1978).

——, *Mosaics of the Greek and Roman World* (Cambridge 1999).

Eco, U., "Mirrors," in *Iconicity: Essays on the Nature of Culture*, ed. P. Bouissac, M. Herzfeld, and R. Posner (Tübingen 1986) 215–38.

Edwards, C., "Beware of Imitations: Theatre and the Subversion of Imperial Identity," in *Reflections of Nero: Culture, History and Representation*, ed. J. Elsner and J. Masters (London 1994) 83–97.

Elsner, J., *Art and the Roman Viewer* (Cambridge 1995).

——, "Caught in the Ocular: Visualising Narcissus in the Roman World," in *Echoes of Narcissus*, ed. L. Spaas (New York 2000) 89–110.

Emigh, J., *Masked Performance: The Play of Self and Other in Ritual and Theatre* (Philadelphia 1996).

Etienne, R., *Le quartier nord-est de Volubilis* (Paris 1960).

Fanon, F., *Peau noire, masques blancs* (Paris 1952).

Flower, H., *Ancestor Masks and Aristocratic Power in Roman Culture* (Oxford 1996).

Fuss, D., "Interior Colonies: Frantz Fanon and the Politics of Identification," *Diacritics* 24 (Summer/Fall 1994) 20–41.

Gleason, M., *Making Men: Sophists and Self-Presentation in Ancient Greece* (Princeton 1995).

——, "Mutilated Messengers: Body Language in Josephus," in *Being Greek under Rome: Cultural Identity, the Second Sophistic and the Development of Empire*, ed. S. Goldhill (Cambridge 2001) 50–85.

Goldhill, S., ed., *Being Greek under Rome: Cultural Identity, the Second Sophistic and the Development of Empire* (Cambridge 2001).

Goldman, A., "Comparative Identities," in *Borders, Boundaries and Frames: Essays on Cultural Criticism and Cultural Theory*, ed. M. Henderson (London 1995) 107–32.

Grigson, G., *The Goddess of Love* (London 1978).

Grimal, P., *Les jardins romains*, 2nd ed. (Paris 1969).

Hales, S., "How the Venus de Milo Lost Her Arms," in *The Hellenistic World: New Perspectives*, ed. D. Ogden (London 2002).

——, *Roman Houses and Social Identity* (Cambridge 2003).

Hall, S., "The Question of Cultural Identity," in *Modernity and Its Futures*, ed. S. Hall, D. Held, and T. McGrew (Cambridge 1992) 273–325.

Hallesten, K., "In Exile in the Mother Tongue," in *Borders, Boundaries and Frames*, ed. M. Henderson (London 1995) 64–106.

Havelock, C. M., *The Aphrodite of Knidos and Her Successors* (Ann Arbor 1995).

Henderson, J., *Pliny's Statue: The Letters, Self-Portraiture and Classical Art* (Exeter 2002).

Henderson, M., ed., *Borders, Boundaries and Frames: Essays on Cultural Criticism and Cultural Theory* (London 1995).

Henrichs, A., "'He Has a God in Him': Human and Divine in the Modern Perception of Dionysus," in *Masks of Dionysus*, ed. T. Carpenter and C. Faraone (Ithaca 1993) 13–43.

Hinks, R. P., *Catalogue of the Greek, Roman and Etruscan Paintings and Mosaics in the British Museum* (London 1933).

Horn, H. G., *Mysteriensymbolik auf dem Kölner Dionysosmosaik* (Bonn 1972).

Huskinson, J., "Theatre, Performance and Theatricality in Some Mosaic Pavements from Antioch," *Bulletin of the Institute of Classical Studies* 46 (2002–2003) 131–65.

Jashemski, W., *The Gardens of Pompeii*, vol. 1 (New Rochelle 1979).

Johnston, D., "Some Mosaics and Murals in Roman Tripolitania," in *Roman Provincial Wall Painting of the Western Empire*, ed. J. Liversidge, British Archaeological Reports International Series 140 (Oxford 1982) 193–206.

Keene Congdon, L. O., *Caryatid Mirrors of Ancient Greece* (Mainz 1981).

Koloski-Ostrow, A. O., "Violent Stages in Two Pompeian Houses: Imperial Taste, Aristocratic Response and Messages of Male Control," in *Naked Truths: Women, Sexuality and Gender in Classical Art and Archaeology*, ed. A. O. Koloski-Otrow and C. L. Lyons (London 1997) 243–66.

Kondoleon, C., *Domestic and Divine: Roman Mosaics in the House of Dionysos* (Ithaca 1995).

Lassus, J., "Mosaïques de Vénus," in *La Mosaïque Gréco-Romaine*, vol. 1 (Paris 1965) 175–90.

Leach, E. W., *The Social Life of Painting in Ancient Rome and on the Bay of Naples* (New York and Cambridge 2004).

Lehmann, P., *Roman Wall Paintings from Boscoreale in the Metropolitan Museum of Art* (Cambridge, Mass. 1953).

Lévi-Strauss, C., *The Way of the Masks* (London 1983).

Ling, R., *Roman Painting* (Cambridge 1991).

Little, A., *Roman Perspective Painting and the Ancient Stage* (Kennebunk, Me. 1971).

Mack, R., "Facing down Medusa (An Aetiology of the Gaze)," *Art History* 25 (2002) 571–604.

Manderscheid, H., *Die Skulpturenausstattung der Kaiserzeitlichen Thermenanlagen* (Berlin 1981).

McCarty, W., "The Shape of the Mirror: Metaphorical Catoptrics in Classical Literature," *Arethusa* 22 (1989) 161–95.

Michel, D., "Bemerkungen über Zuschauerfiguren in pompejanischen sogenannten Tafelbilden," in *La Regione Sotterata dal Vesuvio. Atti del Convegno Internazionale 1979* (Naples 1982) 537–98.

Napier, A., *Masks, Transformation, and Paradox* (Berkeley 1986).

Neal, D., *Roman Mosaics in Britain*, *Britannia* Monograph Series 1 (London 1981).

Osborne, R., "The Ecstasy and the Tragedy: Varieties of Religious Experience in Art, Drama and Society," in *Greek Tragedy and the Historian*, ed. C. Pelling (Oxford 1997) 187–212.

Otto, W., *Dionysus: Myth and Cult* (Bloomington 1965).

Pajaczkowski, C., "The Ecstatic Solace of Culture," in *Other than Identity: The Subject, Politics and Art*, ed. J. Steyn (Manchester 1997) 101–12.

Parker, A., and E. K. Sedgwick, eds., *Performativity and Performance* (New York and London 1995).

Pernet, H., *Ritual Masks: Deceptions and Revelation* (Columbia, S.C. 1992).

Peters, W., and P. Meyboom, "The Roots of Provincial Painting: Results of Current Research in Nero's Domus Aurea," in *Roman Provincial Wall Painting of the Western Empire*, ed. J. Liversidge, British Archaeological Reports International Series 140 (Oxford 1982) 39–59.

Picard, G.-Ch., "Le couronnement de Vénus," *Mélanges d'archéologie et d'histoire* 57–58 (1940–46) 43–108.

Platt, V., "Viewing, Desiring, Believing: Confronting the Divine in a Pompeian House," *Art History* 25 (2002) 87–112.

Porter, J., "Ideals and Ruins," in *Pausanias: Travel and Memory in Roman Greece*, ed. S. Alcock et al. (Oxford 2001) 63–92.

Rehm, R., *The Play of Space* (Princeton 2002).

Richlin, A., "Making up a Woman: The Face of Roman Gender," in *Off with Her Head! The Denial of Women's Identity in Myth, Religion and Culture*, ed. H. Eilberg-Schwartz and W. Doniger (Berkeley 1995) 185–213.

Said, E., *Orientalism* (London 1978).

Sardar, Z., "British, Muslim, Writer," in *Other than Identity: The Subject, Politics and Art*, ed. J. Steyn (Manchester 1997) 63–82.

Schilling, R., *La religion romaine de Vénus* (Paris 1982).

Sharrock, A., "Looking at Looking: Can You Resist a Reading?," in *The Roman Gaze: Vision, Power and the Body*, ed. D. Frederick (Baltimore 2002) 265–95.

Slater, N. W., "Passion and Petrification: The Gaze in Apuleius," *Classical Philology* 93 (1998) 18–48.

Smith, R. R. R., *Hellenistic Sculpture* (London 1993).

Stewart, A., "Reflections," in *Sexuality in Ancient Art*, ed. N. B. Kampen (Cambridge 1996) 136–54.

Steyn, J., ed., *Other Than Identity: The Subject, Politics and Art* (Manchester 1997).

Strocka, V., *Die Wandmalerei der Hanghäuser in Ephesos*, Forschungen in Ephesos 8.1 (Vienna 1977).

Suleri, S., "Criticism and Its Alterity," in *Borders, Boundaries and Frames: Essays on Cultural Criticism and Cultural Theory*, ed. M. Henderson (London 1995) 171–84.

Thébert, Y., "Private Life and Domestic Architecture in Roman Africa," in *A History of Private Life*, vol. 1: *From Pagan Rome to Byzantium*, ed. P. Veyne (Cambridge, Mass. 1987) 313–410.

Thompson, M. L., "Programmatic Painting in Pompeii" (Ph.D. diss., New York University 1960).

Too, Y. L., "Statues, Mirrors, Gods: Controlling Images in Apuleius," in *Art and Text in Roman Culture*, ed. J. Elsner (Cambridge 1996) 133–52.

Vermeule, C. C., *Greek Sculpture and Roman Taste* (Ann Arbor 1977).

Vernant, J.-P., *Figures, idoles, masques* (Paris 1990).

Vernant, J.-P., and F. Frontisi-Ducroux, *Dans l'oeil du miroir* (Paris 1997).

Wallace-Hadrill, A., "Pliny the Elder and Man's Unnatural Luxury," *Greece & Rome* 37 (1990) 80–96.

——, *Houses and Society in Pompeii and Herculaneum* (Princeton 1994).

Webster, T. B. L., *Monuments Illustrating New Comedy*, 3rd ed. (London 1995).

Whitmarsh, T., "Greece Is the World: Exile and Identity in the Second Sophistic," in *Being Greek under Rome: Cultural Identity, the Second Sophistic and the Development of Empire*, ed. S. Goldhill (Cambridge 2001) 269–305.

Wiles, D., *The Masks of Menander: Sign and Meaning in Greek and Roman Performance* (Cambridge 1991).

Wiseman, T. P., "*Conspicui postes tectaque digna deo*: The Public Image of Aristocratic and Imperial Houses in the Late Republic and Early Empire," in *L'urbs: espace urbain et histoire (Ier siècle av. J.-C.– IIIe siècle ap. J.-C.): actes du colloque international organisé par le Centre National de la Recherche Scientifique et l'École française de Rome (Rome, 8–12 mai 1985)*, Collection de l'École française de Rome 98 (1987) 393–413.

Zanker, G., *Modes of Viewing in Hellenistic Art and Poetry* (Madison 2003).

Zanker, P., *Eine Kunst für die Sinne: zur Bilderwelt des Dionysos und der Aphrodite* (Berlin 1998).

13 ◆ THE IMAGE OF THE FAMILY ON SEPULCHRAL MONUMENTS IN THE NORTHWEST PROVINCES

Henner von Hesberg

Images of families represent the smallest social group of a society. In this sense, they provide information about the society in general, the valid definitions of its roles and designations. This is one of the reasons why, since late medieval art, such images represent one of the favorite subjects of painting and sculpture.[1] The theme of the family and its individual members—as in the whole of the Roman Empire—continuously recurs on the sepulchral monuments of the northwest provinces. And yet differences due to various factors, such as the diverse types of monuments, quickly become evident. The possibilities offered by a relief are different from those of a sepulchral building. Apart from this, there are regional, temporal, and social distinctions.[2] The forms developed in the Danubian area are quite different from those in the northwest provinces, but there are many differences to be seen within a single concentrated area as well.[3] The monuments of the first century A.D., for instance, show the families in a stately way, whereas the monuments of the second and third century A.D. express the feeling of unity prevailing among its members. In addition, the families of Roman veterans as well as other social groups merit consideration. Furthermore, a methodologically convincing analysis must take into account the kinds of representations: statues, for instance, convey different messages and conditions than busts or reliefs.[4]

These difficulties may be clarified by the following example: the grave monument of the veteran (*miles*) L. Poblicius in Cologne, presumably erected ca. A.D. 40, represents the family of the deceased (fig. 1). Two men are depicted dressed in a toga, each holding a book scroll in his right hand. Placed in front of them was a *scrinium* for such scrolls. Only the lower section of a female statue survives, making its original design unclear (fig. 2). The statue bears a certain resemblance to the large Herculaneum type, but it also demonstrates clear variations, such as in the garments and the hand, which is not wrapped in cloth. As shown by H. Gabelmann, the little girl is wearing the toga (fig. 3).[5]

By comparison, the image of a family on a monument in Igel (near Treves), erected by the family of the Secundini ca. A.D. 220–30, is of a clearly different type (fig. 4). Three men are shown, the smallest one in the center. He and the one to his left wear togas and are joined in a handshake. The third figure, on the left side, is turned toward the scene and is wrapped in a cloak (*paenula*). The two men on the outside would originally have held scrolls. The three medallions placed above are

For the translation of the text and corrections, I would like to thank B. Takats and S. Bell, for fruitful discussions T. Hölscher and P. Noelke, and for illustrations the Rheinisches Landesmuseum Bonn, the Römisch-Germanisches-Museum Cologne, and the Landesmuseum Mainz.

[1] For the image of the family in the medieval period, see Weber-Kellermann 1976, 29–137.

[2] Frova 1975; Frenz 1985, 1–41; Diebner 1989, 15–57; Hatt 1986, 111–242; Kleiner 1987, 73–88; Hope 2001, 1–14.

[3] Schober 1923, 67–132; Kremer 2001, 383–90.

[4] Ghedini 1980, 91–148; Pflug 1989, 78–91; Kockel 1993, 11–14; Trillmich 2001, 21–29.

[5] Precht 1979, 61–64, pls. 1–3, 19–22; Gabelmann 1979, 232–35, figs. 19–20; Andrikopoulou-Strack 1986, 9–19, fig. 1.

Fig. 1. Monument of Poblicius. Cologne, Römisch-
Germanisches Museum (photo Museum).

Fig. 2. Wife of Poblicius, Monument of Poblicius. Cologne,
Römisch-Germanisches Museum (photo Museum).

of great interest as well: they represent beardless faces, but, even taking into account the limited indications of their clothing, it is not clear whether they are male or female. The inscription suggests an interpretation of the two men in the scene as the brothers Securus and Aventinus, who erected the monument, whereas the smaller figure may be seen as one of the sons of Securus, extending his hand to bid farewell to his father. The medallion in the center possibly represents the father of both brothers, Publius Secundinus, while that on the left might show Pacata, the deceased wife of Aventinus, and the individual on the right may be Macedo, the second son of Securus.[6]

The differences between the two monuments mentioned here are very evident. The monument in Cologne shows an abstract series of statues, which—elaborated in a more precious material such as marble or bronze—might equally have been placed in the Forum (figs. 1–3). The scene represented in Igel deals with the subject of parting. The medallions placed above it indicate another aspect. The deceased are commemorated in their portraits, and, as shown by the turning of their heads and by their composition, they are closely connected to those represented below (fig. 4). Thus the contents of the scene are determined by the representation of emotion and reverence.

[6] Dragendorff and Krüger 1924, 62–65, fig. 34, pl. 5; Mehl
1997, 60–61.

Fig. 3. Daughter of Poblicius, Monument of Poblicius.
Cologne, Römisch-Germanisches Museum
(photo Museum).

Fig. 4. Monument of the Secundini. Igel (after Dragendorff and Krüger 1924, pl. 2).

These are the circumstances that lead to the question I shall try to answer in the following discussion. In the first instance, it will be shown that the attributes of these images are characteristic of their respective periods, parallels to which can be found on other monuments as well. Secondly, this chapter will look at the way in which social roles are constructed and confirmed in the Roman provinces and, thirdly, the reasons for their change. In what way did the character of the family change and consequently the kind of role played by their individual members, or is it a change in the way the family is regarded that leads to a different means of their representation in the respective media? In addressing these questions, this discussion will concentrate on women and children, for it is their bonds with one another that are traditionally accentuated in representations.

THERE ARE OTHER examples that demonstrate that the conventions of representation seen in the sepulchral monument of Poblicius are typical in a general sense and are not reserved exclusively for this type of monument. In the case of a monument from Nickenich (near Andernach on the Rhine), a mother and child appear in the center, while a man wearing a toga is represented in the niche on the right and a man wearing a tunica and pallium is shown on the left. The woman is dressed in the local (possibly Celtic) tradition, the costume of the Menimane, with a neck scarf and her hair held

Fig. 5. Woman with child, Monument of Nickenich.
Bonn, Rheinisches Landesmuseum, inv. no. 31.87
(Landschaftsverband Rheinland/Rheinisches
Landesmuseum Bonn).

Fig. 6. Gravestone of Bella. Cologne, Römisch-Germanisches
Museum, inv. no. 62.274 (photo Museum).

by a scarf and a *torques* around her neck. Her son is clad in a tunica and pallium, wears covered shoes, and holds a scroll in his upraised left hand (fig. 5).[7]

While the connection between the mother and child is represented as closer—that is, in a manner that the monument of Poblicius cannot imitate (due to the position of its columns)—the element of stateliness prevails. Even though the boy is holding his mother's hand, both figures are staring rigidly outward toward the viewer. This arrangement is even more puzzling given that metropolitan monuments, such as the frieze of the Ara Pacis, clearly represent the close attachment between mother and child by the gestures of their hands and by the fact that they look at each other.[8] Thus, there was neither a lack of models nor of appropriate conceptions. The grave reliefs from Rome and Italy are represented in the same manner.[9]

This is also supported by a third example. On the tombstone, erected ca. A.D. 10–20 in Cologne for Bella, a woman from the Celtic tribe of the Remians (the area around modern-day Reims), the

[7] Neuffer 1932, pls. 2–3; Wild 1968a, 200–201, fig. 22; Bauchenss 1975, 91–94, pl. 34; Gabelmann 1979, 242–44, fig. 24; Andrikopoulou-Strack 1986, 42–43.

[8] Simon 1967, 18–22, pls. 13–23; Settis 1988, 416–24.

[9] Zanker 1975, 290–97, figs. 23–32; Frenz 1985, 156, no. 146, pl. 62.1; Varone 1989, 11, fig. 4; Pflug 1989, 179–80, no. 59, pl. 16.2; Hope 2001, 62–73.

deceased is also looking out of the picture, without paying attention to her newborn baby in her right arm (fig. 6).[10] Although emotion could have easily been made the theme of the image, this is clearly not the case. At the same time, these monuments demonstrate that one might follow the same pattern in representing both Roman and local women.

Each of these representations is concerned with two respective roles: one is the relationship between mother and child; the other is the specific role of the mother with respect to the child. According to the definition of Peter Berger and Thomas Luckmann, "we can properly begin to speak of roles when their kind of typification occurs in the context of an objectified stock of knowledge common to a collectivity of actors. Roles are types of actors in such a context."[11] The inhabitants of the Roman border provinces along the Rhine had a definite idea of how a mother and child were expected to interact. Apart from this, however, the additional roles of the woman and the child were included as well, for "by playing roles, the individual participates in a social world. By internalizing these roles the same world becomes subjectively real to him. . . . The representation of an institution in and by roles is thus representation par excellence, on which the other representations are dependent."[12] One of these roles is represented by "linguistic objectification" and, we might add, is no less important than the figurative one. All media take part in this process. But as T. Hölscher has pointed out, pictures construct roles simplistically while, at the same time, incorporating their significant details. They demonstrate, in simplified form, the way in which one would like to be understood.[13]

In this context we may pose the question of how these roles take shape. For two cultural traditions, the Roman and the local, are confronting each other and interacting in the setting of the province. It may be expected that their social institutions—that is, the roles among themselves—were quite different from each other. For the local perspective there is only the indirect evidence supplied by archaeological traces and written records by Romans, which are usually influenced by their own point of view.[14] The well-known descriptions by Caesar (*B Gall.* 6.19.21) of the Celts and Germans provide an account of their different roles. The description of family life within the Germanic tribes by Tacitus (*Germ.* 17–20) was explicitly formulated in a way that criticized the Roman situation, which means that it was supposed to ascertain certain types of behavior and general values. Based on this agenda, the ethnological value of these statements is very limited.[15]

Contrarily, barbarian women are depicted on Roman victory monuments.[16] But in these contexts, they remained within the specifically Roman typology, lest the role of Roman soldiers be put into doubt through scenes of their violence toward powerless individuals. Nor are the women ever depicted in the specific cloth of an indigenous tribe so as to avoid offending their respective feelings.

These roles include two aspects: on the one hand, they determine the area of activity of the individual whose role is described, which—in the case of a woman—is the family. There she acts as the keeper of the household, as the wife, mother, and so forth. In the case of a child this is the

---

[10] Galsterer and Galsterer 1975, 75 n. 310, pl. 67; Gabelmann 1979, 224, fig. 10; Riedel 1998, 311, fig. 3.

[11] Berger and Luckmann 1966, 69f.

[12] Berger and Luckmann 1966, 69f.

[13] See his contribution in this volume.

[14] See n. 28 below. Schoppa 1958, 289–91, pl. 57.4 (indigenous goddess from Poitiers); von Kurzynski 1996, 41, 59.

[15] Perl 1990, 181–89.

[16] Gemma Augustea: Kähler 1968, pls. 14–15; Hölscher 1988. Barbarian woman in Mainz: Frenz 1992, 59, no. 4, pl. 3. She wears a dress of unknown type (cf. Tac. *Germ.* 17.1–2) but without any details of a special indigenous costume: von Kurzynski 1996, 68–71; cf. Gergel 1994, 197–207. Compare also a group in which a soldier attacks a barbarian woman; from the necropolis of Langres: Joly 2001, 269, fig. 102.

act of playing or of learning but also of demonstrating the qualities of a future adult. On the other hand, the forms of self-representation determine—as can be seen on representations on sepulchral monuments—the normality of the role. They define the kind of social interaction and usually express it with positive connotations; that is to say, in the sense of a good mother, an alluring but also faithful wife, a promising and obedient child, and so forth. Here quality is defined in the relationship between the individual persons, which encompasses aspects of their gender, social behavior, and ethnicity.[17]

The images avail themselves of traditional formulas, which circumscribe both status and interaction. In this relationship, the convention of the role is somehow correlated with the standardized types of images. It would be quite instructive, however, to consider new motifs or radical changes. Apart from these, one might expect that the population of the provinces is above all using Roman images. So we have to ask to what extent independent role models could develop under these conditions. There are various difficulties associated with this line of inquiry: for instance, the use of prototypes demonstrates the acceptance of certain bearers of prototypes for roles. On the one hand, they are slightly altered, and this opens up the question of how they are accepted in the provinces. On the other hand, there are different possible images to choose from in order to create a unique and, in a certain sense, filtered approach to the memory of the deceased. And yet the pictures remained in an utterly traditional frame of self-representation.[18]

I shall start with the portrait of the daughter from the monument of Poblicius (fig. 3). As H. Gabelmann has observed, she is oddly wearing a tunica and a toga, with a bracelet (*armillae*) on her right arm. In addition, he explains that this is evidently to accentuate the status of the child as a free Roman citizen.[19] The day before their wedding young girls put away the toga with a purple stripe (*praetexta*). In this context, the representation is largely oriented to the girl's role as the daughter of a Roman citizen before her marriage. Clothes and jewelry stand for prosperity. The representation of the mother was adjusted to the so-called large Herculaneum type (fig. 2). The great abundance of clothing, which is distinguished by its repetition, is additionally illustrated by the deployment of the folds on the ground and by her grasp upon the garment as well as further accentuated by its contrast to the representation of a very small foot. I would suggest that we have here, in a provincial context, an example of a new interpretation of the prototype in which the details are accentuated in a distinct way.[20]

The upper part of the body and the head are destroyed. The head, however, might be imagined to be very similar to the one in Treves, where the sculptor worked hard to create a fashionable hairstyle (seen in its curls and artificial conception).[21] The back of the head was apparently covered by a cloak pulled over like a veil.

Alongside these examples, which are oriented directly toward Roman-Italian models, there are quite a few deviations. I begin with a female statue found in Aachen-Burtscheid, now in the Rheinisches Landesmuseum Bonn (fig. 7). According to H. Gabelmann, the statue was part of a sepulchral monument of a kind similar to that of Poblicius from approximately the same period.[22]

---

[17] Zanker 1975, 300–307; Zanker 1976, 598–605; Giuliani 1986, 25–51; Zanker 1992, 340–49; Hope 2001, 17–24.

[18] Hope 2001, 88–91.

[19] Gabelmann 1979, 233–34, figs. 19–20.

[20] Compare it with a similar process in other fields: Zanker 1983, 44–47.

[21] Polaschek 1971, 122–25, figs. 3–4; Andrikopoulou-Strack 1986, 175, pl. 20.2.

[22] Bauchenss 1978, 51–52, no. 57, pls. 33–35; Gabelmann 1979, 209–17, figs. 1–7.

Fig. 7. Statue of a woman from Aachen-Burtscheid. Bonn, Rheinisches Landesmuseum, inv. no. D 1131 (Landschaftsverband Rheinland/Rheinisches Landesmuseum Bonn).

She is wearing a tunica and pallium and therefore greatly resembles a type of representation that is, in turn, well known from Italy. There is, however, an additional attribute in her left hand, a purse shaped like a bracelet. This form is very rare, and most of the existing examples come from Gallia.[23] Apparently this is a particular sign, introduced locally, in order to emphasize a certain quality of the woman, such as her wealth or good housekeeping. So we see a varied mixture of Roman and indigenous elements in the expression of different values. The problem lies in decoding that system since it is not possible to make a clear distinction between sign and meaning.[24] Regional forms of clothing, for instance, do not rigidly suggest an interpretation of foreigner status.

The same is true for a small statuette of a woman in the Römisch-Germanisches Museum in Cologne, somewhat damaged on the surface but on the whole well preserved, with vestiges of red coloring (figs. 8–10).[25] She is adorned with an article of special indigenous origin, a breastplate fixed with a necklace that we find on figures in Mainz and Bonn.[26] The composition is very similar to the statue from Aachen-Burtscheid (fig. 7), with her right hand grasping the cloth and the left hand holding an object, perhaps also a purse bracelet. Judging by its dimensions, the statuette should

[23] Gabelmann 1979, 244–47, fig. 25.

[24] Compare a similar phenomenon on, e.g., eastern gravestones: Pfuhl 1905, 52–59; von Hesberg 1988, 312–21; Breuer 1995, 15–38, 66–100.

[25] Lehner 1918, 218 no. 581, pl. 14.3.

[26] Neuffer 1932, 25; Bauchenss 1978, 51, no. 56, pl. 33; Böhme 1985, 428–29, fig. 4. Perhaps that can be connected to a ritual of indigenous origin: Puttock 2002, 115–17.

*Figs. 8–10. Votive statuette of a woman. Limestone,
H. 32.5; W. 14.4 (at plinth); D. 10.3 (at plinth).
From the Apellhofplatz. Cologne, Römisch-
Germanisches Museum, inv. no. 33.43 (photo
Forschungsarchiv Römische Plastik Cologne).*

be a votive, perhaps from a girl or a woman to a goddess.[27] Stylistic cues indicate a date in the first half of the first century A.D.[28] So it is a very early example for that type of dedication and illustrates that self-representation in grave or votive sculpture used the same prototypes.

This recourse is reflected in a still more characteristic and direct way in the case of a regionally used form of clothing. Until recently, this aspect was treated more as an antiquarian interest, to clarify how the different parts of cloth were combined and from what indigenous prototypes they originated.[29] Thus, they are principally understood as a particular resistance to Roman costumes. Two forms can be discerned in the Rhineland: the costume of the so-called Menimane (fig. 11), named after the wife of Blussus, a naval merchant from Mainz from the Tiberian period.[30] The clothing consists of an undergarment with long sleeves, around the neckline of which a scarf (*focale*) is tucked. The main garment on top of these is fastened on the shoulders with two fibulas. Another fibula gathers the garment on the chest, thus forming heavy cloth folds. On top of this the woman wears a coat that covers her left arm and shoulder. The right hand holds the seam of the coat. The contrast among the colors of the different parts of the clothing is certainly of significance. The undergarment of a statue from Ingelheim in Wiesbaden was light green, the garment above this was of a light red, whereas the coat and the bonnet were colored in a darkish gray.[31] Very often there is also a sort of local jewelry—that is, a ring twisted around the neck (*torques*) and bracelets. A further characteristic attribute of the costume is the hairstyle, with the hair parted in the middle and, at both sides, two thick plaited braids forming a loop wound up in a spiral, which is covered by a bonnet. The costume of the so-called matron-deities represents a certain simplification—there is no overgarment, and a fibula on the chest is clasped to the heavy coat. Here too the hair is covered by a bonnet. The earliest example for this dates to the reign of the emperor Claudius.[32]

The fibula and bonnet indicate that it is not a Roman costume. This is a situation discussed quite often, above all with regard to questions of Romanization. These discussions have revealed a characteristic image for Gallia Belgica, and here especially the regions of Treves and Metz. Men wearing the toga are found relatively seldom on sepulchral monuments: only 19 from among 300 examples. Here most of the exceptions are exclusively found in the first century A.D. and in the late antique period.[33] But on the whole, a form of dress influenced by local traditions was the one that prevailed. In the Rhineland, this picture is probably not as clear but is in general similar. In any case, the form of clothing does not correspond to the legal status of the represented person. It is true that a togatus represents a citizen of the Roman Empire, but the opposite conclusion does not hold true—any individual wearing a local costume is not necessarily bound to be a provincial person lacking all civil rights.

The images considered up to now reveal that the role models are changing. According to the preserved monuments, it is of greater importance for a male inhabitant to demonstrate by his form of dress that he is also a holder of civil rights, but this is not an absolute value. We do not have direct insight—to quote Berger and Luckmann again—into the "fundamental process of habitualization and objectivation as the origins of institution" of the roles, as must have taken place in the period

[27] Kyll 1966, 50–51; Spickermann 1994, 451–56 (without any consideration of the votive material).

[28] Gabelmann 1979, 225–28, figs. 10–13.

[29] Garbsch 1965, 3–118; Wild 1968a, 210–17; Wild 1968b, 72–73; Böhme-Schönberger 1995, 3–6; Freigang 1997, 299–309; Faust 1998, 75–77; Martin-Kilcher 1998, 197–99, 219–39.

[30] Wild 1968a, 170–73, fig. 4; Bauchenss 1975, 85–89, pl. 33.2; Wild 1985, 393–99, pl. 2; Boppert 1996, 53–59, no. 2, pls. 6–7; Böhme-Schönberger 1995, 3–7, figs. 1–4.

[31] Wild 1968a, 188, fig. 14; Bauchenss 1975, 87–88, pl. 35.1; Gabelmann 1979, 238–40, fig. 21.

[32] Andrikopoulou-Strack 1986, 74–80.

[33] Freigang 1997, 299–309.

Fig. 11. Monument of Blussus. Mainz, Landesmuseum,   Fig. 12. Young girl from Mainz. Mainz, Landesmuseum,
inv. no. S 146 (photo Museum).   inv. no. S 1079 (S 952) (photo Museum).

from Augustus to Tiberius, although later "behavioural typisations" cannot be excluded.[34] In any case, it becomes evident that, as opposed to great parts of the Roman Empire, the regional traditions were included in an evident and marked way. And yet the special regional forms do not interfere with the generally valid typologies. On the contrary, their peculiar duality becomes evident. The way that provincials definitely hold on to their own forms but, at the same time, accept the paradigms of the existing Roman role models confirms their importance and validity in a special way. When seen from a special folkloristic perspective, the roles offered by Roman civilization are completely accepted despite the existing differences.

Discussion of some examples may explain this thesis. Women wear the local costume, it is true, but in essence it follows the Roman standards of value. Thus, to provide one example, the body is covered, displaying very few of its charms, even though Caesar and Tacitus wrote that the Germanic women dressed very freely, that their dresses were without sleeves, and that even the adjoining part of the breast remained uncovered.[35] The monuments in question, however, are from regions of a mainly Celtic tradition. Even so, we may assume that there the definition of the role of women differed to a great extent from that valid in the Roman-Italian surroundings within Germania. The garments worn by the women represented on the images exhibit, above all, an abundance of cloth, as seen in the different articles of clothing. This is supported by the rich jewelry that enhances most of the representations. Furthermore, the way in which a garment is worn expresses that the woman pictured is carrying this out in the appropriate manner—that she has put on the garment in accordance with

---

[34] Berger and Luckmann 1966, 69.

[35] Caes. *B Gall.* 6.21.5; Tac. *Germ.* 17.1; Perl 1990, 97, 180–82.

the conventions, decorously covering herself. The representation of breasts is reduced to sketchlike impressions and nearly omitted altogether, as seen, for instance, on the monument from Mainz (fig. 12). This means of representation is not, however, due to a presumed lack of skill on the part of the artist, for he might just as well have chosen quite different forms. Neither does this depend on the age of the woman represented, which in any case is indicated in a very vague manner. The cloth clasped in the center by a fibula could have had the effect of specially accentuating the breasts, as a bodice would have done, but—as seen in the figures from Wiesbaden—the artist has strived for rather the opposite. The folds of the garment have the same effect as frills.

An exception is provided by the representation of Menimane herself, which gives its name to this type of representation (fig. 11). On this monument, the left strap has slipped onto her arm and there reveals her breast. Beneath this, one has to imagine the undergarment in a special color that contrasts with the color of her body. Thus the exposure represents only a quotation from Graeco-Roman art, as seen mainly in representations of Venus.[36] Apparently this is an additional component, as found quite frequently in Roman-Italian sepulchral relief—that is, the depiction of physical female beauty. Allusions to it can already be deduced from the aforementioned elements, such as clothing, jewelry, and hairstyle, but sensual physical beauty, too, is included in these details. As evidenced by numerous references in inscriptions and epitaphs for the deceased, this did not violate any taboo.[37] Here the varied and contrasting aspects of the female role were sensibly combined in one and the same image without coming into conflict with one another. The primary characteristic could be assumed by very different values, which could be represented in a more conspicuous form.

One of these values is domesticity, which is referred to by different means. So a married couple is seated on a bench upholstered in a manner similar to the interior of a house.[38] In addition to this, a small dog with a little bell around its neck is sitting on Merimane's lap. This type of image evokes a series of other associations, as we learn from antique literature as well as other sources, about the care of an animal or the luxury of possessing a pet dog.[39] In a similar way, a man, such as the owner of the so-called Weisenau monument, may hold a dog as well.[40] At the same time, objects like a distaff with ball and thread held in the hand are associated with domesticity and diligence, for the activity of spinning wool could only be carried out at home.[41] On the tombstone from Mainz of earlier date, the female subject holds it in a rather demonstrative manner before her breast (fig. 12).[42] These details are worked out in a clearer way than in many Italian prototypes, demonstrating again how the roles are constructed in the pictures.[43] Some of the attributes, on the other hand, may have had a significance that is difficult to understand, such as the flower in the hand of the man on the Weisenau monument[44] or the pineapple on another relief from a tombstone in Mainz.[45]

[36] Böhme-Schönberger 1995, 3. For the different types of Venus, compare Brinke 1991, 126–31.

[37] E.g., compare the stele of Egnatia Gaiae in Rimini: Pflug 1989, 163–64, no. 30, pl. 7.1. Inscriptions: von Hesberg Tonn 1983, 214–15.

[38] Von Hesberg Tonn 1983, 220–21.

[39] Petron. *Sat.* 71.11.

[40] Bauchenss 1975, 85–86, pl. 30.1; Boppert 1996, 48–53, no. 1, pls. 1–2.

[41] Von Hesberg Tonn 1983, 221–22.

[42] Schoppa 1958, 288–89, pl. 57.3; Wild 1968a, 200, fig. 21; Boppert 1996, 69–71, no. 12, pl. 16.

[43] Compare a similar phenomenon in the imperial portraits in the provinces: Zanker 1983.

[44] For his earlier interpretation as a gardener: Boppert 1996, 52. For the flower as indication of the veneration of the tomb: Sinn 1987, 54–56; Kockel 1993, 55; von Hesberg 2002, 46–48. He evidently died after his wife, as shown by the mask that covered his head during his lifetime: Boppert 1996, 52.

[45] Boppert 1995, fig. 4.

Even the association between women and men, children, or slaves corresponded to the patterns as they were known in Italy. As indicated above, the different members of the family are placed next to each other in a strikingly emotionless fashion. Only barely noticeable turns of the body, such as on the sepulchral monument from Weisenau for instance, indicate the couple's attachment.[46] The most important quality of the role that the represented persons are trying to communicate is that of their representative appearance in public. This appearance, in turn, entails the appropriate controlled behavior.

In spite of the differing costume and peculiar jewelry, the persons represented follow the Roman value system, which again forms a constituent part of the roles of the different social groups.[47] This applies above all to women and children, whereas men obviously express certain liberties, such as being seated (as seen on the sepulchral monument in Weisenau). This, in turn, leads to a stronger limitation on their representative quality, and for this reason fewer examples may be stated for Italy.

This system of values is not compromised, however, by costume and its component parts. Whether clad in tunica with pallium or wearing the costume of Menimane (fig. 11), the role retains its determinant character. This might be compared to the modern range of clothing possibilities that do not necessarily allude to different roles and new values. The resort to folkloristic patterns in dressing (as may be found in some regions of Germany) may be quite appropriate for one's rank and quite suitable for attending the opera. In this way, a special local tradition is articulated, as is a pride in demonstrating it perhaps, and this I would suppose is a sign of local identity. At the same time, this identity only finds validation through membership within a larger one, that of the Roman Empire.[48] But this identity exists only in reference to the husband, for women of local origin married to Romans could represent themselves in Roman garments as well, like the person of Bella cited above (fig. 6),[49] or a certain Louba, a woman of Ubian origin, perhaps with an indigenous type of clothing,[50] or a sculpture of an unknown woman from a tomb building on Luxemburger Straße in Cologne (perhaps she was the indigenous wife of a rich Ubian or Roman).[51] As all of these examples illustrate, it is only by questioning the conventions related to the form and manner of dressing that clothing may violate the rule. On the monuments in question, such a possibility is excluded in advance by their context. As is revealed by their attributes and their social interaction, these women act in full accordance with Roman rules.

As far as the images allow such interpretation, roles—as represented in Roman culture within the field of the family—are not impaired by the integration of the local population, at least not with regard to the roles of women and children in the first century A.D. Some of the peculiarities could possibly be exhibited in a more extensive manner, as for instance in the jewelry, which is not represented on Roman monuments very often. (For there its demonstrative display would have been interpreted as luxury.)[52] However, such deviations from the standard could be integrated into these roles, as this was a type of customary adornment in the provinces, albeit one with its own conventions and limitations (a lack of precious stones or inability for conspicuous display).

[46] Boppert 1996, 48–53, no. 1, pls. 1–2. Sometimes the status of the deceased is difficult to define: Böhme-Schönberger 1995, 3 n. 8.

[47] Schenke 2003, 51–61, 168–71.

[48] Garbsch 1965, 10–11, 23 (local references in special forms of bonnets); Böhme-Schönberger 1995, 11; Boppert 1995.

[49] See n. 10 above.

[50] For Louba, see Noelke 1977, 7–9; Müller 1977, 19, 111, no. 325, pl. 98.

[51] Wild 1968b, 17 pl. 17.2; Andrikopoulou-Strack 1986, 173, pl. 19.2.

[52] In the relief sculpture in Italy, women are represented with only a few objects of jewelry: Lenertz 1992, 56–57; Schenke 2003, 102–13.

As THE COMPARISON with the monuments of the second and third century from the beginning of this chapter was intended to illustrate, the representation of roles changed over the course of time. I think it could be quite easily demonstrated that the roles do not change completely, however, for certain fundamental values that were already accepted in the first century A.D. were expressed in the same way. This becomes evident when considering the forms of dress, postures, and placement of figures vis-à-vis one another. Even the characteristics of a certain folkloristic tradition recede into the background. And yet the family finds a new definition in these images. The relationship among the different individuals is now defined by emotions to a much greater degree.[53] This does not, however, indicate a basic change in the institution of the family. It reflects, moreover, a certain shift of meaning. The first century A.D. sought to find in the definition of roles a reference to the public image of the community. The family was ranked below that. During this time the togati prevailed. Women and children presented themselves as if statues in the forum. This characteristic was called into question by additions like the dog, the spindle, etc., but, on the other hand, it was further accentuated by the rigidly frontal position, which was always regarded as an especially provincial disposition.

In the second and third century, the other representations also give a general idea of domesticity, of schooling, as well as of the private amusements of men and women.[54] The reason why the roles attain a different quality lies in the change of the individual's relationship to the family and to society as a whole. The value of the family as a focus increases, as does the value of those particular qualities that are regarded as characteristic of it: solidarity, intimacy, and responsibility. I would like to conclude that, fundamentally, it was not the roles as such that changed but only the classification of their meaning against the background of comprehensive social change. These representations at least suggest that their purchasers now saw the sense of their respective roles primarily within the closer field of the family, thus offering possibilities of perception and of visualization that broke away from the old ideals of stateliness.[55]

[53] Von Massow 1932, 125–59, figs. 76, 106; Freigang 1997, 318–25; Hope 2001, 76–81.

[54] Mehl 1997, 64–69; Freigang 1997, 323–29, 363–64.

[55] For the general change in tombs: Zanker 1992, 350–58.

Works Cited

Andrikopoulou-Strack, J.-N., *Grabbauten des 1. Jahrhunderts n. Chr. im Rheingebiet*, *Bonner Jahrbücher* Beiheft 43 (Bonn 1986).

Bauchenss, G., "Römische Grabmäler aus den Randgebieten des Neuwieder Beckens," *Jahrbuch des römisch-germanischen Zentralmuseums, Mainz* 22 (1975) 81–95.

———, *Zivile Grabdenkmäler*, *Corpus signorum imperii romani*, Deutschland 3.2 (Bonn 1978).

Berger, P. L., and T. Luckmann, *The Social Construction of Reality: A Treatise in the Sociology of Knowledge* (Garden City, N.Y. 1966).

Böhme, A., "Tracht und Bestattungssitten in den germanischen Provinzen und in der Belgica," in *Aufstieg und Niedergang der römischen Welt*, ed. H. Temporini (Berlin and New York 1985) 2.12.3:423–55.

Böhme-Schönberger, A., "Das Mainzer Grabmal von Menimane und Blussus als Zeugnis des Romanisierungsprozesses," in *Provinzialrömische Forschungen. Festschrift G. Ulbert*, ed. W. Czysz, C.-M. Hüssen, H.-P. Kuhnen, C. S. Sommer, and G. Weber (Epelkamp 1995) 1–12.

Boppert, W., "Zur bildlichen Darstellung der einheimischen Bevölkerung in Mainz auf Grabdenkmälern des 1. Jhs.," in *2. Internationales Kolloquium über Probleme des provinzialrömischen Kunstschaffens. Vorträge der Tagung in Veszprém (14.–18. Mai 1991)*, ed. M. Praznovsky (Veszprém 1995) 91–95.

———, *Zivile Grabsteine aus Mainz und Umgebung*, *Corpus signorum imperii romani* Deutschland 2.6 (Mainz 1996).

Breuer, C., *Reliefs und Epigramme griechischer Privatgrabmäler* (Cologne, Weimar, and Vienna 1995).

Brinke, M., *Kopienkritische und typologische Untersuchungen zur statuarischen Überlieferung der Aphrodite Typus Louvre-Neapel*, Antiquitates 1 (Hamburg 1991).

Diebner S., *Reperti funerari in Umbria a sinistra del Tevere*, Archaeologica 67 (Rome 1989).

Dragendorff, H., and E. Krüger, *Das Grabmal von Igel* (Trier 1924).

Edmondson, J., T. Nogales Basarrate, and W. Trillmich, eds., *Imagen y Memoria—monumentos funerarios con retratos en la Colonia Augusta Emerita* (Madrid 2001).

Faust, W., *Die Grabstelen des 2. und 3. Jahrhunderts im Rheingebiet*, *Bonner Jahrbücher* Beiheft 52 (Bonn 1998).

Freigang, Y., "Die Grabmäler der gallo-römischen Kultur im Moselland," *Jahrbuch des Römisch-germanischen Zentralmuseums, Mainz* 44 (1997) 278–440.

Frenz, H. G., *Römische Grabreliefs in Mittel- und Süditalien*, Archaeologica 37 (Rome 1985).

———, *Bauplastik und Porträts aus Mainz und Umgebung*, *Corpus signorum imperii romani*, Deutschland 2.7 (Mainz 1992).

Frova, A., "Monumenti Funerari Romani di Luni," in *Archaeologica. Scritti in Onore di A. Neppi Modona*, ed. N. Caffarello (Florence 1975) 297–305.

Gabelmann, H., "Die Frauenstatue aus Aachen-Burtscheid," *Bonner Jahrbücher* 179 (1979) 209–50.

Galsterer, H., and B. Galsterer, *Die römischen Steininschriften aus Köln* (Cologne 1975).

Garbsch, J., *Die norisch-pannonische Frauentracht im 1. und 2. Jh.*, Münchner Beiträge zur Vor- und Frühgeschichte 11 (Munich 1965).

Gergel, R. A., "Costume as Geographic Indicator: Barbarians and Prisoners on Cuirassed Breastplates," in *The World of Roman Costume*, ed. J. L. Sebesta and L. Bonfante (Madison 1994) 191–209.

Ghedini, F., *Sculture greche e romane del Museo Civico di Padova*, Collezioni e musei archeologici del Veneto 12 (Rome 1980)

Giuliani, L., *Bildnis und Botschaft* (Frankfurt 1986).

Hatt, J.-J., *La tombe Gallo-romaine—recherches sur les inscriptions et les monuments funéraires gallo-romains* (Paris 1986).

Hesberg, H. von, "Bildsyntax und Erzählweise in der hellenistischen Flächenkunst," *Jahrbuch des deutschen archäologischen Instituts* 103 (1988) 309–65.

———, "Il profumo del marmor—cambiamenti nei riti di seppelimento e nei monumenti funerari nel 1. sec. d.C.," in *Espacios y usos funerarios en el Occidente Romano*, ed. D. Vaquerizo Gil (Córdoba 2002) 34–49.

Hesberg Tonn, B. von, *Coniunx Carissima—Untersuchungen zum Normcharakter im Erscheinungsbild der römischen Frau* (Stuttgart 1983).

Hölscher, T., "Gemma Augustea," in *Kaiser Augustus und die verlorene Republik: eine Ausstellung im Martin-Gropius-Bau, Berlin, 7. Juni–14. August 1988*, ed. W. Dieter-Heilmeyer (Mainz 1988) 371–72.

Hope, V. M., *Constructing Identity: The Roman Funerary Monuments of Aquileia, Mainz and Nimes*, British Archaeological Reports International Series 960 (Oxford 2001).

Joly, M., *Langres*, Carte archéologique de la Gaule 52.2 (Paris 2001).

Kähler, H., *Alberti Rubeni dissertatio de Gemma Augustea*, Monumenta Artis Romanae 9 (Berlin 1968).

Kleiner, D. E. E., *Roman Imperial Funerary Altars with Portraits*, Archaeologica 62 (Rome 1987).

Kockel, V., *Porträtreliefs stadtrömischer Grabbauten* (Mainz 1993).

Kremer, G., *Antike Grabbauten in Noricum*, Sonderschriften des österreichischen archäologischen Instituts 36 (Vienna 2001).

Kurzynski, K. von, *". . . und ihre Hosen nennen sie bracas." Textilfunde und Textiltechnologie der Hallstatt- und Latènezeit und ihr Kontext*, Internationale Archäologie 22 (Espelkamp 1996).

Kyll, N., "Heidnische Weihe- und Votivgaben aus der Römerzeit des Trierer Landes," *Trierer Zeitschrift für Geschichte und Kunst des Trierer Landes und seiner Nachbargebiete* 29 (1966) 7–114.

Lehner, H., *Die antiken Steindenkmäler des Provinzialmuseums in Bonn* (Bonn 1918).

Lenertz, R. A., "Die statuarische Selbstdarstellung der Frauen in den Vesuvstädten" (Magisterarbeit, Universität zu Köln 1992).

Martin-Kilcher, S., "Gräber der späten Republik und der frühen Kaiserzeit am Lago Maggiore: Tradition und Romanisierung," in *Bestattungssitte und kulturelle Identität*, ed. P. Fasold, T. Fischer, H. von Hesberg, and M. Witteyer, Xantener Berichte 7 (Cologne 1998) 191–252.

Massow, W. von, *Die Grabmäler von Neumagen* (Berlin and Leipzig 1932).

Mehl, A., "Wirtschaft, Gesellschaft, Totenglauben: Die 'Igeler Säule' bei Trier und ihrer Grabherren," *Laverna* 8 (1997) 59–92.

Müller, G., *Die römischen Gräberfelder von Novaesium*, Novaesium 7, Limesforschungen 17 (Berlin 1977).

Neuffer, E., "Ein römisches Familiengrabmal bei Nickenich," *Germania* 16 (1932) 22–28.

Noelke, P., "Grabsteine aus dem römischen Neuss," *Neusser Jahrbuch* 4 (1977) 7–9.

Pelletier, A., *La femme dans la société gallo-romaine* (Paris 1984).

Perl, G., *Tacitus, Germania*, Griechische und lateinische Quellen zur Frühgeschichte Mitteleuropas 2 (Berlin 1990).

Pflug, H., *Römische Porträtstelen in Oberitalien* (Mainz 1989).

Pfuhl, E., "Das Beiwerk auf ostgriechischen Grabreliefs," *Jahrbuch des deutschen archäologischen Instituts* 20 (1905) 47–96, 123–55.

Polaschek, K., "Zur Zeitstellung einiger römischer Bildnisse im Landesmuseum Trier," *Trierer Zeitschrift* 34 (1971) 119–42.

Precht, G., *Das Grabmal des L. Poblicius*, 2nd ed. (Cologne 1979).

Puttock, S., *Ritual Significance of Personal Ornament in Roman Britain*, British Archaeological Reports British Series 327 (Oxford 2002).

Riedel, M., "Frühe römische Gräber in Köln," in *Bestattungssitte und kulturelle Identität*, ed. P. Fasold, T. Fischer, H. von Hesberg, and M. Witteyer, Xantener Berichte 7 (Cologne 1998) 307–18.

Schenke, G., *Sein und Schein—Schmuckgebrauch in der römischen Kaiserzeit: eine sozio-ökonomische Studie anhand von Bild und Dokument*, Monographs on Antiquity 1 (Louvain 2003).

Schober, A., *Die römischen Grabsteine von Noricum und Pannonien*, Sonderschriften des österreichischen archäologischen Instituts 10 (Vienna 1923).

Schoppa, H., "Keltische Einflüsse in der provinzial-römischen Plastik," *Bonner Jahrbücher* 158 (1958) 268–94.

Settis, S., "Die Ara Pacis," in *Kaiser Augustus und die verlorene Republik: eine Ausstellung im Martin-Gropius-Bau, Berlin, 7. Juni–14. August 1988*, ed. W. Dieter-Heilmeyer (Mainz 1988) 400–425.

Simon, E., *Ara Pacis Augustae* (Tübingen 1967).

Sinn, F., *Stadtrömische Marmorurnen* (Mainz 1987).

Spickermann, W., *"Mulieres ex voto." Untersuchungen zur Götterverehrung von Frauen im römischen Gallien, Germanien und Rätien* (Bochum 1994).

Trillmich, W., "De altar a tabernáculo: evolución, tipológica y artística de un modelo de representación funeraria," in *Imagen y Memoria—monumentos funerarios con retratos en la Colonia Augusta Emerita*, ed. J. Edmondson, T. Nogales Basarrate, and W. Trillmich (Madrid 2001) 19–36.

Varone, A., "Stele funerarie del Museo dell'Agro Nocerino," *Rivista di studi pompeiani* 3 (1989) 7–28.

Weber-Kellermann, I., *Die Familie: Geschichte, Geschichten und Bilder* (Frankfurt am Main 1976).

Wild, J. P., "Clothing in the North-Western Provinces of the Roman Empire," *Bonner Jahrbücher* 168 (1968a) 166–240.

———, "Die Frauentracht der Ubier," *Germania* 46 (1968b) 67–73.

———, "The Clothing of Britannia, Gallia Belgica and Germania Inferior," in *Aufstieg und Niedergang der römischen Welt*, ed. H. Temporini (Berlin and New York 1985) 2.12.3:362–422.

Zanker, P., "Grabreliefs römischer Freigelassener," *Jahrbuch des deutschen archäologischen Instituts* 90 (1975) 266–315.

———, "Zur Rezeption des hellenistischen Individualporträts in Rom und in den italischen Städten," in *Hellenismus in Mittelitalien*, ed. P. Zanker, 2 vols., *Abhandlungen der Akademie der Wissenschaften zu Göttingen* 97 (Göttingen 1976) 2:581–619.

———, *Provinzielle Kaiserporträts—Zur Rezeption der Selbstdarstellung des Prinzeps*, Bayerische Akademie der Wissenschaften, München, Philosophisch-historische Klasse, Abhandlungen 90 (Munich 1983).

———, "Bürgerliche Selbstdarstellung am Grab im römischen Kaiserreich," in *Die römische Stadt im 2. Jh. n. Chr.*, Kolloquium Xanten 1990, ed. H. Schalles, H. von Hesberg, and P. Zanker, Xantener Berichte 2 (Cologne 1992) 339–58.

14 ◆ MUSES AS MODELS:
LEARNING AND THE COMPLICITY OF AUTHORITY

Inge Lyse Hansen

This chapter will examine a particular group of images that represents one of the most popular decorative choices on sarcophagi in the period between the mid-third and early fourth century A.D.—depictions of learned couples, or Muses and philosophers. Around the middle of the third century the only other narrative choice more popular on sarcophagi was depictions of hunting, superseded in sheer numbers only by imagery of seasons and of bucolic scenes.[1] The reading of these images will focus on the possibilities for (self-)representation that this rich body of material offered to the patrons of the sarcophagi, and for this reason much of the discussion will be centered on examples in which portrait features have been added to the figures of the learned men and women. I am particularly interested in the interaction between the individual and the model in whose guise he or she is depicted: how the figure of learning acts as a role model for the individual, how learning is presented as a model of behavior conditioning the representative range for the individual, and how the act of appropriating particular characteristics casts the individual as a model worthy of emulation.

In the following I will focus on the depictions of learned couples and in particular on the role played by the Muses in these depictions as models for women. As a female model that could be used as a foil for the rendering of portrait features, the Muse is the most popular choice of figural decoration in the third century—more popular even than Venus or the other figure to gain an exceptional popularity in this period, Ariadne. Therefore, the Muses must have represented an attractive role model for contemporary patrons and a potent iconographic scheme for the imaging of Roman women during that period. As in practically all of the narrative schemes, for which the rectangular format of a sarcophagus is so eminently suited, the viewing of these learned men and women is undertaken by multiple spectators—internal and external to the relief field.[2] What I want to propose here is that the relationship between the internal viewers offers a key for the reading of these depictions for the external viewers.

My aim in the following is twofold: first, to show how the imaging of women as Muses can be placed within the same social framework as their male counterparts—that is, a particularized reading specifically of the Muses as (role) models for individual women; second, to suggest that these reliefs offer a wider rhetorical reading based on the relation among the internal viewers in the reliefs, the formal arrangement of the compositions, and a comparison with other motifs popular during this period—that is, a symbolic reading in which the depicted individuals themselves appear as role models for their descendants and other viewers of these sarcophagi.

My thanks to the conference speakers and participants for the stimulating conversation offered in response to this paper, and to those who read early drafts of it, in particular Janet Huskinson, Natalie Kampen, and Bert Smith, as well as Jane Fejfer, Jessica Hughes, and Sharon Salvadori, all of whom offered invaluable comments and corrections. All mistakes naturally remain my own.

[1] Ewald 1999. Cf. Trimble 2002, 507 and D'Ambra 2001, as well as Fittschen 1972 and Huskinson in this volume.

[2] Sharrock 2002, 266–67.

Fig. 1. Sarcophagus front with seated couple and eight standing Muses.
Vatican Museums (photo Anger, DAIR, inst. neg. 1993 Vat 1019).

Fig. 2. Strigillated sarcophagus with three individual figural fields.
Porto Torres, Basilica of S. Gavino (photo Koppermann, DAIR, inst. neg. 1966.2174).

Patrons as Pendants: The Muse and Philosopher as Counterparts

Figures 1 and 2 illustrate some of the most common pictorial schemes for the depiction of learned couples.[3] In figure 1 a couple is portrayed seated facing each other within the rather shallow picture space of the sarcophagus front; around and behind them are eight Muses clearly identifiable by the feathers in their hair and by their individual attributes. The man, who is dressed in a himation, raises one hand as if in address and holds a book-scroll in the other; more scrolls are placed on the ground by his feet. The woman holds a lyre, which she seems to have been handed from the Muse standing in front of her, and below her chair is a kithara, presumably belonging to the Muse standing behind

[3] Figure 1: Vatican Museums, Museo Pio Clementino, Cortile Ottagono (inv. no. 976); ca. A.D. 255–70. For further details, see Ewald 1999, 173, no. E6, pls. 51.2, 52.2, 53.2; Wegner 1966, 57–58, no. 138, 131, pl. 68; Wrede 1981, 290, no. 250; and Zanker 1995, 270–71, fig. 146. Figure 2: Porto Torres (Sardinia), Basilica of S. Gavino (crypt); ca. A.D. 240. See further Ewald 1999, 156, no. C9, pl. 27.1; Wegner 1966, 40, no. 81, 137, pls. 76a, 81b, 82c/d; Wrede 1981, 287–88, no. 244.

her. One of the Muses is missing from the scene, and so, though depicted formally without any of the attributes of a Muse, the seated woman must be seen as the ninth, completing their number. Figure 2 is a more economical version of the same idea. On this strigillated sarcophagus now in Sardinia, two standing figures—a bare-chested philosopher in a himation and a female figure (possibly with portrait features) in a pose common to the Muse Calliope—frame a central couple. The male figure of this couple is represented in a manner almost identical to the learned man in figure 1, whereas the female figure is shown standing with her legs crossed and her elbow leaning on a column—a pose associated with the Muse Polyhymnia.

The two images also illustrate why the Muse representations, and the Polyhymnia pose in particular, have been seen as problematic. The hierarchical organization of the internal viewers gives a predominance and narrative emphasis to the couple at the expense of the goddesses and professional philosophers. This is more clearly expressed in the Vatican relief (fig. 1) in which the Muses are entirely engaged with the two mortal figures, whereas the couple is engaged in a dialogue with each other. Representing the mortal woman in the guise of a Muse in this way renders her status in relation to the seated man ambiguous: is she his personal muse who inspires him to produce great works?[4] Or is the kithara meant to indicate her own proficiency in the traditional female accomplishments of the elite?[5] Equally, the internal relationship between the couple (as in fig. 2) often situates him in a more active role. Is he supervising the teaching of his pupil-wife, or is she simply an iconographic foil for highlighting his learned status?[6] In this case it is somewhat unclear whether he is speaking to anyone but himself.[7] In recent years, the image of the male figure in these reliefs has been the subject of much innovative work. In particular, Björn Ewald's monograph, *Der Philosoph als Leitbild*, has given substance to these depictions as a corpus and has added greatly to the contemporary contextualization of their meaning. The increasingly nuanced picture and the broadened interpretative scope gained by recent research enable us to apply similar approaches in reading the depictions of the Muses.[8]

The cultural and social context of late antiquity that informs the creation of these images has been described by Peter Brown as a sharply pointed pyramid open at the base.[9] On the one hand, social differentiation is more marked than earlier, with a senatorial elite in the west that is estimated to be five times as rich as that of the first century.[10] On the other, there is an unprecedented opportunity for upward mobility at most social levels. It is the developments of the third century that created many of the conditions for this. In A.D. 212 Roman citizenship was extended to provincials, while even the emperors themselves might be of obscure social backgrounds. Around 260 the senatorial aristocracy was excluded from holding military commands, and the posts filled with professional officers of non-aristocratic rank.[11] The third century saw a rise in the status of not only military men but also the administrators of the empire, and the expanded bureaucracy would

[4] Zanker 1995; Huskinson 1999.

[5] Ewald 1999, 51–52; D'Ambra 2001, 365.

[6] I.e.,, much as Plutarch advises his friend Pollianus to be the "guide, philosopher and teacher" to his wife Eurydice (*Mor.* 145a). On the ideal of the husband as a teacher of his wife, see Hemelrijk 1999, 31–36.

[7] Zanker (1995, 271) notes this but does not elaborate.

[8] Cf. n. 2 above, to which should be added also Huskinson 1999 and Zanker and Ewald 2004, in particular 236–38.

[9] Brown 1971, 32.

[10] Brown 1971, 34.

[11] Brown 1971, 24; Hopkins 1965, 17; Diocletian was a son of a freedman from Dalmatia; Galerius was a former cattle herdsman from Carpathia. The rising status of the military is evident also in the inclusion of legionaries among the privileged class of *honestiores* in A.D. 240; this new class now comprised the top privileged groups of senator, *equites* and *decuriones* (now unified also with the legionaries).

Fig. 3. The so-called
Plotinus sarcophagus.
Vatican Museums
(photo Faraglia, DAIR,
inst. neg. 1935.1981).

have provided ample opportunities for middle-class upward mobility and for cultural identification through adherence to traditional classical learning.[12]

The new and extrovert emphasis on the status of learning is evident in images where the seated learned man has adopted the frontal pose normally associated with magistrates and rulers (cf. the so-called Plotinus relief: fig. 3).[13] It is interesting how late third-century imagery represents a reformulation of traditional symbols for entirely contemporary purposes without necessarily representing a break with the inherent meaning behind these symbols. Classical learning now gains meaning as a symbol of career opportunity and at the same time reinforces traditional norms and values as a common cultural language.[14] Indeed, learning becomes a symbol signifying both *otium* and *negotium*.[15] Hence the image of the learned man can also be found as part of the way a fully rounded Roman aristocrat is depicted, as on the so-called Brother Sarcophagus now in Naples.[16] Here the same man is represented four times in various guises: on the far left in the new-style *toga contabulata* (or banded toga) indicative of magisterial office; in the center in the pallium of a learned man, and in another new-style toga with a shoulder umbo, characterizing him as a fashionable Roman citizen; and on the far right in a heavily draped toga in the style of the early empire. In the latter aspect he is also depicted as part of a wedding scene, and the slightly old-fashioned aspect of the toga underscores his adherence to traditional values and virtues.[17]

[12] Hopkins 1965, 16–19; Brown 1971, 29–32; Zanker 1995, 279.

[13] Figure 3: Vatican Museums, Museo Gregoriano Profano (inv. no. 9504), ca. A.D. 280. On this sarcophagus fragment, see also Ewald 1999, 167–69, no. D3, pls. 42–43; Wegner 1966, 47, no. 116, 130, pls. 64b, 70–71; Wrede 1981, 290–91, no. 252; and Zanker 1995, 279, fig. 150.

[14] Ewald 1999, 58–60, 78, 131; Trimble 2002, 510; D'Ambra 2001, 365; Zanker 1995, 277–78.

[15] Ewald 1999, 59; Trimble 2002, 509; Zanker 1995, 282. Cf. Hopkins (1965, 18–19), who identifies the continuity

of an aristocratic ethos in the reward system as being part of what prevented a revolution based on a professional bourgeoisie.

[16] Naples, Museo Archeologico Nazionale (inv. no. 6603); see Ewald 1999, 200–201, no. G9; Zanker 1995, 279–81, fig. 151; and see further Hölscher's contribution in this volume.

[17] A description of the same composite depiction of a single person can be found also in a private honorific context. A painting of the emperor Tacitus (A.D. 275–76) in the villa of the Quintilii depicted him respectively as *togatus*, *chlamydatus*, *armatus*, *palliates*, and *venatorio habitu* (in toga, military cloak, armor, Greek mantle, and hunting outfit); SHA, *Tac.* 16.2.

Fig. 4. Front panel of a columnar sarcophagus. Vatican Museums (photo Anger, DAIR, inst. neg. 1993 Vat 0701).

Establishing the composite nature of the image of the learned man and its value as a depiction of a socialized persona enables us to do the same for the image of the learned woman. In the Plotinus relief (fig. 3), three figures are given portrait features: the central man and the two women in the poses of Polyhymnia and Calliope, respectively. Both women are veiled; the former holds a fold of the veil close to her face in the manner of the *pudicitia* gesture; the latter holds a book-scroll. The three form a cohesive, almost closed unit, seemingly unaware of the three philosophers included in the depiction. What is particularly interesting in this image is the attitude of equilibrium between male-female and public-private spheres that this relief projects. The classic bare-chested philosopher figure in himation on the far left is balanced on the right by a figure who must originally have been intended to be a Muse but who was adapted to depict another sage by the addition of a bearded male head.[18] The low-relief head of the philosopher by the seated man's right shoulder is balanced by an extravagant knotted curtain. Of all the subsidiary figures the latter is the only one appearing to communicate into the closed unit of the portrait figures, and it is tempting to read him as a symbol of exemplary council. If this figure suggests exemplary behavior in public affairs, the *parapetasma* may denote a complementary exemplary domestic life. The depiction, in other words, establishes a series of balancing and inter-related symbols: philosopher-Muse, male-female, public-private. In this, the two women contribute to the articulation of the official image of the ideal family as much as the seated man does.

Similarly, in a sarcophagus relief of ca. A.D. 240 now in the Vatican Museums (fig. 4), the male and female figures in two three-figure groups are represented as mirroring each other in drapery arrangement and gesture.[19] Paul Zanker has suggested that the subtle differences between these two figure groups indicate that they should be read as images referring to philosophical and rhetorical learning, respectively: the tightly wrapped mantle enveloping the right arm may denote an orator, whereas the looser type leaving the arm free to gesture may indicate a teacher.[20] The values

[18] Ewald (1999, 168) suggests that the lower part of this figure, with the detail of the visible long female undergarment, may not belong to the relief. However, other features give this figure a distinct feminine air, including the pronounced right breast framed within the drapery fold and the soft curvature of the hips, which is accentuated on the left side by the arrangement of the folds of the pallium.

[19] Figure 4: Vatican Museums, Museo Pio Clementino,

Cortile Ottagono (inv. no. 871), ca. A.D. 230–40. For further details on this relief, see Ewald 1999, 171–72, no. E1, pls. 48–49; Wegner 1966, 55–56, no. 135, 132–33, pls. 55a, 57–58, 63a, 100a; Wrede 1981, 287, no. 243; and Zanker 1995, 275–76, fig. 148.

[20] Zanker 1995, 275–76. A similar interpretation has been proposed by R. R. Smith for the drapery arrangement in statues from Aphrodisias: the looser drapery type leaving

of tradition and the discipline of the good citizen, as well as the all-embracing concept of learning, are here significantly reflected in the manner of representation of the women as well. In both of the two three-figure groups there is a correspondence in the arrangement of the drapery between the seated man and the standing woman facing him. On the left, both are shown with their right arm wrapped in an arm-sling fold and held tight toward the chest; on the right, both are depicted gesturing and wearing drapery of loose and rich folds. In the iconography of the representation there is therefore a convincing correspondence in the imaging of learned men and women.

Indeed, in the cases where a woman is shown in the guise of a specific Muse (as in figs. 2–3), the overwhelming preferences are for Calliope and Polyhymnia. Calliope is the foremost of the Muses associated with epic poetry; Polyhymnia is the Muse of word and narration. In a sense, these figures most closely embody the aspects of rhetoric, teaching, and discourse that are identified in the motif of the male figure.[21] In fact, if these particular Muses are shown with an attribute, it is always a book-scroll: the attribute that, together with the pallium, is used to characterize the learned man.

Viewed as a model for women, the goddess can, in other words, be interpreted along very similar lines to that posed by the image of the philosopher-style figure for men. This is particularly clear when women are depicted alone or in the company of other women. The visual authority invested in these images is as explicit as it is in depictions of learned men, and the book-scroll as an attribute becomes as ubiquitous for depictions of women as it had been for men. When not accompanied by a male partner, women are often depicted in a standing pose reminiscent of the stance of Calliope, but turned frontally toward the viewer of the relief, and most often at the center of the composition.[22] At the same time, significant differences occur in the depictions of men and women in these reliefs. For instance, the frontal seated pose reminiscent of magisterial status is never used for women.[23] Further, the pose of Polyhymnia gives her an aspect of listening to rather than discoursing with her male companion. Since this relative passivity of women only occurs when they are depicted in the company of men, it must indicate an intent to depict the values of a traditional ideal couple and serves as a qualifying nuance to the greater narrative visibility given to women in this period.[24]

Yet this less extrovert role also situates these women in an implied relationship similar to that of philosophers to magistrates; that is, in an advisory function in which the two appear as complementary.[25] The indirect influence exerted by the philosopher, and his position as outside the political system, is in many ways similar to the access of influence and position of Roman women.[26]

---

the arm free is characterized as "the posture of speaking, of calm, modest address," the more tightly wrapped version as "a public posture of reserve and discipline, waiting to speak and act" (Smith 1998, 66). On draped Roman female statuary, see also Davies in this volume.

[21] A point also noted by Ewald (1999, 129).

[22] These observations are discussed in more detail by Janet Huskinson (1999, 197–200), whose incisive article also discusses how the association with the Muses represents an important body of evidence for the increased visibility of women in the arts of the third century.

[23] Though depictions of women seated in a three-quarter pose, like seated philosophers, do occur; cf. Kranz 1954, 229, no. 181, pl. 74.7. This sarcophagus depiction of a woman, in which the face has been left as a boss, is directly comparable with that of a seated male figure, possibly with portrait fea-

tures; Kranz 1954, 229–30, no. 183, pl. 74.6. Both sarcophagi are in Rome (though without provenance) and dated between the late third and early fourth century A.D.

[24] Cf. Hansen forthcoming a; Huskinson 1999.

[25] A contemporary example of the interplay between learning/philosophy and politics can be found in Constantine's erection of ancient statues of Muses in the senate in Constantinople; Zos. 5.24, cf. Mango 1963, 57. However, the same tradition is also found in Hellenistic Alexandria, especially the position of the *Museion* within the royal palace; Strabo 17.1.8, cf. Welch 2003, 25.

[26] Dixon 1983; Flory 1997, 120–21. Cf. Dio's (57.12.3) description of Livia: "except that she never ventured to enter the senate chamber or the camps or the public assemblies, she undertook to manage everything [. . .] for in the time of Augustus she had possessed the greatest influence."

The gendered image is therefore constructed not solely on the basis of a contrasting relationship of active masculinity to passive femininity but also on a relative relationship in which learned women interact with men, just as learned men interact with political authority.[27]

Between Viewers and Viewed: The Complicity of Auctoritas

A set of moral values, social connotations, and cultural contexts can, in other words, be established for both the male and the female models of philosophers and Muses. In this the learned couple appears as a model of social aspiration within a framework of Roman cultural values, which offers the individual patrons an image through which to project a visual identity of themselves. The few sarcophagi for which the social status of the patron can be identified—for example, by inscription—suggest that the cultured image of learning had a broad social target group: from a commander in the praetorian guard to a pimp.[28] The popularity of the Muse sarcophagi is clearly not restricted to being a descriptive evaluation of the attainment of cultural accomplishments but rather as an indication of the desire to be seen as partaking in the moral values exemplified by learning. These images consequently lend themselves to a wider symbolic interpretation. From the particularized reading of these images, I want to suggest that a wider symbolic interpretation can be constructed for the narrative choice of these reliefs as a whole (and, indeed, around other "mythological" sarcophagus depictions)—in this case, particularly the virtue, or ideal, of *auctoritas*.[29]

In the previous section, the emphasis was deliberately placed upon depictions of couples and, indeed, the internal relationship between the two suggests that the reliefs should be read as emblematic articulations of this cardinal virtue. The imposing aspect of the seated couple facing each other from either end of the relief field, as in figure 1, confers a sense of control upon their visual world, in which the Muses themselves are reduced to a series of caryatids upholding and affirming their constructed cultural universe. As discussed earlier, the two dominate the picture field by effectively excluding any of the other internal viewers in the scene and by maintaining eye contact only between themselves. The symmetrical arrangement of the two emphasizes the formalized aspect of the scene, and their relationship appears as one of authoritative respect. The same can be found in the figurative scenes that concentrate entirely on the primary protagonists (figs. 2–4). Indeed, a reading of this nature suggests that the idiom of the standing Polyhymnia type figure with seated male himation figure exemplifies a rhetoric of authority and *concordia*.

The particular formal aspects of this type of imagery are especially clear when compared to other types of mythological narratives popular in the third century, such as the scenes of Ariadne and Dionysus (fig. 5).[30] The depictions of this couple represent some of the most explicitly erotic of the scenes of couples.[31] This is not simply due to the full or partial nudity of the female figure or her

[27] For a more detailed discussion on gendered iconographic relationships on sarcophagi of this period, see Hansen forthcoming a; Hansen forthcoming b.

[28] Respectively the sarcophagus of L. Pullio Peregrino (Rome, Museo Torlonia, inv. no. 424) and the sarcophagus of M. Sempronius Nikokrates (London, British Museum, inv. no. Sc. 2313, GR 1805.7-3.152); Ewald 1999, 152, no. C1, 216, no. I7.

[29] *Auctoritas* as an inherent value in these depictions has been

identified also by Zanker (1995, 277–79).

[30] Figure 5: Paris, Louvre (inv. no. 1346), ca. A.D. 230–40. See Baratte and Metzger 1985, 138–42; Matz 1968–75, 394–97, no. 222, pls. 234, 237–45; Wrede 1981, 210, no. 50. See also Zanker and Ewald 2004, 306–12 for a discussion of the motif in general.

[31] The erotic quality of Ariadne is evident also in literary references to her; cf. Catull. 64.50–264; Nonnus *Dion.* 47.271–94; Prop. 1.3.1–20, 2.3.17–20; Xen. *Symp.* 9.3–7. See also Clarke

*Fig. 5. Sarcophagus with Ariadne and Dionysus. Paris, Musée du Louvre
(photo Bildarchiv Foto Marburg, neg. 180.354).*

half-reclining, open body posture with one or both arms raised above her head but more particularly to the quality of the gaze between the protagonists. Ariadne is approached by Dionysus and gazed upon by him; indeed, the significance of the gaze is often highlighted by the presence of a satyr or cupid who draws back her drapery and quite literally reveals her to him. Even set off-center (as in fig. 5) and within the melee of the Dionysiac group, the force of this gaze renders the protagonists as an identifiable unit. The tension that is thus created within the composition implies a complicity that may be read as both erotic and united. In this connection it is particularly interesting to note that the roles are not intrinsically gender-determined and can be reversed (as in the Luna and Endymion reliefs in which the female characters act as the desiring agents).[32]

Another popular motif of this period is the hunt, here exemplified in figure 6, a scene in which the figure of Virtus was designed with the potential for adding portrait features and in which the face is still left as a boss.[33] Her status within the narrative is twofold: on the one hand, she exemplifies the courage evidenced by the heroic horseman; on the other, she is the personification of Virtus herself. In the vast majority of the reliefs of this type the female figure follows the male rider, and as internal viewers in the scene they therefore do not have eye contact with each other. Rather, they share a common point of focus in their concentration upon the attacking animal, which emphasizes their unity of purpose. Similarly, the strong framing diagonals create a V-shaped composition of the two figures that sets them apart as an entity within the relief decoration. Unlike scenes depicting Muses or Ariadne, there are no reliefs in which Virtus is shown without her male companion. This

---

1998, 68–70 (and figs. 7, 23, 34, 69 for explicitly sexual scenes making use of the gesture/pose of Ariadne/Rhea Silvia) and Sichtermann 1992, 33–35. Links can also be established between sleep and death and between sleep and eroticism, as in the Barcelona papyrus's rendition of the story of Alcestis (lines 117–25 and 86–90 respectively); cf. Marcovich 1988, 33 and 39. Similarly R. Mitchell (1991, 224–35) has observed the links between death and defloration in the *Aeneid*.

[32] The sarcophagus in the Vatican Museums (Museo

Gregoriano Profano, inv. no. 9558) juxtaposes desire and desirability explicitly in its double depiction of Mars/Rhea Silvia and Luna/Endymion; cf. Sichtermann 1992, 150–51, no. 99, pl. 62.3.

[33] Figure 6: Rome, Museo Capitolino (stairwell), ca. A.D. 250–60. For further details on this sarcophagus, see Melucco 1963–64, 21, no. 10, pl. 12.27 and Wrede 1981, 323, no. 339.

Fig. 6. Lenos *sarcophagus with lion hunt. Rome, Museo Capitolino (photo Singer, DAIR, inst. neg. 1973.0240).*

suggests a desire to counter her masculine appearance and characteristics with a male presence to highlight her essential femininity, much as her presence emphasizes his masculine characteristic of courage. Qualifying the female presence in this way is very similar to doing so for the figures of the Muses when in company of a philosopher. As in the depictions of the Muses, the ambiguous status of the female figure provides a fuller and more complex description of both of the figures.[34]

A comparison of the depictions of learned couples with the visual renderings of the mythologized couples, such as Ariadne-Dionysus and Virtus-rider (figs. 5–6), highlights the appearance of the former as images of composure and authority. If, from this point of view, these reliefs are read as emblematic of *auctoritas*, the depictions of Virtus and rider are much more straightforward—that is, as exemplifications of *virtus*.[35] The narratives pertaining to Ariadne and Dionysus, on the other hand, are more ambiguous. The sensuous tension between the two figures, combined with the interchangeable gendered emphasis of the gaze, makes an interpretation of these as exemplifications of *pietas* the closest analogy—that is, as devotion or even as reciprocal "well-wishing duty."[36]

Common to all of these representations, and common to a great many of the other funerary depictions of this period, is the inherent emphasis on *concordia*. Indeed, throughout it has been evident how the unity of the couple, and their appearance as an indivisible unit, is an integral element in these images. The dual symbolism thus contained within the representations illustrates

[34] Another type of battle scene that is used as a locus for the attribution of portrait features in this period is the depiction of Theseus and Penthesilaea. In these, *virtus* as a virtue appropriate for women is as explicit as in those of Virtus and rider. Similar to these, the former counters her warrior characteristics by depicting the moment of greatest *concordia* between the two—i.e., the moment of her death, when they realize their love for each other. For illustrations, see Grassinger 1999, nos. 119, 122, 125, 127, 130–31, 137; see also Hansen forthcoming b.

[35] Examples of women being described positively as possessing *virtus* include Porcia, the daughter of Cato the Younger and the wife of Brutus, who is said to have lacked neither wisdom nor courage, and Epicharis, who defied her torturer, Nero, and the general expectation of female weakness by showing herself to be braver than a man (Plut. *Cat. Min.*

73.4; Tac. *Ann.* 15.57). More often, however, the heroic females are described as possessing the virtue of *fides*, as in the narratives of loyal wives narrated by Appian, Cassius Dio, Pliny, Plutarch, Tacitus, Valerius Maximus, and Velleius Paterculus. *Fides* is also attributed to women in exceptional circumstances: Ovid, in exile, ascribes the virtues of *pudica*, *probitas*, and *fides* to his wife and likens her to the heroines Andromache and Penelope; Statius claims that only good fortune prevented Pricilla from showing her endurance in the face of adversity (Ov. *Tr.* 5.5.41–45; Stat. *Silv.* 5.1.66–70, 125–31).

[36] The definition "well-wishing duty" has been proposed by Richard Saller (1994, 113), quoting Cic. *Inv. rhet.* 2.161. I.e., as a mixture of desire (devotion) and socialization (duty), which was seen as being a natural trait and based on reciprocity; Saller 1994, 105–14.

how the intended content is not necessarily a single aspect but is a composite whole. The narrative abstraction that is a characteristic of this period—that is, the emphasis on a single significant moment within an overall narrative structure or the use of individual motives disassociated from their normal narrative context—also supports this view. Individual motives can be combined and juxtaposed as emblematic fields and together be built up into a composite depiction of exemplary virtues. For instance, a woman holding a book-scroll may be depicted with a Muse and a philosopher, or she may be shown alone framed by panels depicting attacking lions. A portrait of a woman with a book-scroll may be juxtaposed by the figure of Ariadne. Or the depiction of a couple may be the locus of composite attributes: the book-scroll, the Mars-Venus gesture of her touching his upper arm or shoulder, and the feminine motif of the drapery slipping off her right shoulder.[37]

A complex symbolic reading of these depictions demands a particular engagement by the external viewer of these reliefs—that is, by the audience of these pieces. Since the visual narratives require an evaluative reading in order to be understood, external viewers are drawn in to the narrative and into the act of narration in these depictions and hence are placed in a position inviting them to see themselves as complicit in the events.[38] For instance, in the depictions of Ariadne and Dionysus the emphatic gaze of the internal protagonists mirrors the spectator's viewing of the depicted scene.[39] In this, the internal viewer can be seen as the mediator, or even substitute, between the external spectator and the character gazed upon. In the act of viewing these reliefs, the spectator is offered the possibility of identifying simultaneously with the desiring agent and the desired object. Similarly, in the representations of scenes of hunting as evidence of *virtus*, the external viewer may identify with both the attainment and the possession of this virtue: with the figure of the hunter and with the figure of Virtus. The shared focus of the two protagonists on the attacking animal and their close physical proximity render them a single unity in which there is no essential difference between acquisition and exemplification of virtue, and hence no essential difference between emulation and aspiration for the viewer faced with this image. In front of the depictions of learned couples, the external viewer is placed in a position of dialogue with these. The compositional arrangement of the learned couple—whether framing a central scene or occupying the center of the field—invites the external viewer to appear as a participant figure within the tight figure groups on the relief. The depictions of the frontal standing figure (cf. the outer figures in fig. 2) or a bust portrait of the deceased are in many ways the more straightforward articulations of this dialogue between internal and external viewer. Here the depicted person is seen to speak almost directly to the viewer in a seemingly one-to-one dialogue. However, the implied relationship between the internal viewers (or different picture fields, as the case may be) in this type of depiction is similar to those found in the compositions with multiple figures arranged across the entire sarcophagus front. The friezelike compositions with the couple seated at opposing ends of the picture field (fig. 1) propose a conversation between the two protagonists into which the external viewer enters as a central mediator. The internal emphasis inviting the spectator to identify with the couple, rather than with the "real" Muses or philosophers, creates an implied three-figure group extending outside the picture field to encompass the external viewer. From this position the

---

[37] For illustrations of these examples, see Stroszeck 1998, 132–33, nos. 204 and 209 (among others); Kranz 1954, 195–96, nos. 37 and 41.

[38] In certain funerary monuments, the intent to engage the viewer is made particularly explicit by the inscriptions, which directly address the viewer: cf. Koortbojian 1996.

However, the iconographic relationship here is subtler and more complex than that found in the epigraphic material: the viewer is not engaged as a listener but as part narrator (cf. Hansen 2002).

[39] See also Koortbojian 1995, 141.

latter not only partakes in the discourse of teaching and learning between the couple but may relate to the figures of learning as evidence of a common cultural context and the attainment of virtue and social status. The tight figure groups mainly consisting of two to three figures, as in the central fields of figures 2 and 3, accentuate this audience involvement by drawing the viewer in to a closed group with an invitation to participate in a particularized and select conversation. As in the depictions of Ariadne and Dionysus, where the gaze between the internal figures creates a mediating effect allowing the spectator to identify with both figures simultaneously, so the dialogue between the figures here establishes the possibility for the external viewer to identify with the idea of being at once in an advisory and in a magisterial role. In the dialogue established between the internal and external viewers there is no intrinsic difference among advising, teaching, and learning, and the spectator may identify with all these aspects simultaneously.

Muses as Models

As examples of role models, the images of learned men and women are at once gendered and generalized. When examined as particular narratives, the depictions of male and female figures are qualified and nuanced to highlight aspects appropriate respectively to men and women. Or rather, the more extrovert visibility of women in this period is tempered in joint depictions in order to highlight gendered accomplishments and to situate the couple within a framework of traditional morals and virtues. Simultaneously, the embodiment of *concordia* articulated in the unity of the couple renders the male and female depictions intrinsically similar in content. The context of social aspiration and ideas of cultural belonging inform these depictions universally and create a framework in which the *exemplum* of *auctoritas* is presented as an acceptable ideal and desirable model for men and women alike. The unity of the couple, highlighting the qualities shared between them, further creates the basis for a symbolic reading of the relief as a whole. The choice of models situates the patrons of these reliefs within a framework of aspirations and values that can be read as characterizing individual traits and as exalting their status. The particular role model in this way represents an image of achievable aspirations and the possession of status and virtues in the self-imaging of the patron. The complicity between the two invests the couple as an entity with symbolic connotations in which the individuals are characterized as participants within the narrative of their own funerary commemoration.

Such a reading posits a congruity between the model and the portrayed individual in which the depiction no longer speaks solely about the patron but also to the viewer of the image. The person for whom the sarcophagus was intended now appears as a role model for the spectator: first, by appearing as the embodiment of exemplary virtue and, second, by representing a series of values requiring the participation of the viewer in the evaluation of their meaning. The complicity of authority, which constitutes the real role model, is—in other words—both a dialogue between the internal viewers and between these and the external spectator.

Works Cited

Baratte, F., and C. Metzger, *Musée du Louvre. Catalogue des sarcophages en pierre d'epoque romaine et paléo-chrétienne* (Paris 1985).

Brown, P., *The World of Late Antiquity* (London 1971).

Clarke, J. R., *Looking at Lovemaking: Constructions of Sexuality in Roman Art 100 B.C.–A.D. 250* (Berkeley 1998).

D'Ambra, E., Review of Ewald 1999, *American Journal of Archaeology* 105 (2001) 365–66.

Dixon, S., "A Family Business: Women's Role in Patronage and Politics at Rome 80–44 B.C.," *Classica et Mediaevalia* 34 (1983) 91–112.

Ewald, B. C., *Der Philosoph als Leitbild. Ikonographische Untersuchungen an römischen Sarkophagreliefs* (Mainz 1999).

Fittschen, K., Review of Wegner 1966, *Gnomon* 44 (1972) 486–504.

Flory, M. B., "The Meaning of *Augusta* in the Julio-Claudian Period," *American Journal of Ancient History* 13.2 (1997) 113–38.

Grassinger, D., *Die mythologischen Sarkophage, die antiken Sarkophagreliefs* 12.1 (Berlin 1999).

Hansen, I. L., "The Metamorphic Moment: Heroic Biographical Narratives on Roman Sarcophagi," in *TRAC 2001. Proceedings of the Eleventh Annual Theoretical Roman Archaeology Conference, Glasgow 2001*, ed. M. Carruthers et al. (Oxford 2002) 113–24.

———, "A Mythological Mirror? Imaging Ideal Couples on Third-century A.D. Sarcophagi," in *Social Construction and Social Control of Women in the Classical World*, ed. G. Davies (Swansea forthcoming a).

———, "Marital Concord and the Conformity of Male-Female Virtues on Late Roman Sarcophagi," in *Public Roles—Personal Status. Men and Women in Antiquity (Proceedings of the Third Nordic Symposium on Gender and Women's History in Antiquity)*, ed. L. Larsson Lovén and A. Strömberg (Sävedalen forthcoming b).

Hemelrijk, E. A., *Matrona Docta: Educated Women in the Roman Elite from Cornelia to Julia Domna* (London 1999).

Hopkins, K., "Elite Mobility in the Roman Empire," *Past and Present* 32 (1965) 12–26. Reprinted in *Studies in Ancient Society*, ed. M. I. Finley (London 1974) 103–20.

Huskinson, J., "Women and Learning: Gender and Identity in Scenes of Intellectual Life on Late Roman Sarcophagi," in *Constructing Identities in Late Antiquity*, ed. R. Miles (London 1999) 190–213.

Koortbojian, M., *Myth, Meaning, and Memory on Roman Sarcophagi* (Berkeley 1995).

———, "In *commemorationem mortuorum*: Text and Image along the 'Street of Tombs'," in *Art and Text in Roman Culture*, ed. J. Elsner (Cambridge 1996) 210–33.

Kranz, P., *Jahreszeiten-Sarkophage, die antiken Sarkophagreliefs* 5.4 (Berlin 1954).

Mango, C., "Antique Statuary and the Byzantine Beholder," *Dumbarton Oaks Papers* 7 (1963) 53–75.

Marcovich, M., *Alcestis Barcinonensis, Mnemosyne* Supplement 103 (Leiden 1988).

Matz, F., *Die dionysischen Sarkophage, die antiken Sarkophagreliefs* 4 (Berlin 1968–75).

Melucco, A. V., "Sarcophagi romani di caccia al leone," *Studi miscellanei. Seminario di archeologia e storia dell'arte greca e romana dell'Università di Roma* 11 (1963–64) 7–60.

Mitchell, R. N., "The Violence of Virginity in the *Aeneid*," *Arethusa* 24 (1991) 219–37.

Saller, R. P., *Patriachy, Property and Death in the Roman Family* (Cambridge 1994).

Sharrock, A., "Looking at Looking. Can You Resist a Reading?," in *The Roman Gaze: Vision, Power and the Body*, ed. D. Fredrick (Baltimore and London 2002) 265–95.

Sichtermann, H., *Die mythologischen Sarkophage: Apollon bis Grazien, die antiken Sarkophagreliefs* 12.2 (Berlin 1992).

Smith, R. R. R., "Cultural Choice and Political Identity in Honorific Portrait Statues in the Greek East in the Second Century A.D.," *Journal of Roman Studies* 88 (1998) 56–93.

Stroszeck, J., *Löwen-Sarkophage. Sarkophage mit Löwenköpfen, schreitenden Löwen und Löwen-kampfgruppen, die antiken Sarkopagreliefs* 6.1 (Berlin 1998).

Trimble, J., "Understanding Muse and Philosopher Imagery" (review of Ewald 1999), *Journal of Roman Archaeology* 15 (2002) 507–10.

Wegner, M., *Die Musensarkophage, die antiken Sarkophagreliefs* 5.3 (Berlin 1966).

Welch, K., "A New View of the Origins of the Basilica: The Atrium Regium, Graecostasis and Roman Diplomacy," *Journal of Roman Archaeology* 16 (2003) 5–34.

Wrede, H., Consecratio in Formam Deorum. *Vergöttlichte Privatpersonen in der römischen Kaiserzeit* (Mainz 1981).

Zanker, P., *The Mask of Socrates: The Image of the Intellectual in Antiquity*, trans. A. Shapiro (Berkeley 1995).

Zanker, P., and B. C. Ewald, *Mit Mythen leben. Die Bilderwelt der römischen Sarkophage* (Munich 2004).

15 ◆ DEGREES OF DIFFERENTIATION:
ROLE MODELS ON EARLY CHRISTIAN SARCOPHAGI

Janet Huskinson

What happens to traditional role models in an altered social context, and how far did new social groups choose to distance themselves from these old exemplars as they sought to create their own identities? Did they introduce models of their own, and if so how did these serve to integrate or differentiate the new groups within wider society?

Questions like these are central to tracing how role models functioned in the Roman world. They bring the element of temporal change to another major question of how various subgroups sought to claim social inclusion, if not empowerment, by identifying themselves with particular traditional role models. As other chapters in this volume will show, this process was regularly used for people such as freedmen, women, and children, while even emperors hankered after more potent imagery by identifying themselves with gods and heroes. But it is perhaps less easy to find a period in time that clearly shows how emergent subgroups in Roman society used role model imagery as a means of articulating their new position in society. For this reason the Christian community in third-century Rome makes a particularly useful study as it grew as a distinctive social subgroup within the city. In the process of identifying themselves as such, Christians began to develop their own specific visual culture, introducing religious images of their own while adopting and adapting figures and motifs from the art that surrounded them. But this development could not have been straightforward since Christians were subject to persecution at various times in the third century, which must have affected their wish to be clearly visible as a separate social group. Not until the Peace of the Church in 313 did they have the security to develop this social visibility to the full, and in the course of the fourth century they became a dominant force in Rome. So these various historical factors make this an interesting testing ground for exploring how new groups in society made use of role model imagery.

As a focus for this investigation I have chosen to look at some figures that appear on sarcophagi used by the Christian community at the time. Although it is ultimately impossible to be certain of the beliefs held by those who used or viewed them, sarcophagi provide good evidence about role models because funerary commemoration as a genre was an important vehicle for self-representation: it offered special opportunities for people to represent ideals that were valued by themselves as individuals and also by the society in which they lived. This was also true for Christian patrons at this time. These earliest Christian sarcophagi used conventional designs in the arrangement of their figurative elements. Thus Christian strigillated sarcophagi followed contemporary fashions by filling separate panels at the corners and/or center of the front with one or two figures.[1] There were

I would like to thank the organizers of the conference and the Arts Faculty of the Open University for financial support. All photographs are published by kind permission of the German Archaeological Institute in Rome.

[1] For contemporary types: Koch and Sichtermann 1982, 74, fig. 2. For Christian examples: *RS* 1 nos. 759, 760, 817, 985. Brandenburg 2004 is an interesting recent review of early Christian sarcophagi in Rome and their patrons.

also frieze designs decorated with biblical narratives (usually in highly abbreviated forms) or by juxtaposing allegorical figures, such as the Good Shepherd, praying woman (*orans*), and allegorical subjects (such as the philosopher, to be considered below).

Taking selected examples of each type of figure—described for convenience here simply as "secular" and "biblical"—this chapter will consider how they might have operated as role models and how Christians used them as a means of self-definition. By the term "role model" I mean here a figure chosen not merely to commemorate the individual dead but to offer a collective example to the Christian community in terms of beliefs and the conduct of their lives. And here literary references from the bible or from later works of exegesis can be of great help in complementing or supplementing our understanding of the visual image.

Secular Role Models

The examples chosen for discussion in this group are images of men and women associated with learning: the philosopher and his female companion, and married couples or single figures shown with attributes such as the pallium and scroll or accompanied by Muses. The empirewide interest in *paideia* had inspired a good deal of self-representation in terms of learning and classical culture, and these had been popular figures on Roman sarcophagi in various combinations and designs since the second century.[2] As Hansen shows in this volume, they were associated with traditional Roman qualities such as *concordia* and *auctoritas*; and by the mid-third century they had become part of an extensive repertoire of images evoking the virtues of a reflective and peaceful life in fairly general- ized "feel-good" terms.[3] This group also included the Good Shepherd (carrying a sheep across his shoulders) and the *orans*, which were based on figure types found in secular art of earlier periods and which were both capable of specifically Christian interpretations. Just how far individual examples of each figure should be seen as specifically Christian needs to be argued for each case, but in the context of this discussion it is important to focus on their general capacity for Christian meaning (which was certainly developed further in Christian art of the fourth century).[4] As I shall argue, it is this potential for Christian meaning combined with the secular traditions of their past that makes these figures so useful as role models here.

Given its popularity as a signifier of social status and aspirations, it is not surprising that Chris- tians took up the theme of learning when they too became patrons of sarcophagi. And as Christian influence increased in the last decades of the third century, these conventional figures were given a new context through the addition of other imagery that had a specifically Christian value. As we shall shortly explore, these developments involved some ideological issues for Christian role models, but it is also the case that there were some practical needs at stake. In the need to create a Christian iconography craftsmen adapted existing figure types for new uses (for instance, the philosopher type was used for Christ the teacher).[5] In the rather uncertain economic and religious climate of the time there must also have been some commercial advantage in depicting generic themes like learning that could be meaningful to a wide range of customers.

A sequence of examples can trace how these developments unfolded for each of the main images of learning, as their conventional figures came to be matched with elements that could be

[2] See Zanker 1995, 267–331; Ewald 1999; Huskinson 1999; and Hansen in this volume.

[3] E.g., Ewald 1999, 79.

[4] Cf. Klauser 1958; Klauser 1959; Klauser 1960; Ewald 1999, 64, cf. 132.

[5] Zanker 1995, 291–92.

Fig. 1. Sarcophagus from Rome showing a woman with scroll and Good Shepherd figures (RS 1 no. 1004)
(photo Boehringer, DAIR, inst. neg. 59.448).

given Christian meaning. Single figures of ordinary men and women shown with attributes of learning such as the pallium or the scroll were very common in the later third century.[6] On sarcophagi decorated with conventional subjects such as the Seasons, they occupied the center as full-length figures or as busts in roundels, or they filled the corner panels of strigillated designs. Men and women were treated similarly, but it is interesting to note how these representations of "learned" women increased in number from the mid-third century.[7] Some strigillated sarcophagi of the late third or early fourth century show a woman with two Muse companions in the center and conventional images (of seasonal cupids and Cupid and Psyche) at the corners.[8] Contemporary with these is a fragmentary sarcophagus from San Lorenzo in Rome that reduced the Muses in the central scene to smaller statuelike figures and that replaced the conventional figures with a Good Shepherd at the corner; the woman holds a scroll, while her blocked out facial features show that this was intended to be a personal portrait (in the event left unfinished).[9] A slightly later strigillated sarcophagus also has Good Shepherds at each corner, this time flanking the single figure of a woman who holds a half-opened scroll and gestures as if expounding a text (fig. 1).[10]

A final example of this type replaces this "learned" figure with an *orans* with scroll box at her side: one corner panel depicts a Good Shepherd and the other a bearded philosopher in skimpy pallium and holding a scroll.[11] Single philosopher figures are frequently found occupying this corner position on "non-Christian" sarcophagi, and there are a few other cases in which one is paired up with a Good Shepherd (fig. 2).[12]

Another popular representation of learning on sarcophagi was a symmetrical composition that portrayed a man and woman (presumably a married couple) sitting facing each other, holding scrolls or musical instruments and each with "learned" companions such as Muses or philosophers.[13]

[6] Ewald 1999, 34–37 for historical development.

[7] Huskinson 1999.

[8] Ewald 1999, 190, nos. F11 and F12.

[9] *RS* 1 no. 696.

[10] *RS* 1 no. 1004; also nos. 396 and 837.

[11] *RS* 1 no. 912.

[12] *RS* 1 no. 744.1 (end third century).

[13] For the history of this motif: Ewald 1999, 48–53. Also Zanker 1995, 271–77; Huskinson 1999, 193–94; Hansen in this volume.

Fig. 2. Sarcophagus showing male bust with Good Shepherd and philosopher figures (RS 1 no. 744.1)
(photo Boehringer, DAIR, inst. neg. 59.428).

Fig. 3. Sarcophagus showing man and woman facing a Good Shepherd in central mandorla (RS 1 no. 945.1)
(photo Sansaini, DAIR, inst. neg. 60.1325).

Hansen has discussed elsewhere in this volume how these compositions often used the gaze of internal viewers as a means of encouraging external viewers to identify with their "role models," and this would have also applied to Christians who viewed these sarcophagi. Figures of potential Christian significance are also introduced into the designs. The Good Shepherd is presented as the focus of the couple's preoccupation with learning, occupying the center of strigillated sarcophagi (fig. 3).[14] This is done in a more thoroughgoing way on a sarcophagus from the Via Lungara in Rome that placed a Good Shepherd and an *orans* figure at the center of the frieze design, between the seated couple.[15]

[14] *RS* 1 nos. 817, 945 (both from the last decades of the [15] *RS* 1 no. 66.
third century).

Fig. 4. Sarcophagus from S. Maria Antiqua, Rome (RS 1 no. 747) (photo Boehringer, DAIR, inst. neg. 59.421).

A group of figures that was simple in its composition but quite complex in its flexible interpretation was the pair of the philosopher and female companion.[16] Particularly popular in the late third century, its variations show a Muse, or an ordinary woman in the pose of a Muse, as a source of inspiration or as a listener or pupil, while the philosopher himself might be learning from her or teaching. About a third have portrait features. The group is most common at the center of strigillated sarcophagi, with figures of ordinary men and women (the couple represented in the center as the philosopher and his Muse?), stereotypical philosophers at the corners. These get replaced by figures capable of a Christian reading—shepherds, especially the Good Shepherd type, and the *orans*.[17] Just as the men and women in the corner panels had given a context in which to understand the particular significance of the philosopher and woman at the center, so did these figures, but in Christian terms. Here the philosopher sits as a reader or teacher, while the woman is likely to be learning from him. The culmination (ideologically speaking) of this development is represented by a frieze sarcophagus from S. Maria Antiqua in the Roman Forum, where Christian biblical figures (Jonah and the whale and the baptism of Jesus) seem to spell out the content of this learning: by devoting themselves to learning and prayer, the couple are now involved in the process that leads via baptism to the hope of everlasting life (fig. 4).[18]

To sum up, Christian significance was added to these conventional figures of learning partly because the Good Shepherd and *orans* fitted so easily into the repertoire of supporting images to do with the "good life." Especially on strigillated sarcophagi (where the separate panels made this easy), these images were mixed and matched to convey ideas about peace, fulfillment, and spirituality (for instance), which provided a context for the central subject of learning. Alongside Seasons, shepherds, fishermen, and philosophers, these Christian allegorical figures introduced the possibility of Christian religious readings, confirmed on the S. Maria Antiqua sarcophagus by the addition of biblical scenes. But this iconographical development did not happen in a sudden change or in a smooth, relentless progression to Christian images. Even allowing for the difficulty in dating many sarcophagi with great precision, it is still clear that conventional and Christian treatments of the learning theme coexisted in the last decades of the third century. It seems to be the case that

[16] Ewald 1999, 42–47 about the development of the group.

[17] E.g., also *RS* 1 no. 994 (*orans* and Good Shepherd); Ewald

1999, 157–58, no. C13 (semi-*orans* and a shepherd).

[18] *RS* 1 no. 747; Ewald 1999, 46.

Fig. 5. Sarcophagus with scenes of Jonah, Museo Pio Cristiano, Rome (RS 1 no. 35)
(photo Boehringer, DAIR, inst. neg. 61.330).

Christians simply developed versions that added their own religious values to the conventional scenes—values that did not detract from the traditional ideals attached to learning in the Roman Empire but that gave them a new purpose, as means to a Christian spiritual experience. As is shown (though in different ways) by later examples from the fourth century, the theme of Christian learning had arrived to stay.

It is therefore not surprising to find figures of learning being used to provide meaningful role models for Christians in the late third century. Being to hand in the existing funerary repertoire, this imagery was convenient, and above all for Christians it was able to commemorate ordinary people and their aspirations in terms that biblical scenes could not. Despite its conventional background it could be used in a Christian context to provide models of how Christians should conduct their life, through prayerful learning (symbolized by the *orans*) and by loving their neighbor (the Good Shepherd).

Biblical Role Models

It would appear that Christians began to decorate sarcophagi with biblical scenes from around the middle of the third century. As in catacomb painting many of the episodes they chose for this were from Old Testament stories of God's saving intervention or were of miracles recounted in the Gospels. The religious "messages" of these episodes were reinforced by the usually highly abbreviated style of narrative composition, which highlighted essential moments in their presentation: thus the cycle of scenes depicting the story of Jonah reinforces the themes of salvation from death (being thrown out of the boat; being ejected by the whale) and peaceful rest (reclining under the gourd) (fig. 5). Particularly on frieze sarcophagi "highlights" from a whole variety of biblical scenes would be juxtaposed, sometimes along with allegorical figures (the Good Shepherd and *orans*) to present a cumulative message to the viewer. Within the general theme of salvation the different stories had interpretations of their own to be included, which are also to be found in contemporary Christian writings (even if it is not always appropriate to transfer literary interpretations directly to the visual images). Biblical scenes like these were a powerful means of self-definition for the Christian community: by relying on specific knowledge and understanding of the scriptures, they bound Christians into a common experience of their past and hope for the future. At the same time they excluded outsiders who did not have this knowledge.

As the S. Maria Antiqua sarcophagus showed, Christians still had the chance to follow the conventional practice of adding their own portrait features to allegorical figures like the *orans* or philosopher. In this way they claimed these figures as role models for themselves, just as earlier generations had done with mythological figures on sarcophagi. But this did not happen on biblical sarcophagi, where portrait features are never given to biblical figures.[19] So whereas it was possible for an individual Christian man to portray himself on sarcophagi as a philosopher type devoted to the true learning, he could not directly represent himself as a Jonah or Daniel in quite the same way. Instead we can find other devices used on sarcophagi that suggest particular engagement with the biblical figures: for instance, the deceased may be portrayed in the midst of biblical figures[20] or shown half-turning toward them as if a firsthand witness,[21] or occasionally links are made through the use of inscriptions.[22] These are only modest devices, yet they serve to reinforce the kind of connection between individual Christians and biblical role models that is also found in contemporary writings and in prayers.[23]

A central element in this linking of contemporary believers with biblical figures is the theme of God's saving grace. This was the paramount theme in the earliest Christian funerary art, in catacomb paintings and on sarcophagi. The salvation narratives they depicted were central to Christian experience as proofs of God's power to save and give new life to believers. This is also illustrated by the way in which the epistles of the New Testament often exhort contemporary Christians by reminding them of the examples set by great figures from the biblical past. The Epistle to the Hebrews, for instance, contains a long list of Old Testament figures who in their time were witnesses to faith, a faith that in the present day "gives substance to our hopes and makes us certain of realities we do not see."[24] Elsewhere they are quoted as witnesses to the value of endurance: according to the Epistle of James: "if you want an example of patience under ill-treatment, take the prophets who spoke in the name of the Lord; remember 'We count those happy who stood firm.'"[25]

Faith and endurance are certainly important lessons exemplified by the two cases chosen for discussion here, namely Jonah and the Three Young Hebrews in the fiery furnace, who were all saved from death because of their faithfulness to God. These Old Testament subjects were both very popular in the earliest Christian art of third-century Rome and were often juxtaposed in the decoration of sarcophagi.[26] In scripture both stories have more than one episode, but in the abbreviated narrative approaches of third-century sarcophagus art one alone was often enough to recall the full message to the Christian viewer and to emphasize its essentials.[27]

---

[19] Wrede 1981, 156.

[20] E.g., *RS* 1 no. 67.

[21] E.g., *RS* 1 nos. 77, 130 (lids): further instances of the use of the internal viewer to indicate the "role model" to external viewers: see Hansen's chapter in this volume.

[22] E.g., *RS* 1 no. 46 (start of the fourth century): the *orans*, pendant figure to the Good Shepherd on the other corner, is identified by the name inscribed above her head as the woman commemorated in the central panel.

[23] See Finney 1994, 282–86.

[24] Heb. 11 (trans. New English Bible 1970).

[25] James 5:10–11 (trans. New English Bible 1970).

[26] E.g., *RS* 1 nos. 130, 664, 674; Gerke 1940, 186–87.

[27] Episodes: Jonah being thrown out of the boat in his flight from God, being swallowed and then ejected by the whale, and his rest under the gourd tree; the Three Hebrews refusing to worship Nebuchadnezzar's image and then surviving unharmed their martyrdom in the furnace.

Fig. 6. Fragment of a sarcophagus lid showing the Three Young Hebrews and the Angel of God (?) in the fiery furnace and Noah (RS 1 no. 834) (photo Sichtermann, DAIR, inst. neg. 64.1713).

Jonah had met his death in trying to flee God's orders to go to preach in Nineveh, but his resurrection from the belly of the whale showed how someone who had been sinful and disobedient could still gain divine forgiveness and be restored to life to fulfill God's purposes.[28] In particular the story was seen as an example of resurrection: even in the Gospel according to Matthew, Jesus quoted the three nights Jonah spent in the dark belly of the whale as a "sign" of his own coming death and resurrection, and this concept was used and developed in many later Christian writings.[29] So on these sarcophagi it is not hard to see that the story appears as a sign that God would do the same for the deceased and their families; Jonah's salvation from death is an example of God's own power to save the faithful (despite their intrinsic sinfulness) and to use their restored lives to further his purposes. As well as providing this model for Christian hope, the story of Jonah was also interpreted by Christian writers of the second and third centuries as demonstrating God's mercy and concern, not just in saving the disobedient yet faithful Jonah but also in looking to the conversion of the gentile Ninevites. The universalism of this concern was developed by later Christian writers, after the Peace of the Church, but it possibly also underlies some of these early visual representations.

For historical reasons messages of peace and salvation must have been especially important to third-century Christians, who had experienced times of persecution for their faith and refusal to obey imperial orders to sacrifice to other gods. This would seem to give a particular relevance to the story of the Three Young Hebrews saved by God from death in the fiery furnace, to which they had been condemned by Nebuchadnezzar after they refused his command to worship an idol.[30] Indeed, the popularity of their survival unharmed in the flames as a subject in catacomb painting and on sarcophagi testifies to its importance as a model of the salvation to be gained by those who were faithfully committed to worshiping the one true God (fig. 6). The scene of their refusal to worship the idol did not start to appear in art until later, at the end of the third or early fourth century. (Its appearance is hard to date precisely in relation to the Peace of the Church in 313, but the earliest surviving examples are possibly before it—that is, at a time that remembered the persecution of Christians under Diocletian.) The relative lateness of its appearance seems

---

[28] Jon. 1 and 2.   Beradino 1992, 1:449–51 s.v. Jonah.

[29] Matt. 12:40. For references to early Christian writings: Di   [30] Dan. 3. For the imagery: Carletti 1975.

rather surprising because of the obvious historical resonance of the episode, particularly since so many Christians had been condemned for refusing to obey imperial orders to sacrifice. Christian writers had been quicker to make this link between the scriptural event and what was currently happening to their community: even at the start of the third century Tertullian (*On idolatry* 15.8–9) had explicitly quoted the Three Hebrews as "that example" (*illud exemplum*) of Christian believers who had to draw the line between idolatry and the proper respect due to authorities (15.8–9). He pushed the link even further by turning the idol erected by Nebuchanezzar into an image of the king himself and equating the biblical event with the contemporary imperial test of sacrifice. When the scene does appear on sarcophagi, it is notable that it follows this literary twist, so all surviving examples depict the idol as an image of Nebuchanezzar himself.[31] By doing so, they turn him into an explicit symbol of all emperors hostile to Christianity, as it were a negative role model for rulers, contrasted with the positive models offered to faithful Christians by the Three Young Hebrews.[32]

A little later on, after the Peace of the Church, the scene of the refusal to worship Nebuchanezzar's idol is often found on sarcophagi contrasted with yet another positive counterpart—the adoration of the Christ child by the three Magi who had defied King Herod.[33] On these examples the emphasis has shifted from salvation narrative to commitment to the worship of the one true God (produced by the juxtaposition of these two otherwise unrelated episodes) that would have reminded Christians of their experiences of their own recent martyrs, increasingly celebrated in the martyr cults of the fourth century. These were homegrown role models who had also defended their faith to the death.

In sum, these biblical figures on sarcophagi were role models in the sense that they showed how God would reward those who were faithful witnesses to him in the communities in which they found themselves. More specifically, in terms of salvation, they were *exempla resurrectionis*, proofs offered to believers that their God would save them as he had saved these scriptural figures in the past. In the words of Tertullian, "as a guarantee of God's omnipotence to work resurrection he rescued Jonah from the whale, the Hebrews from the desert, and the three Hebrews from the furnace."[34] And there are also signs that as circumstances changed for the Christian community with the Peace of the Church in 313, these biblical models could be used to remind Christians of their own recent martyrs, thereby offering models of Christian behavior from the Church's own more recent past.

Conclusions

These cases have shown that role models offered to Christians on these late third-century sarcophagi come from two different traditions—biblical and secular—and work slightly differently. Essentially the biblical examples require a more directed reading, while the secular may be interpreted in various ways and on various levels.

---

[31] E.g., *RS* 1 nos. 160, 324, 351, 596; *RS* 2 no. 184 (lids, mainly fragmentary).

[32] Tertullian, *On Idolatry* 15.8–9; Origen, *Exhortation to Martyrdom* 33.

[33] E.g., *RS* 2 nos. 20, 63, 150.

[34] Tertullian, *On the Resurrection of the Flesh* 58.

As was discussed above, the secular figures of learning belonged to a large group of images to do with the cultured life that had been popular throughout the Roman world in the second and third centuries, and in that context their meaning was often rather general or was polyvalent. But on these sarcophagi they were able to pick up on the Christian associations of figures such as the Good Shepherd or *orans* with which they were juxtaposed and so gain the possibility of new, specifically Christian religious meanings. With little change to their conventional depiction they thus came to offer models for ideal Christian activities of learning, teaching, and contemplative reading. By contrast the biblical images on these sarcophagi were Christian creations, and though they were as widely popular in Christian funerary art as the philosopher and Muses had been in non-Christian settings, their interpretation was tied in with a specifically Christian teleology and scriptural exegesis.

Despite these background differences each type of role model (secular and biblical) suggests that Christian patrons of these sarcophagi were aware of a crucial spiritual distinction between themselves and their non-Christian contemporaries. This was their certain hope of an everlasting life in Christ. Undoubtedly this was the central message of biblical characters such as Jonah and the Three Hebrews who were presented to contemporary Christians as historical proofs of God's promises of salvation. The very illustration of their stories would be enough to direct Christian viewers to remember them as examples and take them as models for their own hope of redemption from sin or worldly adversity: to use the words already quoted from the Epistle to the Hebrews about faith, this process of giving visual form to exemplary biblical figures "gives substance to our hopes and makes us certain of realities we do not see."[35]

On the secular sarcophagi the same hope is also effectively conveyed in more personal terms by the continued convention of adding individual portrait features of the deceased to figures of philosophers and learned women, now represented in the context of Christian imagery (as on the sarcophagus in S. Maria Antiqua). This identified them as active participants in Christian life and belief. This underlying sense of hope persistently differentiated Christian funerary imagery from non-Christian and in their fullest interpretation gave these particular figures an exclusive value as Christian religious role models; only Christian believers would have fully appreciated their message of hope. Ultimately these models were therefore intended only for a Christian audience: the biblical imagery had really been so from the start, but with the secular figures of learning we can see the development of traditional role models to the point where they could convey a specific value to the new Christian audience.

On one level these are private role models, for individual commemoration, yet on another they provide interesting evidence for how Christians saw their collective position in the wider society of Rome. For what they suggest is that Christian patrons had a certain degree of positive ambivalence about their relationship with the community as a whole and so adopted a choice of role models that promoted different views. The use of biblical exemplars suggests separation from surrounding society. By evoking scriptural history to reinforce contemporary hope and endurance, these figures set the Christian audience apart and identify it as a separate religious community. Jonah and the Three Hebrews were all distinguished from contemporaries by their faithfulness to the true God; but they represent more than mere separation from surrounding society, as in fact all of them were actually aliens far from home (as Jonah had found himself in Nineveh to preach against its sinful life, while the Three Hebrews were in exile in Babylon). In a similar way early Christians were figurative aliens from their heavenly home, often trying to work for their faith in rather hostile

---

[35] Heb. 11:1 (trans. New English Bible 1970).

circumstances; and so they may have been empowered to continue their witness by the example of these biblical figures who were saved by God to continue as instruments of forwarding his purpose in godless places.[36]

By contrast the use of the secular images of the philosopher and other learned figures seems to reflect some degree of Christian assimilation to wider society. In choosing such traditional and familiar images as their starting point, Christian patrons were aligning themselves with society in general and expressing a share in some of its conventional values. Even when they added specifically Christian elements, they might have expected that non-Christians would continue to view the images sympathetically, without necessarily fully understanding the new religious values that had been introduced. (Perhaps too some non-Christians found it quite acceptable to use this Christian imagery on sarcophagi of their own: we should not fall into the trap of assuming that imagery always is a direct indicator of the religious affiliation of the deceased.)

As well as this ideological sharing there was a practical one: masons must have appreciated imagery that appealed to as many customers as possible, and if conventional figures such as the philosopher and learned woman could also sell their sarcophagi to the growing number of Christians in Rome, then so much the better for trade. Certainly, as we have seen, the physical process of including the traditional figures in new Christian compositions was not artistically difficult, and this practicality is another aspect of shared culture at this time to be remembered.

Factors like these are a reminder that in their daily life third-century Christians were regularly confronted by questions to do with their assimilation and differentiation within the wider community. This situation provided scope for the kind of role models that could allow them to identify with acceptable aspects of the surrounding world—for example, by celebrating learning or a good marriage—while also indicating their Christianity. Thus images that combine secular and Christian religious models (such as the combination of Muses and the Good Shepherd or philosopher and *orans*) should be seen as commemorating both aspects of these Christians' lives rather than representing what, on the face of it, looks like an almost ambiguous commitment to Christianity.[37] In the earlier twentieth century such mixed images were often described as "crypto-Christian" on the grounds that they hid their Christian significance behind a near-conventional appearance.[38] This interpretation presupposed that artists had a specific intention to conceal and that Christian patrons were defensive about expressing their beliefs outright, aware of how these would mark them off from other viewers. But rather than tokens of such a "closet Christianity" these images are perhaps better understood as a way of representing simultaneously some of the many (sometimes conflicting) facets of contemporary Christian life in a way in which the biblical scenes, with their directed religious readings, could not. So by adding elements of their own to a traditional model (rather than simply discarding it), Christians did not totally separate themselves from ideals of surrounding society. In fact this fusion of symbolism provided them with new role models for the various compromises required in their daily life: by linking figures of learning and culture to religious symbols, they brought these aspects of their lives into a Christian spiritual dimension.

All these matters relate to a major question about the emergent "visibility" of the Christian community in Roman material culture at this time. It has been argued that there is really no evidence of a distinct Christian material culture before the late second century, not because the Christians

---

[36] Jon. 3; Dan. 5:28–30.

[37] E.g., *RS* 1 nos. 66, 696, 817.

[38] Cf. Finney 1994, 288–89 for summary of use.

did not have any but because it was indistinguishable from that shared by society as a whole.[39] Why did things begin to change, then, in the early third century? Some scholars have suggested ideological reasons (for instance, a desire to express their beliefs in visible form); others have argued that Christians had not achieved sufficient socioeconomic stability before then; yet others have noted the need for artists and craftsmen to develop the new imagery. Whatever the reasons for it, the fact remains that it was not until the early third century that signs emerged of a distinct Christian material culture. From the middle of that century these sarcophagi were part of this development, and it is not therefore surprising that their images of role models reflect different approaches to relating Christianity to the culture that surrounded it. As this chapter has shown, for role models they offered two sets of exemplars, one from the bible and one from popular secular ideals. The former reflected the Christian community's needs to draw on its private internal source of spiritual strength through images recalled from its scriptural past. As new artistic creations that meant little to outsiders, they served to distance Christians from the rest of society, giving them models to encourage faithfulness and the work of conversion, and above all they served as proofs of personal resurrection. By contrast the latter allowed Christians to look outward to see how to make the most meaningful use of models existing in the wider world and to combine them with aspects of their own religion.

[39] E.g., Finney 1994; Rutgers 1997. Also Snyder 1985, 9–11 for theoretical perspectives on "visibility" and material culture.

Works Cited

Brandenburg, H., "Osservazioni sulla fine della produzione e dell'uso dei sarcofagi a rilevo nella tarda antichità nonché sulla loro decorazione," in *Sarcofagi tardoantichi, paleocristiani e altomedievali (Monumenti di antichità cristiana XVIII)*, ed. F. Bisconti and H. Brandenburg (Vatican 2004) 1–34.

Carletti, C., *I tre giovani ebrei di Babilonia nell'arte cristiana antica*, Quaderni Vetera Christianorum 9 (Brescia 1975).

Di Beradino, A., ed., *Encyclopaedia of the Early Church*, trans. A. Walford (Cambridge 1992).

Ewald, B. C., *Der Philosoph als Leitbild. Ikonographische Untersuchungen an römischen Sarkophagreliefs* (Mainz 1999).

Finney, P. C., *The Invisible God: The Earliest Christians on Art* (New York and Oxford 1994).

Gerke, F., *Die christlichen Sarkophage der vorkonstantinischen Zeit* (Berlin 1940).

Huskinson, J., "Women and Learning: Gender and Identity in Scenes of Intellectual Life on Late Roman Sarcophagi," in *Constructing Identities in Late Antiquity*, ed. R. Miles (London 1999) 190–213.

Klauser, T., "Studien zur Entstehungsgeschichte der christlichen Kunst I," *Jahrbuch für Antike und Christentum* 1 (1958) 20–51.

———, "Studien zur Entstehungsgeschichte der christlichen Kunst II," *Jahrbuch für Antike und Christentum* 2 (1959) 115–45.

———, "Studien zur Entstehungsgeschichte der christlichen Kunst III," *Jahrbuch für Antike und Christentum* 3 (1960) 112–33.

Koch, G., and H. Sichtermann, *Römische Sarkophage*, Handbuch der Archäologie (Munich 1982).

RS 1 = *Repertorium der christlich-antiken Sarkophage*, Band 1: *Rom und Ostia*, ed. F. W. Deichmann, G. Bovini, and H. Brandenburg (Wiesbaden 1967).

RS 2 = *Repertorium der christlich-antiken Sarkophage*, Band 2: *Italien mit einem Nachtrag, Rom und Ostia, Dalmatien, Museen der Welt*, ed. J. Dresken-Weiland (Mainz 1998).

Rutgers, L., Review of Finney 1994, *Jahrbuch für Antike und Christentum* 40 (1997) 245–49.

Snyder, G. F., Ante Pacem: *Archaeological Evidence of Church Life before Constantine* (Macon, Ga. 1985).

Wrede, H., Consecratio in Formam Deorum. *Vergöttliche Privatpersonen in der römischen Kaiserzeit* (Mainz 1981).

Zanker, P., *The Mask of Socrates: The Image of the Intellectual in Antiquity*, trans. A. Shapiro (Berkeley and Los Angeles 1995).

16 ♦ THE PHILOLOGICAL, THE FOLKLORIC, AND THE SITE-SPECIFIC: THREE MODELS FOR DECODING CLASSICAL VISUAL REPRESENTATION

John R. Clarke

The history of art, although a relative newcomer among the humanities, has a rich historiography—not least because it came of age in the twentieth century, when all of the humanistic disciplines were striving for increased rigor. The application of empirical approaches in the social sciences—especially in psychology, sociology, anthropology, and linguistics—inspired art historians to expand their methodologies. New genres of art history, including the psychology of art, social art history, and interdisciplinary approaches that wedded art history with cultural anthropology or even linguistic science, rapidly vied for a place alongside the fundamental and time-tested methods of connoisseurship and formal analysis.[1] If the discipline of art history originally developed from the work of the archaeologist and curator, whose job it was to examine the object to determine its authenticity, date, and meaning, the new art history looked beyond these basic concerns to investigate how the object fit into social, political, and cultural contexts.

The "role models" that are the subject of this chapter are not only those that surface in Roman art and literature but also the individuals who, much later, study and reconstruct the Romans according to their own models and milieu. In this chapter I look at how these *methodological* models have affected the interpretation of classical art. It is a case-study analysis in which I chart how several scholars in the modern period attempt to "decode" the same enigmatic painting using three different investigative models or hermeneutics: what I call the philological, the folkloric, and the site-specific. Each approach produces a different account of how visual representation functioned in ancient Rome. As will become apparent, each of these models reveals as much about the researcher's mentality as it does about the mentality of the ancient Romans who originally looked at the image.

Seen from another point of view, these methodological models also reflect the milieu that formed scholarly attitudes—especially since the image is a "pornographic" one. For this reason, it seems, scholars recoiled from publishing it, curators refused to exhibit it to the public, and no one went out on a limb to adopt a personal voice in discussing it.[2] The personal voice in modern art historical/archaeological scholarship is a comparatively recent phenomenon.[3]

My focus is the painting of an ass mounting a lion found at Pompeii around 1855 (fig. 1). This fresco adorned the exterior facade of a commercial establishment variously identified as a bordello, a tavern, and a gaming house, located in Regio VII, insula 6. The building occupies a corner, and its facade consists of two wide openings framed by three piers (fig. 2). The ass-lion painting decorated the pier in the middle, between doorways 34 and 35. There were two other images on the facade:

---

[1] For the situation around 1970: Kleinbauer 1971; for the new Roman art history: Brilliant 1998; Altekamp, René, and Hofter 2001; Smith 2003; Donohue and Fullerton 2003; Kampen 2003.

[2] For the implications for a scholar publishing a pornographic image, see Bonnet 2000.

[3] Hallett 1997; Shanks 1997; Zanker 1994.

Fig. 1. Ass mounting a lion fresco from Pompeii VII, 6, 34–35. Naples, Museo Nazionale Archeologico, inv. 27683 (photo M. Larvey).

Fig. 2. Pompeii, Tavern at VII, 6, 34–35 (photo M. Larvey).

a painting of Mercury decorated the corner pier, to the viewer's left, and an image of Dionysus decorated the pier to the right. Today only traces of plaster remain.

But because the excavator judged the sexual imagery of the ass-lion fresco offensive, he had it detached from the pier (along with the gladiatorial graffiti beneath the offending image) and sent it off to the Raccolta Pornografica of the Museo Archeologico Nazionale in Naples, where it remains to this day.[4]

It is an image that still surprises the modern viewer and elicits laughter. The ass—normally the prey of the powerful carnivorous lion—has overcome the lion in a most vigorous and sexual way. Not only has the artist depicted intercourse between two animals of very different species; he has portrayed

[4] Ass Mounting Lion while Crowned by Victory, from Pompeii VII, 6, 34–35. Naples, Museo Nazionale Archeologico, inv. 27683, H. 137 cm, W. 74 cm. Sampaolo 1997 (with previous bibl.); De Caro 2000, 41–45.

a male ass anally penetrating a male lion. A goddess is present as well. Victoria swoops in on her outspread wings to crown the ass with her right hand while holding the palm of victory in her left.[5]

If a central element of humor is the surprise that comes from overturning the expected, the Victory-ass-lion painting overturns the expected in three ways. The ass mounts a lion; their intercourse is homosexual; and Victory, a goddess who presides over the triumphs of gods and humans, crowns an ithyphallic ass.

The Philological Model (1860–1950): Minervini, Fioirelli, and Matteo Della Corte

The earliest approaches to deciphering this painting were philological. By this I mean that they sought out classical texts to explain the image. Giulio Minervini set out the details of the philological argument in his article of 1859; Giuseppe Fiorelli accepted Minervini's interpretations, and then—nearly a century later—Matteo Della Corte recapitulated and elaborated Minervini's entire argument, adding little to it. Our philologists saw in the fresco the metaphorical enactment of a famous historical event: the battle of Actium.[6] Augustus, the ass, overcomes Anthony, the lion. All three scholars based their claim on two passages that tell the same story of an omen seen by Augustus on the dawn of the battle: Suetonius, *Divus Augustus* 96,[7] and Plutarch, *Vita Antonii* 65. Plutarch's version is somewhat fuller than Suetonius's:

> Octavian on the dawn of the day of the battle of Actium left his tent and while on his way to see the ships he met a man driving an ass. This man, upon being asked by Octavian what his name was said: "My name is Eutychus [Good Fortune] and this ass is called Nicon [Victory]." Therefore Octavian, after his victory, adorned that place with the ships' rostra and also placed there an ass and a man in bronze.[8]

In order to get from these two classical texts to the "solution" of the Victory-ass-lion painting from Pompeii, it was not enough to cite this passage to identify Augustus with the ass. To justify making Antony into the defeated lion, our three philological scholars remind us that Antony (1) proclaimed himself the son of Hercules, who killed the Nemean Lion; (2) celebrated his victory at Pharsalis by going through the streets of Rome in a chariot pulled by lions; (3) adapted the image of a lion with a sword in its paws for some of his coins; and (4) in coins minted at Lyon, used the types of the Victory and the lion. Minervini adds the supposition that we see in the image of the ass penetrating the lion the visual representation of one of the obscene ditties recited by soldiers who accompanied their generals in triumphal processions.[9]

---

[5] On the iconography of Victoria, see Hölscher 1967; for the crown, Rumscheid 2000.

[6] Minervini 1859; Fiorelli 1875, 437–38; Della Corte 1951, 25–30; Della Corte 1965, 169–72, nos. 309–12. According to Helbig 1865, L. Stephani (*Comptes-rendus des séances de l'Academie des Inscriptions et Belles-Lettres* 7 [1863] 235 n. 5) opposed Minervini's interpretation, holding that the painting simply showed the victory of the ass's fertility over that of the lion. Helbig's reference to Stephani, repeated in the literature, is incorrect; I failed to locate it. Helbig 1865 catalogues all three paintings from the facade (no. 10 [Mercury], no. 23 [Dionysus], no. 1548 [ass-lion-Victory]) and questions Minervini's interpretation.

[7] Suet. *Aug.* 96: *Apud Actium descendenti in aciem asellus cum asinario occurrit: homini Eutychus, bestiae Nicon erat nomen. Utriusque simulacrum aeneum victor posuit in templo, in quod castrorum suorum locum vertit.*

[8] Καίσαρι δὲ λέγεται μὲν ἔτι σκότους ἀπὸ τῆς σκηνῆς κύκλῳ περιϊόντι πρὸς τὰς ναῦς ἄνθρωπος ἐλαύνων ὄνον ἀπαντῆσαι, πυθομένῳ δὲ τοὔνομα γνωρίσας αὐτὸν εἰπεῖν· "ἐμοὶ μὲν Εὔτυχος ὄνομα, τῷ δ'ὄνῳ Νίκων." διὸ καὶ τοῖς ἐμβόλοις τὸν τόπον κοσμῶν ὕστερον, ἔστησε χαλκοῦν ὄνον καὶ ἄνθρωπον.

[9] Suet. *Iul.* 49.4; Dio Cass. 43.20; Juv. 10.36–46; Mommsen 1887–88, 1:412; Richlin 1992, 229 n. 9; Cèbe 1966, 24–25, 32, 92–93, 96; Beard 2003.

The appeal of this philological explanation is immediately clear. It transforms an odd and uncanny sexual image into an allegory of a historical event by making Augustus into the ass and Antony into the lion: a well-known reversal in history takes allegorical form when two animal characters reverse their natural roles. What is more, the ass-Augustus gets rewarded for his act of overturning nature by receiving the crown of victory from none other than the goddess herself.

The biggest problem with this interpretation is how we get from an omen that is essentially verbal (an *asinarius* named Good Fortune and his ass named Victor) to a representation that is visual. Although the verbal omen took the visual form of a bronze monument memorializing it (if we believe Suetonius and Plutarch), the artist of our painting was illustrating a story of an omen. He was not creating an alternative symbol for Augustus. Put another way: How did the artist of our painting come to make Augustus into an ass, as it were? And when they looked at the image of the ass, did people think that they were looking at an allegorical substitution for Augustus himself? The identification of the lion with Antony is even more problematical since the texts of Suetonius and Plutarch do not introduce the lion at all.

The second problem with the Minervini–Fiorelli–Della Corte interpretation is that it does not take into account either where the image was or what the intended viewers knew. The Victory-ass-lion painting was part of a decorative scheme on the facade of a commercial building. When the building was excavated, a layer of white plaster covered the painting; shortly after excavation, a fortuitous rainfall caused the plaster to detach and reveal the painting. All that can be said with certainty is that the painting was covered sometime before the eruption of Vesuvius.

Minervini, however, wishes to date the painting close to Actium, some time around 31 B.C. In his scenario, the painting appealed directly to Augustus's veterans who settled in Pompeii after the civil wars. Minervini asserts that they knew the story of the omen and proposes that they had even made up an obscene song: "a crude jibe at Augustus, and a savage satire at the expense of his conquered adversary: *Asinus Actiacus Antonii leonem devicit* ('The ass of Actium subdued the lion of Antony')."[10] But when Claudius became emperor, the painting had to be canceled since Mark Antony was his maternal grandfather.

Close examination of the pier beneath the painting along with the piers beneath the painting of Mercury and that of Dionysus casts grave doubts on Minervini's date (see fig. 2). Although the two shop spaces are built in concrete faced with irregular, fist-sized pieces of tufa and limestone, all three piers present the same familiar construction technique. Deep brick and tufa quoins tie each pier into its respective wall. This is a common technique used to stabilize walls, and especially doorways, that had sustained damage in the earthquake of 62.[11] Since the three paintings rested directly on plaster attached to these tufa-and-brick piers, they probably date after 62. What is more, at the time of excavation the plaster and the color of the paintings of Mercury and Dionysus were in good condition—not what one would expect for a painting exposed to the elements for 110 years. In fact, these two paintings, left in place rather than being removed to the Naples Museum like the Victory-ass-lion painting, disappeared soon after they were excavated. Facade paintings were not very long-lived.

But why was the Victory-ass-lion painting covered? The canceled erotic paintings that decorated apodyterium 7 of the Suburban Baths at Pompeii suggest an alternative scenario to Minervini's for the cancellation of the Victory-ass-lion painting. At some time before the eruption, the owner of the Suburban Baths had a painter cover the erotic vignettes with a bland Fourth Style scheme.

[10] Minervini 1859, 70.   [11] Maiuri 1942; Richardson 1988, 379–81.

Jacobelli speculates that their sexual obscenity may have been offensive to the new public morality that came in with Vespasian in A.D. 69.[12] A similar cleanup may have accounted for the cancellation of the Victory-ass-lion picture, especially considering that the images of the gods Mercury and Dionysus were left untouched.

From the accounts of Minervini, Fiorelli, and Della Corte, it is clear that scholars who use the philological model want art to illustrate or illuminate history—the history known from the preserved texts. They assume that classical texts explain who the Romans were. Never mind that all the texts that have come down to us are elite texts, touting the values of elite men (or the writers who worked for them). The philological has little room for the voices of non-elite, ordinary people—let alone the voices of any women of any class.

The philological/historical model is also a trickle-down model. By this I mean that if Actium is on the minds of elite writers, it must be on the minds of elite Romans. In turn, the art that the elites commission puts Actium and Augustus's glory in the minds and hearts of non-elite Romans. Therefore, even in a town like Pompeii, if a patron commissions a painter to put the Victory-ass-lion painting on the facade of his humble establishment, the idea of Augustus's victory over Antony is so pervasive that even an ordinary person thinks—Yes! This is an allegory of Augustus whipping his rival!

The Folkloric Model (1950–1980): Mingazzini and Kenner

Beginning in 1950s, two folkloric interpretations of our painting surfaced. Using the methodology of structuralism, they searched for fables and images that contained interactions between asses and lions—or other strange reversals in the animal kingdom. Mingazzini puts forward his interpretation in a 1953 festschrift honoring Ludwig Curtius.[13] Mingazzini rejects the Actium allegory. To set up his folkloric interpretation, he mentions several lamps with images of reversals in the animal world that must, he maintains, refer to lost fables. Among the images of the upside down world inhabited by animal characters, he includes a lamp where a stork holds a scale with two pans. A mouse in one pan outweighs an elephant the other.[14] Another image, much repeated on lamps, is that of a human-looking fox trying to catch a crow in a tree with lime twigs.[15]

He then relates a modern fable about an ass and a lion that he says is bandied about among the farmers of Sicily and Magna Graecia. The ass and the lion, traveling along the same route, agree to take turns carrying the other one across each river they come to. It's the ass's turn first, but when both are in the middle of the river, the lion sinks his claws into the ass so that he won't be swept away by the water. When the ass complains, the lion replies that it is his nature to use his claws, and he can't do otherwise. So when they come to the next river, and it's the lion's turn to carry the ass, in the middle of the river the ass penetrates the lion with all his might. When the lion complains, the ass says, *armis utitur quisque suis* ("one uses whatever weapons one has"). Mingazzini concludes that this folk tale, although not recorded in ancient literature, was the one known to the painter of the Pompeian Victory-ass-lion picture.[16]

[12] Jacobelli 1995, 80–82.

[13] Mingazzini 1953.

[14] Walters 1914, 90, cat. no. 595, pl. 16.

[15] Loeschcke 1919, 400–401, cat. nos. 473–83, pl. 12; Walters

1914, 104, cat. no. 686, pl. 24 claims that the three sticks held up by the fox are "flutes."

[16] Although twenty of the fables of Aesop involve the ass, and three of them include the lion, none recounts this story; Chambry 1927, nos. 262–81.

Fig. 3. Lion mounting an ass. Terracotta lamp
(after Loeschcke 1919, pl. 12, 484).

Fig. 4. Lion on top of ass. Mold from Magdalensberg
(photo G. Khevenhüller, after Kenner 1970, fig. 3).

As proof that this fable existed in antiquity, he illustrates a first-century A.D. lamp from Vindonissa depicting a lion on top of an ass (fig. 3). There are several problems with Mingazzini's reading of this image. Loeschcke believes that the lion is attacking, or bringing down, the ass rather than riding him.[17] In the Pompeian fresco the ass is on top of the lion, so that—even if we accept the lion as riding the ass—the lamp would, at best, have illustrated the first half of the story. What is more, there is no figure of Victory in either the lamp or in Mingazzini's fable. Finally, there is no indication of water either in the Pompeian fresco or on the lamp.

Yet, to be sure, the biggest problem is that of extrapolation. How do we get from the present-day fable all the way back to the first century A.D.? Minervini also knew the modern tale of the ass penetrating the lion.[18] But what neither Mingazzini nor Minervini knew was that a version of the story had already found its way into high literature in Giordano Bruno's 1582 comedy, *Candelaio*.[19] Bruno's use of the fable in his play gets us back to the sixteenth century and to popular folklore of the time, showing the story's long life. Are we then correct in supposing that it was in circulation in some form in the first century, even though none of the fables of Aesop or others tell it?

The problem of extrapolation becomes even more acute in Hedwig Kenner's much more extensive study of the phenomenon of the world-turned-upside-down in Graeco-Roman antiquity.[20] In 1865 Wolfgang Helbig claimed to have seen in a private collection a lamp—unfortunately no longer extant—that showed the image of the ass penetrating the lion, but without the Victory.[21] Kenner mentions Helbig's lost lamp and then goes on to compare the fresco from Pompeii with a mold found in the Celtish-Roman settlement of Magdalensberg in Kärnten. The mold itself, found by a farmer in 1910, is now lost, but a positive made from the mold shows a parallel but arguably quite different representation with an ass on top of a supine lion (fig. 4). It is a scene from the circus

[17] Loeschcke 1919, cat. nos. 484–88, pl. 12; another lamp of the first century is a less ambiguous representation of a lion bringing down an ass: Heres 1972, cat. no. 136 (Antikensammlung, Staatliche Museen zu Berlin, TC 6315.89).

[18] Minervini 1859, 69.

[19] Bárberi Squarotti 1964, act 2, scene 5, lines 65–66. I thank Hilary Gatti for this citation.

[20] Kenner 1970.

[21] Helbig 1865, 383–84, no. 1048.

or amphitheater, for to the left is an animal handler wearing a short tunic with a wide belt; he holds a lance in his right hand. Here the lion is welcoming the stallion's penetration. The animals join mouths, mimicking a kiss. What is more, the lion lies on his back, assuming a position well known from images of human sexual intercourse.

Even with all these differences, Kenner assumes that this representation is close enough to the Victory-ass-lion painting to mean about the same thing. She sees the Pompeian painting and the mold displaying a parallel structure: whereas in nature the lion is the predator of the ass, in both visual representations the ass/stallion and lion are copulating using positions that humans do. She then expands her search to include any image where animals act like humans. Although Kenner does not acknowledge it, assumptions and her methodology come from structuralist thinking in anthropology. In particular, comparative mythography, as practiced most famously by Claude Lévi-Strauss, informs Kenner's approach.[22]

What Kenner finds is what her method expects to find: that the structure of the world-upside-down is pervasive in the ancient Mediterranean. Because she reads the Pompeian fresco not as a transparent reference to a specific historical event (as our philologists did) but as one among many expressions of a deeply rooted folkloric construction circulating around the ancient Mediterranean, she robs the ass and lion image of any claim to uniqueness. It becomes an image that surfaces from a plenum of popular imagery in which animals overturn the order of the human world by doing what humans do. Kenner's is an exercise in substitution, and her book a compendium of images of animals acting like humans. For example, Kenner's search takes her to Egypt, where many papyri and tomb paintings show animals carrying out human actions. The famous Turin papyrus gives animals human dress, pose, and activities. Reversals of the ass-lion variety occur as well. In several images, for example, cats wait obsequiously on an enthroned mouse.[23]

The value of Kenner's structuralist-folkloric work is in the way that it frames the Victory-ass-lion fresco in relation to other scenarios of inversion in both art and myth. She sets up parallels. But the problem lies in her interpretation. She proposes that the Victory-ass-lion picture, because it shows the order of nature upside down, is about a special realm where such things could happen. It is a world where, as in the biblical phrase, the ox beds down with the lion. It is a paradisiacal world. So in her search for the deeper meaning Kenner has ennobled the image, making it into a precursor to Christianity, or at least to the philosophical underpinnings of what comes to be Christianity. The burlesque image becomes a model for the supposed Roman quest for an answer to the meaning of life.

The visual evidence that both Mingazzini and Kenner marshal is nevertheless quite useful if we think about what kind of imagery was circulating. For it encourages us to think that the artist who got the job of decorating the facade of this Pompeian establishment could have had visual models, like the lamp from Vindonissa or the Magdalensberg mold, that helped him to conceive the Victory-ass-lion image. Whether he had a sketch of the three figures in a model book, or whether he copied them from small-scale objects like lamps or carved gemstones, he was not inventing from scratch. But, in the absence of other representations that have *all* the elements (Victory crowning ass that penetrates lion), we must credit our Pompeian artist with a new invention for the facade of Pompeii VII, 6, 34–35.

[22] Sinclair Bell notes that Kenner's approach may have been influenced by the late nineteenth- and early twentieth-century colonial experience in Africa: Mielke 1990.

[23] For animals performing as humans on gemstones, see Piccottini 1990. Piccottini believes that rings showing such reversals (on this ring, a mouse driving a *cisium* drawn by chickens) were apotropaic. I wish to thank Sinclair Bell for this reference.

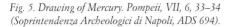

*Fig. 5. Drawing of Mercury. Pompeii, VII, 6, 33–34
(Soprintendenza Archeologici di Napoli, ADS 694).*

The Site-specific Model (1980–Present): Fröhlich and Clarke

So far we have seen two different scholarly models at work: the philological/historical model and the structural/folkloric model. The third model is the site-specific/contextual model: in the case of the Victory-ass-lion picture, the model used by Thomas Fröhlich and myself.[24]

In a certain sense, the site of Pompeii compels many art historians to become contextualists. A trek through the city, with remains of paintings decorating the facades of both fancy and humble buildings, makes it clear that even the humblest image occupied a specific location in the skein of streets and alleys and spoke to the people who passed by that place or who frequented it.[25] The Victory-ass-lion painting decorated a building on a corner just one block west of the forum. Although its removal preserved it, the rest of the painted program that passersby would have seen, as well as the numerous graffiti found on the structure, is gone.

It is possible to reconstruct the program using the verbal descriptions and measurements provided by Helbig and Fiorelli and a drawing of the Mercury on the left-hand pier. The drawing, executed by Nicola La Volpe before 1859, shows Mercury with *petasus*, winged shoes, and caduceus and an unusually flat *marsupium*, or purse (fig. 5). An image of Dionysus pouring wine down the panther's mouth was on the right pier. Beneath him was the graffito LIB LIBER, an alternate name for Dionysus in the Roman world.[26]

Other graffiti, recorded in *CIL* 4 1626–49, tell us something about the people who wrote things

[24] Fröhlich 1991; Clarke 2003b, 9–13. For a history of the contextual approach, see Burke 2002.

[25] Favro 1996; Kellum 2000.

[26] Bruhl 1953, 133–44; Collins-Clinton 1977; North 1996.

on the facade. We find names, and one MYSTIS near the image of Dionysus labeled LIB LIBER, and a certain RESTIT*ut*[us] who *f*ELAT. Della Corte, who was fond of jumping to sexual conclusions, interprets the graffito VENUS ES VENUS as the celebration of a prostitute named Venus, who according to him was the proprietor of this *casa allegra*.[27] Recently his interpretation resurfaced when the signpost for the Pompeii Audio-Guide went up, naming the space Caupona di Venere.

We also have someone writing below the gladiators, CARMINIBU[S] CREDO. In addition to these names and activities, under the Victory-ass-lion picture are three images of gladiators (fig. 6). They include depictions of a Thraex, a Murmillo, a Retiarius. The fourth image is a sketchy gladiatorial helmet.[28]

A site-specific, contextual interpretation of the Victory-ass-lion painting must begin with the function of the building. At the time of excavation, Minervini questioned whether 34 and 35 housed separate enterprises since there is no internal doorway in the wall that divides the two spaces. But both spaces had stairways to the upper story, connected externally, at least, by a common balcony. What is more, if we accept that all three piers received their fresco decoration at the same time, it is likely that the three images—Mercury, Victory-ass-lion, and Dionysus—were meant to be read together. Even if the artist adapted these images from a repertoire that was in circulation among wall painters, he chose these three because of what he knew about the intended use of the building.[29]

We have to think what went on there. If it was a bordello, as Della Corte suggests, then we

[27] Della Corte 1951, 25; Della Corte 1965, 171–72, nos. 312a and 312b.

[28] Langner 2001, cat. nos. 775 (Thraex), 782 (Murmillo), 829 (*retiarius*), 975 (helmet). For definitions of these types,

see Ville 1981.

[29] For workshops and the use of pattern and model books at Pompeii, see Moormann 1995, 61–298.

*Fig. 7. Facade
painting. Pompeii,
V, 6, 1–2 (Pompeii,
Archivio Fotografico
della Soprintendenza,
A14, courtesy of the
Ministero per i Beni e
le Attività Culturali—
Soprintendenza
Archeologica di Pompei).*

have to consider why the ass is more important than the lion.[30] Since the ass is penetrating a lion, not a lioness, it would be hard to read the scene as an allegory of a human male mounting a human female. It's certainly not a very flattering representation if it's supposed to stand for lovemaking between human beings. What we find in bordellos, as I have elaborated elsewhere, are images that romanticize the rough-and-ready sexual action that went on there.[31] If the ass-lion intercourse is supposed to announce sex-for-sale in the interior of the building, it is an anomalous image without parallel. For this reason I find it difficult to agree with Fröhlich that the image refers to the erotic activities of a bordello.[32]

Fröhlich also states that the images of the two gods, Dionysus and Mercury, lent a sacral character to the facade.[33] In view of the many pairings of these two deities on the facades of commercial establishments, I hesitate to see them as religious images; I think that they were meant to bring good fortune to the establishment and its clientele.[34] Rather than being sacral images, they are propitious images.

An old photograph of the facade of another building (never excavated in its entirety) provides a plausible model for reconstructing the lost deities on VII, 6, 33–34. Like our building, V, 6, 1 was a commercial establishment and occupied a street corner at the Via di Nola and Vicolo delle Nozze d'Argento (fig. 7). Mercury, on the left-hand pier, appears in profile striding to the right, with *petasus*, flowing mantel, and a caduceus in his left hand. In front of him is an *omphalos* with a serpent wound around it. A drunken Dionysus, supported by a satyr with a thyrsus, decorates the right-hand pier. Dionysus gives a crouching panther a drink from the kantharos he holds in his right hand.[35]

[30] Della Corte 1951, 25–27; Della Corte 1965, nos. 309–12.

[31] Clarke 1998, 196–206; Clarke 2003a, 60–67.

[32] Fröhlich 1991, 65.

[33] Fröhlich 1991, 65–66.

[34] In other contexts, as Sinclair Bell points out, Mercury can be an unstable figure. See Binder 2003; Allan 2004.

[35] De Vos 1991; Sogliano 1906, 155–56, fig. 5; Boyce 1937, 110, no. 6; Fröhlich 1991, 318–19, cat. no. F34. Fourth Style. Like the establishment at VII, 6, 34–35, the image of Dionysus covers a pier in *opus listatum*, indicating a date after the earthquake of 62.

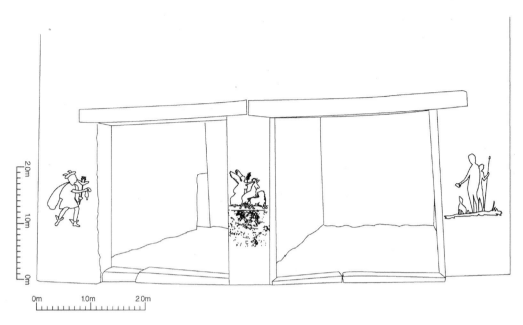

Fig. 8. Reconstruction of facade with paintings. Pompeii, Tavern at VII, 6, 34–35 (drawing J. R. Clarke).

By using the facade painting from V, 6, 1–2 as a model, and combining it with La Volpe's drawing, and the descriptions and measurements furnished by Minervini, Fiorelli, and Helbig, we can reconstruct the facade—and in so doing the spatial context—of our establishment (fig. 8). It is not difficult to understand the pairing of Dionysus and Mercury; they appear together in almost every space that can be identified as a tavern in Pompeii. A particularly eloquent representation, from a shop on the Via dell'Abbondanza, is not a facade painting but rather a *lararium* within the shop.[36] It gives us the combination of Mercury, on the left (here with a full money bag), and Dionysus giving his panther a drink on the right. In between we have the familiar representation of the Genius sacrificing. The two Lares flank him.[37] As the context shows, this *lararium* lines up with the serving counters. Dionysus is the god of wine, so he is the proper god to invoke in a place where you consumed wine and caught his enthusiasm. Perhaps in our building at VII, 6, 34–35 the tavern-goer's prayer or hope was to consume enough wine to get happy but not so much as to get sick, to dim his wits at the gaming table, or, worst of all, to blunt his sexual prowess in the lovemaking room.[38]

Mercury with his *marsupium*, or moneybag, is ubiquitous at Pompeii. He is both the god of commerce and, like Priapus, a phallic protector deity. On the facade of Verecundus's shop, Mercury is there, ensconced in his little temple, above the image of a woman selling shoes.[39] He's there to make the shop turn a profit. On the facade of our tavern, he's there to help with another kind of money matter: gambling.

But, seemingly, there's an odd twist to our Mercury. If we trust La Volpe's accuracy, Mercury's *marsupium* looks empty. Rather than bulging with coins, it is unusually thin, suggesting that it is either nearly or completely empty.[40] If he has lost his money or has yet to make his money, the god

[36] Sampaolo 1990.

[37] Boyce 1937; Orr 1978; Fröhlich 1991.

[38] On lovemaking and drinking, see Purcell 1994.

[39] Clarke 2003b, 106, fig. 61.

[40] Sampaolo 1995, 683, cat. no. 132.

who is supposed to bring money is empty-handed. Here I think the painter was connecting the Victory-ass-lion scene with Mercury. In both cases the tables are turned. Just as Mercury has lost his money, so the lion has lost his dominance. As the ass mounts the lion in a twist of fate, so Mercury, bringer of wealth, comes up empty-handed.

What both paintings encode is the reversal of fortune. It *is* the world-turned-upside-down. It's the world where the goddess Fortuna guides the fates of the ordinary people who gambled for money—and perhaps gambled for love—in the tavern. And Dionysus, presiding over the right side, in Roman thought the auspicious side, is there to give his blessings to the goings on. It's his wine that intoxicates and incites the grandiose behavior of humans—the very behavior that leads to Fortune's upsets.

Finally, we shouldn't leave out the graffiti below the image of Victory, the ass, and the lion. Here we get a taste of what some of the hangers-on around the doorway were thinking about. Now it would be lovely if we had some graffiti commenting on the image above. What we have instead are graffiti with images and names of gladiators. In a certain sense the gladiator graffiti contain an oblique reference to the Victory-ass-lion painting in that they are about victory: the power of the stronger gladiator over the weaker one. Each shows the ass, as it were, who triumphed, *vicit,* over the lion. It is the power of one gladiator's sword over another's. One could even attempt to interpret the swords as symbols of the phallus and therefore of sexual superiority. But in this context I am inclined to say that these graffiti of gladiators—ubiquitous at Pompeii—were just what was on the graffiti writers' minds at the moment. Or they were simply images they knew how to draw.

If the images of Mercury and Dionysus-Liber were placed there for good luck, this hoped-for luck extended to all the activities that went on there. If it was a tavern where people gambled, they counted on Fortune to give them the luck—and power—to mount the lion, as it were, and to win the games of dice, *alea,* or whatever game of chance they were playing.[41] And if it was a tryst they were after, the image served its purpose as well. In the end, the ensemble of images on the facade of the establishment spelled winning—or at least being on the good side of the gods.

Interpretive Strategies of the Future: Multivalent Messages

And now to return to role models in classical scholarship. The painting hasn't changed, at least not since its detachment from the building at VII, 6, 34–35. It now takes pride of place in the new installation of the Raccolta Pornografica in the Naples Museum. The painting hasn't changed, but scholarly approaches have. We started with analyses that considered the image in relation to elite texts and elite ideas: the trickle-down model of classical scholarship as framed by Minervini, who first proposed that the painting was an allegory of Actium. We then considered scholarship that cast a wider net: Mingazzini's lost fable and Kenner's paradisical world-turned-upside-down, two examples of what I call the anthropological or comparative folklore approach. Then we looked at the Victory-ass-lion picture through the lens of the contextual or site-specific model. Notice that we started with discussions of the image studied in isolation and ended up with the image put back into its original physical and social uses.

Studying any image in isolation means studying it as a picture, often looking at a photograph or engraving of the image rather than the original. It is the kind of research you can carry out in a photo archive—what some scholars disparagingly refer to as "motif hunting." The idea is that if

---

[41] Ihm 1890; Purcell 1995.

MAKING OF IMAGE		TRANSMISSION OF IMAGES	
WHO IS PATRON?	WHO IS ARTIST?	VIEWER ADDRESS	WHO IS VIEWER?

Patron's social status:
Elite
Non-elite:
  freeborn
  freedman
  slave
  foreigner
	Training and ability	Location of image:
		  street
		  temple
		  dining room
		  tomb
		  house
		  tavern
		  latrine
		  in moving procession
			Viewer's social status:
			Elite
			Non-elite:
			  freeborn
			  freedman
			  slave
			  foreigner

Patron's gender role
Patron's motivations:
  advertisement of goods or services
  commemoration
  entertainment
  mediation–to resolve community tensions
  appeasing gods or propitiation
  competition or one-upmanship
  announcement of status or wealth
  apotropaic/admonition
  civic benefaction
		Viewing context
		–seen while:
		  working
		  walking
		  standing
		  praying
		  dining
		  shopping
		  mourning
		  visiting
		  defecating
		–seen with what other images?
			Viewer's gender role
			Viewer's past experience
			–image seen before in:
			  temple
			  forum
			  theater
			  coin
			  house
			  pattern book
			  procession or triumph

		Size and scale of image:
		  close viewing
		  distant viewing	

Patron's understanding of image:
  knows/does not know model or referent
	Has models:
	  understands/does not
	  understand models
	Has no models:
	  invents from observation
	  invents through pastiche
			Viewer's understanding of image:
			  knows/does not know model or
			  referent
			  believes/does not believe image
			  is a god or goddess

		Cost and medium of image	
Literate/illiterate	Literate/illiterate	Writing/no writing on image	Literate/illiterate
Patron's occupation or profession			Viewer's occupation or profession

Fig. 9. Chart: A model for the making and transmission of visual representation in ancient Roman visual culture (after Clarke 2003b, fig. 3).

you can find images that look like the one you've isolated for your study (in this case the ass and lion image from Pompeii), you've made a discovery. If you can find a classical text to pin on those images, you're Minervini. If you can find a folkloric idea to pin those images on, you're Kenner or Mingazzini.

What do I want to pin my image to? It's the notion, common to all poststructuralist thinking, that meaning is not stable but rather dependent on who the readers are: what equipment, so to speak, they bring to the imagery. A contextual approach wants to know what the original viewer knew or might have known about the visual representation.

What a Pompeian viewer brought to the Victory-ass-lion painting will have varied according to his or her class, gender role, past experience, beliefs, and much more (fig. 9). Starting with this assumption, it is possible to reconstruct, at least in part, what a Pompeian viewer understood about the Victory-ass-lion image by analyzing what coexisted with it on the facade (here Dionysus-Liber, Mercury, and the graffiti) and where else images like those on the facade appear. As a further step, going beyond what I have done here, I could create "viewer scenarios" that imagine how particular viewers—say, an elite man, a male slave, or a freedwoman—might have brought their own experiences to the interpretation of the image.[42]

[42] For a discussion of viewer scenarios, see Clarke 2003b, 9–13; examples of viewer scenarios, Clarke 2003b, passim.

But even using a combination of site-specific analysis and viewer scenarios, I can only describe a zone of possible meanings rather than "solving" the Victory-ass-lion painting. What I hope to have shown through this case study is that the search for a *single* key that explains the meaning of an image—whether it is based on the study of texts, folklore, or archaeological context—can only result in unbalanced interpretations. If the semantic dances performed by Minervini, Della Corte, or Mingazzini look weird to the scholar of the twenty-first century, it is because their scholarly culture expected them to "solve" images definitively—and then defend their interpretations to the death.

Perhaps today's scholars can learn a lesson in humility from the excessively deterministic methods of our elders. The crossing of disciplines that has enriched humanistic studies should teach us to expect and embrace multivalent interpretations of visual representations from the past. If the New Art History has learned anything from anthropology, feminism, sociology, reception theory, and cultural studies, it is that the meanings of any single visual representation are anything but fixed and eternal.

As for my own interpretation of the Victory-ass-lion image, a new discovery tomorrow—textual or visual—could modify it, but what would stand is the contextual, site-specific part of my analysis. I believe that site-specific observations that take into account the variables outlined in my chart will continue to be useful as our knowledge of an image widens through new discovery and research. You could sum up my own scholarly model with the motto, "Context first and last."

Works Cited

Allan, A., "From *Agônistes* to *Agônios:* Hermes, Chaos and Conflict in Competitive Games and Festivals," in *Games and Festivals in Classical Antiquity*, ed. S. Bell and G. Davies (Oxford 2004) 45–54.

Altekamp, S., M. René, and M. K. Hofter, eds., *Posthumanistische Klassische Archäologie. Historizität und Wissenschaftlichkeit von Interessen und Methoden. Kolloquium Berlin 1999* (Munich 2001).

Bárberi Squarotti, G., ed., *Il Candelaio di Giordano Bruno* (Turin 1964).

Beard, M., "The Triumph of the Absurd: Roman Street Theatre," in *Rome the Cosmopolis*, ed. C. Edwards and G. Woolf (Cambridge 2003) 21–43.

Binder, G., "Verkehrte Welt: Gott Mercurius als Mensch in Rom? Gedanken zu Horaz, Carmen 1, 2," in *Gottmenschen*, ed. G. Binder, B. Effe, and R. F. Glei, *Bulletin archéologique du Comité des travaux historiques et scientifiques* 54 (Trier 2003) 45–65.

Bonnet, C., "'L'immortalité appartient an Sage.' Franz Cumont et l'art érotique," *Dialogues d'Histoire Ancienne* 26 (2000) 77–97.

Boyce, G. K., *Corpus of the Lararia of Pompeii, Memoirs of the American Academy in Rome* 14 (Rome 1937).

Brilliant, R., "The New Roman Art History," *Journal of Roman Archaeology* 11 (1998) 557–65.

Bruhl, A., *Liber Pater: Origine et expansion du culte dionysiaque à Rome et dans le monde romain, Bibliothèque des Écoles françaises d'Athènes et de Rome* 176 (Paris 1953).

Burke, P., "Context in Context," *Common Knowledge* 8 (2002) 152–77.

Cèbe, J.-P., *La caricature et la parodie dans le monde romain antique, Bibliothèque des Écoles françaises d'Athènes et de Rome* 206 (Paris 1966).

Chambry, É., *Ésope: Fables* (Paris 1927).

Clarke, J. R., *Looking at Lovemaking: Constructions of Sexuality in Roman Art, 100 B.C.–A.D. 250* (Berkeley 1998).

———, *Roman Sex: 100 B.C.–A.D. 250* (New York 2003a).

———, *Art in the Lives of Ordinary Romans: Visual Representation and Non-elite Viewers in Italy, 100 B.C.–A.D. 315* (Berkeley 2003b).

Collins-Clinton, J., *A Late Antique Shrine of Liber Pater at Cosa, Études préliminaries aux religions orientales dans l'empire romain* 64 (Leiden 1977).

De Caro, S., ed., *Il gabinetto segreto del Museo Archeologico Nazionale di Napoli* (Naples 2000).

Della Corte, M., *Cleopatra, M. Antonio e Ottaviano nelle allegorie storico-umoristiche delle argenterie del tesoro di Boscoreale* (Pompei 1951).

———, *Case ed Abitanti di Pompei*, 3rd ed. (Naples 1965).

De Vos, A., "V 6, 1," *Pompei: pitture e mosaici* (Rome 1991) 3:1099–1101.

Donohue, A. A., and M. Fullerton, eds., *Ancient Art and Its Historiography* (Cambridge 2003).

Favro, D., *The Urban Image of Augustan Rome* (Cambridge 1996).

Fiorelli, G., *Descrizione di Pompei* (Naples 1875).

Fröhlich, T., *Lararien- und Fassadenbilder in den Vesuvstädten: Untersuchungen zur "volkstümlichen" pompejanischen Malerei, Mitteilungen des deutschen archäologischen Instituts, römische Abteilung,* Supplement 32 (Mainz 1991).

Hallett, J. P., and T. van Nortwich, eds., *Compromising Traditions: The Personal Voice in Classical Scholarship* (London 1997).

Helbig, W., *Wandgemälde der vom Vesuv verschütteten Städte Campaniens* (Leipzig 1865).

Heres, G., *Die römischen Bildlampen der Berliner Antiken-Sammlung, Deutsche Akademie der Wissenschaften zu Berlin* 3 (Berlin 1972).

Hölscher, T., *Victoria Romana: Archäologische Untersuchungen zur Geschichte und Wesensart der römischen Siegesgöttin von den Anfängen bis zum Ende des 3. Jahrhunderts n. Chr.* (Mainz 1967).

Ihm, M., "Römische Spieltafeln," in *Bonner Studien: Aufsätze aus der Altertumswissenschaft. Reinhard Kekulé zur Erinnerung an seine Lehrthätigkeit in Bonn, gewidmet von seine Schulern,* ed. M. Ihm (Berlin 1890) 223–39.

Jacobelli, L., *Le pitture erotiche delle Terme Suburbane di Pompei* (Rome 1995).

Kampen, N. B., "Writing Histories of Roman Art," *Art Bulletin* 85 (2003) 171–86.

Kellum, B., "The Spectacle of the Street," in *The Art of Ancient Spectacle*, ed. B. Bergmann and C. Kondoleon, Studies in the History of Art 56, Symposium Papers 34 (Washington, D.C. 2000) 282–99.

Kenner, H., *Das Phänomen der verkehrten Welt in der griechisch-römischen Antike* (Klagenfurt 1970).

Kleinbauer, E., ed., *Perspectives in Western Art History* (New York 1971).

Langner, M., *Antike Graffitizeichnungen: Motive, Gestaltung und Bedeutung, Palilia* 11 (Wiesbaden 2001).

Loeschcke, S., *Lampen aus Vindonissa* (Zurich 1919).

Maiuri, A., *L'ultima fase edilizia di Pompei* (Rome 1942).

Mielke, A., "Fremde Welt—Verkehrte Welt: Zu Bestialisierungstendenzen der Hottentotten in Reisebeschreibungen und Satire," in *Begegnung mit dem "Fremden." Grenzen-Traditionen-Vergleiche. Akten des VIII. Kongresses der internationalen Vereinigung für Germanische Sprach- und Literaturwissenschaft (IVG)*, ed. E. Iwasaki, vol. 7 (Tokyo 1990) 365–71.

Minervini, G., "Nuove scavazioni di Pompei, rimpetto al Foro civile, e nella continuazione del vicoletto detto di Augusto," *Bullettino Archeologico Napolitano,* new series 7 (1859) 68–71.

Mingazzini, P., "*De pictura quadam pompeis reperta et de fabula ab ea nobis tradita*," *Mitteilungen des deutschen archäologischen Instituts, römische Abteilung* 60 (1953) 150–52.

Mommsen, T., *Römisches Staatsrecht*, 3 vols. (Leipzig 1887–88).

Moormann, E., ed., *Mani di pittori e botteghe pittoriche nel mondo romano: tavola rotonda in onore di W.J.Th. Peters in occasione del suo 75.mo compleanno, Mededeelingen van het Nederlands Historisch Instituut te Rome* 54 (Assen 1995).

North, J. A., s.v. Liber Pater, in *The Oxford Classical Dictionary*, ed. S. Hornblower and S. Spawforth, 3rd ed. (Oxford and New York 1996) 854.

Orr, D., "Roman Domestic Religion: The Evidence of the Household Shrines," *Aufstieg und Niedergang der römischen Welt*, ed. H. Temporini (Berlin and New York 1978) 2.16.2:1557–91.

Piccottini, G., "Ein Renngespann auf einem römischen Fingerring aus Völkermarkt, Kärnten," *Nikephoros* 3 (1990) 705–8.

Purcell, N., "Women and Wine in Ancient Rome," in *Gender, Drink and Drugs,* ed. M. McDonald (Oxford 1994) 191–208.

———, "Literate Games: Roman Urban Society and the Game of *Alea*," *Past and Present* 147 (1995) 3–37.

Richardson, L., *Pompeii: An Architectural History* (Baltimore 1988).

Richlin, A., *The Garden of Priapus: Sexuality and Aggression in Roman Humor*, rev. ed. (New York 1992).

Rumscheid, J., *Kranz und Krone. Zu Insignien, Siegespreisen und Ehrenzeichen der römischen Kaiserzeit, Istanbuler Forschungen* 43 (Tübingen 2000).

Sampaolo, V., "I. 8, 8: Termopolio," in *Pompei: pitture e mosaici* (Rome 1990) 1:805–25.

———, in *Pompei: pitture e mosaici. La documentazione nell'opera di disegnatori e pittori dei secoli XVIII e XIX* (Rome 1995) 683, cat. no. 132.

———, "VII 6, 34–35," in *Pompei: pitture e mosaici*, 10 vols. (Rome 1997) 7:207–9.

Shanks, M., "Archaeological Theory: What's on the Agenda?," *American Journal of Archaeology* 101 (1997) 395–99.

Smith, R. R. R., "The Use of Images: Visual History and Ancient History," in *Classics in Progress: Essays on Ancient Greece and Rome*, ed. T. P. Wiseman (London 2003) 59–102.

Sogliano, A., "Relazione degli scavi fatti dal dicembre 1902 a tutto marzo 1905," *Notizie degli scavi di antichità* (1906) 148–61.

Ville, G., *La gladiature en Occident des origines à la mort de Domitien, Bibliothèque des Écoles françaises d'Athènes et de Rome* 245 (Rome 1981).

Walters, H. B., *Catalogue of the Greek and Roman Lamps in the British Museum* (London 1914).

Zanker, P., "Nouvelles orientations de la recherche en iconographie. Commanditaires et spectateurs," *Revue archéologique* (1994) 281–93.